The
Human Resources
Program-Evaluation
Handbook

The Human Resources Program-Evaluation Handbook

Jack E. Edwards
U.S. General Accounting Office

John C. Scott
Applied Psychological Techniques, Inc.

Nambury S. Raju
Illinois Institute of Technology

The opinions expressed in this book are those of the authors and do not necessarily reflect the views of the U.S. General Accounting Office or the Federal government.

SAGE Publications
International Educational and Professional Publisher
Thousand Oaks ▪ London ▪ New Delhi

9-11-7

For information:

Sage Publications, Inc.
2455 Teller Road
Thousand Oaks, California 91320
E-mail: order@sagepub.com

Sage Publications Ltd.
6 Bonhill Street
London EC2A 4PU
United Kingdom

Sage Publications India Pvt. Ltd.
B-42, Panchsheel Enclave
New Delhi 110 017 India

Printed in the United States of America

Library of Congress Cataloging-in-Publication Data

The human resources program-evaluation handbook / [edited by] Jack E. Edwards, John C. Scott, Nambury S. Raju.
  p. cm.
Includes bibliographical references and index.
ISBN 0-7619-2396-9 (Cloth)
  1. Personnel management—Evaluation—Handbooks, manuals, etc.
2. Employees—Training of—Evaluation—Handbooks, manuals, etc. 3. Human capital—Cost effectiveness—Handbooks, manuals, etc. 4. Manpower planning—Evaluation—Handbooks, manuals, etc. 5. Organizational effectiveness—Evaluation—Handbooks, manuals, etc. I. Edwards, Jack E. II. Scott, John C. (John Carlson), 1955- III. Raju, Nambury S.
HF5549.17.H86 2003
658.3′007′2—dc21

                                        2003008110

This book is printed on acid-free paper.

03   04   05   06   10   9   8   7   6   5   4   3   2   1

Acquisitions Editor:	Al Bruckner
Editorial Assistant:	MaryAnn Vail
Copy Editor:	Patterson Lamb
Production Editor:	Diane S. Foster
Typesetter:	C&M Digitals (P) Ltd.
Proofreader:	Toni Williams
Indexer:	Molly Hall
Cover Designer:	Janet Foulger

Contents

Glossary: Definitions of Technical and Statistical
  Chet Robie

  Nambury S. Raju

Preface

During the last 10 years, private- and public-sector organizations have come under increased pressure to do more with less. Although many novel—as well as traditional—methods have been used to identify assessment and implementation strategies for increasing the efficiency and effectiveness of human resources (HR) in organizations, little has been done to document the strategies that were used to achieve these goals. At most, organizations and the program evaluators in those organizations have provided case studies.

Although the technology of organizational program evaluation has advanced rapidly, there are many individuals who, despite their formal methodological training, need guidance in how to assess HR programs. This handbook provides a practical, user-friendly, but scientifically rigorous guide to HR program evaluation.

To a great extent, the quality of program evaluation information and the decisions and changes resulting from such assessments depend on the rigor employed during the process. Recent technological and methodological advances as well as changes in the demographics of the workforce pose challenges to program evaluators. This handbook provides a program evaluation team with content-specific guidance for most major types of HR programs. The guidance for each chapter/program includes an overview of the content area, general instructions regarding how to assess the effect and efficiency of a specific program, real-life examples that draw on the chapter authors' personal experiences, identification of potential pitfalls, and additional references for "best practices."

Our book is unique because of the way that it brings the science of program evaluation to practitioners *and* the practical considerations of conducting real-life program evaluations in organizations to the academic/research community. To bridge the science-practice gap that is sometimes present, each chapter was written by at least two authors with different orientations—usually a practitioner and an academician. Moreover, the authors are employed in a wide range of organizational roles: university professors, internal HR staff, consultants from large and small firms, and personnel from state and federal governmental agencies. The strengths resulting from having authors with such diverse perspectives parallel the benefits that come from evaluation teams with complementary training, experiences, and approaches to program evaluation.

What Are the Goals for the Book and Who Are Its Intended Users?

The handbook provides readers with a guide for enhancing the effectiveness and efficiency of HR programs. In general, most business books emphasize general knowledge about a content area or how to *implement* a program. There is *no* source specifically designed to assist individuals who are responsible for *evaluating* or *enhancing* existing HR programs. Therefore, the goal of this book is to provide a reader with an in-depth source for information about state-of-the-art procedures for evaluating and improving HR programs in organizations.

The handbook should be of interest to three types of readers:

1. individuals (e.g., personnel specialists and consultants) who are charged with assessing the effectiveness of an organization's HR programs,

2. managers and policy makers who utilize the resulting information, and

3. graduate students (and therefore their academic faculty) who are interested in careers in HR, personnel management, organizational behavior, indus-trial-organizational psychology, or program evaluation.

A Few Words of Thanks

Our foremost thanks go to the chapter authors. Without them, we had no book. They are the ones who have generously given of their time and expertise. It amazed us how much insight the authors were able to incorporate into the 30 manuscript pages that we were able to allot each author. Truly, each chapter could be easily expanded into a whole book, but the authors distilled their guidance into a succinct, but very readable chapter.

We also wish to express our appreciation to the many people at Sage who helped us see this book to its completion. MaryAnn Vail, Diane Foster, and Al Bruckner supplied much encouragement and assistance in helping us to finalize our project, convincing us that we had made a good choice in working with Sage. Their belief in the need for the book kept us on course, and the excellent editorial assistance by Patterson Lamb improved our ability to convey a clear message.

Finally, the number of hours spent preparing our book took us away from other portions of our lives. We'd like to thank the following people who understood when we were unavailable because we were working on this book. Those people are Deborah Edwards, Mary Edwards, Harold Edwards, Susie Hoke, Patti Groves, Betty Goluchowski, Kimberly Scott, Justin Scott, Jeremy Scott, Marijke Raju, Indira Hanley, and Saroja Raju.

—Jack, John, and Nam

PART I

Framework for Human Resources Program Evaluation

CHAPTER 1

Overview of Program Evaluation

Dale S. Rose

E. Jane Davidson

Program evaluation can be an invaluable tool for professionals interested in maximizing the potential for human resources (HR) programs as a value-added function within the modern organization. By focusing on the strategic role of human resources in the value chain, HR professionals can use well-conducted evaluations to distinguish among interventions that make a worthwhile contribution to an organization's competitive advantage, those with promise, and those that aren't really worth pursuing. Though program evaluation has its foundation in a rich history of academic inquiry, we have taken an approach in this chapter that emphasizes the practical side of HR evaluation. Although we certainly do not eschew rigor and experimental control in evaluating programs, we find that fitting research methods to business necessity results in the most useful and timely information. We provide frequent examples, point out real-world challenges as well as opportunities, and emphasize a balanced approach to designing, implementing, and utilizing evaluation in which practical and technical considerations are equally important.

Traditionally, HR programs have been treated as more of a luxury than a necessity. Although many authors have questioned the appropriateness of thinking about HR strictly as a liability rather than an asset, this approach continues to pervade common practice. Some authors have made inroads toward a more balanced approach. For example, Kaplan and Norton (1996) introduced the popular Balanced

Scorecard, which clearly demonstrates the link between benefits from employee behavior and bottom line indicators. Also, the recent linkage research that has demonstrated ties between HR activities and broad-based financial outcomes has been promising (e.g., Rucci, Kirn, & Quinn, 1998). Thus, whereas some progress has been made in demonstrating the more tangible benefits of strategic HR initiatives, the lack of comprehensive and systematic methods for doing so has left such initiatives disproportionately vulnerable to cost cutting.

Program Evaluation in Human Resources

In contrast to the use of scorecards (which cover a breadth of organizational indicators) and other more narrowly focused methods (which we mention later), a more comprehensive and systematic approach to measuring, documenting, and communicating the value of HR is to utilize formal program evaluation. Unlike other methods, program evaluation is a tool that when used well (a) determines the quality or value of programs that have been, or are being, implemented; (b) explicitly considers the alternative interventions available; and (c) includes assessment of financial and/or nonfinancial impact.

Program evaluation is a systematic process for determining the merit of alternative activities that have been or are being implemented, usually for the purpose of selecting a preferred option for future implementations. A program is a set of activities designed to accomplish something of value to an organization. Examples of programs in this context include a benefits package, a personnel selection system, a 360-degree feedback program, a mentoring program, and a culture change effort. Program evaluation is useful for decision makers who must choose whether to (a) modify an existing program, (b) expand or eliminate an existing program, or (c) select an alternative program that will more effectively accomplish pressing business objectives.

The most common form of program evaluation is program monitoring and documentation (i.e., checking whether the program is on time, on target, and on budget relative to identified goals). To determine whether the program is on target, one would likely be interested in examining progress against stated outcome goals, such as decreased turnover, increased customer satisfaction, or increased sales. A more thorough evaluation strategy that goes a step beyond monitoring would also include an open-ended exploration of any unintended effects (or implementation/process issues) that had not been foreseen at the design stage. For example, a program might be significantly more time-consuming than is appropriate for its users (an unforeseen time cost), or unanticipated outcomes might ripple through other parts of the organizational system (Senge, 1991). The evaluator may also examine the efficiency, ethicality, and legality of the means by which those outcomes were achieved.

In its highest form, evaluation should go further and consider the organization's strategic goals. A *strategic evaluation* would do all the above with (a) deliberate links to organizational strategy (Martineau, 2001; Rose, 2001) and (b) tough comparisons with alternative activities that might produce effects of similar value (Scriven, 1991). Thus, the bottom line in strategic evaluation is whether the program represents the most cost-effective use of available resources to produce outcomes of the greatest possible strategic value to the organization and its stakeholders.

Evaluation Myths

Despite the growing interest in formal evaluation of HR programs, we still see several roadblocks that prevent some organizations from committing to this results-based method of decision making. These roadblocks come in the form of commonly held beliefs about evaluation and research that prevent decision makers from using formal evaluation and leave them instead with informal methods that are prone to bias, judgment errors, and myopia. In our experience, when formal evaluation is either not used (or it is used but runs into difficulties), the primary culprit is not poorly designed research so much as misplaced expectations born of a variety of myths about the evaluation process.

Myth 1: It Is Impossible to Measure . . .

Nearly all evaluators have stories about the myths that we encounter, but perhaps the most common is the notion that "it is impossible to measure (insert just about anything here)." Some managers won't even consider conducting a formal evaluation because they assume the issues involved just can't be measured. The truth is that reliable and accurate measurement of human behavior is often difficult, but not impossible.

For example, consider the wide range of measures available to the HR manager today. We have very sophisticated measures of employee satisfaction, customer satisfaction, individual and department-level competencies, organizational commitment, and even the amorphous organizational culture. Certainly, measurement of complex constructs can require a high degree of creativity as well as expertise in assessment techniques. The basic skills required for this kind of evaluation include an understanding of organizational change, techniques for research design, statistical analysis, assessment methods, and a familiarity with measurement theory and various evaluation methods. The more sophisticated an evaluation becomes, the greater the depth of knowledge required in each of these areas. Often managers assume that because *they* do not see how to measure something, it cannot be done. This is equivalent to people's assuming that because their financial lives are too complicated for any one of them to successfully complete his or her own tax return, no one can. In fact, this is why we have accountants—to help us see and do what we cannot. The same issue faces many evaluations. When things get complex, they just may require an expert with the skills to do what seems impossible.

Myth 2: There Are Too Many Variables to Do a Good Study

Often managers have the sense that so many different things impact a particular goal that it isn't possible to tease out the effect of any one program. For example, we once faced a client who wondered how we could know that a particular management training program caused employee satisfaction to increase when any number of other related programs could have made the difference. In fact, when we measure any aspect of human behavior we can never be 100% sure that X causes Y, but there is a wide range of methods that can be used to tease out effects of specific programs to an appropriate level of certainty, given the context. In this case, we increased our confidence in causality by randomly assigning groups to the early training group (January/February) or the late group (April/May) and then comparing results measured in March before the second group was trained. The randomization procedure was actually seen as a benefit because it was the fairest way to determine who received the training first and who had to wait. Even when it is not possible to use random assignment and other experimental or quasi-experimental techniques, a range of alternative methods (both qualitative and quantitative) exists for understanding causal links (Davidson, 2000, in press).

Myth 3: No One Is Asking for Evaluation, So Why Bother?

A third myth that has baffled many evaluators is the notion that since no one outside of HR has specifically asked for an evaluation, it is not necessary. We once heard this argument from a vice president of HR at a large company who followed with the statement, "We're smart people. Everyone here assumes that because we have Ph.D.s our programs are great." Though we have no doubt that HR managers develop programs with the best of intentions, it is equally true that the best-laid plans go awry. Just as we recognize that even top performers in the organization can take their performance to the next level, so too does a very good program often have room for improvement.

More often than not, there is more than enough room for improvement to make the payoffs of an evaluation well worth the investment. Without systematic evaluation, one is left with the assumption that a program is fully effective and no means by which to identify how it might be enhanced. For example, an effective 360-degree feedback program may improve performance for 60% of the managers who participate, but how much greater impact might such a program have if an analysis were done of the 40% who gained little? Perhaps half of those who struggled with the program might have gained considerably more with something as simple as supplementing their feedback with a list of relevant employee development resources.

Even if the program is working extremely well, it is always in danger of being cut when times are lean unless there is documented evidence of its impact. The point is, don't assume a program that *should* work well actually *did* work well or that its value is obvious without hard evidence. Find out, and document its value!

Myth 4: Negative Results Will Hurt My Program

Perhaps the greatest myth of all is the notion that negative results will hurt a pet program or cast doubts on the HR department in general. Many programs are never evaluated, or an evaluation is conducted, but the results are buried in an effort to avoid hearing "bad news." Often political considerations are thought to outweigh the need to know the truth about a program. The pitfalls here are obvious. Untold resources have been expended on programs that are of little benefit in the name of not hearing bad news. Even more important, these poorly performing programs are almost always found out eventually, and the length of time they have been allowed to continue despite dismal track records reflects very poorly on the department concerned. In our experience, finding out a program's flaws—and then working proactively to address them—can be far more valuable in the long term than finding out how great a program is in an effort to sell it.

Many top-performing companies advocate deliberately pushing the envelope in order to achieve "fast failure." For example, as Jack Welch—former CEO of General Electric—argued, firms that experiment with something new and reach failure before their competitors have the chance to be the first to learn about a new product, market, or technology (Slater, 2001). There is no reason that the same attitude about experimentation and learning should not be applied to innovation in HR.

In describing these myths, it should be clear that we can not only use program evaluation for continual improvement of current programs, but we can also apply what we learn from our successes and failures to maximize our chances of success in future efforts. In addition, evaluating HR programs can be an important form of organization development. By helping program managers define their program goals clearly, to link these goals to business strategy, and then to measure their progress toward these goals (as well as any unintended outcomes), evaluation can encourage a level of accountability and results orientation that can profoundly influence organizations in their quest to create value. When we add to the equation the notion of benchmarking HR programs against the most innovative and cost-effective ideas in the industry, we have a potentially very powerful mechanism for staying on the cutting edge of strategic HR.

Key Distinctions

Rather than detail the fairly extensive range of evaluation typologies, we present here a brief description of approaches to evaluation that HR managers may find useful. For those interested in finer distinctions or more theoretical background for these approaches, Worthen, Sanders, and Fitzpatrick (1997) and Stufflebeam (2001a) present good summaries of a range of evaluation philosophies and approaches.

Process Versus Outcome Evaluation

One important distinction in evaluation approaches is the contrast between process evaluation and outcome evaluation. Process evaluation assesses aspects of a program specific to program content, delivery, and/or implementation. Generally, process evaluation focuses on the program itself, rather than the recipients. For example, process evaluation of a customer-service training program would consider issues such as whether (a) the content was job relevant, (b) trainees attended all sessions, and (c) trainers were effective in their delivery. Outcome evaluation, on the other hand, focuses on the results achieved by the program. Considerations for our fictitious training program would include whether trainees applied what they learned, and whether these new skills are benefiting the organization (e.g., whether customer service improved).

Process and outcome evaluations are occasionally used separately; however, it is preferable to include both components in any evaluation. To illustrate the need for *both* process and outcome evaluations, consider the evaluation one of us conducted for a new performance bonus system in which high-performing employees were paid a 5% to 20% bonus, based on the extent to which they exceeded yearly performance objectives. No significant improvement (either statistical or practical) was found in employee motivation or performance after implementation of the new bonus system. Conclusion: the program is a failure, right? Further inquiry uncovered a critical glitch in the implementation of the new system (i.e., process evaluation). A significant number of managers had not set performance objectives for their direct reports, deciding instead to pay everyone (good and poor performers alike) a 5% bonus! Some others had set unachievably high objectives (referred to in the organization as walk on water targets), which nobody had seriously tried to achieve. Here, process evaluation uncovered precisely why the intervention was doomed to failure—inconsistent implementation had virtually wiped out the program's motivational properties.

A particularly important evaluation issue related to implementation inconsistency occurs when experimental or quasi-experimental methods are being used to compare organizational units or groups who have received an intervention with those who have not. Any comparison of these two groups implicitly assumes that the intervention has been fully implemented in the "treatment" group and not at all in the "control" group.[1] As the example described above illustrates, the reality is that different managers in different parts of the organization may implement programs to widely varying degrees. This means that a straight comparison between units would likely lead to the faulty conclusion that the intervention had no effect—an invalid conclusion because the degree of implementation is no longer a yes/no variable (implemented vs. not implemented) but one that ranges all the way from "not at all" to "fully implemented." Does this mean that it is now impossible to tell whether the program had any effect? Not at all. Professional evaluators have numerous strategies available for dealing with problems like this, as well as with tricky issues such as delayed effects (e.g., Lipsey, 1990).

Program Improvement Versus Program Selection

Program evaluation can be conducted for different purposes. The two most common distinctions of purpose are between program improvement and program selection. As the names would imply, program selection evaluation is useful for selecting among alternative programs. For example, should we use 360-degree feedback or coaching seminars to enhance manager effectiveness (or perhaps both)? In contrast, program improvement evaluation is initiated to identify facilitators and barriers within a particular program so that adjustments can make the program more effective. Evaluations of HR programs may be used for both purposes—to determine whether program improvement is a viable option (and if so, where improvements can be made), or whether an alternative intervention (or none at all) might be a better investment.

Of course, one would use both process and outcome evaluation when conducting either program improvement or program selection studies. For example, suppose we were planning to conduct a program improvement evaluation of an executive coaching intervention. A good quality evaluation would ask both process questions (e.g., about the quality of the program content and delivery) and outcome questions (e.g., transfer of training, downstream impact of the intervention). Similarly, if we were to conduct a program selection evaluation of the same program—for example, to see whether executive coaching or 360-degree feedback would be a better investment for the organization—such an evaluation should also include both process and outcome questions (see Table 1.1 for examples).

Program Evaluation Versus Utility Analysis

Utility analysis is often mistakenly seen as a form of program evaluation. The basic idea in utility analysis is to calculate the utility, or dollar value of savings, expected from implementing a program. The method is typically used for personnel selection systems when a validity coefficient is available. Considerable literature has been devoted to refining the ways in which utility is computed, but the underlying goal for all utility methods is to estimate the potential dollar gains that would result from using a particular hiring system. (See the Glossary for more technical information on utility analysis.)

Some authors have questioned the practicality of utility analysis as a sole means for evaluating HR programs (e.g., Latham & Whyte, 1994). We suggest that utility analysis is often a useful tool but should not be considered a complete evaluation. Utility analysis examines only one outcome (expected dollar savings) rather than examining a range of intended and unanticipated outcomes (not all of which can be reduced to monetary terms). Thus, whereas utility analysis would address the narrow question of anticipated financial benefits to be realized by implementing a program, it would not adequately address the program's broader strategic impact, including ripple effects that can occur throughout the system.

Table 1.1   Example Questions for the Evaluation of Executive Performance Improvement Interventions

Purpose of Evaluation	Type of Evaluation Question	
	Process Question	*Outcome Question*
Program Improvement	How well does the content covered correspond to executives' most pressing performance problems?	How effectively do executives who complete this program apply their new knowledge and skills on the job?
Program Selection	How does the breadth and depth of coverage compare with that in a 360-degree feedback intervention?	How do direct reports' assessments of their supervisor's performance change 6 months after the program?

Who Does Program Evaluation?

Informal evaluation is typically done by those who implement or are impacted by a program, whereas formal evaluation has a much wider range of parties who might be involved in a systematic assessment. Formal program evaluation may be conducted by (a) the individuals or teams who designed, developed, and/or implemented the program (e.g., HR staff); (b) others from the organization (often program sponsors); (c) external evaluation contractors; or (d) a combination of these. Table 1.2 highlights some of the distinctions among these options, as well as key considerations for deciding who should evaluate a particular HR program.

Each of the three types of evaluators comes with both an upside and a downside, but all three are certainly capable of conducting useful evaluations to fulfill the varying needs HR has at different times. The main point in this analysis is to suggest that when working with any of these types of evaluators, consumers of the evaluation should be conscious of the potential pitfalls and take steps to address them. For example, one can ameliorate the potential problems of working with an external evaluator by finding an experienced evaluator who specializes in HR evaluation (but not program implementation) and thus is not as motivated to recommend changes that will result in more program-related consulting work. Also, to prevent the loss of evaluation knowledge after the project, you might have an evaluation coach or facilitator who works to build the evaluation capacity of the organization during evaluation (e.g., Fetterman, Kaftarian, & Wandersman, 1996; Patton, 1997; Preskill & Torres, 1999). The major challenges to using HR staff as evaluators can be addressed by having an evaluation specialist within the HR department—that is, someone whose sole focus is evaluating HR programs and who has considerable experience with formal evaluation. Keep in mind, however, that when working with HR staff as evaluators, internal politics and perceptions of biased motivations may be difficult to overcome. Not much can be done to address the issues with using other internal staff as evaluators. However, it is critical to

(Text continues on page 13)

Table 1.2   Advantages and Disadvantages of Different Types of Evaluators[2]

	Types of Program Evaluators		
	HR Staff	Other Internal Staff	External Evaluation Consultants
Knowledge of the organization and HR's history with the program	(+) Have in-depth knowledge of both the organization and its history with HR program being evaluated.	(+/–) Have in-depth knowledge of the organization but may have limited knowledge of HR program specifics.	(–) Will lack this knowledge initially if it is the first time that they have worked with the organization.
Knowledge of industry best practices for specific HR program and program evaluation techniques	(+/–) May be aware of program best practices but unlikely to have evaluation-specific expertise. Without specific evaluation expertise, may use inappropriate evaluation methods.	(–) Are unlikely to know about best practices for an area outside their expertise—including both evaluation and the program area.	(+) High level of evaluation-specific skills as well as exposure to the various practices of multiple clients and best practices for program being evaluated.
Credibility with decision makers and stakeholders	(–) Decision makers may question motivations for conclusions (e.g., self-serving bias). Depending on HR's history in the company, may have their expertise and therefore credibility underestimated by their organizational peers.	(+/–) May partially compensate for their lack of HR and evaluation expertise by being (a) a high-level stakeholder, (b) a representative of stakeholder groups, and/or (c) seen as having no vested interest in the program's success.	(+) May have higher credibility because the organization formally picked them for their evaluation objectivity and expertise with the HR program. However, even external consultants are not immune to general positive bias.
Potential constraints to a frank evaluation	(–) May not be totally objective because the program belongs to the HR department, and a negative assessment may reflect badly on the department (or even get them fired).	(+) May have fewer direct reasons for biasing the evaluation outcome than do the other two types of evaluators, unless (as is often the case) they have a need to keep HR on their good side.	(+/–) May be more frank because they are not constrained by internal politics. However, objectivity may be limited if they (a) want repeat business or (b) helped design the HR program being evaluated.
Fresh perspective	(–) May have little experience outside HR or outside the organization, which	(+/–) May have limited experience outside the organization but bring a useful perspective	(+) Have spent time in other organizations, so can review the program with these other

(Continued)

Table 1.2 Continued

	Types of Program Evaluators		
	HR Staff	*Other Internal Staff*	*External Evaluation Consultants*
	could limit options explored. Could also be overly conscious of former constraints or traditions that no longer apply.	from outside HR. Might consider internal constraints/norms, but could generate new ways of looking at things.	examples in mind. Not bound by internal constraints/traditions and are likely to push for new ways of looking at issues.
Time and dollar cost of the evaluation	(+/–) May work on pieces of the evaluation as part of their normal HR program duties, and program familiarity may result in more rapid completion of those pieces. But most HR personnel do not have extensive evaluation expertise, so will require more time on the evaluation learning curve and may in the end not deliver the most valuable analysis without expert assistance.	(–) Take time away from their normal job to do the evaluation (opportunity costs); doing work outside one's area of expertise (both content and evaluation expertise) probably results in poorer return relative to cost. But can take back to the home unit a better understanding of HR's strategic role.	(+/–) May charge a higher daily rate than the cost of in-house employees, but evaluation expertise (a) means less time spent on the evaluation learning curve and (b) can help minimize the opportunity costs associated with internal staff involvement. Evaluation skills are not retained in the organization.
Design of a practical implementation plan for program changes	(+) May attempt to limit the changes because of internal HR turf concerns. However, involvement of HR staff in the evaluation (or at least the design of recommendations) is probably the most effective way to get practical changes and maximum buy-in and follow-through.	(–) Probably have limited HR-specific knowledge and thereby have limited ability to design the plan to fit with other HR programs.	(+/–) Experience outside the organization plus content expertise may contribute innovative ideas from elsewhere. However, may have insufficient knowledge of political and budgetary constraints to design something practical, unless there is substantial input from HR and the rest of the organization.

Table 1.2 Continued

	Types of Program Evaluators		
	HR Staff	Other Internal Staff	External Evaluation Consultants
Program evaluation and HR program knowledge left in the organization after the evaluation	(+/–) Keep some evaluation expertise in-house because a member of the HR staff will have been a member of (or a liaison to) the evaluation team, but the amount of knowledge gained will be limited unless the evaluation process has been facilitated by a knowledgeable evaluator.	(–) Will lose their HR knowledge as a result of disuse, and transfer of new evaluation skills will probably be limited because transfer is to new content domain.	(–) Take their knowledge with them when they exit the organization, *unless* additional consulting occurs, or unless the evaluation is conducted in participatory mode (with HR staff involvement).

include these stakeholders on any evaluation team as they often provide invaluable perspectives and will help the evaluation stay focused on business needs.

The best of all possible worlds is for organizations to support an internal evaluation unit that cuts across all functions (see Love, 1991; Sonnichsen, 2000) and supplement this with occasional external evaluations to inject a fresh perspective. Internal evaluation departments are typically given considerable latitude within organizations for providing critical feedback and often are isolated from functional units, so they experience none of the internal pressures for positive findings bias. To date, this approach to evaluation has not become commonplace; however, an increasing emphasis on accountability for results may lead to an upswing in these internal evaluation teams.

Choosing Criteria for Success

Kirkpatrick (1959a, 1959b, 1960a, 1960b) pointed out that evaluation should consider several different *types* of effects that programs may have. Though first introduced in the context of training evaluation, Kirkpatrick's four levels of evaluation data—(a) participant reactions, (b) learning, (c) behavior change, and (d) results—provide a useful framework for any evaluation. More recent thinking in training evaluation extends Kirkpatrick's work by exploring different linkages between the levels (Alliger & Janek, 1989) and expanding the learning level to include cognitive, affective, and skill-based outcomes (Kraiger, Ford, & Salas, 1993). In our experience,

Kirkpatrick's levels are quite intuitive and can be applied to a wide range of HR programs in that nearly all such programs are targeted at creating organizational change through individuals.

The most popular and widely used evaluation tool is a Level 1 reaction survey administered after participating in a program (usually some form of training). Though these surveys are widely used, they are also widely dismissed. This is unfortunate because knowing what people think of a program can provide essential process feedback for making improvements. Having seen untold numbers of these forms, however, we believe that some attention to thoughtful design and measurement standards could go a long way toward improving the usefulness of the data they collect. Just as a simple example, far more useful information could be obtained by moving away from satisfaction ratings and addressing the extent to which specific, work-relevant needs were met. In our experience, satisfaction ratings are often inflated so badly that simple average scores are nearly impossible to interpret.

Generally, learning (Level 2) is fairly straightforward to measure and interpret by comparing pretest average scores to posttest averages. Levels 3 and 4 become somewhat more complex. Measuring Level 3 (behavior change on the job) almost always involves use of qualitative methods such as interviewing or on-the-job observation, but we have also found success with specific behavioral checklists. Level 4 (results, or impact on the bottom line) is the Holy Grail of HR program evaluation.

Strategic use of Kirkpatrick's four levels is not simply a matter of picking one or two of the levels and assessing performance on those. The real power of the levels is the ability to trace impacts all the way from program implementation down to the bottom line. After all, good intervention content and delivery/implementation (which a good Level 1 evaluation would assess) is valuable only insofar as it leads to actual learning (Level 2). Knowledge and skill acquisition, in turn, have value to the organization only when it is actually applied on the job to enhance performance (Level 3). And improved performance on the job is meaningless unless it adds at least some demonstrable financial and/or strategic value to the organization in terms of short-term performance and/or long-term potential (Level 4).

Although the downstream impacts of an HR intervention (Levels 3 and 4) clearly represent the most strategically important evaluation questions, the upstream information (Levels 1 and 2) is essential for demonstrating that it was in fact the program (and not something else) that caused improvements in individual, business unit, and/or organizational performance. When times are lean and budgets are under pressure, HR managers need all the evidence they can muster to demonstrate the value their best programs are adding to the organization. Otherwise, HR programs are seen as "nice if we can do them, but no real strategic value" luxuries that are first to fall under the ax when times are tough.

Practical Design Considerations

When choosing a research design, keep in mind that the alternative to the imperfect study is usually no systematic analysis at all. Standards of proof for any evaluation are completely context specific. Therefore, you should provide only the level of confidence that is necessary, rather than throwing in the methodological kitchen sink. As with statistical concerns, a good idea is to involve an expert in research design who is sensitive to the realities of doing evaluation in organizational settings. Large organizations may have HR research departments with evaluation specialists who can assist with such considerations, but organizations without such resources should seek outside counsel.

Standards of Proof

100% certainty is an unachievable and unnecessary goal in HR program evaluation. As in a criminal or civil trial, the evidence needs to be sufficiently compelling to satisfy the relevant standards of proof in that context (e.g., beyond reasonable doubt or the balance of evidence). Similarly, in evaluation, it is necessary to produce a body of evidence that will stand up to scrutiny and is commensurate with the relative costs of Type I (erroneously attributing a coincidental change to the program) and Type II errors (erroneously concluding that an effect caused by the program was coincidental). Additional information about Type I and Type II errors can be found in the Glossary.

An important first step for the evaluator is an information needs assessment to establish the degree of certainty to which conclusions about causality must be drawn. Preferably, this should be addressed when assessing the feasibility of evaluating the program. Specifically, one must consider (a) what information is needed, (b) to what degree of certainty, and (c) within what time and budgetary constraints. Note that clarifying these issues is not simply a matter of asking the program manager (or evaluation client) what he or she thinks is needed; helping to determine information needs for a client who is uncertain about them is an important part of the evaluator's job.

Designing an Adequate Evaluation

Recently one of us completed a study and cautioned that the results did not constitute incontrovertible proof of the program's effect. In preparing for the next study in the same organization, the client requested a proposal for the perfect study that would leave no doubt about the program's effectiveness. The complexity of organizations makes doubt something we must live with. Program evaluation utilizes a number of methods, including experimental, quasi-experimental, and qualitative designs, none of which alone can provide unquestionable proof of a program's effectiveness (for more detailed description of these research methods see Phillips, 1997). Evaluation designs typically involve some sort of observation (interviews, focus groups, tests, surveys, etc.) before, during, and/or after a program is implemented. Conclusions about the programs are dependent on the validity of causal inferences regarding documented changes. None of these inferences are perfect, but by using some tried and true techniques, we can be increasingly confident about the results.

A common concern about nonexperimental studies is that they do not adequately account for *all* extraneous factors that may influence the impact of a particular program. As Sackett and Mullen (1993) have pointed out, however, "there are alternatives to true experimental design which can, under some circumstances, be of value and may be better than no evaluation at all" (p. 622). Some of those alternatives include causal tracing techniques that can employ a blend of qualitative and/or quantitative methods to build a plausible case for causation (Davidson, 2000, in press).

The important thing to remember when evaluating HR programs is that the choice is not between complex, rigorous, high-budget experimental research and cheaper but weaker quasi-experimental or completely nonexperimental studies. Rather, the choice is between doing an imperfect study that nevertheless meets the needs of HR or not doing a study at all. When no systematic program evaluation findings are available, potentially expensive decisions may be based on whatever data are available, including individual testimonials, the persuasiveness of a salesperson or marketing materials, or internal political concerns. Thus, findings from systematic and well-thought-out qualitative and mixed method nonexperimental designs may be a dramatic improvement over unsystematic alternatives.

Measurement Issues

Though we can never be 100% sure of our conclusions, there are some guiding principles that every competent evaluation study should include to improve our confidence in the findings. In consideration of space, we discuss only two issues related to accuracy of measurement and do not delve into the fairly extensive world of research design. For those interested in a more detailed treatment of research design, we refer you to Chapter 7 of Phillips's (1997) book on training evaluation.

Reliability and Validity

Two critical tenets of effective measurement are reliability and validity. Though detailed treatment of these concepts is available in Robie and Raju's chapter, some mention of their application to the evaluation process is useful here. Measures used in evaluating programs must be both reliable and valid. Unfortunately, HR evaluators can easily overlook these considerations when developing both quantitative and qualitative measures for evaluations, especially under challenging time and resource constraints. An instrument with good validity is one that measures what it is supposed to measure (e.g., a measure of coaching skills should actually provide an accurate indication of an individual's ability to help others enhance their performance, not public speaking ability or general charisma).

Reliability refers to the consistency of a measure (i.e., getting the same results under a variety of conditions). We need assessments that have a high degree of reliability so we can be confident that if we were to observe the same skill level for the same person under several conditions we would get essentially the same result. We want to be sure the results we get on the assessment are a true measure of the individual's ability (on coaching skills, for example) and are not caused by the unique conditions under which the person was observed, interviewed, or tested.

Validity in evaluation is one step more complex than validity of the measures used. Not only does the evaluation need to accurately gauge different levels of performance on relevant criteria, but it also needs to have a sound basis for determining how meritorious these results are. In other words, evaluators not only have to present results (just as applied researchers do), but we also have to explicitly ascribe *value* to them in the context of the organization's strategic goals. The step from saying "there was a 15% decrease in turnover" to "this is an exceptional result, given the organization's strategic needs and current market conditions" has to be based systematically on a robust mix of quality information, appropriately combined.

The reliability of an evaluation goes beyond the reliability of measures. For the HR practitioner, the reliability of the evaluation may also mean that another evaluator would have drawn more or less the same conclusions, while validity would mean that those conclusions were accurate and clearly justifiable. To ensure good reliability and validity of the evaluation overall, strong evaluations use a meta-evaluator to assess the quality of the evaluation, cross-checking findings as necessary. In the wake of recent corporate scandals highlighting the fallibility of auditors (e.g., Enron and Arthur Andersen), the use of meta-evaluators (and meta-auditors, for that matter) has become increasingly important.

Quantitative and Qualitative Data

Often we run into managers with a strong bias for quantitative data. Managers are trained to focus on the bottom line, and generally the bottom line involves numbers. We frequently hear statements like "We want the hard facts," "Show us the numbers," and "We don't want any of that touchy-feely stuff, just straightforward objective data." The meaning and value of data are based to some extent on judgment or opinion, but people often get seduced into thinking that once information is converted into numbers it is somehow more objective than it was when it was words! Turnover is a good example. It sounds objective because it is based on numbers, and it has direct financial implications, but there are about a dozen ways to compute turnover (e.g., see Cascio, 1991). For instance, should the turnover figure include people leaving to attend school or change careers? Should it include people who are demoted? What about layoffs or people who are let go and then rehired as subcontractors?

The bias in favor of quantitative data can be counter-productive in program evaluation in cases where qualitative data are more appropriate (see Patton, 1990). Qualitative data are more useful than quantitative data when (a) the evaluator needs to obtain the unique perspectives of the participants or (b) we are asking questions about a program for which a wide range of unpredictable responses or outcomes are possible and are not known at the outset of the study. Conversely, quantitative data are more appropriate when the evaluator knows in some detail what questions to ask and needs to access a large number of respondents. Even then, quantitative questions should be augmented with respondents' open-ended comments. One of the most important questions to ask at the end of any survey or interview is "Can you think of anything else about this program I should know that we did not already discuss?" Failing to ask this question amounts to assuming you have thought of everything—seldom true, even for very experienced evaluators.

The relevant question is not whether to use quantitative *or* qualitative data, but rather how to use *both* in a way that will provide the clearest and most accurate conclusions. Including the right combination of qualitative and quantitative data is crucial to reliable and valid measurement of program impact. It is far more important to find answers to the questions that mean the most to your organization than to insist on seemingly objective quantitative measures.

Costs and Benefits

Like many HR programs, evaluation is often seen as an unnecessary expense drawing away resources that could be used for the organization's "real" business of manufacturing products or delivering services. Certainly, costs are associated with doing evaluation, just as costs are associated with having a good HR function. In both cases, it is necessary to carefully consider the kinds of resources that the organization can reasonably commit—and that will yield the greatest strategic benefit. In this section, we discuss the various kinds of benefits that HR program evaluation can bring and the cost-benefit trade-offs associated with choosing among the options in any particular case.

HR needs to work through two steps (preferably with the assistance of an evaluation expert who has broad knowledge of the field) when deciding what approach should be used for conducting an evaluation in any particular case. The first step is to clearly identify exactly what HR (and the organization as a whole) needs from an evaluation, in both practical and strategic terms. Is the focus on improving an existing program, gathering evidence about its overall cost-effectiveness, or building the organization's (or HR's) knowledge base or capacity to learn? The second step is to map out the evaluation options that will substantially meet those needs—preferably including a range of cost options—and to discuss the trade-offs among the costs and benefits. The purpose of this second step is to decide which blend of evaluation approaches or designs will provide the greatest strategic value within the organization's practical constraints (time, budget, availability of staff time, etc).

Identifying Human Resource Needs

The use of evaluation in organizations brings with it three broad categories of benefits. The first benefit is useful information to help with program improvement or streamlining. This might be the case with a relatively new and experimental program that the organization is unfamiliar with. After all, how many new interventions work perfectly the first time? Early evaluation can mean the difference between a new program's being able to "find its feet" in a reasonable length of time versus floundering for so long that it never reaches its full potential before it is discontinued. Improvement-oriented evaluation can also be useful for taking a new look at a mature program to see whether tried-and-true methods could be improved on in light of recent advances in the field or whether different approaches are needed because of changes in strategy or workforce needs.

The second potential benefit of evaluation to HR is the provision of evidence about program effectiveness or value. This may be used for accountability, for example, when the organization needs to ascertain what return it received on the investment it made in HR (or in a particular program). Evidence about effectiveness may also be produced proactively to build credibility for the program or for political leverage (such as justifying budget requests). Information about relative value/effectiveness is also necessary for making good program selection decisions (e.g., comparing interventions to see which should be implemented more widely).

The third major payoff of evaluation is as a knowledge-generating mechanism that allows HR to experiment with different ways of doing things and learn about what works best, for whom, and why. Learning can occur at two levels: (a) gathering information about the relative effectiveness of various innovations so that it is retained in organizational memory, and (b) "learning how to learn"—building the capacity of the HR unit to generate useful knowledge for itself and for the wider organization.

HR will, at different times, have a need for each of the above benefits (and sometimes two or three of them simultaneously) with respect to many of the programs and systems it implements. If there are multiple potential benefits, these should be listed and prioritized. Having thought through these priorities, HR will then need to consider the various evaluation design options.

Considering Cost-Benefit Trade-Offs

There are many different approaches to conducting an evaluation, each of which brings with it different combinations of the above benefits, as well as different kinds of costs. Although mapping out all the possibilities cannot be done here, the following brief discussion will highlight some of the main considerations. A competent evaluation specialist will be able to identify many more options that will fit a particular situation, and HR practitioners are encouraged to use such expertise when making decisions about evaluation approaches. Table 1.3 details some of the key considerations relating to each of the benefits to HR of conducting an evaluation, an example of an evaluation approach that is likely to best address each benefit, and the main financial and nonfinancial costs associated with that approach. One of the most difficult trade-offs organizations need to make occurs when evaluation knowledge and skills or buy-in/commitment to findings are key. In such cases, substantial staff involvement in the evaluation process is frequently the most effective strategy, but one that comes with a cost—considerable staff time spent away from regular assignments. In many cases the payoff will clearly outweigh this cost; but in other cases, compromises will need to be made.

Table 1.3 Costs and Benefits of Evaluation

Benefits to HR	Considerations/ Assumptions	Potentially Powerful Evaluation Approach	Main Costs (money and nonmoney)
1. Incremental program improvement	Staff commitment to implementation of improvements often crucial; if improvements are more incremental than transformational, external expertise may not yet be required	Internal/self-evaluation (HR staff design and conduct own evaluation)	Staff time spent designing and conducting evaluation; additional time often needed due to lack of evaluation expertise; opportunity costs associated with drawing staff away from regular assignments
2. Documenting effectiveness OR transformational program improvement	Perceived independence of evaluator often (though not always) important	Independent evaluator conducts systematic assessment	Evaluator's consulting fee (will represent less time than total with staff involvement—expertise allows faster completion of work, as does lack of consensus decision making during evaluation); minimal staff time (providing information to evaluator, assisting with making contacts)
3a. Generating knowledge for organizational learning 3b. Building HR capacity for learning	Evaluation questions often extend beyond "what works" into understanding why (may require use of theory-based evaluation and more complex methodologies); important to impart knowledge and skills to staff	Involve evaluation specialists in conducting initial evaluation training and then in facilitating an actual evaluation to coach staff members in applying skills. Include creation of knowledge management system for future use	Evaluator's consulting fee; considerable staff time and opportunity costs (time away from regular assignments); knowledge management system may require IT expertise

Concluding Comments on Costs and Benefits

HR departments are currently endeavoring to answer the demand from other business units that they demonstrably add value to the organization's bottom line and are also having to try new strategies that meet the needs of the organization.

Inevitably, cutting-edge innovations seldom work perfectly the first time they are tried, nor are the benefits of even the best programs usually intuitively obvious to those outside HR. Given these considerations, two of the more immediate potential costs of not conducting evaluations include (a) needing a longer time to bring innovative interventions up to their full potential, which has budgetary consequences as well as an impact on HR's perceived ability to design high-quality programs, and (b) being armed with little more than anecdotal evidence about program effectiveness when tough questions are being asked at the senior level.

In the longer term, organizations often fail to leverage the potential for generating and reflecting on powerful new knowledge about what works when it comes to attracting, developing, and retaining the lifeblood of the organization (its people). By critically examining the successes and failures experienced while trying out interventions, policies, and strategies related to people management, HR can be in a much better position to design more effective programs and to contribute to organizational longevity and effectiveness.

Clearly, there are many substantial benefits of proactively conducting good evaluations that will arm HR with answers to questions sought by other organizational stakeholders as well as HR practitioners and that will build its ability to design ever more effective HR interventions. As a general rule of thumb, it is a good idea to allow for 10% to 20% of the total cost of an intervention as budget for evaluation (whether done internally or externally). Evaluation budgets should be set at a level that yields the maximum possible return on investment for HR as well as for the organization as a whole.

The alternative to systematic evaluation is to assume that the HR staff will somehow be able to divine where, when, and how the programs need to be improved—and will be able to convey this convincingly to other organizational stakeholders without the benefit of hard evidence. The risk with such an approach is that HR ends up in a *reactive* role, wherein systems are changed and improved only when the crescendo of complaints from the other organizational stakeholders gets loud enough to force some action. Clearly, if marketing were operating like that with respect to meeting their customers' needs, the organization would struggle to survive.

The HR department of the new millennium needs to take a proactive role, innovating and experimenting with new ways of doing things and having good methods available for sorting out which of these are the best. By linking these activities to organizational strategy, the HR department has a real opportunity to prove itself as a value-adding strategic partner to the business units it serves.

Utilization

It may seem obvious, but actually using what you learn from an evaluation is a critical component of the process. Having invested considerable resources to understand the impact a program may or may not be having, it is critical that HR managers take advantage of this knowledge and apply the findings by fixing program problems, eliminating poor performing programs, or expanding effective programs to new settings.

Evaluation Readiness

The old adage that "you can lead a horse to water, but you can't make it drink" is all too appropriate for program evaluation. Organizations must have at least a base level of evaluation readiness if program evaluation is to have any level of success. Essential ingredients include a de-emphasis on political decision making, an openness to change, and a general orientation toward continual improvement. Among organizations in which these characteristics are not well developed, it may be a good idea to start small with a highly participative low-stakes evaluation to gradually introduce the idea of using evaluation data to assist in decision making and educate organizational members about what is involved and why.

Communicating Results

One of the major goals of any study is to communicate the successes of a program and the needs for change. Even the most elegant evaluation design can be poorly communicated, leaving the study useless for most audiences. Clearly communicating study findings involves three basic concepts: (a) keep it simple; (b) keep it brief; and (c) use language, measures, and presentation methods that fit the audience. Only on rare occasions should statistics be presented in detail. Rather, they should be included in a full report (preferably in an appendix) and available to the interested reader. As Cascio (1991) pointed out, "the language of business is dollars, not correlation coefficients" (p. vii). For instance, regardless of your statistical brilliance, we do not recommend sharing with managers the finding that a new selection test predicts 16% of the variance in performance ratings for new hires. It may be more useful to point out that turnover has been reduced by 53% since introducing a new selection system, for an estimated savings of $320,000 in turnover costs companywide. Of course, this turnover example is susceptible to several alternative explanations, but no doubt you will have collected considerable process data to support your conclusions.

It is usually impossible (not to mention unadvisable) to avoid the use of statistics in evaluation, but it is essential to use statistics only as tools for creating clearly communicable information. Recent research on the most effective methods of communicating statistical results to managers has demonstrated the importance of using data that are clear, to the point, easily understood, and presented in a way familiar to employees (Kuthy & Svyantek, 1996). Equally important in evaluation is the ability to condense a large amount of detailed information into a concise summary of results. Here are the rules of thumb: For a report to managers, you need a two-page bullet-point summary. For senior managers, you need one page. And for the CEO, you need a concise profile summary of the program's performance on 5 to 10 dimensions.

Applying Findings

The results of a good evaluation study will help guide important decisions about your organization or program. The real benefits of evaluation occur when positive findings are used to guide program enhancements and negative findings are used for program development. Ideally, evaluation results should be used as one step in a continual improvement process. Keep in mind, however, that this process relies on a staff dedicated to understanding and using evaluation findings—and who are recognized for doing so.

To ensure the maximum usefulness of evaluation results, all constituents with an interest in the program should (where possible and appropriate) be included in a presentation of the results and be provided copies of a full report or an executive summary. Often it is useful to allow certain groups to review the results before they are made public. This can allow internal stakeholders to understand the results and formulate strategies for addressing areas of concern before others within the organization begin asking for program changes. During this process, however, it is essential that a continual improvement orientation be taken so that the data can be used for development rather than punishment. Otherwise, evaluation findings will be resisted, attacked, and then buried. Also, when dealing with highly sensitive programs, evaluators may want to consider the potential for leaking such early results. In these situations, it is not uncommon to present findings orally for preliminary discussions, but to withhold written documentation until the official release date.

One difficulty often faced by evaluators is the question of "who is the evaluation client or consumer?" This is equally true for internal and external evaluators as well as program managers who are conducting self-evaluation. Without careful attention to this issue, evaluation can easily become a tool for advancing individual agendas. This issue should be clearly sorted out prior to commencing the evaluation, as should several other matters including ownership of data, confidentiality issues, and rebuttal procedures. For a comprehensive checklist for evaluation contracting, see Stufflebeam (2001b).

Even with careful planning, the identity of the client can become a moving target, especially in fast-moving organizations. With changing personnel, mergers, and even shifting goals and strategies, you may need to renegotiate the evaluation contract to adapt to these organizational realities. Similar to admonitions by organizational development specialists, it is essential that evaluators, when determining evaluation criteria and appropriate standards, see *the organization as a whole* as the client. In order to maintain focus on the organization as the client, both internal and external evaluators need to be extremely careful not to adopt the agenda of one particular group of stakeholders. Rather, it is the evaluator's responsibility to ensure that all relevant perspectives are included and that all evaluative conclusions are well founded in fact and transparent with respect to any assumptions used. Evaluators need to be aware of their own assumptions and biases, take measures to balance these with other perspectives, and avoid evaluations in which their own strongly held views conflict with the basic tenets of the program.

Conclusion

Program evaluation is a tool for decision makers with an as yet unrealized potential for HR programs. If evaluation is done well, it should allow HR managers to more fully understand and clearly communicate the link between HR interventions and the strategic direction of an organization. Using existing knowledge about specific evaluation techniques and applied research in general, program evaluation can provide invaluable feedback for HR managers to improve and select among a wide range of programs. Success in conducting practical and valuable evaluation greatly depends on getting past the myths and fear of evaluation, being clear about the purpose for the study, and being realistic about implementation issues related to organizational readiness and capacity.

Note

1. This issue is sometimes referred to as "workforce saturation" and has been described in more detail elsewhere (Rose & Fiore, 1999).

2. All the above assessments are general conclusions designed to caution organization members considering a program evaluation. The conclusions could vary widely from those provided above depending on the organization's staff or the consultant. For example, if the HR staff or the consulting firm has a recognized expert for the particular type of program being evaluated, the general statements may prove incorrect. We recommend a team approach that uses various types of evaluators to benefit from the advantages of each type of evaluator and minimize their disadvantages.

References

Alliger, G. M., & Janek, E. A. (1989). Kirkpatrick's levels of training criteria: Thirty years later. *Personnel Psychology, 42,* 331–342.

Cascio, W. F. (1991). *Costing human resources: The financial impact of behavior in organizations.* Boston, MA: PWS-Kent.

Davidson, E. J. (2000). Ascertaining causality in theory-based evaluation. In P. J. Rogers, T. A. Hacsi, A. Petrosino, & T. A. Huebner (Eds.), Program theory in evaluation: Challenges and opportunities [Special issue]. *New Directions for Evaluation, 87,* 17–26.

Davidson, E. J. (in press). Linking organizational learning to the bottom line: Methodological issues, challenges, and suggestions. To appear in T. E. Kramer (Ed.), Linking organizational learning to the bottom line [Special issue]. *The Psychologist-Manager Journal.*

Fetterman, D. M., Kaftarian, S. J., & Wandersman, A. (1996). *Empowerment evaluation: Knowledge and tools for self-assessment and accountability.* Thousand Oaks, CA: Sage.

Kaplan, R. S., & Norton, D. P. (1996). *Translating strategy into action: The balanced scorecard.* Boston, MA: Harvard Business School Press.

Kirkpatrick, D. L. (1959a). Techniques for evaluating training programs. *Journal of American Society for Training & Development, 13,* 3–9.

Kirkpatrick, D. L. (1959b). Techniques for evaluating training programs: Part 2—Learning. *Journal of American Society for Training & Development, 13,* 21–26.

Kirkpatrick, D. L. (1960a). Techniques for evaluating training programs: Part 3—Behavior. *Journal of American Society for Training & Development, 14,* 13–18.

Kirkpatrick, D. L. (1960b). Techniques for evaluating training programs: Part 4—Results. *Journal of American Society for Training & Development, 14,* 28–32.

Kraiger, K., Ford, J. K., & Salas, E. (1993). Application of cognitive, skill-based, and affective theories of learning outcomes to new methods of training evaluation. *Journal of Applied Psychology, 78,* 311–328.

Kuthy, J. E., & Svyantek, D. J. (1996, April). *Probability versus statistical significance terminology as an aid in making business decisions.* Presented at the 11th annual conference of the Society of Industrial and Organizational Psychology, San Diego, CA.

Latham, G. P., & Whyte, G. (1994). The futility of utility analysis. *Personnel Psychology, 47,* 31–46.

Lipsey, M. W. (1990). *Design sensitivity: Statistical power for experimental research.* Newbury Park, CA: Sage.

Love, A. J. (1991). *Internal evaluation: Building organizations from within.* Newbury Park, CA: Sage.

Martineau, J. W. (2001, April). *Is there a role for strategic evaluation in I-O interventions?* Practitioner forum at the 16th annual conference of the Society of Industrial and Organizational Psychology, San Diego, CA.

Patton, M. Q. (1990). *Qualitative evaluation and research methods* (2nd ed.). Newbury Park, CA: Sage.

Patton, M. Q. (1997). *Utilization-focused evaluation* (3rd ed.). Thousand Oaks, CA: Sage.

Phillips, J. J. (1997). *Handbook of training evaluation* (3rd ed.). Houston, TX: Gulf Publishing.

Preskill, H., & Torres, R. T. (1999). *Evaluative inquiry for learning in organizations.* Thousand Oaks, CA: Sage.

Rose, D. S. (2001, April). *Strategic evaluation: Methods for assessing the impact of industrial/organizational psychology interventions on business critical objectives.* Presented at the 16th annual conference of the Society of Industrial and Organizational Psychology, San Diego, CA.

Rose, D. S., & Fiore, K. E. (1999). Practical considerations and alternate methods for evaluating human resources programs. *Journal of Business and Psychology, 14,* 235–251.

Rucci, A. J., Kirn, S. P., & Quinn, R. T. (1998). The employee-customer-profit chain at Sears. *Harvard Business Review, 76*(1), 83–97.

Sackett, P., & Mullen, E. J. (1993). Beyond formal experimental design: Towards an expanded view of the training evaluation process. *Personnel Psychology, 46,* 613–627.

Scriven, M. (1991). *Evaluation thesaurus* (4th ed.). Newbury Park, CA: Sage.

Senge, P. M. (1991). The fifth discipline: The art and practice of the learning organization. New York: Doubleday Currency.

Slater, R. (2001). *Get better or get beaten.* New York: McGraw-Hill.

Sonnichsen, R. C. (2000). *High impact internal evaluation: A practitioner's guide to evaluating and consulting inside organizations.* Thousand Oaks, CA: Sage.

Stufflebeam, D. L. (2001a). Evaluation models. *New Directions for Evaluation, 89.*

Stufflebeam, D. L. (2001b). Evaluation contracts checklist (online). Available: http://www.wmich.edu/evalctr/checklists/contracts.pdf

Worthen, B. R., Sanders, J. R., & Fitzpatrick, J. L. (1997). *Program evaluation, alternative approaches and practical guidelines* (2nd ed.). New York: Longman.

Suggested Reading

Phillips, J. J. (1997). *Handbook of training evaluation* (3rd ed.). Houston, TX: Gulf.

Preskill, H., & Torres, R. T. (1999). *Evaluative inquiry for learning in organizations.* Thousand Oaks, CA: Sage.

Scriven, M. (1991). *Evaluation thesaurus* (4th ed.). Newbury Park, CA: Sage.

Sonnichsen, R. C. (2000). High impact internal evaluation: A practitioner's guide to evaluating and consulting inside organizations. Thousand Oaks, CA: Sage.

Wholey, J. S., Hatry, H. P., & Newcomer, K. E. (Eds.). (1994). *Handbook of practical program evaluation.* San Francisco, CA: Jossey-Bass.

Evaluation Resources

American Evaluation Association *http://eval.org*

AEA Business & Industry Topical Interest Group *http://www.evaluationsolutions.com/aea-bi-tig/*

The Evaluators' Institute *http://www.erols.com/cwisler*

Internet-Based Resources for HR Evaluation

Downloadable evaluation and research tools (U.S. Dept. of Energy) *http://www.t2ed.com/*

Evaluation Checklist Project (The Evaluation Center, Western Michigan University) *http://evaluation.wmich.edu/checklists/*

Online Evaluation Resource Library *http://oerl.sri.com/*

Practical Assessment, Research, and Evaluation (online journal) *http://ericae.net/pare/*

CHAPTER 2

Job Analysis—The Basis for Developing Criteria for All Human Resources Programs

Peter Y. Chen

Jeanne M. Carsten

Autumn D. Krauss

A well-conducted job analysis provides fundamental information for optimally planning, coordinating, and implementing human resources (HR) programs. A job analysis is a method by which a job (i.e., one of many positions that share similar activities) is *objectively* and *systematically* broken into behavioral components such as duties, tasks, and activities (Brannick & Levine, 2002) that can be generalized across situations and over time. In addition, job analysis identifies observable knowledge and skills as well as verifiable abilities and other personal characteristics needed to perform the job. Knowledge, skills, abilities, and other characteristics (KSAOs) of a job are independent from personal characteristics of incumbents (Harvey, 1991). That is, a job rather than employees who perform the job is the focus of a job analysis.

A comprehensive, high-quality job analysis provides descriptive (i.e., how a job is done), prescriptive (i.e., how a job should be done), and predictive (i.e., how a job will be done) information about the critical tasks of a job and the KSAOs required to perform these tasks. This information allows HR professionals to engage in competent HR practices. For instance, an HR professional is able to establish legally defensible promotion criteria if required KSAOs for the target position are identified from a well-planned and well-documented job analysis. HR programs developed without an analysis of critical tasks and KSAOs are like skyscrapers built without a solid foundation.

A job analysis program should be ongoing and forward thinking—aiding in the development of strategic HR plans and cost-effective programs. Such an approach also allows HR professionals to create new positions when needed or combine jobs into a job family, which is a collection of jobs that share similar important work activities (Harvey, 1991). This chapter describes a proactive job analysis approach and how it may be applied within an organization. The discussion is organized into five sections. First, we describe uses of a proactive job analysis program. The second section links needs assessment and job analysis, while the third section describes how to conduct a job analysis program. In the fourth section, we survey several job analysis applications. Finally, we summarize key elements of a successful job analysis program accompanied with a list of evaluative criteria, which are presented throughout the chapter.

Uses of a Proactive Job Analysis Program

There are two reasons for an organization to invest resources in utilizing job analyses. First, job analyses are strongly recommended in the *Uniform Guidelines on Employee Selection Procedures* (1978) and favorably viewed in the courts (Sparks, 1988). Although there is no statute that mandates a job analysis, several laws (e.g., Americans with Disabilities Act or ADA; Equal Pay Act) do require job information that has to be derived from some systematic study of the job (Brannick & Levine, 2002). Second, the job analysis is an inherent part of management (Ghorpade, 1988) that serves four major HR functions: staffing, evaluating and rewarding performance, enhancing effectiveness, and promoting safety and health. Each function is separately discussed below.

Staffing comprises workforce planning, recruitment, selection, and placement. Workforce planning includes the forecasting and preparing of workers for the future. Job analyses identify the tasks performed and the KSAOs possessed by the current workforce or required in the future workforce as well as predict and explain how and why employees move from job to job and organization to organization. This information helps organizations develop strategic recruitment plans before facing a labor market shortage, an internal realignment, a turnover problem, or a "right-sizing" situation. Furthermore, it ensures that personnel selection or placement strategies are practical, efficient, and legally defensible. In a later section, we describe in detail how to identify these critical tasks and correspondent KSAOs to be used for different HR programs.

Job analysis offers valuable information about performance criteria on which an equitable reward system can be based. It helps organizations identify the critical KSAOs possessed by superior job incumbents and the tasks they perform, which are then used to develop performance criteria. These criteria can be utilized for the purposes of evaluating performance, rewarding performance, and providing feedback. Furthermore, we can compare two or more jobs based on tasks involved, KSAOs required, education/licensing necessary, and so on. The identified similarities and differences can be used to determine each job's relative worth and to construct job families.

A third major role of job analysis is to enhance effectiveness by optimizing individual and team performance and organizational structures, which can subsequently improve productivity. The incorporation of identified KSAOs into ongoing training and career-planning programs provides opportunities for individuals and teams to develop new skills and consequently increase performance. An organization often restructures its units so that it possesses adequate flexibility to cope with rapid changes and new challenges. To ensure the success of restructuring programs, an organization needs to identify (e.g., through selection, recruitment, evaluation, and training) people with the requisite KSAOs to direct the restructured units.

Finally, job analytic information can be used to promote worker safety and health by identifying job contexts or tasks that are less likely to lead to injuries or accidents. In addition, this information can aid in matching an individual with the job and organizational unit most likely to increase the individual's physical or psychological well-being. The findings from a job analysis can also be used to modify workflow and physical layouts to increase safety and efficiency.

Assessing the Need for a Job Analysis Program and Preparing for It

Facing pressures from global competition, service-quality challenges, and the technological revolution, HR professionals must take a strategic perspective and proactively link job analysis to business needs. They must ensure that the budgetary and personnel investments of job analyses add value to the organization. Specifically, HR professionals must show that resources invested on job analyses result in informational products that can be used to the fullest degree.

Before time and resources are invested, HR professionals should establish either formal or informal advisory panels to identify organizational needs and to increase project acceptance. In addition, HR professionals need to assess organizational readiness by identifying constraints that might influence the success of collecting job information (Hakel, Stalder, & Van De Voort, 1988). For instance, several months prior to the deadline for filing taxes can be extremely busy for tax accountants. This seasonal demand clearly impedes quality job information from being collected.

It is critical to articulate how job analysis results will help an organization reach its short- and long-term business goals so that support for the job analysis program will extend beyond the HR department. To illustrate, an organization's training division was expected to achieve the short-term goal of operating at a profit within six months after a recent "right-sizing." One specific expectation was to sell training products to other business units and other companies. Obviously, traditional responsibilities of the training staff expanded from training design and delivery to also include marketing, sales, customer service, and so on. An immediate challenge the division faced was to either identify and train internal staff or recruit and select external candidates to execute these new responsibilities. With the aid of job analysis, the organization's HR professionals easily identified which KSAOs incumbents should possess to fulfill their new responsibilities, which KSAOs distinguished superior from average incumbents, what specific tasks were involved in each training responsibility, and what KSAOs were lacking in the current personnel pool.

While planning a job analysis, HR professionals should decide what practical criteria will be used to evaluate the job analysis program. These criteria include whether both the goals of the job analysis and the expectations of the involved parties were met, how well the job analysis program was linked to business goals, and whether the job analysis reached an adequate level of thoroughness. In addition, they should plan when and how these criteria will be measured. HR professionals should also determine how the job analysis program/results will be evaluated in terms of the organization's strategic and tactical goals and the stakeholders' expectations.

Before conducting a job analysis, HR professionals should determine what criteria will be used to assess the accuracy and consistency of the resulting information. For instance, the job analysis plan should state a minimum required level of agreement among the subject-matter experts (SMEs) who will provide the job information. The plan should also include methods for identifying SMEs who tend to provide erroneous information and for evaluating the accuracy of the job analysis results.

Conducting a Job Analysis Program

While planning a job analysis program, HR professionals often ask, "What is the best approach?" This question can be considered from three perspectives: legality, comprehensiveness, and practicality. Regarding legality, according to Ghorpade (1988), neither the *Uniform Guidelines on Employee Selection Procedures* (1978) nor the courts have expressed any preference for a particular job analytic method. It is the quality of job analysis information that determines the level of legal defensibility for an organization.

A good job analysis should provide comprehensive information pertaining to the four major HR functions previously described. In other words, a job analysis should supply sufficient information about needed KSAOs and tasks prior to the development of HR programs. Job information will not be useful if it is either unreliable or invalid. In job analysis, reliability addresses the extent that job information from SMEs is similar and consistent at different times for the same job. Validity addresses the extent that job information derived by different job analysis approaches is similar and job information provided by SMEs is accurate. In other words, inferences from job information such as the importance of a task as well as the skills required to perform the task are accurate. Eventually, the validity of a job analysis program should be evaluated in terms of how well it serves different goals such as the development of selection tests, the creation of performance evaluation criteria, or the determination of rewards. For recent in-depth discussions about this issue, refer to Harvey and Wilson (2000) and Sanchez and Levine (2000). Note that these two indispensable criteria (i.e., reliability and validity) have often been overlooked, and adequate evaluations of job analysis results have seldom been performed even though unreliable or invalid job analysis information can lead to undesirable consequences.

A practical approach to job analysis uses standardized procedures so that information about different jobs can be compared to one another (Brannick & Levine, 2002). In addition, it should be suitable for analyzing different jobs, cost-efficient, acceptable to the job analysts, ready for use, and easily used. In addition, it should require both the least amount of people involved and the least training for job analysts while providing reliable and valid job information.

In the remainder of this section, we describe how to select job analysts, who should be recruited as SMEs and the source of these SMEs, and which data collection methods should be used to collect job information. After that, we present step-by-step procedures for conducting a job analysis based on suggestions by Brannick and Levine (2002), Harvey (1991), and Mitchell, Alliger, and Morfopoulos (1997). A job analysis procedure that is tailored to an organization's needs is flexible, cost-effective, and efficient enough for HR professionals to collect critical KSAOs, tasks, and other information needed for the four major HR functions described earlier. By understanding the procedures used to collect this information, HR professionals will be cognizant of the critical components of the job analysis program and be capable of selecting a job analysis provider, should an external consultant be used to implement the program.

Competence of Job Analysts

Based on budgetary and time constraints and in-house expertise, HR professionals may choose internal staff or external consultants to conduct the job analysis. The main mission of job analysts is to provide organizations with valid, accurate, and reliable information about jobs (Ghorpade, 1988). Because the quality of job information relies, in large part, on the skills and abilities of job analysts, selection of competent job analysts is essential. Competent job analysts should possess adequate training and work experience as well as the following KSAOs: oral/written communication, planning and coordination, interpersonal relations, observation, interviewing, rapport building, and basic knowledge of reliability and validity. More information about job analysts' KSAOs, training experience, or job characteristics can be found via the online (*http://online.onetcenter.org*) Occupational Information Network (O*NET), under the title of "job and occupational analyst," and from Van De Voort and Stalder (1988).

Sources and Number of SMEs

After job analysts have been selected, decisions must be made with respect to the selection of SMEs and the number of SMEs needed. Without having competent and credible SMEs, we will have little faith in the job analysis information that they provide. Job analysis information is often derived from SMEs' judgments. The reliability and validity of their judgments are likely influenced by both social and organizational factors as well as cognitive factors such as lack of motivation, social desirability, carelessness, and information overload (Lindell, Clause, Brandt, & Landis, 1998; Morgeson & Campion, 1997; Sanchez & Levine, 2000). Realistically, it is difficult to recruit SMEs who are completely free of personal bias.

As a rule of thumb, SMEs should include experienced job incumbents and immediate supervisors who have considerable experience and knowledge about the job. Gael (1988) considered job incumbents and their immediate supervisors the best sources to address job content issues and provide job information. Compared to experienced job incumbents, their immediate supervisors tend to have a broader perspective pertaining to the interrelationships among project teams and among departments as well as the directions and goals of the organization.

Other SMEs include job analysts, higher level managers, trainers, customers, and jobholders from other parts of the organization who interact frequently with the staff occupying the jobs being analyzed. Inevitably, SMEs within or between sources will see the same job differently; these discrepancies can reveal meaningful information and thus should not be regarded as errors or biases. For instance, customers or supervisors will likely provide information about how the job *should* be done. This information is vital for strategically planning a new type of job or developing new performance criteria for the current job. Information from different business groups also assists in identifying the tasks and KSAOs required for the job in a project/product team setting.

Given the expected discrepancies in information that often appear among SMEs, Gael (1988) suggested that six to ten SMEs who know the job of interest well are needed to generate reliable information. During the planning and execution of a job analysis, HR professionals also need to ensure that SMEs are representative in terms of gender, race, age, job location, and so on. There are two reasons that representative SMEs should be recruited. Empirical studies in the job analysis literature have not reached a definitive conclusion pertaining to the effects of the SMEs' characteristics (e.g., race or sex) on the quality of the job analysis (Harvey, 1991; Harvey & Wilson, 2000; Sanchez & Levine, 2000; Spector, Brannick, & Coovert, 1989). Second, the presence of representative SMEs is desirable from a legal perspective because diverse SMEs will add to the credibility and fairness of the job analysis (Ghorpade, 1988).

Methods of Collecting Information

In their comprehensive summary, Brannick and Levine (2002) listed 11 ways to collect information on job tasks, KSAOs, or both. These methods include observing an incumbent performing the job, interviewing individual SMEs, interviewing a group of SMEs, having technical conferences, conducting surveys, writing work diaries, recording or videotaping job actions, reviewing records, reviewing literature, studying equipment design specifications, and doing the work oneself. Because each method offers a unique perspective of the job, we recommend using several methods whenever possible to obtain a comprehensive and accurate view of the job.

Choices of the above data collection methods often reflect practical constraints and personal preferences. Regardless of the types or number of methods chosen, these methods should complement one another so that both task- and worker-oriented information can be obtained. Task-oriented information describes the job in terms of the duties, tasks, and activities required by the job. In contrast, worker-oriented information describes the job by indicating the KSAOs that are required to perform the job tasks. We discuss these types of information more after we provide an example in which multiple methods are used to analyze the job of network programmer.

Prior to or during a job analysis, job analysts can collect information about network programmers from a combination of the following approaches:

- Performing or observing the job at different points of time and locations with the aid of questionnaires (e.g., Position Analysis Questionnaire [PAQ], McCormick, Jeanneret, & Mecham, 1989)
- Interviewing an individual or group of SMEs about what tasks and KSAOs are required
- Using an electronic or mechanical device such as a videotape recorder or computer records
- Asking network programmers to describe in detail the activities that they engage in during a typical day or week
- Consulting with experts (e.g., computer scientists)
- Reviewing professional articles, magazines, or books
- Reviewing databases (e.g., Occupational Information Network [O*NET]) or work records (e.g., studying the meanings and functions of networks or acquiring a basic understanding of programming languages)
- Studying equipment specifications (e.g., knowing the functions of server or network cards and how the network programmers interact with them)

Two of the methods above—questionnaires and the O*NET database—require further elaboration because of their popularity and availability.

Questionnaires

There are many off-the-shelf job-analysis questionnaires. In addition, questionnaires can be developed from scratch based upon SME input. To be maximally effective, a job analysis questionnaire should be structured and standardized when administered to a group of SMEs such as several incumbents. It should also be written at a level appropriate to the reading skill of the people who will be completing it. Job analysis questionnaires can be distributed to SMEs in person, by mail, by phone, or through the Internet and are regarded as the most efficient and indispensable tool to collect job information, particularly when there are large samples of SMEs working at different geographical locations (Gael, 1988).

Some questionnaires list possible tasks and ask SMEs to rate each task's relative importance or frequency for the target job. Typically, these lists were generated from interviews of SMEs, observations of job incumbents, reviews of records or diaries, and other sources of task-oriented job information. Two tasks performed by the previously described network programmer are "to inspect the server to determine whether repair, replacement, or upgrade is necessary for efficiency of data transfer" and "to examine server security by simulating hackers' attack algorithms." Each task is evaluated with regard to how much time is spent per week engaging in the task, how difficult the task is to perform, and so on (Brannick & Levine, 2002). Information in the well-known *Dictionary of Occupational Titles* (*DOT*; U.S. Department of Labor, 1991) was compiled primarily from task-oriented questionnaires.

In contrast to task-oriented questionnaires, other job analysis questionnaires are worker-oriented and emphasize KSAOs of the job incumbent. Examples of KSAOs for a network programmer include "skills to repair, replace, or upgrade cooling fans in a server" and "JAVA programming skills for intra- and extranet data exchanges." KSAOs are evaluated using criteria such as "how important are these characteristics for distinguishing superior programmers from average programmers," "how important are these characteristics for selecting candidates," and "how practical is it to expect job candidates to possess these characteristics" (Brannick & Levine, 2002).

The Position Analysis Questionnaire (PAQ) (McCormick et al., 1989)—a commercially available, worker-oriented questionnaire that has received rigorous scrutiny and generated much empirical research—has demonstrated satisfactory validation evidence. The Worker Rehabilitation Questionnaire and the Occupational Preference Inventory use modified PAQ items to design jobs for disabled or injured workers and to help workers identify career preferences, respectively. Other off-the-shelf job analysis questionnaires that have received empirical scrutiny include the job components inventory (Banks, Jackson, Stafford, & Warr, 1983), functional job analysis scales (Fine, 1989), and the Personality-Related Position Requirements Form (Raymark, Schmit, & Guion, 1997).

O*NET Database

Recognizing the shortcomings of the *DOT* and facing rapid changes in the labor market and workplace, the U.S. Department of Labor (1993) initiated the development of a system to enhance and disseminate the job information database. About a decade later, the online O*NET was released. This database contains job information on over 1,100 representative occupations and describes these occupations with regard to six aspects: worker characteristics, worker requirements, experience requirements, occupational requirements, occupational-specific requirements, and occupational characteristics (Peterson et al., 2001).

Worker characteristics refer to incumbents' abilities, work styles, and occupational values and interests that are important for the job. For instance, the O*NET indicates that abilities such as oral or verbal expression/comprehension and mathematical reasoning are important for a network programmer (under the title of computer programmer in the O*NET). *Worker requirements* refer to developed attributes such as the knowledge, skills, and education required by a job. For instance, network programmers should possess the following skills: programming, writing, reading comprehension, critical thinking, information organization, problem identification, active listening, and active learning. *Experience requirements* focus on training and licensure and are linked to work activities. According to the O*NET, network programmers should have a minimum of two to four years of work-related skill, knowledge, or experience. *Occupational requirements* refer to generalized work activities under work and organizational contexts. In contrast, *occupational-specific requirements* stress the specific tasks/duties performed and tools used by a particular type of worker. Examples of general work activities for network programmers based on the online O*NET are interacting with computers and providing consultation and advice to others. Examples of specific tasks for network programmers include analyzing, reviewing, and rewriting programs, and using workflow charts and diagrams. Finally, *occupational characteristics* are related to labor market-relevant information such as employment outlook and earnings. As the current version of O*NET does not provide this information, users need to conduct their own searches about the labor market within America's Career InfoNet (http://www.acinet.org/acinet/).

O*NET is considered a valuable resource for HR professionals for several reasons. First, the database is continuously updated and replenished every five years. Second, the O*NET is free to the public via the Internet. Third, it provides information beyond KSAOs and tasks obtained from traditional job analyses by focusing on six interrelated aspects of the job. Fourth, the database utilizes well-researched HR theories including Hackman and Oldham's (1976) job characteristics model and Holland's (1973) vocational choice theory. Finally, it integrates many existing databases such as the Standard Occupational Classification System and the Guide for Occupational Exploration.

Steps to Collect Job Information

The job analysis program presented here incorporates five data collection methods: observing, interviewing, conducting surveys, reviewing records, and reviewing literature. Brannick and Levine (2002) suggest that such an approach can provide the following types of individual job or team-level information about jobs:

- Organizational structure (e.g., thick or thin layers of management) and philosophy (e.g., technology-enabled or technology-driven)
- Formal and informal authorities or responsibilities (e.g., budget or merit-raise decisions)

- Services or products related to the job (e.g., tax preparation or technical support)
- Professional standards (e.g., ethical principles for members in the Academy of Management)
- Licensing (e.g., dental hygienist certification) and other government mandated requirements (e.g., continuing education requirement or training)
- Job contexts (e.g., temperature levels facilitating or inhibiting task completion)
- Equipment or tools involved (e.g., computer or microscope)
- Competency standards (e.g., processing a contract within 24 hours)
- Personal job demands (e.g., lifting or physical endurance requirements)
- Critical tasks and activities
- KSAOs
- Work flow

If the choice is made to outsource the job analysis project, asking different vendors the extent to which they will provide the above information can help when deciding whom to employ. Given the numerous methods to obtain job information, using only organizational records (e.g., training manuals, job descriptions, performance evaluation standards, company annual report), public databases of information (e.g., O*NET), and an observation of the target position tends to yield insufficient information about the job of interest. However, information obtained from these methods offers excellent clues about what the job entails and what subject matters deserve special attention in later interviews and surveys.

Observation is appropriate throughout the job analysis to resolve inconsistencies in information received from other sources. It can be structured or unstructured depending upon the extent to which the target behaviors to be observed are predetermined versus undefined. A recent trend has been to utilize unstructured observation rather than structured observation, because unstructured observation allows for an in-depth understanding of complex phenomena whereas structured observation is restricted by predetermined categories of interest. Although unstructured observation offers the opportunity to view serendipitous behaviors, the resulting data are difficult to interpret and classify and also tend to be less reliable (Martinko, 1988). Observation can also be conducted in a less intrusive or a less participatory manner, as close involvement tends to increase demand characteristics and alter incumbents' behavior patterns. Nevertheless, adequate stratified sampling of locations and times when observing job incumbents with technological aids (e.g., recording devices) can result in rich data not available by other methods.

Task Generation Interviews and Survey

At the first meeting, job analysts lead a group of 6–10 SMEs to generate the tasks that a job entails. Initially, each SME spends about two hours to independently create 30 to 100 task statements. Task statements should be specific, clear, concise, and written according to the format that consists of an actor (the job incumbent), an action (the activity of the actor), an object of the action (the target that is the focus of the action), and the business-relevant purpose(s) of the action. However, the actor is generally omitted from the task statements.

SMEs tend to write broad or vague statements. To improve the quality of task statements that SMEs generate, job analysts should provide a few examples and a practice period. It should be emphasized that the level of specificity in generating task statements depends on the purpose of the job analysis (Brannick & Levine, 2002). For instance, task statements can be somewhat broadly written if the main purpose of the analysis is either performance appraisal or selection. However, task statements should be more specific if the goal of a job analysis program is to design training programs or create operation specifications. After each SME generates task statements individually, the group of SMEs compiles, reduces, and adds task statements, with an end goal of 100 or fewer statements, although the number may vary contingent upon the level of specificity.

The final task statements are used to construct a task questionnaire, which is in turn used to identify which tasks are considered to be important or essential. Brannick and Levine (2002) recommend that large, representative samples of incumbents as well as other SMEs be used to provide ratings. Should there be practical constraints, they suggested selecting a panel of SMEs with broad experience in the job under study. It is less desirable to use the same group of SMEs who generated the tasks because they may have personal preferences for certain tasks.

SMEs are asked to rate each task statement using one or more of the following four scales, depending on the focus of the job analysis and the structure of the questionnaire:

- Task difficulty—Difficulty of learning a task correctly: 1 = considerably easy to learn, 2 = easy to learn, 3 = intermediate, 4 = hard to learn, and 5 = considerably hard to learn
- Task criticality—Consequence of performing a task incorrectly: 1 = consequences of error are of little importance, 2 = consequences are of some importance, 3 = consequences are moderately important, 4 = consequences are important, and 5 = consequences are very important
- Time spent—Time spent per week doing a task: 1 = under one fifth of the time, 2 = one fifth to less than two fifths of the time, 3 = two fifths to less than three fifths of the time, 4 = three fifths to less than four fifths of the time, and 5 = four fifths and over four fifths of the time
- Task essentiality—Necessity of the task to accomplish goals: 1 = considerably marginal to fulfill organization-relevant goals, 2 = marginal to fulfill organization-relevant goals, 3 = more or less necessary to fulfill organization-relevant goals, 4 = necessary to fulfill organization-relevant goals, and 5 = considerably necessary to fulfill organization-relevant goals

The sum of the scales of task difficulty, task criticality, and time spent determines the importance of the task.

Two of the above rating scales, task essentiality and task criticality, are relevant when determining the essential functions of a job, an important element in Title I

Table 2.1 Example of Task Ratings by Two Hypothetical Subject-Matter Experts

Tasks	TD	TC	TS	TE
SME: John Doe				
1. Revise system codes to prevent hacker attacks	3	5	1	4
2. Conduct various hacker simulations once a week to identify any system flaws	1	3	1	3
3. Examine firewall settings to filter any external executable files	4	5	2	5
SME: Jane Doe				
1. Revise system codes to prevent hacker attacks	3	4	2	5
2. Conduct various hacker simulations once a week to identify any system flaws	2	2	2	2
3. Examine firewall settings to filter any external executable files	5	4	3	5

Note: TD = Task Difficulty. TC = Task Criticality. TS = Time Spent. TE = Task Essentiality.

of the ADA. The ADA protects employees and job applicants with disabilities if they can perform the essential functions of a job; therefore, the determination of a job's essential functions is imperative (Cascio, 1994). Essential functions of a job are defined as fundamental or primary job duties that fulfill organization-relevant objectives. Essential functions are not necessarily the same as important tasks. Although there is no concrete way to define the essential functions of a job, in practice, a task is considered an essential function if it meets one of the following three criteria (Mitchell et al., 1997): (a) serious consequences exist if the task is performed incorrectly, which can be identified from the task criticality rating, (b) over 70% of the job incumbents report performing the task *and* spending an above average amount of time per week performing the task, and (c) no other employees are available to cover the task. To determine whether a task is considered an essential function of a job, a composite score of essential function is derived based on the sum of the task essentiality and task criticality scales.

Table 2.1 shows how two SMEs rated three network programmer tasks. (Usually, it will take less than 90 minutes for SMEs to supply the ratings.) The task importance value assigned by SME John Doe for Task #1 is 9—the sum of his ratings for task difficulty, task criticality, and time spent. On the other hand, the essential function value derived from SME John Doe for Task #2 is 6—the sum of his ratings for task criticality and task essentiality. Following the same procedure, job analysts would compute importance and essential function values for each task statement and rank order the values to identify the tasks that are most important and essential. Essential functions are not discussed in the remainder of this chapter, as the concept is not relevant when determining worker-oriented characteristics of a job.

Task statements can be grouped into functional categories, each of which shares a common duty or job function. In practice,[1] job analysts create the functional categories with brief descriptions. Next, SMEs independently assign each task statement to a category. Disagreements among SMEs about the task-category assignment can be resolved by discussion afterward.

Job analysts should assess the reliability and validity of SMEs' ratings. In practice, this can be done by randomly inserting 5 to 10 task statements unrelated to the job throughout the questionnaire before SMEs supply their ratings. The number of these job-unrelated statements judged as critical by SMEs forms a careless index or false reporting index (Green & Stutzman, 1986). Careless SMEs (e.g., those who endorse more than 20% of the job-unrelated statements) can be identified, and their data can be discarded.

There are many sophisticated statistical procedures to examine the agreement or reliability among SMEs (Cornelius, 1988). We present two simple techniques that can be easily performed using spreadsheets. The first technique calculates an agreement index for each task statement using the standard deviation of its importance index. A small standard deviation suggests a high agreement among SMEs. For example, we calculate the standard deviation of the importance values of the 10 SMEs for Task #1 (15, 13, 15, 14, 12, 12, 15, 11, 12, and 13) and Task #2 (15, 15, 9, 14, 12, 15, 15, 12, 12, and 13). The standard deviations are 1.48 and 1.99, respectively. Although both tasks have the same importance value (132), there is less agreement among SMEs for Task 2 than for Task 1. An examination of the values for Task 2 shows one SME gave a rating (9) quite different from the ratings of other SMEs. Before throwing his or her data out of the final analysis, we need to check for any clerical errors, misunderstandings, or other explanations.

The other technique assesses the consistency among SMEs by calculating the relationship between each pair of SMEs across the 100 task-importance values. High intercorrelations among SMEs' ratings indicate that the SMEs' judgments are consistent and reliable. Spector et al. (1989) reported that the intercorrelations from prior empirical studies have ranged from .46 to .79, with an average and median of .62 and .63, respectively. A high-quality job analysis should attempt to achieve intercorrelations among SMEs' ratings above .60.

KSAO-Identification Interviews and Survey

A job analysis would be incomplete if critical KSAOs were not identified. KSAOs are imperative for developing or designing selection instruments, compensation structures, performance evaluation programs, competency models, and so on. Only those tasks judged to be important in the prior task ratings are listed under each function category and used in the KSAO-identification interviews. An example is shown in Columns 1 and 2 of Table 2.2. In the third column, SMEs write all the KSAOs required for each function category, with a goal of generating 30 to 100 KSAOs overall. As seen in Table 2.2, SMEs determined that seven KSAOs are needed to perform the function of "system security maintenance."

To facilitate the identification of KSAOs, taxonomies such as 50 categories of generic human abilities (Fleishman & Reilly, 1992), 107 job-related personality characteristics (Raymark et al., 1997), or 53 managerial competencies (Tett, Guterman, Bleier, & Murphy, 2000) can be used as examples. After the SMEs identify the KSAOs, all KSAOs are compiled and revised for each function category. It usually takes about 2 hours for SMEs to complete KSAO identification. The linkages

Table 2.2   Example of Linkages Between Tasks and KSAOs Generated by SMEs

Function Categories	Tasks	KSAOs by SMEs
Maintain System Security: Maintain external and internal safeguard devices at the optimal condition to ensure security of network system.	A. Revise system codes to prevent hacker attacks. B. Conduct various hacker simulations once a week to identify any system flaws. C. Examine firewall settings to filter any external executable files.	1. Demonstrate ability to apply general rules to specific problems to come up with logical answers. 2. Write ASP, JAVA, and SQL computer programs. 3. Generate different approaches to solve problems and to implement ideas. 4. Use mathematics to develop simulation algorithms. 5. Adapt equipment and technology to serve user needs. 6. Install equipment, machines, wiring, or programs to meet specifications. 7. Provide example of written expression.
Category 2 . . .	Tasks . . .	KSAOs . . .

between a function category (or tasks) and their correspondent KSAOs provide HR professionals with a comprehensive framework for developing HR programs.

Similar to the task survey, a panel of SMEs rates each KSAO on a questionnaire using one or more of the following scales:

- Necessary to possess–Should a newly hired employee possess this KSAO? NO = A newly hired employee does not need to possess this KSAO, and YES = A newly hired employee should possess this KSAO.
- Practical to expect–Is it practical to expect this KSAO in the labor market? NO = It is not practical to expect that most applicants possess this KSAO in the labor market, and YES = It is practical to expect that most applicants possess this KSAO in the labor market.
- Consequence–What is the degree of detrimental consequence if this KSAO is ignored in selection? 1 = to a very little extent, 2 = to some extent, 3 = to a moderate extent, 4 = to a great extent, and 5 = to a very great extent.
- Competence–To what extent does this KSAO distinguish the superior from the average employee, compared to other KSAOs? 1 = to a very little extent, 2 = to some extent, 3 = to a moderate extent, 4 = to a great extent, and 5 = to a very great extent.

Different combinations of the above scales serve different HR functions. We discuss applications of various combinations in the next section.

Table 2.3   Example of KSAOs Rating by Two Hypothetical SMEs

KSAOs	Necessary	Practical	Consequence	Competence
SME: John Doe				
1. Show ability to apply general rules to specific problems to come up with logical answers	Y	Y	3	5
2. Write ASP, JAVA, and SQL computer programs	Y	Y	4	2
3. Generate different approaches to solve problems and to implement ideas	Y	Y	3	5
4. Use mathematics to develop simulation algorithms	N	N	1	4
5. Adapt equipment and technology to serve user needs	N	Y	2	3
6. Install equipment, machines, wiring, or programs to meet specifications	N	Y	1	1
7. Provide example of written expression	Y	Y	1	2
SME: Jane Doe				
1. Show ability to apply general rules to specific problems to come up with logical answers	Y	Y	3	4
2. Write ASP, JAVA, and SQL computer programs	Y	Y	4	1
3. Generate different approaches to solve problems and to implement ideas	Y	Y	2	5
4. Use mathematics to develop simulation algorithms	N	N	2	4
5. Adapt equipment and technology to serve user needs	N	Y	2	2
6. Install equipment, machines, wiring, or programs to meet specifications	N	N	1	2
7. Provide example of written expression	Y	Y	1	2

Assuming that the seven KSAOs described in Table 2.2 are needed to perform the duty of maintaining system security, SMEs independently rate each KSAO with the above scales, as shown in Table 2.3. After all SMEs complete their ratings, job analysts perform the consistency analyses described earlier for the task-generation phase of the job analysis.

Brannick and Levine (2002) recommend that at the end of a job analysis program, a report should be prepared that documents the process (e.g., advisory panels, involved SMEs), evaluation criteria (e.g., careless index), outcomes (results of tasks and KSAOs questionnaires), and uses of the job analysis (how the outcomes are applied to HR functions). Advisory panels and SMEs should be invited to review and comment on the report to ensure accuracy and increase their support. Any necessary revisions should follow. HR professionals should maintain a codebook describing any outcome data, and data should be safely stored in an easily retrievable place.

Applications for Job Analysis Results

In this section, we illustrate how to apply the job analysis information to four HR applications: selection, training, performance evaluation and competency modeling, and employee well-being—one application from each of the four functions cited at the beginning of this chapter. We also briefly discuss job classification at the end of this section although we do not provide as much detail as for the four applications mentioned above. Note that job information can also be applied to other HR uses such as compensation, the generation of required KSAOs for a future job position and the selection of team members.

Application to Personnel Selection

According to Brannick and Levine (2002), three criteria must be met to identify those KSAOs to be considered in a personnel selection program. First, a clear majority of SMEs (i.e., more than 50%) must consider the KSAO necessary for a newly hired employee to possess. Second, a clear majority of SMEs must judge that job applicants with such a KSAO are available in the labor market. Third, the average rating for a KSAO on the "consequence" scale must be 1.5 or greater.

As shown in Table 2.3, HR professionals do not need to develop selection devices that assess KSAOs such as "written expression" or "use mathematics to develop simulation algorithms," because these KSAOs do not meet the three criteria cited in the previous paragraph. In contrast, selection devices should be developed to assess KSAOs (e.g., writing ASP, JAVA, and SQL computer programs) that meet the three criteria. For instance, HR professionals can initially screen job candidates from an applicant pool by asking them to submit a portfolio that consists of ASP, JAVA, and SQL computer programs that they have previously written.

Other selection devices developed from the KSAOs can further be used to rank the applicants from best to least qualified. For example, KSAOs such as "ability to apply general rules to specific problems to come up with logical answers" and "ability to generate different approaches to solve problems and to implement ideas" are necessary to possess, are practical to expect in the applicant pool, and cause trouble if ignored in selection. Assessment devices such as psychological test batteries (e.g., cognitive ability tests), situational tests (e.g., problem-solving tasks), or work samples (e.g., job candidates actually performing important tasks like revising/debugging system codes) that measure these KSAOs can be effectively used to select the most qualified candidates for the target position.

Application to Training

To decide which KSAOs should be the foci of training, two worker characteristic scales, "necessary to possess" and "competence," are employed. If a KSAO is considered not necessary for a newly hired employee *but* is judged to be a marker to distinguish superior from average employees (i.e., an average rating of 1.5 or above), it should be considered while developing training programs. Take the KSAOs "use mathematics to develop simulation algorithms" and "adapt equipment and technology to serve user needs" as examples. Because these KSAOs are not necessary for newly hired employees to possess but employees with these skills tend to be more competent, training programs pertaining to these KSAOs are needed. For instance, training developers can design simulated exercises based on the critical tasks described in Table 2.2 (e.g., conduct various hacker simulations to identify system flaws or set up firewall settings to filter any external executable files) in order to aid employees in acquiring the correspondent KSAOs.

In addition to facilitating the development of valid training content, job analysis information assists organizations in developing succession plans for incumbents (e.g., sale representatives) who attempt to pursue different career goals (e.g., network programmer, purchasing officer). Needs assessment questionnaires, consisting of important tasks and required KSAOs of various jobs, can be retrieved from the HR information system and individually developed and tailored for the incumbents. After completing the needs assessment questionnaires, incumbents can then recognize their strengths and weaknesses for different jobs they may attempt to pursue. Hence, career development plans or career networks are established systematically.

Application to Performance Evaluation and Competency Modeling

Both important tasks (or functional categories) and the KSAOs that distinguish superior from average employees (an average competency rating of 1.5 or above) can be used to develop performance evaluation forms. For instance, for each selected KSAO (e.g., use mathematics to develop simulation algorithms), different levels of behaviors to accomplish the correspondent tasks (e.g., "conduct various hacker simulations once a week to identify any system flaws") can be generated. Employees can be evaluated based upon the frequency that they engage in these behaviors.

Over the past several years, the practice of competency modeling has grown dramatically (Shippmann et al., 2000). To date, a consensus among HR experts has not been reached with respect to the actual meaning of "competency." Nevertheless, different definitions of "competency" all indicate that it comprises KSAOs and other personal attributes that distinguish superior from average employees. Job analysis typically focuses on the tasks a job entails and the KSAOs needed to perform the tasks. In contrast, competency modeling emphasizes generic and broad KSAOs, which are not linked directly to specific tasks (Brannick & Levine, 2002). Although job analysis and competency modeling may apparently be different, the latter can easily be developed from the former, but not vice versa. Specifically, job analysis information such as detailed KSAOs that distinguish superior from average employees (an average competency rating of 1.5 or above) and important tasks (or functional categories) can be easily categorized into broad competency areas (e.g., creative thinking, adaptation), contingent upon the level of application (i.e., divisionwide, departmentwide, or organizationwide) and level of detail needed.

As pointed out by Brannick and Levine (2002), the use of broader rather than narrower KSAOs may be more applicable to broader jobs with ill-defined boundaries. A few caveats should be noted here. First, empirical evidence has shown that presumably "cost-effective" and "flexible" holistic ratings usually do not converge with decomposed ratings. Butler and Harvey (1988) asked highly trained professional job analysts, who routinely administered the PAQ in their jobs, to directly rate 32 broad PAQ dimensions or competencies (i.e., a holistic rating task). In addition, they also rated 189 detailed KSAOs in the PAQ, which in turn produced the same 32 dimensions (i.e., a decomposed rating task). Statistical analyses indicated near-zero convergence between the holistic and decomposed dimension ratings. Shippmann et al. (2000) indicated that a common pitfall among many competency models is that they tend to look alike and attempt to overgeneralize to all jobs within an organization (denoted as "core competencies"). In reality, these core competencies are not equally useful for all jobs throughout levels (e.g., loan officers and tellers), business units (e.g., sales and accounting), or regions (e.g., Asia and Europe) within an organization.

Application to Employee Physical and Psychological Well-Being

Job analysis information such as job contexts, equipment, KSAOs, and tasks has long been used to identify job hazards (e.g., noise, air, temperature, vibration, and repetition), physical abilities requirements (e.g., strength or endurance), and task demands (e.g., heavy lifting or pushing). In addition, KSAOs and tasks including physical or psychological demands reveal the amounts of pressure and strain that employees may experience in their daily tasks. This information can be applied to redesign jobs. Furthermore, it has been shown in HR literature that employees tend to be satisfied with their jobs and perform well when their interest and ability match the tasks and KSAOs that their jobs require. To identify the extent that employees' interests and abilities match those required by their jobs, incumbents can rate the task and KSAO questionnaires based on how much they prefer to perform or utilize each task or KSAO, respectively. This information is invaluable for HR programs such as employee development, job rotations, and so on.

Other Applications

As stated earlier, job analysis information can also be applied to other HR functions such as classifying jobs, generating required KSAOs for a future job position, or selecting team members. We will only briefly discuss job classification as an example of these peripheral applications. Job classification is to classify jobs into a job group or a job family on the basis of similarity of tasks and/or KSAOs. In practice, the development of competency models, training programs, selection procedures, performance evaluation criteria, career development processes, job evaluation methods, or compensation methods often requires the specification of similar jobs. To classify multiple jobs into a job family, we often need a large number of task or KSAO items, and SMEs from different jobs are required to rate all these items. After that, we can use either Q-type factor analysis or a hybrid approach (a Q-type factor analysis followed by a cluster analysis) to form job families (see Colihan & Burger, 1995, for a detailed discussion of these statistical approaches).

Once the job analysis information is integrated into an HR application, the process is not finished. A proactive job analysis program requires ongoing monitoring of the job to assess the impact of any changes. Many jobs (e.g., retail clerk or janitor) are very stable, with little change in work behaviors over time. Other jobs, particularly those linked to technology, change at a much faster pace. If you are not sure of the extent that changes impact a job, you can conduct a "mini" job analysis. A single group of SMEs could review the work behaviors and KSAOs of the prior job analysis and assess whether they accurately reflect the current job. When judging whether a job analysis needs to be redone, it is important to consider the HR application(s) in which the information is used. If the job analysis supports selection, changes in the job will require a new job analysis. If the information is used in training, you may be able to merely update training materials to reflect procedural changes, and add the information to your job analysis report.

Conclusion

No single job analysis approach is appropriate for all HR programs or situations. Consequently, a flexible job analysis program enables an organization to capitalize on the approach providing the greatest benefit for a particular situation. Regardless of the circumstances, a job analysis program should ensure high-quality information that meets the organization's needs and administrative efficiency in gathering and analyzing the job information. When job analyses are frequent and serve as the foundation of HR programs and initiatives, the speed and ease with which information is gathered and applied also become critical criteria to be considered.

Using the techniques and considerations described in this chapter will increase the likelihood that HR programs start with well-founded criteria for development, implementation, and evaluation. Best practice organizations have integrated HR systems based on job analysis information (sometimes called competency-based systems). Linking HR systems in this fashion makes it easier for both managers and employees to understand the HR systems and to use them appropriately. In Table 2.4, we provide an evaluation checklist that can be used to evaluate job analysis programs along different stages.

Note

1. Cranny and Doherty (1988) noted a statistical flaw that occurs when categorizing tasks by factor analysis (or using any similar statistic) based on task importance values and have suggested other strategies.

Table 2.4   Proactive Job Analysis Program Evaluation Checklist

- Have you established advisory panels to identify organizational needs?
- Have you assessed organizational readiness?
- Are the goals of the program clear?
- Do the goals of the program correspond to business goals?
- Do stakeholders agree on business goals and expectations accomplished by a job analysis?
- Has the program received support from stakeholders?
- Have you assessed the accuracy and consistency of the program?
- Have you identified SMEs who may provide erroneous information?
- Has the program met all or most of the practical criteria?
- Do job analysts meet the selection criteria?
- Have you used the suggested criteria to select external consultants? Should the program be outsourced?
- Do you have representative SMEs?
- Did you use multiple methods to collect job information?
- Does the program yield critical individual job or team-level information about jobs?
- Is the job analysis information reliable?
- Is the job analysis information valid?
- Has the program accomplished business goals and met stakeholders' expectations?
- Is the program flexible enough to meet other units' needs?
- Have you documented the process, evaluation criteria, outcomes, and uses of the program?
- Have you solicited comments about the report from the advisory panels and SMEs?
- Have you created a code book describing any data collected from the program?
- Are data safely stored and easily retrievable?

References

Banks, M. H., Jackson, P. R., Stafford, E. M., & Warr, P. B. (1983). The job components inventory and the analysis of jobs requiring limited skill. *Personnel Psychology, 36,* 57–66.

Brannick, M. T., & Levine, E. L. (2002). *Job analysis: Methods, research, and applications.* Thousand Oaks, CA: Sage.

Butler, S. K., & Harvey, R. J. (1988). A comparison of holistic versus decomposed rating of position analysis questionnaire work dimensions. *Personnel Psychology, 41,* 761–771.

Cascio, W. F. (1994). The Americans with disabilities act of 1990 and the 1991 civil rights act: Requirements for psychological practice in the workplace. In B. D. Sales & G. R. VandenBos (Eds.), *Psychology in litigation and legislation* (pp. 175–211). Washington, DC: American Psychological Association.

Colihan, J., & Burger, G. K. (1995). Constructing job families: An analysis of quantitative techniques used for grouping jobs. *Personnel Psychology, 48,* 563–586.

Cornelius, E. T., III. (1988). Analyzing job analysis data. In S. Gael (Ed.), *The job analysis handbook for business, industry, and government* (Vol. I, pp. 353–368). New York: Wiley.

Cranny, C. J., & Doherty, M. E. (1988). Importance ratings in job analysis: Note on the misinterpretation of factor analysis. *Journal of Applied Psychology, 73,* 320–322.

Fine, S. A. (1989). *Functional job analysis scales: A desk aid.* Milwaukee, WI: Sidney A. Fine.

Fleishman, E. A., & Reilly, M. E. (1992). *Handbook of human abilities: Definitions, measurements, and job task requirements.* Palo Alto, CA: Consulting Psychologists Press.

Gael, S. (1988). Subject matter expert conferences. In S. Gael (Ed.), *The job analysis handbook for business, industry, and government* (Vol. I, pp. 432–445). New York: Wiley.

Ghorpade, J. (1988). *Job analysis: A handbook for the human resource director.* Englewood Cliffs, NJ: Prentice Hall.

Green, S. B., & Stutzman, T. (1986). An evaluation of methods to select respondents to structured job-analysis questionnaires. *Personnel Psychology, 39,* 543–564.

Hackman, J. R., & Oldham, G. R. (1976). Motivation through the design of work: Test of a theory. *Organizational Behavior and Human Performance, 16,* 250–279.

Hakel, M. D., Stalder, B. K., & Van De Voort, D. M. (1988). Obtaining and maintaining acceptance of job analysis. In S. Gael (Ed.), *The job analysis handbook for business, industry, and government* (Vol. I, pp. 329–338). New York: Wiley.

Harvey, R. J. (1991). Job analysis. In M. D. Dunnette & L. M. Hough (Eds.), *Handbook of industrial and organizational psychology* (Vol. 2, pp. 71–163). Palo Alto, CA: Consulting Psychologists Press.

Harvey, R. J., & Wilson, M. A. (2000). Yes Virginia, there *is* an objective reality in job analysis. *Journal of Organizational Behavior, 21,* 829–854.

Holland, J. L. (1973). *Making vocational choices: A theory of careers.* Englewood Cliffs, NJ: Prentice Hall.

Lindell, M. K., Clause, C. S., Brandt, C. J., & Landis, R. S. (1998). Relationship between organizational context and job analysis task ratings. *Journal of Applied Psychology, 83,* 769–776.

Martinko, M. J. (1988). Observing the work. In S. Gael (Ed.), *The job analysis handbook for business, industry, and government* (Vol. I, pp. 419–431). New York: Wiley.

McCormick, E. J., Jeanneret, P. R., & Mecham, R. C. (1989). *Position Analysis Questionnaire.* Logan, UT: PAQ services.

Mitchell, K. E., Alliger, G. M., & Morfopoulos, R. (1997). Toward an ADA-appropriate job analysis. *Human Resource Management Review, 7,* 5–26.

Morgeson, F. P., & Campion, M. A. (1997). Social and cognitive sources of potential inaccuracy in job analysis. *Journal of Applied Psychology, 82,* 627–655.

Peterson, N. G., Mumford, M. D., Borman, W. C., Jeanneret, P. R., Fleishman, E. A., Levin, K. Y., Campion, M. A., Mayfield, M. S., Morgeson, F. P., Pearlman, K., Gowing, M. K., Lancaster, A. R., Silver, M. B., & Dye, D. M. (2001). Understanding work using the occupational information network (O*NET). *Personnel Psychology, 54,* 451–492.

Raymark, P. H., Schmit, M. J., & Guion, R. M. (1997). Identifying potentially useful personality constructs for employee selection. *Personnel Psychology, 50,* 723–736.

Sanchez, J. I., & Levine, E. L. (2000). Accuracy or consequential validity: Which is the better standard for job analysis data? *Journal of Organizational Behavior, 21,* 809–818.

Shippmann, J. S., Ash, R. A., Battista, M., Carr, L., Eyde, L. D., Hesketh, B., Kehoe, J., Pearlman, K., Prien, E. P., & Sanchez, J. I. (2000). The practice of competency modeling. *Personnel Psychology, 53,* 703–740.

Sparks, C. P. (1988). Legal basis for job analysis. In S. Gael (Ed.), *The job analysis handbook for business, industry, and government* (Vol. I, pp. 37–47). New York: Wiley.

Spector, P. E., Brannick, M. T., & Coovert, M. D. (1989). Job analysis. In C. L. Cooper & I. Robertson (Eds.), *International review of industrial and organizational psychology* (pp. 281–328). New York: Wiley.

Tett, R. P., Guterman, H. A., Bleier, A., & Murphy, P. J. (2000). Development and content validation of a "hyperdimensional" taxonomy of managerial competency. *Human Performance, 13,* 205–251.

Van De Voort, D. M., & Stalder, B. K. (1988). Organizing for job analysis. In S. Gael (Ed.), *The job analysis handbook for business, industry, and government* (Vol. I, pp. 315–328). New York: Wiley.

Uniform Guidelines on Employee Selection Procedures. (1978). *Federal Register, 1978, 43, No. 166,* 38290–39309.

U. S. Department of Labor. (1991). *Dictionary of occupational titles* (4th ed., rev.). Washington, DC: Government Printing Office.

U. S. Department of Labor. (1993). The new DOT: A database of occupational titles for the 21st century. Washington, DC: Author.

Suggested Readings in Job Analysis

Brannick, M. T., & Levine, E. L. (2002). *Job analysis: Methods, research, and applications.* Thousand Oaks, CA: Sage.

Fleishman, E. A., & Reilly, M. E. (1992). *Handbook of human abilities: Definitions, measurements, and job task requirements.* Palo Alto, CA: Consulting Psychologists Press.

Gael, S. (Ed.). (1988). *The job analysis handbook for business, industry, and government* (Vols. I & II). New York: Wiley.

Ghorpade, J. (1988). *Job analysis: A handbook for the human resource director.* Englewood Cliffs, NJ: Prentice Hall.

CHAPTER 3

Criteria for Human Resources Program Evaluation

Stephen David Steinhaus

L. A. Witt

Managers invest considerable financial and human resources in developing and implementing program initiatives to execute their business and organization strategies. In this regard, they often expect that significant criteria of success will be achieved. Criteria may focus on issues such as financial performance, time saving, customer satisfaction and retention, employee satisfaction and retention, advantages to employees, materials utilization, skills development, time to market, cycle time, cost, and inventory management. Measures like these are often used as the criteria in a program evaluation project. Ultimately, a program evaluation will only be as good as the measures, or criteria, that are used to assess actual effectiveness relative to the intended impacts.

How do managers know whether an initiative in which they have invested is paying off? In practice, a common answer is through anecdotes—others say it seems to be working. Such anecdotal reports typically reflect more of a subjective orientation than fact. Nonsystematic research like this can be particularly flawed for a variety of reasons, including (a) particular characteristics of the samples used, (b) bias of those who have the mixed goals of program accountability and assessment, (c) clarity of the questions asked, (d) interpretation of feedback received, and (e) methods used to develop conclusions.

An approach to program evaluation that is more scientific is often the best way to move past challenges associated with strictly anecdotal information. Of course, we recognize that most organizations may not have internal "scientific" expertise to conduct program evaluation research. The important thing is that criterion measures are systematically identified, collected, and analyzed. We suggest that the art and science of program evaluation often comes down to the degree to which there is a clear and well-defined focus on criteria that are measurable, practical, and meaningful.

In this chapter, we discuss some of the challenges facing Human Resource (HR) program evaluators and offer some suggestions. We begin by describing common approaches and pitfalls and then proceed to discuss the importance of well-planned criteria, ways to identify metrics, and characteristics of effective metrics. At the end, we present issues to be considered when planning implementation.

Common Approaches and Pitfalls

In practice, it is quite tempting for managers to immediately assume the use of criteria that have been used elsewhere. A common approach to identifying criteria is to gather whatever information is generally considered to be important, is commonly available, or comes immediately to mind. The good news is that these are very important considerations for selecting criteria. However, if it stops there, HR program evaluation results will likely be questionable or difficult to interpret.

One Measure to Serve All Masters

In our experience, managers often assume that if a measurement is important elsewhere, it should also be used as a criterion in the program evaluation. For example, managers associated with training programs for sales representatives often immediately conclude that available revenue data will serve as effective program criteria. Data that are collected elsewhere and determined to be a key organization metric should, of course, be considered. However, there are problems with stopping there and adopting such data wholesale as criteria in program evaluation.

The obvious problem with automatically using data that are used elsewhere is that they may not be directly related to the HR program objectives. For example, if a training program was designed to reduce customer complaints by reducing wait time, revenue data would not necessarily be the best criterion for determining its effectiveness.

In some cases, a program that is being evaluated may be conceptually, but not directly, related to commonly used performance measures. There might be a downstream or indirect effect, as when customer service training impacts customer satisfaction that in turn impacts revenue over the long term by enhancing customer retention. In a case like this, research may not be sensitive enough to identify the downstream effects as an impact from the training. In this particular case, revenue data may be looked at relative to customer satisfaction but not directly as a function of the training. The best model might be to first link customer service training to customer satisfaction and then link customer satisfaction to revenue. The model must be identified first, and then the criteria developed around it.

Findings might suggest that a particular program is not yielding a return on investment. However, in some cases, these findings may merely suggest that the right things are not being measured—or that the measures are inadequate. Without a clear model linking a program to systematic criteria, the research likely will not be sensitive to changes, or measurement may be confounded by other variables.

In summary, we believe that predefined, available organizational data should be considered but not necessarily selected as evaluation criteria. On the other hand, such data may be directly or indirectly used in the criterion measurement. In an indirect sense, the data may be used as a conceptual basis for the criteria or as a secondary variable in the analysis. Secondary variables are often extremely valuable for assessing moderating influences between two other variables. Criterion data must be clearly and unambiguously linked to a program's goals and objectives.

Getting Past the Obvious

In addition to automatically selecting measures because they are perceived as being important in the organization, it is also common to select measures out of convenience. We have found it common for managers to look around and ask, "What can we measure here?" Most often, this translates into something that can easily be counted. Of course, the obvious should not be overlooked; however, if we encourage this tendency and stop there, we will probably select measures that are convenient but might not have much to do with our initiative.

For example, what criteria might be applied to evaluate a technician training program? In a case that we were involved with, managers advocated the criterion of the number of equipment installations that the technicians performed per day. Clearly, this information would be readily available and would appear to be a good measure of productivity. One problem, however, is that the measure does not factor in the quality of the installations. The technician with the most installations could also have the lowest quality. In fact, if technicians were informed that this was the criterion of performance, they would likely focus on speed so as to deliver as many installations as possible. Such a focus would actually be counter to business strategy if speed led to unacceptable quality levels. A balanced approach would be to consider not only speed but also quality by focusing on the percentage of installations not needing rework.

Also important is for project managers to go from their past and current views of success and consistently evaluate criteria relative to timely issues. In this regard a view toward the latest circumstances and expected future changes needs to be considered. Past and current data may not always be useful for evaluating future success. In some cases, criteria may have to change even after being implemented as technology and organizational goals change.

Ramifications of Selecting Poor Criteria

The HR law of effect suggests that people will do what you pay them to do, if they can figure out what they are being paid to do. Translated to program evaluation, the HR law of effect suggests that programs will deliver the performance outcomes that will be measured. Given the expense and time required to develop and implement a program initiative, it is surprising when the identification of criteria in a program evaluation is done hastily with little thought or discussion. Project participants and stakeholders should be informed that the criteria represent key goals of the organization and therefore appear to deserve the attention that other high-level strategy receives. Criteria that are not well thought out and carefully selected can create a number of challenges:

- Difficulty in clearly demonstrating direct, causal relationships between the program objectives/goals and criteria. In cases where there is strong yet indirect impact, it is often difficult to isolate the effects of the program on the criteria using statistical and manipulative techniques. This could lead to erroneous conclusions about a program's effectiveness or lack thereof.

- Lack of stakeholder buy-in and commitment to results. This often is the result when stakeholder interests are ignored, program developers proceed in a biased manner to protect their interests, results are not communicated effectively, or stakeholders perceive that the research is biased or particularly self-serving in support of the program evaluation project managers.

- Excessive time and costs of the program evaluation. In some cases, a program evaluation effort may actually be disruptive to key organizational goals if not well planned and executed. This may happen, for instance, when researchers ask for mounds of reports to be generated from an organization that has other priorities.

- Motivating employees to achieve goals that are counterproductive to an organization's goals. This may happen, for instance, when time to complete a task does not take quality into account.

- Difficulty in specifying conclusions. If the relevant questions are not asked, the relevant answers remain unknown. It is critical that the criteria are clearly and directly linked to the program objectives and goals. If the data are based on numerous assumptions and are unclear, it will be difficult to parcel out effects and make meaningful conclusions. Additionally, it is important to account for potential moderator variables such as season, level, and location from which the data are collected. A moderator variable is a third variable aside from the direct variables of interest that partitions a variable into subgroups that better reveal impacts on the dependent variable (Baron & Kenny, 1986). *In the worst case, one might erroneously conclude that a program did or did not have an impact because of inadequate criterion data.*

Although the natural tendency is to go after criterion data that are important and easily accessible, there are numerous other characteristics to be mindful of. The next section of this chapter specifies factors to watch out for when developing criteria.

Box 3.1   Checklist of Characteristics Associated With Good Criteria

---

CRITERION BENCHMARKS

Reliability and Measurement Issues

❑ Are the criterion measures reliable and valid? Would the measures be stable across individuals and circumstances? Are they truly measuring what they were intended to?

❑ Are the measures strictly based on actual observations as opposed to assumptions, intuition, and judgments?

❑ Will the criteria yield data that can be effectively summarized? If qualitative data are used, can they be digested in a manner that will yield definitive findings?

Relevance Issues

❑ Will the criterion data be credible and meaningful to key stakeholders? Will the data be simple enough and relatively devoid of untenable assumptions?

❑ Has the starting point for identifying the criteria been of *value to the organization*, as opposed to return on investment (ROI)? Although ROIs might be effective criteria, the first point to consider should be "what criteria can we use to determine value to the organization?" This *may* then lead to ROI as the next point.

❑ Are the criterion data structured in a way that it will potentially reveal they focused on answering the one question as to whether the program is effective or not?

Practicality Issues

❑ Are the costs and efforts associated with developing, implementing, and analyzing the criteria balanced with their expected benefits?

❑ Are the targets and the results of the program evaluation realistic—or may they be perceived as grandiose by stakeholders?

❑ Will key stakeholders buy into and support the criteria used?

Characteristics of Good Criteria

As stated earlier, the identification, development, and deployment of effective criteria reflect both art and science. In general, benchmarks for good criteria include reliability, relevance, and practicality. Box 3.1 lists several benchmark characteristics associated with good criteria. These benchmarks may be used to guide the criterion development and as a checklist to evaluate the effectiveness of the ultimate measures.

Reliability, Validity, and Other Measurement Factors

Several measurement factors are important to consider when developing criteria. Chief psychometric characteristics include reliability and validity. As a precondition to these, measures should be defined in clearly observable terms and be free from bias. Measures may be defined in qualitative or quantitative terms. Each of these issues is described in more detail below.

Reliability and Validity

Two fundamental measurement principles are reliability and validity. Reliability focuses on the accuracy or precision of measurement. Synonyms for reliability include dependability, stability, consistency, predictability, and accuracy (Kerlinger, 1973). One key aspect of reliability is the stability of the measure. If we were to measure something twice, to what extent could we expect to find similar results? A poor measuring stick would be expected to yield different values on different occasions (e.g., perhaps due to a lack of clarity in the tick marks). Imprecise or nonspecific wording used in an interview question as part of program evaluation criteria may yield different individual interpretations on different occasions. Such an interview question could yield unreliable information from different interviewers, for different respondents, or at different times. In terms of reliability, criterion measures should be consistent from one situation to the next and be representative of key organization objectives (Landy & Trumbo, 1980).

A second key psychometric concept and goal is validity. Validity can be described as the degree to which we are measuring what we think we are measuring (Kerlinger, 1973). Reliability may be strong indicating that something is measured well, but low validity would suggest that we are not measuring what is intended. In the example stated earlier, the number of installations per day made by a technician by itself is lacking as a valid measure of performance effectiveness. A more valid measure would be number of installations that do not need rework within a specified period, because it more accurately assesses the underlying true business concept of interest—impact of the program on technician efficiency and quality.

A measure can be reliable without being valid but cannot be valid without being reliable. Validity is paramount. Lack of validity implies that an area of interest is not being effectively isolated and measured. This may occur when the selected criterion does not measure what is actually intended (e.g., using abandonment rate in a call center as a measure of customer satisfaction). This may also occur when the process inadvertently measures unintended phenomena.

Validity can be considered at the macro and micro level. At the macro level, one could view the degree to which the criterion measure reflects the primary program objectives. At the micro level, one would look at the components of the criterion measures (e.g., questions in a follow-up survey). Both should be considered. To illustrate this point, we offer the example of an HR program designed to align the company's culture with its business strategy. The first phase of the program involves communication about the implementation of a new performance appraisal system. How can the HR manager assess the impact of the first phase of the program? At the macro level, the question is what should be measured. If communication is handled though employee meetings, then one measure might be the number of employees in attendance at the mandatory meetings. In this case, success may be declared if 95% of the employees attended the meetings. However, if the ultimate aim were strategy-culture alignment, then the attendance measure would be inadequate. Such a count would not tap the extent to which employees understood or "bought into" the new system. A more valid approach at the macro level would be to assess employee understanding of the to-be-implemented performance management system through a survey or focus groups.

If these issues are measured by a survey or focus groups, then the validity of the criteria can be assessed at the more micro level by viewing the questions asked. Survey and focus group items with high validity are generally ones that (a) focus on single issues, (b) are written as unambiguously as possible, (c) are directly linked to the key criteria, and (d) require little interpretation by the respondents.

Measures Based on Clearly Observable Events

One thing that has been shown to particularly impact reliability and validity is the degree to which the measure is observable. It is quite common to confuse judgments with conclusions based on fact. Of course, left to their own devices, different observers are likely to arrive at different judgments and personal conclusions. This could be a key source of unreliability and hence low validity.

In a focus group measuring employee attitudes, an observer may come to the conclusion that employees are angry because of the emotions expressed. Of course, interpreting emotions is often highly subjective. In the example of aligning a performance appraisal with a desired organization culture, it might be that angry emotions expressed in a focus group have more to do with frustration with other events in the organization (e.g., managers' neglect of appraisals). To optimize validity of measurement, employees could be asked specific questions regarding their feelings about the announcements, and then a hand-count could be taken to quantify and compare responses. Researchers could then look into the actual percentage of employees surveyed who identified with a particular orientation. Wherever possible, it is important that measures are based on observation rather than assumption, judgment, and intuition.

Measurable

Measurement theory presupposes a scale that will reveal more or less of a particular construct. For example, in customer service, how can customer anger be effectively measured? Of course, this cannot be measured by something as concrete as a ruler.

Criterion measurements can either be quantitative or qualitative. Quantitative measurements simply count the occurrence of a particular event (e.g., the percentage of employees believing that a new system will be an improvement over an old one). In training evaluation, a quantitative measurement would be the number of correct responses on an end-of-course test, which would assess the extent to which the knowledge was acquired. Quantitative measures yield relatively straightforward interpretations compared to qualitative measures and are often simpler to explain to stakeholders.

Qualitative measurements, on the other hand, generally involve open-ended data that do not directly provide data in a quantitative form. Narrative feedback would be an example of qualitative data. Unless the collection and processing of qualitative data are well planned and understood, the evaluator may end up with mounds of verbatim comments and other input that become impossible to digest, summarize, and communicate. In cases like this, we have heard comments like "after reviewing all the responses we received, it seemed like people were saying that they liked the program." Sample comments and anecdotes, albeit not always representative, are often offered.

In many cases, qualitative measures may indeed be some of the most appropriate criteria in a HR program evaluation project. For example, when an initiative to elevate customer service levels from extremely poor to acceptable has been introduced, a process to measure the qualitative variable of anger may be important. This might involve focus groups before and after the initiative. To interpret and summarize the magnitude of anger, an evaluation team might develop a methodology that gives them specific operational guidelines for when a comment should be interpreted as anger. Additionally, they could take each comment and evaluate the magnitude of anger using a behaviorally anchored rating scale in which each angry comment was evaluated relative to specific descriptions or behaviors. They could then quantify the qualitative data by indicating the number of instances of anger, the average magnitude of anger, and the themes toward which the angry comments were targeted.

Freedom From Bias

One other important measurement consideration that deserves special attention is bias. As criterion measures are constructed, program designers need to be alert that measures are not biased toward different groups. As an example, researchers need to ensure that wording on a survey and in focus groups is equally understandable by members of different cultural subgroups.

In addition to the content of the measures, one, of course, needs to be alert to approaching the evaluation without stereotypes about a particular group. If there are clear research findings that, for instance, show differences between males and females, this could be built into the evaluation design. However, it is very important to ensure that differences between subgroups are not assumed.

Relevance

Although the measurement factors described above are the backdrop of good science important to the researcher, it is important that in its pursuit we do not lose the forest for the trees. Box 3.1 indicated that relevance is a second category of criterion characteristics that must be kept in mind. The issue of relevance as discussed below includes the development of criteria that (a) are meaningful to stakeholders, (b) focus on value to the organization, and (c) are actionable.

Meaningfulness to Stakeholders

The meaningfulness of human resources evaluation results to key stakeholders is as important as reliability, validity, and other measurement characteristics previously discussed. Stakeholders can be thought of as those who have a vested interest in results and will make decisions based on them. Stakeholders may include key leaders and decision makers, program sponsors, implementers and participants, researchers, and job analysts.

Although importance need not be the primary consideration in identifying meaningful criteria, keeping it in mind is critical for avoiding stakeholder ambivalence. If the criteria alone are not particularly salient to stakeholders, they should at least be presented in a context of other variables that are important to stakeholders. At times, researchers with a scientific orientation become so interested in showing connections between variables that they lose sight of the practical goals. If the program evaluation results are intended to communicate information to stakeholders and influence their decisions, then criterion variables need to be selected with the stakeholders' concerns in mind.

Another thing to be wary of is the extent to which the criterion measurements are based on overly complex formulas, untenable assumptions, and/or very rough estimates. Unless the results can ultimately be presented in simple terms that stakeholders can readily understand, there will be little buy-in and support. Equations and approaches should be presented so that stakeholders can understand the supporting assumptions and see clear links between different components.

It is also critical that the magnitude of results is highly credible. An esteemed colleague of ours indicated that she had conducted several utility analyses to assess the return on investment (ROI) of several employee selection systems. When she showed the results to top management in her company, they expressed a feeling of disbelief indicating, "the savings appeared equal to the United States national debt" at the time (in the 1980s).

In a similar vein, we were once asked to conduct an ROI analysis on a training course in which employees on a critical job were trained to perform one of the fundamental activities of the company. The training was for installers in the area of basic telecommunications installation. During the process of seeking a mathematical model to express the value of the course in dollar terms, we realized that any result other than the multibillion dollar revenues of the company would be erroneous. This training was so critical that the company could not survive without it. ROI in and of itself was irrelevant. Ultimately, methods of evaluation other than return on investment approaches were pursued.

Focus on Value as Opposed to Return on Investment as a Proxy Measure

Frequently, stakeholders are quick to focus on financial indices of ROI as the ultimate HR program evaluation measure. However, financial measures of ROI may be too elusive, overly complex, or, simply as suggested above, not as relevant as it at first might appear. In a training program that provides critical knowledge needed to do the job, the criteria may simply be how much knowledge was obtained and how that knowledge enhanced performance. Financial measures might not be particularly relevant, depending on the level of analysis. If a financial orientation were preferred, the better evaluation design might include criteria that are focused on potential approaches to reduce delivery costs of the training program. The focus on training costs would also be the more appropriate approach in evaluating the financial criteria associated with the earlier example of basic installation training for installers. The issue of whether there is an ROI is somewhat moot; the real financial question, if any, is whether costs can be reduced.

Although a return on investment analysis is often desirable, sometimes the best place to begin is with the stated focus on *value to the organization.* If this is used as a starting point, the conclusion might indeed be that the best way to express value is in terms of ROI. This would especially be true in most cases where there are anticipated changes in revenue as a function of an intervention.

In other cases, however, the starting point related to the issue of value might lead to criteria other than ROI. For example, when assessing a new teamwork program that supports the specific strategic initiatives of an organization, a study using financial measures would likely be quite costly and could well yield ambiguous and somewhat irrelevant results. A better route to the appropriate criteria would be to investigate the value of the teamwork program to the organization. If clear links are made between the strategic initiatives and success in an area like cross-functional team effectiveness, then the program effectiveness findings are likely to be more accurate and meaningful than when the focus is strictly on financial outcomes. Once again, if a financial orientation is desired in a case like this, it might indeed be beneficial to evaluate program costs, rather than return on investment per se as a criterion.

Actionable Results

Typically, HR program evaluation is seen as part of a "one shot deal" that yields an all-or-nothing assessment of whether the program is effective. To optimize the value, criteria should be selected and measured in a way that assesses different levels of effectiveness in different areas and, hence, is aimed at facilitating program improvement. In this regard, it is often best to think of the criteria in a program evaluation as part of a continuous improvement process. One conclusion might be to eliminate a program based on results. However, if designed correctly, there is the possibility for several highly beneficial improvements based on the program evaluation criterion data.

As criterion data are gathered and analyzed, they should be instructive as to how the program may be refined and refocused to improve. To accomplish this, each criterion should be developed and explored relative to potential improvement opportunities. With each piece of data, the researcher should be prepared to focus on specific improvements. For instance, a training evaluation program may have criteria focused on training modules, each with different employee performance objectives. The data obtained could then be used to target the modules that will be the focus for improvements. Overall, the value of the research may be optimized if criterion data directly reveal program improvement opportunities in addition to overall measures of program effectiveness. In summary, criteria should focus on specific potential targets for improvement.

Practicality

A final characteristic of the criterion to consider is the degree to which the measurements are practical to obtain, analyze, and communicate to others. One of the first considerations is whether the costs associated with the criterion measurement justify the potential benefits. Another key consideration is whether the criteria are realistic and will be credible to others. Additionally, it is important to consider the degree to which the criterion is developed in consideration of organization politics.

Practicality and Costs

It is important that the cost associated with building and implementing the criterion measurement process is justified by the benefit of the results. Program evaluation criteria are commonly identified as a "wish list" by researchers and stakeholders without much regard to the expense of the data collection and analysis. The costs of developing, implementing, and analyzing the criteria need to be incorporated into the study design.

We have witnessed occasions when the costs of collecting and analyzing the criterion data appeared to outweigh the benefits from the evaluation results. The balance between collecting extensive, highly customized criterion data and using existing data must be considered. As suggested earlier, using existing data may compromise the program evaluation, as the focus is not necessarily on the data that the initiative is designed to impact. On the other hand, highly customized criterion measurements may be excessive in costs and efforts required. This is especially true when the program evaluation results are unlikely to cause major change in the initiatives. For example, a program that is etched in stone and is not likely to be changed much because of the needs of the business would not likely warrant costly criterion measures. In the end, the use of existing data, customized data, or anything in between should be balanced relative to the expected value of the results.

Realistic and Credible Goals

In many cases, some members of the program evaluation team also developed and implemented the program. This is often quite appropriate, as the people who prepared the initiative are those who know the issues and nuances best and therefore are in the best position to develop the program evaluation. Practically speaking, given limitations of resources and division of labor and expertise in organizations, only so many people are qualified and available to prepare the initiative and conduct the program evaluation. When program developers are involved in the development and/or implementation of the evaluation, it is important that participants are alert to, and consequently minimize, self-serving objectives.

Because there is often a pride of authorship, as well as ownership of the initiative and ongoing accountability, a program evaluation runs the risk of being overzealous in its goals. It is not uncommon in cases like this for the program evaluation to be presented as securing extremely high paybacks for the organization. As stated when discussing meaningfulness of measurements, this is likely to come off as somewhat grandiose to stakeholders. For this reason, it is advisable to have more modest targets and goals that may, nevertheless, be proudly presented if they are achieved. As indicated earlier, declaring that a particular program had savings greater than the national debt is likely to yield a great deal of suspicion no matter how scientific the methodology.

Organization Politics

One additional aspect of practicality is the political acceptability of the criterion. If decision makers and program implementers do not like the criteria, they may compromise (and potentially sabotage) the evaluation effort.

People behave at work like they do outside of work. That is, they often make decisions based on feelings instead of relevant facts, and then they develop justifications for their decisions. It is imperative to the success of evaluation efforts that key constituencies in and outside the organization agree with and buy into the criteria selected. A psychometrically sound and relevant criterion whose implementation is resisted is likely to sabotage the program evaluation effort. Of course, we are not suggesting that the criterion measurement be compromised or distorted by politics—but rather, that the criteria are simultaneously effective for measuring program impacts and well accepted by stakeholders.

Practical Steps in Criterion Development and Implementation

There are several steps in establishing the criteria in a program evaluation study. These steps involve the development and implementation of the criteria and the analysis and presentation of results. Figure 3.1 presents an illustration of the complete process flow in developing and implementing program evaluation criteria. Clearly, each of these steps should be built into any broader initiatives that are simultaneous. Thus, if a needs analysis is conducted simultaneously with the development of a program evaluation plan (which is common when developing a training program), data may be gathered at the same time for both purposes.

The time required for the complete criterion development and implementation process will likely vary depending on the scope of the program and the level of the evaluation. The longest part of the process is generally the data collection. This is because of the time needed to run the program and collect enough criterion data. On average, evaluators might expect to spend two months on planning the evaluation, two

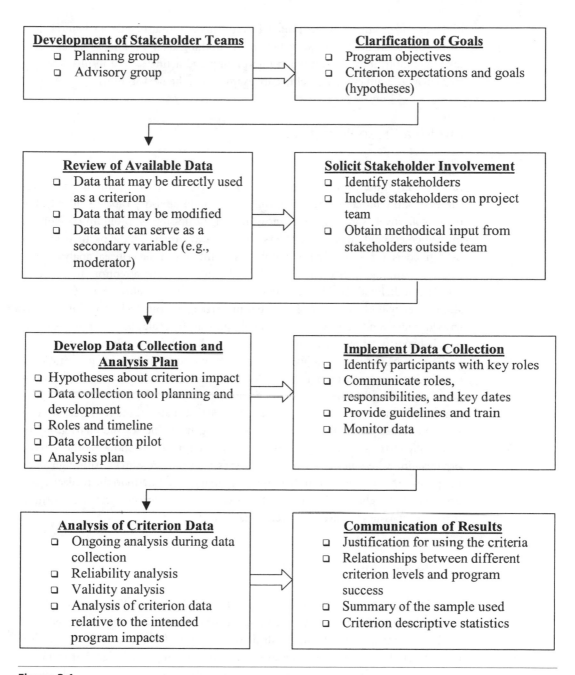

Figure 3.1

to six months on data collection, and another two months on data analysis and communication. This estimate is based on overlapping evaluation steps, not consecutive calendar months. Data collection might also be considerably longer if long-term effects of the program are being studied (e.g., assessing performance a year after employees complete training). On the other hand, program evaluation time could be minimized to accommodate organization constraints. In time-demanding situations and on smaller projects, more limited, less conclusive results based on whatever time and resources are available may be better than nothing at all—as long as stakeholders take limitations into account when interpreting and acting on the results. The key steps in a program evaluation effort are examined in the next sections.

Involve a Broad Project Team

As with all research efforts, a team that is diverse in experience, expertise, and functionality should be assembled. This may involve a small core team that conducts the evaluation and a broader team that serves in an advisory capacity. Ideally, the teams collectively should include measurement professionals, program developers, implementers, and other stakeholders. In many ways, each of these participants can be defined as a core stakeholder with a vested interest in the criteria, analyses, and findings. Although it is often somewhat difficult to get the attention and time of different individuals within the organization, once they realize their stakeholder status, they will likely be very interested in participating in each step. Participants should understand that they will be taking part in the evaluation of a program, in which, by virtue of their stakeholder status, they have considerable interest.

Because of the resources involved and the ubiquitous nature of organizational politics, we suggest that a step in the development of the team include the composition of a team charter. A charter is a document that specifies the mission and general plan for the evaluation team, and it includes estimates of the resources needed and milestones anticipated. Once senior management blesses the charter, it can essentially serve as a "hunting license" that team members can show to others in the organization when they approach them for assistance or resources. Although a key purpose of the charter is to confirm senior management buy-in to the project, a by-product of the charter development process is that it forces members to think through key issues in advance of taking action.

Clarify Program Goals and Expected Impacts

As stated in the previous section of this chapter, significant effort must be placed on clarifying the goals and expected impacts of the initiative being evaluated. The goals and anticipated outcomes will drive selection of the questions asked. Very often, a list of goals and impacts is available from the program design. For instance, training course objectives are likely to be available from the course development materials.

Even when objectives are available, it is often necessary to translate them to establish the criteria for program evaluation. It is important with the objectives in hand to then ask how they will be observed. In many cases, we must also ask not simply what the participants will be able to do at the end of the program, but perhaps more importantly what they will be able to do after they leave the program. For example, objectives for influencing skills training may include being able to present cogent arguments to others at the end of the course. Program evaluation, on the other hand, may focus on transfer of training by observing how well trainees can influence others after they leave the course.

Program evaluation should also go beyond the program objectives to assess the impacts of the objectives. For instance, a program designed to increase customer service skills may focus on the number of customers who retain service before and after the training.

Review All Available Data

Although available data may not be sufficient as criteria, such information is often a good starting point. In this regard, all available data should be identified and reviewed.

Available data may be used as is or modified. In an example cited above, separate data regarding number of installations and number of installations needing rework would perhaps be most effectively combined to express number of correct installations. Additionally, the unit of analysis may be modified. Instead of looking at number of correct installations for a newly trained technician per year, the focus could be on the average number of correct installations per day. Similarly, data may be adjusted to ensure an apples-to-apples comparison. This is often done for seasonality so that time-related effects are minimized. In the current example, the criterion might be the ratio of the average number of correct installations (x) completed by newly trained technicians to the average number of installations (y) completed by experienced technicians at their same location in the same time period (e.g., x/y).

As indicated earlier, even available data that are not used as criteria per se should be considered for the analysis. If the data are easily accessible, they may be combined in the total database and considered in subsequent/additional analyses such as a moderator analysis (Baron & Kenny, 1986).

Involve Stakeholders Other Than the HR Program Evaluation Team

The evaluation team may not represent the full range of views and input of stakeholders. Therefore, it is almost always advisable to consult with stakeholders outside the evaluation team to achieve broad involvement. First identify them by listing each internal or external group that would be impacted or would have an interest in the results of the program. Once the stakeholder groups are identified, individuals from each should be asked for their representative input. In some cases, it is important to seek specific individuals as key stakeholders.

Input from stakeholders can be obtained through focus groups, face-to-face interviews, phone interviews, surveys, and e-mail. The particular method chosen should be based on the information that is desired. Additionally, the plan should be adaptable to the time availability, location, and resources of the stakeholder participants.

Prior to meeting with stakeholders, a pool of questions and areas of inquiry should be specified. This pool may then serve as a structure and guide for the meetings. Questions may be selected based on stakeholder expertise and interest and the information that is needed at any given point in the data collection process.

Develop Data Collection Strategy and Tools

Once all available information is reviewed and initial stakeholder input is obtained, a detailed criterion development plan should be prepared. The plan should cover (a) how the criteria fit with the complete program evaluation, (b) available data that will be used, (c) the different data collection tools that will need to be developed, (d) roles and responsibilities in the data collection, (e) the timeline, and (f) how the results will be analyzed.

In accordance with a rigorous and sound evaluation plan, analyses should be clearly defined prior to collecting the data. At a minimum, the evaluation plan should include the intended effects and impacts of the program. More elaborate evaluation plans could map out the complete model of expected causes and effects. Once hypotheses are formed, specific analysis should be decided on even prior to data collection. It is helpful to have all individuals involved in the analyses and interpretation to agree on the method of analysis prior to data collection.

A variety of data collection methods and tools are available to evaluate the criteria. Methods include worksheets to collect and manipulate available data, interview and focus group protocols, rating forms, and performance assessments. Remember that the data collection goals and plan should drive the selection of data collection tools and not vice versa.

Very often a pretest of the different tools and procedures is instructive before they are finalized. This is particularly important when numerous focus groups, surveys, or rating forms will be used to collect the data. To ensure that participant time is best used and that the data collection format yields the data as planned, the pretest can provide valuable information to make adjustments as needed. We have found from pretests that even the most carefully designed interview and survey questions present multiple and unintended meanings. For example, historical context sometimes drives interpretation of questions in ways the program evaluation team did not anticipate.

As part of the data collection plan, once the tools are identified, a strategy should be determined for database development and analysis. As the data are collected, they should be input into a database with clearly defined variables.

Implement Data Collection

The first step in the data collection should be to solicit the involvement of others who will be involved. As with any organizational initiative, the evaluation team should initially seek the support of key organizational leaders. The appeal should be strictly based on the value that the evaluation is expected to add—to serve as a basis of ensuring that the new program is effective and, where possible, of finding ways to improve it. This step should be taken as part of the development of the team charter. We have seen many occasions in which HR program evaluation teams waited until their plans were set in stone to visit an organization's "gatekeepers" to request access. About 40% of the time, they were rejected. With no access, there was no evaluation. A lot of time and effort had been wasted.

Roles, responsibilities, and goals of each participant in the data collection process should be clearly identified and communicated. Participants should receive all relevant tools and be fully informed as to what is expected. Explicit, definitive, and clear milestones should be established, and for reasons of organizational politics, these should be congruent with the global milestones laid out in the evaluation team's charter. Additionally, data collection details need to be specified to avoid data misunderstandings and to ensure efficiency.

It is critical that participants understand exactly any specific requirement of data collection—for example, in some evaluations, data collectors must group and label forms that they receive (e.g., indicating where the forms were completed). Additionally, it is important that the data providers realize the exact format required for the data. This includes the unit of analysis (e.g., days versus weeks) and the format of the data files. We have seen cases when one person sending in data had used weeks and another person used days without specifying this in the data file—a misunderstanding that threw the data analysis into a complete state of disarray. Formatting the database is often necessary so that the analyst can understand what is where and also to efficiently combine data from different sources.

Data providers should receive clear direction and guidelines on exactly what they need to do and provide. Given the importance of details, the guidelines should be written in a concise and simple manner to avoid misunderstandings and ensure that items are not overlooked. Additionally, training is recommended. Training may be done through a meeting, conference call, or video. Periodic monitoring is also important.

The bottom line is that evaluation staff need to know from the outset exactly what they are going to do with the data when they receive them. This clarity drives collection design and process.

Employees involved in providing information also need to understand what involvement is expected and what the results will be used for. If the data are for program evaluation, employees should be clearly informed that the information will be used only at the aggregate level and that their individual data will be kept confidential.

Analyze Criterion Measurements

The criterion data will need to be analyzed alone and with other criterion data. As the initial data come in, they should be visually inspected to ensure that nothing has gone astray from the plan. One key test upfront is to ensure that all data are in the expected range of values. It is wise to analyze the variability of the data to assess the degree to which there is some differentiation for different variables. Anything unexpected should be investigated and followed up. This review process should be continued through the end of the data collection. If there are any misunderstandings regarding what is being asked for from different groups, this can be detected early.

At the end of this monitoring, the database would be expected to be "clean" when all data are believed to be accurate. We have succumbed to the temptation of conducting analyses before thoroughly cleaning the data. This scrubbing is laborious, highly detailed, and unpleasant work; but in every case when we conducted analyses before cleaning the data, we lived to regret our decision. Such problems as the misplacement of one column of data and the inclusion of numbers outside the possible range of values (e.g., a "9" when the possible range was from "1" to "5") are not rare and can drastically affect the integrity of the evaluation. Cleaning the data is somewhat like sterilizing surgical instruments—a monotonous task that is critical to the long-term viability of the activity.

When analyzing the criterion data, the reliability and validity of the data should be assessed. Several techniques exist for assessing reliability. A statistical process would be to investigate the internal consistency of the data (Guion, 1998). Similarly, their validity should be assessed. Information about the different types of validities and the appropriateness in specific situations may be found in Guion (1998). Individuals with statistical/psychometric expertise and validation expertise may be consulted for guidance in matters of reliability and validity.

Very often the program evaluation will yield several different measurements. Separate key measurements of interest to stakeholders should each be presented. This may include some measurements that show support for program objectives and others that do not. Of course, both sides of the picture need to be clearly and faithfully represented. Additionally, results should be spoken about collectively. Bottom line conclusions and action items from all the results should be specified.

Communicate Results

When communicating results, separate attention should be paid to explaining the findings for the various criteria. Stakeholders are typically very interested in the criteria, as these are the linchpins for any declarations about the success of a program.

Particular issues to communicate should include an overview of the justifications as to why the particular criteria were used. This part of the communication, while serving as a recap to many, should link different aspects of the program to the different criteria. The communication should emphasize how the criteria differentiate between different levels of program success or lack thereof.

Results should also document who was used in the sample for the data collection. The most important thing in this regard is to show that a wide and representative sample was used. This often includes basic demographics such as race, age, and gender. Most important, information about the organization should be included involving the degree to which participants from different locations and business units were included.

The communication materials should also include a basic summary of the criterion data. This often covers basic descriptive statistics reviewing the means and variability of different criterion variables. These data may also be presented for different subgroups.

The most important findings should be individually specified. Additionally, these findings should be summarized. Specific overall conclusions and recommendations should be clearly and distinctly communicated. It is advisable to present bottom line conclusions first. While secondary conclusions may be summarized, detail should simply be included in background materials provided to an audience.

We suggest that results be presented not only in writing but also in "dog and pony show" meetings using clear, descriptive graphics and an engaging presentation. Many decision makers, of course, evaluate results based on reasons beyond the empirical results. Data seldom speak for themselves. Considerable effort in preparing the visual aids and storyline is as important as verifying the integrity of the data. Stakeholders like a show, and they like a show with a happy ending. Often, some will not like the ending and will be lying in wait for the appropriate moment to spring to the attack. We invite you to consider always having two presenters. In many cases, the second person will remain quietly on the sidelines. In others, the second person can take the floor when a difficult question is posed and distract the audience while the primary person has time to think of an appropriate response or recover from the attack. We also suggest that a pilot presentation be done in front of a friendly audience to identify problems prior to the actual presentation.

Final Comments

This chapter points out how important careful planning, development, and implementation of criteria are to HR program evaluations. An evaluation will only be as good as the measures used to assess effectiveness and achievement of program goals.

Evaluation criteria are often viewed as central to the final evaluation of a particular program. As pointed out in this chapter, criteria included in program evaluation results may also be viewed as the beginning of a continuous improvement program. Thus, the criterion results should not be viewed as threatening to project developers and stakeholders—as the sword by which a program lives or dies—but rather as part of a process to drive increased program effectiveness. In this regard, it is important to also consider criterion measurements and variations of them as tools that can be used to consistently monitor and improve program results and impacts even well after the initial evaluation effort. In this regard, the process map provided in Figure 3.1 can be viewed as a continuous network of diagnostic and communication feedback loops rather than a more limited cycle with a beginning and an end.

References

Baron, R. M., & Kenny, D. A. (1986). The moderator-mediator variable distinction in social psychological research: Conceptual, strategic, and statistical considerations. *Journal of Personality and Social Psychology, 51,* 1173–1182.

Guion, R. (1998). Some virtues of dissatisfaction in the science and practice of personnel selection. *Human Resource Management Review, 8,* 351–365.

Kerlinger, F. N. (1973). *Foundations of behavioral research.* New York: Holt, Rinehart and Winston.

Landy, F. J., & Trumbo, D. A. (1980). *Psychology of work behavior.* Homewood, IL: Dorsey Press.

Suggested Readings on Criterion Development

Fernandez-Ballesteros, R., Vedung, E., & Seyfried, E. (1998). Psychology in program evaluation. *European Psychologist, 3,* 143–154.

Gredler, M. E. (1996). *Program evaluation.* Englewood, NJ: Prentice Hall.

Hanser, L. M. (1997). Criterion development in Project A. In R. F. Dillon (Ed.), *Handbook on testing* (pp. 256–273). Westport, CT: Greenwood Press.

Hinn, D. M., Benson, A. P., & Lloyd, C. (2001). *Visions of quality: How evaluators define, understand, and represent program quality* (Advances in Program Evaluation, Vol. 7). New York: JAI Press.

Laurence, J. H., Wall, J. E., Barnes, J. D., & Dela Rosa, M. (1998). Recruiting effectiveness of the ASVAB career exploration program. *Military Psychology, 10,* 225–238.

Posavac, E. J., & Carey, R. G. (1997). *Program evaluation: Methods and case studies* (5th ed.). Englewood, NJ: Prentice Hall.

Schalock, R. L. (2001). *Outcome based evaluation* (2nd ed.). New York: Kluwer Academic/Plenum Publishers.

Torres, R. T., & Preskill, H. (1999). Ethical dimensions of stakeholder participation and evaluation use. In J. L. Fitzpatrick and M. Morris (Eds.), *Current and emerging ethical challenges in evaluation. New directions for evaluation: A publication of the American Evaluation Association, No. 82* (pp. 57–66). San Francisco, CA: Jossey-Bass.

PART II

Staffing

CHAPTER 4

Recruitment

Michael M. Harris

Elliot D. Lasson

T raditionally, the recruitment function has been relegated to a relatively minor role in the hiring process. When the recruitment aspect was systematically considered, the primary focus was on identifying and using the sources (e.g., print ad and college campus) that were likely to produce the most promising candidates. Two major trends in the late 1990s, however, changed the importance of the recruitment component rather dramatically. First, significant changes in the labor market sometimes produced far more job openings than applicants. In turn, this produced serious shortages of workers in certain growing occupations. Second, with the the advent of the Internet employees could easily and very quickly search for, identify, and apply for large numbers of jobs with a minimum amount of effort. As a result, an organization seeking to fill a job opening cannot assume that there will be a surfeit of candidates to choose from. In many cases, just the opposite is true. Even if a number of candidates do apply for a job opening, no longer will the organization's first or second choice candidates automatically accept a position. These considerations have, in turn, led those in charge of recruitment to recognize that recruitment covers far more than just which source to use; rather, recruitment must address a wide range of activities and processes.

This chapter is divided into three major sections. First, we provide a basic overview of the major recruitment steps and review research on reasons that applicants choose to apply for and accept jobs. Next, we discuss recruitment sources—both traditional

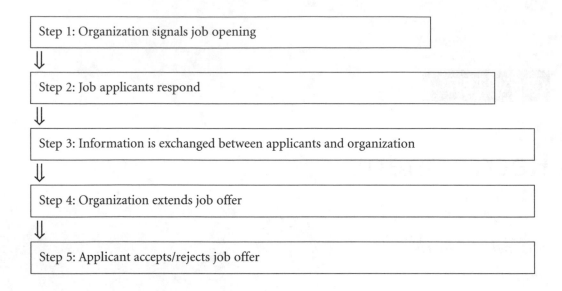

Figure 4.1 Model of Recruitment Process

and Internet-based approaches. Finally, we discuss four types of recruitment evaluation measures and their pitfalls.

Understanding the Recruitment Process

We define recruitment as organizational practices and policies developed for the primary purpose of motivating applicants to apply, remain in the candidate pool, and accept job offers. In keeping with this definition, and for the purpose of helping to understand the recruitment process, we depict the basic steps in a recruitment process in Figure 4.1. As shown in Figure 4.1, we assume that the recruitment process begins with a signal or announcement by the organization of a job opening, which in turn produces job applicants (Step 2). The third step involves an exchange of information between the organization and the applicants. In this step, the organization may obtain further information from applicants (e.g., what is traditionally referred to as the selection process), and applicants may obtain more information from the organization (e.g., ask about the nature of the job and visit the organization's plants or facilities). Offers for employment are made by the organization in the fourth step of the process and either accepted or declined by the applicants in the fifth step of the recruitment process.

Even though applicants may fail to apply to as many as one third of the job openings they review (Barber & Roehling, 1993), there has been little research on the reasons applicants choose to apply for some jobs but not others. To simplify this discussion, we divide the research into two approaches: The research that focuses on the *factors* that people consider in choosing to apply for jobs and accept offers, and the research that addresses the *process* that potential applicants use in determining whether to apply and accept an offer. What little research has been performed focuses mostly on the former question and has addressed two topics: the effects of organizational image or reputation and reactions to the recruitment message. Although limited in scope, research suggests that applicants may base their decision to apply on organizational image (Barber, 1998). Similar conclusions may be made with regard to recruitment message. Although there has been a dearth of well-done field research, there is some good evidence to suggest that applicants heavily base a decision to apply on the salary that is offered, the geographic location of the job, and diversity policies. None of these factors are particularly surprising.

What is perhaps more interesting is *how* applicants decide to apply, or not apply, for a particular job and whether they accept or decline a subsequent job offer. Although most of the research has used traditional decision theory models (e.g., subjective expected utility models), image theory (Beach, 1990; Mitchell & Beach, 1990) may be a more useful way to think about whether applicants choose to apply or not apply for a job. Briefly stated, image theory assumes that people "adopt and implement plans to reach goals in order to satisfy principles" (Mitchell & Beach, 1990, p. 16). Image theory further assumes that decision makers use a two-step process. In the first step, decision makers conduct a *compatibility test* to determine whether the option meets their basic principles and values. The compatibility test is assumed to be a fast and superficial screen of the options. For example, imagine that Mary sees an advertisement for an opening with a cigarette manufacturer. If one of Mary's principles is to be involved only with socially responsible organizations for the betterment of human life, she may very quickly decide not to apply for this job. Job advertisements, on the other hand, for a nonprofit organization such as the United Way, may pass Mary's initial screen and she may choose to apply. Because applying for a job may entail relatively low costs and one can always apply for multiple jobs, there may be relatively little need to screen more carefully.

In the second stage, the *profitability stage,* job searchers use more sophisticated decision rules, such as a subjective expected utility model, in which the value of each option in terms of costs and benefits is assessed. It may only be at the interview stage or job offer stage that a job seeker uses such a careful and deliberate process.

Perhaps the major significance of applying image theory is that at the job announcement stage, job seekers will make quick screening decisions about applying based on whether the job fits their fundamental principles and values. Applicants are not likely to apply to organizations that do not fit these. Although we know of no research on this issue, we suspect that organizational reputation may play a powerful role in the decision to initially apply for a job.

Recruitment Sources

Before we begin to discuss the different recruitment sources, it is helpful to consider why different sources may produce different results in terms of the program evaluation criteria described later in this chapter. One explanation is that candidates from certain sources know more about the organization than candidates from other sources. For example, candidates who are recruited through friends who work at the organization will receive key information about the organization that enables them to more accurately choose whether to apply. Such candidates also may be less likely to suffer from unrealistic expectations.

A second explanation is that candidates from some sources are more qualified for the job than candidates from other sources. Specifically, an employee of the organization may be more likely to recommend a highly qualified friend and will refrain from suggesting a marginally qualified person. A third explanation is that certain sources are more effective in generating "passive" candidates than are other sources. A passive candidate is an applicant who is not actively searching for a new job. Such applicants may be highly successful, well-rewarded employees who are content with their current positions. Alternatively, candidates who are actively searching may be on average less qualified; otherwise they would have more quickly found jobs. Sources that produce passive candidates therefore may be more effective than sources that generate "active" candidates.

Despite the arguments for why one source may be superior to another, generally there is no one single best source of job applicants. Rather, the best source will depend on various factors such as the job type, the amount of experience needed, and the location of the company.

Because there are many different sources of applicants, it is helpful to organize them into a smaller number of categories. We will divide the sources into two categories: traditional and Internet sources. For each approach, you will learn about the source's strengths and weaknesses, followed by some general suggestions. Note that the ratings on these sources are based on our experience and review of the literature. In practice, the relative strengths and weaknesses will be affected by many factors, and these ratings are merely rough estimates.

We focus on five features of each source as described below:

1. Quality ratio: The number of qualified candidates compared to the number of total candidates. Some sources may provide many candidates, of which only a handful are likely to be qualified; other sources may provide far fewer candidates, but most of them may be qualified for the job.
2. Speed: The relative quickness from start to finish of our Figure 4.1 model.
3. Meet equal employment opportunity (EEO) needs: The relative effectiveness of the source in terms of legal history and the degree to which it is likely to generate a diverse group of applicants with regard to such demographics as ethnicity and gender.
4. Degree of personalization: How personable and customized the source is. For example, a source that refines its message to the particular individual is viewed as high on personalization. Although this index is generally not considered in the recruitment literature, we believe it may play an important role in attracting candidates.
5. Cost: The relative costs of the source in terms of managerial time and other expenses, such as job posting.

Table 4.1 Summary of Strengths and Weaknesses of Major Recruitment Sources

Source	Quality Ratio	Speed	Meet EEO Needs	Degree of Personalization	Cost
Employee referral	Good	Average	Poor	Good	Good
Print ad	Poor	Average	Good	Poor	Average
Search firm	Good	Good	Average	Good	Poor
College campus	Good	Poor	Average	Average	Average
Radio	Poor	Average	Average	Poor	Average
Job board	Poor	Average	Poor	Poor	Good
E-recruiting	Good	Average	Poor	Good	Poor
Relationship recruiting	Good	Poor	Average	Average	Average

The strengths and weaknesses for each recruitment source are summarized in Table 4.1.

Traditional Sources

Employee Referrals

Using employee referrals is a common approach in a competitive labor market as they offer a number of advantages. Research supports the contention that employee referrals produce the best candidates. Thus, the quality ratio is likely to be high. Employee referrals also provide a high degree of personalization because the employee will be able to fine-tune and customize the message to the candidate. Finally, we judge this as being a good (i.e., low) cost source because a payout is made *only* when a candidate is successfully hired. Recent studies indicate that a $1,000 payment to the employee who did the recruiting is about typical in this area. For an employee candidate who will earn $30,000, this represents only about 3% of the candidate's starting salary.

Employee referrals are rated as average on speed. The major potential disadvantage is in regard to meeting equal employment opportunity (EEO) needs. Employee referrals tend to maintain a workforce that reflects the demographic characteristics of the existing workforce. Thus, a predominantly white, male workforce that relies heavily on employee referrals is likely to generate a white male candidate pool. Conversely, an organization that has a diverse workforce may use this recruitment source with minimal problems meeting EEO needs.

Print Ad

A print ad refers to advertising in newspapers, trade magazines, and newsletters. The print ad is probably one of the most widely used traditional sources. Because we use the term *print ad* to represent a wide range of publications, print ads can differ greatly in terms of the numbers and types of applicants they draw. Local newspapers can be quite effective in drawing clerical, service, and production employees who are actively seeking jobs. Similarly, trade magazines and newsletters may be one of the most effective means of drawing professional employee candidates from a national and even global pool.

Because print ads can differ widely, depending on whether they appear in a local newspaper or in a trade magazine, it is rather difficult to draw any general conclusions about their advantages and disadvantages. Print ads do have one major potential advantage, namely, meeting EEO needs. Specifically, use of print ads will help verify that the company conducted an appropriate search and has the potential to draw a diverse group of applications. In terms of cost and speed, we believe that print ads are about average. The two major drawbacks are quality ratio and degree of personalization.

Search Firms

Search firms, or as they are sometimes called, headhunters, play an important role in the recruitment area. Search firms generally operate on either a contingency basis, where they are paid if the person they find is hired, or on a retainer basis, where they are paid a fee for the search regardless of whether anyone is hired. Usually, the latter is for higher level executive (e.g., chief executive officer [CEO]) or professional (e.g., medical doctor) jobs.

A headhunter brings several advantages to the recruitment process. First, the headhunter focuses on a select group of candidates, thus the quality ratio is likely to be high. The process is also likely to be fast. In addition, the degree of personalization is quite high. Because a headhunter can also focus on diversity, we believe that this source should be rated average in terms of meeting EEO needs. The major shortcoming here is cost. The typical fee for a search firm is one third of the first year's annual salary. For a $50,000 position, this would be a $17,000 fee, which would be higher than most other recruiting sources (Pawlik, 1998).

College Campus Recruitment

Another traditional recruitment source is college campus recruitment, which offers one major advantage and one key disadvantage. In terms of advantages, college campuses provide large numbers of recently trained graduates in highly sought-after fields—such as information technology and accounting—who can be easily screened for grade point average and so forth. Thus, this source provides a high quality ratio. We believe that college campuses are average in terms of meeting EEO needs, degree of personalization, and costs. Much will depend on the nature of the college campus (e.g., the minority population) and the organization's proximity to the institution. The greatest potential weakness is the speed, which we rate as low. We rate the speed low for two reasons. First, college campus hiring is highly cyclical; in the summer and fall, for example, there will be relatively few candidates to hire. Second, students may be interviewing with several different organizations and may want to see what the alternatives are before accepting a job offer, further slowing down the hiring process.

Radio Ads

Although television and radio ads are somewhat similar, we will focus solely on radio ads because of their relative prevalence. In general, radio ads do not have one single major strength. They are considered about average in speed and meeting EEO needs. In terms of cost, radio may be lower (i.e., less expensive) than one would expect, and overall we rate the cost as average. Radio allows organizations to target their ads to some extent; people who listen to rock stations, for example, tend to differ in a variety of ways from people who listen to classical music stations. Radio ads have two major disadvantages. In terms of personalization, radio delivers the same basic message to all potential candidates; thus, it is rated poor on this dimension. Also, the quality ratio is likely to be fairly poor as many unqualified people are likely to apply.

Internet-Based Approaches

In the last few years, the Internet has had a major impact on recruitment. In a very short period of time, it has become a major source for job applicants. Although the use of the approach varies widely, The Good Guys, a West Coast Electronics chain, obtains between one fourth to one third of its employees from this source (Frost, 1997). There are many different approaches to Internet recruitment, but we focus on three basic types: job boards, e-recruiting, and relationship recruiting.

Job Boards

An early approach to Internet-based recruiting was the job board. Monster Board (*www.monster.com*) was one of the most successful examples of this approach. Basically, the job board is much like a newspaper listing of job opportunities, along with resumes of job applicants (Harris & Dewar, 2001). The job board's greatest strength is the sheer numbers of job applicants listing resumes; according to some estimates, job boards contain 5 million unique resumes (Gutmacher, 2000). Although initially a highly successful approach, the standard job board is currently not highly valuable. As shown in Table 4.1, it is poor in quality ratio, meeting EEO needs, and degree of personalization. The major strength of job boards is the low cost. Their speed is considered to be average.

E-Recruiting

A completely different approach to Internet-based recruiting focuses on the recruiter searching online for job candidates (Gutmacher, 2000). Sometimes referred to as the meta crawler approach (Harris & Dewar, 2001), e-recruiters use the Internet to ferret out potential job candidates. For example, in a technique called flipping, recruiters use a search engine, like Altavista.com, to search the Web for resumes with links to a particular company's Web site. Using a technique known as peeling, e-recruiters may enter a corporate Web site and peel it back to locate lists of employees. Finally, using a technique known as x-raying, e-recruiters may locate company Web sites not generally accessible to the public (Silverman, 2000).

The major advantage of this technique is the potential to find outstanding passive candidates. In addition, because the e-recruiter chooses whom to approach, this method will generate far fewer candidates and especially far fewer unqualified candidates. Thus, the quality ratio is good, as is the degree of personalization. On the negative side, the effectiveness of this technique is likely to decline over time (Harris & Dewar, 2001). Second, some of these techniques may constitute hacking, which at a minimum may be unethical and possibly illegal. Because it is intensive work, we deem this technique poor (i.e., high) in costs. This technique is also considered poor in meeting EEO needs.

Relationship Recruiting

One of the relatively newer approaches to Internet-based recruitment is called relationship recruiting (Harris & Dewar, 2001). A major purpose behind relationship recruiting is to develop a long-term relationship with passive candidates so that when they decide to enter the job market, they will turn to the companies and organizations with which they have developed a long-term relationship (Boehle, 2000). This technique is highly dependent on customer relationship management techniques. As an example, relationship recruitment relies on the Internet to learn more about Web visitors' interests and experience and then provides regular updates about careers and their fields of interest. When suitable job opportunities arise, an e-mail may be sent to them regarding the opportunity. (For an interesting example, see www.futurestep.com.) Similar to the headhunter approach, relationship recruiting is high on quality ratio. However, the use of the Internet provides the capability of developing such relationships at a medium cost. We rate the technique as being poor on speed and average on the other three features.

Evaluating the Recruitment Function

Before we examine the details of evaluation, here are three general suggestions: First, we generally recommend that a committee of line managers, human resources (HR) staff, and possibly others be included in conducting the evaluation. There are several reasons for this recommendation, but perhaps the most important is that including people who are familiar with the organization will provide valuable input into such areas as what the key criteria are for the evaluation. Another major reason for using a committee is that the conclusions agreed on by several knowledgeable people will usually have greater credibility than those drawn by one individual.

Second, for some of these evaluation measures, you must decide whether to obtain quantitative information (e.g., from surveys) or qualitative information (e.g., from focus groups). There are advantages and disadvantages for both approaches. The quantitative approach allows for more scientific accuracy and may be faster and easier to collect. Participants may be more willing to complete an anonymous survey. The qualitative approach, on the other hand, may lead to the discovery of issues not previously considered and allows for probes and follow-up questions. Ideally, both methods will be used.

Finally, we generally recommend that a neutral third party be used to collect any data (e.g., applicant reactions) external to the organization. A neutral party may be viewed as more trustworthy by respondents. If so, respondents will be more likely to respond honestly than if the data were gathered by a representative of the organization.

We have organized our discussion of evaluation measures into four categories: recruitment outcomes, applicant predictors/criteria, subjective recruitment measures, and organizational reputation. Recruitment outcomes include the lag time between an organizational announcement of a job opening (Step 1 in Figure 4.1) and applicants accepting a job offer (Step 5), as well as the costs incurred by the organization in hiring job candidates. Applicant predictors (e.g., tests, interviews, and other measures of qualifications) and criteria (e.g., job performance ratings and tenure) rely on comparisons of the relative advantages and disadvantages of different recruitment sources. Subjective recruitment measures focus on *applicant* reactions (e.g., to the recruiters who do the interviewing, the site visit, and the recruitment process overall). Finally, organizational reputation addresses applicant as well as nonapplicant perceptions of the organizational image.

Using Recruitment Outcomes for Evaluation

Recruitment outcome measures are the most commonly used measures for evaluating the recruitment function. The three major recruitment outcome variables are cost, time, and quality ratio (Cascio, 1998). We also include a fourth variable from Table 4.1—meet EEO needs (e.g., percentage of minority and female applicants).

Not surprisingly, cost or cost-per-hire, which refers to the costs of the recruiting source, is of critical value. Given the complexity of this measure, we devote more attention to it below. A second variable worthy of tracking is time. Typically, the shorter the time frame between beginning the recruitment process and the hiring of applicants, the more effective the recruitment source is considered to be. Because of the many steps involved in a recruitment process, it is probably helpful to assess the amount of time involved at each step.

The quality ratio is the percentage of qualified applicants generated by the recruitment process. Although traditionally the recruitment function has focused on the simple *number* of candidates generated by the recruitment process, we believe that the focus should be on the percentage of qualified applicants. Finally, the percentage of applicants who are members of minority, female, or other underrepresented classes may be essential in meeting various regulations and corporate goals. Examining the percentages at each stage of the recruitment cycle may also be helpful, to determine whether a problem exists at any particular point (e.g., a large percentage of candidates drops out at a particular stage). Because estimating time, quality ratios, and EEO impact is fairly straightforward, we focus here on estimating costs.

Assessing Costs

Each step in the recruitment process is likely to have some kind of cost associated with it. A careful examination is needed to determine where the costs lie and what the estimate of each cost is. Referring to Figure 4.1, the cost items discussed next may be relevant.

In Stage 1, each signal or announcement has an associated cost. For example, a manager spends time writing and submitting an ad to the newspaper. The cost of the manager's salary and benefits therefore should be calculated. During Stage 2, application submissions, the organization must process these applications or resumes that are received on paper or electronically. Both equipment costs (e.g., tracking software prorated across multiple recruiting efforts) and labor costs for the administrative tasks must be included in these calculations. Information exchange in Stage 3 involves organizational costs such as interviewer time for interviewing, as well as travel expenses and time. The candidates also incur a variety of potential costs (e.g., travel, meals, and hotels) that the organization may reimburse. In Stage 4, deciding which candidates will and will not receive offers takes employee time. In addition, some organizations make use of employment contracts that applicants accepting job offers must sign. Such contracts may require the use of legal counsel, which has associated costs.

Next, one should determine as precisely as possible what the costs are for each of these factors. While the costs for some items may be more readily available than others (e.g., the cost of a drug test may be easier to estimate than how much managerial time was spent), it is important to get the best estimates possible. For labor costs, it is best to break the estimate down into two parts. First, estimate the amount of time spent on the task. For example, estimate the number of hours spent interviewing. Second, calculate the cost per hour of employee time (this should include the cost of salary and benefits). Then, multiply the number of hours by the cost per hour of employee time (recruiters, clerical staff, managers, and so forth). Don't forget that the numbers often differ by how many applicants there are. If 100 candidates interviewed, for instance, and the average interview consumed 1.5 hours and the average labor cost is $45.00 per hour, then the proper estimate for the interviews is $100 \times 1.5 \times \$45.00$, or $6,750.00.

Advantages of Estimating Costs

The primary advantage of estimating costs is that this is a key factor in making HR decisions. Also, managers will always ask about the costs of any HR program. Finally, cost represents a metric that any manager can understand.

Potential Concerns in Estimating Costs

We anticipate three possible concerns in estimating costs. Different people may arrive at different estimates of the costs. For example, people may estimate the costs of software differently, particularly if they have different opinions on how often it will be used in the future. The best thing is to have each committee member independently estimate the costs and be prepared to explain exactly what the basis is for the estimate. It is also recommended that accounting experts be included in helping to estimate the costs. Only by identifying assumptions can agreement be reached.

Recruitment outcomes have a narrow focus. A recruitment source that is quicker, is cheaper, and has a high quality ratio at each stage of the cycle may not necessarily produce the best applicants in terms of performance, tenure, and other important measures of performance (Harris & Dewar, 2001). Decision makers must therefore not emphasize this measure to the exclusion of others.

Recruitment outcomes may be among the most objective, but they can also be manipulated. If recruiters, for example, were judged on speed, they might be tempted to oversell the job and make job offers to less qualified individuals.

Using Applicant Predictors and Criteria for Evaluation

Researchers have focused on applicant predictors (e.g., test scores) and criteria (e.g., job performance ratings) as ways to evaluate the recruitment process (Breaugh, 1981). The rationale behind this approach is that if the organization is using a valid predictor, it would be reasonable to compare different recruitment sources to determine which provides better candidates. Alternatively, one could use criterion measures (i.e., job performance measures), such as turnover rates, performance evaluations, and absenteeism, to compare different recruitment sources. As with predictors, research has shown that criteria may differ by source (Barber, 1998).

Assessing Predictor and Criterion Results

The program evaluation team should investigate five aspects of the predictors and criteria.

1. They should determine the key predictors that the organization currently uses to make hiring decisions. These may include selection tests, drug tests, interview ratings, or other possible predictors. Measures should reflect important organizational factors in hiring.

2. Similarly, they should determine key criteria, such as job tenure, performance measures, and absenteeism rates, that the organization currently uses to reflect job outcomes. These are often measures that are kept in HR databases. The team should examine all performance measures deemed important to the organization.

3. Where necessary, the evaluation team should request additional predictor or criterion measures. In some cases, such as the interview, the organization may not

currently be producing numerical ratings. In that case, the team should request that a measure be developed for the evaluation process. For example, an interview guide may be created that interviewers will use to rate each candidate on multiple dimensions (e.g., interpersonal and technical skills). Similarly, some criterion measures may be derived for the first time, such as absenteeism or turnover information.

4. The relative importance of each predictor in predicting the criteria should be assessed. In addition to looking at each predictor and criterion separately, it may also be beneficial to have a single, composite rating for each candidate based on the predictors. This is particularly true when some recruitment sources appear better on one predictor and worse on another predictor. It is generally recommended that predictors and criteria not be combined as they are assessing quite different things; instead, the predictors and criteria should be analyzed separately.

5. The evaluation team should compare different sources (e.g., print ads versus employee referral) in terms of averages and standard deviations. Statistics should be used to compare the different ratings across sources. In addition to looking at mean differences by predictor, the team may also find it useful to look at standard deviations for each source. Thus, sources with more variability might be reexamined. It may also be useful to break the analyses down by demographics (e.g., race and gender) to determine whether different sources produce candidates of different quality.

Advantages of Evaluating Predictors and Criteria

If the question is which source provides the best candidates, an employee predictor-criterion approach represents a direct way to determine an answer. A second advantage of this approach is that there is both a short-term and a long-term perspective. For example, one can determine whether a source that is most effective in terms of short-term considerations (e.g., which source produces employees who are most effective in the first year of tenure) is also most effective in terms of long-term considerations (e.g., which source produces employees who are most effective five years after their employment begins). Finally, particularly with the trend toward HR information systems and database development, many organizations collect information that will enable them to easily gather and analyze such data.

Potential Concerns When Evaluating Predictors and Criteria

One potential concern is that these measures do not explain why one source is better than another source or help pinpoint problems. For example, a job fair may be producing poor candidates because the recruiters do not represent the organization well. This evaluation method will not reveal that kind of information, so it will not lead to a correction of the problem. Another potential assessment concern is that comparing results with other organizations would be difficult, given that different organizations typically have different predictors and criteria. A third concern is that criteria may not reflect the recruitment process as much as they reflect other factors (e.g., rating errors, good supervisors, and effective pay policies).

Using Applicant Perceptions
of the Recruitment Process for Evaluation

Gathering applicant perceptions of the recruitment process became popular in the 1970s and 1980s. Research that has used such measures has focused on the degree to which Step 3 (information exchange between applicants and the organization) in Figure 4.1 affects subsequent steps. This research may be summarized as follows: "negative recruitment experiences . . . [are] enough to completely eliminate the organization from further consideration" (Rynes, Bretz, & Gerhart, 1991, p. 515) and therefore applicant perceptions are important to use in evaluating the recruitment process.

Assessing Applicant Reaction

Although applicant reaction to the recruitment process is probably a multidimensional variable, we believe that a key factor in understanding this is the degree of personalization. Specifically, we believe that the more the recruitment message and process is customized to fit the particular issues and concerns of each applicant, the more successful the recruitment effort will be. This is particularly challenging today, given the level to which mass media (e.g., print ads and Internet) dominate the recruitment scene. The program evaluation team should investigate the following three aspects of applicant reactions:

1. Determine the key components/dimensions in the recruitment process. One potentially important component is the behavior of the hiring manager. In addition to personalization, research shows that perceived competence (e.g., is the hiring manager effective in conducting the interview?) and informativeness (e.g., did the hiring manager speak of the job in great detail?) are important to applicants. Other aspects of the recruitment process should also be examined. The value of the company's Web site, with regard to how informative it was and how easy it was to use, should be surveyed. The nature of the site visit, including meetings with other employees, should be assessed by including questions regarding the amount of information shared and the quality of the accommodations (e.g., hotel and meals). These measures may be either qualitative or quantitative.

2. Determine when to collect measures. An applicant's rating of the recruitment process may change dramatically, depending on when one obtains the measures. We recommend that information be collected both immediately after applicants go through the recruitment activities and after they are hired. If possible, it may be helpful to get information from those who were not made job offers as well. Because of the sensitive nature of the questions, a focus group may not be feasible. Survey methods, particularly using the Internet and a neutral third party, may be more revealing.

3. Analyze results. It is particularly important that data be analyzed in several different ways. First, it is important to compare different groups of applicants, including those who accept offers and those who do not accept offers, to determine whether the

recruitment process appears related to job offer acceptance. Second, it may be helpful to compare results across departments to determine whether some departments are more effective than others. Finally, for organizations doing extensive amounts of hiring, it may be useful to compare different hiring managers to determine whether some are more effective than others and whether recruitment training may be in order. Minor differences may be meaningless; focus on large differences.

Advantages of Assessing Applicant Perceptions

The major strength of this approach is that it will help diagnose problems in the recruitment function. If, for example, recruiters are perceived by applicants as being ineffective, then programs can be undertaken to address this issue. Second, compared to applicant predictors/criteria, applicant perceptions will be far less affected by outside circumstances, such as supervisory practices, because applicant perceptions focus quite directly on the actual steps in the recruitment function.

Potential Concerns in Assessing Applicant Perceptions

Applicant perception measures may indicate that the recruiting process is well run, but that does not guarantee that the best candidates are hired. Other factors may be operating, such as competitors who pay more. In addition, this approach does not include potential applicants who choose not to apply. It only focuses on those applicants who did apply and completed the survey. Again, this measure focuses on the recruitment processes, not the factors that determine whether someone will even choose to apply. Finally, applicants may be concerned that their individual responses will be identified and therefore they will be reluctant to report how they actually feel about the recruitment process. Or, being busy on the job search, they may not respond. Lack of a response or use of a socially desirable response may be problems.

Using Organizational Reputation for Evaluation

In more recent times, with the tight labor market and a greater emphasis on life-work issues, organizations have begun to understand that organizational reputation, or image, is increasingly important in terms of recruiting. Because this is a relatively new approach compared to the three previously described, we discuss organizational reputation in a bit more detail. We first define what we mean by reputation. Then, we discuss how to measure reputation in the recruitment context.

Organizational reputation has been defined in a variety of ways, but most experts (Gatewood, Gowan, & Lautenschlager, 1993; Berkson, Harris, & Ferris, 1999) have suggested that reputation refers to one's reaction to the organization as a whole. For present purposes, this is the definition we are using. Several questions should be answered before assessing reputation. One question is whether and how organizational reputation differs from attributes of a specific job, such as pay and type of work. We assert that it does differ. Another question is whether the term *reputation* means different things, depending on whether one is considering the issue from the perspective of a job candidate, a consumer, or an investor. We believe that the reputation of an organization may have widely different meanings depending on the perspective taken, and therefore it is important to obtain this information from actual applicants as well as from potential applicants who choose to not apply.

A third issue is whether reputation is best measured as a single component or as multiple components. Although most researchers have merely attempted to measure reputation as a single concern (e.g., Turban, Forret, & Hendrickson, 1998), there have been attempts to examine its different components (Cable & Graham, 2000). For present purposes, we recommend that overall as well as specific aspects of reputation be evaluated. For example, *Fortune* magazine annually publishes a list of the top 100 companies to work for and includes employee satisfaction survey ratings, turnover rates, and other similar indices in making these ratings.

Assessing Organizational Reputation

To measure reputation, the following steps are suggested.

1. Obtain the names of organizations you compete with for new employees. This may be determined by finding out where applicants have interviewed in the past and where employees go after they leave your organization. To avoid missing names, generate a list using as many sources as possible (e.g., former and current employees, and recruitment experts). The list should contain no more than a few top companies that are viewed as the most significant competitors for talent.

2. Develop a list of survey questions. Ideally, you would use a general question, such as "overall, what is the reputation of company X as a place to work," as well as some specific aspects (e.g., "what is the reputation of company X for promotional opportunities?"). Some specific areas to include are pay and benefits, training opportunities, managers/supervisors, promotion opportunities, and work/life balance. We suggest that each competitor be rated on each question. That way, a quantitative comparison can be made between your organization and the competition.

3. Determine how data will be gathered. The main question here is what method will be used. This is an area where a focus group may be quite valuable, though a follow-up quantitative survey will provide valuable information as well.

4. Determine which respondents to use. It may be tempting just to use current employees in completing the survey, but by using only applicants who are hired, you run the risk of not understanding the perceptions of candidates who turn down job offers and others who are not offered jobs or who did not apply. Respondents may, however, be concerned about anonymity.

5. Analyze results by different groups. Results should be analyzed and reported by different demographic and recruitment groups. By the former, we mean comparing gender, ethnicity, and possibly other groups to determine whether differences exist. In

terms of recruitment groups, the comparisons could contrast the responses of applicants who accepted jobs, applicants who turned down job offers, and potential applicants who did not apply to the company. Such information may be highly useful in determining why certain individuals choose not to work for your organization.

Advantages of Assessing Organizational Reputation

A major advantage of assessing organizational reputation is that the resulting data may provide valuable insights as to why some potential candidates choose not to apply at all or to withdraw their application at a later date (e.g., Ryan, Sacco, McFarland, & Kriska, 2000). Another advantage is that assessing organizational reputation reminds all employees that their actions and behavior have a wide impact on the success of the organization.

Potential Concerns When Assessing Organizational Reputation

Two concerns come readily to mind. First, organizational reputation is not routinely measured, especially in the recruitment context. HR practitioners may have difficulty justifying their collection of such data. Second, organizational reputation reflects just one factor in the recruitment process. In addition, this measure is rather removed from the actual recruitment activities and practices conducted by most organizations.

Conclusions

We have reviewed four categories of measures that may be used to evaluate an organization's recruitment program. We would like to draw attention to three important points in closing. First, based on the advantages and disadvantages of each of our four categories of measures, there is obviously no one best measure to use; different measures help analyze different components of a recruitment program. Thus, we assert that all four types of measures that have been described here are valuable. Even when there may appear to be overlap between different measures, what they tell us may be quite different. For instance, although time lag between steps may be measured both objectively (recruitment outcome) and subjectively (applicant reactions), they measure different aspects (e.g., one is objective, the other is perceptual) and therefore both types of measures may be valuable.

Second, we note that it may be useful to evaluate the recruitment function separately for different groups. For example, it may be valuable to analyze female candidates' reactions to the recruitment process separately from male candidates' reactions as we suspect that different demographic groups may have different reactions to recruitment efforts. This is particularly true if there is a segment in which recruitment has been difficult in the past.

Finally, we have presented our measures in a relatively simplistic fashion. Others (e.g., Boudreau & Rynes, 1985) have argued for applying much more sophisticated techniques (e.g., utility analysis) for estimating the dollar value of alternative recruiting sources. Indeed, using utility analysis, Boudreau and Rynes demonstrated that, depending on one's assumptions, conclusions as to which recruitment source was superior could change radically. However, Barber (1998) warned that one should be cautious about basing decisions about recruitment on the results of utility analysis due to the many estimates that are involved. One must therefore be careful in judging the results of any evaluation of the recruitment process.

References

Barber, A. E. (1998). *Recruiting employees.* Thousand Oaks, CA: Sage.

Barber, A. E., & Roehling, M. (1993). Job posting and the decision to interview: A verbal protocol analysis. *Journal of Applied Psychology, 78,* 845–856.

Beach, L. R. (1990). *Image theory: Decision making in personal and organizational contexts.* Chichester, England: Wiley.

Berkson, H. M., Harris, M. M., & Ferris, G. R. (1999). Enhancing organizational reputation to attract applicants. In R. W. Eder & M. M. Harris (Eds.), *The employment interview handbook* (pp. 83–98). Thousand Oaks, CA: Sage.

Boehle, S. (2000, May). Online recruiting gets sneaky. *Training, 37,* 66–74.

Boudreau, J., & Rynes, S. L. (1985). Role of recruitment in staffing utility analysis. *Journal of Applied Psychology, 70,* 354–366.

Breaugh, J. (1981). Relationships between recruiting sources and employee performance, absenteeism, and work attitudes. *Academy of Management Journal, 8,* 612–619.

Cable, D. M., & Graham, M. E. (2000). The determinants of job seekers' reputation perceptions. *Journal of Organizational Behavior, 21,* 929–947.

Cascio, W. (1998). *Applied psychology in human resource management.* Upper Saddle River, NJ: Prentice Hall.

Frost, M. (1997, May). The internet's hire purpose. *HRMagazine, 42,* 30–32.

Gatewood, R. D., Gowan, M. A., & Lautenschlager, G. J. (1993). Corporate image, recruitment image, and initial job choice decisions. *Academy of Management Journal, 36,* 414–427.

Gutmacher, G. (2000, October). Secrets of online recruiters exposed! *Workforce, 79,* 44–50.

Harris, M., & Dewar, K. (2001). *Understanding and using web-based recruiting and screening tools: Key criteria, current trends, and future directions.* Pre-conference workshop presented at the annual meeting of the Society for Industrial and Organizational Psychology, San Diego, CA.

Mitchell, T., & Beach, L. (1990). " . . . Do I love thee? Let me count . . . ": Toward an understanding of intuitive and automatic decision making. *Organizational Behavior & Human Decision Processes, 47,* 1–20.

Pawlik, B. (1998, September). Recruiting a recruiter: Seven steps to success. *HR Focus, 75,* S13-S14.

Ryan, A. M., Sacco, J. M., McFarland, L. A., & Kriska, S. D. (2000). Applicant self-selection: Correlates of withdrawal from a multiple hurdle process. *Journal of Applied Psychology, 85,* 163–179.

Rynes, S., Bretz, R., & Gerhart, B. (1991). The importance of recruitment in job choice: A different way of looking. *Personnel Psychology, 44,* 487–521.

Silverman, R. E. (2000, October 3). Raiding talent via the web. *The Wall Street Journal,* pp. B1, B16.

Turban, D., Forret, M., & Hendrickson, C. (1998). Applicant attraction to firms: Influences of organization reputation, job and organizational attributes, and recruiter behaviors. *Journal of Vocational Behavior, 52,* 24–44.

Suggested Reading in Recruitment

Barber, A. E. (1998). *Recruiting employees.* Thousand Oaks, CA: Sage.

Cascio, W. (1998). *Applied psychology in human resource management.* Upper Saddle River, NJ: Prentice Hall.

Harris, M. M., & Fink, L. S. (1987). A field study of applicant reactions to employment opportunities. *Personnel Psychology, 40,* 765–783.

Rynes, S., Bretz, R., & Gerhart, B. (1991). The importance of recruitment in job choice: A different way of looking. *Personnel Psychology, 44,* 487–521.

CHAPTER 5

Setting Standards

Andrew J. Falcone

Nambury S. Raju

T o determine the level of performance in any human endeavor ultimately means setting a standard of performance. How can one judge the performance of an individual on a task or the efficacy of a procedure without knowing what the standard of performance is? Some point of reference is needed to be able to determine whether a person or a procedure meets an acceptable level of performance, or benchmark. Without a standard, there is no way to measure the quality of any aspect of human performance or the performance of objects and procedures.

Many organizations set standards for various aspects of life. For example, Underwriters Laboratories (UL) sets standards of minimum performance for electrical appliances, and the Occupational Safety and Health Administration (OSHA) sets standards of performance for worker safety. Likewise, state licensing boards set performance standards for various professions by requiring a psychologist, physician, or pharmacist to meet standardized requirements before these professionals can practice. The standards that regulate title and practice typically include examinations. All of the standard setting entities in the foregoing discussion are in fact setting cut scores for various aspects of life, and the absence of such standards would seriously limit the development of our culture. Standards are an inescapable necessity of an organized society.

Setting Standards for Program Evaluation

In the context of program evaluation for human resources (HR), the establishment of standards plays a crucial role in determining how a program will be judged and ultimately what recommendations are made. Standard setting lays the foundation for determining whether a program provides a sufficient return on investment or meets key stakeholder objectives. If not, it needs to be modified to better meet these requirements. Standards also direct the methodology of the evaluation process and will therefore significantly impact the outcome of any program evaluation.

The establishment of standards is inextricably linked to the development of criteria, which was discussed in Chapter 3. Once the evaluation criteria have been developed, it is necessary to establish the performance levels on these criteria against which the HR program will be evaluated. Depending upon the particular HR program being evaluated, these standards can be developed using a variety of techniques; in some cases (e.g., selection), the development of standards is governed by a set of professional and legal guidelines. One such set of professional guidelines is the *Standards for Educational and Psychological Testing* (American Educational Research Association [AERA], American Psychological Association [APA], & the National Council on Measurement in Education [NCME], 1999) which is intended to "promote the sound and ethical use of tests and to provide a basis for evaluating the quality of testing practices" (p. 1).

A critical piece of information in any assessment procedure is the cut score, a minimum value that examinees or applicants must attain to be chosen for further consideration in a selection process. If this cut score or decision rule is used as intended, organizational decision makers will treat individuals in a fair and standardized manner and thereby avoid arbitrariness, preferential treatment, or capriciousness. This treatment of standard setting and its evaluation will be presented from a criterion-referenced examination perspective since standards should be absolute and not relative (norm-referenced). In the realm of licensing examinations, the most prevalent standard-setting procedures are those based on the Angoff method (Plake, 1998; Sireci & Biskin, 1992). Shepard (1980) captured the essence of criterion-referenced testing with the following statement:

> Criterion-referenced testing has an important connotation of absolute, rather than relative interpretations of achievement. For this reason, the most obvious method for setting standards has been to inspect test content and to decide what percentage of correct answers looks like evidence of mastery. In this way, only the merit of the questions and the expectations of the examiners determine the standard rather than the performance of the examinees. (p. 452)

In the evaluation of standard-setting procedures for written or performance-based examinations, the existence of a criterion-referenced procedure is imperative. In the development of a criterion-referenced examination, the content validity strategy is normally the only approach used. If the assessment instrument (e.g., a set of examination items) representatively samples the content of a job in terms of the necessary tasks for effective performance of that job, it is said to possess content validity. Content validity differs from criterion-related validity in at least two very important ways. In a content validity approach, a *new* measure is constructed from the "ground up" to be inexorably tied to the content domain of the job. It is true that job analyses are usually performed for a criterion-related validity study, but the emphasis is on the validation of an *existing* measure and not on the development of a new one as is the case with a content validity approach. The second major way in which these two approaches to establishing validity differ is that a content validity approach relies exclusively on the presence of subject matter experts (SMEs) and their expert judgment throughout the job analysis, item writing, examination development, standard setting, and item analysis. With the content validity approach, typically no validity coefficient or other metric equivalent is utilized to establish validity, as is the case with criterion-related validity. Usually no correlational analyses are performed to establish content validity; instead, validity is inherent in every phase of development of a content valid examination.

For the HR practitioner, the content validity approach has vast applicability. Specifically, setting cut scores for work sample tests, as well as licensure and certification examinations, typically follows an examination development path that embraces the content validity approach. The content validity approach is an examination development procedure that is required for the criterion-referenced test. The standard-setting procedures used to determine the cut scores for these types of examinations is the focus of this chapter. In criterion-related validation studies, cut scores can be determined using statistical regression procedures (see Chapter 6 in this book; these procedures will not be described here).

Criterion-Referenced Versus Norm-Referenced Approaches

Criterion-referenced examinations are designed to assess the mastery/nonmastery of a requisite body of knowledge or a given content domain (e.g., nursing, electrical contracting, network engineering). Licensure as an electrician or certification as a network engineer will require the use of a criterion-referenced examination. Scores on criterion-referenced examinations indicate what an individual knows and can do. A minimum level of competence is determined without considering the performance of others. An individual's mastery is not based on the performance of those who happen to be taking the examination at the same time. The benchmark standard of performance is based on what is required for the job in an absolute, fixed sense.

Criterion-referenced testing avoids the inherent, primary pitfall associated with norm-referenced testing, that of an examinee passing a standard based on the performance of others. Because ability levels of individuals can shift over the course of time, the norms of an examination will likewise change. The unintended effect could be that people might be certified or hired at varying levels of competency; stated another way, people could be certified or hired without having demonstrated a minimum level of competency. Because the ability level of the examinee is determined relative to the performance of other examinees taking either the same or a parallel form of an examination, a norm-referenced standard will be variable, as it is based on a variable ability distribution.

With criterion-referenced development procedures, the test is essentially validated against itself without any statistical linkage to an external criterion, as is the case with the criterion-related validation approach typically used in employee selection. When external criterion data (e.g., performance ratings or number of sales) are *not* available, the criterion-referenced approach of developing and validating a test should be used. The concept of internal (criterion-referenced/content validity) versus external (norm-referenced/criterion-related validity) criteria is one of the most critical concepts in this chapter if one of the criterion-referenced approaches to standard setting is to be used. These "absolute" methods of standard setting (Angoff, Nedelsky, etc.) are the preferred and professionally correct approaches to determining a standard, or cut score for a criterion-referenced examination. If external criteria are available, either a criterion-referenced *or* a norm-referenced cut score approach can be used. Even though a test publisher may provide norms and/or suggest a norm-referenced cut score for an existing measure, a criterion-referenced standard-setting approach can still be used. There is nothing technically wrong when the HR practitioner buys an existing examination from a publisher and then has SMEs set a criterion-referenced cut score for the examination. Table 5.1 provides an overview of the methods that are central to this discussion. It is crucial to understand the interrelationships between criterion-referenced examinations and norm-referenced examinations, the inherent validation strategies central to each type, and the standard-setting procedures associated with each. Because these examination *development,* examination *validation,* and standard-setting methods (see Table 5.1) are all interrelated, this association must be examined before the evaluation of standard setting can take place.

Table 5.1 lists the two major approaches to examination development, the validation methods associated with each, and the standard-setting methods linked to each type of examination. For example, a work sample test and an end of training examination are criterion-referenced examinations that are constructed through content validity procedures. Standard-setting methods such as those described by Angoff, Nedelsky, and others should be used to set the cut score. As an alternative approach, it is technically possible to further validate a work sample test against an external criterion such as performance appraisal scores if a criterion-related validity approach is desired. In general, criterion-referenced examinations do not need performance-based external criteria as "proof" of their validity, if content validity procedures are followed. There are no alternative approaches to standard setting for criterion-referenced examinations. The norm-referenced approaches to standard setting should not be used to establish the cut score with a criterion-referenced examination. Doing so is contrary to everything that we have said about the absolute standards that must be used with criterion-referenced examinations.

For norm-referenced examinations, the customary validation method is criterion-related, whereas the standard-setting methods can be regression-based, banding, or others. Although aptitude tests do possess content validity, they are generally

Table 5.1   Examination Development Methods and Associated Standard Setting Methods

Examination Development Method	Typical Approach		Alternative Approach	
	Validation Method	Standard-Setting Method	Validation Method	Standard-Setting Method
Criterion-referenced (e.g., work sample tests, psychology licensing exam)	Content (internal criteria)	Angoff, Nedelsky, Bookmark, Jaeger (i.e., a fixed, absolute standard)	Criterion-related (external criteria)	Alternative methods are not typical
Norm-referenced (e.g., verbal, numerical, mechanical, spatial, aptitude exams)	Criterion-related (external criteria)	Statistical regression procedures, banding, extreme groups, one SD below the mean (i.e., a variable, relative standard)	Alternative methods are not typical	Angoff, Nedelsky, Bookmark, Jaeger (i.e., a fixed, absolute standard)

not considered to have the same degree of content validity as a criterion-referenced examination, which can show clearly that the items representatively sample the content of the job. Because of this, an alternative validation method is not listed in Table 5.1. As stated earlier, it is technically feasible and highly desirable to derive a criterion-referenced cut score for a norm-referenced examination.

Nonmeasurement Aspects of Standard Setting

Although standard-setting procedures can be followed, the end result will always encompass more than the final cut score. It will be the collective conscientiousness of what has been taught in our society since the days of grade school and high school, as well as the desire to do what is appropriate for the profession. Concerns about consumer protection, concerns about practice regulation and limiting the number of people in a profession are some of the ingredients that are the essence of standard setting. The political aspects include the potential impact on affected individuals: collection of a credential that might allow the acquisition of a new job, a promotion in a current job, an increase in job prestige, a salary increase, increased respect from similar professions, and professional turf protection. Perhaps Cizek (2001) best described this interplay: "Standard setting is perhaps the branch of psychometrics that blends more artistic, political, and cultural ingredients into the mix of its products than any other" (p. 5). Although Cizek states that there are some subjective components to criterion-referenced standard setting, it is important to understand that the cut score resulting from one of the procedures described in this chapter is an absolute standard. Even though there are some artistic and political aspects to these criterion-referenced standard-setting procedures, the cut score will not be based on the examination performance of a group of individuals. It will be derived independently of such performance.

Evaluation of the Standard-Setting Program

In the evaluation of performance standards—namely, that of cut scores—three vital elements must exist prior to the development of a cut score. These elements are (a) appointment of a committee of SMEs for project oversight and participation, (b) job analysis, and (c) development of examination specifications based exclusively on the results of the job analysis.

Subject Matter Expert (SME) Selection

Regardless of the standard-setting method utilized, a common requirement must be the use of SMEs who are job incumbents, supervisors or trainers of job incumbents, or personnel otherwise knowledgeable about the job in question. Certain characteristics should be met regarding the selection of the SMEs who will eventually set this standard. The *Standards for Educational and Psychological Testing* (AERA, APA, & NCME, 1999) state that their qualifications should be documented and that "well-qualified judges can apply their knowledge and experience to reach meaningful and relevant judgments that accurately reflect their understandings and intentions" (p. 54). The qualifications of SMEs are also addressed in Standard 4.21 by pointing out that "the judgmental process should be designed so that judges can bring their knowledge and experience to bear in a reasonable way." Unfortunately, no other guidance is provided as to what must be considered in the selection of individuals who will be setting the cut score. The most important characteristics to consider in selecting SMEs for a standard-setting enterprise are job experience and competency, geographic representation, and number of SMEs.

Job Experience and Competency

In prior work conducted by the authors, they found that the most important competency factors to be considered when selecting an SME committee are as follows:

- Licenses, certificates, or other credentials
- Earned degrees (e.g., academic, trade, or technical)
- Short-term training (e.g., specialized nondegree courses, workshops, seminars, etc.)
- Prior experiences (e.g., as a supervisor, consultant, an instructor, or a trainer)

- Publications or conference presentations
- Current position, grade, or rank in the organization
- Various on-the-job special appointments or projects

SMEs who have completed formal education and/or training in the last one to two years can bring the needed current knowledge perspective to the process. However, they can also be somewhat out of touch with the competency levels of those individuals for whom they are about to set the standard of performance. These recent college graduates or recently trained individuals are inclined to have higher and sometimes inaccurate expectations of performance for job applicants or incumbents and will likely set a higher cut score. During the examination item-review process, this type of SME may believe that all individuals who will eventually take the examination are as knowledgeable as he or she is. With this attitude and perception, the SME will see the examination items as easier than they might be to the examinees and might give the items high ratings, which will lead to a higher cut score, a higher failure rate for the examination, or a higher rejection rate of job applicants. At the other end of the continuum are the SMEs with a great deal of experience but many years away from formal training and other educational experiences. These individuals bring a different perspective as they work with, supervise, and otherwise have substantial knowledge of the competency levels of the individuals the examination is designed to assess. Their approach to evaluating item difficulty and applicant/incumbent ability tends to be more realistic, but they will also sometimes render unrealistically high ratings. This may be a subconscious effort to (a) limit the number of individuals coming into the profession or (b) disqualify some qualified applicants who might be hired or promoted, because some highly able new hires could somehow threaten their own job security. In general, the more experienced SMEs will have a more accurate picture of the incumbent ability levels and will vary their item ratings in accordance with the varied item difficulty. Regardless of the level of experience and the associated tough- or tender-minded approach of the SME, the point of the foregoing discussion is actually about making sure that varied levels of experience are represented on any standard-setting committee.

In the event of a challenge to the examination standard-setting process, individuals setting the standard must be considered true SMEs whose qualifications are beyond reproach and not subject to challenge. To be able to assess and determine the minimum competencies needed for a job or profession, the SME must have job proficiencies that are well beyond the minimum level. Lack of appropriate capabilities will become apparent (e.g., as large differences in opinions about how critical some of the items are for indicating competency) during the standard-setting process when examination items designed to assess these competencies are being discussed.

Geographic Representation

"This is the way we do it at the Chicago facility; therefore, you should know the answer to this question, or you do not deserve the job or the credential." This type of remark demonstrates that one must be careful in setting a standard on an examination in which some of the items may be tapping job content that applies to only some job locations. A thorough and *national* job analysis should minimize this problem by identifying any location-specific requirements. The varying tasks; knowledge, skills, abilities, and other characteristics (KSAOs); or job condition requirements can be detected with subgroup analyses of the job analysis data (preferably a task inventory) or by conducting focus groups at various locations. With the task inventory approach, the process of removing regionally specific job content can be based on empirical ratings for importance or significance to the job. If you are using the same examination for all geographic locations of a given job, the examination must match the content of the job at the various locations. If the examination is to be used only at a specific location, regardless of how dissimilar the local job may be from the "same job" at another location, it will be quite acceptable to use a local examination for a local job.

When an employee fails an examination by one point, the one item on the examination that addresses a job task that is not performed at a given location can be challenged. Including SMEs from various organizational locations on the standard-setting committee can effectively identify location-specific requirements before a cut score is determined. If the regional SMEs agree that the job is highly similar at the various locations, then a national examination and its associated cut score can be put into place. Regional SMEs from the different locations can, and frequently will, reach a consensus regarding the common tasks that a job possesses. If this consensus is reached, then the examination can be put to use at the national level. As long as the examination is assessing what is common to the job at all locations, the examination can be used at all locations. The unique tasks from the midwest or the northwest that could lead to unique examination questions can be empirically purged from the job description or content outline for the purposes of the examination. The disadvantage of making the job analysis/examination relationship homogeneous is that the examination may be covering a reduced part of the job since it is limited to only the common tasks of the job at all locations. Expert judgment will have to be used when considering the extent to which the job has been cleansed of the unique tasks. A question that must be answered is "what percentage of the job is the examination now covering?" Care must be taken to prevent the use of an examination that covers only a small percentage of what the employee does on the job. Minimum competency cannot be ensured if the examination covers, for example, only 30% of the job.

Number of SMEs

Regarding the number of SMEs, Jaeger (1991) states: "Participants should be selected through procedures that permit generalization of their collective recommendations to well defined populations." He further says that the number of participants should be of a sufficient quantity that their estimation of the standard would be the same as that of the standard estimated by the entire population of SMEs. In this same article, Jaeger recommended calculating the number of SMEs based on the standard error of the mean (SE_{mean}) of the ratings and the standard error of measurement (SEM) of the examination. He suggested that the SE_{mean} be no larger than one fourth the size of the SEM. The criterion of one fourth the SEM was achieved with 13 SMEs in Jaeger's hypothetical example.

These sample size recommendations also appear to be consistent with similar recommendations suggested by HR professionals (Maurer, Alexander, Callahan, Bailey, & Dambrot, 1991). Given that sample size and standard errors are inversely related, others (Kane, 1994; Mehrens & Popham, 1992) have concurred that the number of SMEs should be large enough to ensure an acceptably small standard error. However, Norcini, Shea, and Grosso (1991) have argued that as few as five SMEs can yield acceptable results. In summary, one can consider the problem of how many SMEs to use as being directly related to the margin of error that you are willing to live with. The exact number of SMEs required is directly related to the degree of precision desired. In the experience of the authors, a realistic number appears to hover in the 12–15 range, with a point of diminishing returns being reached when this range is exceeded. However, with well-trained SMEs it is possible to achieve rating stability and repeatability with less than this stated range.

Job Analysis

Job analysis information should be the basis for any HR activity, and it is the essential foundation in the developmental chain that ultimately leads to a cut score. Because a cut score will be used to make a pass/fail or hire/no hire decision, a job analysis is required to ensure that the standard being set does indeed relate to job performance. Job analysis provides a technique for establishing the foundation for content validity. The objective of a job analysis is to define a job in terms of the behaviors necessary to perform it at a minimum level of proficiency. Of course there are many methods of job analysis, but for content validity to be established, task-oriented approaches are clearly the most preferred. Tasks are written in a way that directly addresses what the worker does while not necessarily listing the underlying aptitudes. Examples of task-specific, job-content oriented statements are "identify supplies and equipment for cardiac procedures" and "prepare a bid document for a new construction project."

Examination Specifications

The examination specifications, or test blueprint, is a detailed record of an examination's current and subsequent development. Information contained in the specifications should include (a) content categories and task-related information resulting from a job analysis; (b) knowledge, skills, abilities, and other job characteristics; (c) distribution of items in each content category; (d) percentage of items in each content category; (e) total number of items; (f) distribution of the cognitive complexity levels of the items; (g) types of items used; (h) number of pretest items; (i) intended examinee population; and (j) time limit. If the standard-setting process is to have a content valid link between the job analysis and the examination, this

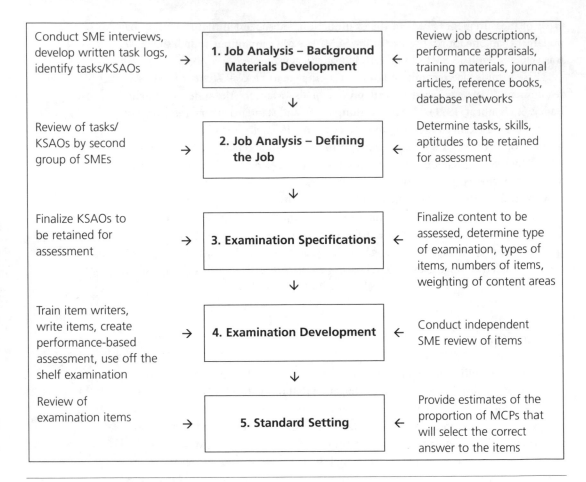

Figure 5.1   Content Validity Steps Leading to Valid Standard Setting

document is vital. A graphical summary of the content validity process resulting in a valid standard being set is provided in Figure 5.1.

This diagram illustrates the developmental process of a criterion-referenced examination. Listed in the center column are the major steps in the process, with the end result being that of a criterion-referenced cut score. At each phase of this five-step process, the associated activities that must be performed are listed in the left and right columns. The course of development must begin with a job analysis, then the determination of the specifications, the writing of the items or performance-based assessments, and finally, the determination of the cut score. This process establishes the chain of content validity.

Standard-Setting Procedures

A single point/score must be selected in the distribution of test scores to serve as the division point for a mastery/nonmastery or a hire/no hire decision. This outcome is accomplished by collecting the judgments of SMEs about the level of knowledge needed for someone to be classified at or above a given standard. This is one of the most critical parts of the entire developmental chain of events in the creation or validation of an examination. There is no perfect, agreed-upon way to determine this magical number, but there are numerous criterion-referenced standard-setting procedures available (Angoff, Ebel, Nedelsky, Hofstee, Jaeger, Bookmark, borderline group method, contrasting groups method, etc.) to the HR practitioner. The most commonly discussed standard-setting methods based on the evaluation of examination content are the Nedelsky (1954), Angoff (1971), Jaeger (1978), Ebel (1979), and Bookmark (Lewis, Mitzel, & Green, 1996) methods (Mills, 1995). All of these procedures require SMEs to rate examination items. With the exception of the Jaeger method, an estimation of the difficulty of each item is also required before an SME can render an item-passing estimate. Some of these methods are described below.

Angoff Method

The most ubiquitous criterion-referenced standard-setting procedure is the Angoff method (Cizek, 1996; Meara, Hambleton, & Sireci, 2001; Mills & Melican, 1988; Plake, 1998; Sireci & Biskin, 1992;). This method, also sometimes called the modified Angoff method, can be employed with essentially any type of item format (e.g., multiple-choice, situational sets, and constructed response formats), or with performance-based examinations or simulations for which an SME rates the difficulty of the task to be completed on the examination. In the evaluation of a cut score that has been determined by the Angoff approach, several steps must be present. These steps are delineated after a brief introduction to this procedure.

This technique typically begins with several hours of training for the SMEs, with considerable emphasis given to a concept known as the "minimally competent practitioner (MCP)" and its variants: "minimally competent person," "minimally acceptable person," "minimally competent examinee," "borderline proficient," or "borderline competent." One of the following statements is typically provided when eliciting SME ratings: "The minimally competent examinee must at least know the concept presented in this item;" or "The minimally competent examinee would be expected to know the concept presented in this item;" or "In your judgment, what is your best professional estimate of the proportion (or percentage) of minimally competent examinees who will answer the question correctly?" The purposes of this procedure are to (a) help the SMEs focus on the competency level of the MCPs and (b) determine the probability that the MCP will answer each item on the examination correctly. The core of the procedure rests on the ability of the SME to evaluate the difficulty level of the item and then estimate the probability that the MCP will answer that item correctly.

The following steps should be present in some form when conducting or evaluating the proper use of the Angoff method.

1. A committee of SMEs should be appointed.

2. The SMEs should discuss the eligibility requirements of future examinees and the examination's purpose.

3. The SMEs should discuss the job analysis information for the target job(s).

4. The training should delineate characteristics that an MCP would possess. These characteristics could include education, training, and personal qualities (e.g., dependability, degree of detail orientation, and professional ethics). This part of the training is intended to aid in the development of the definition of the MCP.

5. The training should also cover a review of the examination specifications.

6. The SMEs should identify aspects of the job that would be difficult for an MCP to perform. This is done by examining each task separately.

7. The examination developer collects ratings from SMEs:
   a. SMEs read each item without the key being provided
   b. SMEs estimate the difficulty of the item for the MCP
   c. SMEs rate each item individually
   d. The key can then be presented to the SMEs
   e. Initially, individual ratings are discussed and justified to the entire committee
   f. Extreme ratings are discussed so that SME convergence is achieved

It cannot be stressed enough to the SMEs that the ratings they are providing are their best professional estimate of expected performance by an MCP, *not the entire population of examinees.* This is so because the entire population will contain a much broader range of ability and will not be limited to those who are borderline competent. Rating inflation can occur when the SMEs act as though they are setting the standard of performance for the most able in the profession or job. Sometimes it is difficult to convince SMEs that the cut score should be set at a level that might, for example, pass air traffic controllers or emergency room nurses who are less than brilliant. But the Angoff cut score is set to screen individuals who are competent at the minimum level into a profession or job.

8. The examination developer periodically discusses the ratings with the SMEs. This feedback to SMEs often pertains to extreme ratings or ratings that are consistently deviant from the ratings of the other SMEs.

9. A statistical analysis of the rating data should be used to determine the cut score. This analysis should include individual item means, individual SME means, the grand mean of all items across all SMEs, the standard error of the grand mean, and confidence intervals in which the "true" cut score would fall at an acceptable probability level.

10. The entire process should be documented in a technical report.

Ratings can be elicited from SMEs with the following question: "If a group of 100 minimally competent examinees were taking the examination, how many would select the correct answer to the item?" If an item is determined to be quite easy, an SME might render a rating of .90 (i.e., 90% of MCPs could be expected to answer the item correctly). Conversely, if the item is determined to be difficult, the rating could

Table 5.2   Angoff Rating Data From 10 SMEs

Item	SME										Item Mean
	1	2	3	4	5	6	7	8	9	10	
1	.50	.45	**.60**	.55	.45	.50	**.70**	**.40**	.60	.45	**.52**
2	.70	.70	**.75**	.65	.70	.65	**.80**	**.60**	.60	.75	**.69**
3	.65	.60	**.70**	.75	.65	.70	**.75**	**.60**	.75	.60	**.68**
4	.70	.75	**.90**	.80	.75	.70	**.55**	**.65**	.75	.75	**.73**
5	.80	.75	**.90**	.75	.70	.65	**.60**	**.75**	.70	.70	**.73**
6	.80	.80	**.85**	.80	.70	.85	**.65**	**.75**	.70	.75	**.77**
7	.75	.70	**.70**	.75	.75	.70	**.90**	**.70**	.70	.75	**.74**
8	.55	.60	**.65**	.60	.55	.60	**.75**	**.50**	.60	.65	**.61**
9	.70	.80	**.80**	.75	.70	.75	**.60**	**.70**	.60	.75	**.72**
10	.60	.70	**.75**	.60	.70	.55	**.80**	**.65**	.70	.70	**.68**
SME Mean	**.68**	**.69**	**.76**	**.70**	**.67**	**.67**	**.71**	**.63**	**.67**	**.69**	

be .30 (i.e., 30% of MCPs could be expected to answer the item correctly). Listed in Table 5.2 are typical ratings from 10 SMEs for a 10-item multiple-choice examination. The values in the table are the estimated proportion of MCPs who will select the correct answer to a given item. Since these are four-option multiple-choice items, the examination developer would expect 25% of the examinees to guess the correct answer. Therefore, SMEs should not be permitted to render a rating of less than .25.

Because the mean ratings of all SMEs can be compared, as well as the mean rating of each item, some conclusions can be drawn. For example, Item 1 is a somewhat difficult item, with a mean rating of .52. The 10 SMEs are telling us that, on average, they expect an MCP to get this item correct slightly more than half the time. For some professions or jobs, having several items rated at this level might indicate that the anticipated difficulty level is too high for the given examinee population and perhaps should not be included on the examination. The cut score for this 10-item examination is simply the overall sum of an 100 individual SME ratings divided by the total number of ratings, or 68.45/100 = .6845 (68.45%). For a 10-item examination, 68.45% of 10 is 6.85, which rounds to 7, therefore the cut score is 7. For a 100-item examination with a mean rating of .6845, the raw cut score would be 68. Whether the length of the examination is 100-items, 150-items, etc., the cut score will be .6845 multiplied by the total number of items and rounded to the nearest integer. It should be noted that for increased accuracy in the calculation of the cut score, the mean of all individual ratings for all items should be used, and not the row, or column means of the data file.

Useful information can also be gleaned regarding the harshness or benevolence of the SMEs. Looking down the third column of Table 5.2 shows that this SME tended to give higher ratings to the items than did other SMEs. This SME estimated that the expected pass rate would be 76%, whereas SME 8 estimated it at 63%. SME 3 would be considered tougher than SME 8 because her mean rating of 76% for these items would produce an examination cut score of 76% if her ratings were the only data that were used. SME 8 would be considered more lenient because his ratings average 63%, and this of course is a lower cut score. For whatever difficulty level the examination is intended, a cut score of 63% is easier to attain than a cut score of 76%. Concerning SME 7, if an interrater reliability coefficient was calculated between SME 7's ratings and those for each of the other SMEs, the inconsistencies of this SME would be evident. Although the mean rating of this SME is reasonable, he is so inconsistent with the other nine SMEs that his interrater reliability coefficient will be low. As a result, SME 7's ratings should be removed from the data file.

The Angoff method or a variation of it has many positive characteristics (see Cizek, 1996; Meara et al., 2001; Plake, 1998; Sireci & Biskin, 1992) that make it the most popular criterion-referenced standard-setting technique in use today.

1. It can be used effectively with essentially any item format including positively worded multiple-choice, negatively worded multiple-choice, complex multiple-choice, complex true/false, k-type items, binary response items such as true/false and alternate response, situational set/word problems, constructed response items, and items associated with performance-based examinations.
2. It does not place as heavy a cognitive demand on SMEs as do some of the other approaches.
3. It can be used with new items for which item analysis data (p-values, item-test correlations, and item parameters from item response theory [IRT]) do not exist.
4. SMEs can be trained in the method relatively quickly (2–3 hours).
5. Rating sessions can proceed quickly (approximately 2 hours for 100 items).
6. Data collection and cut score computation are easily accomplished.
7. The method can be used for standard setting for (a) criterion-referenced examinations developed through the content validity method or (b) norm-referenced examinations developed using criterion-related validity methods.

Nedelsky Method

Much like the Angoff method, the Nedelsky method is another approach to standard setting that focuses on the examination item as the unit of analysis. Also like the Angoff method, it requires the 10 development/training procedural steps identified earlier. The Nedelsky method requires an SME judgment about each wrong answer (distractor) of an item, in contrast to the Angoff method, which considers the item key (right answer) as the focal point. With the Nedelsky method, the task of each SME is to evaluate the difficulty of the item based on the quality of the distractors and to identify which of them the MCP would recognize as being incorrect. The Nedelsky method places a heavier demand on the SMEs because the rating process requires them to consider the attractiveness of each of the wrong answers; therefore, all elements of the item (the stem, the key, and the distractors) must be considered. This procedure makes the assumption that the examinee eliminates whatever distractor(s) he or she can and then guesses randomly from the remaining

Table 5.3   Nedelsky Rating Data From One SME

Item		Options			Number of Options Not Eliminated	Estimated Passing Probability
1	~~A~~	B	C	D*	3	.33
2	~~A~~	~~B~~	C*	D	2	.50
3	~~A~~	B*	~~C~~	~~D~~	1	1.00
4	A*	B	~~C~~	~~D~~	2	.50
5	A	B*	C	D	4	.25
6	A	B	~~C~~	D*	3	.33
7	A*	~~B~~	~~C~~	D	2	.50
8	~~A~~	B*	~~C~~	~~D~~	1	1.00
9	~~A~~	B	C*	~~D~~	2	.50
10	A	~~B~~	C*	D	3	.33

*–Key   **Cut Score = .524**

options. Table 5.3 provides an example of a single SME's data for a 10-item examination. It becomes immediately apparent that a primary difference between this method and the Angoff method is that the Angoff approach requires the SME to provide only an estimated overall passing probability for the item, without *express* consideration of the distractors. Although the SME may be performing the mental operation of eliminating the distractors in determining the item difficulty, it is not a feature of the Angoff data collection component or the cut score calculation as is the case with the Nedelsky approach.

After an SME reads the item without the benefit of the key, he or she identifies the option an MCP will probably eliminate. The results for a single SME based on a 10-item examination are displayed in Table 5.3. Listed in the sixth column of this table is the number of options for each item that this SME estimated could not be eliminated by the *examinee*. As can be seen, the number of options that cannot be eliminated becomes the crucial component of the estimated passing proportion for that item. For example, Item 3 has been determined to be a very easy item as this SME estimated that the MCP could eliminate all three of the distractors (indicated by the strikethroughs). The calculation of the estimated passing probability for this item is 1/1 = 1.00. Item 5 is a much more difficult item as the SME has determined that no distractors could be eliminated. The estimated passing probability is therefore 1/4 = .25. As was the case with the Angoff method, the lower bound of selecting the key is 25%, based on examinee guessing at random for a four-option item. For space considerations, only the data from a single SME are provided; therefore, the cut score for this "10-item examination" is merely the sum of the individual item ratings divided by 10, or 5.24/10 = .524 (5.24%). Once again, had there been 10 SMEs for this 10-item examination, the division of the sum of the ratings would have been by 100. For the 10-item examination the raw cut score is 5; if it had been a 100-item examination with a mean rating of .524, the raw cut score would be 52.

Although the Nedelsky procedure can yield a reliable, well-conceived cut score, it does have some limitations. First, it can be a very slow process due to the burden placed on the SMEs. Training SMEs and gathering ratings for a 100-item examination can take a full day. Second, the method is limited to use with only multiple-choice items. Third, it does not work as well as other procedures with certain item types, such as the negatively worded item shown in the following example:

Which of the following cities is NOT located east of the Mississippi River?

> A. Atlanta
> B. Cleveland
> C. **Kansas City**
> D. Birmingham

As an SME reads this item, he or she must remember that because this is a negatively worded item, any of the cities east of the Mississippi are *not* correct answers. The task for an SME then becomes evaluating that the farther the cities are to the east of the Mississippi, the more likely the MCP will evaluate the response as wrong. Fourth, the method assumes that examinee test-taking behavior proceeds by eliminating the distractors, then by randomly guessing the correct answer from the remaining options; but Melican, Mills, and Plake (1987) pointed out that this is not necessarily true.

Fifth, the most serious concern is perhaps that the passing probability estimates are limited exclusively to .25, .33, .50, and 1.00 for a four-option, multiple-choice item. Limiting the ratings to these four discrete categories ignores the entire range of probability estimates that can theoretically vary from .00 to 1.00. Because of this, the Nedelsky approach almost always results in a lower cut score than the Angoff method. Despite these constraints, the Nedelsky method remains popular in certain professions, although its popularity has declined in recent years (Mills, 1995).

Bookmark Method

A fundamentally different and quite sophisticated approach (Lewis et al., 1996; Mitzel, Lewis, Patz, & Green, 2001) has recently emerged. It takes advantage of item analysis data by arranging all of the items on an examination in order of difficulty before they are presented to SMEs. Mitzel et al. (2001) stated the following:

> In the bookmark procedure, the judgment task is to specify a cut score at a chosen location, which divides items into two groups. Participants are instructed to try to find the point that divides items that should be mastered, from those that are too difficult for a minimally competent student at a given performance level. (p. 260)

The cut score location is determined by placing a "bookmark" among the items at a division point where the MCP would be likely to answer the most difficult item correctly with a probability of success at a minimum of .67. Simultaneously, this bookmark is at the point where the easiest item would be answered incorrectly, but at a probability of success of less than .67. The probability of answering an easier item incorrectly is less than .67 because it is an easier item. While item statistics (i.e., p-values) from classical test theory may also be used, this method is typically IRT-based; and it uses item parameters and ability-scale location as they relate to examinee proficiency (Hambleton, Swaminathan, & Rogers, 1991). The response probability level of .67 (2/3) has been adopted by the developers of this procedure and is typically applied. The implementation of this rule means that an examinee who has a test score at the cut score point will have a .67 probability of answering that item correctly. When this item difficulty location is agreed upon, along with its associated proficiency scale, an equivalent standard scale score can also be derived as the cut score point. When the bookmarking is complete, there are two groups of items, with one set having a .67 or greater probability of mastery for a MCP, and the other set having less than a .67 probability of mastery for a MCP.

Procedurally, the items are presented to the SMEs in a booklet with a rank order arrangement based on the scale locations determined by an IRT calibration. The easiest items are placed in the front of the booklet, and items increase in difficulty as the SME works toward the back of the booklet. IRT scaling permits item characteristics and examinee proficiency estimates to be placed on the same scale. Given the assumptions of IRT, this process has the inherent advantage of having an examinee score provide a theoretical probability of getting an item correct. Once the cut score is established, the examinee will have a .67 probability of correctly answering an item that is also at that cut score, as determined by the IRT probability of a correct answer for that item. The bookmark method was developed for use in educational assessment. It has been used to set student proficiency cut scores for K–12 grade-level achievement tests in the public education sector and has indeed found its most prominent use there. Because of this, the actual bookmarking process as it relates to the various grade levels and their associated content (subjects) will most likely proceed in a slightly different manner than would likely be the case for determining the cut score in an applied personnel selection or professional credentialing setting. With that said, the bookmark method of standard setting can be extended to selection tests with some minor adjustments in the way the bookmark data are collected, reviewed, and summarized from the SMEs during the "three round review process" discussed next.

The process of collecting the bookmark difficulty level judgments from the SMEs proceeds in three rounds, with each round designed to refine the judgments expressed in the previous round and foster an increasing consensus among the SMEs. During round one, they are asked to determine and discuss what KSAOs would have to be applied by the examinee to correctly answer the item, and why each item is progressively more difficult than the previous one. In brief, during this very crucial first round, the heart of the discussion is centered on the content and skills that must be mastered to answer the item correctly and the initial placement of the bookmark for each of 10 SMEs. For example, at the end of round one, the bookmarks might be placed at items 55, 56, two at item 57, 61, 64, 65, 67, and two at item 69 as the proficiency point for 10 different SMEs in a test booklet for telecommunications equipment installers. At the beginning of round two, each SME is provided with the bookmark placements from each of the SMEs in round one so that all SMEs are aware of each others' bookmark location. The discussion now shifts to the content that must be mastered for proficient examinee performance within this 15-item range (55–69), which will contain the final cut score point. Round two includes not only a discussion of these potential eight different cut points but also a discussion of all items within this 15-item range and their associated content and difficulty level. It concludes with the placement of another set of bookmarks for each SME, which now may be reduced, for example, to a 7-item range. In an applied personnel setting, these data should then be presented to a larger secondary group of SMEs for the beginning of round three, whereas the same group of SMEs should be used for rounds one and two. During the third round, the bookmark placements are once again discussed and refined, the final judgments tabulated, and a final cut score determined.

As was the case with the Angoff method, the bookmark system can be used with essentially any type of selected response (SR) or constructed response (CR) item format. In comparing the Angoff method to the bookmark approach, Plake (1998) rightly points out that the Angoff approach *tends* to function better with multiple-choice items despite attempts to generalize the approach. We would agree with her with the exception that the Angoff approach can and does work well with performance-based examinations and simulations in the applied selection and placement setting, as has been the experience of the senior author of this chapter.

A major limitation of the method would be that it cannot be used for a newly developed examination in which IRT item analysis data are unavailable. Perhaps this difficulty can be circumvented by collecting item analysis data through a field test of the examination before it is used in a "live" setting and determine the cut score from this field test data. The field test would have to be administered to a representative sample of the population who would eventually take the examination, with a sample size sufficient for an IRT calibration. Whether an organization or professional credentialing body would be willing to commit the resources for this undertaking is another matter. The Angoff, Nedelsky, and other item-centered judgmental approaches do *not* have the limitation of requiring item analysis data to set the cut score. These methods can be, and very frequently are, conducted without the use of item analysis data because of their use with newly written or modified items in which item p-values and IRT-based item parameters may not be readily available.

Summary

The Underwriters Laboratories sets standards of minimum performance for electrical appliances, and the Food and Drug Administration (FDA) sets standards for the evaluation of pharmaceuticals and medical devices. Standards are also needed for evaluating the quality of human performance. This chapter describes several standard-setting procedures (e.g., Angoff, Nedelsky, and Bookmark methods) currently popular among test developers and HR professionals. These cut score procedures are designed for use with criterion- referenced, content valid tests or measuring devices. Important practical issues associated with the implementation of these methods are described and discussed.

References

American Educational Research Association, American Psychological Association, & National Council on Measurement in Education. (1999). *Standards for educational and psychological testing.* Washington, DC: American Psychological Association.

Angoff, W. H. (1971). Scales, norms, and equivalent scores. In R. L. Thorndike (Ed.), *Educational measurement* (2nd ed., pp. 508–600). Washington, DC: American Council on Education.

Cizek, G. J. (Ed.). (2001). *Setting performance standards: Concepts, methods and perspectives.* Mahwah, NJ: Lawrence Erlbaum.

Cizek, G. J. (1996). Setting passing scores. *Educational Measurement: Issues and Practice, 15*(2), 20–31.

Ebel, R. L. (1979). *Essentials of educational measurement* (3rd ed.). Englewood Cliffs, NJ: Prentice Hall.

Hambleton, R. K., Swaminathan, H., & Rogers, H. J. (1991). *Fundamentals of item response theory.* Newbury Park, CA: Sage.

Jaeger, R. M. (1978, Spring). *A proposal for setting a standard on the North Carolina High School Competency Test.* Paper presented at the spring meeting of the North Carolina Association for Research in Education, Chapel Hill, NC.

Jaeger, R. M. (1991). Selection of judges for standard setting. *Educational Measurement: Issues and Practice, 10*(2), 10.

Kane, M. T. (1994). Validating the performance standards associated with passing scores. *Review of Educational Research, 64,* 425–461.

Lewis, D. M., Mitzel, H. C., & Green, D. R. (1996, June). Standard setting: A bookmark approach. In D. R. Green (Chair), *IRT-based standard setting procedures utilizing behavioral anchoring.* Symposium conducted at the Council of Chief State School Officers National Conference on Large-Scale Assessment, Phoenix, AZ.

Maurer, T. J., Alexander, R. A., Callahan, C. M., Bailey, J. J., & Dambrot, F. H. (1991). Methodological and psychometric issues in setting cutoff scores using the Angoff method. *Personnel Psychology, 44,* 235–262.

Meara, K. C., Hambleton, R. K., & Sireci, S. G. (2001). Setting and validating standards on professional licensure and certification exams: A survey of current practices. *CLEAR Exam Review, 12*(2), 17–23.

Mehrens, W. A., & Popham, W. J. (1992). How to evaluate the legal defensibility of high stakes tests. *Applied Measurement in Education, 5,* 265–283.

Melican, G. J., Mills, C. N., & Plake, B. S. (1987, April). *Accuracy of item performance predictions based upon the Nedelsky standard setting method.* Paper presented at the annual meeting of the National Council on Measurement in Education, Washington, DC.

Mills, C. N. (1995). Establishing passing standards. In J. C. Impara (Ed.). *Licensure testing: Purposes, procedures, and practices* (pp. 219–252). Lincoln, NE: Buros Institute of Mental Measurements.

Mills, C. N., & Melican, G. J. (1988). Estimating and adjusting cutoff scores: Features of selected methods. *Applied Measurement in Education, 1,* 261–275.

Mitzel, H. C., Lewis, D. M., Patz, R. J., & Green, D. R. (2001). The bookmark procedure: Psychological perspectives. In G. J. Cizek (Ed.), *Setting performance standards: Concepts, methods and perspectives* (pp. 249–281). Mahwah, NJ: Lawrence Erlbaum.

Norcini, J. J., Shea, J., & Grosso, L. (1991). The effect of numbers of experts and common items on cutting score equivalents based on expert judgment. *Applied Psychological Measurement, 15*(3), 241–246.

Nedelsky, L. (1954). Absolute grading standards for objective tests. *Educational and Psychological Measurement, 14,* 3–19.

Plake, B. S. (1998). Setting performance standards for professional licensure and certification. *Applied Measurement in Education, 11,* 65–80.

Shepard, L. (1980). Standard setting issues and methods. *Applied Psychological Measurement, 4,* 447–467.

Sireci, S. G., & Biskin, B. J. (1992). Measurement practices in national licensing examination programs: A survey. *CLEAR Exam Review, 3,* 21–25.

Suggested Readings in Setting Performance Standards

Cizek, G. J. (Ed.). (2001). *Setting performance standards: Concepts, methods and perspectives.* Mahwah, NJ: Lawrence Erlbaum.

Cizek, G. J. (1996). Standard setting guidelines. *Educational Measurement: Issues and Practice, 15*(1), 12–21.

Mills, C. N. (1995). Establishing passing standards. In J. C. Impara (Ed.), *Licensure testing: Purposes, procedures, and practices* (pp. 219–252). Lincoln, NE: Buros Institute of Mental Measurements.

Schoon, C. R., & Smith, I. L. (1996). Standard setting. In A. H. Browning, A. C. Bugbee, Jr., & M. A. Mullins (Eds.), *Certification: A NOCA handbook.* Washington, DC: The National Organization for Competency Assurance.

CHAPTER 6

Evaluating Personnel Selection Systems

Scott B. Morris

Russell Lobsenz

P ersonnel selection systems are designed to yield data relevant to making effective personnel decisions. The primary goal of a personnel assessment program is to increase the likelihood of hiring a skilled, productive, and dependable workforce that will give the hiring company a competitive advantage. No selection system will be able to determine with absolute certainty which employees will be most effective, but the standard for evaluating a selection procedure should not be perfect prediction. Rather, the goal should be to develop the most effective system possible, given the available alternatives and the practical constraints of the employment setting. The purpose of this chapter is to present methods for evaluating personnel selection systems, which can provide information on the current level of effectiveness and serve as the basis for system improvements.

Selection systems can use a wide variety of assessment methods, including multiple choice tests, interviews, work samples, self-report questionnaires, and review of training and education. Common to all these methods is that they involve systematic procedures for obtaining and scoring a sample of examinee behavior. We use the term *test* to refer to any measure that is used as a basis for an employment decision.

Program evaluation can occur at different stages of the implementation of a selection system and for a variety of purposes. Selection systems are often evaluated during the development of the system. In other cases, the evaluation team will be brought in to evaluate an existing system. For example, when faced with a potential lawsuit, an organization's lawyers may request a review of evidence supporting the job-relatedness and fairness of hiring practices. The evaluation may also be performed for the purpose of ongoing monitoring of the system. Over time, job requirements can change due to technological advances or changes in the organization's priorities. Changes can also occur in the availability of qualified applicants in the labor market. Therefore, it is important to reevaluate the appropriateness of selection systems periodically.

The nature of the program evaluation will be influenced by the purpose of the evaluation. When designing a selection system, the evaluation team will need to conduct research on the technical quality of selection methods and the appropriateness of test administration and decision-making procedures. In contrast, when reviewing an existing system, much of the evidence regarding these issues will presumably be available in existing technical reports. Although the activities of the evaluation team in the two cases may differ (i.e., designing vs. reviewing research), the principles guiding the evaluation effort will be essentially the same. To properly interpret the available evidence, the evaluation team needs to have a thorough understanding of the different evaluation criteria and the research methodologies used to evaluate selection systems.

Program Evaluation Process

Prior to commencing the evaluation, individuals involved in or affected by the selection program should be identified (e.g., management, job applicants, and human resources [HR] staff). Different stakeholders often have different priorities, and a comprehensive program evaluation will be responsive to the needs and interests of all stakeholders. The next step is to form the evaluation team, making sure that team membership represents the interests of all relevant stakeholders. Next, the evaluation team must identify the evaluation criteria and determine appropriate evaluation methods for the selection setting.

Forming the Evaluation Team

The evaluation of a selection system will draw upon a variety of different types of information, ranging from technical aspects of the tests to practical issues of system administration. In general, no one individual will be well suited to evaluate all aspects of the selection system. A more comprehensive and credible evaluation will result if the evaluation team includes diverse perspectives and areas of expertise.

A representative of the HR department will typically have the broadest perspective on the system and therefore would be best suited to lead the evaluation team. In addition, because HR representatives interact with all business units/functions, they usually have a broad network of contacts within the organization from which to draw participants for the evaluation research. The leader of the evaluation team should have a full understanding of the entire HR system and should be aware of the resources, staff, and facilities available to conduct evaluation research.

Many aspects of the program evaluation will involve complex technical issues such as psychometrics (e.g., reliability and validity) and legal defensibility. The evaluation team either will be responsible for overseeing research on these issues or will review research conducted by others. In either case, at least one individual trained in psychometrics and test development should be included on the evaluation team. Ideally, this individual should have a doctoral degree in industrial/organizational psychology, educational measurement, or a related field. Similarly, at least one member of the team should have extensive expertise in employment law.

Care should be taken to ensure that all members of the evaluation team are willing to provide an objective evaluation of the selection system. For example, the individuals who developed a selection system may not have the most objective views on the weaknesses of the system. Similarly, HR representatives may be hesitant to criticize a system that is supported by their supervisors. Under such circumstances, an external consultant may be better suited to conduct all or part of the evaluation.

Representatives of all relevant stakeholders should be consulted during the program evaluation and should be considered, when appropriate, for membership on the evaluation team. To keep the size of the evaluation team to a manageable number and use the organization's resources most effectively, some of the members might participate only in certain phases of the evaluation in which they have particularly relevant backgrounds or perspectives.

One of the key stakeholders is upper management. The primary function of a selection system is to help the organization accomplish its strategic objectives. Therefore, it is important for the evaluation team to fully understand the organization's business strategy and the role of HR in that strategy. Buy-in from upper management will also facilitate obtaining the resources needed to conduct a thorough program evaluation.

Job applicants and current employees also have a considerable stake in the selection system and are likely to emphasize criteria that may be overlooked by other constituencies. Organizations may be reluctant to include union representatives or recent applicants on the evaluation team, fearing that providing these individuals access to test content or scoring procedures could compromise test security. However, attempts should be made to include individuals on the evaluation team who are sensitive to employee and applicant issues, and to seek input from these groups (e.g., perceptions of test fairness) at appropriate points in the evaluation process.

Evaluation Criteria

The evaluation team should examine all aspects of the selection process, including the psychometric quality of selection tests, procedures for making selection decisions, and test administration practices. Much of the evaluation of the selection system will involve an analysis of the psychometric quality and appropriateness of selection tests. First, the evaluation team should examine evidence of reliability, that is, whether the assessment procedure provides precise and consistent measurements. Second, the evaluation team should examine evidence of validity, or the extent to which the inferences drawn from the test are appropriate.

In addition to examining the tests themselves, the evaluation team should also consider how test scores are used in making selection decisions. Several methods exist to determine passing scores and to combine information from multiple tests. The evaluation team should review decision-making practices to ensure that they are well justified and applied consistently for all applicants. Similarly, the evaluation team should examine test administration practices, such as the conditions under which testing occurs, test scoring methods, and maintenance of test results. Criteria for evaluating test administration practices include whether practices promote standardization of testing conditions, accurate recording of results, and respect for the rights of examinees.

Two other important evaluation criteria are fairness and utility. The evaluation of both issues crosses all aspects of the selection system (psychometrics, test administration, and selection decisions), and therefore each will be discussed separately. A selection system would be unfair if non-job-related factors, such as gender or ethnicity, influence decisions. Related to the concept of fairness, the evaluation team should consider whether selection practices are legally defensible. Utility refers to whether use of the system results in benefits to the organization that outweigh the costs of testing.

Specific evaluation methods and professional standards have been developed for each of the evaluation criteria. The following sections provide a more thorough explanation of the evaluation criteria and specific methods for evaluating the reliability and validity of tests, decision-making procedures, test administration practices, fairness, and utility.

Reliability

The *Standards for Educational and Psychological Testing* (American Educational Research Association [AERA], American Psychological Association [APA], & National Council on Measurement in Education [NCME], 1999) defined reliability as the consistency of measurements. No employment test is perfectly reliable because measurement error operates to cause scores to vary or be inconsistent from time to time and situation to situation. For example, differing levels of anxiety, fatigue, or motivation may affect an applicant's test results across repeated administrations. In addition, test performance may be impacted by differences in the testing environment, such as room temperature or noise level. Reliability is the degree to which test scores are unaffected by measurement errors.

Estimates of test reliability are based on the analysis of test scores. Typically, test responses of applicants during the selection procedure will provide the best data for reliability analysis. However, this may not be feasible if the number of applicants is small. Other samples, such as current incumbents, can be used if they are reasonably similar to the applicant pool. In addition, because reliability analysis is a standard part of the test development process, estimates of reliability will often be available from validation reports or test manuals. In such cases, the evaluation team should carefully review the methods used to generate the reliability estimates.

Types of Reliability Estimates

There are five common approaches to estimating the reliability of a test: test-retest, alternate forms, internal consistency, inter-rater, and generalizability theory. Because each approach defines error in a distinct way, the procedures may result in dissimilar reliability estimates when applied to the same test. Therefore, it is imperative that the evaluation team knows what approach was used and to be cognizant of which approaches result in higher (and lower) estimates.

Test-Retest Method

Test-retest reliability is the degree to which the same test yields similar results from one assessment occasion to another, in the absence of intervening growth or learning. Shorter time intervals result in a greater potential for "carry-over" effects, when the first test administration influences the second (Allen & Yen, 1979). If candidates recall answers they provided on the first administration of a test and repeat them on the second administration, the correlation between observed scores on the two administrations will likely overestimate the test's reliability. Conversely, an underestimate of the test's reliability will result if the time between test administrations is so long that the characteristic being measured changes during the interim period.

Alternate Forms Method

Typically, it is not possible for a test to include all possible questions related to a subject area. Consequently, test scores will be influenced to some degree by the particular sample of items included on the test. Sometimes, multiple versions of a test are created with different items but are intended to measure the same ability. Alternate forms reliability is established by correlating scores on two versions of a test that were both administered to the same group of examinees. If the two forms are administered with a time interval between administrations, the resulting correlation coefficient indicates the test's reliability across forms, as well as over time. When the tests are administered immediately following one another, only alternate forms reliability is estimated. A high alternate forms reliability coefficient provides strong evidence that the different versions of the test are measuring the same thing. A low alternate forms reliability coefficient is less clear. It might indicate a high degree of measurement error. Alternatively, a low reliability coefficient might indicate that the two forms are measuring different things and therefore cannot be used interchangeably.

Internal Consistency Methods

It is often not practical to develop alternate forms of a test or have the same examinees participate in two test administrations. Internal consistency methods, such as coefficient alpha (see Pedhazur & Schmelkin, 1991), estimate reliability based on the association among items within a test. This method requires only a single administration of one test, which is probably why it is the most common method used in applied settings. Estimates of internal consistency account for error due to the particular sample of items included on a test—typically the largest single component of measurement error. Internal consistency will be high when test items all measure the same thing. Consequently, this approach may not be appropriate for assessment methods with multidimensional content. In addition, internal consistency reliability can be inflated when factors other than actual ability on the characteristic being tested create similarity among responses to different items. For example, on speeded tests, the fact that some items are not completed tends to increase the correlation between items, resulting in an overestimate of internal consistency.

Inter-rater Reliability

Many assessment methods (e.g., interviews and assessment centers) are scored using expert judgment. When selection procedures involve subjective scoring, the idiosyncrasies of the raters represent another potential source of error. Inter-rater reliability is estimated by having two judges or experts each rate the same set of examinees on a particular dimension. The correlation between the two sets of ratings provides the estimate of inter-rater reliability.

Generalizability Theory

Generalizability theory (Shavelson & Webb, 1991) provides an alternative framework for conceptualizing and investigating the reliability of test scores. Rather than choosing among the reliability indices described above, reliability is defined flexibly in each setting, depending on the factors that are likely to influence scores in that setting. Generalizability theory allows the researcher to separate out the impact of multiple sources (items, raters, time, etc.) of measurement error, but also to combine all of these sources into one overall estimate of reliability.

From the perspective of generalizability theory, reliability is not something inherent in a test, but rather, it depends on how a test will be used (Murphy & Davidshofer, 1991). For example, if test scores are meant to reflect a stable characteristic of the individual, it is important to evaluate whether test scores can be generalized across time. On the other hand, if the purpose of the measurement is to evaluate an individual's standing at a particular point in time, changes across time would not be included as a source of measurement error.

Interpreting Reliability

When reviewing reliability evidence, the evaluation team must determine whether the level of reliability is sufficient to support the use of a test. Reliability evidence can take several forms, such as a reliability coefficient or a standard error of measurement (SEM). In either form, reliability information must be interpreted in light of the design of the study used to collect the reliability information.

Reliability Coefficient

In general, higher reliability coefficients indicate more repeatable or stable test scores. There are no stringent rules for determining what is acceptable reliability for a test. Reliability should be interpreted in light of how the reliability coefficient was estimated, as well as the reliability of available alternative tests. Reliabilities above .80 are generally considered acceptable, although this value should not be used as an absolute cutoff. Higher levels of reliability are desirable if selection decisions are based on a single test score, whereas tests with substantially lower levels of reliability are often able to contribute to selection decisions when used in conjunction with other measures.

Standard Error of Measurement (SEM)

The SEM can aid in the interpretation and communication of reliability evidence because it demonstrates the impact of reliability on the interpretation of test scores. The SEM is inversely related to the reliability of a test: a higher reliability will result in a smaller SEM. The SEM can be used to estimate a confidence interval within which a person's true score is expected to fall. We can say that for 95% of the candidates, their true scores will fall within $+/- 1.96$ SEMs of their observed scores. For example, for an individual with a score of 90 on a test with a SEM equal to 3, the confidence interval would range from 84 to 96. Such an interval provides an indication of how much an individual's score might change if he or she is tested on a different day or using a different version of the test.

Effect of Study Design

Characteristics of the reliability study can affect the size of the estimate. The program evaluation team should pay close attention to the following issues when interpreting reliability coefficients:

- The sources of error estimated by the reliability coefficient
- The conditions under which data were collected (e.g., length of time that passed between administrations of a test in a test-retest reliability study)

■ Whether the group on which reliability data were collected was sufficiently similar to the test takers (in terms of educational level, age, etc.)

Validity

A second important feature when evaluating a test is validity. Validity refers to the appropriateness of inferences drawn from test scores, and the process of validation involves gathering evidence to support these inferences (AERA, APA, & NCME, 1999). Validity is not something inherent in a test. Rather, a test's validity is established with respect to a specific purpose. For example, a job knowledge test may be valid for predicting performance in entry-level accounting positions; however, the same test may not be valid for predicting performance in senior-level accounting positions.

As illustrated in Figure 6.1, a variety of inferences can be involved in linking test scores and job performance (Binning & Barrett, 1989). A fundamental concept in the model is that neither tests nor job performance measures are perfect indicators of the variables of interest. Therefore, the evaluation team needs to distinguish between the test (the predictor measure) and the underlying theoretical variable the test is intended to measure (the predictor construct). A similar distinction is made between an individual's actual job performance (the job performance construct) and the recorded measure of job performance.

Figure 6.1 illustrates several types of evidence that the evaluation team can use to examine test validity. Criterion-related evidence establishes an empirical relationship between test scores and a measure of job performance (link 1), which should be combined with evidence that the performance measure adequately reflects actual job performance (link 4). Another approach, referred to as construct validity, relies on evidence that the test is a good measure of the intended knowledge, skill, or ability (link 2) and that this characteristic is essential for successful job performance (link 3). A third type of evidence, content validity, focuses on the overlap between the tasks or knowledge utilized on a test and those required on the job (link 5). A fourth type of validity evidence is validity generalization, a form of criterion-related validity evidence (link 1) in which the relationship between test scores and job performance measures is obtained from past research in similar settings. As illustrated by Figure 6.1, there is no single best way to establish test validity. Instead, the evaluation team should strive to obtain as many different kinds of evidence as possible.

The following sections provide a detailed description of these four types of validity evidence. A common element of each approach is the reliance on job analysis to define job content, establish ability requirements, or develop performance criteria. Although a thorough review of job analysis methods (see Harvey, 1991; and the job analysis chapter in this volume) is beyond the scope of this chapter, the importance of carefully defining the job and linking its requirements to the test should not be minimized.

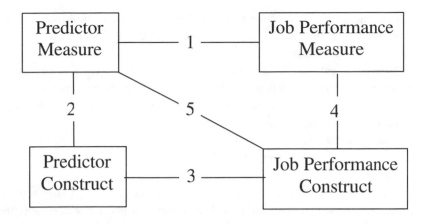

Figure 6.1   Conceptual framework for types of validity evidence.

SOURCE: From Binning, J. F., & Barrett, G. V. (1989). Validity of personnel decisions: A conceptual analysis of the inferential and evidential bases. *Journal of Applied Psychology, 74,* 478–494. Copyright 1989 by the American Psychological Association. Adapted with permission. No further reproduction authorized without written permission of the American Psychological Association.

Criterion-Related Validity

Criterion-related validation involves showing a statistical relationship between a test and a criterion measure. To be useful, criterion measures should assess relevant job activities or behaviors, which ideally would be identified through a comprehensive job analysis (Society for Industrial and Organizational Psychology, Inc., 1987). Indeed, to be effective, criteria must not be chosen out of convenience but rather should be selected because they are job relevant, reliable, and free of bias.

When reviewing criterion-related validity evidence, the evaluation team should determine whether the study used a predictive or concurrent design. In a predictive validity study, there is a time interval between the collection of test score data and criterion data whereas in a concurrent validity study, there is no such interval. Because the predictive design examines predictions of future performance based on the test scores of applicants, it more closely parallels the way tests will be used for selection. However, for tests of stable characteristics, such as general abilities, predictive and concurrent designs are likely to provide similar results (Barrett, Phillips & Alexander, 1981; cf., Guion & Cranny, 1982). Because the concurrent design allows larger samples to be collected more quickly, it is often a more practical alternative.

The degree of association between a test and criterion is expressed by a validity coefficient (i.e., correlation coefficient). An evaluation team should assess validity in terms of both statistical significance and the magnitude of the correlation. Validity coefficients theoretically range from +1.00 to −1.00; however, because no single test can fully predict job performance, validity coefficients for individual predictors rarely exceed 0.50. More typical validity coefficients for employment tests are in the neighborhood of between 0.20 and 0.30. The use of multiple tests can improve prediction but only when the different tests are designed to measure unique facets of performance.

Validity coefficients should be interpreted in light of the practical constraints of research in organizational settings. For the sample sizes commonly observed in validation research, significance tests have extremely low power (i.e., a small sample study will often result in a nonsignificant validity coefficient, even for a test that is valid). Unless sample sizes are very large, nonsignificant results should be interpreted as uncertainty regarding the job relatedness of a test, rather than as evidence that the test is not valid.

This situation is further aggravated by other factors such as unreliability and range restriction, which tend to artificially lower validity estimates. Selection researchers often use statistical corrections to compensate for the effects of unreliability and range restriction. Therefore, when interpreting a validity coefficient, it is important to understand which corrections, if any, have been applied.

High reliability is a necessary but not sufficient condition for high validity. If a measure contains a lot of random error, it is unlikely to correlate with other measures. Statistical corrections can be used to compensate for the measurement errors that are likely to occur in both selection tests and outcome measures (e.g., job performance ratings). However, the standard practice is to correct only for unreliability in the outcome measure. This correction provides an estimate of the validity that the test would have demonstrated if a perfectly reliable measure of performance were available. Unreliability in the test will also result in lower validity. However, because selection decisions are made using the actual test, with its associated measurement error, estimating the validity of a perfectly reliable test is not relevant to the evaluation of the selection system.

Another concern in validation research is range restriction, which occurs when the sample used to compute the validity coefficient has substantially less variability on the test than is found in the applicant population. Direct range restriction occurs when the test under investigation is used to make selection decisions. When this occurs, performance measures are available for only those individuals with high scores on the test, and the reduced variance in test scores tends to lower the observed correlation. Range restriction can also be indirect when selection is based on a test that is correlated with the test being validated. Corrections for several kinds of range restriction are discussed in Sackett and Yang (2000).

Content-Oriented Validity

Content validity involves demonstrating that the test is a representative sample of the content of the job as determined through a comprehensive job analysis. Content validity is often used with work sample, simulation, or job knowledge tests when the content of the test can reasonably be viewed as a sample of work behavior. For example, the content validity of a word processing test would be supported by evidence that the test involves the same types of documents and word processing software used on the job. With more abstract characteristics, such as personality or general cognitive ability, a content-validation strategy alone would probably be insufficient because the content of the test items often bears no direct similarity to the job.

Content validity can be assessed through an evaluation of the test development plan or a review of test content. In most cases, this involves having subject matter experts (SMEs) compare the content of a test against the requirements for the job. An evaluation team should pay careful attention to the composition of the SME panels used to validate assessments. The SMEs should be sufficiently knowledgeable to provide accurate information about job requirements. In addition, the sample of SMEs should be diverse enough to fully represent all members of the relevant workforce.

When evaluating content validity evidence, the evaluation team should consider the relevance and representativeness of test content. Each component of the test should be essential to successful job performance. Furthermore, a test should fully cover the domain of skills or behaviors it was designed to assess. A common measure of content relevance is the content validity ratio (CVR; Lawshe, 1975). Several SMEs judge whether each item on a test is essential for the job. The CVR reflects the degree of agreement among SMEs regarding the relevance of an item. The CVR can range from −1.00 to 1.00, where a value of 1.00 indicates perfect agreement that the item is essential, and 0.00 would occur when 50% of the SMEs rate the item as essential.

Construct Validity

Construct validity evidence generally involves using theory to specify a pattern of expected relationships among variables and then obtaining empirical evidence to confirm the predicted pattern. Construct validity is generally not determined from a single study. Instead, it reflects the integration of multiple types of evidence, including empirical research, theory, and expert judgment. In employment settings, evidence is needed that the test adequately represents the intended construct and that this construct is important for effective job performance. An evaluation team might encounter methods such as the following if construct validation were used to substantiate the use of some tests in the organization.

■ Showing that the test is strongly correlated with other measures of the same construct (convergent evidence) and less strongly related to measures of distinct constructs (discriminant evidence). This evidence will be strongest when the convergent evidence is based on different measurement methods, and discriminant measures include reasonable alternative hypotheses about the determinants of individual differences on a test. For example, the construct validity of a written mechanical reasoning test would be supported by a strong correlation with a performance-based mechanical reasoning test and a lower correlation with a measure of verbal ability.

■ Providing evidence from a factor analysis[1], in which one would evaluate the pattern of correlations among test items to verify the test's hypothesized structure. For example, if a personality measure is designed to assess the Big 5 personality traits, a factor analysis should reveal five factors, with items loading on the appropriate factors.

■ Theory or past research suggesting the importance of the predictor construct for effective job performance. For example, a measure of leadership style would be supported to the extent that it assesses critical behaviors identified in a well-established theory of leader effectiveness.

Although construct validity evidence is critical to evaluating whether a test measures what the user intended it to measure, it is rare to see such evidence in applied settings. The major obstacle preventing the accumulation of construct validity evidence is the need for large samples from which to collect test score data. Furthermore, it is often hard to justify the time and cost of administering convergent or discriminant measures that are not intended to become part of the final selection battery. However, if validation researchers approached construct validity as the process of accumulating evidence across multiple studies, the demands of conducting the research would not rest on individual organizations. The existing literature often addresses some aspects of construct validity, and an evaluation team can collect additional data in their organization to strengthen and expand on the available evidence.

Validity Generalization (VG)

Often, conducting a validation study is impractical due to limited budget, time, or sample size. Under these circumstances, it may be more feasible to use professionally developed assessment tools for which documentation on validity already exists. In this situation, the evaluation team may be in a position of either reviewing or conducting a VG study. VG involves determining whether a previously validated test can be used to select employees for similar jobs in a different organization or setting.

The use of a professionally developed test without a local validation study rests on two types of evidence (Hoffman & McPhail, 1998). First, there must be evidence that the test is valid in other settings. VG methods (Hunter & Schmidt, 1990) have been developed to aggregate validity evidence across a large number of small-sample validation studies, providing substantially more precise estimates of predictor-criterion relationships. When interpreting the results of a validity generalization study, an evaluation team should examine the variability of results across studies and identify job, organization, and applicant pool characteristics that moderate the level of validity.

Second, it is important to evaluate whether this validity can be faithfully "transported" to the current assessment setting. Job analysis data should be used to verify that the organization's job is similar to the jobs used in past research in terms of work behaviors and knowledge, skill, and ability requirements. In addition, the target group on which the test was originally validated should be similar in background and demographic characteristics to applicants in the current setting.

Selection Decisions

In addition to the technical quality of selection tests, the evaluation team should examine how tests are used to make selection decisions. Reaching a final selection decision involves a number of important choices, including how to combine multiple sources of information, how to set cutoff scores, and whether to use banding or ranking procedures. It is generally not possible to show that a particular decision rule is valid. If selection tests are valid, any reasonable procedure for hiring on the basis of these tests would be valid. That is, the procedure would select employees who have a greater chance of success on the job than those who were not selected. Still, evidence should show that the chosen decision-making procedure is reasonable and consistent with the purpose of the selection system.

Cutoff Scores, Ranking, and Banding

Test scores can be used in any number of ways to reach hiring decisions. Candidates may be required to achieve predetermined cutoff scores, they may be ranked according to their scores and selected "top-down," or score bands may be created reflecting score ranges corresponding to distinct levels of performance.

The choice between top-down selection and the use of a cut score should be based on the nature of the characteristic measured by the test. Top-down selection is appropriate when there is a linear relationship between test scores and job performance, such that individuals with higher scores will tend to demonstrate better performance. In other situations, employment tests are used to screen out those applicants who do not possess a minimum level of proficiency (e.g., basic reading comprehension). Here, it would be more appropriate to establish a single cutoff score, above which applicants are further evaluated using other assessment methods. A variety of methods have been developed to establish cut scores corresponding to minimum qualifications, based either on criterion-related validity evidence or judgments about test content (Cascio, Alexander, & Barrett, 1988).

The use of cut scores or banding procedures is often justified as a way of reducing adverse impact (i.e., difference in passing rates) against minority groups. The adverse impact of a test will typically be greater with a ranking procedure and lower with a cut score that is set at the minimum proficiency level. However, use of a low cut score would result in a large pool of candidates from which the organization must choose using other methods. The use of a cut score will result in lower adverse impact for the overall selection decision only if these other methods have less adverse impact than the selection test. In addition, setting a low cut score tends to reduce the utility of the test. Banding is often seen as a compromise between the two extremes (Campion et al., 2001), reducing some of the adverse impact associated with the ranking procedure while still maintaining a good portion of the test's utility. However, the effectiveness of banding at reducing adverse impact may be negligible unless preferential treatment is given to the minority group within each band, a practice that could be viewed as illegal (sometimes called reverse) discrimination.

Combining Scores From Multiple Employment Tests

Many assessment programs use a variety of tests and procedures in their assessment of candidates. When examining a multiple-component selection system, the evaluation team should assess not only the individual components but also how the information will be combined to form an overall decision.

Generally speaking, there are two approaches—mechanical and judgmental—for combining information from multiple assessment procedures. Mechanical approaches rely on explicit rules or formulas to integrate two or more sources of information. Judgmental strategies, on the other hand, require the decision maker to subjectively evaluate all of the assessment information and then form an overall evaluation. In most cases, mechanical approaches are preferred because they are less apt to introduce error due to decision-maker idiosyncrasies or biases that may enter into the decision-making process.

For mechanical approaches, it is important to evaluate the relative weight that is given to various test components. Each test could be given equal weight, or optimal weights could be determined empirically based on a regression analysis. It is also possible to develop weights using judgments by SMEs regarding the job relevance of different predictors (Arthur, Doverspike, & Barrett, 1996).

For judgmental integration strategies, it is important to evaluate the ability of the decision maker to effectively use the available information. The decision maker should have a good understanding of the role of each component of the selection system. Training of decision makers and the development of explicit instructions or evaluation forms can help to demonstrate that the resulting decisions are comprehensive, fair, and free of bias.

Test Administration Practices

Procedures for administering and scoring tests and maintaining records all impact the effectiveness of the system. The evaluation team should review the relevant policy and procedure manuals to determine whether test administration policies are clearly defined and promote standardization of assessment methods and testing conditions. The evaluation team should also consider the qualifications and training required of staff who administer and interpret tests.

Administrative procedures should cover all stages of the testing process. The evaluation team should consider the following issues:

- What information about selection tests (e.g., test content and format) is provided in advance to applicants? Do all potential applicants have access to this information?

- Is the testing environment free of distractions?
- Are test instructions and time limits adequate, and are they administered consistently to all applicants?
- Are test-scoring procedures designed to be as objective as possible?
- How is the security of test data protected?
- How are test results stored, and do policies regarding who has access to test scores adequately protect the privacy of applicants?
- Is there an appeal mechanism through which applicants can challenge test results or selection decisions?
- Under what conditions and after what time lag can applicants retake selection tests?
- In what ways can testing practices be altered to accommodate the needs of individuals with disabilities or different linguistic backgrounds? How do applicants request accommodations, and how are these requests evaluated?

A review of professional standards regarding test administration is provided in the Test Administration, Scoring and Reporting chapter in the *Standards* (AERA, APA, & NCME, 1999).

Fairness, Bias, and Discrimination

The evaluation team should review selection tests and administrative procedures to ensure that the selection system does not unfairly discriminate against particular demographic groups. Historically, racial and ethnic minorities, women, and individuals with disabilities, among others, have had limited access to the most desirable employment opportunities. There is a growing recognition that employers have an ethical—as well as a legal—responsibility to provide fair access to all members of a diverse labor market.

There is no universally accepted definition of fair selection practices (AERA, APA, & NCME, 1999). For example, the fact that African Americans and Hispanics tend to score lower than White Americans on general cognitive ability tests suggests to some that these tests are unfair, since their use would tend to screen out most members of the minority groups. Others have argued that the use of such tests would be fair if there are true differences in ability or potential performance, but would be unfair if the differences were an artifact of the test. Testing professionals tend to focus on fairness in terms of technical considerations, such as the absence of bias. However, assessments of fairness ultimately reflect value judgments and will be subject to different interpretations in different social or political settings. Therefore, an evaluation team will want to examine the issues of fairness from several perspectives, including evidence of test bias, avoidance of illegal discrimination, and perception of fairness.

Bias

Measurement specialists have operationalized the concept of fairness in terms of bias, or systematic errors of measurement or prediction. If two individuals have the same level of ability, they should receive the same test score (plus or minus random measurement error). However, if members of one group tend to obtain lower scores than individuals with the same level of ability from another group, then the test is biased. Bias can be examined both for individual test items and for the test as a whole.

Item Bias

Item bias analysis is typically performed during test development in order to identify and remove biased items before a test is used. One approach is to review the test for (a) content that may be unfamiliar or offensive to some demographic groups and (b) the appropriateness of the reading level required by test items and instructions (see Guion, 1998, pp. 447–449, for a guide to item content review). A wide variety of statistical techniques, often referred to as differential item functioning (DIF) analysis, can also be used to identify biased items (Holland & Wainer, 1993).

Test Bias

Test bias refers to group differences on test scores that do not correspond to an external criterion, such as job performance. A common method for assessing test bias is to perform a moderated multiple regression analysis (Cohen & Cohen, 1983) to examine whether there are differences across groups in the ability of the test to predict job performance.

The regression analysis can distinguish three types of bias. First, the relationship between test scores and job performance might be stronger for the majority group than for the minority group. Second, the test may be less accurate at predicting performance for the minority group, as indicated by more extreme prediction errors. A third type of bias would occur when group differences on the test overestimate differences on the job. That is, given the same level of job performance, members of the minority group would tend to score lower on the test than members of the majority group.

Although moderated multiple regression is a common approach for evaluating test bias, the evaluation team should be aware of the limitations of this method. The analysis requires large sample sizes (Aguinis & Stone-Romero, 1997) and makes assumptions about the data that may not be appropriate in all settings (Aguinis, Petersen, & Pierce, 1999; DeShon & Alexander, 1996). In addition, the analysis depends on the availability of a comprehensive and unbiased measure of job performance. If there is bias in the performance measure (e.g., if supervisors rate minority employees unjustifiably lower), tests for bias based on the regression analysis may be misleading.

Illegal Discrimination

Whereas bias is a technical property of test scores, discrimination refers to whether selection practices meet specific requirements established in employment laws. A selection system could be illegal, even if there is no evidence of item or test bias. In the United States, it is illegal for employment decisions to discriminate on the basis of ethnicity, national origin, gender, religion, age, or disability (see Gutman, 2000, for a review of equal employment laws). Consequently, an evaluation team will want to determine whether selection systems are nondiscriminatory and will stand up to scrutiny by the legal system. In the following, the term *protected group* is used to refer to any group covered by current equal employment law. It is important to keep in mind that the law protects both men and women and all ethnic groups, even members of the majority group.

Most employment discrimination cases involving selection systems fall under one of two legal theories: disparate treatment and disparate impact. Disparate treatment applies when an individual is subjected to different or more stringent selection criteria because he or she is a member of a protected group. An example would be basing a selection decision on an interview in which different questions are asked of men and women. The evaluation of legal defensibility under the disparate treatment theory should focus on how selection decisions are documented and whether decisions can be linked to a systematic assessment process that is applied consistently to all applicants.

Disparate impact refers to the use of a selection system that tends to disproportionately screen out members of a protected group. A system is discriminatory if (a) it produces adverse impact, that is, a substantial discrepancy in results across groups, and (b) the system is not job related. The best way to defend against disparate impact discrimination claims is to justify the job-relatedness of the selection system, using any of the validation methods described above. In addition, the evaluation team should determine whether attempts were made to identify alternative selection methods that would also be valid but that would have less adverse impact (U.S. Equal Employment Opportunity Commission, Civil Service Commission, Department of Labor, & Department of Justice, 1978).

Even if tests are job related, it is important to monitor adverse impact statistics. Two types of data can be used to assess the degree of adverse impact produced by a selection system. Workforce composition analyses compare the proportion of a minority group in the workforce to the proportion in the relevant labor market (e.g., data obtained from U.S. Census Bureau reports). Workforce flow analyses focus on the proportion of protected group applicants who are hired or pass a test compared to the passing rate for the majority group. Because population data cannot take into account factors such as job choice, the use of workforce composition analysis may misrepresent the pool of actual applicants. The individuals who apply for an opening will better represent the actual labor pool from which a company can hire. However, if workforce flow data are not available, or if recruiting practices deter minority applications, the evaluation team may still be able to make relevant comparisons using population data.

The most common approach to adverse impact analysis is based on the 4/5ths or 80% rule suggested by the *Uniform Guidelines* (U.S. Equal Employment Opportunity Commission, Civil Service Commission, Department of Labor, & Department of Justice, 1978). The adverse impact ratio is defined as the selection rate for the minority group divided by the selection rate for the majority group. The degree of adverse impact is considered to be substantial when the adverse impact ratio is less than 0.80.

A limitation of the 4/5ths rule is that it does not account for sampling error. The result can change dramatically across different administrations of a test, simply due to the sample of individuals who make up the applicant pool. Under many common conditions (e.g., when only a small number of applicants are hired), the 4/5ths rule will often indicate adverse impact when none exists in the population and may also fail to indicate adverse impact when it does exist (Morris & Lobsenz, 2000).

Because sampling error is often a concern, an evaluation team might find it useful to supplement the 4/5ths rule with a test of statistical significance. A discussion of adverse impact significance tests can be found in Morris and Lobsenz (2000) and Morris and Collins (2001). Unfortunately, because all significance tests have low power under typical conditions (Morris, 2001), their value is limited. The evaluation team may be able to develop a more complete understanding of the adverse impact evidence through the use of alternative approaches such as confidence intervals (Morris & Lobsenz, 2000) or by aggregating adverse impact statistics across multiple test administrations (Morris & Henry, 2000).

Perceived Fairness

Even if an organization follows all professional and legal standards for fair selection practices, this will not guarantee that the examinees will perceive the system as fair. Therefore, if such perceptions have not been previously gathered, the evaluation team might survey recently selected employees to learn of their reactions to the selection system. When applicants perceive selection as unfair, they will be more likely to pursue legal action against the company. Furthermore, they will be less likely to accept a position if offered and may demonstrate lower initial job performance if hired (Gilliland, 1994). Because the purpose of testing is to screen out applicants, some level of dissatisfaction is probably unavoidable. However, theories of procedural justice suggest that fairness perceptions can be enhanced by informing applicants that selection procedures are job related and rely on standardized decision rules.

Utility Analysis

The development and administration of selection systems is often quite costly, and organizations need to make decisions about the level of financial resources to invest in assessment methods. Organizations must determine whether the benefits of a system outweigh the cost of implementation or how to choose between a more expensive assessment method and a cheaper but less valid alternative. Utility analysis addresses these questions by quantifying the value of a selection system to an organization.

Utility analysis is a systematic procedure for considering costs and anticipated payoffs of decisions. It provides a common metric for evaluating alternatives, without which costs and benefits cannot be directly compared (e.g., a $50,000 investment to increase validity from .20 to .30). A common solution is to express the value of selection in dollars.

A variety of methods has been developed to evaluate the utility of selection systems (Cascio, 2000). One of the most common approaches is the Brogden-Cronbach-Gleser model, which estimates the utility (in dollars) of a selection system by considering a number of factors, including the number of persons hired, criterion-related validity, and the cost of testing.

The biggest challenge for this method is the need to estimate the standard deviation of job performance in dollars (SD_y). For some jobs, performance can be readily measured in dollar terms (e.g., sales volume). However, often SD_y must be estimated indirectly, and a number of strategies have been developed for this purpose (Cabrera & Raju, 2001). Often, these estimation strategies rely on questionable assumptions, and they can sometimes produce estimates of utility that are not viewed as credible by managers (Latham & Whyte, 1994). Alternate ways of operationalizing utility, such as increases in productivity or reductions in turnover, may be just as meaningful to organizational decision makers.

Conclusion

An effective personnel selection system will benefit all members of an organization by ensuring an effective workforce, matching applicants with jobs that best fit their capabilities, and providing an efficient system for the management of the selection process. Evaluation of the quality of selection tools and administrative procedures is important not only for the design of the system but also for refining existing practices. The development of an effective personnel selection system is best viewed as an ongoing process, in which periodic research is used to further enhance system effectiveness and adjust to changes over time.

Note

1. Factor analysis refers to a statistical technique that attempts to identify the underlying variables that account for the correlations between test scores. For a detailed treatment of factor analysis, the reader is referred to Pedhazur and Schmelkin (1991).

References

Aguinis, H., Petersen, S. A., & Pierce, C. A. (1999). Appraisal of the homogeneity of error variance assumption and alternatives to multiple regression for estimating moderating effects of categorical variables. *Organizational Research Methods, 2,* 315–339.

Aguinis, H., & Stone-Romero, E. F. (1997). Methodological artifacts in moderated multiple regression and their effects on statistical power. *Journal of Applied Psychology, 82,* 192–206.

Allen, M. J., & Yen, W. M. (1979). *Introduction to measurement theory.* Monterey, CA: Brooks/Cole.

American Educational Research Association, American Psychological Association, & National Council on Measurement in Education. (1999). *Standards for educational and psychological testing.* Washington, DC: Authors.

Arthur, W., Doverspike, D., & Barrett, G. V. (1996). Development of a job analysis-based procedure for weighting and combining content-related tests into a single test battery score. *Personnel Psychology, 49,* 971–985.

Barrett, G. V., Phillips, J., & Alexander, R. A. (1981). Concurrent and predictive validity designs: A critical reanalysis. *Journal of Applied Psychology, 66,* 1–6.

Binning, J. F., & Barrett, G. V. (1989). Validity of personnel decisions: A conceptual analysis of the inferential and evidential bases. *Journal of Applied Psychology, 74,* 478–494.

Cabrera, E. F., & Raju, N. S. (2001). Utility analysis: Current trends and future directions. *International Journal of Selection and Assessment, 9,* 92–102.

Campion, M. A., Outtz, J. L., Zedeck, S., Schmidt, F. L., Kehoe, J. F., Murphy, K. R., & Guion, R. M. (2001). The controversy over score banding in personnel selection: Answers to 10 key questions. *Personnel Psychology, 54,* 149–185.

Cascio, W. F. (2000). *Costing human resources: The financial impact of behavior in organizations* (4th ed.). Cincinnati, OH: South-Western College Publishing.

Cascio, W. F., Alexander, R. A., & Barrett, G. V. (1988). Setting cutoff scores: Legal, psychometric, and professional issues and guidelines. *Personnel Psychology, 41,* 1–24.

Cohen, J., & Cohen, P. (1983). *Applied multiple regression/correlation analysis for the behavioral sciences* (2nd ed.). Hillsdale, NJ: Lawrence Erlbaum.

DeShon, R. P., & Alexander, R. A. (1996). Alternative procedures for testing regression slope homogeneity when group error variances are unequal. *Psychological Methods, 1,* 261–277

Gilliland, S. W. (1994). Effects of procedural and distributive justice on reactions to a selection system. *Journal of Applied Psychology, 79,* 691–701.

Guion, R. M. (1998). *Assessment, measurement, and prediction for personnel decisions.* Mahwah, NJ: Erlbaum.

Guion, R. M., & Cranny, C. J. (1982). A note on concurrent and predictive validity designs: A critical reanalysis. *Journal of Applied Psychology, 67,* 239–244.

Gutman, A. (2000). *EEO law and personnel practices.* Thousand Oaks, CA: Sage.

Harvey, R. J. (1991). Job analysis. In M. D. Dunnette & L. M. Hough (Eds.), *Handbook of industrial and organizational psychology* (2nd ed., Vol. 2, pp. 71–163). Palo Alto, CA: Consulting Psychologists Press.

Hoffman, C. C., & McPhail, S. M. (1998). Exploring options for supporting test use in situations precluding local validation. *Personnel Psychology, 51,* 987–1003.

Holland, P. W., & Wainer, H. (1993). *Differential item functioning.* Hillsdale, NJ: Lawrence Erlbaum.

Hunter, J. E., & Schmidt, F. L. (1990). *Methods of meta-analysis: Correcting error and bias in research findings.* Newbury Park, CA: Sage.

Latham, G. P., & Whyte, G. (1994). The futility of utility analysis. *Personnel Psychology, 47,* 31–46.

Lawshe, C. H. (1975). A quantitative approach to content validity, *Personnel Psychology, 28,* 563–575.

Morris, S. B. (2001). Sample size required for adverse impact analysis. *Applied HRM Research, 6,* 13–32.

Morris, S. B., & Collins, M. (2001, April). *Testing for adverse impact when sample size is small.* Paper presented at the 16th annual conference of the Society for Industrial and Organizational Psychology, San Diego, CA.

Morris, S. B., & Henry, M. (2000, April). *Using meta-analysis to estimate adverse impact.* Paper presented at the 15th annual conference of the Society for Industrial and Organizational Psychology, New Orleans, LA.

Morris, S. B., & Lobsenz, R. (2000). Significance tests and confidence intervals for the adverse impact ratio. *Personnel Psychology, 53,* 89–111.

Murphy, K. R., & Davidshofer, C. O. (1991). *Psychological testing.* Englewood Cliffs, NJ: Prentice Hall.

Pedhazur, E. J., & Schmelkin, L. P. (1991). *Measurement, design, and analysis: An integrated approach.* Hillsdale, NJ: Lawrence Erlbaum.

Sackett, P. R., & Yang, H. (2000). Corrections for range restriction: An expanded typology. *Journal of Applied Psychology, 85,* 112–118.

Shavelson, R. J., & Webb, N. M. (1991). *Generalizability theory: A primer.* Newbury Park, CA: Sage.

Society for Industrial and Organizational Psychology, Inc. (1987). *Principles for the validation and use of personnel selection procedures* (3rd ed.). College Park, MD: Author.

U.S. Equal Employment Opportunity Commission, Civil Service Commission, Department of Labor, and Department of Justice. (1978). Uniform guidelines on employee selection procedures. *Federal Register, 43,* 38290–38315.

Suggested Readings in Personnel Selection

American Educational Research Association, American Psychological Association, & National Council on Measurement in Education. (1999). *Standards for educational and psychological testing.* Washington, DC: Authors.

Cascio, W. F. (1997). *Applied psychology in human resource management* (5th ed.). Englewood Cliffs, NJ: Prentice Hall.

Guion, R. M. (1998). *Assessment, measurement, and prediction for personnel decisions.* Mahwah, NJ: Lawrence Erlbaum.

Murphy, K. R., & Davidshofer, C. O. (1991). *Psychological testing.* Englewood Cliffs, NJ: Prentice Hall.

Society for Industrial and Organizational Psychology, Inc. (1987). *Principles for the validation and use of personnel selection procedures* (3rd ed.). College Park, MD: Author.

CHAPTER 7

Selecting Managers and Executives

The Challenge of Measuring Success

Rob Silzer

Seymour Adler

Recently a New York financial services organization was in financial trouble. Revenues were stalled and earnings were declining. The trend had been going on for four or five years with annual commitments from the executives to reach goals that never were reached. Finally the board of directors took action and hired a new chief executive officer (CEO) from the outside, who, in turn, quickly replaced the entire executive team using an extensive executive selection process (including broad recruiting, extensive interviewing, and executive level psychological assessments). In the name of team alignment, the new CEO hired only executives who agreed with her strategy of significant cost cutting but who also had strengths and limitations similar to her own. While she wanted to impact organizational performance, she also insisted on complete fidelity to her approach and style.

After two years, revenues remained stalled but the earnings stabilized. The board asked one of the authors to help evaluate the success of the CEO and the other new executives to decide whether they should stay or be replaced. Since the board was interested in determining the performance effectiveness of each executive, it was important to specify the results that had been expected from each executive while also considering the changing circumstances that the executives faced during their two years. Board members disagreed on the expected and actual performance for each executive. For example:

- What can an executive be expected to accomplish the first two years in a position?
- Was stopping the slide in earnings enough to keep the current CEO in place?
- How do you factor in the impact of a strong-willed CEO, who tended to micromanage the performance of individual executives?
- What emphasis should be placed on group versus individual contributions?
- How do you account for the constraints of a narrowly focused business plan on an executive's performance (e.g., if the major focus is on cost cutting what can be reasonably expected from sales and marketing efforts)?
- What weight should be given to the CEO's evaluation of an executive?

Ultimately the board decided to extend the CEO's contract and set a clear objective for significantly growing the revenues even though they knew her real talent was for cost cutting. The evaluation of the other executives was heavily influenced by the CEO's perception of whether they were fully aligned with her approach and "on the team." The strong reliance on the view of a single person to evaluate executive success is not uncommon, particularly if the CEO has strong opinions and is forceful in expressing them. In hierarchical organizations the immediate manager usually controls the evaluation of a reporting manager or executive. In many cases, this process serves the limited and short-term needs of the immediate manager but often serves the needs of the organization poorly and overlooks the broader performance contributions and the future potential of the individual.

In this case, the CEO and her handpicked executive team failed over the next two years to grow the revenues. Looking back, it now seems apparent why this happened and why the evaluation of executive selection success was flawed. The most glaring problem was what one executive once called "mono-variable-itis." That is, the over-reliance on a single variable to set a direction or to make a decision. The CEO was narrowly focused in her evaluations and missed the opportunity to retain executives who had the skills to grow revenue. And the board relied too much on her opinion of the executives.

This example highlights the challenge of objectively evaluating executive selections in situations where politics and power can overwhelm a more rigorous and thorough evaluation process.

This chapter discusses the range of issues that should be considered in evaluating the effectiveness of a management or executive selection process. In particular, we review selection context and then cover approaches to evaluating four components of a management or executive selection process: selection design, administration, decisions, and outcomes.

In general, the approach to evaluating management and executive selection programs should follow logical program evaluation steps such as specifying evaluation questions, identifying stakeholders and resource requirements, designing an evaluation plan, collecting data, analyzing and interpreting the data, communicating findings, and leveraging the conclusions to impact the business. We will not spend any time here discussing these general standard steps. For further information on general evaluation steps, please see chapter 1 in this book and Scott, Edwards, and Raju (2002). We also do not focus much on management/executive assessment methods and selection approaches. For that, we would direct you to Hollenbeck (1994), Jeanneret and Silzer (1998), and Silzer (2002b).

Selection Context

Before we discuss evaluation approaches, it is important first to consider the context and the complexity of selecting managers and executives in organizations, factors that make management/executive selection much more challenging to evaluate than other selection efforts.

Context of Management and Executive Roles

Over the last 25 years, as external consultants, we both have worked on innumerable management and executive selections. Each selection is unique in some way, and these differences must be considered when evaluating the success of the selection. A number of factors can contribute to the uniqueness.

Role Complexity and Change

Twenty years ago, it was not uncommon to find lengthy written job descriptions for management and even executive positions. However, in the 1980s, organizations significantly changed in an effort to redesign the company and regain competitive advantage. Organizations eliminated not only written job descriptions but also the view that managers had a limited, standard, and unchanging set of duties. Managers and executives were being expected to do whatever was necessary to "get the job done" and produce results. They were now responsible for outcomes rather than processes. The performance demands on managers significantly increased, and their role became much more complex. They were given a broader mandate and more latitude in how they accomplished their goals. By the 1990s, managers and executives were also expected to handle frequent changes in strategies, operations, and even products and services in order to keep up with the fast-paced shifts in the global marketplace. The focus of management and executive evaluations moved from fulfilling job responsibilities to delivering results and demonstrating performance competencies.

Management Versus Executive Positions

Executives made the transition to complexity and change even before managers. They were the ones who had to face the investment community, the board, and the shareholders to defend their actions and demonstrate each quarter how they were staying ahead of the market and the competition. In addition, executives were being heavily recruited from the outside to breathe life into aging organizations or to start up brand new organizations and were held personally responsible for the results. While CEOs had to meet unrelenting expectations and goals, they also gained increased power to shape or create the organization. They not only were allowed to do this, they were eventually expected to do it. This meant that the other executives had to be responsive to the CEO's every idea, request, and demand. So their jobs were defined by the expectations of the current CEO; as a result, their roles constantly changed and became even more complex and challenging. Ultimately this made each executive position different, given the variances in business strategies, objectives and culture, CEO's expectations, and marketplace competition. Today while both management and executive positions are more complex than they used to be, it is the executive positions that are typically the most distinctive.

Impact of the Individual

Along the way individuals were given much more latitude to pursue their jobs in their own way. This allowed them to redefine their role and interject their own personality and behavioral preferences into their leadership approach. This is most evident in executive and CEO positions that expect the incumbent to be charismatic, visible, and influential to a wide range of constituencies and audiences (Hollenbeck, 1994; Silzer & Hollenbeck, 1992). As a result, executive roles are regularly being redefined based on the incumbent's skills, personality, ideas, experience, and preferences. This shift has also occurred in management roles but to a slightly lesser extent. Managers are now encouraged to understand and leverage their peculiar skills and abilities. Of course, they are given more latitude in their behavior if they deliver results, while those who have trouble delivering are often subjected to a behavior improvement plan (which is essentially a behavioral change process). In general, though, both managers and executives are allowed and encouraged to modify their job positions based on their individual skills and abilities.

Selection Considerations

Management and executive selections are different from other types of selections.

Multiple Stakeholders

The number of individuals with a vested interest in a particular selection decision increases the higher the position is in the organization. At the management level, the stakeholders with an interest in the selection include direct and indirect reports, key peers, the immediate manager, and maybe the next higher skip-level manager. At the executive level, it includes the larger organization, all the other executives, the CEO, the board, shareholders, and the outside investment industry. But it might also include the local community, the industry leaders, business partners, clients, and vendors. Each of these stakeholders has a different perspective and a different set of needs. Each may have different selection expectations and goals. For example, executive peers may be looking for someone who is cooperative and open to influence. The board and the stakeholders may be looking for someone who can quickly take control and deliver results against goals. In contrast, the CEO may prefer to fill the position with someone who will follow through on decisions and see business issues in the same way as the CEO. These differences impact the way stakeholders evaluate the selection process itself. The CEO may want complete control over the screening process of anyone who reports directly to him. The board may want a more open process with multiple, independent assessments, including perhaps the involvement of an outsider professional assessment expert. This lack of consensus often results in a complicated and drawn-out executive selection process and may be a key reason for the high level of executive failure.

Sequential Selections and Candidates

Executive and management positions are usually filled one position at a time because of their uniqueness and significance. Each position is so different from any other that grouping them together in a selection process or summarizing across them for a selection evaluation study is difficult.

In addition, candidates are typically seen sequentially rather than simultaneously. That is, the selection decision makers are often asked to make a decision about the first candidate before they have seen a second candidate. Often they are encouraged to compare the candidate against the "position requirements" (even though these are rarely written down). This approach may constrain the decision-making process and prevent the comparison of one candidate against other candidates.

Levels of Fit

Selection at the executive level, in particular, is a complex challenge and requires the consideration of at least four levels of selection fit (Silzer, 2002a):

1. *Person-position fit.* Matching the executive to the needed skills and abilities, the strategic mandate of the role and the expectations of the immediate manager while also matching the position to the candidate's skills, career interest, and role requirements.
2. *Person-group fit.* Matching the candidate to the executive team and peers while also matching the group to the candidate's skills and leadership style.
3. *Person-organization fit.* Matching the candidate to the business strategies, organizational culture, and CEO's leadership style while also matching the culture to the candidate's skills and style.
4. *Person-country culture fit.* Matching the executive and the country culture in terms of the executive's openness to experience, cultural sensitivity, and need for support with the country culture's characteristics and dynamics.

An executive selection program may effectively evaluate some levels of fit but not others.

Evaluating Selection Design

Evaluation of selection design for managers and executives begins with the identification of competencies hypothesized to relate to performance. Then we assemble or develop tools that are hypothesized to validly measure candidates on these target competencies. In evaluating the process, we need to examine two questions: Are candidates being assessed on the right competencies? Are the assessment tools measuring the target competencies?

Evaluating Target Competencies

Several approaches could be used to evaluate whether the selection process is focusing on the right set of competencies, those that are relevant to effective performance. Assuming your selection process is based on a competency model of some sort, that model can be compared to other models for comparable positions. The objective of that comparison would be to identify areas in which your model either is deficient (i.e., you have neglected a potentially important competency) or irrelevant (i.e., you have included a competency that really is not essential to success on the job). Books, articles, and Web sites can provide competency models for managerial and executive positions (e.g., Spencer & Spencer, 1993). One model in the public domain is the Office of Personnel Management's Mosaic model (www.opm/mosaic.gov).

A more rigorous approach is to conduct a subject matter expert review of the target competencies. Depending on the level of the position being filled, appropriate subject matter experts may include recruiters, senior executives, outside consultants, and even clients. Subject matter experts should be asked, either individually or as members of a panel, to evaluate whether each target competency is relevant to performance in the target position. At the most senior executive level, the subject matter experts may be a board-level subcommittee to ensure that the CEO, chief operating officer, or chief financial officer selection process is focused on the right attributes. These evaluations are best collected on rating forms that can then be analyzed quantitatively to determine the degree of consensus around the relevancy of the competency. Various indices of consensus have been developed; one popular index is the content validity ratio (Lawshe, 1975). At the very least, qualitative information can be collected through interviews and used to arrive at a judgmental assessment. For documentation purposes, these qualitative comments and evaluations should be summarized in writing on a competency-by-competency basis.

At times, it is possible to use performance appraisal data to evaluate the competencies assessed during the selection process. The managers falling into the top and bottom quartiles are identified based on overall performance ratings. These two groups can then be compared on specific dimensions of performance and potential. The dimensions on which superior performers truly shine when compared to poor performers are key differentiators. The competencies that relate to these dimensions of performance and potential should be the focus of the assessment process.

In evaluating whether a selection process is assessing candidates on the right dimensions, it is important to look beyond the competencies currently required for successful performance. Especially at senior levels, success is significantly affected by the degree to which a candidate's values, aspiration, and style fit the prevailing organizational culture (Silzer, 2002a). Also, selection is inherently a future-oriented activity; you are assessing people for their capacity to meet the demands of the target position, as those demands will challenge them a year or two or three in the future. This is especially true for the selection of those who will have to sense, adapt to, and lead in the face of forces for change. Input from the most senior levels in the organization—and from Board members themselves when selecting at the most senior level—is needed to capture these strategic competencies.

Evaluating Assessment Tools

Managerial and executive assessment processes typically rely on a variety of tools, as target positions are complex and selection at this level is a high-risk decision. Virtually all management and executive selection processes include an interview, often several interviews. Research (e.g., Campion, Palmer, & Campion, 1997) has demonstrated that the validity of the interview increases with a more structured interview process in terms of what questions are asked and how responses are evaluated. Notwithstanding this research, executive-level interviews tend to be quite unstructured. Most management and executive selection involve some sort of evaluation of experience and education. Many processes include psychological testing of abilities (e.g., critical thinking) or personality. In the United States, personality traits are almost always assessed through self-report inventories (sample item: "I am attracted to adventure and risk"—agree or disagree?). In Europe, projective tests like the Rorschach inkblot, incomplete sentences, or Thematic Apperception Test are more common. At the managerial level in Europe, in France and Germany in particular, graphology, or handwriting analysis, is often used in an effort to assess personality traits in prospective managers (Levy-Leboyer, 1994).

These strong cross-cultural differences in preferred selection tools are often paralleled by strong differences in organizational culture around these preferences. A major cosmetics manufacturer had always hired its division managers through both a series of interviews and an assessment center process, in which senior managers served as assessors. The organization's culture placed a strong value on warm personal relationships and "good social chemistry." Managers felt that the opportunities afforded by the assessment process to get to know and become comfortable with the candidate were critical to accurate selection and successful onboarding. However, the selection process was costly and time-consuming; much management time was invested in interviewing and assessing candidates and cycle times stretched to 3 or 4 months. Moreover, senior managers were aware that the process was not yielding accurate selection decisions. Nonetheless, efforts by the human resources (HR) department to introduce a more rigorous, objective, and well-validated but "colder" set of tools—a biodata inventory and a remote, professionally operated, telephone-based simulation—were met with strong resistance from the end-user hiring managers. The methods to be used in the proposed process were seen as incompatible with the core and long-standing cultural values of the organization. In contrast, the former Bell operating companies, like SBC and BellSouth, had a long tradition of using objective testing and simulations. The tradition derived from their origins in the engineering-oriented culture of AT&T, where these tools were adopted in the 1950s for managerial selection. These cultural values and traditions need to be carefully considered in evaluating a selection process.

As for all psychological measurement, tools for assessing prospective managers and executives must be evaluated on their psychometric characteristics, primarily their consistency and accuracy as measuring instruments. It is important to emphasize that evaluations of a test's validity should be based on the test's established empirical record of job-relatedness and not on testimonials or popularity. An initial step should be to search the literature for objective reviews of the test. One long-standing source of such reviews is the *Buros' Mental Measurements Yearbook,* now in its 12th edition (Conoley, Impara, & Murphy, 1995). Another potential source is the journal, *Educational and Psychological Measurements.* The Web simplifies the search for formal reviews, informal (and often questionably reliable) users' comments, and bulletin boards that include content relevant to testing.

A critical step is to review any test manuals for reliability and validity information. Beyond data on the test's reliability and validity, test manuals often include other information (e.g., reading level and descriptions of normative populations) relevant to assessing a test's suitability. For instance, a test that discriminates average from above average intellectual ability may not be sensitive enough to differentiate the above average from the brilliant. In a highly preselected group of gifted candidates for a division manager position, such a test will be unsuitable. Particular attention should be paid to validation studies conducted on populations and industries similar to the target context. The accumulation of such validity studies can create a case for validity transportability or validity generalization.

How do you draw on this information to evaluate a selection process? One of us was recently asked by the HR director of a large financial services firm to evaluate an existing managerial selection process that included a battery consisting of three published paper-and-pencil tests. The firm had never done a local validation of this battery. One of questions we were asked to address was this: Does the company need to invest in conducting a local study to be confident of the tests' validity for selecting its own managers? Fortunately, the test publisher included the results of six validity studies in the test manual with some description of the managerial jobs incorporated in these earlier studies. Networking on the Web yielded two additional validation studies on these tools (though, undoubtedly many more existed—for discussion of this "file drawer" problem in generalization research see Rosenthal, 1995). As a first step, we mapped the firm's managerial competency model onto the descriptions of the managerial jobs included in prior research. The mapping strongly suggested that the population on which the prior validation record was built was relevant to the target population in the client company (e.g., all positions had strong people management responsibility, similar average age and education, and jobs in service industry). Validity generalization formulas (see Hunter & Schmidt, 1990, for examples) yielded an estimate of .22 as a minimum (at the 90% confidence level) validity coefficient likely to be produced if a local validation study was actually performed. That level of validity was both statistically and practically significant. Our recommendation to the HR director was not to invest in a local study and instead to proceed with using the test battery with confidence in its validity based on the accumulated track record of the tools.

One obvious but occasionally overlooked step in evaluating the suitability of tests is to actually read the test carefully. Ask: Is the content suitable to the target population or will the test come across as inappropriate, irrelevant to the job, or intrusive? Some tests of critical thinking skills ask respondents to analyze passages about nature or teen gangs whereas others provide business cases and business journal articles. Some tests of quantitative reasoning use SAT-like items ("Train A left station B traveling 75 miles an hour . . . ") while other tests ask about supply-and-demand curves and the interpretation of market research results. In recruiting top talent it is important that the selection process not only be as valid as possible but also appear as credible as possible. A projective personality test like the Rorschach does not, on the surface, appear job related, even if there are data correlating test scores with job performance. In contrast, candidates can readily observe the job relevance of assessment centers and simulations, especially if customized to the target position. This face validity inspires credibility, whether or not supported by actual criterion validity, and is one reason that assessment centers have been popular for so long as tools in managerial assessment.

The test should also be as fair as possible. Clearly, an evaluation of fairness includes examining any data on the test's adverse impact (e.g., differential pass rates, mean score differences, and differential validity) across different demographic subgroups. Here, too, evaluation should go beyond the data to include a close reading of test content. It is important to ensure that test items are not offensive to respondents based on their ethnicity, age, gender, race, religion, sexual preference, disabilities, and other factors. Into the 1980s, organizations administered the original Minnesota Multiphasic Personality Inventory (MMPI) to managerial and other job candidates, even though it had been developed in a very different culture in 1940–1941. That version of the MMPI included items like "I am very strongly attracted to members of my own sex" and "everything is turning out just like the prophets of the Bible said it would." Several years ago, we asked a senior executive at a major investment bank what he looks for when he hires. Without a hint of self-consciousness, he emphatically said that he looks for people (no, he did not say "guys"; he was sensitized to that) who played team contact sports like football or lacrosse.

An evaluation of the suitability of tools used in selection must include consideration of cost. Obviously, all else being equal, cheaper is better. The first consideration is the cost of acquiring the tools themselves. Published "off-the-shelf" tests of ability, biodata, or personality are relatively inexpensive, with per test fees as low as $4 or $5 and rarely higher than $100. The investment in custom designing and validating a standardized test is often prohibitive, particularly at the executive level, because of the relatively few selection opportunities over which to amortize initial research and development costs.

Time is money, we are taught. At the levels that senior executives are compensated, a little time translates into lots of money. As a result, a major criterion for evaluating selection program design is length, or better, efficiency. Shorter is better. One of our colleagues once suggested that we evaluate selection programs in terms of "validity per minute." There are clear diminishing returns in most selection programs. Adding a fifth or sixth hour to a selection battery will add very marginally to the overall accuracy of the battery but impose a considerable burden on those tested. This is especially true if the tools administered in that fifth or sixth hour are essentially similar to those administered earlier in the battery. It is worth questioning the common practice of sending an executive candidate through eight or ten interviews if the interviewers are all using similar questions and evaluating similar characteristics against similar standards.

Labor and travel are other major cost factors. The administration of objective tests requires little to no low-cost clerical labor, particularly if it is administered on a computer. The administration of customized face-to-face assessment center exercises or an in-depth background interview typically involves considerable time investment in preparation, execution, and analysis from high-priced talent, whether by senior managers or Ph.D. psychologists. Travel costs for candidates and for their assessors need to be considered. In multisite organizations, executive candidates are almost always brought to corporate headquarters, or at the very least regional headquarters, for assessment. Travel-related costs can add thousands of dollars to the cost of selection. For that reason, several companies are turning to remote assessment tools to screen candidates before bringing them to headquarters for final evaluation. For example, one major financial services firm evaluates candidates for certain branch office positions on a series of professionally administered, telephone-based job simulation exercises. Only those candidates who qualify on this remote screen are brought to regional or national headquarters for in depth interviewing. Motorola uses an engaging Web-based leadership simulation that includes e-mail, voice messages, and live telephone conference calls to assess managers around the world, substantially reducing administrative costs associated with the program.

In assessing the cost-benefit of a selection battery, all these cost factors must be considered. The expense of executive candidate assessment can be high; costs of over $10,000 per candidate are not uncommon. Some sources of cost are often overlooked—such as the time that senior decision makers invest in interviewing and evaluating candidates and the candidate's time if he or she is internal to the organization. However, the benefits of accurate selection need also to be evaluated. We should remember the enormous impact of bad decisions made by a small member of business executives at Enron, WorldCom, and other corporations. In assessing candidates for powerful executive positions, a valid selection process (i.e., one that reduces the probability of choosing the wrong person) has utility at almost any cost.

Evaluating Selection Administration

Selection validity and reliability can be compromised with poor administration design and implementation, and the process used for selecting managers and executives often is less structured and more inconsistently administered than other selection processes. In addition, organizations and candidates are very sensitive to how the process is conducted, particularly at the executive level. Organizations want to handle the selection process in a professional manner without offending strong candidates who are alert to possible slights to their ego and want to be treated not only fairly but also with a good deal of respect. Since management and executive candidates are usually seen sequentially, there is some tendency to individualize the process and tailor it to the specific candidate (Frisch, 1998). Unfortunately this often diminishes the standardization and reliability of the selection process.

Design of Selection Administration

Once the person requirements for the position have been identified and appropriate selection tools have been developed or chosen then the administration process should be created. Frequent selection administration components include the following:

- Written person requirements for the position
- Standard administration schedule and guidelines
- Test, inventory, and simulation materials as well as guidelines for administration and scoring
- Interview materials, assignments, and guidelines for administration and scoring
- Pre-assessment work materials sent to the candidate
- Standard communications to participants, interviewers, and selection staff
- Designated location and facilities
- Schedules for candidates and clear staffing assignments for the selection staff
- Materials and guidelines for providing feedback to the organization and to the participant
- Form for making notes on administration variances for a candidate
- Summary form for integrating all evaluative data on a candidate
- Form for recording decisions on the participant

The appropriate evaluation standard is that the same components and administration process should be applied to all candidates for the same position. The evaluation process should focus on whether these components were specified ahead of time in writing and whether they were systematically implemented by an administrator adequately trained on the guidelines. From our own personal experience and from some research evidence (Schmitt, Schneider, & Cohen, 1990), we know that the lack of consistent administration in a selection process can cause deterioration in the selection validity. The main reasons for inconsistent administration are a poorly trained administrator and a lack of written administration guidelines to follow.

Records and Documents

The approach to evaluating the administration process post hoc usually relies on reviewing written records and documents or on contacting the people in the organization involved in the process and the candidates, if possible. Frequently selection documents are not systematically stored inside an organization. Program evaluators should try to gain access to as many of these documents as possible. Also, they should check with the internal recruiters and HR staff for available records.

A member of the evaluation team should review these records for standard and consistent record keeping and some evidence that the selection process was administered in a reliable and consistent manner. Often a selection psychologist may need to get involved in the evaluation process if psychological tests were used. A checklist should be developed that allows the document reviewer to systematically audit the process. In some instances, with a large number of cases assessed, only a sample needs to be selected for review.

Part of the administrator's responsibility during the selection process is to make sure that the selection data and forms collected during the process are complete and accurate when the folder is given to the selection decision maker. The selection folders must also be kept confidential and in a secure location.

A backup evaluation approach is to contact those involved in the selection and collect their input post hoc through interviews or questionnaires. Possible sources of these data include candidates, the external recruiter, the internal recruiter, the HR manager, the hiring manager, internal interviewers, the selection administrator, and any outside consultants or assessment psychologists involved in the selection process. Here is a checklist to use for this evaluation:

1. Describe the selection process that was used with this candidate.
2. Were there any variances from the usual selection process and administration?
3. Were there any complaints or concerns from anyone about this particular selection?

Most of the data collected will be qualitative and may be difficult to summarize across selection cases because of the unique nature of each case. When a large sample of selection cases is included in the evaluation the qualitative data can be converted to numerical or categorical variables and analyzed statistically.

Implementation of the Selection Process

There is usually little information captured during a selection that is related to how well a selection process was implemented. We encourage client organizations to have the selection administrator take notes on any problems, concerns, or variances that come up during a selection and how they were handled. However, this is rarely done.

Usually it is difficult to evaluate post hoc the actual implementation process used for each candidate. Often the evaluation team must resort to follow-up interviews with the participants and the selection staff. Typically, external participants are reluctant to participate in these interviews. If the selection decision has not yet been made they don't want to jeopardize their selection chances and if they have been rejected they have little interest in spending any more time with the organization. Internal candidates who are not selected also may have reservations about discussing the selection process since they don't want to jeopardize their careers. Successful candidates are often the only source of feedback, but they often have a positive spin on the whole selection process and may overlook any shortcomings. They got the brass ring and really don't care that the merry-go-round wobbled a bit in the process. The selection staff can be a mixed source of feedback because they often have difficulty remembering the specifics of the selection process with a particular candidate.

There should be a documented reason for any process variances that occur. A selection expert is usually in the best position to decide whether the reason justifies the variance from the guidelines and whether the variance will have any impact on selection validity. In our experience, the CEO, the hiring executive, or other executives typically reserve the right to change the interview schedule at any time to accommodate their own needs. However, there are more serious variances, for example, inaccurate timing or scoring of psychological tests, inconsistent instructions for simulations, inappropriate questions being asked during an interview. Most administration variances will be minor and probably seem reasonable, given that the process can be somewhat flexible (i.e., number of interviews and the order in which selection components are presented). The administrator should understand the differences in the severity of variances and know when to be flexible and when to hold the line on an administration guideline.

Clearly our first responsibility as evaluators should be to ensure that the administrative process was implemented to optimize selection reliability and validity and to reflect professional standards and integrity. This can be a challenge if the organization has little knowledge or interest in professional standards or selection validity. In fact, it is a pleasure, and something of a surprise, to work with an organization that not only understands selection validity but also supports its importance. Capital One Financial is such an organization that strongly advocates designing and implementing a reliable and valid selection process for managers and executives and supports the effort needed to ensure that this happens.

Typically executives think about how well the process has served the pragmatic needs of the executive and the organization. They are likely to be interested in the following questions:

1. Did the process produce people that the hiring executive thought were strong candidates?
2. Was the process flexible enough to accommodate organizational preferences, constraints, and last minute changes?
3. What is the perceived credibility of the process, the selection staff, and the HR manager in charge of the selection?

Such organizations are often more interested in the face validity and the credibility of the process than in its empirical validity. Executives will cite a single good or bad selection decision as the basis for their evaluation of the whole selection process. And of course the CEO's opinion carries enormous weight. In contrast, evaluators should determine the effectiveness of the entire selection process from the organization's perspective.

Another important perspective to consider is that of the participants. Their perspectives about fairness and other issues can be biased by the final selection decision so it is much better to survey them immediately at the end of the process— before the decision is made. Some questions that a participant is likely to consider when deciding on fairness include the following:

- Did the process meet my understanding and expectations of what would happen?
- Was I treated fairly and in the same way as other candidates?
- Did I get an opportunity to discuss or demonstrate my skills and talents?
- Was I treated with respect?
- Was the process structured and efficiently managed?
- Was I provided with sufficient information on the position and what the organization was looking for in a candidate?
- How well did the organization design the selection process to accommodate my own requests or constraints such as my limited availability?
- Did the selection staff demonstrate appropriate behavior, credentials, courtesy, and professionalism?
- Was the process sufficiently rigorous and comprehensive to let me show my talents and abilities?
- Were the communications from the organization clear and adequate?

These review efforts should provide some indication of how well the selection process was administered. At the very least a conclusion can be reached on whether the process was administered in a reasonably structured, reliable, and consistent way and whether the number of inappropriate variances was within acceptable tolerances.

Evaluating Selection Decisions

Three key components should be reviewed in evaluating the selection decision making: data interpretation, data integration, and selection decisions.

Data Interpretation

The raw data collected during the selection process are scored and interpreted in terms of the relevant selection dimensions or competencies. Sometimes this results in actual ratings on the dimensions for each of the selection components (tests, interviews etc.). The critical focus for evaluators is how well the raw data are reflected in reliable and valid interpretations.

Several different types of raw data are collected during a management/executive selection such as test scores, interview notes, and simulation ratings. It may help to think of the data as either actual behaviors (actual candidate behavior in the interviews and simulations) or behavioral indicators (test scores and self-report interview information). Each requires a different approach to scoring and interpretation. The best way to evaluate both approaches is to observe administrators, staff, and psychologists as each actually scores and interprets the tests, role plays, in-baskets, or interviews.

More typically, evaluators must try to reconstruct the scoring and interpretation process after it has been completed based on written records. Occasionally, organizations retain audio- or videotapes of interviews or role plays or paper copies of exercise materials like in-baskets that can be independently rescored later to evaluate the reliability and validity of initial assessment decisions.

Behavioral Indicators

Test scoring is usually the easiest to evaluate because there are usually scoring keys and guidelines. The tests can often be rescored, and the scoring error rate can be determined over the population of candidates. However, the interpretation of the test scores should be looked at carefully to ensure that the appropriate comparison normative groups have been used. In addition, the interpretations need to be consistent with the constructs that underlie the test. This can be difficult to evaluate post hoc because particular test interpretations are frequently not specifically documented.

Interpreting self-report information from the candidate can be a challenge as the information comes from a biased source. If possible, evaluators should look at both the types of questions asked and the data that are collected. Behavioral example questions have been demonstrated to produce more objective, less biased behavioral information than more subjective, self-evaluative questions such as likes and dislikes or strengths and weaknesses. The more potentially verifiable the self-report information, the more accurate and objective it is likely to be.

Actual Behavior

Behaviors that the candidate shows in interviews (e.g., interpersonal and communication skills) and in behavioral simulations (e.g., skills demonstrated in a role-play or group discussion exercise) should also be assessed. Evaluating the collection and interpretation of these data is made more difficult when the raw data are in the form of handwritten staff notes that are often hard to read and poorly organized. Sometimes these data are collected in structured rating forms, which are then easier to evaluate. Sometimes the best that evaluators can do is to review the conclusions of the interviewer or simulation rater to determine whether they are objective and behavioral. Evaluators might consider the following:

- Does the rating form focus on behavior related to the relevant dimensions or competencies?

- Is the form structured in a way to capture the candidate's behavior reliably?
- Has the interviewer or rater adequately completed the form, and does it capture enough behavior to allow some reasonable and valid conclusions?

Evaluators should outline a checklist of things to pay attention to when reviewing each candidate folder and then summarize the checklist data across numerous cases if possible. A similar checklist could be used to observe data interpretation *in situ.*

Data Integration

After the raw data are scored and interpreted, the conclusions from each selection component need to be integrated into some overall conclusions on the skills and abilities of the candidate against the relevant requirements for the position. In reviewing the data integration step, evaluators should look at the relationship between the candidate data from the selection components (either in the form of raw data, interpreted conclusions, or structured ratings) and the final integrated conclusions and overall evaluation of the candidate's skills and abilities. Key points to look for include these:

- Is there a structured process or form for integrating the data?
- How well do the post-integration conclusions reflect or summarize the original data from the selection components?
- Does some information get overweighted or underweighted in the conclusions?
- Do the ratings of some assessors have disproportionate influence on the overall profile?
- Are the conclusions reasonable and fair?

Evaluators should try to determine how reliable and structured the integration process is. This can be difficult if the selection process does not capture both the component conclusions (or dimension ratings) and the integrated ratings (across components). Sometimes an integration sheet is used which captures both in a sort of multitrait multimethod matrix, similar to an assessment center ratings matrix (Thornton, 1992). The dimension ratings for each component are captured in columns, and the integrated dimension ratings are in the last column. In this process, a selection staff person responsible for the integration first reads all the original data and reviews the dimension ratings from each component. Then the staff looks at all component ratings for a single dimension across the dimension row and decides on the final integrated dimension rating. The staff person does this for each of the relevant dimensions. Evaluators are unlikely to find such clear guidelines or such a structured approach for most management and executive selections. More commonly, a HR manager collects data from each of the selection components (often orally in telephone conversations), takes short notes, and somewhat subjectively decides on the candidates' skills and abilities. This approach is likely to compromise the reliability and validity of the integration process.

Evaluators should develop a checklist that focuses attention on the following:

- How systematically are the conclusions and dimension ratings data from the components captured?
- Is there a structured, objective, and reliable process for combining the data on a particular dimension across the components into an overall rating or conclusion on that dimension?
- How valid are the overall dimension ratings or conclusions, based on the raw data or interpretations from the components?

The internal validity of the selection process can be calculated if there are numerical dimension ratings for both the components dimension data and the overall integrated dimension conclusions. Evaluators can then statistically correlate the component ratings with the overall ratings to answer such questions as:

- Do the component ratings on a dimension correlate with the overall dimension rating?
- Which components seem to have more influence on the overall rating?
- Is there sufficient variance in the ratings from each component to produce any validity?
- Does the internal validity vary depending on the staff person doing the integration?

When the ratings data are available, this analysis can follow the internal validation process used to study assessment centers. When such data are unavailable, evaluators must first reconstruct how the integration process was handled and then try to determine the related reliability and validity. In either case, it is advisable to use a checklist of key indicators of reliability and validity when reviewing a particular selection integration process.

There are many decision points in a selection process:

- What variances in the administration process should be allowed?
- What participant comments and behavior in the interview and simulations should be recorded or explored?
- What data should be included and how should they be weighted in interview or simulation decisions?
- What test scores should be included and how should they be weighted in test interpretations ?
- What ratings on a dimension from various selection components should be included and how much weight should they be given in the overall dimension ratings?
- How should evaluators weight the overall ratings on a candidate, the various selection fit issues, and the profiles of other candidates when deciding whether to hire a candidate?

In making this last decision, several hurdles should be considered:

1. How well did the candidate's overall skills, abilities, and experience match the stated requirements for the position?
2. How well does the position match the candidate's needs and interests?
3. How well does the candidate fit when considering the broader range of executive fit issues?
4. How does the candidate compare with other known candidates?
5. Is the preferred candidate strong enough to be effective in the position or do we need to look at additional candidates?

There are, of course, different styles of decision making and there is an extensive literature discussing the merits of clinical versus mechanical data integration, multiple hurdles versus compensatory decision approaches, profile discriminability, and individual differences between decision makers. However, decision making in management and executive selections is usually unstructured and unsystematic, primarily because of the number of variables involved and how much the variables change with each candidate and selection decision (i.e., the number and identity of decision stakeholders, the number and identity of final decision makers, the business or strategic urgency related to the position, and the availability of other competitive candidates). For this reason executive selection decisions rarely follow a standard process.

Sometimes the decisions are carefully documented. If the overall dimension ratings are also documented, then evaluators can statistically correlate them with the final selection decisions to assess the internal validity of their decisions. However, even then there are likely to be innumerable additional variables affecting the decision that are not documented. So it is unlikely that a comprehensive internal validity study on executive selection decisions can be completed.

More likely there is little documentation of the decision-making process. On occasion, evaluators might be fortunate enough to observe several actual decisions being made. More likely, evaluators may need to interview the key people who were involved in several selection decisions. The best people to interview or survey include the hiring manager, the HR manager or recruiter who shepherded the selection process, and the psychologist who might routinely participate in executive or management selection.

Evaluators should identify some benchmarks of effective decision making and include them in a checklist (or an interview outline). Listed below are some of the key things to look for:

■ How systematically were the data from the selection components recorded, scored or rated, interpreted, and considered?
■ Were there any consistent systematic steps taken to reach a selection decision?
■ Was there any effort to be objective and systematic when considering all available data and information?

- Were there multiple, independent, objective decision makers who reviewed the same participant data?
- Was there any process for having decision makers justify their decisions with available data and logical reasoning?

Evaluators may be fortunate enough to interview a significant number of people related to the selections but will probably be unable to cover a large number of selection cases. The evaluators may need to focus the interviewee on a particular candidate in order to avoid generalities unrelated to any specific situation. In either case, the resulting data may be summarized as selection trends rather than hard and fast evaluation conclusions.

Evaluating Selection Outcomes

In a certain sense, the question of evaluating the accuracy of selection decisions is straightforward: Are those who are selected significantly more likely to succeed on the job than those not selected? The complications in answering this question for managers and executives are both conceptual and practical.

On the conceptual level, the key complication is in defining the success criterion. The nature of managerial and executive work is complex. It is very difficult, if not impossible, to conceptualize an executive's performance in isolation, in the way we can isolate the work of a salesperson, a schoolteacher, or a production team leader. More than for those deeper in the organization, the performance of those close to the top is affected by the economy, market conditions, competitors, unexpected technological developments, and the performance of those around them inside the organization. "Hard" performance criteria are particularly contaminated at this organizational level by factors independent of an executive's personal level of performance.

On the practical level, for all but the very largest of companies, senior-level hiring is a low-volume, high-risk activity. As a consequence, traditional predictive criterion validation is not feasible. There are too few hires to provide statistical rigor to any study, and the risks of hiring unqualified candidates for powerful positions are too high for most organizations to absorb just for the sake of program evaluation. Moreover, assessment costs are often so high that organizations are not willing to invest in testing incumbents as part of a concurrent criterion study.

Of course, there are situations where these practical constraints are not an issue. For example, the selection processes for branch management positions in larger banks or store managers in large retail chains may allow for the application of standard validation methods, including concurrent and even predictive criterion-oriented studies. But what can be done to evaluate managerial and executive programs in the more typical environment? The answer lies in the combined use of a number of inherently flawed methods, perspectives, and measures.

One of the best sources of data is archival information on those who have been assessed in the past. Over time, even in situations of relatively low-volume hiring, a sufficient number of cases for reliable analysis may accumulate. Of course, the nature and completeness of available archival data can limit the analysis. On a going-forward basis, a comprehensive database should be designed to store future assessment data. All available assessment data can then be compared to criterion data that are either stored, as well, in existing databases or files or specially collected for the evaluation effort.

Individual-level criterion data against which selection judgments can be compared include both "softer" and "harder" information. Softer criteria include performance ratings, ratings of potential, and multirater survey data (even if collected for developmental purposes). Harder individual-level criteria include number of promotions, rate of salary increase (total increase over the number of years since being selected), and bonus and stock option awards.

The major shortcoming in evaluating selection process outcomes against these criteria is the absence of a comparison group, that is, those for whom such performance data are available even though they were judged to be unsuitable for the management or executive position. Of course, even more rare are data on "false negatives" (i.e., those rejected by the selection process who in actuality would have been successful if hired or promoted). It is a rare instance when a rejected applicant becomes a publicly acclaimed "star" at a competitor. Should this happen, it would surely be worth a bit of self-critical investigation to determine what if anything in the selection process might have led to this possible oversight. Recognizing these limitations, there are still retrospective analyses that can shed light on the accuracy of selection outcomes. One of us recently had the opportunity to sit with a senior executive and review his perceptions of why five relatively recent executive-level hires were considered failures. Many of the causes related to faulty on-boarding (i.e., an initial assignment that was poorly defined or of marginal value and visibility), poor management direction, and business developments that could not have been anticipated. But some of the factors associated with failure related to characteristics of the new hires that could have been detected before a selection decision was made. In one case, there was clear evidence during the assessment process that the candidate was very independent and tended to act decisively without conferring with others. This candidate was a poor fit with the corporate culture that was highly collaborative. These shortcomings were downplayed during the final decision-making process in the face of the candidate's strong intellectual abilities, executive presence, and excellent presentation skills. In another case, the new executive failed because of poor planning skills. The selection process simply failed to assess these critical skills.

Collective criteria can shed light, albeit imperfectly, on the accuracy of a selection process. For example, two regions of a large manufacturer may have different procedures for selecting plant managers. The relative financial performance across these regions, controlling for factors unrelated to managerial quality, can be compared

Recently Bristol Myers Squibb used a longitudinal approach to evaluating a new leader development and promotion process. Prior to implementing the new process, senior executives were asked a simple question: If you left tomorrow, how many managers are ready to succeed to your position? Two years after implementing the new process, senior executives were asked the same question. The number of managers ready to step into succession roles had increased dramatically, enhancing the executive talent pool at Bristol Myers Squibb significantly, reflecting the success of the new process. Similarly, when implementing a new managerial and executive selection program, hiring managers can be asked to evaluate the quality of hires over the prior 2 or 3 years. They can then be resurveyed on the same question some 2 or 3 years after program implementation.

On a more informal basis, if you are responsible for selection, you should be talking with the "consumers" of your "services" on a regular basis to elicit their evaluations on what is working effectively and ineffectively from their prospective. This input can provide ideas for continuous process improvement, not just around the accuracy of selection outcomes but for elements of the process itself.

Conclusions

To complete the evaluation process, it is important to take the final steps of summarizing, communicating, and implementing the results. In particular, the results should be summarized and communicated in way that will influence senior managers and get their support for implementation. We recommend two key guidelines to follow when presenting results to executives: (a) keep the communication focused and brief, and (b) connect the results and the recommendations to organizational priorities and goals. The recommendations should be kept to no more than three high-level issues. Be sure to target the needs of the stakeholders to the selection process while also emphasizing the issues that will really make a difference and have an impact on the organization. It is also helpful to lay out clear decision choices so they know the options you are asking them to decide between and the benefits and downsides of each. Most executives will respond favorably if you are thoughtful in how you communicate with them. Frequently they will leave others to take responsibility for framing an action plan once the decision has been made.

A comprehensive evaluation of management/executive selection can be hampered by the single-event nature of the selections, a lack of consistency in the design and implementation, and the limited availability of archival records. As a result, it may often be difficult to use statistical evaluation tools. Evaluators may ultimately need to use sound judgment and reasoning to determine the effectiveness and success of the selections.

For those companies that have effectively evaluated and validated management/ executive selections, the benefits can be substantial. Companies such as The Hartford and Capital One Financial are benefiting from well-validated management selection programs. This not only strengthens the management talent pool but also provides a definite competitive advantage. A while ago, one of the leading grocery chains was interested in evaluating the effectiveness of the management assessment process that was used to select all managers. The assessment included a competency-driven interview, a battery of personality inventories and cognitive tests, and a role-play simulation. The internal study concluded that the success rate of management selections based solely on interviews by senior managers (without the psychological assessment) was about 60%. This is probably a fairly typical success rate for these unstructured, wandering interviews. However, when a psychological assessment was added to the process, the selection success rate jumped to 85%. Such a success rate is rather remarkable, particularly if it can be sustained over the long term. The evaluation process revealed the most predictive parts of the selection process and allowed the organization to emphasize them and drop the nonpredictive elements. This not only increased the performance level of the whole management team, but it also resulted in substantial cost savings. What executive wouldn't support that? Just think of the contribution you can make to your own organization by initiating your own evaluation initiative.

References

Campion, M. A., Palmer, D. K., & Campion, J. E. (1997). A review of structure in the selection interview. *Personnel Psychology, 50,* 655–702.

Conoley, J. C., Impara, J. C., & Murphy, L. L. (Eds.). (1995). *The twelfth mental measurements yearbook.* Lincoln, NE: Buros Institute of Mental Measurements.

Frisch, M. H. (1998). Designing the individual assessment process. In R. Jeanneret & R. Silzer (Eds.), *Individual psychological assessment: Predicting behavior in organizational settings* (pp. 135–177). San Francisco, CA: Jossey-Bass.

Jeanneret, R., & Silzer, R. (Eds.). (1998). *Individual psychological assessment: Predicting behavior in organizational settings.* San Francisco, CA: Jossey-Bass.

Hollenbeck, G. P. (1994). *CEO selection: A street-smart review.* Greensboro, NC: Center for Creative Leadership.

Hunter, J. E., & Schmidt, F. L. (1990). *Methods of meta-analysis: Correcting error and bias in research findings.* Newbury Park, CA: Sage.

Lawshe, C. H. (1975). A quantitative approach to content validity. *Personnel Psychology, 28,* 563–575.

Levy-Leboyer, C. (1994). Selection and assessment in Europe. In H. C. Triandis, M. D. Dunnette, & L. Hough, L. (Eds.), *Handbook of industrial and organizational psychology* (2nd ed., vol. 4., pp. 173–190). Palo Alto, CA: Consulting Psychologists Press.

Rosenthal, R. (1995). Writing meta-analytic reviews. *Psychological Bulletin, 118,* 183–192.

Schmitt, N., Schneider, J. R., & Cohen, S. (1990). Factors affecting validity of a regionally administered assessment center. *Personnel Psychology, 43,* 1–12.

Scott, J. C., Edwards, J. E., & Raju, N. S. (2002). *The art and science of measuring success.* Workshop presented at the annual conference of the Society of Industrial and Organizational Psychology, Toronto, Canada.

Silzer, R. (2002a). Selecting leaders at the top: Exploring the complexity of executive fit. In R. Silzer (Ed.), *The 21st century executive: Innovative practices for building leadership at the top* (pp. 77–113). San Francisco, CA: Jossey-Bass.

Silzer, R. (Ed.). (2002b). *The 21st century executive: Innovative practices for building leadership at the top.* San Francisco, CA: Jossey-Bass.

Silzer, R., & Hollenbeck, G. P. (1992). *Executive assessment.* Workshop presented at the annual conference of the Society of Industrial and Organizational Psychology, Montreal, Canada.

Spencer, L. M., & Spencer S. M. (1993). *Competence at work: Models for superior performance.* New York: John Wiley.

Thornton, G. C. (1992). *Assessment centers in human resource management.* Reading MA: Addison-Wesley.

Recommended Readings on
Management and Executive Selection

Hollenbeck, G. P. (1994). *CEO selection: A street-smart review.* Greensboro, NC: Center for Creative Leadership.

Jeanneret, R., & Silzer, R. (Eds.). (1998). *Individual psychological assessment: Predicting behavior in organizational settings.* San Francisco, CA: Jossey-Bass.

Silzer, R. (Ed.). (2002a). *The 21st century executive: Innovative practices for building leadership at the top.* San Francisco, CA: Jossey-Bass.

PART III

Evaluating and Rewarding Employees

Performance Appraisal and Feedback Programs

Janet L. Barnes-Farrell

Angela M. Lynch

Performance appraisal and feedback programs (often simply referred to as performance appraisal systems) have the potential to serve a host of valuable roles in work organizations. Performance information drawn from appraisal systems can serve as the basis for a variety of important organizational decisions, with both positive (e.g., promotions, talent identification, and merit awards) and negative (e.g., downsizing and terminations) implications for individual workers. It can also be used for developmental planning efforts by individuals and departments. Because the information drawn from performance appraisal systems has the potential to have significant short-term and long-term consequences for workers, it is important that organizations have a plan for evaluating whether their performance appraisal and feedback systems function effectively. To this end, in this chapter, we hope to accomplish three main goals:

1. Articulate goals and concerns of major stakeholders in performance appraisal programs, and identify evaluation issues that should be addressed with respect to these concerns
2. Describe important features of the measurement function of performance appraisal and identify key questions that evaluators should consider as they review the performance measurement "piece" of the appraisal program

3. Describe the role of communications in an effective performance appraisal system and identify key questions to consider when evaluating the effectiveness of the communications function in the appraisal system

Goals of Appraisal and Feedback Systems

Plans to evaluate an appraisal system must systematically recognize the differing concerns various stakeholders bring to the table when they consider what the appraisal system is intended to accomplish and whether it is meeting those objectives. Three general groups of stakeholders can be identified in most organizations: organizations, appraisers, and workers. The various stakeholder groups may have quite different goals and standards for a "good" appraisal system.

Organizational Perspectives and Goals

Typically, organizations have multiple goals for a performance appraisal and feedback system. Surveys of organizations that conduct formal performance appraisals on a regular basis indicate that most organizations try to offset the high cost of developing and implementing an employee appraisal system by using the information that is generated from the appraisals for a variety of organizational purposes (Cleveland, Murphy, & Williams, 1989). The following list is not exhaustive, but it represents the wide variety of organizational functions that can benefit from data generated in performance appraisals.

- Input to human resources (HR) control systems: Information from performance appraisals can be used to make decisions about the allocation of rewards or other important outcomes, such as downsizing decisions.
- Legal defense of HR decisions: Performance measurements from an appraisal system can be used to document the appropriateness of selection, promotion, termination, and pay allocation decisions when there are legal challenges.
- Identification of potential: When appropriately designed, performance appraisals can be used to identify organizational members with the potential to move into other organizational roles.
- Identification of group training/development needs: Performance appraisals can reveal gaps between target performance levels and current performance levels for units and departments; this is extremely useful information for the identification of training needs.
- Individual feedback and development: The basis for most coaching and development efforts is a performance appraisal designed to emphasize the identification of individual performance strengths and weaknesses.
- Team feedback and development: In organizations that emphasize team-based operations, the goal of appraisal efforts may be to assess collective team performance strengths and weaknesses and provide feedback for team development purposes.

- Criteria to guide development and evaluation of selection systems: The content of appraisal instruments can be used as input for developing selection tools for hiring new staff members; the appraisals themselves can be used as standards against which to judge the effectiveness of those tools.
- Understanding of individual and team contributions to organizational effectiveness: Examination of the relationships between performance measures and more global measures of organizational effectiveness can help organizations understand the impact of individual workers' behaviors on the organization's performance.

It is tempting to think that the "ideal" performance appraisal system is one that addresses as many of these goals as possible. However, in practice the attempt to get as much "bang for the buck" can backfire because there is no single "most effective" approach to measuring performance. For example, a performance appraisal approach that does a good job of differentiating one worker from another—which would be ideal when the goal of the appraisal system is to identify workers who are most deserving of a promotion or merit raise—is less likely to provide the kinds of individual diagnostic information that are useful when the purpose of the appraisal is to provide feedback for coaching and development purposes. A program evaluation team should also understand that the goals of a performance appraisal system can be in conflict with one another and that such conflict can produce poor results. For example, a manager who wishes to promote a particular person may downplay important development opportunities. In this case, the recipient does not receive the guidance that may be helpful in the higher level position. Furthermore, in team environments, performance appraisal systems that emphasize differences among workers may only serve to interfere with the spirit of cooperation that is critical to effective team functioning.

For these reasons, organizations should be encouraged to prioritize the most important goals for their performance appraisal systems. The system should be designed to emphasize those goals; similarly, evaluations of the system should keep the intended purposes of the performance appraisal system in mind. From the standpoint of evaluating the appraisal system, this implies that three key questions should be asked:

1. Have the primary goals of the appraisal system been articulated and communicated to appraisers and workers whose performance will be appraised? Evidence for this can often be found in training materials and in documentation that is provided to appraisers and workers when the system is rolled out each year. The goals of the system must be clear to the users and recipients of the system as well as the designers of the system!

2. Is the design of the appraisal system aligned with the primary goals of the system? For example, if a primary goal of the appraisal system is to encourage improved team performance, measurement and feedback should focus on team behaviors and outcomes rather than individual workers' performance strengths and weaknesses. Similarly, if a primary goal of the system is to provide developmental feedback, the evaluation team should look for evidence that the measurement

system gathers information on which workers can act (e.g., information about specific competencies or information about behaviors) and look for evidence that the feedback system is designed to link performance measures with discussion of strategies for action on those performance areas that need attention. If a primary goal of the system is to make defensible promotion or termination decisions, there should be clear evidence that the measurement system is directly relevant to specific job requirements and evidence that appraisers are qualified to make high quality judgments about performance. This is discussed in more detail later in the chapter.

3. What efforts have been made to minimize conflicts between competing goals of the appraisal system? The political and cultural environment in which performance appraisal takes place can place strong demand characteristics on the behavior of those who use the system. Evaluation teams should look for evidence that these demands will not interfere with appraisals. For example, if the system is primarily intended to serve developmental purposes, an evaluation team could look for evidence that developmental feedback is handled *separately* from compensation decisions. It is extremely difficult for appraisers to provide candid developmental feedback when that feedback has the potential to harm talented personnel. It is important that those who design and implement the system identify potential areas for conflict and address them through structural means (e.g., separate systems for developmental appraisal/feedback and decision making) and/or process interventions (e.g., appraiser training that addresses these issues). This may pose special challenges for multinational organizations carrying out appraisal in a variety of national settings.

Appraisers' Perspectives and Goals

Appraisers bring personal goals and motives to the appraisal situation that may conflict with organizational goals for performance measurement. They may be much more concerned with minimizing the time devoted to the appraisal process, with maintaining harmonious working relationships, or with minimizing legal and political liabilities than they are with the quality and accuracy of performance judgments. Appraisers play a crucial role in effectively implementing a performance appraisal and feedback system, so evaluation of the appraisal program must also address the extent to which it meets their needs. Common goals and concerns of appraisers that should be considered during a program evaluation include the following:

■ Individual feedback and performance management: Managers who take their roles as performance coaches seriously view performance appraisal as "data" for discussion during coaching and development sessions. To do this effectively, the appraisal system must help them to gather diagnostic information about workers' performance strengths and weaknesses.

■ Time demands: A critical concern for appraisers is the amount of time required to carry out performance appraisal activities. Appraisal almost always takes place in an environment that includes significant competing demands on an appraiser's time and attention. To put it bluntly, many managers experience significant work overload; they simply don't have time to get everything done. Furthermore, the consequences of devoting less time to the appraisal process are often less salient than the consequences of devoting less time to other work responsibilities. Thus, many appraisers have real constraints on their time that create situations where they are not *able* to devote large blocks of time to appraisal tasks, and they are not *willing* to reallocate precious time to these tasks because there are few incentives (and many disincentives) to do so. Furthermore, managers often have so many formal direct reports that it is not feasible for them to engage in elaborate, systematic observation of all workers' performance. They may choose to focus observational efforts on workers who appear to have performance difficulties; alternatively, they may choose to focus most of their observational resources on the identification of talent. The practical problem for those who design, implement, and evaluate appraisal systems is to recognize how to save time without sacrificing the quality of performance measurement.

■ Usability: A related issue is the complexity of the system. Evaluating system usability and complexity would focus on answering the following questions. Is the system easy to understand and use? Will the performance appraisals provide useful information for structuring feedback sessions? Will appropriate training be provided to appraisers so they understand how to use the system properly? Do the requirements of the appraisal system conflict with daily tasks? For example, keeping a behavioral diary may be a useful way of providing an up-to-date record of important performance information about each worker for whom a manager must provide performance ratings. However, in organizations with flat structures, managers may have responsibility for so many workers that this becomes an impractical task.

■ Managing worker motivation: Performance appraisals can be used to document the need for a "kick in the pants" or encouragement for efforts in the right direction. This is a sensitive issue because appraisers and organizations can be held legally accountable for recorded appraisals. For this reason, truly useful performance management information is often downplayed in formal appraisals. This can be frustrating for managers and workers alike because information critical to performance improvement and maintenance goes unstated. The value of maintaining regular informal feedback channels to ensure that workers get "the whole picture" cannot be overstated. Thus, an important question to ask about an organizational appraisal system is whether it also supports and rewards informal, candid discussions of performance between managers and those they supervise.

■ Maintaining harmonious interpersonal relationships: Appraisers, whether they are managers, fellow team members, or subordinates, generally need to be concerned with maintaining constructive daily working relationships. Appraisal systems that threaten to disrupt such relationships by focusing on differences between workers or focusing on performance problems are not likely to be well accepted by appraisers.

■ Obtaining and maintaining resources: Performance appraisal measurements are sometimes used to demonstrate the need for additional resources; similarly they provide a means of maintaining current resources. Conservative performance ratings may mask the potential of a "star"; overly generous performance ratings may represent a strategy for retaining staff if it is unlikely that money will be budgeted for a replacement should the worker be terminated.

■ Impression management: Information from the performance appraisal program can be used for positive upward reporting of the contributions of the appraiser's group. Positive appraisals reflect well on managers as well as those whose work is assessed in the appraisal; likewise, negative appraisals may reflect poorly on the manager who conducts the appraisals.

■ Documentation of issues/problems: For managers, formal performance appraisal systems sometimes serve as an important vehicle for documenting the history of performance problems. Although managers are understandably reluctant to record negative information about workers, a formal record of performance problems and attempts to resolve those problems provides important protections for managers if they find themselves in the difficult position of recommending discipline or termination.

Workers' Perspectives and Goals

As "targets" of performance appraisal and recipients of performance feedback, workers bring yet another perspective to the table. Evaluations of appraisal systems that fail to consider the recipient's perspective are missing some key information about the success of the system. Positive recipient reactions to an appraisal program are particularly important if one of the goals of the appraisal system is to provide workers with feedback about their performance and work with them to improve their performance.

■ Do workers want to have their work appraised? Although workers often express apprehension about formal performance appraisals, they value feedback about their performance, and want reward systems to reflect their individual contributions, so evaluations of appraisal systems should include an assessment of the extent to which workers perceive that these goals are met. Workers must also bear some responsibility for seeking feedback about their performance. The appraisal system should communicate the worker's role in seeking informal feedback and providing input to supervisors on a regular basis, and build in key checkpoints for both supervisor and worker to ensure that this is happening. This becomes particularly important in matrix organizations, organizations that rely heavily on cross-functional teams, and organizations in which geographically dispersed work teams complicate the appraisal process for supervisors and workers.

■ Fairness and accuracy of performance appraisal: In addition to a concern with the outcomes of performance appraisal, the manner in which performance appraisals are conducted is of great concern to workers and therefore to the evaluation team. Each of the following issues contribute to workers' feelings that they have been treated fairly with respect to the appraisal system: (a) the sources of the appraisal should be sufficiently knowledgeable about the worker's performance to give an accurate assessment of performance—this contributes to worker trust in the accuracy of the appraisal; (b) the behaviors being assessed should be important and relevant to work effectiveness—this increases the acceptability of feedback provided to recipients; and (c) the appraisal procedures should be carried out in a fashion that is "just"—that is, the procedures are explained, the rationale and purposes of the appraisal are known, the appraisal system is used consistently for all relevant members of the organization, workers have the opportunity to provide input to the appraisal and discuss the appraisal, and they are treated with respect during discussions of their performance.

■ Opportunities for personal control and impression management: The opportunity to have some control over the impression that they leave is important to workers. This may be particularly relevant when electronic performance monitoring systems (including monitoring of telephone calls and e-mail correspondence, keystroke records, etc.) contribute to the performance appraisal system (Stanton & Barnes-Farrell, 1996).

■ Consequences of performance appraisal: From a worker's perspective, the question is "what, if anything" will be the consequence of this appraisal? If the appraisal is ostensibly developmental, can I expect support to attend training? If it is administrative, are rewards clearly tied to the appraisals? If I complete a self-appraisal, are disagreements between my self-assessment and my supervisor's assessment of my performance discussed?

The extent to which appraiser concerns and worker needs are addressed by the appraisal system can be assessed in several ways. Regularly surveying both users and recipients of the system with respect to the issues and questions raised above will provide important information about managers' and workers' reactions to the system and can be diagnostic in nature. Furthermore, surveys of this nature increase awareness of the appraisal system and communicate the importance of performance appraisal in the organizational value system. Another approach is to appoint a team of appraisers and appraisal recipients to conduct a diagnostic audit of the system from the perspective of each of these sets of stakeholders.

Functions of Performance Appraisal

In the remaining two sections we make a distinction between two primary functions of performance appraisal programs: measurement of work performance and communication of information about work performance. Evaluation of the measurement function of performance appraisal emphasizes design of the system with respect to instruments, user skills, and quality of measurement. The communication function emphasizes context, interpersonal dynamics, and motivation.

Evaluating Performance
Appraisal Measurement Functions

Three classes of issues must be addressed in the design and evaluation of performance measurement systems. Each of these will be framed in terms of the kinds of questions that should be asked by program evaluators. In addition, Figure 8.1 provides a tool that summarizes many of these questions in a compact checklist format. The format is designed for use in discussions with the stakeholders and decision makers concerned with the performance appraisal system.

What Should Be Measured?

Many kinds of criteria find their way into performance appraisal systems. For example, the system may be framed in terms of fairly broad competencies that are part of an organizational competency model, performance areas that are specific to a particular job or job class, individual goals that have been assigned or cooperatively developed, progress with respect to a previous developmental plan, and so forth. Each of these kinds of criteria speaks to somewhat different goals of an appraisal system, so an evaluation of the appraisal system needs to include questions about the appropriateness of each of these criteria to the intended purposes of the system. It also must consider ways of minimizing conflicts between criteria that have somewhat different goals.

The major point here is that it is important that criteria for evaluation of the appraisal system be aligned with the goals of the appraisal. Thus, the first two questions that evaluators must ask are these: (a) What are the primary goals of the appraisal? (b) Is the content of the appraisal consistent with those goals? For example, a clear identification of the primary goals of the appraisal program can be used to determine whether the appraisal system should measure behaviors (e.g., if the purpose of the appraisal is coaching and development) or outcomes (e.g., if the purpose is to allocate rewards). For organizations in which much work is accomplished by teams, it is at this point that consideration should be given to whether the appraisal system should measure team performance or the contributions of individual team members.

A second aspect of the appraisal system that should be examined closely is the extent to which appraisal measures are related to the job for which performance is being measured. This can be evaluated by comparing job analysis information and job descriptions for the jobs covered by the appraisal program with the performance areas covered in the appraisal instrument or by examining documentation that describes how information about job competencies and job responsibilities are accounted for in the appraisal program.

Who Should Measure?

The question of who should measure is important, but often it is taken for granted. Although supervisors continue to have ultimate responsibility for carrying out performance appraisal in most organizations, the system can be designed to

Measurement Function Issues	Y	N	?
Has the performances appraisal system been reviewed and enhanced in the last 2–5 years?			
Have the goals of the system been identified and prioritized?			
Is the appraisal instrument design aligned with the highest priority goals of the appraisal system?			
Are the competencies/behaviors included in the appraisal instruments consistent with competencies, behaviors, and tasks identified from job analyses or an organizational competency model?			
Do multiple sources (e.g., customers, peers, and subordinates) supply input to the performance appraisal?			
Are all appraisers familiar with the recipient's job and performance standards for that job?			
Do all appraisers have adequate opportunity to observe the recipient's performance?			
Are all appraisers trained in the use of the system?			
Are appraisers held accountable for the quality of their ratings?			
Does a second level manager review all the performance appraisals and evaluate their quality?			
Are performance ratings regularly evaluated for evidence of reliability, validity, and rater biases?			
Are performance ratings evaluated for evidence of adverse impact?			
Is the usability and acceptance of the performance appraisal system formally assessed (e.g., with surveys, focus groups, or interviews) every 2–3 years for the following stakeholders? • Appraisers • Recipients • Management			
Communication Function Issues			
Are there at least two feedback sessions each calendar year at 6-month intervals?			
Are new recipients trained in the performance appraisal system and retrained every 1–2 years?			
Is there a prescribed preparation process for the source before the feedback session is held?			
Is there a prescribed preparation process for the recipient before the feedback session is held?			

Figure 8.1   Key Questions to Ask About an Appraisal System

(*Continued*)

Figure 8.1 Continued

Is a diary system used by the source to record specific examples of behaviors to include in the feedback session?			
Are the organization's strategy, goals, and objectives reflected in the performance appraisal Expected Results?			
Do senior managers demonstrate their buy-in by speaking of the performance appraisal system in their remarks about the organization's goals?			
Do recipients have an opportunity to participate in setting expected results for the year?			
Do recipients reference a document summarizing their expected results throughout the appraisal period?			
Do recipients understand how their expected results translate to specific goals and behaviors and how success will be measured?			
Do recipients have an opportunity to participate in the performance appraisal by completing a self-appraisal?			
Do recipients receive guidance on how to perform a self-appraisal?			
Does the output of the performance appraisal feed directly into the other HR systems (e.g., Training and Development, Career Advancement, and Compensation)?			
Do managers meet the scheduled dates for completion of milestones in the appraisal system? Are there incentives and consequences in place for appraiser performance?			
Is a "vocabulary" of performance appraisal terms used widely throughout the organization?			
Do recipients report receiving informal feedback during the year that is based on specific examples of their work?			
Do the formal assessments (including 360 degree feedback) contain a balance of positive feedback and development opportunities?			
Is a plan specifically targeted to the development opportunities created as part of the performance appraisal system and is support provided in carrying out the plan?			
Is there a process that links performance appraisal from year to year that enables the assessment of whether development opportunities have been successfully addressed by the recipients?			

formally incorporate information and appraisals from other sources as well. Potentially valuable sources of information about a worker's performance include supervisors, coworkers, fellow team members on cross-functional teams, internal and external customers, subordinates, and of course the worker whose performance is being assessed. Organizations that incorporate 360-degree feedback as a regular developmental tool may also want to consider whether information from 360-degree feedback should be used solely for developmental purposes or whether it should also be used as input to formal appraisals of performance. This decision must include consideration of the trade-off between acquiring multiple perspectives on worker effectiveness and the willingness of 360-degree feedback sources to be completely candid in their assessments when that feedback is used as part of a formal appraisal system. Critical questions to ask when determining who should contribute information to a performance appraisal include the following:

■ Are sources of performance information in a position to observe relevant behavior? Is there sufficient opportunity to observe performance? If not, what procedures are in place to gather relevant information to "fill in the gaps?" In geographically dispersed organizations and work teams, and for organizations that have increased the role of telework as a way of structuring jobs, this is a particularly important question to ask.

■ Does the appraisal system gather information from all sources that have relevant information to contribute?

■ Are sources of performance information qualified to make informed judgments? Are they familiar with standards and requirements for effective performance on the job? Are they trained to use the measurement system properly? This is not just a matter of ensuring that those who provide performance information "know" something about the worker's performance effectiveness; it is also a matter of calibrating the measurement system so appraisal forms are being used similarly and appropriately by everyone who contributes to the appraisal. Having appraisal training programs in place for everyone who participates in the measurement process is an important indicator that this issue is being addressed.

■ Are sources of performance information motivated to make and communicate accurate judgments? This is a particular concern for sources who may be worried about the impact of giving negative feedback. To ensure that the appraisal system is designed to encourage candid, accurate assessments from all sources, clear explanations of how the information will be used and vehicles for ensuring the confidentiality of information provided by vulnerable parties (e.g., subordinates and coworkers) should be in place. Organizations with personnel in multiple countries must also be alert to cultural differences in willingness to make distinctions among workers or to provide negative assessments. Ratings provided by appraisers in different national settings should be routinely inspected and compared to determine whether appraisers in these settings are using the measurement system differently from appraisers in other countries.

How to Measure?

The question of how to measure work effectiveness has generated hundreds of empirical studies and dozens of specific measurement tools. Important distinctions among measurement tools are probably best classified in terms of (a) appearance and nature of appraisal forms and (b) tasks required of the appraiser.

Appraisal forms can be distinguished in myriad ways—here are just a few: Emphasis on process (behaviors) versus outcomes, complexity (overall assessments of a small number of fairly broad competency areas versus specific assessments of effectiveness with respect to multiple job functions, tasks, and job-specific performance goals); emphasis on distinguishing top performers from others versus emphasis on weeding out weak performers; the number of categories on rating scales (typically ranging from 3-point scales to more fine-grained 9- or 11-point rating scales); and emphasis on quantitative (ratings) versus qualitative (narrative descriptions) performance information.

Perhaps more important, appraisal forms can be distinguished on the basis of what they require the rater to do (Barnes-Farrell, 2001). For example, behavioral observation scales require appraisers to report the frequency of important behaviors; behaviorally anchored rating scales require appraisers to use exemplar behaviors ("behavioral anchors") as benchmarks to guide them in appraising performance. Performance rankings ask appraisers to think about other work group members as the point of comparison in assessing a particular worker's performance. The time demands, cognitive demands, and task demands on appraisers can differ considerably among various performance measurement procedures. However, it is probably no surprise to learn that best practices in performance measurement do not resolve to identifying a single preferred type of appraisal instrument or format. Instead, a program evaluation team should seek answers to two basic questions about measurement tools that form the basis for the appraisal system. First, does the instrument assist appraisers in communicating what they know about worker performance? Second, is the design of the instrument consistent with the goals of measurement? The answers to both of these questions affect the extent to which other standards for high-quality measurement are likely to be met. With these in mind, several criteria for a high-quality measurement instrument system can be used as standards for evaluating the measurement function of an appraisal system.

Accuracy. Accurate distinctions among worker performance strengths and weaknesses and accurate distinctions between workers in terms of their performance effectiveness are goals of many performance measurement systems and might be used as a standard for judging the quality of measurement provided by the appraisal system. However, there are great challenges in assessing accuracy because it implies that there is a gold standard (a "true" measure of performance effectiveness) to which performance ratings can be compared. In practice, this is rarely the case. Instead, we must usually rely on indirect indicators of accuracy, such as evidence that the necessary conditions for accurate appraisal are available. These include an instrument that allows appraisers to communicate what they know about worker performance, appraisers who are knowledgeable about performance standards for the work that is being assessed, appraisers who have adequate opportunity to observe relevant performance, appraisers who are trained in performance measurement, and organizational conditions that encourage and reward careful and accurate appraisal of worker performance.

Reliability and validity of measurement. In general, evaluation of the quality of performance measurements should include an assessment of the reliability and validity of the appraisals produced by the measurement system. Reliability concerns focus primarily on the consistency of those measurements. Several kinds of evidence can be examined, including evidence of internal consistency among ratings that are intended to measure similar aspects of performance, and agreement between appraisers who assess the same workers. Sources of validity evidence include empirical examination of the relationship between performance appraisals and other measures of performance, such as productivity indices, and a thorough examination of overlap between the content of the appraisal instrument and the content of jobs for which it is used.

Rater biases. One well-known concern with performance appraisal systems that rely on managers and others to make judgments about performance effectiveness is the possibility of intentional or unintentional biases in the performance assessments that appraisers provide, such as leniency (overly positive or overly negative ratings), central tendency (avoidance of extreme ratings), and halo bias (failing to differentiate among areas of strength and weakness). This can compromise the quality and use-fulness of the performance measurements, so it is important to examine the performance ratings for evidence of rater biases. Staff members who are trained in testing and measurement can examine appraisals for the entire organization to look for patterns of performance ratings that suggest the presence of rater biases. This information should be inspected on an annual basis, so that problems can be identified and addressed through rater training or redesign of the measurement system. However, a caution is in order with respect to the interpretation of rater biases. Elimination of rating biases does not ipso facto translate into more accurate measurements. For this reason, evaluation of the impact of rater biases on the effective operation of an appraisal system should keep the purposes of the appraisal system in mind. In the case of central tendency and leniency, widespread patterns of rater bias make it difficult to identify performance differences between workers that may be important when promotions or merit raises are at stake. Furthermore, systematic differences among supervisors or among different units in the organization with respect to these biases are problematic if the organization plans to make decisions that require comparisons of workers from different units. Alternatively, in the case of halo bias, high levels of halo make it difficult to detect individual patterns of strengths and weaknesses that can be used for performance development. In multinational organizations, it is also important to recognize that norms and expectations about performance appraisal that operate in different countries can affect the kinds of rater bias that are most problematic. As such, evidence of rater bias should be examined separately for appraisals carried out in different countries. In addition, as mentioned above with respect to accuracy of measurement, it is useful to examine the design of the appraisal system to document the presence of system characteristics designed to minimize bias. Some of these can be determined through examination of training materials; others are probably best addressed by surveying users of the system. Finally, when rater biases persist, it is important to understand why they occur. Sometimes they reflect utilitarian strategies for appraisers to accomplish important goals (such as fostering positive interpersonal relationships or competing for merit money). Conducting focus groups with appraisers may be a useful way of identifying the goals that appraisers try to meet with the appraisal system. If these conflict with top priority organizational goals for the appraisal system, this information can guide interventions that result from the program evaluation.

Legal defensibility. For any performance appraisal system that is used to make important decisions about workers' lives, it is important to examine evidence that the measurement system is likely to survive a court challenge. An evaluation of the legal defensibility of the appraisal system should pay particular attention to the following questions. First, is there any evidence of adverse impact? Specifically, are performance ratings assigned to women, older workers, members of ethnic minority groups, or workers with disabilities systematically lower than performance ratings assigned to other workers? If the answer is yes, care should be taken to examine the appraisal system for evidence that stereotype-driven biases are not the source of these differences. Second, is there a clear link between job requirements and the content of the appraisal system? This can be demonstrated by comparing information from a job analysis to the questions included in the appraisal form. Third, are appraisers well qualified to make accurate judgments about worker performance? Are they familiar with the job in question? Have they been trained to avoid bias in their assessments?

Usability and acceptability to appraisers. Earlier it was mentioned that users of the system should be consulted about the usability of an appraisal system. Examination of usability should include an assessment of ease of use, demands on appraisers' time, and demands on appraisers' judgment capabilities. Appraisers should also be consulted to determine whether the system meets their needs. For example, does it provide the kinds of information that will be useful to them when they coach workers? Another aspect of usability is, of course, the cost of developing and implementing the system, which should be carefully examined, both from the standpoint of development costs and from the standpoint of maintenance costs.

Acceptability to those who are appraised. As pointed out earlier, recipients of performance appraisal will have concerns about the system. They will want to believe that the system produces accurate assessments of their performance effectiveness and that outcomes will be fair. They will also want to be informed about procedures and interpersonal interactions associated with the measurement system, demands on their own time, and the perceived usefulness of the system.

Organizational considerations that support high-quality measurement. Finally, it is important to evaluate whether the performance appraisal system will be allowed to succeed at its task. This is a matter of carefully examining the organizational climate to determine whether it is one that supports high-quality measurement. Of particular interest, is high-quality measurement a valued activity? Is good measurement rewarded? Is performance information used appropriately? Are support mechanisms (e.g., rater training) in place for high quality measurement? For multinational organizations, are there cultural differences in beliefs and norms associated with performance appraisal that are likely to affect the operation of the measurement function in different national locales?

In the following section we move to a consideration of the communications function of performance appraisal. Measurement and communications functions are closely intertwined, and many of the standards and recommendations for the measurement function are echoed in recommendations for evaluation of the communication function. However, communication of performance information also raises a number of unique concerns that should be addressed in the design and evaluation of a performance appraisal system.

Evaluating the Communication Function of Performance Appraisal

The communications function is an essential component of the performance appraisal system. In addition to its primary purpose in guiding individual performance, it has the potential to serve many communications needs of employees and employers alike. Indeed, successful communication in the performance appraisal system can serve as the unifying mechanism among the various HR systems and can provide the linkage of the individual's efforts to the organization's goals and objectives. Through the performance appraisal system, organizationwide goals can be translated into expected behaviors for every employee along with measures to track individual success.

Communication through the performance appraisal system can be considered in two broad categories according to its intended purpose: (a) to provide two-way communication between employees and management of the organization; and (b) to communicate performance expectations and feedback at the individual level. We deal with each of these next. Throughout this section, we describe practices that have been shown through research to promote effective communication and we explain how to evaluate a performance appraisal system for these best practices. The checklist presented in Figure 8.1 also summarizes key questions that can be used to focus evaluations of the communication function.

Corporate Communication Function

The corporate function is the starting point for the effectiveness of the communication function of performance appraisal. It includes the following:

- Senior management communication of strategy, goals, objectives, desired culture, and expectations of employees
- HR systems communication through the link that performance appraisal has with career development, compensation, training, and rewards
- Employee communication to stakeholders in the management chain and HR

The involvement of senior management in the performance appraisal system has a beneficial outcome for the appraisal system, but it appears to work both ways. That is, an effective performance appraisal system can create a more positive view of senior management. This is not surprising. When the system is used effectively to communicate corporate goals, a clearer understanding of senior management objectives is possible; such understanding promotes acceptance. Mayer and Davis (1998) found that implementation of a more acceptable performance appraisal system increased trust of top management. On the other hand, a lack of involvement signals a lack of buy-in from the senior management and is a serious threat to the appraisal system (Longenecker, Sims, & Gioia, 1987).

Evaluation of the corporate communication function of the performance appraisal system begins by asking whether certain prerequisites have been met:

- Do the organization's goals serve as the foundation for work unit goals, which in turn serve as the basis for job requirements and for performance measures for individual workers? Evaluation should assess the linkages among these components by a detailed inspection of a sample of appropriate documents.

- Is performance appraisal prominent in the exchange of information up and down the organization? It should be mentioned when senior executives are describing goals and objectives for the upcoming period. For example, "We will ask each of you to cut costs in your everyday work; it will be included as an objective in your performance appraisal form this year." Throughout the entire organization, management should look to the performance appraisal system as the ultimate repository for the details of expected performance. Evaluation might involve review of a comprehensive sample of senior management communication to assess the tieback to the performance appraisal system for key performance objectives.

- Is the "language of the performance appraisal system" used regularly in the formal and informal exchanges among employees, teams, managers, and others? Terms or shorthand references should be designated so that such exchanges are not cumbersome. Such shorthand, once embedded in the vocabulary of the organization, will be used more easily and will serve to enhance the role of the performance appraisal system. When new projects are launched, a common practice should be to think of ways to include key milestones in the expected results for each individual who will work on the project. Evaluators should ask participants at all levels of the organization if the performance appraisal system is referenced in formal and informal exchanges throughout the year.

- Does the performance appraisal system have regular milestones throughout the year that are met by virtually everyone? Are due dates taken seriously by all? Are there consequences for missing these target dates? The time frame should be a common one that is broadly communicated so that this "to-do" is on everyone's mind at the same time and thus part of the informal communication throughout the organization. Being late should not be considered an option by anyone in the organization.

Individual Performance Expectations and Feedback

The second category of communication is the exchange between the main actors in the performance appraisal communications: manager and employee. The manager sets the stage for the successful exchange between the employee and the organization, and is the conduit for communicating corporate strategy, goals, and objectives and for translating them into actions for the recipient. This is the point at which the communication functions often fail.

Role and Preparation of the Appraiser

The evaluation process should include assessment of whether individual performance is tied back to corporate goals in a way that is clear to the individual. If not, the fault may well be an organizational one: inadequate senior management buy-in. Thus, the importance of the performance appraisal system to the organization plays an important role in how successful the appraiser will be. Do senior managers subscribe to the importance of the performance appraisal system or do they merely provide lip service? Ongoing training in use of the appraisal system is essential to its effectiveness and carries a message of its importance in the organization (Murphy & Cleveland, 1995). There must be an appreciation of the work involved in doing performance appraisals properly, including record keeping throughout the year and careful preparation for the feedback session. Incentives should be designed to recognize excellence in this important function and to provide penalties for late or poor performance. Unless these supports for the performance appraisal are in place, given the heavy workloads that are common today, managers may understandably choose to shortchange this responsibility. The following questions should be addressed by evaluators. Are managers adequately trained to provide feedback and refreshed annually on the appraisal system? Are incentives and consequences in place to encourage appraisers to do this job with care?

Timing and Frequency of the Performance Appraisal Communication

The formal performance appraisal system will likely call for three formal communication events between the manager and employee in the course of the calendar year. The first exchange is to set the expected results in the upcoming appraisal period, the second is an informal mid-year review of how the achieved results match those expected, and third is the year-end appraisal when the formal appraisal is presented, discussed, and recorded. Additionally, there should be opportunity for informal communication on a regular basis. If the employee and manager have a regularly scheduled one-on-one meeting, it should always include an opportunity for informal feedback. No one should be surprised by what is said at the formal appraisal session. This technique is simply good sense; if performance is not up to par, every opportunity should be taken to turn the situation around. Of course, outstanding performance should also be recognized; the positive feedback will serve to reinforce the behaviors and to encourage continued good performance.

Evaluation should address both the formal and the informal performance appraisal communication between the manager and the individual. Have all pre-scribed formal milestones been met for all employees? Does informal communica-tion and coaching about performance take place on a regular basis in the normal interactions between manager and individual? Some characteristics of the formal communications channels can be evaluated by careful examination of the instruc-tions given to managers and documentation that accompanies formal feedback meetings. Other questions about the frequency and nature of formal and informal feedback can be included as items on organizationwide surveys.

Communicating What Is Expected

The first communication event of the performance appraisal is to communicate what is expected of the individual. There are several objectives to be accomplished in this session. Answers to the following questions provide information about how effectively this event is carried out.

1. Does the recipient understand expected results in terms of specific goals and behaviors, including how success will be measured? Are recipients provided with a document summarizing their expected results? Does the employee reference the expected results document outside of the formal discussion with the manager?

2. Does the recipient understand how success on his or her specific objectives would contribute to the success of the manager, business unit or department, and organization? In particular, cooperative goals promote open discussion of issues and foster motivation and acceptance of the appraisal system (Tjosvold & Halco, 1992).

3. Does the recipient know what support is available should barriers be encoun-tered in meeting the objectives specified in the document? This should include support of the manager and the team, and it may also include education and other resources, such as technology.

4. Does the recipient agree with the objectives and feel that the description of what will be expected throughout the period is fair and accurate? Is the recipient welcome to participate in detailing expectations for his or her performance? Cawley, Keeping, and Levy (1998) found a strong relationship between perfor-mance appraisal participation and employee satisfaction with and acceptance of the performance appraisal system.

Communicating How the Individual Performed

Because performance improvement is future oriented, the performance commu-nication between the appraiser and recipient need not be rewarding in itself. The

Figure 8.2   Communicating Performance Information: Steps in the Performance
Feedback Response Process

SOURCE: Adapted from Ilgen et al., 1979.

more pertinent question is whether it has the desired effect: Is performance improved as a result of the communication? Some may argue that for real change to take place a certain level of discomfort with the message is necessary. Ilgen, Fisher, and Taylor (1979) proposed a model in which to consider the factors that affect the success of the communication between the feedback source (the appraiser) and feedback recipient (the employee). A simplified adaptation of their model is shown in Figure 8.2 and organizes the discussion that follows. In the model, the recipient's processing of performance feedback occurs in discrete steps: perception, acceptance, and response. It is based on the premise that to be effective, feedback must be understood, accepted, and acted on in an appropriate fashion. We consider each of the steps in turn, with suggestions about how an evaluation team can recognize whether the necessary features to ensure the success of each step are in place.

Perception. This step pertains to how accurately the recipient perceives the feedback. An essential evaluation question is this: Does the recipient understand how his or her performance is appraised? Features of the source, the message, and the recipient all contribute to the recipient's clear understanding of the feedback the appraiser wishes to convey.

Workers are more willing to pay close attention to feedback from a source if they feel that the source is in a good position to make judgments about their performance. This includes the expectation that the source understands the work and has had the opportunity to adequately judge the performance of the individual being evaluated (Landy, Barnes, & Murphy, 1978).

An increasingly common practice in performance appraisal is to include multiple raters as sources of feedback. This method can enhance the exchange in two ways: by providing input that the supervisor would not have the opportunity to observe first-hand and by corroboration of the feedback among multiple raters (Murphy & Cleveland, 1995). As noted in the discussion of the measurement function, when multiple raters are included in the appraisal system, the evaluation should assess whether the questions posed to raters reflect aspects of performance that they are able to observe and judge in their appraisals.

Three aspects of the message affect this first stage in the feedback process: timing, sign, and frequency. Generally, the shorter the time between the behavior and the feedback, the better for perception. The use of informal feedback throughout the year is crucial and decreases the time between behavior and feedback as well as increases the frequency of the feedback. Although it may not be possible to reduce the time between the behavior and the formal feedback, noting the details of the performance in a diary system will enable the message to be more specific and useful when the time comes to deliver it. Evaluators should look for a high level of informal performance feedback and ask managers if they use any sort of a diary system, even occasionally.

In almost all cases, an employee's performance will have both positive aspects and development opportunities and both should be highlighted. However, positive feedback is more easily perceived and more accurately recalled (Ilgen et al., 1979). Thus, when offering constructive criticism and discussing development opportunities, extra time should be devoted to explaining and using specific examples so that the recipient understands. In the formal performance documents, evaluators should look for both positive comments and development opportunities described and for specific examples of behaviors related to performance.

Recipients enter the feedback exchange with certain notions of what the performance feedback will be. For this reason, it may be important to discuss the recipient's own view of his or her performance, especially if it is at odds with the source's assessment. Self-appraisal can be an excellent preparation step for the feedback exchange, ensuring that the recipient has thought about the dimensions of performance and has searched the appraisal period for examples of performance that support a certain level of achievement. However, to the extent that the self-appraisal is inconsistent with the manager's appraisal, it may interfere with the individual's understanding and learning from the feedback. Recipients are more likely to agree with feedback and incorporate it into subsequent self-appraisals when the feedback is consistent with their self-appraisal (Korsgaard, 1996). The key may be the accuracy of the recipient's self-appraisal. Training recipients in how to conduct an accurate self-appraisal can increase the likelihood that the self-appraisal is a useful step in the process. Evaluators should assess whether self-appraisal is encouraged, whether training is provided on conducting a self-appraisal, and whether agreement on performance levels is reached through the discussion of the recipient and the source.

Acceptance. The source may be the most important factor in whether the recipient accepts the feedback. Characteristics of the source that lead to acceptance are credibility, expertise, reliability, positive intentions toward the recipient, dynamism, personal attractions, and trust in the source's motives (Ilgen et al., 1979). Evaluators should assess whether recipients have a positive view of the source and consider interventions if this appears to be a problem area. Kacmar, Wayne, and Wright (1996) have suggested that managers can be trained in methods designed to cultivate a positive and trustful relationship with their subordinates. Furthermore, training recipients on assertiveness, when coupled with self-appraisal, is associated with positive attitudes toward the appraisal and trust in the manager. Recent research has also shown that appraisers are fairer when interacting with an assertive recipient (Korsgaard, Roberson, & Rymph, 1998). This suggests that evaluators should look for confidence building and assertiveness training in the recipient's training opportunity. Finally, echoing a point made regarding accurate perception of feedback, the message characteristic that will most enhance acceptance is support for the message through very specific examples of the recipient's behavior.

Response. Even if the recipient understands and accepts the feedback as accurate, the job of feedback is far from finished. The recipient must decide to act on the improvement areas cited in the feedback session. The role of the source at this step in the process is to demonstrate personal support for the changes suggested as well as to show the way to other types of support, such as education, people, and technology resources. Evaluators should assess whether recipients take action, receive support, and eventually succeed in areas cited for improvement in the performance appraisal. Effectiveness of the communication function depends on whether the performance improvements suggested are actually achieved by the recipient. This would seem to call for a continuous process in which each year is not considered as a stand-alone event but rather contains a link to the past year to record an assessment of whether development plans were achieved. These data should be captured across the organization so that success of the performance appraisal communication function can be assessed. Evaluators should determine whether a closed loop process exists that links the performance appraisal from year to year.

Summary and Conclusions

The evaluation of performance appraisal and feedback systems requires a careful consideration of the goals of the appraisal system. Both the design and evaluation of the system must be carried out with these goals in mind. Furthermore, a full evaluation of the system will recognize the importance of building the system around the needs and concerns of all three stakeholders in the system: the organization, the appraiser, and the worker.

References

Barnes-Farrell, J. L. (2001). Performance appraisal: Person perception processes and challenges. In M. London (Ed.), *How people evaluate others in organizations: Person perception and interpersonal judgment in I/O psychology* (pp. 135–153). Mahwah, NJ: Lawrence Erlbaum.

Cawley, B. D., Keeping, L. M., & Levy, P. E. (1998). Participation in the performance appraisal process and employee reactions: A meta-analytic review of field investigations. *Journal of Applied Psychology, 60,* 615–633.

Cleveland, J. N., Murphy, K. R., & Williams, R. E. (1989). Multiple uses of performance appraisal: Prevalence and correlates. *Journal of Applied Psychology, 74,* 130–135.

Ilgen, D. R., Fisher, C. D., & Taylor, M. S. (1979). Consequences of individual feedback on behavior in organizations. *Journal of Applied Psychology, 64,* 349–371.

Kacmar, K. M., Wayne, S. J., & Wright, P. M. (1996). Subordinate reactions to the use of impression management tactics and feedback by the supervisor. *Journal of Managerial Issues, 8*(1), 35–53.

Korsgaard, M. A. (1996). The impact of self-appraisals on reactions to feedback from others: The role of self-enhancement and self-consistency concerns. *Journal of Organizational Behavior, 17,* 301–311.

Korsgaard, M. A., Roberson, L., & Rymph, R. D. (1998). What motivates fairness? The role of subordinate assertive behavior on managers' interactional fairness. *Journal of Applied Psychology, 83,* 731–744.

Landy, F. J., Barnes, J. R., & Murphy, K. R. (1978). Correlates of perceived fairness and accuracy of performance evaluation. *Journal of Applied Psychology, 63,* 751–754.

Longenecker, C. O., Sims, H. P., & Gioia, D. A. (1987). Behind the mask: The politics of employee appraisal. *Academy of Management Executive, 1,* 183–193.

Mayer, R. C., & Davis, J. H. (1998). The effect of the performance appraisal system on trust for management: A field quasi-experiment. *Journal of Applied Psychology, 84,* 123–136.

Murphy, K. R., & Cleveland, J. N. (1995). *Understanding performance appraisal.* Thousand Oaks, CA: Sage.

Stanton. J. M., & Barnes-Farrell, J. L. (1996). Relationships among personal control, satisfaction and performance in the use of computer performance monitoring. *Journal of Applied Psychology, 81,* 738–745.

Tjosvold, D., & Halco, J. A. (1992). Performance appraisal of managers: Goal interdependence, ratings and outcomes. *Journal of Social Psychology, 132,* 629–639.

Suggested Readings in Performance Appraisal and Feedback

Ilgen, D. R., & Barnes-Farrell, J. L. (1984). *Performance planning and evaluation.* Chicago: Science Research Associates, Inc.

London, M. (1997). Job feedback: Giving, seeking, and using feedback for performance improvement. Mahwah, NJ: Lawrence Erlbaum.

Murphy, K. R., & Cleveland, J. N. (1995). *Understanding performance appraisal.* Thousand Oaks, CA: Sage.

Pulakos, E. (1997). Ratings of job performance. In E. Whetzel & G. Wheaton (Eds.), *Applied measurement methods in industrial psychology* (pp. 291–317). Palo Alto, CA: Davies-Black. Smither, J. W. (Ed.). (1998). *Performance appraisal: State of the art in practice.* San Francisco: Jossey-Bass.

CHAPTER 9

The Evaluation of 360-Degree Feedback Programs

John C. Scott

Manuel London

An increasingly popular management development tool is 360-degree feedback, also called multisource feedback. However, similar to other human resource (HR) development methods, its effectiveness is rarely evaluated systematically. Organizations jump on the bandwagon assuming that survey feedback results are valuable. Companies suffer through the experience of initially implementing the survey process, often confronting resistance from managers about being evaluated by their subordinates and peers. Long-term reactions and effects are rarely determined systematically, so if the organization continues to use 360-degree feedback, the only evidence for its effectiveness may be anecdotes from vocal participants.

In describing how to evaluate a 360-degree feedback process we focus on three areas: (a) identifying the evaluation criteria, (b) choosing the evaluation methodology, and (c) evaluating the quality and long-term effects. We then provide an example that demonstrates the impact of a 360-degree feedback evaluation on performance improvement and career development and conclude with a program evaluation checklist.

Before reviewing our recommended model for evaluating 360-degree feedback programs, we begin this chapter with an overview of 360-degree feedback. This description covers the administration and use of feedback results, the frequency and methods used in a 360-degree feedback program, and the underlying assumptions of 360-degree feedback.

An Overview of 360-Degree Feedback

The principal purpose of 360-degree feedback is to provide managers with feedback about their performance so that they can set goals for improvement on their current job and for longer-term career development. The feedback provides input for discussion with one's supervisor, coach, mentor, or trainer about strengths and weaknesses.

360-degree feedback is a report of performance ratings from multiple sources (e.g., subordinates, peers, supervisors, customers, and self-ratings). Enough raters from each source should be available (usually at least three) to ensure anonymity. Since the raters represent different elements of a manager's job, different groups may be asked to rate different performance dimensions as well as a common set of performance dimensions. For instance, supervisors may evaluate their subordinate managers' contributions to organization strategy but not necessarily their support of subordinates' development. Subordinates may provide input on this latter topic. Peers may be most appropriate to rate collegial and collaborative work relationships. All raters may evaluate communications, organization, and decision-making skills.

The rating and feedback cycle should not be a one-time, stand-alone event, but part of an ongoing performance management process that includes help with understanding the feedback, using the feedback to set goals for performance improvement and development, and tracking change over time. This process involves employees in performance management as they contribute to establishing the dimensions on which managers are rated, providing the ratings, and helping managers understand and apply the results.

Administering the Program and Using the Resulting Information

Usually, 360-degree feedback is administered by a central office, often the human resources (HR) department. It may be designed for a specific department or the entire organization. Managers receive individualized feedback reports of their ratings, but department heads may receive reports that contain averages that track the overall level of performance in the department and to suggest general training needs. Managers of 360-degree feedback participants will not typically see their direct subordinate's individualized feedback unless the 360-degree feedback system is integrated into the organization's performance appraisal process.

360-degree feedback may also be part of a leadership training program. Participants in such a program are asked to identify peers, subordinates, and supervisors who can evaluate them. Several weeks before the program begins, training administrators send surveys to the identified personnel. Returned surveys are analyzed, and reports are delivered to the participants at the start of the training. The results suggest directions for development. Training activities provide further feedback for learning and goal setting. Trainers are available to help managers interpret and apply the feedback results.

Some organizations use the information from the reports to help make decisions about managers—for instance, about their compensation, job assignments, and readiness for promotion. However, this can be threatening to the feedback recipients. If the data are being used for administrative decisions, raters may be more lenient and less constructive in their feedback, not wanting to unduly influence how their manager is treated. For this reason, an organization may initially use findings from 360-degree feedback surveys for development only. When raters and recipients feel comfortable with the process and recognize its value, an organization may begin using the survey results to make administrative decisions (London, 2001).

Frequency and Method of Delivery

The 360-degree feedback surveys may be administered annually, or possibly semiannually or quarterly. The annual survey may be done for formal administrative purposes. In contrast, a shorter interim survey may contain a subset of items from the annual survey—perhaps targeted to specific issues—or items chosen by the department head. The interim survey may ask about improvement on specific goals that were set as a result of earlier feedback.

Web-based survey development and administration make it easy for respondents to complete and return the survey; this method also eases coding and automatic delivery of results to the managers rated. When managers want feedback, they can select items and provide e-mail addresses for employees to be surveyed. The employees receive an e-mail requesting their participation, with a link to the Web address included with the survey. Their responses are returned via the Web, averaged, and sent in a report to the recipient. Frequent surveys and online development and administration help incorporate the feedback process into the culture of the organization (London & Smither, in press).

Underlying Assumptions About the Benefits of 360-Degree Feedback

London (1997) cited the many benefits of feedback in general, and these also apply to the application of 360-degree feedback. Feedback encourages awareness of one's own behavior on performance dimensions that are important to the organization. It also increases awareness of how a person is viewed by others in different roles. It helps identify development gaps and provides direction for setting development and career goals. Frequent feedback keeps behavior goal-directed. Positive feedback is reinforcing in that it makes recipients feel good about themselves

(DeNisi & Kluger, 2000). Feedback increases employees' ability to detect errors on their own. It enhances learning and encourages seeking knowledge. It shows what is needed to be successful in the organization. It increases the recipient's motivation by demonstrating that effort will lead to performance improvement and positive outcomes, such as merit pay or promotion. In general, feedback increases the salience of information and the importance of feedback in the organization. It communicates to raters and ratees the dimensions of performance that are important to the organization. It can increase the power and control employees feel over their own and the organization's success.

A number of characteristics have been identified as important to giving useful feedback (London, 1997). Feedback needs to be clear, specific, behavioral, and frequent, so the items in a feedback survey need to focus on behaviors. The feedback report should be easy to read and interpret, and it should include clear information about how to decipher company norms and rater disagreement measures (e.g., the range of responses on an item). It should be accompanied by adequate support from the supervisor, coach, or others, to aid in interpreting and applying the results. It should also be accompanied by supportive resources, such as the availability of training programs.

Despite this research demonstrating the benefits of 360-degree feedback, a recent study by Watson Wyatt researchers (Pfau & Kay, 2002) has taken 360-degree feedback programs to task. These researchers contend that multisource feedback systems can actually be harmful to an organization, to the point of adversely impacting shareholder value, unless certain conditions are present. They argue that for these systems to be effective, an organization's culture needs to be supportive of honest, open communication; the competencies being measured need to be specific and aligned with the organization's business goals; and managers need to be trained on how to provide and receive feedback.

These and other criteria for determining whether an organization (a) is "ready" to implement a 360-degree feedback program or (b) has an effective program in place are outlined in the next section. These criteria are designed to help an organization evaluate how well the 360-degree feedback process aligns with their business objectives and impacts their bottom line.

Criteria for Evaluating 360-Degree Feedback Systems

In our model for evaluating a multisource feedback system, we have provided practical and technical guidelines, recognizing that evaluators need to choose how to proceed based upon the purpose of the evaluation and resources available. As with any good research model, the program evaluator needs to establish a well-conceived plan with sound methods. Good planning and methods will yield interpretable evaluation results that have minimal confounds (i.e., the results can be attributed to the feedback and not to situational conditions).

The criteria for evaluating a 360-degree feedback survey should be drawn from four basic areas: (a) survey design, (b) administration and process components,

(c) survey results, and (d) how the feedback process is supported and integrated in a comprehensive development and performance management program.

Survey Design

An evaluation of the 360-degree feedback survey should determine whether the survey items reflect organizational strategies and enhance commitment to the survey feedback process. The items should reflect key managerial competencies, behaviors, and performance outcomes that are important to the organization. The behaviors described in the items should be observable by the raters. The items should be stated clearly. (For example, the item, "Shows leadership skills," would not be of much value because leadership means different things to different people. The item, "Helps subordinates plan career goals," is more specific. The item, "Clarifies department goals at staff meetings," is more behavioral and observable.)

Employees, or at least a group of representative employees, should participate in writing the survey items. Participating in the survey development inspires ownership of and commitment to the rating process and also encourages managers to heed the results. In an international corporation in which the same survey is administered in different languages, the items should be translated and tested for clarity and common understanding. As an indicator of reliability, research should show that raters within sources (e.g., all subordinates) should largely (but not necessarily entirely) agree on their ratings, at least for those behaviors for which the manager is likely to behave similarly for all raters in the group. As an indicator of validity, when objective performance measures exist, research should show that they correlate with the 360-degree judgments.

Process Components

The 360-degree feedback administration process can be evaluated by observing the process and gathering attitudinal data from raters and feedback recipients after the feedback is provided. The evaluation will be slightly different depending on whether the 360-degree feedback survey was introduced as a developmental tool initially to establish trust in the process or introduced as part of the organization's performance appraisal process where ratings are shared with others.

Employees may be reluctant to be honest if they know that their ratings are to be used to make decisions about their manager. In a developmental survey, the ratings should be anonymous. However, raters should feel accountable for providing accurate ratings. Since ratings are anonymous, raters can be held accountable as a group by examining results across departments and measuring the perceived value of the results to the managers receiving the feedback. If ratings do not make sense (e.g., they are uniformly favorable), then the rating process will be called into question (London, Smither, & Adsit, 1997).

Managers may resist being evaluated by their subordinates. They may want to be assured that their survey results will remain confidential. This is important if the results are to be used solely for development. Managers may not be required to share the results, except perhaps with an external coach or trainer.

Another administrative element concerns the format of the feedback report. The managers receiving feedback should perceive that the feedback reports are clear, not confusing. They should feel that there was enough information but not too much. Some feedback reports present means, ranges, and norms for each rater group for every item whereas others present only average ratings for groups of items reflecting the key performance dimensions. Another point is that the feedback should be presented soon after the data are collected. This should be a matter of days or weeks, not months.

The 360-degree feedback process should fit within an integrated performance management and development program that might include coaching, leadership training, supervisory performance review, and follow-up performance measures. Another element of excellent practice is that the formal organizational 360-degree feedback survey is repeated on a regular basis and integrated into the fabric of the organization's HR development system.

Attention should be paid to the cost and efficiency of developing and administering the survey as well as to preparing and delivering the results. Costs can be evaluated in comparison to alternative development tools. For example, the cost of hiring external coaches to help managers process the feedback, establish development plans, and track progress can be compared to the cost of sending managers to a week-long leadership development program. In addition, managers can be asked for their perceptions for the incremental value and cost benefits of the survey results.

Survey Results

In determining the meaning of the 360-degree data and its long-term effects, several factors should be considered: the reliability of the data (interrater agreement), self–other agreement, validity (the relationship between results and external indicators of performance), longitudinal data examining changes in 360-degree ratings over time, and the need for both correlational and experimental design to isolate the effects of 360-degree feedback and other components of development.

Interrater Agreement and Self–Other Discrepancy Scores

Research has shown that ratings by others tend to agree—for instance, subordinate and supervisor ratings are moderately correlated, with correlations often in the .30 to .40 range with a few reaching as high as .60 (Harris & Schaubroeck, 1988). However, self-ratings tend to be inflated. Feedback reports generally provide self-ratings and the average of others' ratings by source and company norms for each item. This allows managers to comprehend the extent to which others agree or disagree with how they view themselves, item by item. Managers may tend to focus on areas of agreement, especially those results that fit their self-views, and ignore areas of disagreement. Consequently, coaches or supervisors who help managers interpret the results should consider the extent to which differences may be attributed to their behavior and the way others react to them. From a practical standpoint, then, the feedback report is a useful catalyst for considering strengths and weaknesses and areas for development. Overraters tend to decrease their self-evaluation at the second administration of the survey after receiving feedback (Johnson & Ferstl, 1999). However, managers who were initially underraters tend to think all is well and then overrate themselves at the second administration.

One way to assess 360-degree feedback results is to examine the unique value of the self-ratings, other ratings, and their interaction in predicting an external, more objective measure of performance (e.g., sales generated or units produced). Regression analysis can be used for this purpose. Across managers, if variance in self-ratings is low because of inflated self-perceptions, then self-ratings will not contribute significantly in the regression equation predicting the objective performance measure. The contribution of the ratings by others across a variety of performance dimensions will show the extent to which other ratings are capturing, in part at least, the objective performance outcome measure.

Relationships Between 360-Degree Feedback and Other Performance Measures

Other, more distal and bottom line measures of performance can be tracked to determine whether the feedback had an effect. These may be objective measures of performance for the individual managers or for the department or organization as a whole. Performance indicators should improve over time, although this may take several years to accomplish. The difficulty with such performance measures is that they are likely to be influenced by many factors other than the feedback. This is why a proper experimental design is important. Having a control group that did not receive feedback but otherwise experienced similar, if not identical, conditions would be necessary.

Isolating the Unique Contribution of 360-Degree Feedback as Part of a Comprehensive Development Program

One of the challenges of program evaluation is to determine the unique effects of the components of a program. This is all the more challenging because the program elements are supposed to be highly integrated. For instance, 360-degree feedback may be part of a leadership development program that includes other assessment methods (e.g., performance in business games) and possibly coaching during and after the program (Brutus, London, & Martineau, 1999). Case discussions, role modeling exercises, and video demonstrations are likely to be included. All these methods may be focused on the same performance dimensions. At minimum, program evaluation forms completed by participants should ask about the perceived value of each of the components. However, overall feelings about results and key elements of the program may pervade attitudes about the other elements.

Experimental designs can be established with comparison groups that systematically vary the interventions applied. For example, to evaluate the usefulness of 360-degree feedback in a leadership training program, one group of managers attending the training program could be randomly assigned to an experimental group receiving the 360-degree feedback at the start of the program. The remaining managers would not receive the feedback until after the training program was evaluated. They might receive their feedback results at a later time after they returned to the office.

To assess the various elements of the 360-degree feedback survey process itself, experimental and control groups could vary in the amount and type of data reported, when managers received the results, and how they received the results (in a desk drop report, in a facilitated group meeting, through an external coach, or as part of a training session).

Methods for Evaluating the Quality of the 360-Degree Program

This section details some of the practical procedures for collecting the data necessary to answer the research questions presented in the previous section so that they can be applied against the criteria for judging the overall quality of the program. To ensure that all the important research questions are adequately answered, evaluators need to decide what information will be collected. The previous section presented a series of questions that will guide the evaluation of an organization's 360-degree system components against best practices. However, these questions should be supplemented with those that are responsive to the information needs of the organization's key stakeholders. The evaluators and key stakeholders must work together to agree on the pertinent questions and the overall evaluation plan.

The next few sections detail several important sources of data for conducting a comprehensive 360-degree program evaluation. Important data sources include archival records, key stakeholders, system users, the 360-degree vendor (if applicable), and information gleaned from other organizations.

Reviewing Archival Records

To effectively evaluate the design components of the survey, copies of the survey and feedback report should be assembled. In addition, the evaluator should gather any documentation that relates to the competency model being assessed by the survey and its linkage to the organization's mission, vision, and values. Any technical documentation that was produced in support of the instrument should be obtained as well, particularly any information related to the psychometrics of the rating scales. If the items have been translated into a foreign language, the procedures for this translation should also be ascertained. Was the instrument back-translated, and were any psychometric analyses run to assess the fidelity of the test translation?

For evaluating the process-related components of the 360-degree feedback program, the program evaluator should collect any materials that provide perspective on the organizational context in which the program was positioned and that furnish information as to the short- and long-term goals of the program. The evaluator will want to gather any available information that describes the stated purpose of the 360-degree feedback (e.g., presentation materials used to "sell" the 360-degree feedback program to management), copies of rater training materials, general communiqués to employees (especially regarding confidentiality and how the feedback results are to be handled), and the credentials of and/or training provided to coaches. The program evaluator should obtain documentation that outlines the process flow (and all variations) of the program, from participant invitation through provision of feedback. Copies of timelines, budgets, and any cost analyses should also be collected.

In evaluating the impact of the survey results, the program evaluator should attempt to assemble external indicators of performance, at both the individual and the organizational level. This information will assist in demonstrating the relationship between 360-degree ratings and performance/bottom line results. Other tangible data such as bonus information, salary, job level, business unit, or demographic information will help to further cut the data and provide more detailed analyses to evaluate program validity and utility. Databases from previous 360-degree feedback administrations should be identified and used along with the current database so that longitudinal data can be examined for changes in 360-degree ratings over time. It may be necessary to enlist the assistance of the company's information systems department for this effort, depending on the state of the data and how it is being stored. The program evaluator should also collect information on how norms and self-other discrepancy scores are calculated and treated.

Stakeholder Assessments

Interviews, focus groups, and surveys involving key stakeholders and system users can provide a rich source of information about the effectiveness and utility of the 360-degree feedback program within an organization. Interviews with executives can elicit information regarding the overall impact of the program and provide input as to how well it is supported by the organization's leaders and the extent to which it has been, or will be, integrated into the company's culture.

Focus groups with the organization's HR staff can provide valuable input regarding administrative issues, user reactions, and lessons learned. The HR organization will typically assign coordinator(s) to help implement and administer 360-degree feedback assessments across its business units or divisions. These coordinators may be uniquely positioned to provide valuable insights into the effectiveness of the 360-degree feedback program. Because the coordinators serve as an interface between HR and the line organization, they are typically responsible for communicating the 360-degree feedback philosophy and helping managers translate that philosophy into practice. HR coordinators are often heavily involved in the initial execution of the 360-degree feedback program when many issues often arise, including perceived or real administrative burdens (e.g., excessive amount of ratings required in a short amount of time, Web-site speed, and written comment requirements), concerns about confidentiality, need for training, competing resource demands, and resistance to the process.

Surveys of raters and feedback recipients can elicit information that covers all phases of the process, including administration, relevance of the assessment dimensions, usefulness of the feedback, satisfaction with the coaching, and impact on behavioral change.

If the organization's 360-degree feedback program is administered by an outside vendor, the vendor should also be included in the evaluation process. Beyond having an "outsider's" unique perspective, the vendor should be in a position to provide comparative data regarding the use and results of the 360-degree feedback program in this context. Although vendors may be expected to put a positive spin on their product, their input about how the system is used may be valuable. In addition, if the vendor is housing the database of 360-degree feedback ratings, the vendor will need to be called on to either prepare the database for analysis or actually conduct the analyses.

Benchmarking Analyses

A benchmarking study can provide valuable information prior to the implementation of a 360-degree feedback program; it can also offer useful data against which an existing program can be evaluated. Information should be gathered about costs, administrative ease, content, process flow, technical information (e.g., scale psychometrics, availability of normative information, research backing, scoring, nature of rating scales, validity, scoring), customer support, links to key organizational outcome variables, feedback reports, and rater training.

A benchmarking study can be time-consuming and require a fair amount of resources to be adequately conducted, so it may be useful to inquire first among contacts within the target industry (including trade associations) as to whether a recent benchmarking study has already been conducted and if the results could be obtained. A literature review is also a sensible initial step that can assist in focusing questions and targeting organizations for participation. In addition to targeting specific industries for participation, "best practices" organizations should also be identified and included as part of the study.

Evaluators of the Survey Program

The key stakeholders involved with and affected by the 360-degree feedback system should be identified and included in the planning and execution of the evaluation. This will help ensure that the specific information needs of the stakeholders are met and establish consensus as to how the results will be used. The following groups should be considered as key stakeholders in a 360-degree feedback program evaluation.

Organizational Leaders

The success or failure of a 360-degree feedback program is highly dependent on the support of the organization's leaders. The impact and value of the program is tied directly to whether these key stakeholders embrace the program and the philosophy that surrounds it. Therefore, the 360-degree feedback program evaluation design should take into account the organizational leaders' input and ensure that their information needs are directly addressed. Because 360-degree feedback programs are often linked to the organization's vision and values, organizational leaders will be in a position to provide a big-picture perspective of the 360-degree feedback program's purpose and goals, which may provide some indication of the long-term viability of the program. Leaders should be asked about the importance they give to evaluation and the type of information they would like about the program's effectiveness. They will probably be interested in collecting information regarding bottom line results, relationship of the 360-degree assessment to objective performance data, participation rates, cost-benefit analyses, longitudinal data, impact of interventions such as coaching and training, and the extent to which the organization's mission, vision, and values have been linked to this process. Leaders should also be asked to identify other relevant stakeholders.

Internal HR Staff

Human resources staff generally play a central role in the implementation and ongoing administration of 360-degree feedback programs. Given this position as the administrators of an organization's 360-degree feedback program, the charge of program evaluation will probably also fall within their domain. That is, HR will likely serve both as a primary source of program evaluation information and the primary evaluator.

The evaluator should consider and deal with any potential conflicts of interest that might arise lest the results of the evaluation be compromised. Internal staff may have a vested interest in ensuring that the program does not receive any negative press and so they may avoid collecting or including such information in the evaluation. It is therefore important to identify potential sources of conflict prior to conducting the evaluation and agree in advance on how to address the challenges associated with this issue.

Another key consideration when the program evaluation is to be staffed internally is the level of competence necessary to conduct it. Taking into account the focus of the evaluation and stakeholder needs, establishing that the evaluator (or evaluation team) possesses the necessary substantive knowledge of and experience with 360-degree feedback is critical. In addition, the evaluator must have the necessary technical competence and objectivity to conduct field research so that the results are meaningful and accepted by the key stakeholders.

External 360-Degree Feedback Assessment Experts

The use of external experts, such as consulting firms or university faculty, can offer certain advantages for conducting a 360-degree feedback program evaluation. In addition to providing substantive knowledge in the area of focus (if properly selected), they are also in a position, based on their experience and perspective as "outsiders," to identify significant components for evaluation that the client may have overlooked. Competent, external experts can also assist the client in establishing the appropriate priority of evaluation questions based on multiple stakeholder concerns, and they can help clients focus the scope of the evaluation and develop realistic expectations regarding what can be accomplished given available time and resources.

Some cautions should also be noted in using external experts to evaluate a 360-degree feedback program. These cautions, similar to those for the internal evaluators, relate to potential conflict of interest. An expert who has a professional or financial interest in promoting a particular 360-degree feedback program may have trouble being objective in planning and interpreting an evaluation of this system. If the vendor of an organization's 360-degree feedback system is also contracted to evaluate the program, determine whether the vendor's financial interests may potentially impact the objectivity of an evaluation plan and interpretation of its results. Where possible, evaluators should not stand to benefit directly or lose financially based on the results of the evaluation. When this is not possible, the potential areas of conflict should be identified and directly addressed in the evaluation plan. In addition, be sure this expert has experience in evaluating multisource feedback systems.

Evaluating the Quality and Long-Term Effects of 360-Degree Feedback

Attitudes About the Process

Data for evaluating a 360-degree feedback program can focus on the program itself—for instance, descriptions of how it was carried out and perceptions of its value. Special surveys can be conducted several weeks, three months, six months, and/or a year after administering a 360-degree feedback survey to ask respondents and feedback recipients about the process. Raters can indicate whether they felt the items were clear, reflective of important behaviors from their point of view, and observable. Also, raters can be asked whether they were honest and whether they were confident that the ratings were anonymous. In addition, they can be asked whether they believe the targets of their ratings valued and used the results and whether they observed a change in performance. Managers who received the feedback can be asked whether they found the feedback helpful, learned something new about themselves, and changed their behavior as a result of the feedback.

One firm asked such questions in a telephone survey of a sample of raters several months after the first administration of the survey. Similar questions can be asked in regularly administered employee attitude surveys. Such surveys are more general and do not necessarily ask raters to evaluate their supervisor or specific managers.

In addition to asking about the 360-degree feedback survey process, questions can be asked about reactions to support tools and processes, such as guidelines for interpreting results, coaching, and training. For instance, if coaches delivered the feedback results, managers can be asked whether the coach took time to understand the manager's position, work group, and task demands. Did the coach help identify performance strengths as well as weaknesses? Did the coach focus on ways the manager can improve performance now, develop needed skills, and encourage career planning? Did the coach follow up over time to see whether the manager's performance actually improved and whether the manager actually carried out the development plan?

Awareness of Performance Dimensions and Performance Management

As mentioned earlier, the 360-degree feedback survey is a way to reinforce other corporate statements about key managerial competencies, behaviors, and performance outcomes. The 360-degree feedback survey should not be the only method for communicating these dimensions, but it should reinforce other messages from the organization to managers and employees (e.g., statements about performance management in training programs, performance appraisal forms, and performance management guidelines for supervisors). As a way to verify the effectiveness of these communication strategies, employee attitude surveys can ask employees to select the major performance dimensions expected of managers in the company.

Creating a Feedback Culture

An evaluation can determine the organization's progress in establishing a feedback, development-oriented organization culture. This is a corporate culture in which 360-degree feedback is welcomed, managers seek feedback on their own, managers are open to processing feedback mindfully (not ignoring or avoiding feedback), work group members discuss performance more frequently and openly, managers ask subordinates for clarification of feedback results, managers talk to their supervisors to get development and career planning advice, and, more generally, managers use feedback to set goals and change behavior. In such an organization, employees and managers continuously receive, solicit, and use formal and informal feedback to improve their job performance (London & Smither, in press). This does not happen with just one administration of 360-degree feedback. Over three to four years of annual surveys, the organization should develop a stronger feedback culture. Apart from the feedback survey, feedback from a variety of sources should become more common as well as more effective in producing behavior change. Ultimately (and ideally), the 360-degree feedback survey may not be needed since giving and receiving feedback, and using the information for performance improvement and career development, are fully incorporated into daily interpersonal interactions.

A challenge for the feedback-oriented organization will be to integrate newcomers into this feedback-oriented culture. New managers may be given the chance to use a 360-degree feedback process in their departments so that they can become comfortable with feedback.

Tracking Change in 360-Degree Feedback Ratings

Another indicator of the effects of 360-degree feedback is change in the 360-degree ratings over time. Research has shown that as 360-degree feedback is administered annually or semiannually, performance ratings tend to improve (Walker & Smither, 1999). However, change scores need to be taken with caution (Golembiewski, 1989). A change in ratings from one time to the next may indicate a true change in performance. Change scores may also be biased by systematic errors. A difference over time could reflect a change in expectations and standards, perhaps because of the attention to performance or expectations that performance would improve. As a result, performance ratings may not change even if actual performance improves. Another possibility is that the users' interpretation or definition of the performance dimensions may change, perhaps because the raters are more experienced or because the nature of performance has changed (e.g., sales goals and indicators may take on different meaning as the product, customer base, competition, or economic conditions shift).

Recognizing these problems with change scores, Martineau (1998) recommended asking raters to evaluate degree of change as well as current performance on each item. Such retrospective ratings of perceived change may not be truly accurate because they are based on a feeling that there has been improvement, and raters may be biased by current feelings. Nevertheless, retrospective ratings are a way to gauge the extent to which change scores are correlated with raters' perception that a change has occurred. Given such measurement problems, a wise approach is to use multiple measures of performance, including ratings of improvement and, when available, objective indexes of departmental performance, such as sales or the volume and quality of production.

Examining Summary Data and Tracking Change Across the Organization

As noted earlier, 360-degree feedback can be averaged across managers in a department or the organization as a whole. This can be valuable for several reasons: It identifies performance gaps that are common across managers in the organization. Training or simply communication from top executives that these are important elements of performance may be needed. For instance, if the results reveal that many managers are evaluated unfavorably by their subordinates on their support for career planning and development, then this performance dimension can be emphasized in training forums, company bulletins, and closer attention by top management in emulating desired leadership style.

Assessing Sensitivity to Others' Ratings

Another component that may influence the impact of 360-degree feedback is the extent to which managers are initially sensitive to others' views of them. Some people are highly sensitive to others' reactions to them, and they vary their behavior in response to the situation. This is known as self-monitoring or public self-consciousness. Self-monitors are sensitive to how others react to them. They understand what others expect of them, and they try to change their behavior to meet others' needs or expectations (Warech, Smither, Reilly, Millsap, & Reilly, 1998). People who are publicly self-conscious compare their behavior to the standard they believe others set for them, and they care what others think about them (Levy, Albright, Cawley, & Williams, 1995).

Evaluations of 360-degree feedback programs might measure personality concepts such as self-monitoring, public self-consciousness, and self-esteem to determine how these individual difference variables affect (in some cases limit, in other cases enhance) the extent to which the feedback is likely to be welcomed and accepted.

Longitudinal Study

In this section, we describe a 360-degree feedback system that evolved from a developmentally based instrument to an integral part of an organization's performance management system (Dowell, Scott, Bennett, & Tross, 1999). In 1994, a research-based health and personal care company with 55,000 employees and net earnings of $3.6 billion faced a number of challenges including a new CEO; projected flat earnings growth; an increasingly complex, competitive market; major products losing exclusivity; and bottom quartile returns to shareholders. As a result of these challenges, the new CEO established some aggressive growth and productivity goals: double sales and earnings by the year 2000 and increase productivity by 5% to 6% per year.

To meet these goals, a fundamental shift in the management paradigm would be required. Specifically, management needed to be operating under a new set of expectations and significant intervention was needed to alter the organization's course over the next 6 years. The intervention in this case was to establish a set of core competencies that were aligned with the corporate goals and to implement a developmental 360-degree feedback program that would establish baseline proficiency on these core competencies and provide road maps for change. The competencies covered such dimensions as strategic leadership, innovation, commitment to excellence, empowerment, rapid decision making, accountability, customer focus, and valuing diversity.

Between 1994 and 1995 the developmentally based 360-degree feedback program was administered to the company's 32 officers and top 500 executives. In 1996, the system was evaluated on a number of components ranging from administrative ease, effectiveness of the feedback, competence of the coaches, confidentiality, extent to which action plans were being developed and acted on, and relevance of the competencies. Evaluation data were collected through focus groups with key stakeholders and surveys of 360-degree feedback participants. In addition, several statistical analyses were conducted to determine the relationship of these competencies to an external measure of high potential, which was drawn from the organization's succession planning program. This program evaluation was conducted conjointly by the organization's Center for Leadership Development and the 360-degree feedback provider.

One of the most important findings from the evaluation was that executives were not following through with their action plans. Given the company's large investment in the process, decision makers determined that steps needed to be taken to ensure accountability in this area. Specifically, a decision was made that the developmentally based 360-degree feedback tool would be changed to a performance-management orientation. Under this system, 360-degree feedback data would be used as primary input for the annual performance appraisal and the manager would be placed in the role of coach. The 360-degree feedback process was also revised to incorporate key responsibility areas along with the core competencies. Thus, a component of the 360-degree feedback process was tailored to the unique responsibilities of each participant and ensured job-relatedness and relevance of feedback. Each executive was therefore rated on both a core set of competencies that were common across all executives *and* on the set of key responsibilities unique to his or her position. This process was then again rolled out to the company's officers and top 500 executives.

A follow-up evaluation of this new system was conducted in 1999 and revealed that no executives ($n = 515$) complained or resisted the change from a developmental to a performance management-based process (an indication of active resistance) and only 2 out of the 515 executives failed to complete the process (an indication of passive resistance). The gap between self-ratings and manager ratings remained essentially the same between the two systems, as did the difference between self- and peer ratings. However, the gap between self- and direct report ratings significantly narrowed after the move to the performance management 360-degree feedback process. The mean ratings were significantly higher on the performance management system across all rater sources.

In examining the relative validity of both the developmental and performance management-based 360-degree feedback programs, evaluators found that both systems similarly correlated with the measure of executive potential.

The results of this evaluation revealed that the initial confidentiality concerns raised when moving from a developmental to a performance management tool were generally unfounded, based on the measures of active and passive resistance. However, the narrowed gap between executives' self- and direct report ratings in the context of performance management may have been reflective of some confidentiality concerns among the manager's direct reports. Ratings were significantly higher across all rater sources on the performance management 360-degree assessment. Inflation of ratings on a performance management 360-degree assessment was not necessarily unexpected, given the link of this process to various personnel decisions, including compensation.

Several significant organizational goals were met through the implementation, evaluation, and subsequent evolution of the 360-degree feedback program from a developmental process to a performance management process. First, the need to raise standards of performance was realized and acted on. Second, leadership development was established as the number one growth priority. Third, the use of a performance management 360-degree feedback program secured the role of manager as a coach within this organization and built accountability into action planning. By the end of 2000, this organization had doubled sales, earnings, and earnings per share. The organization's Center for Leadership Development considered the 360-degree feedback assessment process to have played an integral role in the accomplishment of these organizational objectives.

Recommendations and Conclusion

The evaluation of a 360-degree feedback program should be an ongoing process, not a single-point-in-time event. Organizations trying to determine their return on investment need information that is systematically derived using a sound research design. We have attempted in this chapter to outline, in relation to best practice, the content of the information that should be evaluated as well as the process for collecting and interpreting this information. The checklist at the end of this chapter is presented as a guide in structuring and conducting a 360-degree feedback evaluation.

Note

1. In contrast to an attitude survey that gathers perceptions of the overall organization, a 360-degree feedback survey evaluates the performance of specific managers. Sometimes employee attitude surveys incorporate elements of 360-degree feedback surveys. Attitude surveys may include sections to rate "your supervisor," "the head of your business unit," and "the CEO." When this occurs, the results on these sections can be used to create separate feedback reports for the targeted managers.

Appendix: 360-Degree Feedback Program Evaluation Checklist

Program Evaluation Research Questions

1. Survey Design
   a) What was the source of the survey items contained within the 360-degree feedback instrument?

   b) Were survey items developed to align with organizational mission, vision, and values?

   c) Do the items reflect key managerial competencies, behaviors, and performance outcomes that are important to the organization?

   d) Do the items reflect behaviors that are observable?

   e) Are the items clearly stated?

   f) Was the competency model developed external to the organization? If so, was it linked to the organization's goals and outcome measures? How?

   g) If the items were translated, were they tested for clarity and common understanding? Were they back-translated? Were they assessed for scale equivalence?

2. Process Components

   a) What was the purpose of the 360-degree feedback survey (developmental or performance management)?

   b) Were the ratings anonymous?

   c) Did raters feel accountable for providing accurate ratings? Are raters actually held accountable for their ratings?

   d) Were the survey results confidential?

   e) Did the managers perceive that the feedback reports are clear?

   f) Was there too much information or too little?

   g) Was the administration of the 360-degree feedback survey convenient? How much time did it take to complete a survey? How much time did raters think it should it take?

h) How soon were results available after the data were collected?

i) Did the managers feel there was adequate assistance for using the results?

j) How were the feedback reports distributed?

k) Who delivered the feedback and how was it delivered (e.g., group, individual)?

l) Did participants have access to external coaches or management consultants hired for this purpose?

m) Were courses available within or outside the organization to support developmental needs identified by the survey?

n) Did managers have the option available for just-in-time, self-designed and administered 360-degree feedback?

o) Was the formal organizational 360-degree feedback survey repeated on a regular basis?

p) How integrated was the 360-degree feedback system with the organization's human resource development system?

q) How much did each of these components cost? Were they cost-effective in comparison to alternative development tools?

3. Survey Results

a) Reliability and Self-Other Agreement

i) What was the reliability of the 360-degree feedback instrument? How was reliability estimated (e.g., internal consistency, inter-rater agreement, test-retest)?

ii) Did subordinate, peer, and supervisor ratings agree on items that all these groups should be able to evaluate (e.g., a manager's communications skills)?

iii) How were the difference scores calculated?

iv) How much variation was there on self-ratings?

b) Validity

i) Has validity been established for this instrument?

ii) What criteria were used to establish this instrument's validity?

iii) Were the ratings associated with objective performance measures?

iv) Were ratings associated with organizational outcome measures?

v) Have performance measures improved over time?

vi) Did participants change their behavior as a result of feedback?

c) Isolating the unique contribution of 360-degree feedback system

   i) Were appropriate experimental controls implemented in this evaluation that allowed for meaningful interpretation of the impact of the 360-degree feedback in this setting?

   ii) What controls were utilized (e.g., experimental and control groups) and what cautions should be made about interpreting the results of these analyses?

   iii) Were analyses conducted (e.g., regression analyses) to isolate contribution of rater source in predicting outcome measures?

d) Support Tools

   i) What types of norms were available for this instrument (e.g., internal, external, internal by division, etc.)?

   ii) How clear were the guidelines for interpreting results?

   iii) Was training provided in interpreting the results?

   iv) How effective was this training?

   v) How effective was the coaching?

     – Did the coach help identify performance strengths as well as weaknesses?

     – Did the coach focus on ways the manager can improve performance now, develop needed skills, and encourage career planning?

     – Did the coach follow up over time to see whether the manager's performance actually improved and whether the manager actually carried out the development plan?

Evaluating the Quality and Long-term Effects of 360-Degree Feedback

1. Awareness of Performance Dimensions

a) Were employees aware of major performance dimensions expected of managers in the company?

2. Feedback Culture

a) Was 360-degree feedback welcomed?

b) Did managers seek feedback on their own?

c) Did work group members discuss performance more frequently and openly?

d) Did managers ask subordinates for clarification of feedback results?

e) Did managers talk to their supervisors to get development and career planning advice?

f) Did managers use feedback to set goals and change behavior?

g) Did employees and managers continuously receive, solicit, and use formal and informal feedback to improve their job performance?

h) Was 360-degree feedback supported throughout the organization?

3. Tracking Change Over Time

a) Have performance ratings improved over time?

b) How did raters evaluate change over time?

c) Did performance gaps exist between managers in a department or organization as a whole?

d) Were summary data tracked over time and actually used to refine the evaluation process?

References

Brutus, S., London, M., & Martineau, J. (1999). The impact of 360-degree feedback on planning for career development. *Journal of Management Development, 18*(8), 676–693.

DeNisi, A. S., & Kluger, A. N. (2000). Feedback effectiveness: Can 360-degree appraisals be improved? *Academy of Management Executive, 14*(1), 129–139.

Dowell, B., Scott, J. C., Bennett, A. K., & Tross, S. (1999). *The natural evolution of 360 assessment.* Paper presented at the 14th annual conference of the Society for Industrial and Organizational Psychology, Atlanta, GA.

Golembiewski, R T. (1989). The alpha, beta, gamma change typology: Perspectives on acceptance as well as resistance. *Group and Organization Studies, 14,* 150–154.

Harris, M., & Schaubroeck, J. (1988). A meta-analysis of self-supervisor, self-peer, and peer-supervisor ratings. *Personnel Psychology, 41,* 43–61.

Johnson, J. W., & Ferstl, K. L. (1999). The effects of interrater and self-other agreement on performance improvement following upward feedback. *Personnel Psychology, 52,* 271–303.

Levy, P. E., Albright, M. D., Cawley, B. D., & Williams, J. R. (1995). Situational and individual determinants of feedback seeking: A closer look at the process. *Organizational Behavior and Human Decision Processes, 62,* 23–37.

London, M. (1997). *Job feedback: Giving, seeking, and using feedback for performance improvement.* Mahwah, NJ: Lawrence Erlbaum.

London, M. (2001). The great debate: Should multisource feedback be used for administration or development only? In D. W. Bracken, C. W. Timmreck, & A. H. Church (Eds.), *The handbook of multisource feedback: The comprehensive resource for designing and implementing MSF processes* (p. 368–385). San Francisco: Jossey-Bass.

London, M., & Smither, J. W. (in press). Feedback orientation, feedback culture, and the longitudinal performance management process. *Human Resources Management Review.*

London, M., Smither, J. W., & Adsit, D. J. (1997). Accountability: The achilles heel of multisource feedback. *Group and Organization Management, 22,* 162–184.

Martineau, J. W. (1998). Using 360-degree surveys to assess change. In W. W. Tornow & M. London (Eds.), *Maximizing the value of 360-degree feedback: A process for successful individual and organizational development* (pp. 217–248). San Francisco: Jossey-Bass.

Pfau, B. N. & Kay, I. T. (2002). *The human capital edge: 21 people management practices your company must implement (or avoid) to maximize shareholder value* (pp. 283–291). New York: McGraw-Hill.

Walker, A. G., & Smither, J. W. (1999). A five-year study of upward feedback: What managers do with their results matters. *Personnel Psychology, 52,* 393–423.

Warech, M. A., Smither, J. W., Reilly, R. R., Millsap, R. E., & Reilly, S. P. (1998). Self-monitoring and 360-degree ratings. *Leadership Quarterly, 9,* 449–473.

Suggested Readings in Multisource Feedback

Bracken, D. W., Timmreck, C. W., & Church, A. H. (Eds.). (2001). The handbook of multisource feedback: The comprehensive resource for designing and implementing MSF processes. San Francisco, CA: Jossey-Bass.

Fleenor, J. W., & Prince, J. M. (1997). *Using 360-degree feedback in organizations: An annotated bibliography.* Greensboro, NC: Center for Creative Leadership

Tornow, W. W., & London, M. (Eds.). (1998). *Maximizing the value of 360-degree feedback: A process for successful individual and organizational development.* San Francisco, CA: Jossey-Bass.

Van Velsor, E.V., Leslie, J. B., & Fleenor, J. W. (1997). *Choosing 360: A guide to evaluating multi-rater feedback instruments for management development.* Greensboro, NC: Center for Creative Leadership.

CHAPTER 10

Compensation Analysis

Mary Dunn Baker

An equitable compensation program is based on a pay-setting process that is neutral with respect to demographic group status (e.g., racial/ethnic or gender group). Most pay equity laws and regulations require that similarly situated members of demographic groups receive equal pay for substantially equal work. Equal work is usually assessed by determining whether jobs (a) involve similarly complex or difficult tasks; (b) require similar skills, effort, and responsibility; and (c) are performed under similar working conditions.

U.S. federal statutes and regulations require that employers compensate various demographic groups equitably. For example, the Equal Pay Act of 1963 prohibits gender-based compensation discrimination and Title VII of the Civil Rights Act of 1964 outlaws compensation discrimination based on race, color, sex, religion, and national origin. Similarly, the Age Discrimination in Employment Act of 1967 protects workers age 40 and older from pay discrimination and Executive Order 11246 (1965) bars covered federal government contractors and subcontractors from basing compensation on race, color, sex, religion, or national origin. Besides the federal prohibitions against pay discrimination, many states enforce their own laws and regulations that prohibit compensation discrimination based on demographic characteristics. Virtually all organizations are covered by at least some of the federal and/or state pay-equity laws and regulations discussed above, as well as others (e.g., protections provided to disabled workers through the 1990 Americans with Disabilities Act).

As recent cases illustrate, employers who are accused of violating these laws or who are subject to a compensation investigation by a government agency such as the U.S.

Department of Commerce's Equal Employment Opportunity Commission (EEOC) or the U.S. Department of Labor's Office of Federal Contract Compliance Programs (OFCCP) are at considerable financial risk. For example, in 2002, Coca-Cola paid $4.2 million in back wages to resolve the OFCCP's allegation of pay discrimination against women and minorities. A year earlier, Coca-Cola had settled a race discrimination lawsuit for $192.5 million, $43.5 million of which was for pay adjustments. Judgments, settlements, and other legal agreements to resolve pay equity disputes may also include injunctive relief to prevent future discrimination such as revisions to the employer's pay-setting processes and monitoring future pay decisions for varying lengths of time via periodic reporting of the results of statistical analyses of compensation.

Besides the monetary and injunctive ramifications, allegations of pay discrimination may negatively impact the employer's ability to recruit and retain employees, as well as employee productivity and performance. Consequently, because allegations of pay inequities may be costly in several respects, every organization should have a thorough understanding of its pay-setting system; collect and maintain the data necessary to prepare appropriate pay studies; conduct self-audits to determine whether data reveal patterns of pay differences; ascertain whether there are legitimate, nondiscriminatory explanations for observed pay disparities; and examine its pay practices to ascertain why unexplained compensation differences arise. Experience indicates that the expense of defending against pay discrimination claims is reduced and worker job satisfaction is enhanced when the organization stays apprised of pay patterns revealed by data, corrects well-studied pay differences that remain unexplained, and uses compensation decision-making processes that minimize the creation of disparities.

This chapter presents several methods of analyzing the current compensation of nonrepresented (non-union) employees that are commonly used by government compliance officers and organizations' self-auditors to assess whether compensation decisions are compliant with relevant laws and regulations. The methods of detecting and measuring demographic group pay differences range from the crude to the complex. Most compensation and analytic software packages offer most, if not all, of the procedures that require mathematical computations. Accordingly, this chapter focuses on the concepts underlying these methods and the interpretation and understanding of analysis results, rather than serving as a primer on computing statistics. Further, because a number of organizations have inappropriately implemented pay "fixes" that were based on substantially flawed models and others appropriately attempted to remedy unexplained disparities that reemerged after only a short period of time, this chapter describes common "root causes" of pay differences revealed by pay studies.

Who Should Be Involved in the Preparation of Compensation Analyses?

Any compensation analysis, no matter how simple or complex, should be conducted at the direction of, and in consultation with, legal counsel so as to shield the work product from legal discovery to the extent possible. In many instances, courts have required that self-critical analyses conducted by or for the organization be produced to opposing parties in lawsuits. For similar reasons, the results of compensation analyses should be shared only with those who have a need to know. Legal counsel should provide guidance regarding the publication of any compensation study.

Some compensation software packages that provide simple/casual analysis procedures are user-friendly enough that the analyst needs to have only rudimentary computer programming skills and the knowledge to extract the necessary data from the human resources or payroll information system. However, as discussed below, because simple procedures provide only very preliminary and often misleading pictures of the equitableness of pay, the organization should not rely solely on the outcome of such analyses.

The preparation of an appropriate and more complex compensation study requires extensive knowledge of labor economics and statistics as applied to employment data. Such analyses also require technical knowledge of computer software packages as well as complex computer programming skills that are often required to efficiently extract and manipulate data from human resources and payroll information systems. Therefore, the design and execution of complex compensation analyses is best left to the professional with the requisite education and experience (e.g., labor economist, industrial psychologist, statistician). If the organization does not employ an appropriately credentialed person to competently perform these tasks, then outside consultation should be sought to prepare appropriate analyses and to provide assistance in the interpretation of the results. However, outside consultants should not be expected to work in the dark. In order to efficiently conduct a meaningful pay analysis, the consultant will need the assistance of compensation management and information system personnel, respectively, to gain a clear understanding of the organization's pay-setting processes and the available electronic data. Again, for work product protection reasons, legal counsel should retain the outside consultant, be the conduit through which all information flows to the consultant, and participate in all discussions that the consultant has with the organization's personnel.

Pay Elements Included in a Compensation Study

Most laws and regulations define compensation as any payment made to, or on behalf of, an employee as remuneration for employment. Such remuneration may take the form of wages, salary, overtime pay, bonuses, awards, vacation and holiday pay, commissions, profit sharing, stock options, perquisites, and other benefits. However, when compensation is studied for the purpose of determining whether demographic group differences in pay exist, monetary compensation is generally analyzed separately from perquisites and other nonpecuniary benefits.

Most compensation studies analyze base pay (e.g., regular hourly rate, monthly salary, and annual salary) or total annual compensation (e.g., the sum of base pay, overtime, bonus, and awards). Alternatively, each element of total annual compensation may be studied separately. In all studies, however, it is important to ensure that comparable elements of pay are analyzed for all employees. For example, when base pay is analyzed, the pay rate for all employees must be measured at the same point in time (e.g., December 31, 200X) and at the same frequency (e.g., the pay for every employee is expressed in annual salary terms). When the organization employs both part-time and full-time workers and both "regular" and temporary employees, the analyst should seek professional guidance on appropriate methods for accounting for employment status in pay analyses.

As the elements of base pay (or total compensation) become more complex, the analyst must give careful thought to how the analysis is structured (i.e., whether it is appropriate to include all employees in a given analysis or whether employee subsets should be analyzed separately). For example, in some organizations, the base pay of employees includes premiums or stipends for particular work assignments (e.g., off-site assignment, hazardous duty pay). Unless all employees included in a given analysis are eligible for the premiums, if the pay of all employees is to be studied, then the analyst should remove the value of these elements before conducting the analysis. Alternatively, separate analyses may be conducted for employees who are not paid premiums and for sets of employees who receive each premium type or combination of premiums.

When total annual compensation is analyzed, the analysis should include only those employees who worked the entire year. Generally, employees who were hired or who terminated during the year and those who took leaves of absence without pay should be excluded.

When elements other than base pay are included in total annual compensation, the analysis should include only the employees who are eligible for such compensation. For example, if base pay plus commission is to be studied, then the analysis should include only employees who are paid on a commission basis. (When the commission rate or formula varies from one set of workers to another, the analyst should obtain professional advice regarding appropriate methods of accounting for a variety of commission plans.) If elements such as profit sharing, bonuses, and awards are included in the chosen measure of compensation, then the analysis should include only those employees who are eligible for these pecuniary benefits. The analysis should include eligible employees who received no dollars in profit sharing, bonus, awards, and so on.

Methods of Analyzing Compensation

A pay equity analysis involves the comparison of the actual outcome of an organization's pay decisions and the expected outcome. In a nondiscriminatory compensation system, the expectation is that the pay of comparably situated demographic groups will be similar. Compensation software packages provide a variety of techniques for analysts and auditors to use to assess whether various groups of employees are similarly paid.

Underlying every method of analysis is the assumption that members of the demographic groups whose pay is compared are *similarly situated* with respect to factors that influence pay. When this critical assumption is violated, the analysis may produce nothing more than meaningless statistical artifacts. Before using the outcome of any procedure to draw conclusions regarding the presence or absence of pay equity, the analyst is encouraged to consider the validity of the similarly situated assumption—does the analysis constitute an "apples to apples" or an "apples to oranges" comparison? As illustrated below, to the extent that data permit, the analysis should be structured so that an "apples to apples" comparison is made. As some employers have learned, pay adjustments to remedy disparities exposed by "apples to oranges" models may create, rather than resolve, "real" pay disparities and potentially lead to reverse discrimination lawsuits.

Several of the techniques used to measure differences between the pay rates of demographic groups are illustrated using hypothetical data for active, regular, full-time, salaried, nonrepresented, noncommissioned employees of the XYZ Manufacturing Corporation. In all of the examples, annual salary (annual base pay rate) is studied. The same methods may be applied to other measures of compensation (e.g., total annual compensation, bonuses). Likewise, although the hypothetical analyses provided are all gender-based, these methods may be used to detect pay differences between other demographic groups (e.g., minority vs. nonminority employees).

Simple Pay Equity Analyses

EEOC and OFCCP compliance officers frequently utilize simple methods to measure group differences in pay because they are quick and inexpensive methods of "eyeballing" pay patterns. Casual methods are also used by self-audit analysts because, like government agencies, many organizations do not have the in-house expertise to conduct more complex analyses nor the monetary resources to retain a qualified consultant every time a compensation study is conducted.

Descriptions of casual procedures emphasize that these methods provide only preliminary clues as to the presence or absence of pay equity; are for the purpose of identifying sets of employees whose pay differences warrant further investigation; and produce misleading results if "apples to oranges" pay comparisons are made. Nevertheless, the outcomes of simple analyses frequently serve as the foundation for government agencies' and others' formal allegations of pay discrimination. Knowledge of the claims an adversary may bring helps the organization to prepare for and to develop effective responses to and/or remedies for pay discrimination charges before the allegations are actually levied.

Organizationwide "Raw" Average (Median) Salary Comparisons

The crudest method used to assess the presence or absence of pay equity is an organizationwide (companywide) comparison of the "raw" average or median salaries of the demographic groups. In the absence of pay discrimination, the average (median) salary of both, say, comparable men and women will be in the neighborhood of the companywide average (median) salary. (Because of space limitations, this chapter focuses on average pay comparisons. Many of the simple methods described herein may use median rather than mean pay comparisons.)

Table 10.1 shows that at XYZ, neither the average salary of female nor male employees is close to the overall average salary. The average female salary falls short of and the average male salary exceeds the overall average salary such that the female/male average salary difference is -$13,736 (or approximately -$13.7 thousand).

What can be gleaned from a companywide "raw" average salary comparison? Although this type of analysis is the stuff of which dramatic news headlines are made, such comparisons generally shed little light on the presence or absence of pay equity unless the demographic groups are alike in terms of factors that impact pay. Before relying on the results of this crude analysis, the analyst should carefully examine the pay-determining characteristics of the demographic groups. For example, if women are less likely than men to possess attributes that enhance pay (e.g., work in relatively high pay grades) and are more likely to have characteristics that diminish pay (e.g., work in relatively low pay grades), then the raw overall pay difference overstates the actual difference. If the converse is true, then the raw overall pay disparity understates the actual pay disparity.

What Factors Influence Pay?

Four broad generic categories of factors influence pay. First, the most important determinants of an employee's pay, as demonstrated by empirical research, are the level (e.g., complexity of work and amount of responsibility) and type of work performed (e.g., occupation and working conditions). Labor market forces establish a broad range of pay for a given level and type of work. Where an employee's pay falls within the market-established range depends upon other categories of pay-related characteristics.

Other categories of factors that influence current compensation include the amount and type of work experience, and the amount and type of education, skills, and training the employee possesses. In addition, pay is influenced by the organization's compensation philosophy (e.g., pay for performance; variations in pay structures to compensate for geographic differences in the cost-of-living) and its current and historical budgets (e.g., some departments or functional areas have relatively larger labor budgets than others; some types of employees may have experienced periods of wage concessions or no or low pay increases).

If the analyst finds that the two groups are not similar in terms of legitimate factors that influence pay, then no conclusion regarding pay equity should be drawn from an overall difference in "raw" average salaries. For example, the analyst may find that men and women are distributed differently across levels within the organization. If pay varies by the level at which employees work and demographic groups differ in levels of work, then level differences may explain some or all of the observed overall raw average salary difference.

Table 10.1 Average Annual Salary Analysis by Gender: Overall, by FLSA-Status and by Pay Grade

Employee Group	Total Number of Employees	Average Salary	Number of Female Employees	Percentage of Female Employees	Female Average Salary	Number of Male Employees	Percentage of Male Employees	Male Average Salary	Female/Male Difference in Representation	Female/Male Average Salary Difference
Overall	**1,492**	**$68,935**	**322**	**100.0%**	**$58,164**	**1,170**	**100.0%**	**$71,900**		**−$13,736**
Nonexempt	475	$41,591	142	44.1%	$38,594	333	28.5%	$42,869	15.6%	−$4,275
GR 1	6	$26,983	5	3.5%	$27,520	1	0.3%	$24,300	3.2%	$3,220
GR 2	252	$37,496	72	50.7%	$34,923	180	54.1%	$38,525	−3.4%	−$3,602
GR 3	217	$46,750	65	45.8%	$43,513	152	45.6%	$48,135	0.2%	−$4,622
Exempt	1,017	$81,707	180	55.9%	$73,602	837	71.5%	$83,450	−15.6%	−$9,848
GR 4	206	$52,170	56	31.1%	$51,321	150	17.9%	$52,487	13.2%	−$1,166
GR 5	427	$70,209	81	45.0%	$69,340	346	41.3%	$70,413	3.7%	−$1,073
GR 6	368	$108,913	41	22.8%	$109,010	327	39.1%	$108,901	−16.3%	$109
GR 7	16	$143,081	2	1.1%	$144,200	14	1.7%	$142,921	−0.6%	$1,279

Note: The percentage of females (males) in each FLSA status is computed by dividing the number of females (males) in the status by the total number of females (males). The percentage of females (males) in each FLSA/grade is computed by dividing the number of females (males) in the grade by the total number of females (males) in the FLSA status.

Fair Labor Standards Act (FLSA) Average Pay Comparisons

One very general gauge of the levels at which employees work is their Fair Labor Standards Act (FLSA) status—nonexempt or exempt. Typically, as Table 10.1 illustrates, nonexempt employees are paid less than exempt employees (other things equal) because the nonexempt employees tend to work in lower level jobs than do exempt employees. Therefore, a crude method of accounting for demographic group differences in level of work performed is to examine raw average salary differences for nonexempt and exempt employees separately.

As Table 10.1 shows, female and male XYZ employees are not similarly situated in terms of FLSA status. Approximately 44.1% of the female employees and only 28.5% of the male employees work in the lower paying nonexempt jobs, whereas about 55.9% of the female employees and 71.5% of the male employees work in the higher paying exempt jobs. Although this example shows that gender differences in FLSA category explain some of the overall raw female/male average salary difference, the magnitudes of these pay differences (−$4,275 for nonexempt employees and −$9,848 for exempt employees) clearly indicate that FLSA status does not explain the entire organizationwide female/male average pay difference (−$13.7 thousand).

Average Pay Comparisons by Grade

As many organizations have multiple levels (e.g., pay grades or bands) within an FLSA category, and grade is a more specific indicator of the level of work employees perform, some simple pay equity study protocols recommend that the analyst conduct separate salary analyses by grade (or other indicator of level of work). As Table 10.1 illustrates, when pay increases with grade within an FLSA category and the demographic groups are not similarly distributed across grades, then group differences in grade may explain some or all of the pay differences observed for the FLSA categories.

To determine whether the gender differences in grade within an FLSA category potentially explain FLSA pay disparities, conduct a separate average salary analysis for each grade. The by-grade analyses shown in Table 10.1 reveal that the apparent across-the-board female shortfalls in pay in the nonexempt and exempt ranks are misleading. Indeed, the data show that in nonexempt grade 1 and in exempt grades 6 and 7, the average female is paid more than the average male. In the other grades (2, 3, 4, and 5), the average female pay is less than that of the average male, but in general, the size of the disparities is smaller than the FLSA disparities. Therefore, it appears that a portion of the female/male pay differences among nonexempt and exempt employees is attributable to gender differences in levels of work within FLSA categories.

In some audits initiated by government agencies, the compliance officer declares that grade-by-grade data reveal a pattern of pay discrimination when a specified percentage (e.g., 55%, 75%) of the members of the affinity group (e.g., women) are in grades in which the group is paid less than others (e.g., men). At XYZ, 85% of the female employees are in grades in which women are, on average, paid less than men. Therefore, auditors who take this approach would contend that XYZ's data reveal a preliminary pattern of underpaying women relative to men.

When analysts or auditors find that on a grade-by-grade basis one group tends to be paid less than another, some simple analysis protocols suggest that a casual examination of the groups' other important pay-determining characteristics be conducted to assess whether such factors potentially explain the observed disparities. For example, several software packages offer "eyeball" tests to assess whether group differences in experience with the employer (e.g., years of company tenure or years in the current grade) explain pay differences observed in a set of grades. When the average salary of the affinity group falls short of that of the other group and the affinity group has at least as much experience with the employer as the other group, the grade is flagged as a "problem" area. Some packages also flag grades as having disparate pay when the salary difference is $1,000 or more and the difference in experience is only approximately one year or less. As Table 10.2 shows, none of the XYZ grades with negative female/male average salary differences are "justified" by gender differences in company or grade tenure.

Job Title Cohort Analysis

Some compensation auditors use a job title cohort method of evaluating pay equity that does not involve the calculation of average or median values of salaries or other pay-influencing factors. Advocates of this casual method contend that it is superior to other simple procedures because pay comparisons of employees who work in the same job title constitute more of an "apples to apples" evaluation than pay comparisons of employees who are in the same FLSA status or grade. To conduct a job title cohort analysis, the analyst prepares a chart that shows the demographic status and pay rate as well as the values of selected characteristics of the employees who work in a given job title. An "eyeball" test is applied to ascertain whether observed pay differences appear to be reasonable given differences in other pay-related characteristics such as years in the job and performance rating. (See Chapter 10 in the *EEOC's Compliance Manual* for illustrations of job title cohort analyses.)

Criticisms of Simple Pay Analyses

Social scientists and the legal community have severely criticized the simple methods of compensation analysis described above for two primary reasons. First, many simple analyses fail to account for any pay-influencing factors whatsoever; others consider only limited factors such as FLSA status or grade and company (or grade) tenure. Therefore, these "apples to oranges" comparisons may set off false alarms (reveal "artificial" disparities) or create false senses of security (show "artificially" neutral results).

Second, as discussed below, even in the complete absence of discrimination, it would not be unusual to observe a "small" difference in the pay of the demographic groups. Casual analyses do not provide any test to determine whether the pay

Table 10.2 Average Annual Salaries and Company (Grade) Tenure by Pay Grade and Gender

Pay Grade	Female Average Salary	Male Average Salary	Female/Male Average Salary Difference	Female Average Company (Grade) Tenure	Male Average Company (Grade) Tenure	Female/Male Company (Grade) Tenure Difference	Preliminary Evidence of Female/Male Pay Disparity?	t-Statistic (Number of Standard Deviations) of Salary Difference	Probability that Salary Difference Occurred by Chance	Statistically Significant Salary Difference?
1	$27,520	$24,300	$3,220	2.71 (2.71)	3.78 (3.78)	1.07 (−1.07)	N (N)	—	—	—
2	$34,923	$38,525	−$3,602	7.66 (3.42)	7.11 (2.95)	0.55 (0.47)	Y (Y)	−4.27	0.00%	Y
3	$43,513	$48,135	−$4,622	11.84 (4.36)	10.28 (4.14)	1.56 (0.22)	Y (Y)	−5.11	0.00%	Y
4	$51,321	$52,487	−$1,166	7.01 (2.03)	3.75 (1.92)	3.26 (0.11)	Y (Y)	−1.82	42.00%	N
5	$69,340	$70,413	−$1,073	10.50 (2.33)	9.80 (2.79)	0.70 (−0.46)	Y (Y)	−1.75	46.01%	N
6	$109,010	$108,901	$109	17.67 (3.76)	16.49 (4.54)	1.17 (−0.78)	N (N)	0.05	96.10%	N
7	$144,200	$142,921	$1,279	28.80 (1.30)	23.04 (2.44)	5.76 (−1.34)	N (N)	0.33	77.60%	N

Notes:

1. The t-statistic is not computed when there is only one employee in one or both of the demographic groups.

2. Number (Percentage) of Females in Pay Grade with negative salary difference and similar or more: Company Tenure = 274 (85.1%) Grade Tenure = 274 (85.1%)

3. Number (Percentage) of Females in Pay Grade with statistically significant negative difference = 137 (42.5%)

difference is so large as to be inconsistent with a neutral pay-setting system (statistically significant) or is small enough to be reflective of a nondiscriminatory decision-making process (statistically insignificant). Therefore, when a pay difference is observed, it is important to determine whether the groups' average salaries are "close enough" to be consistent with the outcome of a neutral compensation system.

The analyst can determine whether the average salaries of demographic groups are "close enough" to be reflective of neutral decision making by conducting an inferential statistical analysis. Inferential analyses provide statistics—*the number of standard deviations of the pay difference* or *the probability that the pay disparity occurred by chance*—that are used to assess whether the actual outcome (the pay difference) is "close enough" to the expected outcome (a zero difference) to be consistent with a nondiscriminatory model.

Social scientists and the courts typically conclude that disparities that are approximately two (or three) or more standard deviations, or are associated with probabilities that are 5% (or 1%) or less are not likely to have occurred by chance in a neutral setting. Assuming that the demographic groups are similar with respect to factors that influence pay, these "rare" outcomes are considered statistically significant and do not resemble outcomes consistent with a nondiscriminatory pay-setting process.

Some analysts mistakenly contend that statistically significant pay disparities constitute *scientific proof* of compensation discrimination. A statistically significant difference merely indicates that the difference is not likely to have occurred by chance. If the explanation is not random variation, then what is it? There are three possibilities. First, the observed disparity is entirely attributable to demographic group status (i.e., pay discrimination). Second, the pay difference is totally unrelated to demographic group status, but is entirely explained by legitimate factors for which the analysis did not account and that happen to be correlated with demographic status. Finally, part of the disparity may be explained by omitted factors; the remaining difference is related to demographic status. The unexplained pay disparity that remains after considering other factors may or may not be statistically significant.

Applying Inferential Statistical Tests to Simple Pay Models

In response to the criticisms regarding the lack of tests of statistical significance in casual pay studies, some auditors follow up simple average salary analyses by subjecting the data to an inferential statistical analysis. One of the most commonly used procedures is the *t*-test of a difference between means (or averages).

A *t*-test measures the number of standard deviations of a difference between average salaries. When the *t*-statistic (analogous to the number of standard deviations) is equal to, or greater than, approximately two (or three) and the probability that the difference would have occurred by chance is 5% (or 1%) or less, the pay difference is flagged as statistically significant. Since statistically significant pay differences do not resemble disparities that are likely to be observed in the absence of discrimination, the flag is an indicator that the analyst should examine additional data to determine whether other demographic group differences in pay-related characteristics such as experience, education, and performance are potential explanations for the disparity.

Table 10.2 provides the results of *t*-tests of the differences between the average pay of XYZ men and women by grade. According to the *t*-tests, the female/male pay differences in grades 4, 5, 6, and 7 are not statistically significant. Therefore, assuming that the men and women in these grades are similarly situated with respect to other factors that influence pay, these differences are "close enough" to the expected difference (a zero difference) to be consistent with the outcome of a neutral compensation system.

Table 10.2 also shows that the t-statistics for the female/male pay differences in grades 2 and 3 are statistically significant. Just as with any other salary analysis, before concluding that the grade 2 and 3 pay disparities represent pay inequities to be remedied, the analyst should conduct further research to determine whether these male and female employees are similarly situated with respect to other legitimate factors that impact pay.

Even when inferential statistical tests are applied to simple pay comparisons to determine whether disparities are statistically significant, the analyst is still left with an "eyeball" test to assess whether all or just a portion of the pay difference is explained by casual observations of other pay-related characteristics. Absent the ability to sort out the portion of a difference that is explained by other relevant factors and the ability to determine whether any remaining disparity is statistically significant, making determinations about the need, or lack thereof, for pay adjustments and the amount by which the pay of the adversely affected group should be adjusted, if any, is a risky proposition.

Complex Pay Equity Techniques—Multiple Regression Analysis

Multiple regression analysis is a statistical method that overcomes the primary criticisms of the simple analyses described above, to the extent that data are available. When properly specified and structured, multiple regression analysis enables the analyst to simultaneously filter out of the raw average pay disparity the part that is attributable to demographic group differences in other legitimate measurable factors that impact pay. Further, it allows the analyst to determine whether any remaining disparity is statistically significant.

The analyst has two sets of decisions to make before the multiple regression analysis can be conducted. (1) What explanatory factors are to be incorporated into the regression model? (2) How should the regression analysis be structured (i.e., should an organizationwide regression model be estimated or should separate models be estimated for subsets of employees?)?

Explanatory Factors

For the regression analysis to directly measure the differences between the pay of demographic groups of employees, the model includes a variable that indicates the demographic group to which each employee belongs. For example, if the analysis is to measure the average difference between female and male pay after accounting for gender differences in factors that influence pay, then the model will include a variable that indicates whether the employee is female or male.

The other explanatory variable for which the analysis accounts ideally includes all of the measurable factors (or proxies for the relevant characteristics) that the organization actually considers in setting pay. However, in reality, the factors included in regression models depend, in large part, upon the availability of data.

In most organizations, pay depends upon multiple factors that fall under the four generic pay-determining categories discussed above. Among these factors are level of work, occupation (type of work), the amount and type of work experience within the organization, and relevant prior work experience in other organizations. For some jobs, amount and type of education and the possession of certifications or licenses impact pay. In many organizations, the employee's performance or productivity influences pay (employer's compensation philosophy and budget).

Because many organizations do not collect and maintain the data necessary to quantify all measurable characteristics that influence pay, the factors for which the regression analysis accounts are generally limited. With the exception of the least structured organizations, data are usually available to measure the level within the organization at which the employee works (e.g., grade or band).

Most organizations also maintain the elements necessary to compute the employee's total amount of company experience (e.g., date of hire, service date, credited service date, dates of leaves of absence). However, few organizations have sufficient and easily accessible data to break down total company service into component parts to more specifically measure the amount of the employee's experience by type within the organization (e.g., years in the current grade and other years of company service; or years in the current grade, other years of salaried exempt-service, other years of salaried nonexempt service, and years as an hourly employee). Because the type of work experience that employees have had within the organization tends to have a considerable impact on pay, lack of the data to describe the types of work experience the employee possesses may compromise the ability to make "apples to apples" comparisons.

Some organizations maintain data that can be used to describe the type of work that the employee performs (e.g., occupation category, job family, functional areas or career ladder). When the employer has not already organized jobs into meaningful categories, other data elements may be available (e.g., job title and department name) that allow the analyst to construct variables that describe the type of work.

When employees included in the analysis work in multiple locations (plants or facilities) with cost-of-living differences or varying labor market conditions, it is often appropriate to include location variables in the model. When the organization has separate pay scales for sets of locations (e.g., zones) based on local costs-of-living and prevailing wage rates, location category variables (e.g., high cost area, average cost area, low cost area) may substitute for a separate variable for each location.

Few organizations maintain complete and accurate electronic data on an employee's educational background, possession of relevant licenses and certificates, amount and type of prior work experience and performance/productivity history at the company. As illustrated below, organizations that have the data necessary to describe other important pay-determining factors such as prior experience, education level, and performance history and to decompose total company service into relevant component parts are able to more accurately assess whether demographic group pay disparities exist than companies that have less complete and accurate data.

In addition to the selection of explanatory variables for the regression analysis, the analyst also must determine the form in which each factor enters the model. Typically, categorical characteristics (e.g., pay grade) enter as a set of binary or indicator variables. Noncategorical factors (e.g., years of company or grade experience) generally enter as continuous variables.

The regression procedure most frequently used by compensation analysts (Ordinary Least Squares) assumes that the relationship between salary and each explanatory factor is linear. However, the relationship between some factors and pay is not linear. When nonlinear relationships exist, it is often necessary to transform a variable in order to appropriately capture its relationship with pay. For example, the relationship between company (or grade) tenure and pay is often curvilinear. One method of accounting for the nonlinear relationship between experience and pay is to include two variables for a given measure of experience— experience and experience squared. Analysts who are not well versed in the specification of regression variables are encouraged to seek professional guidance on the appropriate forms in which the explanatory variables enter the model.

How Are Regression Analyses Structured?

Many analysts begin compensation investigations using an organizationwide multiple regression analysis. Table 10.3 provides an XYZ example of a companywide regression model that the analyst used to measure the female/male difference in pay after accounting for gender differences in pay grades and total company experience.

As shown at Table 10.1, on average, XYZ female employees earned about $13.7 thousand less than male employees. To measure the amount by which female and male pay differs after filtering out pay differences attributable to gender differences in pay grade and total company service, the analyst conducted a multiple regression analysis. The model includes a demographic variable (female or not), a set of pay grade variables as well as total years of service along with the squared term (Model 1). Table 10.3 shows that the female coefficient (the female/male pay difference) is −$2,476 (approximately −$2.5 thousand) after filtering out gender differences in grade and company tenure. The t-statistic (analogous to the number of standard deviations) for the female coefficient is −3.862, which indicates that the pay disparity is statistically significant at the three standard deviation level (probability = 0.01%).

Table 10.3   Annual Salary Multiple Regression Analysis

Employee Group	Average Salary	Regression Model	Female/Male Salary Difference (Female Coefficient)	t-Value (Number of Standard Deviations of Salary Difference)	p-Value (Probability that Salary Difference Occurred by Chance)	Adjusted R-Squared	Probability of F	Total Number of Employees	Number of Female Employees
All	$68,935	1	-$2,476	-3.862	0.01%	88.25%	0.00%	1492	322
		2	-$1,395	-2.388	1.70%	91.93%	0.00%	1492	322
Nonexempt	$41,591	2	-$873	-1.560	11.94%	71.22%	0.00%	475	142
Admin/Clerical	$37,800	1	$1,322	1.520	13.21%	78.04%	0.00%	93	75
Mfg. Operator	$38,300	1	-$1,799	-1.826	7.19%	78.62%	0.00%	88	27
Tech. Support	$43,762	1	-$1,765	-2.164	3.13%	66.83%	0.00%	294	40
		3	-$1,364	-1.686	9.29%	67.98%	0.00%	294	40
Exempt	$81,707	2	-$1,819	-2.221	4.01%	87.21%	0.00%	1,017	180
Acct/Finance	$68,190	1	-$6,590	-3.486	0.08%	82.21%	0.00%	94	45
		4	-$3,332	-2.221	4.01%	84.56%	0.00%	94	45
Engr. Support	$70,800	1	-$3,495	-1.733	8.56%	72.11%	0.00%	128	28
Engineer	$94,438	1	$649	0.564	57.33%	82.13%	0.00%	596	88
Field Engineer	$53,731	1	-$2,731	-0.985	32.64%	76.81%	0.00%	128	5
Mfg. Mgt.	$65,050	1	$1,562	0.506	61.47%	77.98%	0.00%	71	14

Model Specifications:

Model 1 accounts for pay grade, years of company tenure, and years of company tenure squared. In addition to the Model 1 variables, Model 2 controls for job family. Model 3 controls for pay grade, years in the current grade, years in the current grade squared, other years of company tenure, and other years of company tenure squared. In addition to the Model 3 variables, Model 4 controls for highest level of education, years of prior work experience, and years of prior work experience squared.

Note: Adjusted R-Squared measures the proportion of variation in annual salaries explained by the salary model. The probability of F indicates whether the salary model is statistically significant (probability of $F \leq 0.05$ or $\leq 5\%$).

Although gender differences in grade and company tenure explain nearly 82% of the −$13.7 thousand raw pay difference, the $2.5 thousand disparity is "too large" to be attributable to random variation.

To illustrate that pay determinants omitted from the regression analysis may explain some of the Model 1 female/male pay difference, consider the following. The approximate −$2.5 thousand female/male Model 1 pay difference does not account for one of the most important factors that influence pay—type of work. XYZ places job titles into job families (collections of job titles that are similar in job content). Table 10.3 shows that average pay varies by job family and that men and women are distributed differently across the job families. Given that a larger percentage of women work in the lower paying job families than men, some or all of the Model 1 −$2.5 thousand female/male pay difference may be explained by gender differences in types of work. To measure the female/male pay difference after accounting for job family (in addition to pay grade and total years of company service), job family variables are added to the regression model (Model 2).

As Table 10.3 shows, Model 2 yields a female/male pay difference of −$1,395, or about $1.1 thousand less than the Model 1 difference, which did not account for gender differences in type of work. Even though gender differences in job family explain nearly 44% of the Model 1 pay difference, the disparity remains statistically significant at the two standard deviation level (t-value $= -2.388$ and p-value $= 1.70\%$). Again, this significant difference indicates that pay is influenced by gender and/or other factors for which the analysis has not accounted that happen to be correlated with gender.

Dangers of Using an Overall Regression Model to Assess Pay Equity

Organizationwide compensation regression models are often inappropriate for purposes of determining whether significant demographic group differences in pay exist and whether salaries should be adjusted to reduce or eliminate an unexplained statistical disparity. First, an overall negative and significant demographic group pay difference implies an organizationwide phenomenon of paying one group less than another. Although such a result will be obtained when adverse pay differences are pervasive throughout the organization, this implication may not be valid. For instance, an overall regression analysis may yield an aggregate negative and significant pay disparity when there are large disparities for some subsets of employees and insignificant (positive or negative) differences for others.

Likewise, when a companywide analysis yields a neutral (statistically insignificant) result, the analyst should not assume that there are no pay disparities anywhere within the organization. An aggregate neutral result may be obtained when there are large negative differences for some employee subsets that are "washed out" by large positive differences elsewhere.

When the analysis yields an organizationwide pay disparity, before relying on the results of an overall regression model to draw a conclusion regarding pay equity, the analyst is encouraged to conduct additional research to determine whether the overall pay difference is truly attributable to an across-the-board pattern or whether there are some employee subsets that are largely responsible for the result. Separate pay analyses for each FLSA status, grade, job family, or location often help the analyst to isolate the employee subsets in which there are disparities of magnitudes that warrant concern.

The analyst should also attempt to determine whether the pay difference the analysis yields is attributable to a general pattern of underpaying a given affinity group or is a reflection of the fact that there are a few "outliers." An outlier is an employee whose actual pay is "extraordinarily" high or low relative to his or her expected salary, given the characteristics for which the model accounts. (Many software packages offer procedures that predict employee pay based on the regression model without a demographic group variable, compare the employee's expected and actual pay, and measure the number of standard deviations between actual and expected pay.) If the overall pay disparity is attributable to a few members of the affinity group who are negative outliers (actual pay is significantly less than expected pay) and a few members of the non-affinity group who are positive outliers (actual pay is significantly more than expected pay), then across-the-board pay adjustments are generally not in order. In circumstances in which it appears that a few outliers are driving the disparity revealed by the model, the analyst should attempt to determine whether there are legitimate reasons for some employees to have salaries that differ dramatically from others who are like them in the factors for which the analysis controls. For example, if education and/or prior experience are not included in the compensation model, perhaps the positive (negative) outliers differ from otherwise similar employees because they have more (less) education or prior experience than their counterparts. The analyst can consult personnel folders to determine whether the outliers differ from others in terms of such characteristics.

However, reasons for outlying salaries may not be apparent in personnel documents. In such situations, compensation analysts (in conjunction with legal counsel) often uncover helpful information via interviews of the managers of the outlier employees. Personnel who are familiar with the individuals and the specific work that they do often provide valuable insight into pay differences that are not explained by computerized data or hard-copy personnel documents. For example, the manager may know that a positive outlier has "star" quality (i.e., highly regarded by experts in the field), possesses a highly sought-after skill that others do not have, performs additional duties or has more responsibilities than otherwise similar employees, or has a history of obtaining other job offers with higher rates of pay which the employer countered. A negative outlier may have a scope of responsibility and a span of control that is narrower than that of otherwise similar employees or have a lower valued skill set or work on less complex projects than others. Discussions with managers about extraordinarily high or low salaries may also alert the analyst to data errors that explain the outlying salary (e.g., the employee's grade was erroneously recorded) or provide clues about the perverse effects that other employment practices have on compensation (see Common Root Causes of Pay Disparities). Once outliers are identified, the analyst should re-run the regression model excluding the outliers. If the resulting demographic group coefficient is insignificant, then there is evidence that the outliers explain the disparity. However, if the demographic group variable remains statistically significant, then the data indicate that outliers are not the whole story.

Besides the fact that overall pay disparities may not be the result of organization-wide pay shortfalls for a given demographic group, an organizationwide regression analysis is not appropriate when the impact that factors have on pay varies from one employee subset to another. For example, if the impact that another year of company service has on pay varies from one grade to another or from one type of work to another, then it is not appropriate to use a single regression model to measure demographic group differences in pay. When this is the case, the model will overstate the value of the characteristic for some employees and understate it for others. Consequently, the analysis may yield a misleading result (overstate or understate the pay difference).

Complex statistical procedures (e.g., F tests of differences between regession equations) are available to ascertain whether the impact that a set of factors has on pay varies from one set of employees to another. The results of these tests are used to determine whether all employees are appropriately "pooled" into a single analysis or whether separate analyses should be conducted for subsets of employees. In most organizations, statistical tests will dictate that, at a minimum, separate analyses should be conducted for nonexempt and exempt employees.

Table 10.3 provides the results of separate regression analyses for XYZ nonexempt and exempt employees. As Table 10.3 shows, on average, nonexempt women arc paid $873 dollars less than nonexempt men who are like them in terms of grade, years of company service, and job family (Model 2). Because the nonexempt female coefficient is not statistically significant (t-value $= -1.560$ and p-value $= 11.94\%$), the data fail to provide statistical support for an allegation that these women are paid less than their male counterparts.

Table 10.3 also shows that, on average, exempt women are paid $1,819 less than exempt men who are like them in terms of the factors for which Model 2 accounts. This pay disparity is statistically significant at the two standard deviation level (t-value $= -2.221$, p-value $= 4.01\%$). Absent other information, this result provides statistical support for an allegation of underpaying exempt women.

Some employment attorneys suggest that organizations counter government auditors' allegations of pay discrimination based on simple/casual by-grade analyses by conducting separate multiple regression analysis for each grade. This approach is appropriate in some circumstances, but because employees in a given grade often perform varying types of work that the market compensates at different rates (i.e., the impact that factors have on pay varies across types of work within a grade), generally the preferred approach is to conduct separate analyses for each job family or other type of work categories. Separate studies for each job family typically constitute analyses more akin to "apples to apples" comparisons than separate analyses for each grade.

The female/male pay differences revealed by separate studies for each XYZ job family are presented in Table 10.3. Although the model for all nonexempt employees suggests that the female/male pay difference is not statistically significant, a review of the results of the separate studies for each nonexempt job family tells another story. In the three job families in which nonexempt employees work, the female coefficient is positive for Administrative/Clerical and negative for Manufacturing Operations and Technical Support. In fact, the Technical Support pay disparity is statistically significant at the two standard deviation level.

Although the all exempt employees' regression analysis shows a negative and significant female/male pay difference, Table 10.3 reveals that this pattern is not constant across the exempt job families. In fact, Model 1 analysis show that the average woman in Engineering and in Manufacturing Management is paid insignificantly more than the average man. In the other four exempt job families, on average, women are paid less than men. Out of the four negative female/male job family pay differences, only one (Accounting/Finance) is statistically significant.

Upon finding statistically significant female/male pay differences for Technical Support and Accounting/Finance, the XYZ analyst identified a few statistical outliers in these two job families. However, removal of the outliers did not eliminate the statistical significance of these female/male pay differences. Therefore, the statistically significant pay disparities in these two job families were not explained by the extraordinarily high or low salaries of a few employees .

In an attempt to ascertain whether the statistically significant negative female/male pay differences for Technical Support and Accounting/Finance were explained by factors for which Model 1 did not account, the analyst reviewed personnel folders of these employees. This review indicated that among men and women who had similar total years of company tenure, the men had more experience in the current grade than the women. Folder reviews of Accounting/Finance employees also revealed that the men were more likely than women to have a bachelor's and graduate degree and that the men appeared to have more years of relevant prior work experience than the women.

To determine whether gender differences in current grade tenure explain the significant result for Technical Support; and current grade tenure, highest level of education, and years of prior work experience explain the significant result for Accounting/Finance, the analyst collected and computerized these data elements. As Table 10.3 illustrates, the Technical Support female/male pay difference decreases from − \$1,765 to − \$1,364 (approximately −\$1.4 thousand) once the analysis accounts for gender differences in years in the grade and other years of company service (Model 3). The − \$1.4 thousand difference is not statistically significant (t-value = − 1.686, p-value = 9.29%).

After filtering out gender differences in grade, years in grade, other years of company service, highest level of education, and years of prior work experience, the statistically significant Accounting/Finance Model 1 pay difference (−\$6,590) was reduced to −\$3,332 (Model 4). However, the Accounting/Finance disparity remained statistically significant at the two standard deviation level (t-value = −2.221, p-value = 4.01%). As evidenced by the Accounting/Finance Model 4 result, the analysis will not necessarily yield an insignificant outcome simply because additional factors are incorporated into the analysis.

Consider Practical as Well as Statistical Significance

The number of standard deviations of a given pay difference increases with the number of observations on which the analysis is based. When the sample size is large, a pay difference that is negligible as a practical matter may be statistically significant. When the sample size is small, a pay difference that is not de-minimus may not be statistically significant. Consequently, the practical significance of a pay disparity should be considered as well as its level of statistical significance. In addition to examining dollar differences in pay, to assess the practical significance of a pay difference, the analyst may find it helpful to examine the percentage by which the groups' pay differs. The percentage difference in pay that is of practical significance depends upon human judgment.

How Well Does the Regression Model Fit the Data?

The analyst should be aware of how well the data "fit" the model. Software packages offer statistics that are useful in assessing the explanatory power of a compensation model. One frequently cited statistic is Adjusted R-Squared, which measures the proportion of the variation in salaries that is explained by the factors for which the model accounts. Adjusted R-Squared ranges in value from 0.0% to 100.0%. A 0.0% Adjusted R-Squared indicates that the explanatory variables included in the model do not explain any of the variation in employees' salaries. A 100.0% Adjusted R-Squared indicates that all variation in pay is explained by the factors for which the model accounts. (Generally, it is unlikely that employment data will explain 100% of the variation in salaries. Therefore, a 100% Adjusted R-Squared usually signals that there is a problem with the data or model and that the results should not be interpreted.)

Table 10.3 provides Adjusted R-Squared values for the regression models estimated for various sets of XYZ employees. For example, Table 10.3 shows that the "goodness of fit" of the Model 1 job family studies ranges from a low of 66.83% (Technical Support) to a high of 82.21% (Accounting/Finance). This range of Adjusted R-Squared values suggests that the factors for which the job family studies account explain a larger proportion of the variation in salaries for some employee subsets than others.

Professional compensation analysts point out that there is no clear-cut level of explanatory power that renders a regression analysis satisfactory. Relatively low Adjusted R-Squared values generally indicate that the factors for which the study accounts have little impact on salary or that the employees included in the analysis are very similar in terms of the explanatory variables (i.e., the variables do not help to distinguish one employee from another). Therefore, a relatively small Adjusted R-Squared is often a signal that important pay-determining variables have been omitted from the model. Interpretation of the results of a regression analysis with a relatively low Adjusted R-Squared statistic should be coupled with consideration for the likely impact that omitted variables would have on the results.

The regression output also provides an F-statistic and its associated probability that is used to determine whether the explanatory power of the model is statistically significant. Generally, when the probability of F is greater than 5%, the model is not statistically significant. Results of statistically insignificant regression models should be interpreted with caution.

Tainted Variables

As discussed above, the compensation study should include variables for as many measurable factors that enter into the pay decision-making process as the data and sample size permit. However, adversaries may claim that some of the explanatory variables are tainted. A tainted variable is a factor over which the employer has control and for which the employer's decisions are alleged to be biased against an affinity group. Consequently, the inclusion of tainted variables may obscure pay disparities. For example, complainants may contend that the incorporation of grade "covers up" pay disparities because the employer initially assigns members of an affinity group to lower pay grades than similarly situated nonaffinity group members or fails to promote affinity group members at the same rate and after the same period of time as nonaffinity group members. Other complainants may maintain that job family variables cause the equation to understate a true pay disparity because the organization channels affinity group members into low-paying occupations and nonaffinity group members into high-paying occupations.

To the extent that data are available, statistical analyses of other pay-influencing employment practices (e.g., initial assignment, promotion, and time until promotion) may be conducted to determine whether there is numerical support for the contention that a given variable or set of variables is tainted. However, many professionals with expertise in compensation analysis contend that key predictor variables that contribute to the explanatory power of the model should not be excluded from the regression equation, even if tainted. If other employment decisions are tainted, then discrimination related to the biased processes should be remedied separate and apart from the compensation analysis so that current salaries reflect the remediation.

Common Root Causes of Compensation Disparities

A number of organizations have discovered through self-audits, government investigations, and/or lawsuits that there are pay disparities that are not attributable to demographic group differences in pay-related factors that can be measured using the available data, and are "too large" to be attributable to chance variation. In an effort to prevent future pay disparities, some organizations launched data collection efforts and commissioned extensive, complex statistical research projects in attempts to uncover why pay differences arise. The most common root causes of pay disparities revealed by these studies are outlined below.

Artificial Pay Differences

Research reveals that in some instances current salary disparities are merely statistical artifacts that are attributable to the lack of information about important pay-related characteristics. In addition to the omitted variable problem, the analysis may also produce misleading pay differences when the human resources and payroll information system contains inaccurate or incomplete information for some employees. Before conducting compensation studies, the available data elements should be reviewed for completeness and accuracy.

Employment Policies and Practices

"Real" pay differences are often rooted in employment policies and practices that are facially neutral but have an adverse impact on particular demographic groups. Some of the policies and practices that give rise to pay differences are outlined below.

Demographic group differences in starting salaries are often a primary contributor to current salary disparities. A review of several organizations' starting salary policies reveals that demographic group differences in starting salaries are often caused by "rules" that govern new hires' salaries. For example, if starting salary offers cannot be more than, say, 10% higher than the candidate's last salary, and the affinity group hires have lower salaries in their most recent jobs than others, then the starting salaries of the affinity group will be lower than those of the nonaffinity group.

In some organizations, current pay disparities arise because the pay raises of one group have lagged behind the rates of increase for other groups. Even when annual percentage differences in pay are relatively small, such differences compound over time and may ultimately create disparities in current salaries, especially when this phenomenon is coupled with starting salary disparities. In some instances, one group receives smaller merit raises than another because their performance ratings are relatively low. When one group consistently receives lower ratings than another, an examination of the performance evaluation program is in order.

Demographic group differences in career paths to the current job explain current pay disparities in some organizations. For example, employees who "worked their way up" from nonexempt jobs to exempt positions tend to be paid less than other employees who entered the organization with an exempt job. In some organizations, this phenomenon is attributable to promotional pay increase guidelines such as "pay increases at the time of promotion are not to exceed 8% without executive approval."

Some pay disparities occur because employees who were recently hired into their current jobs are paid more than others who have considerable experience in the job. "Salary compression" is common in organizations in which internal percentage changes in pay have lagged behind rates of increase in the external market.

Employees who attained their current job via downgrades from higher level jobs are often paid more than otherwise similar employees in the same job. This disparity arises because the demoted employee's pay is not reduced at the time of the downgrade (although the employee's pay may have been "red-circled").

Career paths to the current job may explain demographic group pay differences when one group is more likely to have taken a given path to the job than another. When the available data do not permit the construction of variables that describe the amount and type of experience within the organization that the employee possesses, the analyst is not able to ferret out the portion of an observed pay difference that is attributable to group differences in career paths.

As these examples suggest, an organization that manages actual salaries has a better chance of avoiding pay disparities than one that manages percentage changes in pay. Organizations that set pay based on a review of the salaries of the employee's peers rather than using "guidelines" regarding percentage changes in pay are more likely to have an equitable compensation system than those who do otherwise.

Summary

Virtually all employers are required to comply with myriad laws and regulations prohibiting compensation discrimination. A variety of simple, as well as complex, methods have been used to measure pay differences and to assess compliance with legal requirements. The key to producing a meaningful pay analysis is to compare the pay of employees who are similarly situated in terms of the factors that legitimately influence pay. Pay disparities uncovered by "apples to oranges" rather than "apples to apples" comparisons may present a misleading picture.

Although appropriately specified and structured pay analyses provide valuable information about pay patterns in an organization, the analyst should be aware that no statistical technique can measure pay differences with absolute precision. As Judge Higginbotham stated in his *Vuyanich v Republican National Bank* opinion, even multiple regression analysis is "not a discrimination CAT scanner . . . ready to detect alien discrimination in corporate bodies." The statistical technique "may reveal shadows but its resolution is seldom more precise. Ultimately, the findings of fact . . . are not numerical products and sums but a human judgment that the facts found are more likely true than not true." Before drawing conclusions from pay studies, the analyst should do as much investigatory work as is feasible to assess the accuracy of the data and the completeness of the model and consider the practical significance as well as the statistical significance of the results.

Suggested Readings in Compensation Analysis

EEOC's Compliance Manual, Chapter 10: Compensation Discrimination, www.eeoc.gov/doc/compensation.html.

Haignere, L., Yangjing, L., Eisenberg, B., & McCarthy, J. (1996). *Pay checks: A guide to achieving salary equity in higher education.* Albany, NY: United University Professors. OFCCP's "Analyzing Compensation Data: A Guide to Three Approaches," www.dol.gov/esa/ regs/compliance/ofccp/compdata.html.

Paetzold, R. L., & Willborn, S. L. (1996). *The statistics of discrimination: Using statistical evidence in discrimination cases.* New York: Clark, Boardman Callaghan.

Palmer v. Schultz, 815 F.2d 84, 99 (D.C. Cir, 1987).

Rubinfeld, D. L. (1994). Reference guide on multiple regression. *Reference Manual on Scientific Evidence,* 416–469: Federal Judicial Center.

PART IV

Employee Effectiveness

CHAPTER 11

Conducting Training Evaluation

Miguel A. Quiñones

Scott Tonidandel

R ecent estimates suggest that organizations spend about $55 billion per year on formal training for their employees (Bassi & Van Buren, 1998). However, since many employees learn how to perform their jobs through informal training, this cost estimate is likely to be far below the true cost to organizations. Other estimates suggest that formal training expenditures typically amount to 1.81% of payroll, or around $649 per employee (Bassi & Van Buren, 1999). Approximately 70% of organizations surveyed by Bassi and Van Buren (1998) reported providing some sort of formal training.

The rapid adoption of new technologies accompanied with a shift in workforce demographics is placing an increased demand on organizations. These demands often require training interventions if organizations are to cope successfully. For example, recent moves by organizations to restructure the workplace around teams require that employees possess the ability to work with a diversity of team members. Increasing changes in the way work is done require that organizations maintain a flexible workforce with the capacity to adapt to increasingly complex problems as well as to generate solutions and strategies for dealing with this change. These and other changes in the increasingly global workplace will only serve to increase the demand for training and development.

Most of the training currently being conducted in organizations is focused on job-specific technical skills, management and supervisory skills, computer literacy and applications, occupational safety and compliance, and new employee orientation (Bassi & Van Buren, 1998). The survey by Bassi and Van Buren (1999) also found that most training is still being conducted with traditional classroom-based instructor-led methods. However, they project that the use of more advanced learning technologies will increase dramatically in the coming years. These technologies include computer-based training, intelligent tutoring systems, Web-based training, and virtual reality.

Even though organizations are spending large sums of money on training, less clear is the extent to which these dollars result in changes in the workplace. We do know that training evaluation is often not a top priority in organizations. When evaluations are conducted, they are often in the form of trainee reactions collected at the end of training (Ralphs & Stephen, 1986). In fact, less than 20% of companies surveyed by McMurrer, Van Buren, and Woodwell (2000) reported measuring behavioral and bottom line changes as a result of training. Clearly organizations would be better served if they could determine whether their large expenditures on training are achieving the desired result. It is the hope that this chapter will serve to demystify the training evaluation process and serve as a starting point for training professionals interested in improving the quality of their evaluation process.

Overview of Training Evaluation

Often the focus of most training interventions is on the method of delivery. For example, a number of organizations have begun to examine the Internet as a way of delivering training content to those in need of new skills (sometimes referred to as e-learning). It is difficult to question the appeal of training a large number of employees scattered throughout the world and on completely different schedules without the expense of airfare, lodging, and so on. However, this focus on using the latest "bells and whistles" means that evaluation is often a secondary concern (if it is even a concern at all). This is unfortunate because the barriers to conducting training evaluation can keep organizations from realizing the many benefits resulting from the evaluation process. As part of their plan to overcome these barriers, evaluation teams need to be able to express clearly why training evaluation should be performed.

Training evaluations are seldom carried out in organizations for many reasons. The top ones cited in a survey by Twitchell, Holton, and Trott (2000) were these: (a) evaluations not required by the organization, (b) cost, (c) lack of expertise, and (d) time (see also Grove & Ostroff, 1991). Another important reason is that training departments may be fearful of collecting data that might show their training programs to be ineffective (Kraiger, 2002). These barriers can appear daunting to trainers who are struggling just to maintain their current budgets while keeping up with the ever-increasing demand on their services. It is our hope that this chapter can break down some of these barriers and increase the use of training evaluation in organizations.

Organizations are more likely to require evaluations if they begin to look at training expenditures as investments rather than costs. Educating key organizational leaders on the linkages between an organization's strategy and its training and development activities can serve as a good starting point. If training is seen as one aspect of strategy implementation, key decision makers naturally would want to see evidence that it is having the desired effect. If organizations demand evaluations of other investments such as marketing, technology improvements, and new product lines, training should get the same level of scrutiny.

The cost of conducting training evaluations is often seen as the main barrier to their implementation. As the goal of most training efforts is to design and deliver the training program, the training program budget rarely includes money for evaluation. If money is allocated for evaluation, it is probably the first item that is slashed when the project needs to be scaled back or is over budget. In this chapter, we describe a number of relatively easy methods for conducting training evaluation that do not add a significant amount of money to the overall project. We suspect that the reason evaluation is perceived as being too costly is because it usually involves hiring outside experts to conduct the evaluation.

The perception that outside experts are needed to conduct evaluations is an outgrowth of the lack of evaluation expertise within organizations. This chapter should help to rectify this situation. Conducting solid evaluations that give meaningful information about the effectiveness of a training program does not require an advanced degree or highly sophisticated statistical knowledge. Some investment in time is required for evaluators to become familiar with the concepts presented here, but these concepts are well within the grasp of most training professionals.

The perception that a lot of time is required to evaluate a training program is also a key barrier. This perception needs to be tempered with the knowledge that the largest amount of time is usually spent designing, developing, and delivering the actual training program. It seems to us that spending a little bit of time to ensure that a much larger amount of time is not being wasted is not a tough trade-off to make. If development is done properly, most of the information needed to conduct a proper evaluation is collected during that phase. The amount of time needed to collect data from trainees and analyze it is minimal. In fact, one can usually capitalize on an existing process (e.g., performance management system) to collect some of the data necessary for evaluation.

Those who may be afraid of the outcome of an evaluation possibly misunderstand the purpose of training evaluations. Training design is a continuous process by which training needs are assessed, training programs are developed, and evaluations are conducted. The purpose of this evaluation is to be a feedback loop to training designers so they can make sure that the original goals of training are being met and suggest ways in which training could be improved. Information from evaluations should be used to ensure that limited resources are spent on the most effective approaches. This information should give training professionals the freedom to experiment and try out new methods and approaches. It can also be invaluable when they are arguing for a larger training budget. As most of us know, in these types of battles facts speak louder than words.

A Five-Step Model of Training Evaluation

The purpose of this chapter is to tear down some of these perceived barriers by presenting useful tools and five easy-to-follow steps that can be used to evaluate new or existing training programs. Our five steps are identifying training objectives, developing evaluation criteria, selecting an evaluation design, analyzing change data, and performing a utility analysis.

Step 1: Identify Training Objectives

Training programs are developed for a number of different reasons. Sometimes a manager wants a training intervention designed to deal with a specific problem employee. Organizations can often see training as a way of helping them make the transition to a new work structure (e.g., teams) or process (computer system or automation). Regardless of the original impetus, the first step in designing and evaluating a training program is to determine whether existing training objectives clearly spell out the goals of the program and they are up-to-date.

What Are Training Objectives and Why Do We Need Them?

Training objectives are statements specifying what trainees are expected to know or be able to do at the end of training that they could not do before. Clear and specific training objectives form the bedrock of evaluation. Without them, it would be impossible to know that the goals of training have been met.

Training objectives are typically derived from the data gathered during the needs assessment phase of training design. Although needs assessment methodologies vary, the basic goal is to identify the content of training. For example, needs assessment data can identify the tasks performed in a given job, the level of knowledge required to perform those tasks, and specific motivational or attitudinal characteristics that a person in that job must possess. From this information, the exact focus of the training program can be determined.

Three Components of Training Objectives

Training objectives must be clear and (most importantly) measurable to be effective. They must contain three basic components: a measurable and observable action, criteria for judging how well the action is being performed, and the conditions under which the action is performed.

The first component of a training objective specifies what exactly the trainee is expected to do. For example, a training objective such as "To gain an appreciation for safety in the workplace" does not provide any basis for deciding whether training has had an impact. How does an evaluator know when someone "has gained an appreciation for safety?" On the other hand, a training objective stating that trainees are expected to "Wear their safety goggles" can be easily evaluated by looking at the number of recent trainees who are wearing their goggles.

Box 11.1 Examples of Poor and Good Training Objectives

Poor Objectives

- Learn to use a word processing program
- Gain an appreciation for diversity
- Improve customer service
- Build teamwork skills
- Learn to build Web pages

Good Objectives

- Type a two-page business letter using Microsoft Word without the aid of the help feature.
- State five ways by which diversity helps improve organizational effectiveness.
- Greet customers with a polite smile and hello within 1 minute of their arrival.
- Identify the top three areas of expertise for each team member.
- Produce a Web page with three hyperlinks, two pictures, and one paragraph of text using HTML code.

The second component of training objectives specifies the level of performance expected of trainees. For example, are trainees expected to wear their safety goggles every time or just 80% of the time? Are they supposed to pass a safety knowledge test with a score of 75% or 100%? Similar levels of performance can be specified when others observe the trainees' actions. For example, a training objective could state that trainees are expected to receive favorable customer evaluations from at least 90% of the customers.

The third component describes the conditions under which the action is performed. For example, are trainees allowed to refer to the manual when demonstrating their ability to use a certain piece of software? In general, conditions refer to tools, reference materials, environmental interference (e.g., noise, busy hours), and facilities available or present when the observable behavior is performed. Box 11.1 presents some examples of poor and good training objectives for a variety of training domains.

Writing Training Objectives

The foundation of a good training objective is an action verb. Obviously, the type of action verb used depends on the type of change one expects from trainees. These can include cognitive, affective, and psychomotor changes. For example, cognitive changes would be associated with action verbs such as know, interpret, synthesize, evaluate, and recognize. Affective changes are typically demonstrated by behaviors such as showing an interest in certain activities, accepting individuals different from themselves, volunteering for certain assignments. Psychomotor changes are usually the easiest to specify most clearly because they involve actions such as performs, executes, operates, manipulates, and designs. For a more thorough discussion of training objectives, readers should consult Gagné, Briggs, and Wager (1992) or Mager (1984).

A final issue regarding training objectives concerns what may be best termed "level of specificity." As an example, consider a training program designed to reduce the amount of scrap generated at an assembly plant. A very clear training objective might state "Reduce the amount of scrap from 10% to 5% over the next 6 months." Many training programs are implemented to achieve organizationwide objectives such as increased sales, decreased accidents, or increased innovation, as examples. The difficulty with objectives of this type is that they do not make clear what a specific trainee is supposed to do to achieve the broader objective(s). We recommend that training developers identify the underlying individual behaviors that are related to broader outcomes and use these behaviors to derive training objectives.

Step 2: Develop Evaluation Criteria

Once the objectives of a training program are identified, the next step is to develop metrics or measures to determine whether its objectives have been accomplished. The importance of deriving practical, reliable, valid, unbiased criteria cannot be overstated. After providing information on the importance of good criteria, we give evaluation teams a review of Kirkpatrick's (1994) four levels of criteria as well as more recent evaluation criteria.

Importance of the Criteria

Perhaps the single most important thing to keep in mind when developing evaluation criteria is the old adage that states "What gets measured gets managed." Thus, measures that are convenient to gather but have no demonstrable linkage back to the training objectives can have a lot of undue influence on the perceived success of a training intervention. For example, measuring training success by counting the number of employees who sign up and attend training will likely lead to strong efforts to get the numbers up by offering a "flashy" class or serving lunch and other enticements. Obviously, there is nothing wrong with having employees actually show up for training. The point is that designing a very popular course tells you nothing about whether trainees show any behavioral change back on the job.

A number of criteria can be developed to measure the attainment of a particular training objective. For example, the training objective "knows safety procedures" can be assessed with a paper-and-pencil multiple choice test, a behavioral demonstration of safety procedures, and subsequent supervisor ratings of the former trainee's safety knowledge. Choosing the appropriate evaluation criteria is often a process of balancing the appropriateness of the measure vis-à-vis the training objective with more practical concerns such as time, money, and feasibility. We next discuss a couple of the more widely used evaluation measures.

Kirkpatrick's Levels

Perhaps the single most influential evaluation framework is Kirkpatrick's (e.g., 1994) four-level model. The framework specifies four levels of evaluation criteria that can be used for measuring a number of training objectives. Although much debate has surrounded the appropriate relationship among the various levels (cf. Kraiger, 2002), the framework remains as popular as ever among training practitioners.

The first level in Kirkpatrick's model is concerned with *reactions*—how well trainees liked the training program. The assumption is that if the program was well received, then learning occurred. Reaction measures are typically gathered by having trainees fill out a short questionnaire at the end of training (sometimes referred to as "happy sheets") measuring how well they thought the training was conducted. Reaction measures often separate out reactions regarding the trainer, the training content, and the setting for the training program.

Past research suggests that reactions are by far the most widely used measure of training evaluation (Van Buren, 2001). In fact, reactions are often the only evaluation measure used. This is unfortunate for many reasons. First, the goal of most training programs is not to entertain trainees. Thus, reactions are often far removed from the objectives of the training program. Of course, nobody would question that making sure trainees are satisfied with the quality of training is a good thing. The point is that reaction measures tell you little about the amount of learning and/or behavioral change that has taken place as a result of training.

Another related problem is that reaction measures tend to focus attention on superficial aspects of training at the expense of more important issues. Thus, a disproportionate amount of time may be concentrated on the refreshments to be served or the quality of the visual displays instead of increasing trainee motivation or making sure that the content of training matches the needs of the job.

Perhaps the most important reason for concern about trainee reactions is that trainees are likely to talk to other potential trainees about their experiences. Thus, satisfied trainees can serve a very valuable marketing function.

The second level of evaluation proposed by Kirkpatrick involves measuring the amount of *learning* that occurs as a result of training. Learning typically refers to the acquisition of facts, procedures, techniques, and other information and is often measured using paper-and-pencil knowledge tests. Other methods may include more hands-on demonstrations of knowledge such as picking out appropriate equipment or describing the steps involved in performing a task. Learning can also be measured using supervisory, peer, or self-ratings of knowledge acquisition.

Kirkpatrick's third level attempts to capture actual changes in trainees' job *behaviors*. Presumably, these changes become evident some time after training. Because it is often difficult to track down recent trainees and assess behavioral changes, this level of evaluation is seldom conducted. This is unfortunate because most training objectives are likely to be written in terms of expected behavioral changes back on the job. Behavioral assessments can take the form of observations of recent trainees, self and supervisory ratings or checklists of trained behaviors performed by the trainee, or performance in job simulations.

Often, the ultimate goal of training is to impact organizationwide objectives such as increased efficiency or decreased turnover. This level of evaluation attempts to focus on such results-oriented objectives. Some types of training programs more readily lend themselves to an evaluation of *results*. For example, to evaluate the results of a training program designed to impact the number of accidents, an evaluator can simply compare the frequency of accidents before and after the training program. However, the organizational impact of training on results like increased profit or improved efficiency are often very difficult to gauge because many other factors aside from training simultaneously affect these sorts of outcomes. As a result, training practitioners often focus only on the first two levels of Kirkpatrick's model. Despite the difficulties associated with measuring results, the last part of this chapter presents a methodology for trying to identify the economic impact of a training program on an organization's bottom line.

Additional Evaluation Criteria

The Kirkpatrick model has been widely adopted and represents a useful heuristic for conducting training evaluations. Recently, however, a number of researchers have begun to refine the model by identifying additional criteria that can be used to measure learning. The most notable of these recent models is one developed by Kraiger, Ford, and Salas (1993). In this model, the authors identify three aspects of learning that evaluations could target: cognitive, skill-based, and affective outcomes.

Typical measures of cognitive changes have targeted declarative knowledge and have employed measures such as multiple-choice tests of the content covered in training. However, Kraiger and his colleagues suggest that sometimes training programs are designed to influence knowledge organization or cognitive strategies. Knowledge organization refers to the way individuals perceive the interrelationships among a series of concepts. For instance, research suggests that experts tend to organize knowledge along functional lines (e.g., similar process) whereas novices use surface features to categorize knowledge. Researchers have shown that when trainees' knowledge structures more closely match those of the instructor, they tend to perform better in the class (Goldsmith & Johnson, 1990).

Cognitive strategies refer to the ways individuals utilize their knowledge to solve problems and their awareness of their level of skill relative to the demands of the task. This self-awareness is sometimes referred to as metacognition (e.g., Brown, 1975) and has been implicated in differences between novices and experts in a variety of domains. Individuals who have high metacognitive skills tend to learn more quickly and efficiently and are better at regulating their performance. These individuals not only learn but they also know how to learn.

Skill-based learning outcomes refer to the level of performance that a person is expected to achieve. For example, the objective of a training course may be to introduce trainees to a new skill. On the other hand, sometimes training is aimed at making a skill so overlearned that performance is automatic. For example, industrial plant operators, drivers, and store clerks would be expected to perform the basic functions of their jobs automatically. This would allow them to have excess attentional capacity to perform other tasks, such as interact with customers or plan out a driving route.

Sometimes the goal of training is to change a person's attitude or feelings. For example, orientation courses are often designed to build a sense of commitment or loyalty toward the organization. Training programs can also affect trainees' attitudes toward using a new piece of equipment or their level of motivation at work. For example, diversity training courses are often aimed at changing the way individuals perceive others who are different from themselves (e.g., Chrobot-Mason & Quiñones, 2002). Training has also been shown to influence a person's level of confidence in performing the learned tasks or self-efficacy. Trainees' self-efficacy levels can have an impact on their use of trained skills back in the workplace (Ford, Quiñones, Sego, & Sorra, 1992).

Matching Criteria to Training Objectives

Kirkpatrick's model, as well as the model of Kraiger and his colleagues (1993), presents a wide array of options for evaluating training. The key is to make sure that the specific criteria used match the objectives of the training program. For instance, it is not as useful to know that trainees learned the various definitions of diversity if the goal of training is to reduce the amount of intergroup conflict in work teams. Similarly, it would not be appropriate to expect huge increases in the bottom line from a training program designed to teach safety regulations. What is necessary is to very clearly outline the objective the training is to accomplish and then develop a criterion measure that taps into that objective. Box 11.2 presents some examples of criteria that would be appropriate for a number of training objectives.

Step 3: Select an Evaluation Design

The next step in evaluating the effectiveness of a training program requires choosing an evaluation design. A variety of designs are available that differ in terms of their experimental rigor and the feasibility with which they can be implemented in actual organizations. The following describes various designs available for training evaluation and discusses how one might choose an appropriate evaluation design. The final part of this section discusses practical limitations that evaluation teams might face in implementing an evaluation design.

Classical Experimental Designs

The designs described below vary in the extent to which they allow for firm conclusions to be made regarding the effectiveness of the training program that is being evaluated. The ultimate goal is to be able to say that any observed changes or

---

Box 11.2 Examples of Evaluation Criteria for a Variety of Training Objectives

---

Objective: Type a two-page business letter using Microsoft Word without the aid of the help feature.

Criterion: Typing test in which trainees are given some basic information to be included in a two-page letter. Performance is determined by the speed and accuracy in typing the letter.

Objective: State five ways by which diversity helps to improve organizational effectiveness.

Criterion: Paper-and-pencil test requiring trainees to list five ways in which diversity helps improve organizational effectiveness. The number of statements and the accuracy by which they represent the actual content of the course determines performance.

Objective: Greet customers with a polite smile and hello within 1 minute of their arrival.

Criterion: Observations of trainees in their workplace measuring the time taken to greet customers during a 1-hour period. The extent to which they were smiling would also be recorded.

Objective: Identify the top three areas of expertise for each team member.

Criterion: Group exercise in which team members are required to create a list of each member's areas of expertise. The number of areas of expertise listed per team member measures performance.

Objective: Produce a Web page with three hyperlinks, two pictures, and one paragraph of text using HTML code.

Criterion: Using only an HTML reference manual, trainees are required to create a Web page that links visitors to three specified sites and use two pictures and a paragraph of text provided. Performance is measured by the time used to create the site, the number of links that actually work, and the number of elements used in the final page (2 pictures and 1 paragraph).

---

differences in reactions, learning, behavior, or results are due to the training program and not something else (general learning, self-selection into the program, fatigue, some external event, etc.). The more stringent designs will allow for more definitive conclusions but they may be impractical for a given situation. Thus, evaluation requires one to balance the rigor of the design with the practical constraints of the situation to arrive at the best possible evaluation process for a given situation.

The *posttest only design* consists of a single group of employees who are assessed after completing the training program. Although this design may be useful to ensure that employees are able to perform at some minimum level of competency, the posttest only design provides little if any information regarding the effectiveness of the training program. Even if trainees perform well on the post-training assessment, one cannot determine whether the training program had any impact on trainees' experiences or the trainees themselves changed on the dimensions being assessed. Their performance may simply be a reflection of their previous skill level.

To investigate the amount of change that has taken place, the *pretest-posttest design* requires gathering data for the evaluation criteria (a) prior to participation in the training program and (b) one or more times after training is completed. The two measures can then be compared to see whether any change has occurred as a result of the training program. Despite the additional information afforded by this type of design, making conclusions regarding the effectiveness of the training program remains difficult. A number of alternative explanations, other than the training itself, may be responsible for any changes that are observed. For example, if sales volume increases after a training program, the increase could be due to a more favorable economic climate or a new product launch rather than a useful training program.

To rule out plausible alternative explanations for any changes that might be observed, the use of a control group is necessary. The *pretest-posttest control group design* requires that two groups of employees participate in the training evaluation; however, only one group of employees receives training. The second group does not receive any training but instead serves as a control group and is used for comparison purposes. Both groups are measured before and after the training program and comparisons are made regarding the change observed within the two groups. Typically, the two groups will have roughly equivalent scores on the pre-training measure. Then, if the training program is effective, the group that underwent the training should have higher post-training scores than the control group.

A crucial component of this latter type of design is randomly assigning employees to the two groups. Random assignment is important because it attempts to equalize the two groups along a variety of different dimensions such as their motivation, attitude, and abilities. If random assignment is employed, the only meaningful difference between the two groups should be whether the group received training; thus, any changes observed can be attributed to the training program. Without random assignment, preexisting differences between the groups could be responsible for any changes.

The *posttest only control group design* also requires two groups to conduct the evaluation. One group receives training while the other serves as a control, but only a single post-training measurement is taken. This design is useful if obtaining a pre-training measurement is impossible or if the presence of a pre-training measure could impact respondents. Similar to the previous design with a control group, differences between the two groups on the post-training measure are more meaningful when individuals are randomly assigned to groups. In fact, the lack of any pre-training assessment makes random assignment even more vital for this design.

Alternative Designs

Because organizational constraints can limit the applicability of experimental designs in applied settings, a need exists for alternative designs that are more feasible yet still allow appropriate inferences to be made about the effectiveness of a training program. One difficulty frequently faced by the training analyst is the inability to have a control group.

Under such conditions, a useful alternative design is the *internal referencing strategy* (IRS) (Haccoun & Hamtiaux, 1994). The IRS is similar to a single group pretest-posttest design, but more accurate inferences regarding the effectiveness of the training program can be made because of the unique structure of pre- and post-training measures. The evaluation instruments used in the IRS require that two different sets of items be included on both the pre- and post-training measures. One set of items reflects content to be covered in training. The second set of items is similar in content to the trained items, but the information needed to answer these items is never covered in the training program. To determine whether a training program is effective, one would examine the amount of change exhibited on these two separate sets of items. Evidence of effective training is demonstrated when trainees improve on the trained items but show little or no change on the untrained items. Essentially, the untrained items are serving as a control for the trained items. Note that the IRS design can fail to identify an effective training program under certain conditions. As a result, the IRS approach should supplement but not replace more thorough experimental designs. However, when organizational constraints hinder the viability of a control group, the IRS design is an attractive alternative.

Another design that also does not require a control group is the *rolling group design*. This design is often used when multiple groups of organizational participants are ultimately going to be exposed to the training program, but their exposure is staggered over time. The rolling group design is shown in Figure 11.1.

Using such a design, a group of individuals, who are eventually going to be trained, can serve as a control group until they too receive training. The time lag between groups is dependent on the length of the training program and the frequency with which it is offered. In most cases, the time period involved could be a matter of a few days to a couple of weeks. Training effectiveness is demonstrated when the change from pre-training to post-training is examined. Consistency of the effect across groups allows one to infer that this change is actually due to the training program.

Unequal assignment to training and control groups is another design strategy that will be useful in some training evaluation situations. This strategy, which will help minimize the cost of training evaluation, involves assigning a different number of participants to the training and control groups. For a given number of participants, the statistical power (i.e., likelihood) of identifying an effective training program is maximized when an equal number of participants are assigned to both the training and the control group. However, because training can be very expensive, a more cost-effective strategy may be to use a larger overall number of participants but assign fewer individuals to the training group and a larger number to the control group. Yang, Sackett, and Arvey (1996) presented formulas for determining the optimal ratios of control group size to training group size; the formulas incorporate the differential cost of participation in the training and control groups.

	Time				
	1	**2**	**3**	**4**	**5**
Group 1	Pre-measure	Training	Post-measure		
Group 2		Pre-measure	Training	Post-measure	
Group 3			Pre-measure	Training	Post-measure

Figure 11.1   The Rolling Group Design for Evaluating Training

Selecting an Optimum Design

In general, one should strive for the most rigorous evaluation possible. This typically requires having both pre- and post-training measures, having a control group, and randomly assigning individuals to groups. Unfortunately, in applied settings, a trade-off frequently exists between the quality of the design and the likelihood of implementation. One must often compromise between the most valid form of assessment and more practical issues such as the feasibility of using a control group, the cost of assessment, and the availability of participants. For example, although random assignment is preferred, the cost and logistics of supplying training to individuals instead of intact groups could be a real problem. Additionally, even with random assignment, the effectiveness of a training program could be underestimated because trained people could show untrained people the skills they have learned, thereby decreasing the difference between the training and control group. Also, in an applied setting, the use of a control group may have unintended consequences like affecting the satisfaction of control group members if they perceive that the training gives the other group a leg up on promotions, merit raises, and other organizational rewards.

Because of the difficulties associated with conducting a training evaluation in an applied setting, training analysts must consider these practical issues in their choice of design. Regardless of the design used, the training analysts need to be aware of each design's limitations and take steps necessary to minimize the disadvantages associated with less formal designs. For example, if random assignment is not possible one can examine personnel records or past performance data to look for meaningful differences between the training and control group. Or, if a control group is not available, the IRS can be used to provide some measure of control.

Despite the apparent superiority of the experimental designs, some organizational constraints may enhance the appropriateness of less rigorous designs. Consider an example in which only 20 individuals are available for a training evaluation study. Using a classic experimental design with a control group, 10 individuals would be assigned to the training group and 10 to the control group. With only 10 participants in each group, one's ability to conclude statistically that a training program is effective is severely limited by the small number of participants. In contrast, the IRS design can increase the likelihood of correctly identifying an effective training program because all 20 individuals would be assigned to the training group as opposed to only 10 in the experimental design. In summary, while more rigorous designs are usually preferable, organizational constraints may limit their applicability. Given that organizations need to make decisions about current and future training, alternative or less formal designs are better than no evaluation at all.

Step 4: Assess Change Due to Training

After a design is selected, data can be collected and the impact of the training program can be assessed. To give evaluation teams a greater feel for this step, we provide an illustrative example that highlights three types of analyses and then review considerations in choosing an analytic strategy.

An Illustrative Example

To understand the various procedures that can be used to analyze the data, we begin with an example and assume that a training evaluation study has been conducted using a pretest-posttest control group design. With such a design, three pieces of data are associated with each person in the evaluation: group membership (training or control), a pre-training score, and a post-training score.

In the context of this example, one analytical procedure is to examine differences between the two groups in terms of their *post-training scores only,* ignoring any pre-training information. An independent samples *t*-test could be computed to see whether the two groups differed on the post-training scores. The grouping variable serves as the independent variable, and the post-training score is the dependent variable. Obviously, this method of analysis is required if no pre-training data were collected. However, if pre-training data are available, other types of analyses are also options.

A second type of analysis, called *gain score analysis,* can be performed on the change from pre-training to post-training. To conduct this type of analysis, a gain score for each individual (the difference between their post-training score and their pre-training score) can be computed. Then differences between the trained and untrained groups in terms of their improvement over time can be evaluated, again using an independent sample *t*-test. Note a couple of important caveats concerning this type of analysis. First, the results obtained with gain score analysis will be identical to results obtained using repeated measures analysis of variance (ANOVA), so these two methods are interchangeable. Second, the gain score approach is based on the assumption that a perfect relationship exists between the pre- and post-training measures. To the extent this assumption is not met, the gain score approach will lack some precision. This will become more apparent after we introduce the next analytical approach, analysis of covariance (ANCOVA).

A third alternative to analyzing the present data is to perform an *analysis of covariance* using post-training scores as a dependent variable and pre-training scores as a covariate. As with the previous analytical strategies, group membership is the independent variable. Similar to the gain score approach, ANCOVA attempts to control for the effects of pre-training scores when post-training differences between groups are examined. However, unlike the gain score approach, pre-training scores are not given equal weight as post-training scores, but are instead weighted according to the correlation between the pre- and post-training measures. Thus, whereas the gain score approach assumed a perfect relationship between pre- and post-training measures, ANCOVA takes into account the actual observed relationship between the two.

Choosing an Analytic Strategy

Given the multiple alternatives to analyzing training evaluation data, which procedure should one use? Arvey and Cole (1989) performed a detailed evaluation of each of these procedures under a wide variety of conditions. They found that in virtually all circumstances, the ANCOVA approach was superior to both the posttest only approach and the gain score approach. Specifically, they found that the probability of identifying an effective training program was maximized with the ANCOVA procedure. When conducting training evaluations in organizations, the superiority of the ANCOVA procedure illustrates the importance of collecting pre-training information. Based on these results, whenever possible, posttest only designs should be avoided in favor of pretest-posttest designs.

Although the ANCOVA and gain score approaches take into account pre-training scores, the importance of random assignment has not diminished. Random assignment is still necessary because these procedures fail to control for other relevant variables. For example, although ANCOVA equates groups in terms of their pre-training scores, other important variables such as motivation were never equated. In addition, preexisting differences can never be perfectly controlled because the measures used are imperfect and contain error. As a result, large preexisting differences between groups could lead to improper adjustments and erroneous conclusions regarding the efficacy of a training program. Thus, under ideal conditions random assignment should still be incorporated in the training design regardless of the analytical strategy.

Step 5: Perform a Utility Analysis

The purpose of a utility analysis is to express the benefits of a training program in economic terms. One of the reasons that training professionals have a difficult time competing for resources is because they have trouble translating the impact of their programs into the same metric used by finance, marketing, or operations—namely, dollars. Utility analysis also shows whether the costs associated with developing and implementing a training program are outweighed by the benefits associated with increased productivity, reduced accidents, decreased turnover, or whatever the objectives of the training program happen to be. The details of utility analysis are far beyond the scope of this chapter. The reader is directed to Boudreau (1983) and Cascio (1980, 1987, 1989) for excellent and detailed descriptions of utility analysis. Below are the basic concepts and steps.

Calculating Training Program Costs

The first step in conducting a utility analysis is to calculate the costs associated with the training program. These costs are typically divided into the categories of course development, participants, instructors, and facilities (Mirabal, 1978). If training is outsourced, it is pretty straightforward to determine the costs of the program. If the program is developed in-house, all aspects of development should be taken into account including the time invested by internal staff, costs associated with any interviews or focus-groups with job experts, and needs assessment questionnaires. Other development costs may include handouts, practice equipment, video or CD production, and Web site development and maintenance.

Calculating Program Benefits

The most difficult aspect of calculating utility is determining the dollar value of the benefits associated with training. This calculation is virtually impossible to determine without the type of evaluation data described earlier. Two steps are typically employed to calculate benefit in dollar terms. First, the effect due to training is expressed in standard deviations (effect size or d-value) of the measure of interest (performance, accidents, etc.). For example, if after a customer service training course the trained groups receive an average customer evaluation of 7.5 (out of 10) compared to 5.7 for the untrained group and the standard deviation of all customer evaluations is 2.6, the d-value is calculated as follows:

$$d = \frac{7.5 - 5.7}{2.6} = .69$$

This means that the trained group received customer ratings that were .69 standard deviations higher than the untrained control group.

The second step involves calculating the monetary benefit of this type of increase in customer ratings. Assume that past figures show that every standard deviation difference in customer ratings translates to \$3,500 in sales per employee per year. This figure is often referred to as SD_y as it measures the dollar value associated with a standard deviation difference in the measure of interest. To calculate the overall gains from this customer service course, assume further that 50 employees have gone through the course. To calculate the expected utility due to the training course per year you would multiply the difference in customer ratings due to training by the SD_y and the number of trainees as follows:

$$\Delta U = 50(.69)(3,500) = \$120,750$$

This simplified example shows that this training course would result in an increase in sales of \$120,750 in the first year. It is often difficult to calculate the SD_y for a number of outcomes. For example, how does one put a dollar figure on the resulting increase in tolerance of others after completing a diversity training course? A thorough evaluation can provide some of the data necessary to begin estimating the economic impact of a training intervention.

Calculating the Utility of a Training Program

Utility is calculated by subtracting the training program costs from the training program benefits. A positive number suggests that the training program is a good investment. A negative utility indicates a program that may not be worth the money. The process of calculating utility is complicated by other considerations such as the discount rate and tax write-offs. Cascio (1989) presents a series of formulas that apply capital budgeting analysis to computations of utility.

Another consideration in calculating utility is that training improvements may show a decay over time. Thus, a computed benefit in a given year is not likely to continue into every year the trained employees remain in the company. On the other hand, trained employees are likely to pass along what they learned to untrained employees. This would lead to underestimating the true program utility. Despite these complications, a good faith estimate of utility is likely to go a long way toward justifying the true value of a training program.

Summary and Conclusions

Training is often viewed as an expense rather than an investment. Unfortunately, organizations often fail to evaluate their large training expenditures to get an idea of the effect they are having on organizational effectiveness. We have presented a five-step process of training evaluation that leads to more accurate and diagnostic evaluations. Evaluation should not be viewed as a final judgment on the overall worth of a training program but rather as an integral part of a process of continuous improvement. Evaluation data can be used to pinpoint areas of slippage between training and organizational outcomes. It may be that trainees actually learned the training content but failed to apply it when they returned to their workplace. This situation would suggest that the problem may not lie with the training program itself but with something at the workplace such as lack of peer and supervisor support or inadequate resources required to implement newly learned skills. The references presented at the end of this chapter should guide the interested reader to more detailed information on the many topics presented here. It is our hope that future surveys of training practices begin to show that more and more companies are utilizing training evaluations. Maybe this chapter can serve as a small step in that direction.

References

Arvey, R. D., & Cole, D. A. (1989). Evaluating change due to training. In I. L. Goldstein (Ed.), *Training and development in organizations.* San Francisco: Jossey-Bass.

Bassi, L. J., & Van Buren, M. E. (1998). The 1998 ASTD state of the industry report. *Training and Development, 52,* 21–43.

Bassi, L. J., & Van Buren, M. E. (1999). Sharpening the leading edge. *Training and Development, 53,* 23–33.

Boudreau, J. W. (1983). Economic considerations in estimating the utility of human resource productivity improvement programs. *Personnel Psychology, 36,* 551–576.

Brown, A. L. (1975). The development of memory: Knowing, knowing about knowing, and knowing how to know. In H. W. Reese (Ed.), *Advances in child development and behavior* (Vol. 10, pp. 103–152). San Diego, CA: Academic Press.

Cascio, W. F. (1980). Responding to the demand for accountability: A critical analysis of three utility models. *Organizational Behavior and Human Performance, 25,* 32–45.

Cascio, W.F. (1987). Costing human resources: The financial impact of behavior in organizations (2nd ed.). Boston, MA: Kent.

Cascio, W. F. (1989). Using utility analysis to assess training outcomes. In I. L Goldstein and Associates (Eds.), *Training and development in organizations* (pp. 63–88). San Francisco: Jossey-Bass.

Chrobot-Mason, D., & Quiñones, M. A. (2002). Training for a diverse workplace. In K. Kraiger (Ed.), *Creating, implementing, and managing effective training and development* (pp. 117–159). San Francisco: Jossey-Bass.

Ford, J. K., Quiñones, M. A., Sego, D., & Sorra, J. (1992). Factors affecting the opportunity to perform trained tasks on the job. *Personnel Psychology, 45,* 511–527.

Gagné, R. M., Briggs, L. J., & Wager, W. W. (1992). *Principles of instructional design* (4th ed.). Forth Worth, TX: Harcourt Brace Jovanovich.

Goldsmith, T. E., & Johnson, P. J. (1990). A structural assessment of classroom learning. In R. W. Schvaneveldt (Ed.), *Pathfinder associative networks: Studies in knowledge organization* (pp. 241–254). Norwood, NJ: Ablex.

Grove, D. A., & Ostroff, C. (1991). Program evaluation. In K. Wexley & J. Hinrichs (Eds.), *Developing human resources.* Washington, DC: BNA Books.

Haccoun, R. R., & Hamtiaux, T. (1994). Optimizing knowledge tests for inferring learning acquisition levels in single group training evaluation designs: The internal referencing strategy. *Personnel Psychology, 47,* 593–604.

Kirkpatrick, D. L. (1994). *Evaluating training programs: The four levels.* San Francisco: Berrett-Koehler.

Kraiger, K. (2002). Decision based evaluation. In K. Kraiger (Ed.), *Creating, implementing, and managing effective training and development* (pp. 331–375). San Francisco: Jossey-Bass.

Kraiger, K., Ford, J. K., & Salas, E. (1993). Applications of cognitive, skill-based, and affective theories of learning outcomes to new methods of training evaluation. *Journal of Applied Psychology, 78,* 311–328.

Mager, R. F. (1984). *Preparing instructional objectives* (2nd ed.). Belmont, CA: Pitman Learning.

McMurrer, D. P., Van Buren, M., & Woodwell, W. H. (2000). *The 2000 ASTD State of the Industry Report.* Alexandria, VA: American Society for Training and Development.

Mirabal, T. E. (1978). Forecasting future training costs. *Training and Development Journal, 32,* 78–87.

Ralphs, L. T., & Stephen, E. (1986). HRD in the Fortune 500. *Training and Development Journal, 40,* 69–76.

Twitchell, S., Holton, E. F., III, & Trott, J. W. (2000). Technical training evaluation practices in the United States. *Performance Improvement Quarterly, 13,* 84–109.

Van Buren, M. E. (2001). *State of the industry: Report 2001.* Washington, DC: American Society for Training and Development.

Yang, H., Sackett, P. R., & Arvey, R. D. (1996). Statistical power and cost in training evaluation: Some new considerations. *Personnel Psychology, 49,* 651–668.

Suggested Readings in Training

Gagné, R. M., Briggs, L. J., & Wager, W. W. (1992). *Principles of instructional design* (4th ed.). Fort Worth, TX: Harcourt Brace Jovanivich.

Goldstein, I. L. (1989). *Training and development in organizations.* San Francisco, CA: Jossey-Bass.

Goldstein, I. L., & Ford, J. K. (2002). *Training in organizations* (4th ed.). Belmont, CA: Wadsworth.

Kraiger, K. (2002). Creating, implementing, and managing effective training and development. San Francisco: Jossey-Bass.

Noe, R. A. (2002). *Employee training and development* (2nd ed.). New York: McGraw-Hill.

Quiñones, M. A., & Ehrenstein, A. (1997). *Training for a rapidly changing workplace.* Washington, DC: American Psychological Association.

CHAPTER 12

Succession Management

Michael M. Harris

Manuel London

William C. Byham

Marilyn Buckner

S uccession management may be defined simply as the process of identifying and preparing the right people for the right jobs at the right time. An important element of succession management is ensuring that the company has a pool of candidates ready to assume more responsible positions. This entails estimating future needs for executive talent, identifying candidates, assessing candidates to determine their development needs, establishing development goals, implementing development activities, and tracking learning and readiness for advancement. This is an ongoing, long-term process as managers move through the pool and as the needs of the company change. The focus is not on who is available now for advancement but rather on how many people are likely to be needed for a range of future higher level positions and whether the company will have experienced people ready for advancement when the positions need to be filled.

Although succession management is practiced in most large organizations, relatively little has been written on this topic, particularly from an evaluation perspective. An exception is a recent book by Byham, Smith, and Paese (2002), which described how organizations establish Acceleration Pools[SM] as a method of succession management. The thinking in this book serves as the foundation for this paper. Here, we review the elements of succession management and then focus on the evaluation of succession management programs.

What Is Succession Management?

Byham et al. (2002) defined an Acceleration Pool as "a systematic method for identifying and developing high-potential people to fill targeted levels of management (e.g., senior management, general management). Development of pool members is accelerated through stretch job and task force assignments that offer the best learning and highest-visibility opportunities" (p. 351).

The authors identified four phases of the acceleration pool process for management success:

1. *Nominating, identifying high potentials.* During this phase, managers nominate candidates, and an executive resource board screens them. The board makes the final decision on whom to select for the pool.

2. *Diagnosing development opportunities.* During this phase, the developmental needs of pool members are determined using an assessment center, 360-degree feedback surveys (including supervisor ratings of performance and self-assessment), cognitive tests, personality tests, or a psychological assessment. Assessment results are fed back to the pool members, perhaps with the benefit of coaching. A coach, mentor, or supervisor will help the pool member establish developmental priorities. Competencies for assessment and development include such positive characteristics as adaptability, building strategic relationships, building trust, change leadership, coaching, communicating with impact, cultural interpersonal effectiveness, customer orientation, delegation, financial acumen, energy, learning orientation, marketing and entrepreneurial insight, positive disposition, and team development. The assessment may also ensure that the candidates do not have negative characteristics such as aloofness, arrogance, dependence, distrust, low tolerance for ambiguity, passive aggressiveness, perfectionism, and volatility.

3. *Prescribing developmental activities.* During this phase, the executive resource board decides on a pool member's assignments, special training, or coaching. The board also begins the process of monitoring progress.

4. *Ensuring that development actually takes place and documenting development.* During this phase, pool members develop the needed behavior and knowledge through training and coaching. They apply the new behavior and knowledge in their assignment or a short-term project. Measures of development are obtained to (a) indicate changes in competencies that were targets for development, (b) demonstrate application of learned behaviors and knowledge (i.e., new behaviors were indeed tried), and (c) determine the effects of development on job performance. The developmental experiences and measures are incorporated into pool members' career development portfolios. The pool members meet with a manager and/or mentor to review their progress and set further developmental goals. Note that acceleration pool members manage their own destiny. They set and commit to developmental goals, learn and try new behaviors, and track their own development with an awareness of changes in competencies and areas needing further development. Managers, coaches, and mentors provide guidance, resources, and encouragement.

They help pool members to set clear, realistic, and measurable goals and conduct ongoing measurement. They offer implementation advice and assistance, including help with time management. In addition, they provide feedback and/or help pool members collect and interpret feedback.

5. *Reviewing progress and determining new assignments.* During this phase, the executive resource board audits pool members' progress and decides on a new/next assignment, going back to phase 3. This cycle (phases 3 through 5) continues as the pool member develops and eventually is promoted into positions of increasing responsibility, achieving the organizational level targeted by the pool, and perhaps entering a new pool for even higher level responsibility.

Methods for Evaluating Competencies

Pool members' competency levels can be evaluated in several ways. One method is to use the organization's performance appraisal system to determine employee strengths and weaknesses. The problem is that most of the performance appraisal systems used by organizations are affected by so many other factors that their accuracy is highly questionable. Such systems frequently suffer from problems of leniency, so they don't provide the needed data. A related issue is that individuals who are considered for an acceleration pool are likely to be above average performers to begin with, so the organization's standard performance rating system is unlikely to provide anything beyond uniformly high evaluations.

Another approach for assessing competencies is psychological testing. Although there are many different types of psychological tests, we briefly mention three major possibilities. The first two types, traditionally referred to as paper-and-pencil tests but now often administered over the Internet or through a computerized system, include cognitive ability measures and personality inventories. Cognitive measures evaluate basic skills, such as verbal and mathematical reasoning. Personality measures evaluate five primary traits, such as sociability, openness to new experience, and conscientiousness.

New leadership assessment tools have become available in the past few years as a result of research on what constitutes a successful manager or leader. These personality factors have helped succession planning practitioners better understand the predictors of high-potential managers. Two widely used instruments of this nature are the Hogan Leadership Potential and Leadership Challenge assessments. Unlike other assessments such as a 360-degree survey, these types of tools can be used as selection tools as well as developmental feedback tools. Considerable research with working adults has given many practitioners in Fortune 500 companies the ability to measure the leadership traits that are predictive of success (Hogan & Tett, 2002).

The Leadership Challenge tool is especially interesting in that it is the only proactive measure of derailment. Research on derailment has confirmed the importance of measuring factors that predict career failure and job performance ineffectiveness. Only one part of the story is a candidate's possessing the traits and competencies needed to be a high-potential or a good successor. In addition, it is important for a candidate not to possess many derailment factors. Therefore assessments of both successful traits and derailment factors are needed to fully understand a person's current and future performance. The administrative benefit of these type of instruments is that only the participant needs to complete the assessment, forgoing the administration issue of identifying raters, especially when assessing professionals who do not have direct reports (Hogan & Hogan, 2001). In summary, these new assessments offer the succession planning practitioner more accuracy and depth of information, therefore leading to more predictable and measurable results in succession planning programs.

For the succession planning practitioner in a global organization, recent research has shed more light on the characteristics needed to be a global manager and leader, and these traits are also based on the five primary personality traits. Studies have shown that indeed there is a significant relationship between the five personality traits and the skills necessary to be a successful global manager. These skills include cultural adaptability, international business knowledge, perspective-taking, and the ability to play the role of innovator in conditions of high global complexity.

Multisource (360-Degree) Feedback Surveys

An alternative method that has several advantages is a multisource feedback rating system (sometimes referred to as a 360-degree feedback system), in which individuals are rated by a variety of parties, including subordinates, peers, and supervisors regarding their competencies. Because such rating systems are designed for developmental purposes and because there is a greater degree of anonymity to the ratings compared to performance appraisals, a multisource feedback rating system can be highly useful for assessing strengths and weaknesses. Particularly hepful in a multisource feedback rating system is the fact that multiple parties provide ratings, and the raters have different opportunities to observe the individual at work, over a period of months if not years.

The 360-degree feedback system is generally a survey of behaviors that reflect performance on key competencies. It allows pool members to compare their self-perceptions with perceptions of other groups (direct reports, peers, supervisors, and customers). Ratings and comments are made anonymously to encourage honesty. The advantages of the surveys are that they are simple to administer, yield clear feedback reports, cover a wide array of observable leadership competencies, are available for validation against other standardized measures, provide a basis for clear communication about results, and encourage more frequent communication between the pool member and different rater groups.

Note that multisource feedback rating systems are not immune to shortcomings. One problem is that individuals can be assessed only on competencies that they have had a chance to demonstrate. If the individual has not yet had the opportunity to exhibit that competency, multisource feedback ratings become rather meaningless. A second problem is that multisource feedback rating systems may also be prone to many of the rating errors (e.g., leniency, halo) associated with administrative performance appraisal ratings, particularly if the respondents perceive that negative ratings may affect their relationship with the individual being rated.

Acceleration Centers[SM]

The third type of test is the assessment center. Sometimes referred to as simulation exercise or more recently, an Acceleration Center[SM] by Byham et al. (2002), the purpose of the assessment center is to provide an individual with a realistic context in which competencies can be demonstrated. Byham et al. (2002) defined an acceleration center as a "modern-day assessment center that uses professional assessors, highly realistic job simulations, and a wide variety of other assessment methodologies to accurately diagnose a person's appropriateness for a position as well as his or her development needs. Acceleration Centers compel prospective pool members to deal with issues and situations typical of general manager and executive positions" (p. 351).

Methods may include simulations, 360-degree surveys and interviews, personality inventories, cognitive ability tests, behavior-based interviews (focusing on work experiences related to competencies), and evaluation by a clinical psychologist who can conduct a psychological assessment. Consider a typical acceleration center process: Professional assessors and role players administer exercises and meetings in a "day-in-the-life" format. The exercises might include challenging decision-making tasks with information presented using multiple media (videos of meetings, e-mails, and telephone). Strategy exercises may require reviewing data and developing corporate strategy, a market vision, or another executive-level challenge. Pool members interact with role players, not fellow pool members. An assessor will usually conduct a behavior-based interview focusing on job experiences related to the key executive competencies. The pool members may also complete various cognitive tests and personality inventories as an adjunct to the simulation results. Behaviors are recorded by audio or videotape. Memos, e-mails, and notes made by pool members are collected. The assessors are assigned to work with pool members on different parts of the simulated day. The assessors review the information independently, organizing it by competencies. The assessors then share and discuss their findings and try to agree about the pool member's abilities and developmental needs. One assessor writes a concluding assessment summary report. The report is given to the pool members in one-on-one feedback and coaching sessions. The coach reviews trends in the data, indicates the need for additional information, and begins a list of development priorities. The executive summary of the assessment report or perhaps only the development priority list can be shared with the organization's executive resource board to shape development plans. The data can also be shared with the pool member's immediate supervisor and mentor.

The advantages of the assessment or Acceleration Center are that the simulations can be futuristic, realistic, and challenging. Multiple methods and professional assessors are used to collect the data. Because different assessors are involved in integrating the data, conclusions are derived from different perspectives. The method allows consistency and maintains quality across pool members and locations. Participation in an Acceleration Center is followed up by professional feedback and coaching.

Compared to multisource feedback rating systems, assessment centers offer several advantages. One major advantage is that the assessment center ratings are based on measuring a variety of competencies, including ones that may not yet have been demonstrated at work. Second, standardized exercises and rating scales are used. This ensures greater consistency and accuracy than multisource feedback rating systems may provide.

Assessment center ratings, of course, have some weaknesses compared to multisource feedback rating systems. Probably the biggest obstacle in their use is the cost. Because an assessment center is typically custom designed to assess a specific set of competencies and requires the presence of trained assessors, the expense may be high. However, it is likely to be no higher than the cost of attending a leadership development program. Second, assessment center performance may reflect more of what a person is *capable* of doing rather than what a person really *does* do. In other words, assessment center ratings reflect maximum performance, whereas multisource feedback ratings reflect *typical* performance. Third, questions have been raised as to exactly what assessment center exercises are measuring; there is reason to believe, in other words, that rather than assessing competencies, assessment centers are measuring performance in exercises. This constitutes a problem if the exercises are not closely related to the types of situations that will be encountered in the targeted jobs.

In short, there is no one best way to assess employee competency levels. Ideally, input is obtained from multiple sources to obtain the most complete picture, including an Acceleration Center and a 360-degree feedback survey. Finally, input from the individual is also valuable, particularly in determining interest in moving to a different position or a different location.

Providing Feedback to Pool Members

A key ingredient in setting development goals and tracking improvement is receiving feedback on assessment results and later performance. Pool members must know that they are in the pool of high potential managers and that they are targeted for development and, if successful, further advancement. Being a member of the pool does not guarantee promotion. Also, it doesn't guarantee placement in a particular assignment. The timing of the next promotion and the nature of the position will depend on organizational needs. Pool members cannot be targeted for specific jobs but rather for types of positions or organizational level.

A feedback session with the immediate supervisor, coach, or mentor is a time to review the assessment results and consider priorities for development. The feedback meeting is a time for the pool member to learn more about what positions he or she may fill, understand the purpose of the pool, provide an opportunity to prioritize development goals and activities, and discuss development alternatives.

Determining Appropriate Developmental Activities

An important step in the succession management process is determining appropriate developmental activities. Goals for development depend on both organizational needs for types of talent and the pool members' strengths and weaknesses. Byham et al. (2002) listed four means to develop individuals: (a) assignments, (b) short-term experiences, (c) training/executive education, and (d) professional coaching. In addition to the traditional training/executive education approach, there are many potential ways to develop potential successors. The competency of oral communications, for example, might be improved by having a person assume a one-year job as a trainer (assignment). Alternatively, individuals may improve their oral communications by being the "master of ceremonies" for a company-sponsored dinner (short-term experience). Each method has its own strengths and weaknesses. Development activities must be carefully planned if the trainee is to acquire the targeted competencies. Changing jobs may be more time-consuming and more challenging than attending a two-week seminar. On the other hand, the seminar may be more costly and less effective than moving to a job in which oral communication skills can be practiced and improved on a regular basis.

There are many ways to learn new skills or improve existing ones. What is most important is to design a developmental plan that will enable each pool member to achieve the necessary skill levels.

Succession management is the process of identifying managers who are capable of assuming key positions and preparing these managers for the positions using appropriate developmental experiences. Succession management involves more than just these processes, however. Included in succession management are issues such as deciding which employee to place in a new key role, determining whether to move an employee into a higher level position or hire an outsider and risk losing the employee, and learning how to avoid losing key employees.

Role of the CEO

Byham et al. (2002) emphasized that the success of a succession management program depends on the CEO or the top executive of the business unit. The CEO works closely with the senior executives of the organization to (a) establish desired succession outcomes, (b) demand measurement, (c) ensure alignment with key stakeholders (all the executives affected), (d) create a vision for the succession system and how it will operate, (e) establish the executive resource board, (f) ensure that the best people are nominated for the pool, (g) make succession management activities (e.g., executive resource board meetings) a priority, (h) personally coach senior managers to make decisions that will benefit pool members, (i) be a mentor for at least one pool member, (j) support the pool in all promotion decisions (be certain that pool members were considered for promotion decisions), (k) ensure that diversity goals are met, (l) meet one-on-one with pool members as often as possible, and (m) attend and participate in training events.

CEOs must remember that having a pool is not enough to ensure success. Continued follow-up is necessary from the top down. Also, the CEO must remember that short-term issues are not more important than long-term succession management. The system must be maintained (pool members identified, evaluated, developed, and promoted) even in tough economic times to guarantee that the organization will be ready to take advantage of emerging opportunities. The CEO cannot hope to know all pool members and should not consider only pool members he or she has observed personally. In addition, the CEO must guard against favoring individuals who mirror the CEO in educational background, early career experiences, and other characteristics. The CEO must be patient, allow pool members to learn from their mistakes, and recognize that pool members who handled past challenges successfully may not be automatically ready to handle new challenges (their competencies and development must be targeted to emerging job requirements).

Line Manager Involvement

To have an effective succession management process, both top managers and functional managers must be involved rather than just a representative from human resources. First, having top and line management involved in this process is helpful because it will give the program the credibility and commitment needed to be successful. Second, line manager involvement is essential for gaining input on recommended replacements and for the creation of realistic and meaningful development plans. Without such involvement, the value of the succession management process will be greatly reduced because you do not have commitment to such actions as stretch job assignments and taking pool members off the job for a task force assignment. Top and line management therefore must be active in all the subsequent steps described here and rewards must be defined and provided for active participation in succession management activities.

Identifying the Organizational Level to Be the Target of the Succession Management Process and the Current and Future Requirements

In this step of the succession management process, the organization must determine the organizational level that will be the focus of the succession management process. Usually the level is "general manager" or "strategic management." The job responsibilities and the operating environment of most jobs change too rapidly to allow targeting specific positions. In the past, specific jobs were targeted by succession plans, but today more organizations are focusing on job levels. The size of the organization may very well affect the target level chosen. Very large organizations can have more than one acceleration pool—for example, one pool for each SBU (strategic business unit).

Once the organizational level is identified, the competencies (e.g., skills, experiences) that are required for success in these positions must be determined. Simply identifying the competencies that are *currently* required is not sufficient; the competencies that will be required in the future should also be identified. Today's rapidly changing world means that jobs also experience changes in their requirements. In the utility business, for example, deregulation has forced much more emphasis on marketing as well as public relations skills than has been the case in the past. To focus solely on current requirements may lead to a successor who is not equipped for the job as it will exist when he or she assumes the position.

To identify current and future competencies required for successful performance, input is needed from a variety of parties, including other individuals currently in the position, employees to whom the position reports, and other subject matter experts.

Selection Decisions

Succession management differs from selection and promotion processes in that succession management has a strong developmental component and future orientation. Thus, the goal is not to identify current managers who are ready *now* to fill vacant positions; rather, the purpose is to identify pool members who will be able to fill them in the future on an "as needed" basis. Determining effective developmental activities and assignments that will enable the replacement to assume full responsibility for positions at the target level is therefore a major part of the succession management process.

Pool members need to be evaluated at least annually on their readiness for placement into a higher level position, that is, their growth on competencies, organizational knowledge, job experiences, and successful completion of the assignment. Also, each individual's motivational and personal needs should be considered.

Additional Considerations

Two other aspects to succession management deserve emphasis. First, succession management is an ongoing process. As such, each staffing decision affecting a potential successor must be carefully weighed and considered. For example, if one potential successor is offered a pool position, the effect on another potential successor of not being chosen for that position must be considered. Likewise, a high turnover rate among potential successors must be studied, and changes in compensation, staffing, and other human resource management processes must be reviewed.

Second, in some organizations, for a variety of both legal and business reasons, there may be a focus on identifying and developing women and minority employees for replacement opportunities. Toward that end, organizations have paid special attention to two key issues. One issue is to ensure that qualified women and minority candidates are represented adequately in the succession management process. Specifically, a number of stages may require special attention so that "glass ceiling" barriers are eliminated. Thus, it is important that women and minorities not be ignored when pool members are identified. A second key issue is that appropriate career development experiences must be identified and women and minority candidates must be encouraged to accept such positions, particularly when the positions may differ from those traditionally filled by women and minorities.

Evaluating Succession Management

Three basic types of measures may be used to evaluate succession management: process, reaction, and outcome measures. Examples of these measures are listed in Box 12.1. *Process* measures focus on *how* the succession management is performed. *Reaction* measures examine the perceptions, attitudes, and feelings of pool members, supervisors, coaches, and mentors about the program and its effects. *Outcome* measures refer to the effects of the succession management program on the organization. All three types of measures are needed over time as the program is evaluated and fine-tuned. We consider the application of these measures by reviewing an example of how a succession management program was established to meet the needs of the organization and how its success was tracked over time using data about process, reactions, and outcomes.

A Case Example

The following case example describes how an organization established a succession management program to meet its needs for senior-level managers and how it tracked the success of the program over time using process, reaction, and outcome measures. The case, a composite of several different corporate experiences, focuses on a telecommunications company we'll call APCO Industries. The case begins ten years ago when APCO, with 15,000 employees at the time, was rethinking its corporate strategy in light of changing business conditions in the industry in the United States and the world. Largely a domestic U.S. company, the firm was emerging from a large downsizing in response to a downturn in the economy and a glut of telecommunications services on the U.S. market. The CEO, C. J. Williams, realized that there was tremendous opportunity for opening new markets abroad, and that if APCO didn't act soon, foreign competitors would become industry leaders. However, since APCO's business had been largely confined to the United States, few current managers had experience doing business in other countries. Williams wondered about the skills a manager would need to succeed in a foreign culture and how APCO could find enough managers who would be familiar with the industry and their company and who would have the talent to grow the business in new markets around the globe. Also, would APCO have experienced managers who would be ready to assume top-level positions (heads of business units and leaders of joint ventures) in enterprises that were located in other countries or crossed cultural boundaries by integrating units in more than one country and culture? For

Box 12.1 Examples of Process, Reaction, and Outcome Measures

Process Measures

- Sizing the pool (number of pool members and growth rate of the pool) relative to current and anticipated organizational growth
- Percentage of nominated people selected for the pool
- Average time in the pool before promotion to level targeted by the pool
- Length of time executive positions are open before being filled
- Cross-unit movement
- Creation of developmental positions
- Moving pool members for developmental purposes
- Quality of people in the pool (job performance)
- Number of developmental assignments created for pool members
- Diversity of pool members (in gender, race, geographical region, function, business unit, educational background)
- Percentage of development objectives completed
- Quality of development help/follow-through on development help
- Number of meetings with mentors/coaches/supervisors
- Quantity and quality of feedback
- Learning (knowledge acquired, new behaviors learned) and learning applied

Reactions of Pool Members, Supervisors, Top Executives, and Mentors

- Satisfaction with development opportunities
- Giving development priority
- Motivation for development (to develop oneself/to support pool members' development)
- Satisfaction with development help received/given (e.g., satisfaction with feedback—feedback perceived as accurate and useful)
- Perceived improvements in performance
- Barriers to effective coaching/mentoring
- Perceived value in being a member in the pool
- Perceived return on investment from having the pool

Outcome Measures

- Retention of pool members (voluntary and involuntary turnover)
- Long-term performance of pool members compared to others
- Advancement of pool members (number promoted each year)
- Percentage of positions filled from outside the pool (from outside the organization or from managers not in the pool)
- Effects of learning and new behaviors implemented—changes in pool members' performance (360-degree survey results) over time

SOURCE: Adapted from Byham et al. (2002, Appendix 16–1, pp. 323–326).

instance, who could lead a new venture involving the parent company, a software subsidiary in Sweden, an equipment manufacturing plant in Malaysia, and a sales market throughout the Americas and Europe? Who would be ready to manage a billing operation in Ireland linked to a customer inquiry center in Wyoming? Given this new emerging corporate vision and business strategy, Williams realized that APCO's challenge was to estimate how many managers would be needed in 3, 5, and 10 years in middle and senior levels of management and then design methods to hire the managers when they were needed and/or develop current and recently hired high-potential managers.

For many years prior to this time, APCO had had a management development program. New hires, usually recent college graduates from the best schools, were selected for the program. The program rotated the managers through different line and staff positions every 9 to 18 months as they learned the business. This was an "up-or-out" program. Young managers who were not promoted one or two levels after the first four years were asked to leave. Current, experienced managers were not eligible for the program. The program stopped once the managers reached the first rungs of middle management (second or third level in the seven-level hierarchy). Also, given the company's recent downsizing (10% of its workforce), there were few opportunities for advancement into middle management. Fortunately, the firm was still able to attract the best graduates of the best schools because of the company's excellent reputation and the mild recession limiting opportunities elsewhere. Williams wanted to redirect and restructure the company's management development program. The target needed to be higher level middle and senior management positions. The focus would be a new set of management competencies and experiences with an emphasis on cultural sensitivity and cross-cultural job experiences. The number of managers in the program—an acceleration pool in Byham et al.'s (2002) terms—would be smaller, at least initially, because advancement opportunities would be slower at first. Current managers and new hires would be considered for the pool. The alternative was to hire senior people from outside the organization when needed, and there was no guarantee that mature people who knew the industry and had international experience would be available. The labor market would be highly competitive, if the economy picked up and the anticipated global opportunities developed. The best solution was to initiate a strong internal management development pool.

Williams took a direct interest in the program because he saw that the future of the company's new business strategy depended on having talented managers in senior-level assignments. At Williams's direction, the human resources vice president initiated a search for a "director of succession management" who would report directly to Williams. Mariana Burnham was selected for the position. She had a Ph.D. in organizational psychology, had taught for three years at INSEAD, a highly respected international school of business in France, spoke three languages (English, French, and German), and had spent seven years in the management development department of a multinational pharmaceutical company.

Williams named an executive resource board composed of the heads of all six business units, Williams, the human resources vice president, and Burnham. Burnham's first task was to conduct a "futures" job analysis. She interviewed Williams and other senior executives, including the executive resource board members, about their views of senior-level job requirements given current conditions and strategies for the future. She interviewed the few company executives who were in international assignments. She surveyed information about the industry, and she examined reports about managerial competencies in other firms with strong international businesses. Based on this information, Burnham drafted and then fine-tuned the following list of 13 key managerial competencies and definitions that became the company's management model for selection and development.

1. Strategic thinking—understanding the strategy of the business and setting goals in line with the vision

2. Decision making—readiness to make difficult decisions

3. Communication—generating commitment to the corporate vision and department goals

4. Work standards—high integrity and attention to quality

5. Resilience—ability to overcome barriers; persistence when the going gets tough

6. Openness to new experiences—willingness to understand and accept new ideas and try new experiences

7. Implementing change—ability to effect major organizational changes

8. Team building—developing effective one-on-one and group relationships

9. Cultural sensitivity—understanding and respecting differences

10. Coaching and developing others—supporting subordinates' career development

11. Self-understanding—awareness of one's own strengths and weaknesses

12. Self-development orientation—willingness to seek feedback; desire to enhance one's strengths and weaknesses

13. Knowledge of the business—understanding of key elements of APCO's businesses, including technology, operations, finance, and marketing perspectives

Working with the executive resource board, Burnham determined the approximate right size for the management development pool, which they named simply the APCO Leader Development Pool, referred to by its acronym, ALDP. They estimated that each business unit would need approximately 15 middle- and top-level managers for strategic assignments 3 to 7 years from that point—a total of 90 executive opportunities. Because the pool members would be groomed for management level rather than specific jobs, and thus be potential candidates for several different positions, Burnham and the board decided they would need about 120 pool members to give them the 3:1 selection ratio for each position they desired. Burnham asked each business unit head to nominate 30 managers, from whom they would choose approximately 20 from each unit. Because the units varied somewhat in size, some would have more, and some less. This was done to ensure a good distribution of managerial experience across the different parts of the business. However, Williams emphasized to the executive resource board that these people would be corporate resources. They would not stay in their units, nor would they necessarily be promoted to higher levels of responsibility within their business. Instead, they would be moved to different parts of the company as business needs changed and in relation to their career interests and development needs. Three small subcommittees of the executive resource board were established to review the nominees and make the initial choices. Annual reviews would be conducted of each pool member to assess progress. Also, new people would be added to the pool (and some current pool members asked to leave the program, but not necessarily their jobs) depending on their performance and continued demonstration of potential. A database of pool member information was produced for tracking. It was essentially an expanded personnel file with information about education, work experiences, assessments on the executive competencies, career interests, development goals, and development experiences.

The selected nominees were invited to participate in the program. They were told the purpose of the pool and the opportunities that it might open for them. They were also told they would be expected to move into new job assignments that would likely require relocating, including at least one assignment in another country. Once pool members agreed, they were assessed in several ways. Note that these assessments were conducted for developmental purposes, not evaluation to determine whether they should stay in the program. This alleviated some of the pressure of being assessed and focused the pool members' and executive resource board's attention on establishing development goals and activities.

Three assessment methods were used: (a) a background interview conducted by a clinical psychologist; (b) a 360-degree feedback survey that collected performance ratings from the pool members themselves and their subordinates, peers, supervisors, and customers; and (c) an acceleration center during which trained observers evaluated the pool members' performance in several business simulations. Then each pool member met with an executive coach to review the results and establish initial development goals and plans. Burnham and her staff of three professionals working with a consulting firm had identified a team of external psychologists and coaches to conduct the different components of the assessment.

Burnham met with the executive resource board subcommittees to track the results, goals, and development plans for each pool member. The board needed to sign off on each participant's list of development priorities and planned activities.

During the first 2 years of the ALDP, all the pool members were required to participate in the Business Development Project. This was Williams' brainchild, modeled after a process used by several other major companies. The project began with a 3-day meeting held at an off-site conference center. Williams led each session himself and at least two other members of the executive resource team attended each session. Burnham facilitated the meeting. Thirty pool members participated at a time. The session began with a half-day meeting during which Williams outlined his corporate strategies and held a question and answer session. Next, Burnham divided the participants into groups of five to seven members each. Each group was to formulate a project that would contribute to the corporate strategy. This was not an academic exercise but an actual project that would be reviewed, refined, and ultimately approved by Williams and then carried out by the team during the next 8 months. Williams met with each group periodically during that time. At the end of 8 months, the attendees met again with Williams for 3 days to review what they accomplished and learned. Projects included establishing new product lines, forming new ventures, and improving operations. Many of the projects continued long after the program was completed and some continued to grow and develop into major lines of business.

As each new group of pool members started the project, they were told about prior groups' projects that had been completed or were still under way. After three groups had been through the 3-day start of the program, the company bulletin published a feature story about the projects. This led to a quarterly project report that summarized and tracked the ongoing projects and highlighted their accomplishments and problems. This was circulated throughout the company, and all managers were able to benefit from the experience. Lessons learned, sometimes the hard way, included "listen to your customer," "learn the culture," "don't assume everyone thinks like you do," "people resist change at first no matter what," "double-check your figures," "costs change," "competitors enter the market more quickly than you expect," "don't promise more than you can deliver," "leaders create high-performing teams by building strong relationships with each team member individually," "don't be afraid to ask for feedback," and "listen to what others say are your strengths and weaknesses; you rarely see yourself as others see you."

From the start, Williams wanted to assess the effectiveness of the ADLP and the Business Development Project. If he was going to devote up to a third of his time during the next 2 to 3 years to succession management, working with the executive resource board and the project teams, he wanted to show his board of directors that the acceleration pool would have the intended impact in meeting future executive needs and put APCO ahead of its competitors in the labor market for executive talent. Also, he recognized that this was a long-term endeavor, and he wanted the data to track the benefits of the program over a long time horizon—3, 5, and 10 years out. Burnham agreed that comprehensive assessment was critical. She and Williams would have considerable anecdotal information about the pool members' experiences and feelings. This information could help improve the program, but without meaningful statistics that could be compared over time, she and Williams could not show the effects of management development over time and its value to the company.

Working with Williams and the executive resource board, Burnham developed measures they all agreed were important indicators of success. They included measures of process (how well the pool and the project were going), attitudes (pool members' perceptions of the value of the program), and outcomes (development goals achieved, areas of performance improved, and readiness to assume positions of increasing responsibility). The measures paralleled those listed in Box 12.1. Process measures tracked the size and changes in the pool over time. During the first year, the executive resource board approved 52% of the nominations. Once the purpose of the program and the criteria were clarified and nominating supervisors had a better understanding of the program, 80% to 85% of the nominations were approved. The pool grew from 40 members at the end of the first year and 60 members at the end of the second to 120 at the end of the fifth year. The pool leveled off and stayed at this level for many years.

The distribution of pool members tended to be proportionate to the size of the different business units. At first, all the nominations were from the U.S. offices. Burnham had to request nominations from the different locations around the world. Also, Burnham had to be proactive in requesting more nominations of women, African Americans, and Hispanic managers. She found that managers from these groups tended to be underrepresented in the company. She and the human resources vice president initiated an effort to hire more entry-level managers from these groups. They found that with persistent effort, the percentage of women managers in the company grew from 18% to 42% over 7 years, and the percentage of women in the ADLP grew from 12% the first year to 52% the fifth year, and remained at about half of all pool members. The proportion of people of color in the company and the program also grew over time.

Burnham tracked the development priorities and activities of the pool members. All pool members were interviewed by one of several psychologists, attended an acceleration center, completed a 360-degree survey, and worked with an executive coach to evaluate their results and set goals for development. The most common goals were interpersonal and intrapersonal. The first or second priority for 70% to 75% of the pool members during the first 5 years of the program dealt with improving relationships with others, most often subordinates. Fifty percent to 60% of the pool members recognized the need to learn more about themselves, especially to seek feedback from others regularly, setting this objective within their top five priorities. Other common priorities focused on building relationships with peers and customers and having experiences bringing about major organizational changes. Learning new technology was usually the fifth or sixth priority.

All pool members participated in the Business Development Project. Forty percent attended a weeklong development program run by one of two universities in the United States. During the first 3 years of the program, the pool members had an average of two temporary assignments and one job move requiring relocation. Half the job moves were to assignments in different business units, and a third were to jobs abroad. All pool members moving to another country attended a one-week cultural sensitivity workshop prior to their move. Burnham developed several surveys to tap the reactions of pool members, their supervisors, the executive resource board and other senior executives, and coaches/mentors. The surveys asked about satisfaction with different aspects of the program, including elements of the Business Development Project and developmental assignments. Surveys were administered annually. During the first 5 years of the program, 85% or more of the pool members were satisfied or extremely satisfied with the assessment and development activities, indicating a general positive feeling about the program and its components. Ninety percent or more were satisfied or extremely satisfied with their coach and stated they would select the same coach again. Thirty percent continued to contact the coach after they set their initial development goals. Sixty percent to

70% of the pool members were satisfied with their speed of advancement to their first target organizational level, suggesting a degree of impatience and the need to clarify expectations. This percentage improved somewhat over time as pool members were promoted. Virtually all (99%) of the pool members were satisfied or extremely satisfied with the amount of attention given to development. As an important note, even surveys of employees and managers not in the pool indicated that satisfaction with support for development increased over time, from 35% to 80% satisfied over 5 years. This indicated that the importance of, and attention to, development increased throughout the company as managers devoted increased resources to coaching and developing subordinates, in part, perhaps, as a spin-off of the ADLP. The annual survey of senior managers, including the executive resource board members, indicated that they perceived improvements in pool members' range of abilities and performance and their value to the company.

Results of annual 360-degree surveys and the company's formal performance appraisal indicated that pool members' performance improved each year and improved significantly more than that of managers in the company who were not in the pool. Thirty-seven percent of the pool members nominated during the first 2 years of the pool were promoted to their initial target level after 3 years. Sixty-two percent of the pool members nominated during the third to fifth year of the program were promoted to their initial target level after 3 years, and 78% were promoted after 5 years. Only 15% of vacancies at target levels of middle and senior management were filled from people outside the pool. Five percent of the pool members were taken out of the pool after 5 years without being promoted. Most of them left the company, although they all had the option to stay at their current organizational level with little chance of promotion. Eighty-two percent of the pool members remained with the company five years after being placed in the program, compared to a 75% retention rate of managers overall, and a typical 60% retention rate of managers in the industry. Clearly, the ADLP enhanced retention of the company's most talented managers, giving APCO a competitive advantage as the economy improved and the company grew.

During the first 3 years of the program, Williams continued his close involvement. He maintained his involvement later as well; however, other members of the executive resource board took turns leading the opening session of the Business Development Project. The industry blossomed and APCO grew to 70,000 employees worldwide in only 8 years. When the economy dipped at that point, Williams, now chairman of the board, sustained the level of managers in the pool, insisting that the APCO continue to invest in development of its most talented managers through thick and thin. In 2002, the number of pool members was pared back to just under 100, given a declining economic outlook and a glut of capacity and competition in the industry, but the substance of the program remained strong.

Conclusion

This chapter emphasized the importance of a succession management program in a growing company, described the components of such a program, and indicated how to evaluate it over time. The nature of a succession management program will depend on the needs of the organization. Clearly, the CEO must take a leadership role if the program is to succeed. Succession management is a top-down, not bottom-up, process. Management succession requires identifying managers with potential for advancement, providing assessment and coaching to help the managers in the pool establish development goals, and ensuring a range of developmental experiences. Given differences in organizational objectives, an organization's succession management policies and programs should be evaluated by whether the process is consistent, whether participants and other organizational members react positively, and whether the outcomes demonstrate that the program has the intended benefits. Evaluation is an ongoing process that demonstrates that the company's executive resource goals and the individual executives' goals for development and career advancement have been met.

References

Byham, W. C., Smith, A. B., & Paese, M J. (2002). *Grow your own leaders: How to identify, develop, and retain leadership talent.* Upper Saddle River, NJ: Financial Times-Prentice Hall.

Dalton, M., Ernst, C., Deal, J., & Leslie, J. (2002). *Success for the new global manager.* San Francisco: Jossey-Bass.

Hogan, R., & Hogan, J. (2001). Assessing leadership: A view from the dark side. *International Journal of Selection and Assessment, 9,* 1–12

Hogan, R., & Tett, R. (2002). Leadership personality. In R. Fernandez-Ballesteros (Ed.), *The encyclopedia of psychological assessment* (pp. 548–553). London: Sage.

Suggested Readings in Succession Management

Collins, J. C. (2001). *Good to great: Why some companies make the leap and others don't.* New York: HarperCollins.

McCall, M. W. (1997, August). *High flyers: Developing the next generation of leaders.* Boston, MA: Harvard Business School Publishing.

CHAPTER 13

A Practical Guide to Evaluating Coaching: Translating State-of-the-Art Techniques to the Real World

David B. Peterson

Kurt Kraiger

Our objective for this chapter is to provide a practical framework for examining the effectiveness and the value of organizational coaching programs. The principles we present apply to any type of coaching, although we primarily address one-on-one coaching provided by formally designated coaches charged with helping people gain insight, learn new skills, and improve on-the-job performance.

In an ideal world, the evaluation process is integrally connected to the implementation process, and both are driven by clear purpose and design. Reality, though, is quite a bit different. Kraiger (2002) summarized key factors that diminish the likelihood that any training and development program is evaluated. These factors, which also apply to the evaluation of coaching programs, include the additional costs associated with conducting the evaluation, the evaluator's lack of expertise in statistics or research methods, and a lack of time. In addition to these constraints, coaching may be even more difficult to evaluate because it is individually customized, shrouded in issues of confidentiality, delivered by a range of coaches who rarely follow standardized procedures, and frequently implemented piecemeal rather than systematically throughout the organization. Because of this last point, the typical evaluation process for coaching arises after the fact, when someone observes, "Hey, we're spending a lot of money on this. Let's find out what we're getting for that investment."

Further, the professional practice of coaching is still maturing. Leaders in the field are debating virtually every aspect of coaching, including the very definition itself (Kampa & White, 2002; Peterson & Hicks, 1999; West & Milan, 2001). This lack of consistency makes it essential that users of coaching understand how to evaluate the services they are receiving. This chapter therefore presents a hands-on, practical process for measuring the impact of coaching on the individual participants and on the organization. We begin with an overview of the research that has been conducted on coaching, move to a discussion of the major challenges and issues in evaluating coaching, and conclude with a step-by-step blueprint for designing your own evaluation process. Even though we present a systematic approach to the process, we understand the constraints that operate in most environments and so provide simple and quick options to suit a wide range of needs.

Research on Coaching

Coaching works. That much is simple. Based on dozens of case studies, hundreds of personal testimonials in scores of organizations, and diverse threads of research (Birkeland, Davis, Goff, Campbell, & Duke, 1997; Davis & Petchenik, 1998; Gegner, 1997; Kampa-Kokesch, 2001; McGovern et al., 2001; Peterson, 1993a, 1993b; Thompson, 1986; see also Bloom, 1984), it is clear that coaching has an impact on people and on business results. However, anyone who has worked in human resources (HR) for very long understands that answering the question of whether an intervention works by stating that it has been proven effective in other organizations may not be a sufficient answer. There are two reasons for this. The first is that executives often believe that the effectiveness of certain techniques varies from organization to organization. Therefore, you will want to read the rest of this chapter to learn how to design an evaluation that fits the coaching program in *your* organization. The second reason is that executives evaluate an intervention more broadly than just by its effectiveness or whether it worked (Boudreau & Ramstad, 2003). For many of them to be persuaded that HR programs support business goals, they also require evidence of the impact (did it make a strategic difference?) and efficiency (was it worth the cost?) of the intervention (Boudreau & Ramstad, 2003). Therefore, you will also want to read the rest of the chapter to learn how to conduct evaluations that address the effectiveness, impact, and efficiency of coaching programs.

For now, when we say that coaching works, we are commenting on its *effectiveness* as a method for helping people improve their performance in areas of leadership, communication, interpersonal, and cognitive skills (Peterson, 1993b). Similar to return on investment (ROI), impact and efficiency can only be measured in context, since they depend on the strategic value of improving a specific capability (impact) and the value of a specific person's time (efficiency). This point is discussed in more detail below.

With that in mind, consider the coaching research that has been done. Thompson (1986) is the earliest known study examining behavior change in actual coaching participants. His chief findings, based on 150 managers and executives from a range of organizations, were that participants' bosses reported significant behavior changes due to coaching and that those changes lasted for at least 1 to 2 years following the coaching engagement.

Peterson (1993a, 1993b) studied 370 coaching participants, finding an average effect size of 1.56 or greater on specific learning objectives as rated by participant, manager, and coach. That is, coaching produced an average change of at least 1.56 standard deviation units, roughly the equivalent of moving from the 50th percentile to the 93rd percentile of performance. These results compare favorably to the average effect size of approximately 0.45 reported by Burke and Day (1986) in their meta-analysis of management training and development programs. Based on this comparison, a case can be made that coaching is at least three times more effective than the typical training program in producing results.[1] In addition to measuring improvement on specific coaching objectives (i.e., effectiveness), Peterson obtained measures of overall job performance (i.e., impact). Both boss and participant ratings showed an increase in effect size of .08 or greater for overall performance, indicating substantial incremental value to the organization. These gains were still evident 1 to 2 years after the completion of coaching (Peterson, 1993b).

In 1997, AMOCO Corporation (now part of British Petroleum (BP) conducted a historical evaluation of the coaching they had offered to their executives over the preceding 10 years (Birkeland et al., 1997; Davis & Petchenik, 1998). Noting the problematic nature of this type of research (e.g., poor performers and participants with negative coaching outcomes may have left the organization by the time of the follow-up survey), the authors concluded that "caution should be taken before placing too much stock in any single piece of evidence that was presented. However, throughout the study, the results *consistently* suggested that coaching facilitates the development of skills which positively affects both the individual participant and the overall organization. It is this consistency in results which enables us to reach the conclusion that the individual coaching program has been a valuable investment for AMOCO" (Birkeland et al., 1997, p. 15).

Compared to other AMOCO managers, coaching participants consistently demonstrated improved performance, increased ratings of potential for advancement and 50% higher average salary increases. Also important, participants themselves attributed these results directly to the coaching they had received.

McGovern et al. (2001) conducted one of the first studies to look exclusively at the impact of coaching, examining 100 mid- to senior-level managers at large organizations who participated in coaching. They estimated their coaching to be worth 5.7 times the initial investment, based on a conservative formula for estimating ROI developed by Phillips (1997). Organizational benefits from coaching included better productivity (reported by 53% of participants), quality (48%), organizational strength (48%), customer service (39%), and retention (32%). They also cited improvements in cost reduction (23%) and profitability (22%). Among personal benefits, they reported improved relationships with direct reports (77%) and peers (63%), better teamwork (67%), and increased job satisfaction (61%).

In conclusion, these and other studies (summarized in Kampa & White, 2002; Kampa-Kokesch & Anderson, 2001) provide substantial evidence that well-designed coaching makes a meaningful difference in skill learning, job performance, and organizational results. Nonetheless, we advise caution in generalizing these results— the term *coaching* is used to represent an extensive range of services, and it is doubtful that all providers of coaching will yield comparable results (Kampa & White, 2002; Peterson & Hicks, 1999). In fact, there are examples showing that coaching has not been an effective intervention. One theme in these examples is utilizing a coach who relies primarily on just one methodology for coaching (e.g., 360-degree feedback or other insight-oriented approaches) and does not guide participants through the full development process (see Peterson, 2002, for a more detailed treatment of the necessary conditions for learning). Even when the coaching is well designed and participants are carefully screened, coaching may fall short. Although the average change reported in Peterson (1993b) is substantial, two of the 370 participants did not show any measurable improvement. A final concern is that few studies have connected coaching outcomes to objective measures; virtually all research has been based on self-report and observer ratings. Therefore, it is essential for organizations to conduct some type of evaluation to ensure that coaching is meeting their needs.

Challenges and Issues in Evaluating Coaching

Although research evidence shows that coaching works, these studies also illustrate many of the challenges of conducting quality evaluations of coaching. In this section, we highlight three critical issues in evaluating coaching; in the final section, we lay out a step-by-step process for designing evaluations. In addressing these issues, we draw on existing theory and methods of evaluation in training and organizational development (e.g., Kraiger, 2002; Martineau & Preskill, 2002), previous evaluation research on coaching, and our own experiences working with a variety of organizations.

Purpose

The first challenge in evaluating coaching is determining the purpose: What questions need to be answered and what decisions need to be made? Because evaluation may consume financial resources and participants' time, it should be undertaken with a clear understanding of what is to be learned from the evaluation. Yet more often than not, it is our experience that organizations do not clearly think through the consequences or benefits of evaluation before initiating such efforts. It is said that the unaimed arrow never misses its mark, but in modern organizations, that archer will not get a second chance to shoot.

Kraiger (2002) suggested three primary purposes for evaluation:

1. *Decision Making:* Using evaluation outcomes to change the status of a coaching program, its participants, or its coaches (e.g., continue, expand, or scale back a program, or reassign a coach)
2. *Improvement:* Providing evaluation outcomes to coaches or participants in order to have a positive impact on their participation or to improve the process they are following (e.g., indicate the need for more frequent meetings)
3. *Marketing:* Using evaluation outcomes to encourage adoption of a coaching program by a new organization, garner senior management support, or encourage potential participants to enroll

Deciding on the purpose for evaluation will help to ensure that the right information is collected. For example, if the purpose is to evaluate the quality of the coaches, you will formulate different questions depending on whether you are interested in making decisions about who to use, sharing feedback to improve the quality of their work, or marketing their results to others. For obvious reasons, it is important to consider the needs and preferences of the stakeholders, such as executive decision makers, sponsors of the coaching program, coaches, or potential coaching participants, who will use the data that are collected (Martineau & Preskill, 2002).

Design

The second issue is choosing an appropriate research design. In our experience, even though many of the managers and executives who see evaluation results lack formal research and statistical skills, they are adept at generating alternative explanations for observed effects (e.g., speculating that increased productivity could be due not to coaching but to seasonal variations or staffing changes). Therefore, one of the best strategies for improving the quality of coaching evaluations is to develop a sound research design that minimizes the possibility of alternative explanations.

Thoughtful design makes positive outcomes more compelling. Suppose that a group of 10 newly promoted executives all received coaching for 9 months. At the end of this period, these executives reported an average improvement of 50% in their "sensitivity to the needs of others" and a 40% increase in their "capacity to see the big picture" when making decisions. Although this evidence appears to reflect positively on the coaching program, an obvious counter argument can be made—how do we know that these executives did not develop naturally (on their own) without any benefits from coaching, perhaps because the promotion itself stimulated their development?

Had the organization included a control group—a matched set of executives who were promoted but did not attend training—it would be in a better position to isolate the benefits of coaching. Sometimes such control groups may occur naturally in an organization. However, in other situations, withholding treatment can be unreasonable for political and ethical reasons.

The use of pretest or baseline data is another effective strategy for establishing a context for performance improvement. For example, if the subordinates of our 10 executives rated the interpersonal skills of their bosses as "very effective," this evidence is more persuasive if we know that the same subordinates rated the same bosses as "ineffective" just weeks before the coaching began. However, pretest data may not be available in all evaluations, such as when the need to evaluate occurs *after* the coaching has begun.

When the use of a control group and/or pretest data is not possible, an effective alternative is to use evaluation items as a control (Haccoun & Hamtiaux, 1994). Peterson (1993b) provides an example of this strategy. Two sets of items are used to evaluate the outcome of coaching: Items that measure skills targeted by coaching (e.g., interpersonal skills) are compared with items that measure managerial skills not targeted by coaching (e.g., financial management skills). Both sets of items can be evaluated by ratings or objective performance indices if available. Data showing that coaching-related items improved significantly more than non-coaching items would be strong evidence for the effectiveness of coaching (Haccoun & Hamtiaux, 1994; Peterson, 1993a). In Peterson's (1993b) study, control items in fact showed no significant change when measured at the completion of coaching or at follow-up 1 to 2 years later. This technique can be used even after coaching has been completed, or whenever only post-coaching rating data can be collected. By rating participants on the amount of improvement they have demonstrated, using both sets of items, you can calculate the effect due to coaching.

Thoughtful design consists of anticipating alternative explanations for outcomes and providing a means for rationally arguing whether coaching was the most plausible explanation for the observed effects. As McLinden (1995) noted, organizational decision makers do not expect research to *prove* that a program works but to provide reasonable evidence that the program *could be responsible*. Over time, following a well-designed evaluation process, consistent evidence of improvement from a variety of participants under a variety of conditions can build solid support for the coaching program.

Return on Investment and the Impact of Coaching

This leads into the third challenge: how to show whether coaching makes a difference. Questions about ROI are frequently asked by HR professionals interested in proving to line managers that investments in coaching are worthwhile. Even though it is tempting to cite McGovern et al. (2001) and give a single numerical answer to the question, it is essential to realize that ROI (and any measure of impact) is context specific. For example, using coaching to help leaders in two different organizations improve their ability to think strategically may cost the same (efficiency) and produce the same level of learning (effectiveness) and yet have negligible bottom line impact in one organization and huge impact in the other. These seemingly conflicting results occur simply because the relative importance of strategic thinking to each organization's success is different. For that reason, it is impossible to derive a universally applicable number for "the ROI of coaching."

Although there are methods for estimating the economic value of new behaviors and relating these to program costs (see Cascio, 1982; Phillips, 1997), the most compelling support for coaching comes from analysis of the business impact, effectiveness, and efficiency of the program (Boudreau & Ramstad, 2003).

To understand the potential business impact, you might ask questions such as these: Where does lack of talent limit our ability to achieve strategic business objectives? What skills are most critical to business success, and which of these are in shortest supply? Where would improvement in the organization's talent have the greatest impact on success? It is also crucial to ask about the relative value of the impact, such as, How much would it be worth to achieve that improvement in talent? For example, say the critical issue for senior leadership is the lack of general managers who can think strategically and provide decisive leadership in times of constant change. Senior executives tell you that an effective leader in that role is worth twice what a mediocre leader is worth. If the typical salary in that role is $100,000, it is not unreasonable to contemplate a $50,000 per person investment for the intervention. Getting executives to appraise the value of a performance improvement is one of the keys to determining ROI.

Second, to examine effectiveness, consider the range of solutions (including coaching) that are available for each skill/performance area identified. How effective is each possible solution in generating improvement for that skill? As a broad generality, it is reasonable to say that to produce measurable improvements in performance, coaching is more effective than classroom training, which is more effective than reading a book. Of course, coaching can easily be more expensive than group training, which in turn is generally more expensive than reading a book. Keep in mind that ROI is a function of inputs (investment) as well as outcomes (return), so all costs need to be taken into account, including administrative support and the participant's time. In many instances, the opportunity cost of an executive's time is higher than the actual dollar cost of the book they are reading, or even the training or coaching program they are participating in. In our example, the key question is whether any of these solutions is capable of taking a general manager with mediocre strategic and leadership skills and turning him or her into a strong leader.

Finally, to examine efficiency and arrive at a determination of ROI, consider how to allocate resources optimally to accomplish key objectives. This is a function of the amount of change that is necessary and the financial and nonfinancial cost of the intervention. If only small changes are necessary, less costly and less powerful solutions (such as 360-degree feedback, on-the-job experience, peer coaching, books, or Web-based resources) might be sufficient. When dramatic, rapid change is essential, a powerful solution such as coaching may be the only satisfactory option. At this point, it is appropriate to choose the cheapest solution that can generate the desired amount of change. In our example, coaching could be recommended as long as the total financial and nonfinancial costs (including administration and the manager's time) are under $50,000 per person. The low-cost option of reading a book is unlikely to transform managers into strategic leaders, so even though it is cheap, the ROI in this hypothetical example is virtually zero.

The real question is not what is the ROI of coaching, but what solution is sufficiently effective at the lowest cost to accomplish the objective, whether that is coaching, a book, or a Web-based program. Too many conversations start from the wrong direction, with questions such as these: How do we justify the amount of money we are spending on coaching? Are we getting our money's worth? Searching for ROI is often an attempt to justify a decision that's already been made. Advocates of particular solutions, such as coaching, lose credibility with line executives when they cannot provide the necessary evidence of the program's value. In contrast, credibility comes from starting with the needs of the business and finding useful solutions. Given the type of capabilities we need for our business, what solution produces the change we need at a reasonable cost? This puts the onus on business leaders to determine the value of the need and places HR in the critical role of providing cost-effective solutions.

A Practical Guide to Evaluating Coaching

The previous section of this chapter discusses some of the challenges and issues in planning and conducting an evaluation of coaching programs. This section presents a practical, hands-on approach to evaluation. The key points in this section are summarized in Figure 13.1.

Step 1: Lay the Foundation

As can be seen in Figure 13.1, there are five steps to planning and conducting a successful evaluation of any coaching program. Step 1 sets the stage for an effective evaluation by thinking through the purposes, resources, and challenges of evaluation. Ideally, the evaluation process is designed in tandem with the design of the coaching process. However, the guide presented here can be followed regardless of whether evaluation is sought before, during, or after the coaching has taken place.

First, decide on the purpose for conducting the evaluation. Consider not only the immediate needs, but future needs as well. Well-done evaluations are relatively rare, so consider whether there is a way to leverage the evaluation to meet secondary or future needs related to decision making, marketing, and improvement. For example, the primary purpose of the evaluation may be to provide cost-effectiveness data in the event of anticipated budget cuts, but consider how additional data collected during the evaluation may provide useful feedback to coaches or participants. Explain the purpose to everyone you talk with while planning and conducting these evaluations to refine your focus and to obtain their buy-in. We are aware that HR is occasionally given a mandate by senior management to evaluate a

Evaluation Process Checklist

Step 1: Lay the foundation

 ❑ Decide on the purpose for evaluation
  – Improvement
  – Decision making
  – Marketing

 ❑ Identify the audience for evaluation results
  – Coaches
  – Potential/future coaches
  – Participants
  – Potential/future participants
  – Stakeholders and decision makers

 ❑ Marshal resources for evaluation
  – Financial resources
  – Personnel resources
  – Time resources

 ❑ Anticipate and plan for obstacles
  – Resource-based
  – Motivational
  – Design-based

 ❑ Anticipate and plan for cultural, diversity, and language issues

Step 2: Design the process

 ❑ Choose raters
  – Coaches, participants, bosses, subordinates, peers, customers
  – Other stakeholders

 ❑ Design content for evaluation
  – Coaching objectives for each individual (individually customized and/or common items)
  – Targeted organizational objectives for coaching
  – Aspects of the coaching process and the coach
  – Suggestions for improving the process

 ❑ Choose response scales
  – Yes/no
  – Agree/disagree
  – Current effectiveness
  – Level of improvement
  – Current vs. desired performance

 ❑ Determine data collection process
 ❑ Design evaluation
  – Pretest/posttest options
  – Control/comparison group
  – Item-level controls

Figure 13.1 Evaluation Process Checklist

Step 3: Implement the process

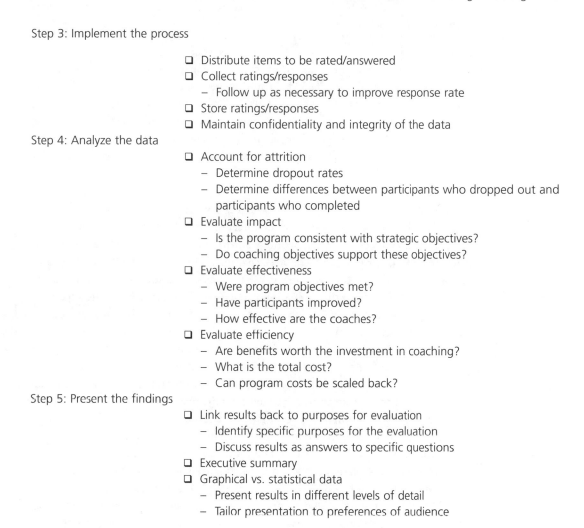

- ❑ Distribute items to be rated/answered
- ❑ Collect ratings/responses
  - – Follow up as necessary to improve response rate
- ❑ Store ratings/responses
- ❑ Maintain confidentiality and integrity of the data

Step 4: Analyze the data

- ❑ Account for attrition
  - – Determine dropout rates
  - – Determine differences between participants who dropped out and participants who completed
- ❑ Evaluate impact
  - – Is the program consistent with strategic objectives?
  - – Do coaching objectives support these objectives?
- ❑ Evaluate effectiveness
  - – Were program objectives met?
  - – Have participants improved?
  - – How effective are the coaches?
- ❑ Evaluate efficiency
  - – Are benefits worth the investment in coaching?
  - – What is the total cost?
  - – Can program costs be scaled back?

Step 5: Present the findings

- ❑ Link results back to purposes for evaluation
  - – Identify specific purposes for the evaluation
  - – Discuss results as answers to specific questions
- ❑ Executive summary
- ❑ Graphical vs. statistical data
  - – Present results in different levels of detail
  - – Tailor presentation to preferences of audience

Figure 13.1   Evaluation Process Checklist

program; it is even possible that such a directive may arrive without a clearly articulated purpose or goal. In such cases, you will often have to play a consultative role in helping senior management clarify exactly what they are trying to accomplish. Be assured that your efforts will be rewarded when you present the results of the evaluation.

Two general questions prompt many of the evaluation efforts around coaching:

1. Does coaching really work? Here, the real question is almost always, Will coaching work in our organization, with our people, to give us the results that we need?
2. Are we getting our money's worth? What's the ROI of coaching in our organization?

Other reasons to conduct evaluation include improving the organization's coaching process (examining factors such as coach and participant selection, coach-participant matching, organizational and managerial support, environmental and organizational obstacles), determining the best pool of coaches for the organization's needs (areas of expertise, knowledge of the organization, cultural fit, perceived credibility by potential participants, etc.), and improving the success rate of those selected to participate in coaching (personal motivation, purpose, organizational support, etc.). For best practices and other important aspects to consider in designing and evaluating a coaching program, see Executive Coaching Forum (2001) and Peterson (2002).

Second, determine the various audiences for the results of the evaluation. Consider who will see the results of the intervention and the type of evidence they require. Will coaches and participants want to know how well they are doing or how effective the program is? Are there champions for coaching within the organization or sponsors for the evaluation? What other stakeholders or decision makers will want to know about the evaluation results? How can evidence of the success of the program be used to enhance the participation of future coaches or participants? As you make decisions about the intended audiences for the evaluation, you will want to understand what they hope to learn from the evaluation and involve them in the evaluation planning process. A belief persists that top executives are primarily influenced by evidence of financial impact such as shareholder value (e.g., Pfau & Kay, 2002); however, an alternative view (Boudreau & Ramstad, 2003; McLinden, 1995) is that organizational decision makers are responsive to logical evidence that HR practices are done well and are logically related to key business objectives.

Third, ensure that there are adequate resources for the evaluation. Presumably, some thought has already been given to the financial and administrative resources required to carry out the evaluation. However, consider the impact on those involved in the program. Will participants or coaches be required to complete multiple and/or lengthy rating forms? Will 360-degree appraisals be given to peers or subordinates of participants? Who else will provide data and how much time will be required to do so? Make sure your expectations are realistic by discussing them with representatives of all who will be involved in data collection.

Fourth, anticipate obstacles you may encounter regarding either conducting the evaluation or presenting the findings. Will you have limited time or access to collect data from coaches or participants? Who will look bad if the results are not positive? Will organizational priorities toward evaluation change? Will the results of the study be met with skepticism? Listing these obstacles during planning may lead to better choices of whom to involve in planning and what level of rigor you should strive for in your research design.

Finally, take steps to anticipate when cultural, diversity, and language issues are relevant. This is another reason to involve a broad set of stakeholders at the outset of the evaluation process, as they may help you identify, for example, how those with different cultural values may perceive the process. Multinational organizations that provide coaching services in various languages need to consider at an early stage how they will gather data from those who speak the nondominant language.

Often, such a process requires translating surveys into a second language and then translating responses back into the original language for analysis and aggregation with other inputs. Disseminating the findings of the program evaluation at the conclusion may involve yet another translation process.

Step 2: Design the Process

After firmly grounding the evaluation, use your analysis and insights to create measures and design the data-gathering process.

First, determine who will provide the information you need. If you are interested in marketing, you will probably want comments from participants and bosses about the value of the program. If you wish to improve the program, coaches, participants, and their bosses can talk about logistics, program administration, communication, organizational support, and the process of coaching itself. If you want evidence of effectiveness, input from participants and bosses is often most compelling; you might even seek objective performance measures that are related to the coaching objectives. Depending on the specific coaching objectives, you may seek input from participants and bosses, as well as their peers, direct reports, and customers, depending on who is most likely to see the relevant behaviors. Organizational sponsors and other stakeholders should also be considered as sources of input.

Second, generate the specific questions and items they will respond to. It often pays to do some homework inside the organization to see whether you can borrow or adapt existing items that have proven their value. In some instances, the evaluation of coaching programs may be supplemented by using existing organizational data such as information on retention, measures of work unit performance, employee surveys, 360-degree evaluation, performance appraisals, or assessment centers.

If your purpose is to gather feedback to improve the coaching process, you might ask similar questions of all parties (recognizing that participants, coaches, bosses, and HR personnel have different needs and expectations and will therefore often comment on different aspects of the program): What recommendations do you have to improve the coaching process? What aspects of the process are most useful? What could be done to meet your needs more effectively? What environmental or organizational barriers, if any, were most detrimental to the process? To ensure a more comprehensive response, include a checklist of issues for each person to either rate or to consider as part of his or her open-ended responses (e.g., clarity of expectations, understanding of the process at the outset, quality and frequency of communication, quality of feedback, confidentiality, scheduling and logistics, length and frequency of meetings, access to other resources; see also Executive Coaching Forum, 2001; Peterson, 2002). For additional depth on the participant perspective, you might ask more specific open-ended questions (e.g., What is most or least useful about the coaching you are receiving? How did your coaching help you achieve better results at work?). Another alternative is to systematically guide them through aspects of the process by having them rate items such as the following:

- Administrative processes and support (e.g., scheduling, communications) have been smooth and responsive.
- My coach tailored the process to address my specific needs and situation.
- My coach has been positive, professional, and supportive.
- My coach understands our organization and its culture.
- My coach was effective in helping me *learn* new behaviors.
- My coach was effective in helping me *apply* new behaviors on the job.
- My manager provided clear, useful feedback.
- My manager was supportive of the coaching process.

To aid decision making or marketing, you may want to evaluate the extent to which participants have learned new skills or improved their performance. The simplest method is to ask about overall outcomes that apply to all participants, such as effectiveness on the job, potential for advancement, and general leadership abilities (e.g., To what extent did coaching improve this person's leadership capabilities?). You may also measure a common set of behaviors related to your organization's values or key learning behaviors, such as these: Actively seeks feedback from others; Takes appropriate risks in order to put learning into action.

Because coaching is individually customized, the most precise evaluation, as well as the most useful feedback for participants and coaches, will be gained by using customized items related to each person's own development priorities. In general, we recommend using both common items (for easy comparison) and unique items (for evaluating individual progress).[2] Representative items include the following:

- Focus your organization on efforts that add significant value to customers.
- Provide strong, decisive leadership despite incomplete and ambiguous information.
- Consider and address the impact of your plans and changes on other business units.

Finally, if marketing is the purpose, items can be included purely to gather information that might appeal to others:

- Overall, this is a high-quality program.
- I would recommend my coach/this process to others.
- The coaching I received was well worth the cost.

Your third decision is to choose the appropriate rating scales to be applied. For example, if the sole purpose of the preceding three items is marketing, it might be best to ask them in a yes/no format so you can say, "99% of participants would recommend this coaching program to others." If your purpose is decision making or improving the process, you need the finer grained information provided by a 5- or 7-point scale.[3]

For rating participants on the amount of improvement they show against their coaching objectives, we recommend choosing from the following rating scales:

■ *Current Effectiveness* (ranging from 1 = Not at all effective, 4 = Acceptable, 7 = Highly effective). This scale is most appropriate when you are able to compare pre-coaching and post-coaching ratings, or make comparisons involving a control group.

■ *Current Versus Desired Performance* (1 = Much less than desired performance, 4 = Equal to desired performance, 7 = Much better than desired performance). This scale may be combined with a current effectiveness scale and is most appropriate when giving feedback is a purpose for the evaluation.

■ *Level of Improvement* (1 = No improvement, 3 = Moderate improvement, 5 = Considerable improvement). This scale is useful for measuring the effectiveness of coaching and is extremely valuable when you are unable to collect baseline performance information (Peterson, 1993a). Because it does not clearly indicate whether a person's performance meets expectations, even when substantial change has occurred, it is most useful in conjunction with one of the other two scales.

Fourth, decide how to collect your data: online, paper-and-pencil surveys, interviews, or through some combination. This, as with all other decisions, should be driven primarily by your purpose. If you are conducting frequent surveys from multiple rater perspectives in widely dispersed areas, online is often easiest. If you are seeking feedback to improve the program design, open-ended questions are most useful. They can be delivered through any vehicle, but interviews allow for deeper discussion and additional follow-up questions. Whatever method you use, be sure to include an explanation of how the information will be used as well as the level of confidentiality and anonymity that you will provide to those responding to your questions.

Fifth, consider the design that will give you the most compelling information for your purpose. For example, pure marketing efforts have less need of rigorous design (pre-/posttesting, comparison groups, item-level controls, etc.) than do evaluation efforts driven by decision making. The point here is to start by carefully designing a thorough and flexible approach to give you all the information you are likely to need. As resource or business factors limit your options, compromises can be made. However, by beginning with an optimal design, you are more assured that the final design will address potential criticisms of the evaluation results.

Recommendations

With such an array of options in front of you, the ideal design is not always clear. Based on our experience balancing typical evaluation needs with the practical realities of data gathering in most organizations, we can offer the following recommendations.

■ For feedback to coaches and participants, and to facilitate open communication with the participant's boss, HR, and other organizational sponsors, use a pre- and post-coaching rating of 8–10 specific learning objectives for each participant. At Time 1, use either the Current Effectiveness or the Current Versus Desired Performance scale. At Time 2 (or at any point during the coaching process), use the

	Strongly Disagree		Neutral		Strongly Agree
1. Overall, this is a high-quality program.	1	2	3	4	5
2. Administrative processes and support (e.g., scheduling and communications) have been smooth and responsive.	1	2	3	4	5
3. My coach and coaching program addressed my specific needs and situation.	1	2	3	4	5
4. My coach has been positive, professional, and supportive.	1	2	3	4	5
5. My coach was effective in helping me *learn* new behaviors.	1	2	3	4	5
6. My coach was effective in helping me *apply* new behaviors on the job.	1	2	3	4	5
7. I would recommend this coaching process to others.	1	2	3	4	5

As a result of my coaching . . .

8. I have a better understanding of my impact on others.	1	2	3	4	5
9. I am more effective on the job.	1	2	3	4	5
10. Others have commented on my increased effectiveness on the job.	1	2	3	4	5
11. I have improved in critical skills that increase my potential for advancement.	1	2	3	4	5
12. I am a more effective leader and/or influencer.	1	2	3	4	5
13. I learned how to keep learning and improving in the future.	1	2	3	4	5

Open-ended questions

14. What are the two or three most important things you personally learned?

15. What were the most helpful and beneficial parts of the program for you?

16. What two things would have made this a more positive and valuable experience for you?

17. Other comments or suggestions:

Figure 13.2   Participant Survey

same scale again plus the Level of Improvement scale. The Time 2 measure can be used even when you do not have Time 1 data.

■ For a simple, all-purpose instrument, use a format similar to Figure 13.2 for participants and Figure 13.3 for the boss and other organizational sponsors. The instrument is designed to be administered at the completion of coaching. Note the range of items and how they can be used to address multiple decision making, improvement, and marketing purposes.

■ If you are interested in ROI and the business impact of the coaching, it is essential to gather information from the boss and/or other organizational sponsors at the outset of coaching (as discussed in the ROI section above) regarding their desired outcomes for the coaching and what they perceive the *value* of those outcomes to be.

	Strongly Disagree		Neutral		Strongly Agree
1. Overall, this is a high-quality program.	1	2	3	4	5
2. The coach and coaching program have addressed our specific needs and situation.	1	2	3	4	5
3. The coach has kept me informed and involved.	1	2	3	4	5
4. The coach was effective in helping this person *learn* new behaviors.	1	2	3	4	5
5. The coach was effective in helping this person *apply* new behaviors on the job.	1	2	3	4	5
6. The coach gave me tactics on how to support this person's development.	1	2	3	4	5
7. I would recommend this coaching service to others.	1	2	3	4	5
8. Considering all aspects of performance, this person is very *effective* on the job.	1	2	3	4	5
9. The coaching and training *contributed* significantly to this person's improved effectiveness on the job.	1	2	3	4	5
10. Overall, I am very satisfied with this person's *progress* in the coaching program.	1	2	3	4	5
11. I am very satisfied with this person's *effort* in the coaching program.	1	2	3	4	5
12. At this point, should an opening appear, this person will be likely to *advance* within our organization.	1	2	3	4	5
13. Others in the organization now feel more confident giving this person's team challenging or difficult assignments.	1	2	3	4	5
14. This person's team is more effective at leading and influencing within the organization.	1	2	3	4	5
15. This person's team gets more done.	1	2	3	4	5
16. Morale in this person's team has improved.	1	2	3	4	5

Open-ended questions

17. What are the two or three changes this person has made that have most impacted your organization?

18. *How* have these changes impacted your organization?

19. What two things would have made this a more positive and valuable experience for you?

20. Other comments or suggestions:

Figure 13.3. Organizational Sponsor Survey

Step 3: Implement the Process

At this point, you implement the decisions made at Step 2—for example, collecting the data using online, e-mail, paper-and-pencil, or interview methods.

It is important to remember here that lack of time by raters is one of the primary obstacles in conducting evaluations (Kraiger, 2002). If you involved stakeholders in the planning process at Step 1, it may be easier to elicit responses from your raters. Recognize that getting timely and accurate ratings will be one of the greatest challenges you face in the evaluation process.

There are four suggestions for improving both response rates and the quality of the data. The first, already stated, is to gain buy-in by involving as many potential raters as possible in the planning of the evaluation and the design of the rating form. For example, you can circulate a draft of the instrument to participants, coaches, and bosses and ask for suggestions for improving the form or adding items. Second, if possible, dedicate time for completing ratings, such as reserving the last 15 minutes of a staff meeting for this purpose. Third, if raters complete the forms on their own time, plan to send one or two follow-ups reminding raters to return the forms by the given deadline. It is usually best to give short initial deadlines, no more than 5 to 7 business days. The longer the initial deadline, the more likely raters are to delay in completing their ratings.

Fourth, it is important to maintain rater confidentiality and protect the integrity of the data throughout the rating process. This is actually a long-term process to build trust and should be managed before, during, and after the data collection process. It is important to answer questions honestly about the purpose for the evaluation and the use of the ratings. It is also critical to safeguard the data and ensure that the data are used for nothing other than the intended purpose.

Step 4: Analyze the Data

This step involves analyzing your data to address the questions raised by the purpose of your study. A tutorial on the techniques of statistical analysis is beyond the scope of this chapter. Instead, our comments are directed at the goals of analysis.

One of the major issues confounding interpretation of results is sample attrition, as it is unlikely that all participants who started the coaching program will have completed it. Calculating the percentage of participants who dropped out can be informative. A dropout rate that is particularly high or low may say a lot about the value participants see in the program or help you identify other obstacles that need to be removed. From the perspective of statistical validity (i.e., can we believe the results?), it is useful to compare participants who dropped out and participants who stayed. Do program dropouts differ from those who stayed in terms of age, gender, ethnicity, program objectives, or type of coach? Occasionally participants will choose to leave the organization as a result of their coaching, which in cases of poor fit may be viewed as a successful outcome of the coaching process. The results of these comparisons may not only address the generalizability of the primary results but provide useful feedback on who is more or less likely to benefit from coaching in your organization, desirable characteristics of coaches, how participants and coaches are paired, or how the coaching can be improved.

For obvious reasons, the analyses you conduct will be based on the measures and design you selected at Step 2. More generally, these analyses should be planned with consideration to the issues of impact, effectiveness, and efficiency addressed in the previous section. To evaluate impact, determine whether the coaching program itself was consistent with the strategic objectives of the organization. Did specific coaching objectives support these strategic objectives? These questions can be answered by rational analysis or judgments by stakeholders. To evaluate effectiveness, conduct statistical analyses of your measures to determine whether program objectives were met and whether coaches improved over the duration of the program. Finally, to evaluate efficiency, consider whether the observed benefits were worth the investment by the organization in coaching. Consider too whether program efficiency can be improved by streamlining some aspects.

A detailed discussion of how to collect data to conduct cost-benefit analyses is beyond the scope of this chapter, but readers interested in detailed presentations are referred to Cascio (1982), Phillips (1997), or Tracey (1992). McGovern et al. (2001) also present a case specific to coaching interventions. A comparison of the costs and benefits of coaching is the most straightforward when both are expressed in the same units of measurement.[4]

According to Tracey (1992), cost and benefit data may be collected from three sources: corporate records and reports, HR department records, and directed accounting surveys and studies. In typical studies, data are collected on both direct and indirect costs. Direct costs include travel expenses, out-of-pocket expenses by participants, and personnel costs associated with the development and maintenance of the coaching program. Indirect costs are items of expense that are not associated with the specific coaching program but are common to multiple HR activities. Examples include fringe benefits (of administrative staff) and overhead.

Note that in contrast to formal training programs, both the direct and indirect costs of coaching programs will be relatively low. However, it is also important to consider opportunity costs, the costs of foregoing other services by participation in the coaching program. Specifically, each hour spent by the participant and coach on coaching is an hour not spent on contributing directly to the primary operation of the business. Thus, it may be appropriate to calculate or estimate time spent in coaching and the hourly salary of participants as costs associated with the program.

Following traditional ROI models, these accumulated costs can be compared to some estimate of the total benefit of the program. Using the same sources as above, it may be possible to estimate reduction in operational costs or errors in job performance, greater individual or unit productivity, or customer retention. For example, after coaching on time management, a manager estimates that she can accomplish her work 15% more efficiently than in the past. Because the investment of her time in coaching was counted as a cost, it is appropriate to count the increased efficiency (.15 times her hourly salary times the length of the intervention) as a benefit.

There are several strategies for comparing costs and benefits including calculating the ratio of benefits to savings (see Cascio, 1982; Phillips, 1997; and Tracey, 1992, for more details). Note too that by using the impact/effectiveness/efficiency approach of Boudreau and Ramstad (2003), it is less important to express the cost effectiveness of the coaching program as a single number than it is to show that coaching creates tangible outcomes, linked to important business goals, while making efficient use of corporate resources.

Step 5: Present the Findings

Finally, present your findings to the relevant audience. Note that you might even choose to disseminate the results of the evaluation more broadly, so that all raters can understand the organizational value of their responses. Regardless of how you present the findings, whether in person or in a written document, be sure the context is clear. On the one hand, this involves linking the results back to the original purposes of the evaluation and to the specific questions that were targeted at the outset of the process. On the other hand, the context requires that the results be interpreted in light of who was enrolled in coaching for what purpose. A coaching program offered to high potentials to use as they wish will undoubtedly generate different findings from a coaching program aimed at potential derailers who are given few choices about their participation.

Other points to sharing your findings are provided in Figure 13.1, so we do not go into additional detail here other than to stress the importance of additional dialog around the results. Present your findings and then talk with your audiences about their reactions. Use your new insights to identify top priorities for action. You may even go back with a clearer or revised sense of the purpose of evaluation. The evaluation process is an ongoing task that benefits from periodic review to ensure that it is serving current purposes well.

Final Comments

Evaluation is primarily about making a *credible case* to support important business priorities. Managers are looking for practical information they can use to achieve organizational objectives and solve problems. The process you design for evaluating coaching must be based on an understanding of the business needs, the types of decisions that will be made, and what your various audiences will find most useful. By considering the need for evaluation early in any coaching process, you can facilitate learning and continuous improvement, and enhance your own value and credibility with your organization's leadership team.

Notes

1. Compare these results to Bloom's (1984) "two-sigma" difference between one-on-one tutoring and classroom learning techniques for children.

2. Although customized learning objectives lead to the best data for the individual, they present a potential secondary problem in the next stage of evaluation—data analysis. There are at least three choices in handling these disparate (i.e., individually customized) pieces of information. (1) Include both individual items and common items in the rating process, using the individual items exclusively for individual feedback and the common items for program-level evaluation. (2) Evaluate each person's progress separately, based on his or her individual ratings, and then combine that information to gauge the overall program. For example, you might conclude that 27 participants showed significant improvement, 12

moderate improvement, 5 no change, and 2 an actual decline. (3) Average all items together as if they were equivalent. Peterson (1993b) concluded, after multiple examinations of the data, that option three is appropriate if all of the coaching objectives are written to express a uniform level of competence. For example, it is *not* reasonable to assume that a rating on "Demonstrates world-class strategic thinking abilities without exception" can be averaged with "Demonstrate strategic thinking in key decisions." An average rating on the former might actually be equivalent to a top rating on the latter.

3. As you will note in the following scales, we recommend using 7-point scales with a range from highly positive to highly negative ratings, such as in the first two scales listed here. When one end point is zero, such as the "No improvement" anchor on the Level of Improvement scale, a 5-point option is sufficient.

4. Alternatively, costs and benefits may be expressed in different metrics, leading to statements such as "a $20,000 investment in executive coaching is related to a 4% decrease in employee turnover or 5% increase in customer satisfaction."

References

Birkeland, S., Davis, B., Goff, M., Campbell, J., & Duke, C. (1997). *AMOCO individual coaching study.* Unpublished research report, Personnel Decisions International. Minneapolis, MN.

Bloom, B. S. (1984). The search for methods of group instruction as effective as one-to-one tutoring. *Educational Researcher, 13,* 4–16.

Boudreau, J. W., & Ramstad, P. M. (2003). Strategic industrial and organizational psychology and the role of utility analysis models. In W. C. Borman, D. R. Ilgen, & R. J. Klimoski,(Eds.), *Handbook of psychology, Vol. 12: Industrial and organizational psychology.* Hoboken, NJ: Wiley.

Burke, M. J., & Day, R. R. (1986). A cumulative study of the effectiveness of managerial training. *Journal of Applied Psychology, 71,* 232–246.

Cascio, W. F. (1982). *Costing human resources: The financial impact of behavior in organizations.* Belmont, CA: Wadsworth.

Davis, B. L., & Petchenik, L. (1998). *Measuring the value of coaching at AMOCO.* Presented at The Coaching and Mentoring Conference, Washington, DC: Linkage, Inc.

Gegner, C. (1997). *Coaching: Theory and practice.* Unpublished master's thesis, University of San Francisco, San Francisco, CA.

Haccoun, R. R., & Hamtiaux, T. (1994). Optimizing knowledge tests for inferring acquisition levels in single group training evaluation designs: The internal referencing strategy. *Personnel Psychology, 47,* 593–604.

Kampa, S., & White, R. P. (2002). The effectiveness of executive coaching: What we know and what we still need to know. In R. L. Lowman (Ed.), *Handbook of organizational consulting psychology* (pp. 139–158). San Francisco: Jossey-Bass.

Kampa-Kokesch, S. (2001). *Executive coaching as an individually tailored consultation intervention: Does it increase leadership?* Unpublished doctoral dissertation, Western Michigan University, Kalamazoo, MI.

Kampa-Kokesch, S., & Anderson, M. Z. (2001). Executive coaching: A comprehensive review of the literature. *Consulting Psychology Journal, 53*(4), 205–228.

Kraiger, K. (2002). Decision-based evaluation. In K. Kraiger (Ed.), *Creating, implementing, and maintaining effective training and development: State-of-the-art lessons for practice* (pp. 331–375). San Francisco: Jossey-Bass.

Martineau, J. W., & Preskill, H. (2002). Evaluating the impact of organization development interventions. In J. Waclawski & A. H. Church (Eds.), *Organization development: A data driven approach to organization change* (pp. 286–301). San Francisco: Jossey-Bass.

McGovern, J., Lindemann, M., Vergara, M., Murphy, S., Barker, L., & Warrenfeltz, R. (2001). Maximizing the impact of executive coaching: Behavioral change, organizational outcomes, and return on investment. *The Manchester Review, 6*(1), 1–9.

McLinden, D. J. (1995). Proof, evidence, and complexity: Understanding the impact of training and development in business. *Performance Improvement Quarterly, 8*(3), 3–18.

Peterson, D. B. (1993a). *Measuring change: A psychometric approach to evaluating individual coaching outcomes.* Presented at the annual conference of the Society for Industrial and Organizational Psychology, San Francisco.

Peterson, D. B. (1993b). *Skill learning and behavior change in an individually tailored management coaching program.* Unpublished doctoral dissertation, University of Minnesota, Minneapolis.

Peterson, D. B. (2002). Management development: Coaching and mentoring programs. In K. Kraiger (Ed.), *Creating, implementing, and managing effective training and development: State-of-the-art lessons for practice* (pp. 160–191). San Francisco: Jossey-Bass.

Peterson, D. B., & Hicks, M. D. (1999, February). *The art and practice of executive coaching.* Presented at the annual conference of the Society of Consulting Psychology, Phoenix, AZ.

Pfau, B., & Kay, I. (2002). Playing the training game and losing. *HR Magazine, 47*(7), 49–54.

Phillips, J. J. (1997). *Return on investment in training and performance improvement programs.* Houston: Gulf Publishing.

Thompson, A. D., Jr. (1986). *A formative evaluation of an individualized coaching program for business managers and professionals.* Unpublished doctoral dissertation, University of Minnesota, Minneapolis.

Tracey, W. R. (1992). *Designing training and development systems* (3rd ed.). New York: Amacom.

West, L., & Milan, M. (2001). *The reflecting glass: Professional coaching for leadership development.* Basingstoke, Hampshire, Great Britain: Palgrave.

Suggested Readings in Coaching

Executive Coaching Forum. (2001). *The executive coaching handbook: Principles and guidelines for a successful coaching partnership* (2nd ed.). Author. (Available at *www.theexecutive-coachingforum.com*)

Fitzgerald, C., & Berger, J. G. (Eds.). (2002). *Executive coaching: Practices and perspectives.* Palo Alto, CA: Davies-Black.

Hargrove, R. A. (1995). *Masterful coaching.* San Diego: Pfeiffer.

Peterson, D. B. (2002). Management development: Coaching and mentoring programs. In K. Kraiger (Ed.), *Creating, implementing, and managing effective training and development: State-of-the-art lessons for practice* (pp. 160–191). San Francisco: Jossey-Bass.

Peterson, D. B., & Hicks, M. D. (1996). *Leader as coach: Strategies for coaching and developing others.* Minneapolis, MN: Personnel Decisions International.

PART V

Team and Organizational Effectiveness

CHAPTER 14

Team Performance

Wendy S. Becker

John E. Mathieu

SABMiller's Trenton facility has been called the brewery of the future, but it started as an experiment in team performance. The plant was built in 1980 but had been mothballed due to excess capacity. When it re-opened in 1991, SABMiller challenged a corporate team to design a totally new workplace based on teams. Today cross-functional and self-directed teams ranging from 6 to 19 people handle everything from brewing to packaging and distribution. Team members handle administration, personnel, safety, quality, productivity, and maintenance. The team approach has yielded a 30% increase in productivity in comparison to SABMiller's other plants, turnover is less than 7%, and absenteeism is less than 2%. The plant has won several awards as an innovative team-based union operation. Managers attribute the success of the facility to its team design, as the plant's physical operating features are identical to SABMiller's other plants (Becker, 2002).

The past decade has witnessed an explosion of interest in teams. High-profile organizations were early adopters, and their successes with teams have spawned much interest. Team designs were seen as a new source of productivity as firms scrambled with domestic and overseas competition. The impact of downsizing, particularly in middle management ranks, challenged organizations to seek new ways of structuring work that did not rely on the traditional hierarchy. Initiatives to empower workers with more decision-making responsibility caught on. An explosion of books and articles in the popular press extolled the virtues of teams. It seems that the time was right for teams.

Recently, we organized a conference entitled "So you've implemented teams . . . Now what?" to examine the efficacy of teams. Experts from organizations that had experimented with teams met alongside academic researchers. We found that organizations were beginning to proceed more cautiously when implementing teams. Even when teams were appropriate, there were problems, most specifically, around how to evaluate team performance.

It is clear that managing team performance continues to puzzle organizations. In fact, an early review found that relevant research on team performance assessment was almost nonexistent (O'Neil, Baker, & Kazlauskas, 1992). Traditional human resource (HR) functions, such as recruiting, selection, performance evaluation, and compensation are designed at the individual employee level, not for teams. This emphasis on the individual contributor reduces the effectiveness of teams and ultimately, of the organization (Reilly & McGourty, 1998).

Teams can be described as "a distinguishable set of two or more people who interact, dynamically, interdependently, and adaptively to achieve specified, shared, and valued objectives" (Morgan, Glickman, Woodard, Blaiwes, & Salas, 1986, p. 3). Teams are more than simply a collection of individuals—they share a common fate, work closely with one another, and ultimately view themselves as an interdependent collective. In other words, real organizational teams are a product of the design of their task work, reward systems, and shared histories with one another. Feeble efforts to "go teams" that are limited to having individuals establish a common team name, complete a few team building activities, and so forth are doomed to failure. Successful team-based organizational designs require a serious commitment to establish and develop organizational support systems designed specifically to promote teamwork (Mohrman, Cohen, & Mohrman, 1995; Sundstrom & Associates, 1999).

Framework for the Chapter

Critical issues surrounding the evaluation of team performance are discussed in this chapter. First, we examine performance evaluation as a general process. We then present a measurement framework that places team performance within the context of the organization. Next, we walk through a five-step process for developing team performance measures. It is important to note that from our perspective, the team owns the evaluation process. Finally, we discuss sources of measurement and how they can facilitate the team process. Before beginning, however, we offer the following caveat:

Team Designs Are NOT Panaceas

A Fortune 100 company opened a consumer products facility with the vision of incorporating state-of-the-art technology and a culture of empowered work teams. Employees were carefully selected and trained in team skills. But installation of the new equipment created unanticipated and lengthy delays.

Employees were focused on individually based tasks, making the team design inappropriate for the start-up phase of the operation. By the time the technology was up and running, it was too late; managers who supported the team culture were gone and corporate support for the team vision had eroded. One manager stated that "we were on our way, but we'll never know if the team strategy could have been successful." (Becker, 2002, p. 31)

Teams should not be seen as the cure-all to every organizational competitiveness challenge. Indeed, both *team interdependence* and *team longevity* determine the applicability of team-based designs and performance evaluation.

Interdependence can exist among coworkers from three different sources: (a) inputs, (b) processes, and (c) outcomes. First, coworkers may need to share resources or *inputs,* whether they are raw materials, information, equipment, or capital. Second, coworkers may have *process interdependence* such that they must coordinate their activities in real time with others. For example, surgical team members must work closely with one another and coordinate their efforts to be successful. Third, coworkers may have *outcome interdependence* in the sense that rewards (both informal and tangible) may be tied to aggregate performance. Thus, even relatively independent contributors (e.g., call center employees) might consider themselves a team if they are rewarded on the basis of aggregate performance. In sum, if a collective of employees does not have to share resources, closely coordinate its actions, or contribute to a common fate in terms of outcomes, there is little to be gained from treating the collective as a team. In fact, team-based outcomes would be counter-productive in such instances.

Longevity of the team also impacts the appropriateness of team designs. For example, teams with very *fluid memberships* pose constraints on team performance evaluation even when rewards are tied closely in time with team accomplishment. Team members may no longer be around when performance-based feedback and rewards become available. In parallel, such feedback may mean little to new members who were not contributors to the team's earlier performances. This situation is common in "crew" arrangements in which the particular configuration of team membership changes quite often (e.g., airline cockpit crews). Teamwork remains critical in such instances, but performance evaluation should focus on the contributions that individual members make to the teams of which they are a part. In sum, team designs can be powerful—but they are not the solution to every problem.

With this caveat in mind, we now turn our attention to performance evaluation, specifically when teammates are highly interdependent and have a reasonable level of membership stability over time.

Performance Evaluation as a General Process

Performance evaluation represents a collection of objective data, judgments, ratings, and perceptions to understand performance better, with the purpose of guiding subsequent actions or decisions (Tannenbaum, 2001). Performance measures include questionnaires, rating forms, interviews, observations, and archival data. Performance measures consist of work-specific behaviors or results (e.g., productivity or scrap records), individual competencies (e.g., knowledge or skills), and employee measures (e.g., employee attitudes or customer satisfaction measures).

Even with the best intentions, performance evaluation is problematic. Common problems include measuring the wrong criteria, trying to do too much, and failing to prepare and support the performance raters adequately. To avoid pitfalls, performance evaluation should be purpose-driven, using the best available science and theory to guide the design of measures. Employees should be involved throughout the development, testing, and rollout phases. Measurement systems have a built-in half-life and need to be reviewed periodically for updating. Careful development of evaluation systems can yield unexpected job performance insights, so it's best to avoid cookie cutter solutions (Tannenbaum, 2001).

Historically, performance evaluation has taken place on an individual employee basis, often in the form of a performance appraisal done annually by the manager. This approach to performance measurement reflects a traditional, hierarchical view of organizational structure in which managers evaluate each employee's individual performance. The manager considers the employee's productivity and work record over a specified period of time. More recently, the employee's competencies or skills may be considered, such as in a skill-based performance system. In addition, customer satisfaction with the employee's work may be considered as part of the appraisal. But there are drawbacks to this traditional, hierarchical approach when the organization is attempting to support teams.

We will never forget speaking to a production employee in an auto parts assembly plant during a job analysis project. The employee was casually reading a comic book while employees nearby struggled with an overload of work on their line. When asked why he did not pitch in to help, the employee replied that his own line was down and while he *could* help the others, it just was not his job. There simply was no benefit to the employee to help others. In this plant, team performance across product lines and shifts was not supported. Therefore, this employee felt compelled to slack off despite his colleagues' desperate need for support.

In team-based organizations, the unit of analysis shifts to the team level. Naturally, individual contributions to the collective good remain important matters to be considered; but as the unique contributions of any given individual become more intermeshed with those of others, the feedback and evaluation systems should shift accordingly. When employees' work is interdependent, focusing on individual performance is a mistake. It encourages people to compete with each other, which suboptimizes team performance. Clear, collaboratively set team goals lead to mutual accountability in work performance (Mitchell & Silver, 1990).

Measurement Framework for Understanding Team Performance

Developing team performance measures requires special considerations beyond the already formidable ones that lurk at the individual level. In short, team measurement systems should be designed to index how different teams can be effective and

---

Box 14.1 Eight Basic Principles of Team-Performance Measurement

1. Capture the team's strategy in the system
2. Align the team strategy with the larger business strategy
3. Ensure that the system yields clear, specific, team goals
4. Ensure that the system incorporates appropriate sources of feedback
5. Focus on the critical few, rather than trivial many indices
6. Ensure that members understand the system
7. Involve customers in the system development
8. See that all member contributions have a "line of sight"

SOURCE: Adapted from Jones & Schilling, 2000.

---

facilitate team development in and of itself. An old management adage is "what gets measured gets attended to, and what gets rewarded gets done."

Capitalizing on this wisdom, we recommend eight basic principles (see Box 14.1) for designing team-based measurement systems, adapted from Jones and Schilling (2000). First, the team's strategy must be represented in the measurement system. Team members should be involved in developing the system, and ultimately "own" their own performance evaluation in order to make this a success. Second, the team's strategy must be integrated with the organization's overall business strategy to facilitate alignment between the business and the team strategy. Third, the team's performance measurement system should consist of clear, specific team goals. Measures should be avoided if they are too complicated for team members to understand or are of interest solely to managers. Fourth, the measurement system should include feedback from multiple appropriate sources to provide a critical focus for the team. The measurement system should help simplify this information, as multiple data from many sources can be overwhelming to the team and create confusion. So the fifth principle is that the measurement system should focus on the critical few rather than the trivial many. Sixth, the system needs to be understandable by team members, as it is important that the team "own" the measurement process. Seventh, the customer's point of view should be included as part of team measurement. Finally, team members must have a clear "line of sight" from their own individual contribution to overall team performance. We observed this recently during a site visit of a successful team facility. Every employee could clearly articulate how his or her work fit into the organization's overall business strategy, to the envy of other managers taking the tour.

The important message to extract from these recommendations is that the team evaluation system should be relevant, both globally and locally. *Global relevance* means that teams do not operate in a vacuum. Their effectiveness must be gauged in terms of how they contribute to the larger system. Just as members' contributions must be evaluated in terms of how they impact the team outcomes, team effectiveness must be evaluated in terms of how it contributes to the over-arching business strategy. Mathieu, Marks, and Zaccaro (2001) coined the term multiteam systems (MTSs) to capture the essence of the emergence of this new form of organization—based on networks or a "teams-of-teams" approach. They argued that the (global) effectiveness of MTSs depends on the effectiveness of their component teams and how well work is orchestrated across teams.

Local relevance means that team evaluation systems must focus on the drivers of team performance that are "close" to team members and subject to their influence. Feedback is valuable only when its connection to the team strategy and goals is clear, when performance "gaps" are vivid (i.e., benchmarking standards are available), and when all members know how their efforts will impact such indices.

To make this effort worthwhile, teams need access to the same kinds of business data that executives use to manage entire organizations. Team access to data is an investment. Just as we pay for expertise when hiring a consultant, we pay a price when we make a commitment to involving team members in their own performance assessment (Brannick & Prince, 1997). But only 12% of the workforce in Fortune 1000 firms has sufficient amounts of the information needed to be highly involved as business partners in their companies (Lawler, Mohrman, & Ledford, 1998). This shortcoming illustrates the huge potential for improvement in the development of team performance. Focusing on team performance allows the team to see itself as a business, with its own problems to solve in order to be successful. It also provides accountability for all team members, as measurement helps to build team pride and ownership of the team's efforts (Jones & Moffett, 1999). In addition, when properly constructed, team performance measures allow constituents external to the team to have input in the team's performance.

Getting Started: How to Develop Team Performance Measures

The team scorecard introduces cause-and-effect into performance measures and helps to translate the organization's business strategy into measurable outcomes for teams (Jones & Moffett, 1999). The idea is that measures of financial results at the organization level must be supplemented with measures of customers' needs, internal business processes, and employee learning and innovation at the team level. For example, the team scorecard concept assumes that employee attitudes are linked to customer satisfaction as teams influence productivity, scrap, rework, and so on. This has an impact on the organization's bottom line financial results. The team scorecard provides a link between the financial results that are important to management and the team's strategy that influences those results (Jones & Moffett, 1999).

Five-Step Process for Developing Team Performance Measures

It is critical to develop a team performance evaluation system that places the team in control of the evaluation. Zigon (1998) outlined a process for developing team performance measures that embrace the team scorecard philosophy. In this section, we offer such a process based in large part on his recommendations. The five steps are these: review existing organizational measures, define team measurement factors, identify and weight team member activities, develop team performance measures and standards, and create a feedback system.

Step 1: Review Existing Organizational Measures

Team performance needs to be integrated within the organization's overall business strategy. Teams do not exist in a vacuum. The team measurement system needs to support the goals of the organization. This involves linking team performance measures directly with organizational measures. That way, team members will better understand how their work fits into the bigger picture. The best way to do this is to involve the team in the development process. Each team member must have a clear "line of sight" from his or her own goals and performance, including team performance goals, to that of the overall business strategy.

The team's operating plan is reflected in its measurement system. Team performance measures should not focus only on team financial measures like profit or return on investment. The team scorecard presents a more comprehensive approach to performance assessment and stresses the importance of including measures of internal business processes, employee learning and growth, and customer needs.

Step 2: Define Team Measurement Factors

Measurement should focus on the processes and outcomes of team performance. Outcomes are the end-state of team activities and responsibilities—"what" they are trying to accomplish. They drive reward systems and must be woven into the fabric of the larger system. Team processes are what members are actually doing to accomplish their goals—they represent "how" the outcomes will be created. Process feedback is "close to the action" and is designed to facilitate quick corrective actions.

Defining team measurement factors requires using techniques such as work process mapping. Work processes are activities that cut across departments and typically provide a value-added product or service to customers, internal or external. An excellent tool for team evaluation is a work process map. A work process map is a diagram in which the boxes represent steps in the activity of the team. Arrows in the diagram represent "hand-offs" between steps.

Step 3: Identify and Weight Team Member Activities

Weights are used to set priorities for the team. Weights help the team understand the importance of various team member responsibilities by focusing the relative importance of results. Weights help to create a shared vision of the team's priorities. Because priorities change in organizations and work group processes change over time for a variety of reasons (e.g., profitability and the introduction of new technology), previously determined weights may no longer be optimal for the teams. Therefore, program evaluators need to examine weights based on the current situation.

One method of establishing weights is to divide 100 percentage points across team responsibilities. The most important results have the largest weights, and the least important have the smallest weights. The idea here is to have team members and other evaluators come to a consensus on the relative importance of different performance facets. The team goals may be weighted alongside individual team member goals, as in the following example:

- **Team Responsibilities (60%)**
  - Shipped products (30%)
  - New product design (10%)
  - Satisfied customers (10%)
  - Effective inter-team coordination/cooperation (10%)
- **Individual Responsibilities (40%)**
  - Facilitated team processes (20%)
  - Performance individual job functions (20%)

The important point to realize from the scheme depicted above is that all team members see a clear line of sight between their contributions and the performance measurement process. Accordingly, to the extent that they are rewarded approximately 40% on their individual performance and approximately 60% on the performance of their team (as outlined above), the HR system will be aligned with the team emphasis. Strengthening the link between the weighted activities and rewards is one of the ways in which normative or summative program evaluation can help organizations to fine-tune the use of teams.

Step 4: Develop Team Performance Measures and Standards

Measures of team performance are used to specify what is important. In general, team performance is represented in terms of quality, quantity, cost, and time. Measures are both numeric and descriptive, and they should be as specific as possible. Numeric measures represent units that can be tracked, such as productivity numbers or annual dollar sales. Descriptive measures define team performance in evaluative statements made by a rater or raters. An example is an evaluative statement from a supervisor, customer, or focus group. In other words, team measures become yardsticks used to judge the team's performance. Box 14.2 provides examples of types of measures to consider for team performance.

Team performance standards represent the range of points on the yardstick that describe performance. Creating performance standards for the team should be straightforward. Objective or numeric standards are often represented as a range of values, such as $24–$35 million of annual sales, or 15%–21% profit. Descriptive or nonnumeric measures outline who will rate this measure, what specific factors will be evaluated, and what indicates that the goal was met. For example, a team performance standard might be stated: "The average customer rating of service will be at

---

Box 14.2 Sample Team Performance Measures

Operational Measures
- Safety
- Information technology enhancement
- Operational efficiency
- Productivity/cycle times
- New product introductions
- Patents
- Cost-saving ideas

Customer Measures
- External customer satisfaction
- Internal customer satisfaction
- Customer recommendations
- Customer loyalty
- Repeat transactions/sales
- Returns
- Recalls

Employee Growth Measures
- Employee satisfaction
- Personal development
- Training costs
- Employee flexibility/cross-training
- Medial costs
- Absenteeism
- Turnover

SOURCE: Adapted from Manas, 1999

---

least 4.5 on a 5-point scale for the next six months." Such information would be collected via traditional customer satisfaction surveys that many companies conduct periodically. Table 14.1 provides further examples of team performance standards.

Step 5: Create a Feedback System

Evaluation of team performance should be designed to provide feedback that is meaningful to teams. Successful teams focus their communications and meetings on performance data (Yeatts & Hyten, 1998). Building on the recommendations from Yeatts and Hyten, we offer six characteristics of effective feedback systems:

Table 14.1   Sample Measurement Report for Retail Team

Results (Weights)	Performance Standards
Profitable Sales (40%)	■ $24–35 million in annual sales ■ 15–21% profit before taxes ■ +/– 5% expense budget variance
New Product Designs (25%)	Corporate VP Marketing's satisfaction that new product designs: ■ maintain corporate feel ■ contain at least 3 products that are different than anything the competition is selling ■ enhance and maintain the corporate image through high quality art, text, and materials Focus groups say the following about the new product designs: ■ the value of the product exceeds the price ■ I would be proud to purchase this ■ They prefer our designs to the competition's designs in a blind preference test ■ Are different than they have ever seen ■ 30–50 ideas generated that are different than those suggested during the last three years
Shipped Products (20%)	■ 90–95% complete orders ■ 96–98% orders shipped within 48 hours ■ reduction in cycle time for entire design/production process from 16 months to 11 months
Signed Retail Outlets (5%)	■ 150–250 new outlets signed ■ $5–8 million in sales from new outlets
Satisfied Customers (10%)	■ Less than 0.5% returns due to defective products ■ Less than $100K in gift returns to retailers

SOURCE: Adapted from Zigon, 1998.

Characteristic 1. Feedback should be specific to the team. The best feedback is relevant to specific team accomplishments rather than an aggregate of company information. For example, information about percentage of on-time deliveries that is specific to the team, rather than the whole department or organization, is preferred.

Characteristic 2. Feedback should be comprehensive but easily understood by all team members. It should consist of multiple measures that reflect team performance, and should be meaningful to team members. Nonfinancial measures should be used when possible. For example, set-up times for changeovers, rather than labor costs, provide useful information that can be understood by all team members.

Characteristic 3. Feedback should be updated as frequently as possible. The usefulness of team performance feedback is lost when the data are not "fresh." As a rule, outdated numbers should not be used for team performance feedback. Recent data are imperative.

Characteristic 4. Feedback should be accessible. In many organizations, performance data are "owned" by management. Information is power, and information that is controlled by management is not accessible to the team. Open channels of communication about team performance data are needed to promote free access to information.

Characteristic 5. Feedback should be designed to emphasize improvement. Team performance measures must be objective, yet fair. Too much emphasis on negative performance may lead to avoidance behaviors and rejection of the information by team members. On the other hand, emphasizing only the positive is of limited usefulness. Feedback information should strike a balance between team successes and team developmental opportunities.

Characteristic 6. Feedback should be globally relevant. The feedback system must emphasize how well the team both meets its local goals and contributes to the larger system. This aspect of the feedback process becomes more and more important as the organizational design moves toward a true team-based approach. Just as emphasizing individual performance can deter people from focusing on team effectiveness, an overemphasis on team effectiveness can lead to dysfunctional cross-team relations. For example, we once worked with a manufacturing plant that placed a high premium on team goal accomplishment—defined, in part, on performance relative to goals per shift. Consequently, shift teams often "ran their machines into the ground" and neglected to perform preventive maintenance, replenish supplies, and so forth. The relieving teams inherited these problems, which generated animosity across shifts and reciprocal neglect. Once the reward system was changed to also emphasize the quality of the "hand-offs" across shifts, teams started working more effectively with one another.

Sources of Measurement in Teams

Outlining what performance dimensions should be evaluated, benchmarked, and used for feedback is the foundation of a team performance evaluation system. The remaining question, however, is this: "How should those performance dimensions be measured?" Below we sculpt a multisource framework for such effort. Care has been devoted to balancing the competing demands of minimizing the efforts needed to gather and index such data while simultaneously maximizing the usefulness of such information. We believe two common mistakes are often committed in an effort to streamline team performance measurement systems. One error is akin to "one size fits all" thinking—in that people lean too heavily on a single source for all information. For example, many rating systems attempt to gauge all performance facets via employee or higher-level management subjective evaluations.

Clearly such an approach is less than optimal when it comes to indexing several performance dimensions such as cycle times, customer satisfaction, and so forth. The other common error is akin to "using what is handy." The temptation is to use measures that are already available—even though they might not fully represent the performance dimension in question. For example, it is tempting to equate "courtesy calls placed" with "customer service" because the former is much easier to count than the latter is to assess.

Table 14.2 overviews a hybrid system that mixes different performance measures by dimensions. At issue here is that HR program evaluators, in concert with team members, should seek to employ measurement sources that are most appropriate for each performance dimension. For example, many traditionally gathered performance indices can easily be incorporated into the team evaluation system (e.g., sales, cycle times, and costs). Care must be taken to ensure that variance in a measure really reflects differences in team performance and not extraneous influences (e.g., sales territories, machine quality, and regional cost differences). Most organizations are savvy at making adjustments for such factors so as to maximize the comparability across regions, shifts, and so forth.

Surveys are perhaps the best source of customer service and satisfaction. Note that as illustrated in Table 14.2, these can be gathered from both external customers and internal customers—that is, employees who work in other teams or units who must coordinate with a team in question. The three right-most columns in the table reflect what is known as multi-rater or 360-degree feedback methods, which involve gathering information about the team and its members from multiple sources: customers, themselves, and higher-level management. Ideally multiple representatives from each of these constituencies participate in the evaluation.

The multi-rater approach helps to avoid problems that exist in traditional performance measurement systems. For example, rater biases can occur when a single rater performs the evaluation. Aggregating data from multiple raters minimizes the bias of a single person. It's also easy for employees to ignore information from a single source in performance appraisal. With multiple-source information, the data become more credible and are more difficult for the employee to dismiss. If targeted appropriately, these systems hone in on which performance factors each perspective is well positioned to evaluate. For example, external customers are not well situated to assess team members' performance of their individual job functions, which may not be visible to outsiders. Similarly, upper-level management is not well positioned to gauge the extent to which team members interact well with each other. The point is that some sources of information are more valuable for indexing different performance dimensions than are others. If thought through ahead of time, the multi-rater approach can actually streamline the rating process. Rather than having "everyone rate everything"—and many raters will know little about certain facets—each source should be asked to evaluate only what he or she knows firsthand.

As a final note, self-reports are also a valuable source of information in teams. Team members are aware of their own key strengths and weaknesses and their past accomplishments, and they can describe specific challenges that they have undertaken. Perhaps more important, large discrepancies between individual self versus

Table 14.2   Sample Performance Dimension X Measurement Source Grid

Performance Dimensions	Records/ Archives	Customer Surveys	Self & Peer Ratings	Manager Evaluations
		Performance Measurement Sources		
Team Responsibilities				
Shipped Products	X			
New Product Designs	X			
Satisfied Customers		X (External)		
Effective Inter-Team Coordination/Cooperation		X (Internal)	X	
Individual Responsibilities				
Facilitated Team Processes			X	
Performed Individual Job Functions			X (Self)	XX

peer assessments of, say, their contributions to team processes can be used to "flag" breakdowns in communication or performance expectations and signal the need for process interventions to get people back on the same track. Accordingly, well-designed multi-rater systems must include support systems for dealing with discrepancies that will no doubt emerge. Such supports could include, for example, the availability of process/feedback facilitators, conflict resolution techniques, and team building interventions.

The multi-rater system described here provides a dynamic, multifaceted view of team and member contributions. Putting team performance measures into practice, however, can be difficult. Members may resist rating each other because of previous negative experiences with performance ratings. Individuals who are unpopular for nonperformance related reasons may suffer negative ratings. The system is subject to abuse if team members make side deals to rate one another favorably. They may fail to see the big picture with respect to organizational goals.

Despite such challenges, multi-rater systems are regarded as fairer than traditional top-down reviews, and if complemented with additional sources of performance evaluation, they should achieve the dual goals of providing timely and accurate information while not becoming overly burdensome to implement and maintain.

The Future of Team Performance Evaluation

We expect that the need for team performance evaluation will expand as organizations move beyond the early adoption phase of experimentation with teams. Already in the twenty-first century, we see that as organizations cope with dramatic external change, structures inside organizations necessarily become more fluid. For example, there is more demand for temporary work teams, such as ad hoc and project teams, placing more emphasis on flexibility and short-term involvement in teams. Thus team performance evaluation will involve every employee as we move to the future.

Multinational organizations increase the prevalence of teams composed of members from different cultures (multicultural teams) as well as members from different countries (global teams). These culturally diverse teams have special training and leadership needs to facilitate performance evaluation. For example, global teams operating under dramatically different compensation systems will challenge the development of systematic team evaluation systems. In addition, unique cultural characteristics and values can inhibit peer evaluations in multi-rater feedback systems. We observed this recently in a multinational project developing a team feedback system; younger engineers were reluctant to "criticize" older engineers in a culture that emphasized respect for elders, even when the older engineers exhibited performance deficiencies.

Less face-to-face time in work teams will continue as a trend, whether in virtual teams, whose members seldom, if ever, meet or in telecommuting and other geographically displaced and mobile teams. Team performance evaluation is magnified exponentially with these physical constraints. The challenge for the team will be to facilitate communication and information exchange through Web-based and e-mail systems in addition to telephone and videoconferencing resources.

Conclusions

The effectiveness of team designs should be evaluated on an ongoing basis, from initial transition to the team model through its evolution to maturity. Ongoing evaluation will ensure that adjustments can be made to the design to make it more effective and better able to achieve its purpose. Attention to team performance evaluation will continue to grow in importance as more organizations successfully transition to team models. HR systems must shift away from exclusive emphasis on individually based performance evaluation to team models. Management support for team performance is critical to long-term team success. Managers who grow and develop new team performance models will be rewarded with stronger organizations.

But team designs are not panaceas or cure-alls. Organizations must carefully evaluate each situation to determine the applicability of team-based performance evaluation. Team interdependence and team longevity are two factors to be considered. Team interdependence may occur with respect to team inputs, processes, and outcomes. If the work does not require that employees share resources, closely coordinate activities, or contribute to a common fate in terms of outcomes, there is little to be gained in evaluating employees as a team. Longevity also impacts team performance. Newly formed teams and teams with "revolving door" members are inappropriate for team-based performance evaluation.

Eight principles that can be used for guidance when transitioning to a team-based performance measurement system were outlined in this chapter. The concept of MTSs or "teams-of-teams" was also described. MTS captures the idea that organizational effectiveness is measured in how well work is orchestrated both across teams and within component teams. Global relevance and local relevance both build on the MTS approach. Global relevance refers to the idea that team effectiveness is measured by how well teams contribute to the larger system. Local relevance refers to the idea that measurement systems must focus on goals that are within team members' control. These concepts are important tools to consider as our understanding of team performance becomes more sophisticated.

The team scorecard process includes five steps for developing team performance measures. This process involves reviewing existing organizational measures, defining specific team factors, identifying and weighting team member activities, developing performance standards, and creating a feedback mechanism. Examples of each of these steps were outlined, along with details for putting them into practice.

As organizations consider sources of measurement in teams, two common mistakes must be avoided: the "one size fits all" mentality and the temptation to use whatever measure is already available, even though it does not adequately fit the performance dimension. We recommend a hybrid system, in which the measurement used is the best source for that specific performance dimension. Customer surveys are often the best source for information about customer satisfaction and meeting customers' needs whereas peer ratings are often the best source of information about how team members contribute to the team process.

As the use of teams matures and becomes more established, we expect new challenges to emerge in the evaluation of team performance. Looking toward the future, we anticipate that individual contributions to team performance will take on more significance at work. This will occur amid a sea of change as organizations continue to look to team designs to cope with competitiveness concerns. Teams with fluid memberships will pose new constraints on measurement issues, as organizations shift team composition to accommodate projects, priorities, and customer demand. Dispersed teams composed of members at remote or global sites will pose new challenges for team and task interdependence. Team performance evaluation holds great promise for organizations that take the time to do it right.

References

Becker, W. S. (2002). *Characteristics of new greenfield plants: An investigation of organizational change.* Paper presented at the meeting of the Academy of Management, Denver, CO.

Brannick, M. T., & Prince, C. (1997). An overview of team performance measurement. In M. T. Brannick, E. J. Salas, & C. Prince (Eds.), *Team performance assessment and measurement: Theory, methods, and applications* (pp. 3–18). Mahwah, NJ: Lawrence Erlbaum.

Jones, S., & Moffett, R. G., III. (1999). Measurement and feedback systems for teams. In E. Sundstrom (Ed.), *Supporting work team effectiveness* (pp. 157–187). San Francisco: Jossey-Bass.

Jones, S. D., & Schilling, D. J. (2000). Measuring team performance: A step-by-step, customizable approach for managers, facilitators, and team leaders. San Francisco: Jossey-Bass.

Lawler, E. E., III, Mohrman, S. A., & Ledford, G. E., Jr. (1998). Strategies for high performance organizations: Employee involvement, TQM, and reengineering programs in Fortune 1000 corporations. San Francisco: Jossey-Bass.

Manas, T. (1999). Making the balanced scorecard approach pay off. *ACA Journal, 8*(2), 13–21.

Mathieu, J. E., Marks, M. A., & Zaccaro, S. J. (2001). Multi-team systems. In N. Anderson, D. S. Ones, H. K. Sinangil, & C. Viswesvaran (Eds.), *International handbook of work and organizational psychology* (Vol. 2, pp. 289–313). London: Sage.

Mitchell, T. R. & Silver, W. S. (1990). Individual and group goals when workers are independent: Effects on task, strategies, and performance. *Journal of Applied Psychology, 75,* 185–193.

Mohrman, S. A., Cohen, S. G., & Mohrman, A. M., Jr. (1995). *Designing team-based organizations.* San Francisco: Jossey-Bass.

Morgan, B. B., Jr., Glickman, A. S., Woodard, E. A., Blaiwes, A. S., & Salas, E. (1986). *Measurement of team behaviors in a Navy environment* (NTSC Tech. Rep. No. 86–014). Orlando, FL: Naval Training Systems Center.

O'Neil, H. F., Baker, E. L., & Kazlauskas, E. J. (1992). Assessment of team performance. In R. W. Swezey & E. J. Salas (Eds.), *Teams: Their training and performance* (pp. 153–175). Norwood, NJ: Ablex.

Reilly, R. R., & McGourty, J. (1998). Performance appraisal in team settings. In J. W. Smither (Ed.), *Performance appraisal: State of the art in practice* (pp. 244–277). San Francisco: Jossey-Bass.

Sundstrom, E., & Associates (1999). *Supporting work team effectiveness: Best management practices for fostering high performance.* San Francisco: Jossey-Bass.

Tannenbaum, S. I. (2001). A strategic view of organizational training and learning. In K. Kraiger (Ed.), *Creating, implementing, and managing effective training and development* (pp. 10–52). San Francisco: Jossey-Bass.

Yeatts, D. E., & Hyten, C. (1998). *High-performing self-managed work teams: A comparison of theory to practice.* Thousand Oaks, CA: Sage.

Zigon, J. (1998). *A seven-step process for measuring the results of work teams.* Media, PA: Zigon Performance Group. (available at www.zigonperf.com)

Suggested Readings in Team Performance

Hitchcock, D., & Willard, M. (1995). *Why teams can fail and what to do about it: Essential tools for anyone implementing self-directed work teams.* Chicago, IL: Irwin Professional Publishing.

Jones, S. D., & Schilling, D. J. (2000). *Measuring team performance: A step-by-step, customizable approach for managers, facilitators, and team leaders.* San Francisco: Jossey-Bass.

Parker, G., McAdams, J., & Zielinski, D. (2000). *Rewarding teams: Lessons from the trenches.* San Francisco: Jossey-Bass.

Thompson, L. (2000). *Making the team: A guide for managers.* Upper Saddle River, NJ: Prentice Hall.

Yeatts, D. E., & Hyten, C. (1998). *High-performing self-managed work teams: A comparison of theory to practice.* Thousand Oaks, CA: Sage.

CHAPTER 15

The Evaluation of Job Redesign Processes

Steven F. Cronshaw

Sidney A. Fine

Job redesign is a process of achieving or restoring balance to an unbalanced situation in a work organization. It is an attempt to restore a wholeness and productivity to a work organization that is or has become incomplete, broken, and unhealthy. Considered from this point of view, job redesign is a natural undertaking akin to healing, which gives dynamic and productive life to a work organization. The question we explore in this chapter is: How does program evaluation enable this healing process of job redesign?

Job redesign is often thought of as a management-initiated intervention conceived and implemented top-down through the management hierarchy. This perspective on job redesign, while common in management circles, is inaccurate. Actually, it can be said that all job assignments undergo natural and spontaneous redesign *initiated and carried out by the workers performing these assignments.* The phenomenon was recently extensively elaborated upon by Wrzesniewski and Dutton (2001). They stated,

> Interactions with others help employees define and bound [sic] tasks by shaping impressions of what is and what is not part of the job. However, job boundaries, the meaning of work, and work identities are not fully determined by formal job requirements. Individuals have latitude to define and enact the

job, acting as job crafters. We define crafting as the physical and cognitive changes individuals make in the task or relational boundaries of their work. (p. 179)

Their article provided a number of examples of this phenomenon in janitorial and kitchen work, nursing, engineering, and hair dressing. It is this natural tendency toward job crafting that provides greatly expanded opportunities to draw in the skills and experience of workers to augment those of management.

When crafting work, each worker brings not only skill and knowledge potentials to the workplace but also his or her personality and adaptive skills. These adaptive skills—to workplace, to work cohort, to pace and physical working conditions, and to management environment—are what make it possible for the worker to become productive and satisfied with a job. They come into play when the worker has an opportunity to make the job his or her own. Worker adaptations are the basis for a work organization to be able to say, "Our workers are our most important resource." The work organization supplies the workplace and its objectives, and the worker effects the job's final design on a more or less continuing basis.

The evaluation of job design is not unlike the evaluation needs that are required in other comprehensive social/behavioral undertakings, for example, delivery of education and social services. What immediately confront the program evaluator are the questions: When and how will I know that I have achieved the overall program goals? What criteria of program effectiveness should I give primary attention to? Pursuing these questions the program evaluator finds that, broadly speaking, he or she has two kinds of criteria that can be the focus of attention (Posavac & Carey, 1992). *Summative criteria* reflect the ultimate outcomes of the program (e.g., reading and math proficiency as shown by periodic tests in education, and the percentage of clients reporting on an annual basis that they are *satisfied* or *very satisfied* with the services received from a social service agency). *Formative criteria* relate to more proximal results of program activity (e.g., midterm grade results of students in an educational program, or social service client reports of debt counselor effectiveness). A major difference in the two types of criteria is that measurement of program effectiveness on formative criteria, which is collected within a shorter time frame, allows adjustments to be made to the program to make it more effective (e.g., by improving teaching methods and curriculum or training debt counselors in client relations). The program improvements made in response to formative evaluation should eventually result in better overall program performance on the summative evaluation criteria.

The concepts of summative and formative evaluation have counterparts in job redesign. Summative evaluation views job redesign as more-or-less a global intervention into a work system by experts to attain predictable business outcomes where the need is to evaluate the effectiveness of job redesign as a whole program following its completion. Formative evaluation is meant to result in changes in the way the job redesign program itself is designed and implemented. For changes to occur, considerable worker involvement is required to provide the flexibility needed to enable incremental improvements in the job redesign process as it unfolds and to make these changes in a timely manner. Formative evaluation would occur when, for example, worker reactions to the job changes are gauged as the job redesign proceeds (perhaps in modifying or adapting aspects of the design by drawing on worker input and accommodating worker concerns). Feedback from the formative evaluation is the key to shaping and modifying the intervention to better achieve its purpose. In fact, it is our belief that formative evaluation is an essential part of any job redesign process and should be woven organically and interactively into that process. Practitioners will probably find summative models somewhat less relevant and useful in job redesign than formative evaluation, although we certainly do not wish to rule out summative evaluation when this is called for. The use of summative evaluation in job redesign is briefly reviewed later in this chapter.

In the following case study, we show how job redesign can engage and involve the people who do the work and can result in outcomes of growth and satisfaction that directly reward worker efforts, as well as improve productivity and efficiency that benefit the work system as a whole. Basically, the emphasis in our approach was to focus on formative criteria, registering change in the satisfaction and possible growth of the workers involved. Our example is a job redesign effort carried out by the first author in an administrative unit of a university department.

Case Study: Job Redesign

The request for the job analysis and evaluation came from the department administrative assistant (DAA), Jean, who was experiencing an increased amount of stress and frustration in her job. Over the previous two years, the department had lost two clerical/secretarial positions because of severe government funding cutbacks at the university, leaving only two staff under Jean's supervision to do the work previously done by four. Understandably, Jean described a situation in which she felt overwhelmed. She reported the following problems:

- Jean was forced to perform work from the two down-sized positions so that the remaining two staff could cope with their workloads, which had also increased.
- The secretarial/clerical staff jobs had become, over time, compartmentalized (disjointed) with little job sharing. When one of the two staff was absent due to sickness or vacation, Jean had to drop her duties and fill in, thus getting behind in her own work.
- Because of the excessive staff workload, Jean was becoming less confident in the quality of the work done—she and her staff needed more time to check the accuracy of their work and think about what they were doing.

- Jean was setting aside important longer term planning and organizing tasks as she fought fires on an hour-by-hour basis. Jean did not have time to initiate and manage systems improvements that would have reduced workload and stress in the longer term (such as the introduction of computerized spreadsheets to improve speed and accuracy in entering and processing student records).
- The remaining two staff members were stressed and frustrated with their inability to cope with the larger amounts of work.

We began the job redesign process by conducting two functional job analysis (FJA) interviews: one with the DAA (Jean) and the other with the incumbents of the staff positions. The resulting two task banks were then rated on 10 FJA scales. (See Fine and Cronshaw, 1999, for an in-depth description of FJA theory and method, and see Fine and Getkate, 1995, for an explanation of the FJA scales and a list of 400 tasks.) We focused much attention on the Worker Instruction (WI) scale as an aid to redesigning the DAA job. The ratings on the WI scale, made on one of eight levels for each task in the DAA job, reflect the mix of prescription and discretion in the respective tasks. Tasks receiving a low WI rating were highly prescribed by standard operating procedures set out by management and required relatively low levels of worker skill and experience. For example, the task of photocopying course outlines and other documents for department faculty was rated at the lowest WI level because inputs, outputs, tools, equipment, and procedures were all specified in the assignment. Other tasks for the DAA received somewhat higher ratings on the WI scale. For example, Jean assisted the department chair in setting up the timetable for undergraduate and graduate courses. This task involves considerably more exercise of discretion and practical judgment, which in turn demands considerably greater amounts of job experience, training, and skill on the part of the worker. On examining the WI ratings of all the tasks in Jean's task bank, we quickly realized that an inordinate amount of her daily working activity was taken up with Level 1 or Level 2 tasks on the WI scale. As a way of reducing the stress and overload in the DAA, we discussed the possibility of moving these tasks from Jean's job to the two secretarial/clerical positions in the department. However, this was not advisable because, as already noted, these two individuals were already overloaded and overworked.

The solution to this situation involved setting up a new position with funds made available through a government program aimed at providing skills training and reentry of individuals to the workforce. Into this position were moved all the WI Level 1 and 2 tasks from the DAA position. A temporary assistant was then assigned to work closely with Jean in performing the low-discretion tasks and freeing Jean up for tasks requiring greater discretion. (For example, Jean focused her attention on tailoring data entry spreadsheets, which, when brought into use, substantially increased the productivity of the department administrative function as a whole.) Subsequently, low WI tasks were moved from the two secretarial/clerical staff positions to the temporary assistant, in a manner analogous to the DAA job redesign, freeing up time in those positions as well.

Our subsequent interview with Jean indicated that the job redesign had the intended effects. By her description, the situation across the administrative function was considerably improved: Jean was able to perform her duties with less time pressure. The two staff members were able to concentrate in a sustained way on a reduced number of higher discretion tasks (e.g., working with professors to improve formatting of tables and text in research manuscripts). And additional time was opened up to cover the duties of anyone who was absent. This had the effect of reducing the feeling that the work had become disjointed and considerably reduced their frustration/stress levels.

Jean also informed us of an unanticipated, yet very positive outcome of the job redesign. A temporary assistant, after gaining experience and performing very well in that position, was promoted to replace one of the secretarial/clerical staff, who had reached retirement age. This former temporary assistant, who had become familiar with the department in that position and willingly undertook more challenging tasks as a temporary assistant, was upgraded to the higher permanent position and, by Jean's account, is rendering excellent service to the department. A new person was hired into the vacant temporary assistant position, which is now staffed on a continual basis. In this way, the job redesign effort brought about a classic win-win situation for both the organization and the worker. The worker was able to develop and grow into a higher skill, higher paid position on an established career path, and the department gained a highly motivated, committed, and productive employee. For us this unexpected, but natural, outcome was the most personally gratifying of all the positive effects of the job redesign.

Five Principles of Job Redesign Evaluation

This chapter represents a departure from much of the existing job redesign literature in that it proposes a pragmatically grounded approach to job redesign and evaluation. It contrasts markedly with a large number of job redesign studies that require the reader to have a strong research bent and a sophisticated understanding of research design. A number of studies of this type, summarized by Champoux (1991), are based on Hackman and Oldham's (1980) job characteristics model. Our pragmatic approach, which is meant to be directly accessible to workers and managers, without the assistance of organization scientists and research statisticians, revolves around five basic principles.

Principle 1: Job Redesign and Its Evaluation Must Be Understood From a Systems Perspective

The above example of an actual job redesign illustrates the domino effect that results from any attempt at job redesign. Jobs, and the persons performing those jobs, do not exist in isolation. They are part of, and interdependent with, a larger work system that includes other jobs and personalities as well as larger system purposes, goals, objectives, and constraints focused on achieving specified outputs. Evaluation outcomes of job redesign therefore cannot be restricted to examining only the focal job that is being redesigned. As well, many outcomes of organizational processes are subject to unpredictable changes inside and outside the work system. Consequently, some outcomes of job redesign can be anticipated in advance, whereas others cannot. This points to the emergent nature of job redesign effects: Good (or sometimes bad) things happen even though they are not anticipated or intended in the original job redesign proposal. If these (often emergent) complexities of job redesign are to be adequately anticipated and handled, it is necessary to understand the job redesign process as impacting on three interrelated and interacting aspects of the overall work system: the work organization, the worker, and the work itself.

The Work Organization as a Systems Component

Job redesign takes place within a structure of work. This structure defines the purpose that the work is ultimately meant to achieve, the goals and objectives of the work system, the constraints limiting the latitude that workers may take, and the rewards that workers may expect for their efforts. The larger work organization also espouses and models a mission and values for everyone in the organization. (The operating values modeled by senior management's behaviors do not always match the espoused values contained in public speeches, company newsletters, and the like.) As any human resources (HR) consultant knows, these values are a two-edged sword: They can aid the job redesign process or seriously undermine it, depending on how worker-friendly and accommodating they are. The work organization also encompasses HR principles, policies, and procedures that have a pervasive impact on worker and management behavior. The job redesign process will have to take full account of these and, in fact, will often necessitate the drafting of new policies and procedures to support the redesigned work. The work organization will also have its own perspective on what job redesign should accomplish and suggest its own criteria against which the success of the job redesign must be evaluated. (See our later section on management criteria for the evaluation of job redesign programs.)

The Worker as a Systems Component

Workers are whole persons, each with a unique history of learning and development within a particular cultural context. Each brings to the job-worker situation a particular set of skills that have been honed through education, training, and experience. Workers bring three kinds of skills with them (Fine & Cronshaw, 1999)—skills that vary in their transferability between job-worker situations.

Adaptive skills enable people to manage themselves in relation to demands for conformity and/or change in the job situation. They are expressed as willingness to adapt to aspects of the work context; for example, time, space, impulse control, authority, and initiative. Adaptive skills have the greatest transferability between job situations. If a worker has a willingness, or even a preference, to exercise a high level of discretion on the job, a job redesign process that enriches the work will be well received by the worker. He or she will exert the necessary effort to get the job done under the new conditions set by the job redesign. If the worker does not have this willingness—the adaptive skill of accepting and exercising discretion across job tasks—the job enrichment will produce a mismatch between what the work context requires and what the worker is willing to provide. The result will be lower worker motivation, morale, and productivity, as well as a tendency to stay away from the job and seek new employment if such is available. (Job enrichment theorists have noted a similar phenomenon whereby workers with a low growth need are affected negatively, or at least are not affected positively, by job enrichment programs.) This mismatch of adaptive skill to job context illustrates the possible occurrence of fundamental conflict between the workers' values and style and the expectations of the work organization. Such a mismatch only hints at the complexities of the interactions among worker, work, and work organization that can make the outcomes of job redesign highly unpredictable and unstable. Organizational evaluation of job redesign that is not flexible enough to allow for the identification of these events, and that does not allow for the revision of the job redesign process to accommodate for them, runs a risk of delivering less than it has promised.

Functional skills are a second category of skills relied on by workers. These are competencies that enable people to relate to Things, Data, and People (Fine & Cronshaw, 1999) encountered in their jobs. These worker functions are a lexicon of worker behaviors that when performed effectively represent the competencies necessary to get the work done. They are organized in three hierarchies from high to low pertaining to Things (11 functions), Data (8 functions), and People (14 functions). In practice, one function from each hierarchy (three in all) is selected to describe the functional skills required by a task. For the range of tasks in an entire job, the three highest functions occurring in the task analysis are used to describe the job. These ratings by functional skill are possible because of the hierarchical nature of the functions. Each function in the hierarchy is defined to include all the lower functions beneath it and exclude those above it (Fine & Cronshaw, 1999, p. 39). In addition, each function is assigned an estimated proportionate weight reflecting the function's proportionate involvement in the job (the three proportions have to add up to 100%). Weighting functions according to their involvement with Things, Data, and People is called a job's orientation (Fine & Cronshaw, 1999, p. 48).

Although these functions are used primarily to describe the requirements of the tasks being performed, they can also be used to describe the skills and competencies of the workers performing those tasks. A worker is capable, of course, of achieving far higher functional levels than are represented by the requirements of a particular job and frequently demonstrates this when given the opportunity (e.g., an assembly line worker taking a leadership position when performing volunteer work with a service club).

Specific content skills are the third category of skills that a worker brings to the job-worker situation. These skills are competencies that enable people to perform a specific job to predetermined standards using equipment, technology, and procedures and relying on functional and adaptive skills. Specific content skills are also expressed as gerunds reflecting specific content areas, for example welding, riveting, carpentering, bricklaying, filing, recording, nursing, and healing. Sometimes they are expressed in terms of broad processes such as assembling, researching, and marketing. There are as many specific content skills as there are unique specialties. Specific content skills are learned on the job in connection with specific tasks or focused self-study to accomplish specific objectives.

The Work as a Systems Component

Job redesign is usually undertaken using a task-based approach. The tasks constitute complete modules of work. Redesign at the task level allows for considerable rigor in the analyzing, dissecting, and reworking of individual tasks combined with great flexibility in rearranging these tasks into a meaningful, productive flow of related work activities. Evaluation criteria for job redesign may be identified with performance of individual tasks (in which case specific content and functional skills, as well as task results, are often targeted for evaluation) or with the performance of a set of interrelated tasks (in which case adaptive skills and outputs provide the most appropriate basis for evaluation).

Principle 2: The Worker Is the Most Significant Factor in Effective Job Redesign

Many consider job redesign to be the exclusive domain of experts and professionals. Engineers study and implement new production machinery and processes; systems analysts install software programs and information systems; management consultants reengineer business processes on an organizationwide scale; and industrial psychologists study the job and give management recommendations on the best way to enrich it. It is a lamentable although commonly known fact that workers are often not in the loop of the job redesign process and are left to their own devices to adapt whatever technological, organizational, or procedural changes management orders them to implement. Although workers are a greatly under-utilized resource in job redesign, we believe that they are the most crucial factor in the success or failure of job redesign. As a result, they should make an active contribution to the evaluation of job redesign by, among other things, helping management to identify the criteria for success of the job redesign, collecting and providing evaluation data, and working with management to utilize the evaluation data in improving the job redesign process.

Those who question our statement that workers are the most significant factor in determining effectiveness of job redesign are advised to note the growing research literature pointing to the gains in organization productivity that result from active and meaningful worker input into the production process. One outstanding example is a meta-analysis conducted by Spector (1986). He statistically combined the results of 88 studies examining the relationships between worker perceptions of control in their workplaces and a number of outcome variables such as performance and motivation. Spector found that "high levels of perceived control were associated with high levels of job satisfaction, commitment, involvement, performance, and motivation and low levels of physical symptoms, emotional distress, role stress, absenteeism, intent to turnover, and turnover" (p. 1005). We further argue that worker input is the most important factor in job redesign because it is the workers who are required by management to make the technology and work arrangements function smoothly and effectively in their area of the production system. After changes are introduced by management, the new arrangements are left to the workers who must make them work over the long term. If all goes well, the workers also draw on their skills to fill in the inevitable gaps between plan and reality and so provide the buffer that allows the new technological and organizational arrangements to fit comfortably and seamlessly within the production system. The workers can also provide much assistance in identifying needed job changes and easing their implementation. In fact, worker input throughout the job redesign process is of great value in making it work more effectively and efficiently. Unfortunately, the opposite appears to be true in many organizations. Many managers take for granted that the workers will simply accommodate to—mold themselves around—the redesign arrangements and so fail to appreciate the pivotal role workers play in job redesign success or failure.

We are not saying that the worker is the only factor contributing to the success of job redesign. Engineers and tradespeople install more efficient and economical machines, computer analysts get information to and from the worker more quickly, and management provides policies and procedures as a contribution to safety and productivity within the new production set up. But, ultimately, it is the workers who must combine all these inputs within the redesigned job and get the work done. This is why we say that the most significant factor in job redesign is the worker and why worker input via formative evaluation is crucial to job redesign.

Principle 3: Job Redesign and Its Evaluation Are Continuous Processes

A common view portrays job redesign as an intervention that is periodically introduced by management to bring the work system up-to-date or as a part of other changes, such as job enrichment and process reengineering. This approach is consistent with the traditional, and probably still prevalent, view that management has a comprehensive and accurate view of work that goes on as well as the final word on how work processes can be improved. In this view, management periodically takes time off from other things, comes down from the Mount with experts in tow, sets things right for the workers, and then leaves them to operate under the new regime until another job redesign intervention is launched, sometimes years later. Anyone who has worked on the shop floor, in the front office, or on the retail floor will immediately recognize that this view of job redesign is naive and inaccurate. As we have already noted, workers craft (redesign) their work informally and on a continuing basis in both small and large ways without management prompting or input and, very often, without their manager's knowledge. This is done largely out of necessity, as well as the natural desire to turn out good work. Workers will also tailor their jobs to personal preferences when their job discretion allows it.

Job redesign occurs de facto on an ongoing basis and is a continuous part of the worker's adjustment and readjustment to the work situation. Management is best advised to participate in this ongoing redesign with the workers, seeking a consensus with them about what job changes should take place. Management is also well advised to solicit ongoing worker assistance in improving and implementing job changes originating from management or even working together to identify better technologies and write new personnel policies (activities usually restricted to management). Job redesign evaluation itself should become a mutual ongoing effort between management and workers with an emphasis on providing quick turnaround of evaluation results. As suggested later in this chapter, worker input during the job redesign is best captured and coordinated with the efforts of management through a joint management-worker committee. When a union is present, it should be represented on the committee as a means of ensuring that the interests of the union's membership are met during the job redesign (often the union's interests will center on the need for management to fairly compensate workers for performing the redesigned work).

Principle 4: A Realistic and Practical Understanding of the Work System Is Needed to Effectively Use Evaluation Results

It is one thing to get evaluation results in a timely manner; it is another to use these results effectively to guide the process of continuous job redesign. Consider the example of a job redesign evaluation conducted during a period when an office staff is converting to a new software package used for word processing and general administration (e.g., bookkeeping). The evaluations, comprising brief interviews with office staff, yield the (not surprising) result that the workers are somewhat stressed with the introduction of the new technology even though they participated in redesigning their jobs around it. In particular, the workers report that they lack the skills needed to operate the new computer system properly. The evaluation results point to a problem but not its solution. For management to respond adequately to this evaluation input within the context of continuous job redesign, it will need to pool its resources with those of the workers to seek answers that do the following:

- Consider the effects of systems interactions (e.g., What other areas or functions, if any, will encounter productivity losses if the office staff cannot use the new computer system properly?)
- Pinpoint the skills that the office staff must have to use the new computer system properly. (These skills, which include functional and adaptive as well as specific content skills, may require a more in-depth response than the usual expedient of offering a computer course.)
- Suggest the right management actions needed to ensure a satisfied and productive workforce (e.g., What type of training is needed? What kinds of manuals and work aids would be helpful? Is an increase in compensation called for to recognize higher levels of skill?)

All of these questions raised by the job redesign evaluation deserve more than an improvised answer or educated guesswork. Further job changes that follow from them should be informed by objective, comprehensive, and accurate data about the work, the worker, and the larger work organization. Job analysis can provide this information. As already noted, FJA deals with each of these components from a system point of view.

Principle 5: Conditions Before and During the Job Redesign Must Be Considered in Evaluation

We have emphasized that worker involvement is key to the success of job redesign. However, management must set conditions of mutual respect and trust before the workers will reciprocate with a wholehearted commitment to participating in job redesign. Management will find these conditions difficult to establish and maintain, but it will see gains toward promoting cooperation evaporate quickly if the workers perceive that management is failing to live up to the principles inherent in a progressive workplace. Even worse, management will not always see this problem coming. For example, actions that they see as innocuous (e.g., sending a job redesign memo to managers without sending a copy to the worker representatives) can invoke negative worker attributions of management's intentions and honesty. When job redesign is undertaken, the need is for a responsive communication setup that will identify any breakdowns in trust and mutual understanding *as the job redesign process unfolds* so these problems can be addressed before the job redesign is fatally compromised. We have previously referred to these communications as part and parcel of the formative evaluation of job redesign.

Worker Criteria for the Evaluation of Job Redesign Programs

We now come to the use of worker criteria as outcomes of job redesign. In a very helpful article on the use of group workshops in participative job redesign, Schweitz et al. (1997) recommended that job redesign be assessed against six criteria. In their words, these criteria represent the "significant determinants" of workers' ability to engage in productive work. We now list these six criteria, which we have found very useful in our own thinking about the evaluation of job redesign, followed by our observations and comments on each.

Adequate Discretion in Decision Making

Schweitz et al. referred to adequate discretion as "elbow room," an apt metaphor for the increased worker latitude that comes with enriched work. Adequate discretion requires management to challenge workers at their present level of skill and to provide the growth opportunities needed for workers to aspire to a higher skill level. It does not mean that workers should be challenged by discretionary tasks beyond their current level of skill—to do so is counterproductive and needlessly stressful to the worker. A good assessment on the *adequate discretion* criterion would involve a close examination of WI ratings across job tasks on the redesigned job, in combination with rated task levels on Things, Data, and People orientation. (Of course, this will require a FJA.)

Let us consider the example of a large retail firm that is implementing a new software system for its warehouse schedulers in a large centralized warehousing facility. The software will automate many of the routine decisions previously made by the schedulers (e.g., automatically sequencing pallets in the delivery trucks in accordance with retailer outlets' order of delivery along customer routes). This change will reduce the amount of discretion required in the related tasks and this will be reflected in lower WI ratings as the task bank is rewritten to incorporate the new job requirements. At this time, the workers participating in the collection of the new FJA data should be asked to give their reactions to the proposed job changes. Their responses in turn become a part of the formative evaluation. For example, the workers may accept the need for management's plan to install new computer software but ask that the software be modified to allow the schedulers to override automated decisions in situations where software mistakes introduce obvious scheduling errors and delays into the system. Used in this way, formative evaluation allows for the reintroduction of worker control into the redesigned job—control that would otherwise be reduced or eliminated by the computerized technology. The redesigned work then incorporates adequate discretion, adds challenge back into the work, and increases the efficiency of the scheduling system. The result is a "win-win" situation for both worker and management.

Opportunity to Learn on the Job and Keep on Learning

This principle is well illustrated in our job redesign example by the part-time temporary assistant who, by taking full advantage of training and learning opportunities presented to her, acquired the skills needed to perform the newly designed temporary assistant job and then transitioned into a full-time secretarial position. This secretarial position in turn represents an entry-level point to a union-protected career path within the organization. Incumbents in this position are frequently transferred laterally between departments, a practice that allows them to broaden their experience and to become candidates for higher level positions (up to the level of DAA). This incident also underscores job redesign's domino effect. When opportunities for learning on the job are provided, and that learning is encouraged and supported, the positive effects for the individual worker and the organization follow that person well beyond the immediate situation. Experience with similar job redesigns in the past and some speculative extrapolation of results into the future time frame will often be necessary to anticipate where and how the cumulative benefits of continued learning will result in job redesign benefits for the individual and the organization.

The FJA task bank, rewritten to reflect anticipated job changes, provides fundamental data for formative evaluation on this criterion. When reviewing the task bank together, workers and managers should ask questions such as these: "What upper-level jobs or team-based roles are now open to the incumbent based on his or her experience and previous performance?" "What skills must be further developed for upward or lateral movement to occur?" "What efforts—both on-the-job and via formal training—is management willing and able to make to give highly motivated workers the learning opportunities and job mobility they desire?" Management will have the answers to most of these questions and should be willing to share this information with the workers. This example illustrates that formative evaluation will point to aspects of job context, as well as job content, that should be changed to maximize learning opportunities for workers impacted by job redesign.

Job Variety

Job variety is present when the worker is asked to perform tasks at varying levels of complexity and differing combinations of emphasis (orientation) in Things, Data, and People skills. These tasks should be at skill levels appropriate to the worker's training and experience. Job variety is motivational to the worker because it offers the unexpected, novelty, and surprise value. It also involves more of the whole person in the job and can even provide an element of play to counteract the tedium and boredom that so often accompanies paid employment. This criterion of job redesign success is relatively easy to measure in summative evaluation if the job is reanalyzed after redesign is complete, but it should also be monitored through formative evaluation. The task bank on the redesigned job should show greater task heterogeneity with regard to rated Things, Data, and People complexity and orientation. As well, job incumbents can be interviewed to assess their reaction to the redesigned work (e.g., "Is it more interesting?" "Does it provide more variety?" "Is there opportunity to provide personal input?"). As with the first criterion (Adequate Discretion), objective data based on job analysis should tell the same story about the job redesign as do the worker reports based on interview data.

Mutual Support and Respect

This criterion represents one of those intangibles—aspects of work context—that, although difficult to measure, are crucial to the success of job redesign. In the first instance, support and respect have to flow from management to the workers as well as exist among the managers themselves—it is only then that a culture of mutual support and respect can flourish throughout the organization. Mutual support and respect will occur only if management adopts a listening stance vis-à-vis its workers. A culture of listening, support, and respect is necessary because workers cannot be expected to extend themselves from their present comfort zones to take on the added discretion and assume the risks required by job redesign if the atmosphere is poisoned by mistrust and suspicion. Mutual support and respect are very much formative criteria in the job redesign process. They comprise a sine qua non that must be met before meaningful participative job redesign can go forward. If interviews with workers and managers or the results of worker attitude surveys indicate that conditions of mutual support and respect are not present, these shortcomings should be attended to, and a suitable environment provided, before the job redesign process proceeds.

Experienced Meaningfulness of the Work

This criterion, originally proposed by Hackman and Oldham (1980) in their classic work on job redesign and enrichment, is another of those somewhat ephemeral, but highly important, human variables in job redesign. Experienced meaningfulness is fundamental to job redesign because work that is experienced as lacking meaning is demotivating of the workers' efforts and alienating of the workers' spirit. Work that is productive and healthy demands an overriding reason for its performance. Meaningful work contributes to a larger whole and is perceived to have a positive impact on and contribution to others. When work has been fragmented to the point that workers begin to lose sight of the contribution they make, worker dissatisfaction and alienation are not far behind. This was the problem contributing to the stress and dissatisfaction of the department secretaries in the case at the beginning of this chapter and addressed through the job redesign. After staff losses due to retrenchment in the department, the secretaries no longer had time to answer student and faculty inquiries completely—compromising their feelings of accomplishment—because they were constantly on the run with other tasks, several of which impinged on them simultaneously. Better than anyone, they appreciated the need to get accurate and complete information in response to front-desk inquiries and were frustrated by their frequent inability to do so. For this, and other reasons, their jobs started to lose meaning and became reduced to earning a paycheck. It was these negative worker reactions, and the amelioration of them, that become the focus of formative evaluation. In this general vein, we recommend that job redesigners stay in touch with workers before, during, and after the process of redesign to ensure that the resulting work is coherent and directs workers toward meaningful outcomes they can point to with pride.

People find work meaningful to the extent that they have the opportunity to contribute to achieving the larger purpose of the organization as well as their own needs. They monitor their ongoing contribution by gauging their efforts against performance standards, their own and those set by management. These performance standards should be identified in the job analysis that, in the formative sense, represents the latest stage of the "work-in-progress" that eventually constitutes the redesigned job. In scrutinizing the performance standards, managers and workers should ask questions such as these: "Are these standards achievable?" "If not, how do managers and/or workers have to adjust their expectations to make them achievable?" "Does the achievement of one performance standard interfere with the achievement of another?" Consideration of these formative questions in the redesign of the work will result in greater felt meaningfulness of the work and a smoother engagement of the worker with the productive system.

A Desirable Future for the Worker

The desirable future for the worker depends on the values the worker holds. Fine and Cronshaw (1999) discussed three areas that provide growth opportunities for workers: compensation, skill and knowledge, and status. All three should be attended to in formative evaluation of job redesign because all three will be directly or indirectly impacted by job redesign. It is very important to hear and address workers' concerns about all three as the job redesign is carried out. Compensation is often a key concern. One job redesign carried out by the first author of this chapter was held up for some time due to sensitivities and anxieties over compensation. At issue was a job that involved oversight and care of office and housing arrangements for a community service organization and its clients. The job incumbent was insistent that the redesigned job be classified as a management job so that she could receive the higher management salary that she felt she was due. Senior management was not convinced that the redesigned job deserved a management-level compensation. Much back-and-forth negotiation was needed to resolve the impasse. Job redesign had highlighted, and brought to the fore, a key growth issue for the employee—the rate of compensation she was owed for the duties performed. A satisfactory level of compensation in turn led to a more desirable future for the worker in terms of her quality of life off the job. If compensation is becoming a major issue emerging from the job redesign process, this question must be addressed between workers (and the union, if one is present) and management in a mutually satisfactory manner. To leave this issue unresolved until the job redesign is complete runs the risk of serious resistance when the redesigned job becomes operational.

If the direction of the job redesign is toward enriched work, workers will likely perceive that opportunities for skill/knowledge growth and higher status (especially vis-à-vis management) have been increased. Their main concern will then be to win the wage or salary that this enriched work deserves (see previous paragraph). Conversely, if the work is being de-skilled, management will have to deal with the consequences of the thwarted growth opportunities that invariably ensue. If the redesigned work is headed toward greater fragmentation and de-skilling, management will have to deal with higher levels of worker dissatisfaction, stress, absenteeism, and turnover after the redesigned job(s) become operational. Many workers do not see a boring, low-status job as having a desirable future and this will become especially apparent in high rates of turnover and the need to pay a wage premium to adequately staff the work that must be done.

The question of desirable future is an intensely personal one and, as previously noted, the responses to a formative evaluation on this criterion will vary depending on the needs of the individual worker. As the job redesign proceeds, workers should be provided with the latest job analysis information outlining job outputs, tasks, performance standards, and skill or ability requirements. Some attempt by management to tentatively place the redesigned job on the compensation grid is also helpful at this stage. Workers, and their union representatives, should be asked questions such as, "Is the pay fair for the work that is done?" "Does this job offer adequate opportunities for skills training and growth?" "Is this the type of job you would be willing to stay in over the longer term?" "If you were to leave this job, what would be the likely reasons?" The answers to these questions will point to aspects of job content and job context that should be targeted in the job redesign or, at the very least, consequences that will ensue, such as worker turnover, if these issues are not addressed.

The job redesign process itself will become more effective, and its ultimate effects more pervasive and sustained, to the extent that the behavior science principles represented by these criteria are organically incorporated into job redesign to shape and focus the process as it unfolds, rather than relying solely on summative evaluation that will point to design improvements only after the job redesign has been completed.

Management Criteria for the Evaluation of Job Redesign Programs

Management, in legitimately representing the interests of the work organization throughout the job redesign process, will focus primary attention on its own set of criteria. Management will tend to view these criteria through a summative lens—they are the "bottom line" outcomes that management is looking for after the job redesign is complete. Yorks and Whitsett (1989) present a good example of this approach. They report summative results for a comprehensive job redesign program across a major life insurance company, in which many employees were impacted by the interventions and were subsequently evaluated on (mainly) management-based criteria such as attendance, turnover, productivity, service, and quality of work. In fact, evaluation results reported in the research literature on job redesign frequently focus on summative evaluation.

When we draw a distinction between worker and management criteria for evaluation of job redesign, we do not mean to imply that workers' and management's interests are fundamentally incompatible—in fact, a good faith effort through job redesign should be made to maximize criterion outcomes for both parties. However, we must be realistic in recognizing that management and workers will come to job redesign with different interests in the outcomes of that process, and these will be reflected in different criteria that each side brings to the job redesign table. With this in mind, we now discuss criteria that management will typically have in mind as outcomes for job redesign.

Reduction of Bottlenecks and Production Problems

Although we would like to believe in the capacity of management to be omniscient and relentlessly proactive, experience tells us otherwise. Job redesign is often directed toward solving immediate and pressing organizational problems rather than being part of a comprehensive, strategic effort aimed at achieving long-term organizational goals. Our case at the beginning of this chapter is a good illustration of how an organizational crisis becomes the stimulus for job redesign. We do not gainsay the value of this type of job redesign—not all organizational problems and difficulties can be anticipated or planned out of the system proactively. Nevertheless, this type of reactive job redesign, however necessary it might be in the short term to keep the goods and services moving to the customer, can have serious shortcomings. Most important, it tends to be reactive in that it responds to accumulated past problems, rather than taking advantage of future opportunities. When possible, it is obviously desirable to proactively anticipate production bottlenecks and problems and engineer them out of the system before they become serious problems. However, the causes of production problems may be deep, multilayered, and largely concealed from management's view by the complexities of the work system and the interactions of its components. As a result, a creative process of job redesign involving the joint perspectives and problem-solving efforts of management and workers will be especially called for. The specific criteria and methods for evaluating this type of job redesign will depend on the production problem addressed and other considerations such as the size of the work unit and the type of technology employed.

Improvement of Work Team Functioning

Sociotechnical theorists propose that the work be designed around self-maintaining work teams following the principle of minimal critical specification or MCS (Davis & Wacker, 1988). (This can be seen as a proactive approach to job redesign, in contrast with the reactive approach in response to bottlenecks and production problems.) Under the principle of MCS, the work team is provided with the constraints imposed by the larger work organization and under which they must operate. The team is then given the discretion to design into the work whatever else it sees as necessary beyond the minimal specification. However, this approach places new demands on workers. As Davis and Wacker (1988) pointed out, tasks done by individual team members now vary from day to day, and each member must perform a wider variety of tasks. This introduces an additional element of uncertainty and instability for job holders—a potential workplace impediment that should be reduced, when possible, through the use of job redesign. Beyond this, we would add that job redesign has the positive effect of increasing the adaptability and resiliency of the work system and the workers in it in so far as it consciously sets about to initiate and build mutual respect and trust through worker involvement.

Davis and Wacker proposed a number of criteria by which to judge the success of job redesign intended to improve team functioning under the MCS model. Some of these criteria, such as the following examples, serve well in the role of formative evaluation:

- Each task group gets timely feedback about task results and information about likely future systems states and results.
- Highly interdependent tasks are grouped together.
- Jobs or teams possess the skills, knowledge, feedback mechanisms, and authority needed to sustain self-regulation.
- Teams perform the social maintenance tasks needed to keep them connected with other teams.

Other management-based criteria, which often play a role in summative evaluation and comprise the basis of team performance evaluation, include productivity, quality, efficiency, yield, maintenance, cost, waste, errors, cross-training, skill acquisition, customer complaints/commendations, machine utilization, and downtime (Davis & Wacker, 1988).

Compliance With Government Laws and Regulations

All organizations have become subject to an increasing number and scope of government regulations, many of which require changes in the way work is done. The Americans with Disabilities Act, as one example, requires employers to offer reasonable work accommodations to those with physical or mental disabilities. Most often, these accommodations will be provided on an individual basis, depending on the type and severity of the disability and the employer's ability to provide the accommodation, short of undue hardship. In these cases, it will be impossible to devise a single set of one-size-fits-all criteria for the evaluation of success of the job redesign. And, most likely, the disabled individual and medical advisors will play a part in deciding with management what those success criteria will be. Job redesign may also be required in response to health and safety legislation by states or provinces. Here the criteria for the success of the job redesign will vary by the (often detailed) requirements of each jurisdiction. State and provincial labor boards will have enforcement mechanisms, including health and safety inspectors, who monitor employers for adherence to these legislatively set criteria.

The Summative Evaluation of Job Redesign

The literature on job redesign emphasizes the use of summative evaluation, mainly using management criteria, and does so to the virtual exclusion of formative evaluation. Summative evaluation differs from the formative approach we have proposed in that it does the following:

- Requires the input, often extensive, of measurement and statistical experts
- Involves the setting up of formal research designs, preferably quasi-experimental or experimental in nature, as the basis for drawing valid inferences about the effects of job redesign interventions
- Places a greater emphasis on bottom line management-defined outcomes of job redesign (e.g., work productivity and wastage rates) than on variables assessing the quality of the job redesign process itself
- Requires large numbers of job incumbents to be included in the evaluation component of the job redesign to ensure the validity and generalizability of the evaluation results
- Reflects the success of the job redesign intervention taken as a whole and when it is completed.

Summative evaluation clearly has a role in job redesign, and this is already well established in the related literature (e.g., see Yorks & Whitsett, 1989). However, formative evaluation as outlined in this chapter has much to contribute to job redesign and should be a part of the redesign intervention, regardless of whether a summative evaluation is planned at a later date.

Bringing Together Worker and Management Criteria in Successful Job Redesign

Although we have discussed worker and management criteria separately, it is most desirable to reconcile the two sets of criteria into a mutual approach to the formative evaluation of job redesign. Under the surface of the activity, we can be sure that the separate criteria will be in the minds of the participants. This is all the more reason for managers and workers to come to a shared understanding of a mutually negotiated set of evaluation criteria before the job redesign begins. Such an understanding could be the beginning of the mutual respect and trust that is essential for the job redesign activity to succeed. In a balanced manner, these criteria need to represent the interests of both parties as follows:

- Job redesign is overseen and steered by a joint management-worker committee. This same committee is also responsible for the evaluation of the job redesign.
- The committee makes a clear statement of what the workers want and what management wants from the redesign activity, and it works out an agreement on which worker and management criteria will be used in the job redesign.

- An agreement is reached on how management proposes to gather the job redesign data. At this point, it is desirable to describe the job analysis method to be used and for management to make an unequivocal commitment to worker input. (One way to assert the need for worker input is to bring forward prior effective adaptations made by the workers in their present jobs.)
- The committee should also be prepared to continuously evaluate the changes being made and to pursue the consequences of the change for training, compensation, and career growth.
- Finally, the committee prepares a work plan before the redesign is initiated and sends it to the appropriate level of management for its approval.

When the work plan is approved, the signing authority will have to commit the necessary budgetary and personnel resources for the job redesign effort, including funding of the evaluation component. Management should be informed that unanticipated needs are liable to arise during the job redesign (such as additional evaluation interviews to gauge worker concerns about an unanticipated side effect of the job redesign), and they should indicate their willingness to make a reasonable commitment of resources to address these emerging concerns.

Conclusions

Job redesign is an ongoing process that is dependent on the inputs of worker incumbents who are oriented to do a good job and achieve the overall objectives of management. Management's interests are best served if, during every stage of the process, it shows an awareness of this fact and involves and supports the workers who are going to implement the redesign through the enlightened use of formative evaluation. Although worker criteria for redesign are more immediate to their own situation—compensation, physical requirements, work satisfaction, and personal growth—it is likely that management criteria relating to productivity and profitability can benefit in the long run by being reconciled with worker interests. When this happens, ongoing evaluation becomes a powerful tool for coordinating the efforts of management and workers in maximizing the outcomes of both parties to the job redesign process.

Participative job redesign has an emergent aspect that has generally gone unrecognized, which makes it impossible to specify a priori success criteria and a comprehensive evaluation strategy. Although practitioners must begin job redesign with a clear picture of the outcomes they wish to achieve, this picture will be insufficient for maximizing the eventual outcomes of job redesign for management and workers. The job redesign team should be open to every opportunity to creatively modify job redesign by drawing on ongoing feedback from formative evaluation, especially from workers, as a way of maximizing opportunities and minimizing problems emerging from the job redesign process. Even formative evaluation criteria themselves will emerge and evolve over time, as will the design of the formative evaluation itself. The complex nature of work, workers, and work organization in effect dictates this by making design omniscience impossible. On the other hand, an open process of inquiry and formative evaluation can lead to new solution possibilities for old production problems—avenues for improved productivity and worker growth that were not apparent at the outset of the job redesign process. Organization evaluation of job redesign is most effective when it explicitly recognizes the need for support and builds in the necessary flexibility to enable the ongoing job redesign process.

References

Champoux, J. E. (1991). A multivariate test of the job characteristics theory of work motivation. *Journal of Organizational Behavior, 12,* 431–446.

Davis, L. E., & Wacker, G. J. (1988). Job redesign. In S. Gael (Ed.), *The job analysis handbook for business, industry, and government* (Vol. 1, pp. 157–172). New York: Wiley.

Fine, S. A., & Cronshaw, S. F. (1999). *Functional job analysis: A foundation for human resources management.* Mahwah, NJ: Lawrence Erlbaum.

Fine, S. A., & Getkate, M. (1995). *Benchmarks tasks for job analysis.* Mahwah, NJ: Lawrence Erlbaum.

Hackman, J. R., & Oldham, G. R. (1980). *Work redesign.* Reading, MA: Addison-Wesley.

Posavac, E. J., & Carey, R. G. (1992). *Program evaluation: Methods and case studies* (4th ed.). Englewood Cliffs, NJ: Prentice Hall.

Schweitz, R., Granata, E., Storjohann, G., Grady, W., Gruenberg, B., & Noble, P. (1997). Could participative design be the answer for us? *Journal for Quality and Participation, 20,* 34–42.

Spector, P. (1986). Perceived control by employees: A meta-analysis of studies concerning autonomy and participation at work. *Human Relations, 39,* 1005–1016.

Wrzesniewski, A., & Dutton, J. E. (2001). Crafting a job: Revisioning employees as active crafters of their work. *Academy of Management Review, 26,* 179-201

Yorks, L., & Whitsett, D. A. (1989). *Scenarios of change: Advocacy and the diffusion of job redesign in organizations.* New York: Praeger.

Suggested Readings in Job Redesign

Fine, S. A., & Cronshaw, S. F. (1999). *Functional job analysis: A foundation for human resources management.* Mahwah, NJ: Lawrence Erlbaum.

Posavac, E. J., & Carey, R. G. (1992). *Program evaluation: Methods and case studies* (4th ed.). Englewood Cliffs, NJ: Prentice Hall.

Yorks, L. (1979). *Job enrichment revisited* (AMA Management Briefing). New York: AMACOM.

Yorks, L., & Whitsett, D. A. (1989). *Scenarios of change: Advocacy and the diffusion of job redesign in organizations.* New York: Praeger.

CHAPTER 16

Organization Development

Allan H. Church

At its core, the field of organization development (OD) is focused on a few straightforward but very important principles. One of these is the underlying belief that data-based feedback (via some mechanism, whether quantitative or qualitative) leads to greater awareness of the present and future states; it thereby drives positive individual behavioral change and as a result larger organizational change as well (Waclawski & Church, 2002). Although other fundamental principles of OD are important for understanding the field in general (e.g., its grounding in systems theory and a values-based normative approach to the types and expected outcomes of interventions in which practitioners should engage), it is this data-based action research perspective that makes the evaluation of OD efforts so compelling, and yet also so challenging. Clearly, if organizational change is the anticipated outcome of an OD intervention, it should be a relatively straightforward process for evaluating the intervention's impact. The challenge, of course, in evaluating OD efforts often depends on semantics (e.g., what exactly does culture change look like?), expectations (e.g., how long does it take to see an organization's culture actually change?), and skill sets (many OD practitioners are not well trained in research design or evaluation methods).

As Hronec (1993) predicted a decade ago, we are increasingly focused on using information (i.e., hard metrics) as our "vital signs" in both driving and evaluating OD-related interventions. As a result of this emphasis, research studies that link various interventions to specific outcomes (e.g., Rucci, Kirn, & Quinn, 1998) are quite popular in the organizational arena. Although historically not a core competency of

OD practitioners, the ability to demonstrate the impact of a change effort on the business (e.g., via reducing turnover, increasing sales or market share, or improving productivity) is receiving increasing attention in actual practice, and managers are being asked more and more frequently to justify their investments in OD, human resource development, and various related training interventions (Cummings & Worley, 1997; Phillips, 1991).

Given this shifting interest in linkage research, why do so many change initiatives have poor or nonexistent evaluation processes in place? One major challenge inherent in evaluating OD efforts is defining exactly what organizational culture change should look like, and when and how it should manifest itself. Because of the complexities and interdependencies involved in large-scale organizational change efforts (e.g., Burke & Litwin, 1992; Porras & Robertson, 1992), it is often challenging to isolate the impact of a complex set of interventions at a single point in time. As a result, some practitioners shy away from impact evaluation entirely. For example, the success of rolling out a major initiative focused on new leadership behaviors will hinge on having visible support and modeling from senior management, reinforcing communication from middle managers, being aligned with the key messages from other systems, and being integrated with rewards and recognition systems (e.g., the performance management process and how promotions are made). If the subsystems of an organization are not aligned (Katz & Kahn, 1978) during a change effort, achieving positive results becomes very difficult.

Aside from the complexities inherent in the field, OD has historically been less focused on evaluation than have many other areas of practice. One reason cited by practitioners over the years is that the evaluation aspect of an OD effort comes at the very end of the project and is often seen as the least interesting or exciting component (e.g., Burke 1982; Porras & Robertson, 1992). Consequently, the evaluation design is an afterthought, and this can result in a less rigorous approach. In addition, an effective evaluation process may well lead to the discontinuation of a given intervention or program an OD professional may be responsible for or may have put a significant level of effort into developing (Martineau & Preskill, 2002; Phillips, 1991). In other words, whether the outcome is positive (success) or negative (failure), the practitioner is likely to be removed from the effort. This potential outcome can result in a lack of objectivity and is one of the reasons some OD consultants recommend that evaluation be conducted by individuals independent from the effort itself (Burke, 1982).

A third reason behind the lack of focus on OD evaluation may be an absence of the appropriate skill sets and consistency in overall approach to doing the work. The contemporary OD arena is characterized by a multitude of individual and independent agents offering customized approaches and specific techniques with widely divergent educational and professional backgrounds and experiences (Church, 2001; Sanzgiri & Gottlieb, 1992). As a result, many OD practitioners may lack formal research design and measurement training, let alone an understanding of various evaluation methodologies. In addition, their approach to the entire consulting process (including the role of evaluation) and the types of interventions they are familiar with is inconsistent.

Despite these issues, many OD professionals (and certainly their internal clients) would also agree that evaluation is a critical component of the change process. We always come back to the question, What do we need to do to conduct an effective evaluation of our efforts? The answer is simple. What is needed is an applied framework for evaluating OD interventions. The purpose of this chapter is to focus on the unique aspects involved in evaluating the impact of OD interventions in contemporary organizational settings. Following an introduction and overview of the field of OD as a data-driven approach to change and some of the complexities involved in understanding the scope of the various types of interventions, the chapter provides a detailed process for evaluating OD efforts that closely mirrors the classic action research–based approach to consulting (Burke, 1982; Nadler, 1977; Waclawski & Church, 2002) that drives much of the work in the field. Next, several case studies of actual OD evaluation efforts are presented. The chapter closes with a call to arms regarding the importance of evaluation for the future of the field of OD.

Overview of Organization Development

To effectively evaluate an OD intervention, first it is important to understand what such an evaluation might look like. Ask practitioners "What is OD?," however, and you will probably receive a different answer from each one you ask. One of the more interesting aspects about the field of OD is the inherent absence of consistency, and therefore clarity, among practitioners regarding its definition, core tools and competencies, and professional boundaries (Church, 2001; Weider & Kulick, 1999). A basis of debate for decades (e.g., Burke, 1982; Friedlander, 1976; Goodstein, 1984; Rothwell, Sullivan, & McLean, 1995), this state of flux and lack of clarity is due in large part to the wide range of influences in the origins of the field.

In general, the field of OD is grounded in a combination of academic theory, applied research methods, and experiential consulting efforts dating back as far as the 1940s (Burke, 1982; Sanzgiri & Gottlieb, 1992). Its roots are quite varied and can be traced to such influences as individual psychology, social psychology and systems theory, group dynamics, theories of participative management, job characteristics and design, survey research methods, and even psychotherapy. Given these perspectives, it should come as no surprise that a recent review of the role behavior of OD practitioners (Gottlieb, 1998) listed such divergent role sets as content expert, diagnostician, trainer/educator, process consultant, and objective observer. Of course, this also means that the range of OD interventions that one might be expected to evaluate is considerably diverse as well.

Taking a more normative perspective, however, some practitioners have argued that at its core an OD intervention or a change effort should represent the implementation of a process of planned change for the purpose of organization improvement. Using the definition offered by Waclawski and Church (2002) for the purposes of this chapter, OD is defined as "a planned process of promoting positive humanistically oriented large-system change and improvement in organizations through the use of social science theory, action research, and behaviorally-based data collection and feedback techniques" (p. 9).

Reviewing the definition in detail from this perspective, there are three basic notions behind all OD efforts: (a) the data-based technique known as action research (Lewin, 1958; Nadler, 1977), (b) understanding interdependencies and systems-level thinking (Burke & Litwin, 1992; Katz & Kahn, 1978), and (c) a normative, humanistic values-based approach to driving organizational improvement efforts (Church, Waclawski, & Burke, 2001; Margulies & Raia, 1990). Although a detailed description of each of these elements is beyond the scope of this chapter, the important point is that information or data regarding how employees think and feel about the present state of their organization—for example, their feelings about senior leadership, company strategy, manager, job, career, work-life balance, and rewards and recognition—is a central component to any OD-related intervention. As a result, data themselves and being able to link those data to other important individual and organizational outcomes are critical for evaluating the success of any significant OD intervention.

One of the interesting consequences of having such a broad context is that many different types of interventions and efforts can be classified under this umbrella. A review of several lists and related typologies of interventions (e.g., Burke, 1982; Cummings & Worley, 1997; Rothwell et al., 1995) reveals a wide range of possibilities that spans three primary dimensions:

1. Type of intervention (e.g., quantitative methods or process-based methods)
2. Level of intervention and intended impact (individual, group/team, subsystem, and total system)
3. Content area of focus (e.g., leadership, culture, conflict management, mission/vision, group dynamics, reward and recognition systems, communication, manager quality, structure, motivation, and performance management)

Table 16.1 provides several examples of these different types of initiatives and interventions and some basic characteristics of each.

Different types of OD interventions require somewhat different evaluation approaches. If there is one truth that can be stated about evaluating OD interventions, it is that there is no one best way. Rather, each approach needs to be tailored to the unique constraints and characteristics of that change program or effort. Moreover, it is important to recognize that larger organizational change efforts often comprise several different but inter-related OD interventions over a series of years (e.g., in an effort to change the overall culture). As a result, one of the very first questions to answer in the OD evaluation process is whether the focus is on the short term or long term and the related implications of each.

Another important aspect in understanding the role of OD evaluation is the underlying consulting framework that drives most practitioners' approaches to doing this type of work. Grounded again in an action research approach, the framework consists of seven different phases: (a) entry, (b) contracting, (c) data gathering, (d) data analysis, (e) data feedback, (f) intervention, and (g) evaluation (Burke, 1982; Church et al., 2001; Rothwell et al., 1995). What is perhaps most apparent here, and as noted earlier, is that the evaluation component of an OD approach is clearly located at the very tail end of the cycle. This often means that little attention is given to the various components (and potential additional resources needed) for evaluation in advance of the overall design of the intervention. Although an effective contracting phase should include a discussion of expected outcomes, resources, and deliverables on both sides of the client-consultant relationship, often the desired "end-state" of an OD effort is less well defined. Questions such as "What does a

Table 16.1   Examples of Different OD Related Interventions

Intervention	Primary Level of Focus*	Description & Expected Outcomes
Whole Systems Change	System	• Large group intervention (often staged as a major event) that brings an entire organization or key decision-makers from all functions, processes, and levels together to create an enhanced future state or to solve a complex interdependent problem.
Organizational Design	System	• Creation of a new and/or revised set of work processes, reporting relationships and cross-function/business/system interdependencies in order to improve overall functioning and performance.
Sociotechnical Design	System	• Participatory approach to changing the design, structure, and process of conducting the work itself that enhances the involvement, ownership and employee-work technology interface (e.g., self-directed work teams, etc.).
Survey Feedback	System	• Fundamental action research-based OD technique used to diagnose the strengths and opportunity areas in a given organization, function or group; surface dissatisfaction with the present state through the sharing of feedback; and action plan around potential interventions that will produce positive change (and thereby transition to the future state).
		• At the individual level this technique is often behavioral focused in nature (e.g., using 360 feedback or multisource feedback, personality assessments, etc.), and when scaled-up is used to drive collective behavior and/or cultural change.
People Systems & Processes	System	• Modifications and enhancements to the formal human resource and performance management systems and tools (e.g., selection, appraisal, rewards, succession planning, communications, etc.) in order to provide greater clarity for employees regarding their development, performance and future career prospects/opportunities.
Leadership Development/ Training	Group	• Individual coaching and/or programmatic development efforts aimed at improving the skills, knowledge, and abilities of leadership in an organization. Often used in conjunction with other tools such as individual assessments (e.g., 360 feedback, personality measures), process consultation, action research, or team building.
Appreciative Inquiry	Group	• Cooperative process through questioning to identify and reinforce the positive aspects of individuals, groups and organizations in order to strengthen a system's capacity for positive potential. The typical cycle includes Discovery, Dreaming, Designing, and Delivery. The AI approach can be applied at many different levels of analysis (e.g., team, group, organization).
Action Learning	Group	• Focused approach for working with a group that creates an interactive laboratory for peer-based learning to solve a specific set of projects or issues.

Intervention	Primary Level of Focus*	Description & Expected Outcomes
Quality of Worklife Programs	Group	• Efforts focused on increasing employee participation, engagement in decision-making, and ensuring better working conditions.
Process Improvement/ Quality Circles	Group	• Targeted intervention to improve the flow and/or output of a specific work process or procedure. Often involves removing redundancies and wasted efforts.
Team Building/ Conflict Management	Group	• Efforts aimed at improving the cooperation, collaboration, and general interpersonal relationships between different members of the same team, or different groups that need to work better together.
Process Consultation/ Coaching	Group/ Individual	• Group facilitation and process coaching to increase effectiveness of team meetings, improve interpersonal skills, and enhance self and process-based awareness.
Job Design/ Enrichment	Individual	• Specific changes made to jobs and/or job families that address the need for more variety, autonomy, and decision-making authority.

*Many system level initiatives rely on group and/or individual level tools (e.g., feedback) to actually achieve system-wide change over time. In addition, many system level tools can also be applied to smaller sub-systems or groups.

SOURCE: Adapted from Burke (1982), Cummins & Worley (1997), Rothwell, Sullivan, & McLean (1995), and Waclawski & Church (2002).

more rewarding culture change look like?" or "How will we know when people are more motivated or when our leaders are significantly better at building talent?" can be difficult to answer without additional work. These types of outcomes are less easily measured and therefore more difficult to evaluate. This is why in many OD efforts evaluation is at best an event that occurs in the consulting process at the end of a project's lifecycle (Martineau & Preskill, 2002).

Despite these issues, it is critical that all types of human process interventions, including OD-related efforts, have effectively structured evaluation components to their design and implementation. If we are ever going to justify the effort and expense associated with these large-scale efforts, it is imperative that practitioners have a clear process for conducting evaluations and a solid understanding of the issues and forces involved. To this end, the following section provides a process for reviewing the basic dimensions of each intervention and building a successful evaluation program.

A Process for Evaluating OD Interventions

As with most applications, to implement a program or intervention successfully, it is important to have a model, framework, or process to follow that clearly outlines the important components and issues involved. One useful way of conceptualizing and upgrading the evaluation component in the OD model is to apply the consulting framework itself to the overall evaluation process. Similar to models suggested by professionals in other fields such as performance improvement, training and development, and human resource development (e.g., Phillips, 1991; Swanson & Holton, 1999), the approach outlined here follows four basic phases:

1. Scoping
2. Designing
3. Collecting and analyzing data
4. Communicating

Each of these phases is described in detail below with relevant examples of organizational applications, potential issues, and success factors.

Scoping

The first phase in any attempt to evaluate an intervention should be the determination of the size and scope of the overall evaluation effort. As OD efforts can range from team-building exercises to complex multiyear change strategies in global organizational settings, the best time to approach evaluation scoping is at the very beginning of the internal or external consulting project—during the contracting stage. As with the OD intervention itself, the nature of the evaluation process will be significantly influenced by the timing needs, budgets, resources, and individuals involved. Therefore it is critical to contract up front for the desired level of evaluation. There are three key factors to consider: (a) what is the purpose of the evaluation, (b) who will conduct the evaluation and who else needs to be involved in the process, and (c) when will it be conducted.

Purpose of the Evaluation

Many OD professionals leave the planning of an evaluation effort until their initiative has been fully launched. Unfortunately, this scenario often results in suboptimal evaluation designs and measures. Certainly if a pre-assessment survey of some sort is to be compared with a post-intervention assessment, it is necessary to have conducted the first measure in advance of (and not concurrent with) the intervention. Although it is difficult to implement a completely controlled experimental design such as an evaluation study given the complexities of organizations and their need to function effectively during a given intervention, it is possible to plan for a well-implemented strategy. Moreover, going through the initial planning process at the outset helps practitioners achieve greater clarity regarding the overall objectives of the intervention itself (Martineau & Preskill, 2002).

Unlike many other types of efforts, most OD-related interventions, particularly those aimed at improving larger systemic issues such as culture or leadership behavior (e.g., Church, Walker, & Brockner, 2002), are driven by external pressures to change (Burke & Litwin, 1992). Mergers and acquisitions, emerging business pressures in a changing competitive landscape, new senior leadership, heightened external scrutiny over systems and processes, or even major structural change or reengineering efforts often require the support of an OD approach and set of tools. Because of this, most large-scale OD efforts are aimed primarily at Kirkpatrick's (1998) levels 3 (behavior change), and 4 (bottom line impact). As a result, the expected outcomes of these efforts can at times be challenging and complex to quantify. It is relatively easy to evaluate a small team-based intervention before and after the event to test for greater cohesion and collaboration, but the complexities inherent in evaluating a multiyear culture change initiative are far more daunting for practitioners

One helpful approach to scoping an evaluation is to start by determining whether the purpose of the evaluation is to be formative, summative, or longitudinal (McLean, Sullivan, & Rothwell, 1995). Although an ideal approach would be to include evaluation components that address all three objectives, reality (as determined by politics, budget, timing, resources, etc.) often dictates that projects can be evaluated on only one or two of these. A formative evaluation strategy is one in which the evaluation is conducted during the OD intervention itself, and the results are used to shape the future direction of that effort. Also known as implementation feedback (Cummings & Worley, 1997), formative evaluations can be quite useful in the OD arena for enhancing the impact of various communication efforts, education and training programs, and senior leadership modeling and messaging during a large-scale change effort. They can also help save an OD intervention from failing if corrective action can be taken midstream.

What formative evaluations do not tell you, however, is the overall impact of the intervention on individuals or the organization as a whole. Summative evaluations (or evaluation feedback), in comparison, are those that follow immediately after the completion of a given intervention or project. Whether based on attitudes (e.g., gathered via a survey or evaluation form) or harder performance metrics (e.g., sales, product shrinkage, or accidents), summative evaluations represent the most classic form of immediate return on intervention investment. Because many OD efforts have nebulous boundaries around when the initiative begins and ends, formal summative evaluation approaches are less easily applied to large-scale change initiatives. They can be used, however, to evaluate various discrete components of a larger integrated effort (e.g., the impact of an executive development program or a new leadership model rolled out via a 360-degree feedback process).

The third type of evaluation strategy, longitudinal, is perhaps the best suited for evaluating the impact of large-scale OD interventions. Completed at some future point following the completion of the intervention, longitudinal designs allow time for new behaviors to form, systems and processes to reach alignment, and individuals to adapt and shape new cultures. Longitudinal evaluations in OD are often challenging to conduct because of other significant changes that tend to occur over time in organizations—such as new senior management, a shift in business direction and focus, or new or multiple consultants. This is one of the reasons that change efforts have been characterized over the last few years as often being in "midstream" (Burke, Javitch, Waclawski, & Church, 1997).

The Role of Evaluator and Key Stakeholders

In conjunction with identifying the purpose of the evaluation, the selection of the individual (or individuals) who will be evaluating the intervention and who else needs to be involved from a stakeholder perspective are also important components to consider at the outset of the OD intervention. Once again, the appropriate selection of the evaluator will be driven in part by the nature and size of the change effort. In some cases, the person conducting the evaluation may also be the OD practitioner (whether internal or external to the company) who designed the effort. Although not ideal from an objective perspective (Burke, 1982), this is often the reality in practice (e.g., due to resource limitations or lack of awareness of the need for objectivity).

If the OD intervention includes a heavy training and development component (e.g., in an effort to provide new tools and key messages for managers regarding their ability to coach and develop employees), the internal practitioner managing the process is often also the evaluator. If, on the other hand, the change effort revolves around a major restructuring and work flow design, the evaluation might need to be conducted by an external third party who would be better able to objectively and independently assess the level of impact and the quality of the work. In addition to the roles of OD practitioner and evaluator, other individuals (i.e., key stakeholders) not directly involved in the effort may also need to be part of the evaluation scoping and design effort. Senior leadership, for example, even if not involved with the details, will often be a key stakeholder in evaluation outcome decisions. As a result, it is advisable for OD practitioners to gain alignment up front regarding who else needs to be involved in the process and at what stages. In an ideal world, the evaluation should always be conducted by someone other than the practitioner responsible for driving the change agenda (Burke, 1982). In most cases, however, the OD practitioner in conjunction with his or her internal client determines the evaluative status of a given consulting project.

Timing of the Evaluation

The final issue in scoping concerns determining when an OD evaluation should be conducted. Timing is always an important consideration, particularly if the evaluation is longitudinal in nature. Very focused change efforts such as an organizational restructuring or team-building exercises suggest natural evaluation points during or immediately following the intervention, but few leaders and managers in organizations have the patience to wait 3–5 years for a culture change initiative to produce measurable results. In these situations, it is often best to work with the client to identify more targeted formative or summative indicators of change during the process. This could include the use of interim data collection among certain populations (e.g., a behaviorally based survey of employees who have been training in some new methodology) or perhaps other types of less intrusive measures (e.g., shifting trends in quality and production rates) among different business units. The objective would be to compare results from those groups of employees with whom OD interventions had already occurred to those from groups with whom interventions had not yet been conducted (e.g., across different divisions, regions, or functions).

Designing

The next major phase in the evaluation process concerns design. Design refers to the entire spectrum of research tools, measures, and considerations that need to be identified and addressed prior to implementation. Decisions to be made at this stage reflect the level of impact needed, the type of assessment instrument or measure (e.g., qualitative vs. quantitative), the nature of the data source (e.g., business metrics, individual employees, external assessments, and existing vs. new data), and the level of detail needed for future analysis and linking research. All of these factors have a significant impact on the evaluator's ability to collect the appropriate information for an effective evaluation approach. As with most research design efforts, the approach to evaluation should be developed using sound research methods and measurement theory, wherever and whenever possible.

Determining the Level of Impact to Evaluate

Generally speaking, the first design question that needs to be answered when creating an OD evaluation strategy is "At what level of impact is the intervention or change effort meant to occur?" Level of impact here refers to the classic Kirkpatrick (1998) framework that when translated into OD terminology (McLean et al., 1995) is reaction (satisfaction level), learning (content mastery), behavior (observable behaviors at work), and organizational impact (bottom line results). At the most basic level, reaction provides a point-in-time snapshot of a set of attitudes and perceptions. Captured using some form of questionnaire, the typical application is a training evaluation form given after the close of the session. This information is helpful to the trainer for modifying the session content or pacing, but it does not provide any long-range information about the impact of training (unless it is administered more than once). Although OD practitioners do not typically think in terms of administering a standard reaction-based evaluation form following a large-scale intervention (though this might be seen as appropriate following a meeting facilitated by a process consultant), an employee survey is a very commonly used form of OD-related reaction level measure. Many HR professionals think of surveys as primarily a means for measuring satisfaction, but organizational surveys are also used by some OD practitioners as a central component in larger change efforts (Church & Waclawski, 2001). Moreover, depending on how the survey is constructed (e.g., based on behaviors as well as attitudes) and how many times it is administered (e.g., before, during, and after a change initiative), it may well provide data that cut across all four levels of evaluation.

The second level of analysis, learning, concerns the extent to which new skills or knowledge have been retained following an intervention. Although again training comes to mind, consider the use of a 360-degree feedback tool in a coaching context. If the manager being coached remembers his or her strengths and developmental opportunities at a later date and is able to use these in preparing an action plan, then learning has occurred. Whether the person takes any action to improve, however, is the realm of level 3—actual behavior change. In many ways, behavior change is at the very center of most OD-related interventions. Whether through process consultation (Schein, 1988) to improve interpersonal and group facilitation skills or multiyear 360-degree feedback and leadership development programs aimed at changing an organization's culture (e.g., Church et al., 2001), the underlying expectation and outcome are individual behavior change. Although certainly observable on an individual level, behavior change is often measured through survey techniques, either via an organizational survey with a behavioral component or via a more focused behavior-based measure such as 360-degree feedback. Behavior change is also observable through other types of assessments such as performance management tools.

The fourth and final level of impact is at the total organizational system level. This is where most if not all large-scale OD interventions are targeted. Whether this type of impact is measured via soft data (e.g., culture change using multiple administrations of an employee survey over time) or harder performance metrics (e.g., reductions in turnover or increased sales), these are organizationwide outcomes that we hope to achieve through our efforts. Some practitioners have had heated debates over the fundamental purpose of OD and whether it should be normative in approach (e.g., Church, 2001; Goodstein, 1984), but for the purpose of this discussion any of these types of business outcomes represent level 4 impact.

Identifying the Evaluation Methods

Once the level of impact is determined, the next obvious design question is the method needed to conduct the assessment. As with most evaluation efforts, the choices are limited to just a few forms of data collection—quantitative measures and qualitative measures. Quantitative measures include tools such as surveys, assessment instruments, and various performance metrics. These are best used when change in a given metric needs to be linked to some other source of data (e.g., financials, sales, inventory, accidents, or turnover). They also work well with large populations because their use makes it relatively easy and inexpensive (particularly using online technology) to reach many people in a short period of time (Church & Waclawski, 2001). Qualitative tools, on the other hand, include interviews, write-in survey comments, focus groups, and observation. Although more time intensive to analyze, they typically provide for rich information including subtleties and contextual data that cannot be obtained any other way. Some researchers feel that OD has historically overemphasized the quantitative/experimental/positivist approach (e.g., Martineau & Preskill, 2002); others have expressed the very opposite (e.g., Cady & Lewis, 2002). A combination of both types of data is probably the best option.

Because organizational surveys can provide both qualitative and quantitative data from a wide range of employees, they are an ideal type of tool for evaluation. Surveys often serve as both the diagnostic (before the intervention) and evaluative (after implementation) tool of choice for efforts directed at changing an organization's culture (Church & Waclawski, 2001). In the SmithKline Beecham merger (Burke & Jackson, 1991), for example, a worldwide survey was used to help drive culture change based on the Burke-Litwin Model. Follow-up surveys were used to assess progress against the change effort over time.

Deciding on Data Source and Level of Detail

Two other factors to consider in the design stage are the source of data needed for evaluation and the level of data detail needed. Data can be internal (e.g., employee opinions, behaviors, financials, or human resource metrics) or external in nature (e.g., rankings, analyst reports, reputation, news articles, or stock price). Evaluation data can also be pre-existing or created new for a given intervention. It is important to plan out at the design stage what types of data already exist, what needs to be generated, and who needs to be involved to do this. The evaluator might want to interview senior leaders during the beginning of a new OD consulting effort. If they have recently been interviewed and those data are available, consider working with that first. Chances are that most organizations will have some form of employee survey results to examine as well.

The last issue to consider with regard to source is the level of detail needed. For example, if a survey is to be conducted prior to a major strategic change in business direction, what level of action planning needs to happen? If those data are to be linked to specific functions, departments, or even individual managers, how is the integrity of these linkages going to be being managed? What is the unique identifier? Although linkage research is one of the most powerful forms of evaluation and can be used to show clearly the level 4 impact link between an OD intervention and changes in culture and performance (Cady & Lewis, 2002; Church & Waclawski, 2001), one key challenge is obtaining the data needed at the right level of detail. For example, in a recent effort in a large retail organization engaged in leadership training, it was possible through careful planning to demonstrate the importance of effective leadership by linking organizational survey results, 360-degree feedback ratings, and store financials such as stock shrinkage and sales.

Collecting and Analyzing Data

Once the evaluation strategy and measures have been properly designed, the next phase is actually obtaining the results. This involves both collecting the evaluation data and analyzing the results to find trends and test for the level of impact. If the scoping and design work have been done with care and attention to the right stakeholders, outcomes, and measurement issues, this phase is primarily an exercise in data analysis. Moreover, the nature of the analysis approach taken should directly follow from the type of information gathered for the evaluation. For example, results from quantitative assessments should be analyzed using both basic descriptive statistics (means, percentages, frequencies, etc.) and multivariate analyses where appropriate (e.g., given the sample size and validity of the instrument used). If data are available for linkage research, then a regression methodology of some manner is probably the best approach. Qualitative data should be analyzed using a content (or thematic) analysis, as well as more traditional nonparametric approaches such as chi-squares.

If, on the other hand, the scoping was not done well or the design was not well constructed, the data collection and analysis phase is where problems will emerge. One potential problem is contaminated ratings (e.g., respondents modifying their information to intentionally change the results). This can be particularly troubling if the survey respondents' demographics do not closely mirror the actual employee population because it suggests that people are not responding honestly. Consider a situation, for example, in which the client knows that a given function (e.g., legal) has only 11 individuals in its headcount, but 35 respondents select the category "legal" as their function on an employee survey—and the ratings from these 35 employees are particularly negative. Another set of issues might emerge from poor measurement design and construction (e.g., survey items that do not provide enough specificity to assess the right level of impact or why the outcome is not as expected) or lack of funding or support from senior leadership to follow through with an evaluation plan. In the end, there are many ways in which evaluators can find themselves stuck in the data collection phase.

Working With International Populations

As with most aspects of the evaluation process, there are several factors to consider during the data collection and analysis phase. The first of these is the degree to which the OD intervention and its subsequent evaluation methods will be applied to international populations. Aside from some fundamental cultural differences in how comfortable people are with responding to questionnaires and the notion of providing feedback in different countries (e.g., Hofstede, 1980; Marquardt, 2002), a host of other technical issues can create difficulty for the evaluator. These include translation issues (e.g., ensuring that different versions of the same instrument are truly assessing the same constructs), technology/access issues (e.g., level of online access vs. paper requirements), and content relevance issues.

The content relevance issue can be illustrated with a simple case of terminology. Rolling out a domestic training initiative around the concept of "diversity" may make perfect sense to employees in the United States, but internationally the program might not work the same way. The term "diversity" might mean very different things in different countries, and the examples of how diversity manifests itself would need to be tailored to each culture. This makes both rolling out the effort and evaluating its impact on the culture complex. It is important to remember that many OD approaches are based on Western values (Marquardt, 2002), and this can often lead to tension and downright failure of an intervention if not properly framed. In some cultures, for example, it is important to be directive and play the expert role in designing an implementation strategy and its evaluation process rather than be collaborative and facilitative. The key to being successful in these situations goes back to carefully contracting the OD effort, designing the evaluation strategy, and determining the desired level of information.

Ensuring Collection of the Right Amount of Data

Another important factor in the implementation process, particularly in formative evaluation approaches, is ensuring that enough data are collected to make a good-quality decision regarding the status and direction of the intervention. In some situations, the first signs of negative feedback might cause the OD practitioner, client, or other key stakeholder to immediately change direction and deviate from the planned intervention. In some cases this shift in approach might be appropriate (e.g., particularly when the evaluation is intended to be formative). For example, you might want to act quickly upon learning that an assessment tool that was intended for development only is being used inappropriately for making selection and promotion decisions. There are other situations, however, when this initial response should be weighted against the level and quality of the data that have been collected. Evaluation data are only as good as the tools used to collect them; so it is always important to consider the source as well when making modifications to a large-scale change agenda.

Similarly, summative and longitudinal evaluation efforts can suffer from a related type of misperception. Any post-hoc assessment of the impact of an intervention (particularly the longer the time lag experienced) can be masked or misrepresented by other factors that may not be in the evaluator's control. Although as noted earlier, linkage research represents some of the most powerful analytics available for evaluating OD interventions, linkage research can lead to erroneous conclusions about the impact of intervention if used improperly. Because large-scale OD efforts often involve many interdependent parts of a social system, it is very difficult to isolate the impact of individual elements. Nonetheless, clients and practitioners often want to jump right to the bottom line and make the causation (vs. correlation) argument. For example, take an organization that experienced significant turnover during the late 1990s. As a result of this concern, the organization implemented a number of improvement programs focused on specific problem areas as identified through various surveys and focus groups with employees. In 2002, after several years with the new programs in place, turnover had declined significantly. Was this because of the impact of the new programs or was it the result of the changing economic and job market landscape? The answer is probably some of both, but without a well-constructed evaluation plan, it will be very difficult to determine the answer.

Communicating

The final phase in the evaluation process is communicating and working with the results to make a positive or negative determination regarding the OD intervention. In formative evaluations, this means using the results to influence the future direction of an ongoing effort (or its continued existence). In summative and longitudinal evaluations, this means making a declarative statement about the impact of a specific effort or set of interventions. This is also the stage at which follow-up recommendations are made. In some cases these might be content or timing based (e.g., recommending the best way to roll out a new vision statement to employees following an OD intervention with senior leadership). In other situations, the recommendations might be evaluation design based (e.g., the results suggest the need to reevaluate at some future date or that another form of evaluation or more data are still needed to demonstrate impact). In general, the important factors in communicating are being able to create a compelling story through data, maintaining balance and integrity, and understanding people's natural reactions to feedback.

Telling a Compelling Story

One of the least well understood but perhaps most important data analytic skills is the ability to tell a compelling story through data (Church & Waclawski, 2001). Whether the source is qualitatively or quantitatively based, just being able to accurately run the numbers and create statistical output are not enough to generate an effective communication plan for an evaluation effort. One of the primary roles of an OD practitioner is to help clients understand their own data and what they mean. Similarly, in evaluating an OD intervention, it is critical that the presentation and communication of the evaluation results be shaped in such a way as to tell a compelling and engaging story about the intervention in question. Although it is very important to maintain the accuracy and integrity of the data, the role of the evaluator in helping clients and other key stakeholders understand what the evaluation results are showing is a very important aspect of the process. An effective evaluator will also help the client understand how that information should be used to shape the direction of current or future OD interventions in the organization.

For example, suppose the evaluator conducts a behaviorally based survey 6 months after the completion of a large multiyear OD culture change effort. As part of this effort, management development training was one of the primary interventions used as a means of communication new messages and skills regarding performance coaching. A question on the follow-up survey reads "as a result of the training, I have seen my manager apply the skills she learned to be a more effective performance coach" and receives a 42% favorable rating (i.e., the percentage of employees indicating they "agree" or "strongly agree" with that statement). Is this showing a positive result (i.e., that 42% of employees report experiencing positive change in their manager's behavior) or a negative finding (i.e., less than half were impacted by the training)? In this example, the OD evaluator needs to set the appropriate context for the interpretation.

Maintaining Balance and Integrity

Related to the issue of telling a compelling story is helping the client (and other key stakeholders interested in the OD intervention) maintain balance and integrity in the evaluation process. Aside from making sure that the results are not misrepresented (e.g., due to pressures to maintain one's current role, level of funding, or consulting status within a given client situation), it is also important that the communication and follow-up efforts surrounding the evaluation process be well balanced. It is important to identify what worked well and what needs improvement. No intervention is perfect and there are always opportunities for enhancement. Nonetheless, some practitioners tend to evaluate either too positively or too negatively, and this tends to skew the interpretation of whatever findings are being communicated. Although partially valid, a mind-set that an intervention either "worked" or "didn't work" misses the developmental spirit of many OD interventions. This is where the values debate in the field sometimes comes into play. Some clients and OD practitioners focus their efforts primarily on bottom line productivity measures whereas others prefer a more normative approach in which the ultimate outcome is a better organization in which to work (and not necessarily a more profitable one). In the end, of course, the issue goes back to appropriate contracting from an intervention standpoint and effective scoping, design, and data collection and analysis from an evaluation perspective. Perhaps that 42% favorable is all that is really needed to demonstrate successful culture change at some level. Whatever the reaction to the data, this is an important area to focus on when communicating results.

Understanding Reactions to Feedback

Speaking of reactions, as every good OD practitioner knows, one of the fundamental tenets of human nature is that people do not like to receive negative feedback. This is true for evaluation results as well as anything else. Even if delivered in a highly sensitive manner, it is likely that clients and practitioners receiving evaluation feedback (particularly if it is for the first time in an effort) will likely become defensive, withdrawn, challenging, or even hostile. Often this progression is described by OD professionals in terms of the classic Kübler-Ross (1969) model of the four stages of grieving: shock, anger, rejection, and acceptance (S.A.R.A. with some practitioners adding H for hope). All communication efforts regarding the evaluation of OD interventions would be well served to help their clients understand and work through this model. It is an important tool for working through feedback from a variety of sources including organizational surveys (Church & Waclawski, 2001) and 360-degree feedback (e.g., Church et al., 2001, 2002).

Several Case Examples

Having reviewed a process-based framework for evaluating OD interventions, it is now appropriate to discuss some short case examples of actual consulting efforts that worked well and those did not work as well from an evaluation perspective.

Case 1: Formative Evaluation Feedback Saves the Day

The first example concerns the effective use of formative feedback to help re-direct the rollout of a multiyear 360-degree feedback and leadership coaching–based change initiative in a large professional services firm. As described elsewhere (Church et al., 2001), the main objective of this effort was to help the firm's executive population (i.e., tax and audit partners) develop the specific relationship and client management skills and behaviors needed to make the transition from operating as traditional accountants to becoming broader strategic business consultants in the eyes of their clients. Driven by external competitive pressures, the change effort involved the development and rollout of a custom set of leadership competencies and a supporting 360-degree feedback process delivered in the context of a multiday developmental coaching program. Although the program was so successful that it ran for 6 years (even after the consulting firm that developed and delivered the first few years of the program was no longer involved) and demonstrated real change in consulting performance over time, there was a pivotal moment during the initial stages of program rollout in which formative feedback saved the entire process and change effort from derailing.

It occurred early in the rollout process. Although the approach to the program design had worked with numerous types of executives and other organizations (e.g., pharmaceuticals, technology, financial services), during the kickoff program and after months of shared preparation the formal mix of lecture, activity, case study, and internal data was simply not working with these types of partners. The senior client was getting edgy and the program material was falling somewhat flat. As soon as the partners received the 360 results from their external clients, however, their interest levels were completely renewed and the program began working again. Evaluations following the program and personal observations on the part of the client and our own team suggested that the content was indeed right but the process needed a major design change. Following that first program, significant changes were made to the overall flow and the role that 360-degree feedback was to play in it (i.e., shifting from one of many tools in the training to becoming the very centerpiece of the program. This included starting off the session with client feedback results and intensive one-on-one coaching focused on specific behavioral improvement). If not for that formative feedback at the right stage in the process this change effort would have been concluded after two or three programs with little lasting impact.

Case 2: A Case of Poor Scoping

The second example is one in which we were involved with a client who fundamentally refused to understand or accept the results from a summative evaluation because he had a much broader personal agenda in mind. Working with another professional services firm (which specialized in management consulting services), we were brought in by a newly hired senior HR professional to provide change management knowledge, skill transfer, and group dynamics learnings for a new hire orientation program he had designed. Although not a large-scale OD intervention, the task was very focused (i.e., help these new consultants understand something about organizational change and about themselves as individuals in groups). In addition, the tools that had been developed to support this type of work were well grounded and had a strong track record of success in other contexts and settings. After what we thought was appropriate contracting and scoping of our evaluation efforts (which consisted primarily of reaction level scales), we went about conducting several of these sessions as part of the new hire program. Unfortunately, every time we conducted a session we experienced hostility from the young MBA-type consultants and negative evaluations at the end of the training. Our client, however, who was focused more on achieving his personal vision and less on its level of fit with his new organization, remained positive about the effort. Despite our suggestion to modify our approach or the objectives overall, he continued to have us work through the same process every time. After several more sessions, we finally decided to end the project ourselves. Although well intentioned, the client simply refused to understand and accept the evaluation feedback. His focus was on having us convey his personal message to the group, and this was not in our understanding of the scope of the project or in alignment with their own perspective. Although staying the course over time might have had an impact on the culture long term, this was an effort we were not able to complete.

Case: 3: Showing That Survey Action Planning Really Works

The third example is of an effective longitudinal evaluation process focused on the impact of organizational survey action planning on bottom line results over time. The case comes from work recently completed at a domestic division of a large multinational food and beverage company. Although the process of conducting organizational surveys for the measurement of employee opinions, attitudes, and preferences has been around for decades, the practice of actually using the results for targeted action planning and OD interventions is still less common (Church & Waclawski, 2001). Part of this is due to inexperience and part is grounded in resistance to the notion that survey action planning really works. The purpose of the evaluation effort in this case was to answer one important question for ourselves and our clients: Does survey action planning really make a difference?

Our approach was simple. We split employees into groups based on their responses to two key survey questions: the extent to which they indicated that (a) the results from the prior survey had been communicated and reviewed in their work group/location, and (b) based on those results, action had been taken on the identified opportunity areas in their work group/location. In short, we looked at whether results were communicated and acted on in a meaningful way. This resulted in four distinct groups of employees:

1. Those who said their managers reviewed their survey results *and then also took action* on their opportunity areas
2. Those who said their managers reviewed the results, but took *no action* afterward
3. Those who said their managers did *not* specifically review the results, but took action anyway on opportunity areas
4. Those who said their manages *did nothing* at all with the survey results

Using these four groups, we then looked at several different aspects of attitude change and business performance–related outcomes. More specifically, we examined employee satisfaction and change on a variety of dimensions at the time of each administration by business unit (1 and 2 years prior and current survey results), and frontline plant-level performance metrics including turnover, lost days due to work incidents, and number of incidents reported. Overall, the results yielded overwhelming support for taking action from survey results on employee attitudes and perceptions over time as well as hard performance metrics. Interestingly enough, the results also indicated that simply sharing survey results with employees but not taking any action was equally as ineffective (and resulted in more negative ratings and outcomes over time) as doing nothing at all. Although OD practitioners have been making the claim for years that survey action planning (not just the survey itself) is what leads to change (Church & Waclawski, 2001), these proved to be important findings for OD-related survey work going forward and for the overall HR agenda in this organization. Longitudinal approaches in OD are often difficult to engineer, but when they can be done the results are very effective for driving new and existing efforts forward.

Conclusion

The purpose of this chapter was to review the specific aspects and challenges involved in evaluating the impact of OD-related interventions in organizational settings and to provide a framework for understanding and driving more effective evaluation in this field. The four-phase model introduced here should prove help-ful in moving the state of OD evaluation efforts forward. Given the significance of the notion of data-based feedback to OD (e.g., via the action research model), it is only fitting that practitioners and those who evaluate their efforts should use vari-ous forms of data to test the impact of a given intervention.

Many practitioners and consultants may argue that OD efforts are too difficult or complex for measuring success or that practitioners are not skilled enough in research methodology, but two things are clear from both existing practice and research and the examples provided above. First, OD interventions can be evalu-ated, both holistically given enough time and in stages following discrete interven-tions. Second, these evaluations should be conducted from a professional ethics perspective. No consultants should be allowed to sell their services without some form of accountability to the quality of their work. One of the core values of the field of OD, then, must be a renewed focus on evaluation. As the field continues to converge on standards of practice and the potential need for future professional-ization efforts (Church, 2001; Weidner & Kulick, 1999), this is one area in which we need to ensure professional competence. Although many criticisms have been directed at the field of OD over the years, it is important for OD's continued vital-ity that practitioners understand the importance of evaluation and build the skills they need to deliver effective reviews of others' work and their own as well. Only by effectively evaluating OD interventions can we truly demonstrate the impact that this work has on organizations.

References

Burke, W. W. (1982). *Organization development: Principles and practices.* Glenview, IL: Scott, Foresman.

Burke, W. W., & Jackson, P. (1991). Making the SmithKline Beecham merger work. *Human Resource Management, 30,* 69–87.

Burke, W. W., Javitch, M. J., Waclawski, J., & Church, A. H. (1997). The dynamics of mid-stream consulting. *Consulting Psychology Journal: Practice and Research, 49*(2), 83–95.

Burke, W. W., & Litwin, G. H. (1992). A causal model of organizational performance and change. *Journal of Management, 18,* 523–545.

Cady, S. H., & Lewis, M. J. (2002). Organization development and the bottom line: Linking soft measures and hard measures. In J. Waclawski & A. H. Church (Eds.), *Organization development: A data-driven approach to organizational change* (pp. 127–146). San Francisco: Jossey-Bass.

Church, A. H. (2001). The professionalization of organization development: The next step in an evolving field. In W. A. Passmore & R. W. Woodman (Eds.), *Research in organizational change and development, 13* (pp. 1–42). Greenwich CT: JAI Press.

Church, A. H., & Waclawski, J. (2001). *Designing and using organizational surveys: A seven-step process.* San Francisco: Jossey-Bass.

Church, A. H., Waclawski, J., & Burke, W. W. (2001). Multisource feedback for organization development and change. In D. W. Bracken, C. W. Timmreck, & A. H. Church (Eds.), *The handbook of multisource feedback: The comprehensive resource for designing and implementing MSF processes* (pp. 301–317). San Francisco: Jossey-Bass.

Church, A. H., Walker, A., G., & Brockner, J. (2002). Multisource feedback for organization development and change. In J. Waclawski & A. H. Church (Eds.), *Organization development: A data-driven approach to organizational change* (pp. 27–54). San Francisco: Jossey-Bass.

Cummings, T., & Worley, C. (1997). *Organization development and change* (6th ed.). St. Paul, MN: West.

Friedlander, F. (1976). OD reaches adolescence: An exploration of its underlying values. *Journal of Applied Behavioral Science, 12,* 7–21.

Goodstein, L. D. (1984). Values, truth, and organization development. In D. D. Warrick (Ed.), *Contemporary organization development: Current thinks and applications* (pp. 42–47). Glenview, IL: Scott, Foresman.

Gottlieb, J. Z. (1998). Understanding the role of organization development practitioners. In R. W. Woodman & W. A. Pasmore (Eds.), *Research in organizational change and development* (Vol. 11, pp. 117–158). Greenwich CT: JAI Press.

Hofstede, G. (1980). *Cultural consequences: International differences in work-related values.* Beverly Hills, CA: Sage.

Hronec, S. M. (1993). *Vital signs: Using quality, time, and cost performance measurements to chart your company's future.* New York: AMACOM.

Katz, D., & Kahn, R. L. (1978). *The social psychology of organizations* (2nd ed.). New York: John Wiley.

Kirkpatrick, D. L. (1998). *Evaluating training programs: The four levels* (2nd ed.). San Francisco: Berrett-Koehler.

Kübler-Ross, E. (1969). *On death and dying.* New York: Macmillan.

Lewin, K. (1958). Group decision and social change. In E. E. Maccoby, T. M. Newcomb, & E. L. Hartley (Eds.), *Readings in social psychology* (pp. 197–211). New York: Holt, Rinehart and Winston.

Margulies, N., & Raia, A. (1990). The significance of core values on the theory and practice of organization development. In F. Massarik (Ed.), *Advances in organization development* (Vol. 1, pp. 27–41). Norwood, NJ; Ablex.

Marquardt, M. (2002). Around the world: Organization development in the international context. In J. Waclawski & A. H. Church (Eds.), *Organization development: A data-driven approach to organizational change* (pp. 266–285). San Francisco: Jossey-Bass.

Martineau, J. W., & Preskill, H. (2002). Evaluating the impact of organization development interventions. In J. Waclawski & A. H. Church (Eds.), *Organization development: A data-driven approach to organizational change* (pp. 286–301). San Francisco: Jossey-Bass.

McLean, G. N., Sullivan, R., & Rothwell, W. J. (1995). Evaluation. In W. J. Rothwell, R. Sullivan, & G. N. McLean (Eds.), *Practicing organization development: A guide for consultants.* (pp. 311–368). San Francisco: Jossey-Bass/Pfeiffer.

Nadler, D. A. (1977). *Feedback and organization development: Using data-based methods.* Reading, MA: Addison-Wesley.

Philips, J. J. (1991). *Handbook of training evaluation and measurement methods* (2nd ed.). Houston: Gulf.

Porras, J. I., & Robertson, P. J. (1992). Organizational development: Theory, practice, and research. In M. D. Dunnette & L. M. Hough (Eds.), *Handbook of industrial and organizational psychology* (2nd ed., Vol. 3, pp. 719–822). Palo Alto, CA: Consulting Psychologists Press.

Rothwell, W. J., Sullivan, R., & McLean, G. N. (Eds.). (1995). *Practicing organization development: A guide for consultants.* San Francisco: Jossey-Bass/Pfeiffer.

Rucci, A. J., Kirn, S. P., & Quinn, R. T. (1998). The employee-customer profit chain at Sears. *Harvard Business Review, 76*(1), 83–97.

Sanzgiri, J., & Gottlieb, J. Z. (1992). Philosophic and pragmatic influences on the practice of organization development, 1950–2000. *Organization Dynamics, 21*(2), 57–69.

Schein, E. H. (1988). *Process consultation Volume 1: Its role in organizational development* (2nd ed.). Reading, MA: Addison-Wesley

Swanson, R. A., & Holton, E. F., III. (1999). *Results: How to assess performance, learning and perceptions in organizations.* San Francisco, CA: Berrett-Koehler. Waclawski, J., & Church, A. H. (2002). Introduction and overview of organization development as a data driven approach for organizational change. In J. Waclawski & A. H. Church (Eds.), *Organization development: A data-driven approach to organizational change* (pp. 3–26). San Francisco: Jossey-Bass.

Weidner, C. K., II, & Kulick, O. A. (1999). The professionalization of organization development: A status report and look to the future. In W. A. Pasmore & R. W. Woodman (Eds.), *Research in organizational change and development,* (Vol. 12, pp. 319–371). Greenwich CT: JAI Press.

Suggested Readings
in Organization Development

Burke, W. W. (1994). *Organization development: A process of learning and changing* (2nd ed.). Reading, MA: Addison-Wesley.

Church, A. H. (2001). The professionalization of organization development: The next step in an evolving field. In W. A. Passmore & R. W. Woodman (Eds.), *Research in organizational change and development, 13* (pp. 1–42). Greenwich CT: JAI Press.

Cummings, T., & Worley, C. (1997). *Organization development and change* (6th ed.). St. Paul, MN: West.

Rothwell, W. J., Sullivan, R., & McLean, G. N. (Eds.). (1995). *Practicing organization development: A guide for consultants.* San Francisco: Jossey-Bass/Pfeiffer.

Waclawski, J., & Church, A. H. (Eds.). (2002). *Organization development: A data-driven approach to organizational change.* San Francisco: Jossey-Bass.

CHAPTER 17

Evaluating Diversity Programs

Paul Rosenfeld

Dan Landis

David Dalsky

T he publication of the Hudson Institute's *Workforce 2000* (Johnston & Packer, 1987) focused attention on the future diversity of the U.S. workforce. The report predicted an increased percentage of minorities and women in the workforce. In 1997, a follow-up report, *Workforce 2020* (Judy & D'Amico, 1997) reinforced these findings. It predicted four major changes for the workplace of 2020: (a) increased technological change, (b) increased globalization, (c) increased proportions of older people, and (d) greater racial/ethnic and gender diversity.

At the organizational level, *Workforce 2000* and its follow-up symbolized a major change: from a focus on compliance with equal employment opportunity (EEO) laws and regulations to something broader, inclusive, and more positive. Most current organizations now view issues related to group differences in the workplace within the framework of *diversity*. While many definitions of diversity exist, a common organizational perspective sees it as referring to differences that employees

AUTHOR'S NOTE: The opinions expressed in this paper are those of the authors. They are not official and do not represent the views of the Navy Department. The authors appreciate the comments of Steve Knouse and Zannette Uriell on an earlier version of this chapter.

bring to the workplace. These differences can be along racial/ethnic, gender, or other dimensions whereby people differ (Thomas, 2001). Whereas diversity originally focused on racial/ethnic and gender dimensions, particularly among those in legally protected classes, it is now viewed more expansively to include age, religion, handicap status, and sexual orientation, and even subjective characteristics such as differences in thinking styles, decision making, and interpersonal orientation.

This heightened awareness of differences is driven by both the realities of an increasingly diverse workforce and an organizational framework that tries to address issues relating to it. The *managing diversity* perspective suggests that fully recognizing and valuing the diversity of its employees will maximize an organization's bottom line outcomes. This viewpoint emphasizes the unique perspectives that a diverse workforce brings to solving organizational problems and enhancing teamwork and productivity. Diversity is not just a good idea; it is good business practice. This perspective also attempts to exploit the growing diversity of the customer base in U.S. and global markets.

To address the increasing diversity of the workforce, most large U.S. corporations have established diversity programs that at a minimum contain diversity training (Ferdman & Brody, 1996). A 1998 Society of Human Resource Management survey found that about three fourths of *Fortune* 500 companies have formal diversity programs and over one third of all U.S. firms have them (Caudron, 1998). Less common is systematic measurement to evaluate organizational diversity programs.

Whereas the claims of organizational diversity programs may echo noble sentiments, demonstrating the impact of a diversity program can be challenging. In theory, a diversity evaluation should indicate whether links exist between aspects of a diversity program and changes in workplace behavior, climate, and productivity. Even for the best diversity organizations, showing a direct link to the bottom line is only rarely achieved. Evaluating diversity programs has become a concern for organizations, but few organizations actually evaluate their diversity programs or make evaluation a priority (Comer & Soliman, 1996).

There is a clear need for diversity programs to include an evaluation component. As Comer and Solimon (1996, p. 473) wrote, "To ascertain if their investments are cost-effective, mechanisms should be in place to measure the success of diversity efforts. However, the fanfare about the imperative of managing diversity has nearly eclipsed questions about efficacy." To facilitate diversity evaluation efforts, this chapter presents a practical, multistep, metrics-based procedure to evaluate an organizational diversity program.

Evaluating Diversity Programs: Barriers and Benefits

Because doing a diversity evaluation often requires that significant organizational resources be expended, it is necessary to determine potential barriers and benefits.

Barriers: Reasons Diversity Programs Might Not Be Evaluated

Although we believe that a fully functional diversity program needs an evaluation component, there are reasons that an organization might not evaluate its diversity program. Barriers such as a superficial commitment to diversity, fear of what might be learned, and the impact, cost, and time involved in evaluation need to be addressed if an evaluation is to be successfully undertaken.

Superficial Commitment to Diversity

Organizations at one end of the commitment spectrum give lip service to diversity but rarely practice what they preach. They have little motivation to expend resources to evaluate their programs as the programs are not that consequential and exist largely for impression management purposes (Rosenfeld, Giacalone, & Riordan, 2002). Often, organizations that need evaluation most are least likely to evaluate their diversity programs. Before attempting an evaluation in these organizations, members of the evaluation team are advised to gain top organizational support and ensure that opinion leaders are on the steering committee as discussed in the program evaluation steps below. Organizations on the other end of the spectrum have extensive, far-reaching diversity programs. We describe some of their efforts in our best practices section. These organizations are also most likely to have in place measurement systems to evaluate their programs.

Ignorance Is Bliss: Fear of What Might Be Learned

Diversity evaluations gather data that may prove embarrassing, divisive, and controversial. As a result, the organization's legal advisors may caution against doing an evaluation. If the gathered data suggest systematic bias or discrimination, the organization may be in legal jeopardy if someone files a lawsuit. For example, employees in one organization claimed religious discrimination in promotion. Their lawyers requested the results of all the organization's surveys during the past 20 years that might in any way be related to the issues raised in the lawsuit. Thus, it is a good idea to involve the legal department in advance to address any hesitancy it may have about conducting a diversity evaluation.

Impact, Cost, and Time Involved in Evaluation

A well-done diversity evaluation will require considerable organizational resources—cost, staff, and time—that many organizations will not want to commit. There is no shortcut or single indicator to quickly summarize how well an organization's diversity program is doing. If organizations seek outside help, the services of expert consultants may entail high fees. One organization we knew of was told that it would cost $13,000 (plus expenses) to bring a renowned diversity consultant in for a few hours—and this was a discount rate! The subsequent diversity evaluation, however, may fail to confirm the expectations of internal personnel who acquired the services. The impact of even a well-designed and executed diversity program may take many years to be realized. Thus, it is not uncommon that early evaluations of diversity programs will find more that has to be done rather than demonstrating the positive impact of what has already taken place.

Benefits: Reasons Diversity Programs Should Be Evaluated

Although there are reasons to avoid evaluating an organizational diversity program, we believe the benefits of an evaluation usually outweigh the costs. This section covers some of the reasons diversity programs should be evaluated and the benefits that evaluation can provide.

Determines Impact, Detects Deficiencies, and Identifies Areas for Improvement

Organizations can spend considerable sums on diversity programs, especially when the costs of training, recruitment, outreach, mentoring, and other efforts are factored in. Program evaluation can determine the impact, if any, of these efforts. In addition, an evaluation can identify, eliminate, correct, or prevent practices that may hinder the success of diversity programs and impact the organization's bottom line. For example, did a prior decision to eliminate the on-site day care center increase turnover among women with children? Diversity evaluations can also help detect areas needing improvement. We are familiar with organizations that have done well with racial/ethnic diversity but have a way to go in areas such as gender and dealing with disabled employees. Subsequent evaluations can determine how much improvement has been made and in what areas progress has occurred.

Signals Commitment

Collecting data increases accountability and signals an organization's commitment to diversity. Indeed, a commitment to measuring all aspects of a diversity program is one of the characteristics of an organization whose diversity program exhibits best practices.

Awareness of the evaluation throughout the organization may signal a commitment from top management. At a minimum, management is committed to spending resources to optimize the organization's diversity program. But this is a two-edged sword. Evaluation will raise expectations among organizational members that something will be done. If nothing happens, then subsequent evaluations may meet with less employee cooperation and participation—the "won't get fooled again" syndrome.

Fends Off the Critics

Though not always fashionable to express publicly, some members do not support an organization's diversity program. In times of economic downturn, skeptics may question the program, its expense, and impact particularly if the organization is undergoing downsizing. A diversity evaluation, especially one that goes beyond just survey results, must demonstrate some value-added (improvements in retention, fewer complaints and lawsuits, etc.) to fend off critics and maintain funding once the "honeymoon phase" is over.

Evaluating Diversity Programs: A Six-Step Plan

Evaluating diversity programs, while having some unique characteristics, includes many of the same steps found in any program evaluation: forming an evaluation team, developing a plan and measures of success, obtaining commitment from organizational leaders, gathering data, analyzing the data, and preparing a report with an action plan.

Step 1. Form the Diversity Evaluation Team

Conducting a diversity evaluation usually requires forming an evaluation team. The human resources (HR) department may coordinate or lead the team, but the types of information needed and the required divergent skills strongly suggest that the evaluation be a team effort. Organizations considering diversity evaluation should determine the advantages and disadvantages of using internal versus external evaluators and decide whether internal, external, or a combination best suits the local organization. Table 17.1 presents several strengths and weaknesses of both internal and external evaluators. Whether the evaluation team is primarily internal or external, an internal steering committee should be established and composed of organization members who are considered objective and credible. The credibility of the team and steering committee is critical if the evaluation and its recommendations are to be seen as something more than just window dressing.

A good diversity evaluation will require resources from throughout the organization. It really cannot be done very well on the cheap. A diversity evaluation will not be thorough if resource restrictions limit its breath or depth. In maintaining the credibility of the evaluation group, it is best to assemble a team with divergent members and differing skills. If outside consultants are hired, they will still need to coordinate with members on the inside for access to needed data and personnel. If the team does the evaluation in-house, it will need to be wide enough in scope so that all the various tasks do not focus on a single member. Whatever the nature of the team, the composition of the members should be diverse—both in demographic background and in skill set. Although the need for a diverse evaluation team seems self-evident, what may easily be overlooked is the need to include

Table 17.1   Internal Versus External Evaluators: Strengths and Weaknesses

	Type of Evaluator	
Attribute	Internal	External
Knowledge of organization's procedures, personnel, decision-making processes, and unspoken roles	+	–
Trusted by the organization	+	–
Credibility as an expert	–	+
Objectivity in evaluation	–	+

NOTE: + indicates potential strengths; – indicates potential weaknesses

majority group members—typically white males—as members of the team. This group is often most skeptical and cynical about diversity programs and needs to be involved and supportive of the effort so that it has credibility with both majority and minority employees.

Internal Versus External Evaluators

The internal consultant knows the organization and its climate, unspoken rules, and traditions. Internal evaluators are more likely to be able to separate diversity efforts done for image purposes and those that are backed by leadership commitment. Being knowledgeable about local perceptions, power, and politics gives internal evaluators an advantage. If the evaluation is being done as window dressing, the internal evaluators may be in a good position to try to change the mind-set of upper management to seeing the advantages of an open and honest process. Of course, there are no guarantees that they will be successful.

Part of a diversity evaluation is the need to understand and evaluate both informal and formal grievance and complaint systems. These may differ from organization to organization and require some time for an outsider to understand. Also, measures of diversity success may include promotion rates and other indicators of career achievement. Internal evaluators are more likely to understand how these work and any constraints that may be operating.

On the other hand, many organizations do not have enough in-house talent with sufficient expertise to handle a diversity evaluation themselves. In many cases, a statistically talented external consultant could do things with data such as promotion/recruitment/selection rates that would be beyond the capability of many internal consultants. Also, although the external consultant may be unfamiliar with the organization's complaint system, even a complex complaint system should be learnable in a week or two. The external consultant may be less familiar with the dynamics of the local organization, but his or her knowledge of what is done in other organizations can often be an advantage for identifying problems and recommending changes.

Even a very talented external consultant may encounter organizations that are worried about outsiders having access to diversity data for fear of exposing their dirty laundry to others. Although reputable external consultants certainly are trustworthy in protecting their client's confidentiality, they are not always viewed by those who have hired them as a trusted insider who will protect the organization's interests. It is clear, however, that a "protect the organization at all costs" philosophy can run counter to doing a good diversity evaluation, so an internal team should attempt to establish firm guidelines with the organization before undertaking the evaluation. This may help prevent someone from subsequently saying the results are too damaging to report simply because they do not like what was found.

Just as biblical prophets were not always respected within their hometowns, so too internal consultants may struggle to be seen as credible experts within their own organizations. The area of organizational diversity has spawned many gurus, visionaries, and icons whose writings and teachings give them exalted status that an insider can never attain.

Our experiences with diversity programs and surveys have taught us that work done by internal consultants has trouble being viewed as objective by many organizational members. Internal consultants may be suspected of having a hidden agenda or being management's pawns. Sometimes an external consultant is hired precisely to demonstrate the objectivity of the process to those who might be skeptical.

It is easy to deliver good news but much harder to tell organizational leaders that things are not going well. The reality of diversity programs is that many do not live up to their lofty claims. It may be easier for an outsider to be objective than someone who has to come to work the next day. Outside evaluators are not totally free from this pressure, however, since they might want to continue working for the organization and have a financial stake in being rehired.

Step 2. Develop the Evaluation Plan and Measures of Success

Often, a team will want to dive into the evaluation immediately after being assigned the task. A more successful course of action is to study the aims of the diversity program and develop a plan to assess how well each aspect of the program has been implemented. Key to this plan is developing preliminary measures of success for each aspect of the program.

Developing the Evaluation Plan

Two common beginner's mistakes are (a) not spending enough time up-front defining the project and (b) trying to do the evaluation too fast. The plan should be tailored to the local organization rather than using a one-size-fits-all approach and blindly adopting something that has been used successfully elsewhere. If possible, the project timeline should include some slack for those times when things go wrong or get delayed (two very common occurrences!), and most important, leave enough time to get the job done right.

Identifying Measures of Success

Both "hard" data (e.g., disciplinary statistics, hiring actions, promotion statistics, training records, and diversity policy statements) and "soft" data (from surveys, interviews, focus groups, and observations) should be used as measures of success. The measures should be selected to determine the level of success for each goal in the diversity program. A general rule is to get as much data as feasible from different sources and use one type of data to corroborate what the other type shows, never relying solely on data from one source to draw major conclusions. If a survey finds that minorities or women feel that promotions are unfair, one would expect some confirmation in actual promotion statistics.

The measures need to be appropriate for the organization being evaluated. Using minority representation as the only measure of success in an organization that is located in a geographic area where few minority members reside or to which few have access may lead to misleading conclusions. This does not mean that one should ignore minority representation rates, but they should be reported against the context of the relevant available labor pool (Edwards & Thomas, 1989). If minority representation were low, one would want to look at recruiting procedures at both the local and the national levels.

Step 3. Obtain Commitment from Organizational Leaders

Top management not only provides the resources to do the evaluation, they also make changes based on the results. Thus, attaining some real rather than superficial buy-in from the organization's leaders should be one of the goals of the entire evaluation process. Early on, the team should meet with a top member of management to gain support from the organization's leadership for the effort. A member of the team should periodically update top management on progress of the evaluation and any barriers that have been encountered in conducting it. With a topic as sensitive as diversity, it is a good idea to avoid any last-minute surprises for the organization's leadership.

Because any program evaluation may start with high expectations but lose momentum over time, the diversity evaluation team should form a "contract" with top management. This should be a clear statement of the evaluation goals, including parameters of what will be assessed and the format and time frame of the final product. Make the evaluation goals both realistic and achievable and do not oversell, especially the first time around. Beware of those who try to please top management by making grand promises that will be difficult to achieve. What is also implicit in the contract (but not always enforceable) is that management will take the results seriously, release some summary of the findings to all organization members, and act on the findings.

Table 17.2   Effectiveness of Data Gathering Methods for Evaluating Various Aspects of an Organization's Diversity Program

Aspect of Program	Method of Data Gathering					
	Policy/Procedure Documents	Demographics	Surveys	Interviews	Observations	Best Practices
Promotions	Medium	High	High	High	Medium	High
Discipline	Medium	High	High	High	Medium	High
Hiring	Medium	High	Medium	Medium	Low	High
Recruiting	Medium	Medium	Low	Medium	Low	High
Training	High	Low	High	High	High	High
Awarding bonuses	Medium	High	High	High	Medium	High

NOTE: High = highly effective; Medium = moderately effective; Low = minimally effective

In addition to top management, it is good to have a sign-off or buy-in from key stakeholders. If the organization is unionized, the involvement of union officers in the process might be vital to the acceptance of the evaluation results by union members. Fear of a lawsuit or grievance often makes legal and labor relations departments reticent about efforts such as a diversity evaluation. The evaluation team should meet with the organization's lawyers sooner rather than later to get their buy-in.

Step 4. Gather Data

The majority of evaluation time will be spent gathering data based on the identified measures of success. The data should come from a variety of sources rather than just one. The most common types of data will be policy and procedure documents, demographic breakouts showing trends over time, survey findings, individual and focus group interviews, naturalistic observations, and best practices from organizations that are recognized as diversity leaders. Table 17.2 presents various aspects of programs and how they might be best evaluated by these different methods of data collection.

Policy and Procedure Documents

Organizations often reveal themselves through their documents, policy statements, rules, and regulations. These archival records and documents should be collected; and the team should make a comprehensive list of diversity programs, policies, training, and other initiatives. It should be determined whether there is a diversity strategic plan or other documents that lay out the organization's vision for diversity. If there is not a specific diversity plan, it is important to know whether the organization's overall strategic planning document includes diversity as a part of its mission and future vision (Thomas, 2001). Many organizations will have a company statement on sexual harassment, but team members should see whether it is displayed clearly in workspaces and signed by the head of the organization or designate. Similarly, the team should gather any statements that exist for discrimination, issues related to disability, pregnancy, child care, and other family-related issues. While the mere existence of such statements does not guarantee a positive diversity evaluation, their absence would certainly raise potential red flags.

Because many organizations promote diversity through festive events honoring various groups, documentation regarding these diversity celebrations should also be collected. These include organization-sponsored events related to African American History Month and similarly designated events recognizing the contributions of Asian Americans, women, Hispanics, American Indians, and European Americans.

During this step, the team should also assess how well diversity is integrated into the organization's HR functions and policies. The team should determine whether diversity training exists, what it entails, and whether everyone (including managers and staff) is required to attend. At one organization we knew of, although diversity training was an annual requirement, it was more likely that staff employees would attend while lower percentages of management showed up. This likely communicated a message that diversity training was not one of the more important organizational functions.

Accountability is an important component of a successful diversity program, so the team will want to know whether the organization's policies and practices make management accountable for diversity outcomes. This requires a determination of whether achieving diversity goals is part of the performance evaluation system and is tied to organizational compensation and bonuses. Also, the evaluation team should learn whether family friendly work policies exist, whether there are flexible work times, and whether the organization has a clear and reasonable pregnancy and maternity leave policy.

In reviewing organization documents and diversity policies, the team should ascertain what the organization spent on diversity efforts. This would include such costs as fees charged by consultants and time away from work to attend diversity training and other company-sponsored events. Also, the costs involved in diversity-related outreach efforts such as targeted recruiting and advertising should be gathered. Costs include direct expenditures, such as how much the organization had to pay in legal fees defending against grievances and complaints and in settling cases, as well as indirect expenses, including the cost to the organization if it had a differentially high turnover among certain groups. For example, there might be a high rate of pregnant women not returning to the organization after giving birth, and this could be tied to a decision to close an on-site day care center. These indirect costs may be hard to pin down as precisely as the cost of hiring a diversity trainer, but an attempt to estimate their impact should be made.

Demographic Breakouts Showing Trends Over Time

An important data-gathering step is to gather and summarize organizational demographics to provide a *diversity snapshot* of the organization. Demographic breakouts might include race/ethnicity, gender, age, handicapped status, and so on. These should be broken out over time to determine any trends that may be occurring. A vestige of the EEO compliance model that focused on underrepresented minorities (e.g., Blacks and Hispanics) and women is that the evaluation team will likely find access to racial/ethnic and gender data easier to obtain than data for groups included under the newer expanded model of diversity. Religion is less often evaluated, but it may be appropriate if potential religious issues are in play (e.g., prayer sessions after work, time off for religious holidays, and discrimination against Muslims following the events of September 11, 2001).

Much of the demographic data will already have been gathered for other organizational purposes. As the diversity snapshot depends on attaining access to this type of information, it is a good idea to have a member from the HR department on the diversity evaluation team. If all of the needed statistics do not exist, breakouts generated for the purposes of the evaluation may need to be requested.

Many of the groups considered in the demographic snapshot will be minorities, so caution needs to be taken when making comparisons based on percentages that involve small numbers. This is especially the case if trend data over time are reported. For example, if there are only three African American women managers in the organization, and one leaves, the turnover in that group will be 33%. Depending on the size of the organization, it is a good idea to be especially cautious in conclusions drawn from percentage data based on groups with fewer than 10 individuals.

In addition to the demographic makeup of the organization, there are other key "hard" data that should be gathered and considered. The team needs to examine data on recruiting (how much was spent, who was interviewed, and who was hired), retention (who stayed with or left the organization), and promotion (what promotion opportunities were available, who applied, and who got the job). The evaluation team should determine whether there were any discrimination and sexual harassment complaints and how they were resolved. On the more positive side, demographic breakouts regarding awards and bonuses (who received them, how much they got, and why) can be contrasted with survey findings about the same issues. Any single year can be misleading, so data from previous years should be included if available.

Survey Findings

A diversity survey is a common technique used in evaluating a diversity program. In some organizations, the diversity survey *is* the evaluation tool—often to the neglect of other steps. Although the survey is a key component in helping evaluate an organizational diversity program, it is by itself only one source of data about how the organization is doing.

Although the diversity survey has become popular in public organizations such as the U.S. government and the military, it often meets with greater resistance in the private sector because of fear that the survey results will be used against the organization in a future legal proceeding. A diversity evaluation team proposing a wide-scale diversity survey in a private company may expect to lock horns with the organization's legal department over the suitability of the survey issue. If the legal arguments are sufficiently strong, the team may need to seek alternatives such as doing diversity breakouts from past surveys (e.g., customer and exit surveys) that were not designed to assess diversity issues but still may offer useful indirect information. Even in the absence of objections from the legal department, the organization's leadership should be made aware of any potential harm that might occur through the diversity survey and what steps are being taken through consultations with the legal department to protect the organization. Working with the legal department has the additional benefit of getting it on-board with the evaluation and sharing accountability for decisions that are made.

With an awareness of these limitations, a diversity survey is a powerful means to provide an accurate snapshot of the state of diversity climate in an organization. The diversity survey shares much in common with other types of organizational surveys including those done as part of program evaluations (see the chapter by Edwards and Fisher, this book). The diversity survey differs from general program evaluation surveys in the types of questions asked, the topic areas covered, and the nature of the analyses conducted.

We have used several different measurement approaches; each of which may prove useful as part of a diversity evaluation survey. One approach *directly* asks employees their views on a number of topics within the diversity area and whether they have personally experienced forms of discrimination or harassment in the past year. Also the effectiveness of diversity training and an evaluation of the organization's other diversity programs could be assessed through questions that specifically ask about training and the various programs.

A second approach *indirectly* assesses diversity success by asking a series of more general organizational questions in topic areas such as climate, organizational commitment, promotions, job satisfaction, supervision, performance evaluations, and so on. Comparisons are then made between key demographic groups, typically racial/ethnic minorities and women. The outcomes for these groups are compared to those of the White male majority and a *gap analysis* is undertaken to see where differences are greatest and where they are minimal. For example, whereas the survey responses overall might indicate positive views of promotion, comparisons between men and women could indicate that women are more negative regarding the fairness of the promotion system and their own chances for promotion. The indirect approach can provide some insight to the state of diversity-related issues without introducing demand cues caused by directly asking about them.

A third approach uses *likelihood of occurrence* (Landis, Dansby, & Tallarigo, 1996). The likelihood of occurrence approach has been used on the Military Equal Opportunity Climate Survey (MEOCS). The MEOCS is a unit-level diversity survey that has been administered to military members in the United States for the past decade and more recently has been adapted and used with civilian and private sector organizations. Whether the events asked on the MEOCS actually occurred is not the focus; rather, this approach attempts to assess the organizational climate for diversity through perceptions of how likely the events are seen as occurring or could be occurring within the organization. This approach uses weather predicting as a metaphor. If you believe that a hurricane is likely to strike a particular city, you might well decide not to buy a home in that locale. It is not important that an actual hurricane has rarely hit that particular area, only that you believe there is a high probability that it will. The interest is in the extent to which members of the organization think that diversity-related behaviors are more or less likely to occur.

As discussed in this book's chapter on organizational surveys, an issue the evaluation team has to address is whether to use a *standard*—same items across organizations—or a *custom-made* survey to which local organizations can add their own specific questions.

The current authors have used both approaches. For example, the standard MEOCS diversity survey allows organizations to measure diversity climate with items and scales that have been tested and validated in many settings and can provide comparison data to help an organization place its diversity survey results in the context of what others have done on the same survey.

Rosenfeld and colleagues (Rosenfeld & Culbertson, 1993; Rosenfeld & Edwards, 1994) have developed an alternative unit-level diversity survey used by the U.S. Navy and Marine Corps that combines standard items but allows local users to add, delete, or modify questions that are scored by a computer program. This approach gives the people who implement diversity programs more flexibility to custom-tailor their diversity surveys to the organization's unique needs, but it also requires survey team members to have some specialized knowledge of survey item construction and analysis that may be hard for them to obtain.

Both standard- and custom-survey approaches have proven successful, but the key is matching the approach to the needs of the organization as well as to the skills of the people implementing the diversity program. There is not one correct answer or approach to be followed.

Individual and Focus Group Interviews

Individual interviews with top management and focus groups with a cross-section of employees are additional sources of useful qualitative material in a diversity evaluation. Experience has taught us that the organization's top leaders are best interviewed individually rather than in groups. The dynamics of gathering individual interview and focus group data are discussed elsewhere (Edwards, Thomas, Rosenfeld, & Booth-Kewley, 1997).

When conducting focus groups as part of the diversity evaluation, one approach is to create homogeneous focus groups made up of 6–12 members of key demographic groups—Whites, Blacks, men, and women. People are often hesitant to discuss diversity issues at all, and the presence of members of other groups (who may be the target of negative comments) may inhibit the discussion. The number of focus groups depends on the organization, and the goal is to cover all key stakeholder groups—supervisors, full- and part-time employees, clerical staff, interns, and others. We recommend that external customers also be interviewed—either individually or in groups.

As in other focus group efforts, a standard set of questions is developed allowing for probes and digressions as warranted by the answers. The questions are general enough to cover a wide range of diversity issues—both positive and negative.

Input should be obtained on what diversity initiatives the organization is doing best and where improvements are needed. The members' views on the organization's diversity climate, how it treats various groups, whether it values diversity, the quality of training, and the complaint system are topics that are usually covered. There will be some overlap in the interview/focus group phase with data gathered in the diversity survey. The difference is that whereas the survey can gather more *quantitative* data about more topics, the interview/focus group stage can flesh out the *qualitative* meaning and provide a context for interpreting other findings.

Because the material gathered in focus groups may be sensitive, it is important to stress the confidentiality of the responses and to impart to other focus group members the inappropriateness of revealing what was said in the group. We have learned from experience, however, that focus group leaders cannot ensure that what was said in the focus groups will not leak and become a source of office gossip. To allow for more sensitive information to be discussed, focus group leaders should provide a way that individuals can contact them privately if they are hesitant to reveal the information during the focus group session.

Naturalistic Observations

An important but sometimes overlooked component of a diversity evaluation involves conducting naturalistic observations within the organization. Here the team takes a more "anthropological approach" and tries to unobtrusively observe what is going on in day-to-day organizational life. Rather than passively watching, the observers should systematically make notes and gather data that can be analyzed later.

Many organizations talk the talk of diversity, but they do not all walk the walk. The observational step can confirm whether there are positive or negative diversity indicators in everyday work affairs. What are the interactions at company social events? What are seating arrangements in the cafeteria? Are there large percentages of certain groups (women, minorities) that do not attend company social events, picnics, and other activities? At one organization we knew of, some women employees felt excluded because they did not feel comfortable attending Friday afternoon drinking events at a local bar where (mostly) male management and male employees socialized.

Observation can also determine the prevalence of potentially offensive comments, jokes, pictures, and e-mails in the workplace. Is inappropriate banter heard in the organization—things such as racial/ethnic jokes or gender-related material (e.g., dumb blond jokes)? If these behaviors occur, who participates? Are they condoned, or does someone note their inappropriateness?

The observation step can show how well the diversity program is being publicized and communicated. Policies on discrimination and harassment should be clearly posted on bulletin boards, in break rooms, and in company newsletters. Materials relating the racial/ethnic celebrations should be easily available. Information about cultural differences and religious holidays should be widely distributed.

Best Practices From Organizations
That Are Recognized as Leaders in Diversity

Diversity programs are very difficult to evaluate in isolation as there is no objective standard about what constitutes success. Therefore, it is important to compare the organization being evaluated to others recognized as being successful. As with all comparisons of this nature, the organization should be assessed relative to the best diversity practices for organizations of similar type and size. Some benchmarking comparisons may be difficult to make because many organizations are reluctant to share specific findings of their diversity assessments with outsiders.

One way to help determine how well the organization's diversity program is doing is to ask those in the outside community for their perceptions of the organization as it relates to diversity issues. This assessment might also ask for perceptions among members of diverse groups as they will often be the targets of the organization's special recruitment efforts. A number of years ago one of us worked on an evaluation of why Hispanics were underrepresented in the U.S. Navy's civilian workforce. From speaking to various stakeholder groups, it quickly became apparent that one of the reasons for the underrepresentation was a negative perception among some Hispanics regarding the federal government. Some interviewees cited the U.S. government's treatment of illegal Hispanic immigrants from Mexico as underlying their apprehension about working for the federal government.

A number of characteristics shared by organizations with the best diversity practices have been published in *Fortune Magazine* (e.g., Johnson, 1998; Mehta, 2000; Urresta & Hickman, 1998). These can be used as benchmarks by the local evaluation team to provide comparative information on how the organization currently stands and where it needs to go.

At the best organizations, *diversity is clearly tied to the organization's strategic plan, vision, and mission statement.* It is integrated into all aspects of the organization's strategic thinking. This is in contrast to the less optimal but more typical practice that finds diversity isolated from the organization's mainstream functions. One large organization we knew of initiated a large effort to do strategic planning for what the organization would look like in the year 2020. That effort gave only lip service to diversity issues. Simultaneously, a diversity strategic planning group, made up mostly of members of racial/ethnic minority groups, was doing a diversity strategic plan for the organization for the same time period. The groups were unconnected, and few members on either panel knew of the other's existence.

Although numbers alone do not always tell the entire story, in the diversity world, numerical representation of minorities and women—particularly in leadership positions—is a commonly used measure of how successful an organization's diversity efforts are. Representation is often among the most controversial aspects of a diversity program because it raises hot button issues related to affirmative action, quotas, and reverse discrimination. Thus, numbers of this sort should always be viewed in context of other factors (availability of group members in the local labor pool, type of job, education, etc.) rather than blindly being used as a positive or negative diversity indicator.

At the best diversity organizations, *minorities and women are well represented in key organizational positions. Fortune* magazine has for the past few years asked the nonprofit Council for Economic Priorities to choose criteria for the 50 best companies for Asians, Blacks, and Hispanics (Johnson, 1998). A number of their criteria revolved around representation of minority members in key organizational positions. In a recent ranking, minorities in the top 50 diversity companies made up 16% of the board of directors, 22% of top officials and managers (national average is 12.4%), and 13% of those receiving the organization's 50 top paychecks. At Bell South Corporation, minorities or women hold 60% of its managerial positions. At Prudential Insurance Company, almost half of management positions are held by women and about 15% of management are minorities.

It is good business practice to seek to establish accountability for organizational outcomes. A best practice characteristic of successful organizational diversity programs is that *managers are accountable for diversity-related outcomes.* Sometimes, the managers' performance evaluations, compensation, or bonuses are tied to successfully achieving diversity outcomes. A measurement-based diversity evaluation can help establish this accountability. A manager whose department showed an increase in diversity climate, better retention, fewer complaints, and other positive indicators obtained through an evaluation would have an empirical basis for being rewarded.

A good benchmark is provided by Prudential Insurance. They have designed and implemented a diversity measurement and accountability system. At Prudential, diversity results are linked to management pay and compensation, with 10% of a manager's bonus being tied to how well she or he achieves diversity goals.

Step 5. Analyze Evaluation Data

Once all the data are gathered, what is the best way to analyze the evaluation data? Our approach tries to avoid the forest-for-the-trees problem by focusing on major trends, prioritizing key findings, and "not sweating the small stuff." To accomplish this, we recommend a technique that has been used in Navy command-level diversity assessments called the *analysis loop.* Here, team members look for trends and disparities in findings from organizational records, demographics, interviews/focus groups, surveys, naturalistic observations, and other data sources. The team looks for patterns and begins to develop a list of findings that are tested, confirmed, and validated by entering and reentering the loop. The analysis loop utilizes the classic program evaluation principle of *triangulation* in which data from multiple measures are used to offset error that may occur from any single data source. Within the loop, things that the organization is doing right—"good news"—as well as potential problems—"areas of concern"—are targeted. The team should develop a prioritized list of findings— those whose existence in one area (e.g., survey data indicating lack of fairness in promotions) is validated by a different data source (e.g., company promotion records).

Based on past experience, we recommend that the team do the following:

- Review all data sources looking for major themes, especially those present in multiple sources.

- Highlight large and medium, positive and negative findings.
- Highlight differences and similarities among racial/ethnic groups, between men and women, and among other key groups (e.g., disabled and nondisabled). For survey data, it may be a good idea to set up a "practical significance" criterion beforehand such that only differences larger than a certain predetermined value (e.g., 10% or 20%) are highlighted as indicating potentially meaningful differences between subgroups. However, these predetermined values need to be applied cautiously in instances where the groups being compared are small:[1]
- Highlight major differences and similarities of the findings to comparable characteristics of relevant outside organizations.
- Synthesize findings from various parts of the evaluation and reenter the analysis loop to resolve any uncertainties.
- Categorize results in a way that tells a story and is easy to follow.
- Determine which findings to include in the presentation or report.

If the team does not have a data analysis expert, consider bringing such a person in to help make sense of the data or to provide some reassurance that the team's conclusions are supportable. However, the analytic techniques and findings should be understandable to all members of the team as it will also have to withstand the scrutiny of management.

Step 6. Prepare an Evaluation Report With Action Plan

Once the data are gathered and analyzed, findings and an action plan need to be presented to key organizational leaders. As with the results of other HR efforts and studies, the best way is with an initial oral presentation followed later by a written report. The action plan should then be implemented and periodically reviewed for any necessary adjustments.

Develop Presentation and Evaluation Report

The oral presentation should review the process, summarize key findings, present conclusions, and make recommendations. The team should present the main findings of the evaluation but not get tied down in excessive details, statistical complexities, or ambiguous results. When in doubt, cut to the chase and keep things simple using graphs over complex tables. The organization of the oral presentation should be guided by the need to tell a clear and coherent story rather than a comprehensive presentation of every single thing that was found. The presentation is the most direct opportunity for the evaluation team to tell top management what they did, what was found, and what needs to be done. If the oral presentation bombs, no one will care what the written report says. The team should have at least one dress rehearsal in which members ask the type of questions that may be asked at the actual presentation.

The written report expands on the oral presentation with a more detailed description of methods, results, conclusions, and recommendations. It can follow the model of an article from a psychology or management journal but still should be written so that a reader unfamiliar with the diversity evaluation could comprehend what was done, found, and recommended. Although organizations may have their own rules about how reports are done, there are some general guidelines worth remembering when developing both the oral and written reports.

- Interpret the results in a way meaningful to organizational leaders rather than to social scientists.
- Prioritize and simplify the results; do *not* give management a stack of findings. More is not always better.
- Summarize data in terms of positive findings/good news, areas for improvement/areas of concern, and recommendations/possible actions.

Develop and Implement Action Plan

Because the diversity evaluation itself is often so time-consuming and tedious, there may be little enthusiasm to continue the process. However, this step is crucial. Regardless of how positive the evaluation is, there will be areas that need to be revisited and successful efforts that should be maintained.

It is important to prioritize recommendations and proposed future actions. The recommendations and proposed actions should try to make the business case for implementation. For example, if the evaluation shows the organization coming up short on EEO complaints, training of managers in ways that might reduce complaints would also save money since legal fees and settlement costs would be reduced. Efforts that cut turnover among minority groups and women would result in reduced recruiting costs to replace these employees. When Aetna life insurance added on-site day care, there was a resulting 50% reduction in turnover among post-maternity mothers. Helene Curtis reduced its new mother turnover from about one third to less than 10% after it introduced a new maternity leave policy.

The action plan should specify proposed actions, target dates, and who will be responsible for implementation. Although many may view the plan as the end of the process, it really signals a beginning to a new phase of the organization's diversity program and continuing efforts to monitor and improve it. Evaluation should be seen as a continual, ongoing process, one that is always returning to make recommendations on program modification. Although enthusiasm may wane for implementing and following up on the action plan, the reality is that if it is not done, the results of the next diversity evaluation will likely continue to show the same problem areas that were originally found. Diversity evaluations often obtain very reliable results: If you do nothing, nothing will change.

A realistic goal for any type of program evaluation is continued improvement with the results of the next assessment showing measurable progress over what the current one has found. This will require that members of the team engage in a periodic review so that needed adjustments can be made to help the organization realize its diversity goals. This periodic review can help prevent follow-ups to the action plan from becoming the forgotten part of the diversity program.

Summary and Conclusions

The title of a workshop at a conference on managing diversity was "what gets measured, gets done." That title captures the essence of this chapter. For diversity programs to move beyond simply being the right thing to do to becoming mainstream HR functions, they need to implement a measurement and evaluation system, one that uses data-based assessment to determine how well the programs are doing and offers corrective actions for subsequent improvement. This chapter has provided the rationale for evaluating diversity programs and offered a step-by-step model for how the diversity evaluation can be effectively carried out.

Note

1. The issue of practical versus statistical significance is a distinction that often causes confusion when one is analyzing diversity evaluation data. Diversity consultant, Dr. Mickey Dansby, noted that statistical significance implies only that the difference between two numbers is stable (i.e., non-zero), not that it has organizational importance. To determine whether an obtained difference has practical significance requires a judgment that the difference is substantial and occurs in multiple evaluation data sources rather than just one.

References

Caudron, S. (1998, September). Diversity watch. *Black Enterprise, 29,* 91–94.

Comer, D. R., & Soliman, C. E. (1996). Organizational efforts to manage diversity: Do they really work? *Journal of Managerial Issues, 8,* 470–483.

Edwards, J. E., Thomas, M. D., Rosenfeld, P., & Booth-Kewley, S. (1997). *How to conduct organizational surveys: A step-by-step guide.* Newbury Park, CA: Sage.

Edwards, J. E., & Thomas, P. J. (1989). Hispanics: When has equal employment been achieved? *Personnel Journal, 68*(6), 144, 147–149.

Ferdman, B. M., & Brody, S. E. (1996). Models of diversity training. In D. Landis & R. S. Bhagat (Eds.), *Handbook of intercultural training* (2nd ed., pp. 282–303). Thousand Oaks, CA: Sage.

Johnson, R. S. (1998, August 3). The 50 best companies for Asians, Blacks, and Hispanics. *Fortune, 138,* pp. 94–96.

Johnston, W. B., & Packer, A. E. (1987). *Workforce 2000: Work and workers for the 21st century.* Indianapolis, IN: Hudson Institute.

Judy, R. W., & D'Amico, C. (1997). *Workforce 2020: Work and workers in the 21st century.* Indianapolis, IN: Hudson Institute.

Landis, D., Dansby, M., & Tallarigo, R. (1996). The use of equal opportunity climate in intercultural training. In D. Landis & R. S. Bhagat (Eds.), *Handbook of intercultural training* (2nd ed., pp. 244–263). Thousand Oaks, CA: Sage.

Mehta, S. N. (2000, July 10). What minority employees really want. *Fortune, 142*, pp. 180–186.

Rosenfeld, P., & Culbertson, A. L. (1993). *Command assessment team survey system (CATSYS): User guide* (NPRDC-TN-94–11). San Diego, CA: Navy Personnel Research and Development Center.

Rosenfeld, P., & Edwards, J. E. (1994, September). Automated system assesses equal opportunity. *Personnel Journal, 73*, 99–103.

Rosenfeld, P., Giacalone, R. A., & Riordan, C. A. (2002). *Impression management: Building and enhancing reputations at work*. London, England: Thomson Learning.

Thomas, G. (2001). *Managing diversity in the 21st century Navy*. Unpublished manuscript. Monterey, CA: Center for Diversity Analysis, Naval Postgraduate School.

Urresta, L., & Hickman, J. (1998, August 3). The diversity elite. *Fortune, 138*, pp. 114–115.

Suggested Reading in Diversity

Hubbard, E. E. (1997). *Measuring diversity results*. Petaluma, CA: Global Insight Publishing.

Keller, J. M., Young, A., & Riley, M. (1996). *Evaluating diversity training: 17 ready-to-use tools*. San Diego, CA: Preiffer.

Knouse, S., Rosenfeld, P., & Culbertson, A. (Eds.). (1992). *Hispanics in the workplace*. Newbury Park, CA: Sage.

Landis, D., & Bhagat, R. S. (Eds.). (1996). *Handbook of intercultural training* (2nd ed.). Thousand Oaks, CA: Sage.

Thomas, R. (1991). *Beyond race and gender: Unleashing the power of your total work force by managing diversity*. New York: AMACOM.

PART VI

Organizational
Communications

CHAPTER 18

Evaluating Organizational Survey Programs

Jack E. Edwards

Bruce M. Fisher

S urveys are common in organizations. A decade ago, Gallup (1988) polled 429 human resource directors and found that 70% of their sample of organizations had conducted an organizational survey during the past 10 years. The widespread use of surveys is not surprising given their applicability for measuring a broad range of worker and work characteristics. For example, they may be used in gathering attitudinal and factual information about cafeteria use, identifying how important a task is in performing a job, and inventorying skills and experiences as part of succession planning. The usefulness of survey information and the large number of consulting firms offering survey services suggest that surveys are at least equally common today. Moreover, some large organizations budget $500,000 or more for a single large survey and tailored feedback of findings to employees.

The widespread use and substantial costs of surveys suggest that organizations should assess the value of their survey programs. A brief lessons-learned assessment after each survey and a periodic assessment of the full survey program can enhance

AUTHOR'S NOTE: The opinions expressed in this chapter are those of the authors and do not necessarily reflect the views of the U.S. General Accounting Office or the federal government.

the benefits received from this method of data gathering. An effective strategy for conducting a program evaluation is to use multiple methods, multiple types of evaluators, and a wide range of criteria (Weiner & Schept, 1998).

This chapter considers those three approaches. The first two sections deal with the methods and evaluators. The third section details criteria that should be reflected in most survey program evaluations. The final section provides summarizing and concluding remarks.

Methods for Gathering Evaluation Data

Ironically, surveys are of limited use in evaluating survey programs. The limited usefulness of surveys for this purpose is especially evident when a survey program suffers from problems such as low response rates and concerns about the confidentiality of responses. The lion's share of the information used to evaluate survey programs is obtained through two methods: reviewing archival records and interviewing primary stakeholders.

Reviewing Archival Records

Survey archives provide a rich base for conducting a program evaluation. Particularly useful archives include copies of previous surveys, timelines and milestones, final budgets, and briefings/reports. The appendix at the end of the chapter shows some of the more common types of information that might be extracted from archives and other sources. A program evaluation team can develop its data gathering form by using the appendix to identify a subset of issues central to its assessment and supplementing those issues with organization-specific concerns.

In addition to time and cost information, program evaluators should be concerned with the survey purpose (e.g., climate assessment or job analysis), who completed it, questionnaire characteristics, distribution/administration methods, data analyses, presentations of findings, and the decisions or actions that were linked to survey findings. Each of these criterion-related concerns is covered in greater depth in a later section.

Using a data-extraction form like that shown in the appendix forces evaluators to be systematic in their assessment of each survey. For organizations that have conducted a large number of surveys during the period of evaluation, entering the data into a spreadsheet and possibly importing it into statistical software provides opportunities to learn about patterns or trends. For example, the records might reveal whether survey usage has increased or decreased over the last five years, who the most frequent sponsors were, and whether some subgroups have been surveyed much more than other subgroups.

In some organizations, archival information may be limited because no one has emphasized it or the budget/staff was thought to be too small for the "extra" task of collecting it. If such records are sparse, their absence will greatly limit the depth of the evaluation. Absence of records does, however, suggest one key recommendation—keep such documentation.

It is tempting to recommend that an organization do a lessons-learned assessment at the end of every survey using the form shown in the appendix, but the time and effort required for such an evaluation may not be optimal for some organizations. The amount of documentation should vary according to survey-program size, organization size, survey-related sophistication of the internal survey staff, and the organization's general philosophy about record keeping.

Interviewing Stakeholders

The versatility of interviews provides another ideal method for gathering information needed for the program evaluation. Decision makers and other primary users of survey information can discuss how well surveys have achieved organizational goals. Foremost among the goals is probably providing high-quality information in a timely, cost-effective manner. Whereas the actual budget and timelines might tell one story, perceptions about the monetary and time costs of a project relative to the perceived worth of the resulting product might tell another story.

Decision makers, survey staff, and rank and file organizational personnel should be asked for their perceptions of how well the survey program accomplishes specific goals. Depending on the organization, these goals might include identifying areas for process improvement, identifying organizational priorities and allocating resources, educating managers on the dynamics of employee morale, facilitating two-way communications through all levels of the organization, enhancing labor-management relations, and linking survey findings to organizational changes.

Evaluators of the Survey Program

Survey programs can be assessed from the perspectives of at least four types of evaluators: internal survey staff, consortia, external organizational survey experts, and organizational leaders. Each type of evaluator emphasizes different criteria and methods, as well as bringing different strengths and weaknesses to a survey program evaluation. Using multiple types of evaluators results in a fuller evaluation than does using a single type of evaluator, much as multiple criteria and multiple methods provide a fuller assessment than a single method or single criterion. An evaluation team with multiple types of evaluators lessens the methodological concerns associated with some types of evaluators while still obtaining the strengths that each type brings to the assessment.

Internal Survey Staff

As might be expected, internal survey personnel should know more about the organization's survey program than does anyone else. At the same time, their vested interest in having the survey program look good might cause some deficiencies to be glossed over.

In an ideal program-evaluation environment, internal survey personnel should be conducting a mini-evaluation after each survey and recording information regarding the criteria listed later in this chapter. Such formative program evaluations are often not done for a variety of reasons, including time constraints, a concern for uncovering internal problems or issues, and limited staff skills in program evaluation. Instead, an organization might elect to do a summative evaluation that covers surveys performed during a specified number of years.

Consortia

Although a consortium itself would rarely be used as part of the evaluation team, it merits inclusion in this section on evaluators because consortia members have information that may be hard to obtain anywhere else. It is desirable to have some standard against which an organization can judge its performance and progress. Some organizations partially address this concern by participating in survey consortia. For example, the Mayflower group is composed of leading organizations from numerous industries, whereas the telecommunications survey consortium restricts membership to only organizations in that industry (see Morris & LoVerde, 1993).

In addition to getting other organizations' findings for the same questions to provide a basis for comparison, consortium participation establishes networks for assessing the quality of an organization's other surveys (i.e., those performed without consortium input). At consortium meetings, member organizations can hear from other representatives about changes in the survey field that should be considered for adoption as best practices in other organizations. Also, personal contacts can provide added information on the general types of surveys being administered, problems encountered, and other concerns.

All of this information offers a context against which an organization's survey program can be judged. The organization can then determine (a) whether it is on the leading edge of surveying, in the middle-of-the-pack, or trailing peer organizations and (b) what, if any, steps are needed to change its relative standing.

External Experts

Many consulting firms and university faculty offer services that include conducting surveys, but fewer will have experience evaluating survey programs. Large organizations with extensive survey programs might go to large human resources consulting firms for their evaluations, but small firms and nonprofit agencies with almost no budget for such evaluations will probably be limited to using university faculty. The criteria listed later will help internal survey staff determine what should be covered in such an evaluation.

If the organization determines that it wants an external evaluation, it is important to select experts who deal routinely with *organizational* surveys. Experts who specialize in *polling and marketing* surveys might make recommendations that would work in their industries but could have detrimental consequences if employed in an organization. Another concern that arises with hiring external experts is the objectivity of the evaluations. Some experts may have their own research agenda or seek to use the problems and recommendations identified in the program evaluation as a stepping stone to added business. Conversely, other experts might underemphasize problems out of a concern for preserving a relationship with a customer.

Organization Leaders

Organizational leaders are a prime source of some types of program evaluation information. Although they may not be able to evaluate many of the statistical and procedural intricacies of surveys, organizational leaders have important views about the costs and benefits of surveys, their timeliness, and links between survey findings and subsequent decisions or actions.

Rank and File Employees

Finally, focus groups with samples of employees can also be an effective avenue for program evaluation. Indeed, employees are quite possibly the only source for an appropriate evaluation of some key issues, such as anonymity, survey administration dynamics (e.g., whether their supervisor would allow them off the job to take the survey), and appropriateness of the reading level of survey items.

Criteria for Judging Survey Program Quality

Over half of this chapter is devoted to the criteria that can be used to judge survey program quality. The criteria are divided into seven general but overlapping areas that cover survey staff characteristics and roughly follow the process found in a single survey. First, consideration needs to be given to the qualifications of the staff who will conduct the survey. Next, the issue of questionnaire quality is discussed. In the third through fifth sections, the generalizability, analysis and presentation, and benchmarking of survey data and findings are reviewed. The sixth section covers the evaluation of the linkage between survey findings and organizational decisions/changes. Finally, time and cost evaluation concerns conclude the discussion of survey program evaluation criteria.

Qualifications of the Survey Staff

An evaluation of a survey program requires the assessment of the qualifications of the people who will be intimately involved with every step in the survey process.

If the staff have shortcomings, those deficiencies can color the quality of all surveys performed under their direction.

The qualifications of survey staff in terms of their training and experience can be readily evaluated. Training can be assessed by examining formalized college instruction taken, attendance at seminars offered through professional associations (e.g., the Society for Industrial and Organizational Psychology or the American Association of Public Opinion Research), and individual study. The training should involve continuous improvement rather than being limited to training early in the staff member's career, with little subsequent exposure to new developments in the survey field. If the training has occurred almost entirely in-house, another important point is to look at the qualifications of the personnel who were supplying the training.

Evaluating experience consists of more than noting the number of years between the times that staff conducted their first and most recent surveys. Each survey has its own idiosyncrasies, problems, and solutions. Even re-administration of a survey requires new decisions such as (a) how to display findings from multiple years instead of a single year and (b) whether or not to improve the wording of an item so as to allow clearer comparisons across time. In addition to considering the number of years of experience, the evaluation team should consider the survey staff's breadth of experiences: methods used to administer surveys (duplicated copies, bubble scan, and computer), distribution procedures (in-person, mail, e-mail, fax, and World Wide Web), and responsibility for each step in the survey (planning, questionnaire development, sampling/weighting, distribution, data analysis, presentation of findings, and post-survey follow-up). By looking at the survey staff's total experience, the evaluation team can help the staff to identify deficiencies and strategies for overcoming those problems. If deficiencies are found, the evaluation should also identify get-well plans.

The evaluation should also consider how the surveys were carried out. For example, were survey personnel treated as interchangeable for all survey steps and organizational subunits (e.g., the sales force)? Conversely, do survey personnel specialize in only one or two survey steps (e.g., questionnaire development or data analyses) or work with only given organization subunits? Although there is probably not a best way to manage surveys in all organizations, the program evaluation may result in identifying more optimum methods for carrying out surveys.

A related issue for survey staff is their reporting relationships. The evaluation should look at the communication and reporting relationships among survey staff as well as the succession planning that goes on in a multi-person survey group. It is equally important to examine the reporting and communication patterns of the survey group with other parts of the organization and outside groups. Poor structure and communication patterns can add needless time, expense, and aggravation to the survey process.

The issue of survey staff qualifications is not restricted to internal staff. Organizations should not assume that they acquired experienced, professionally trained survey staff when they contracted for a survey. The external survey staff may have known little about the organization's industry and may have had little or no formalized training in surveying. Therefore, it is important to determine whether the internal survey staff evaluated the credentials of the consultants who did the day-to-day survey tasks, in addition to looking at the credentials of the survey coordinators.

External consultants may have offered lower-priced services because they used junior-level staff and a previously developed survey (with little or no modification). Using an existing survey has the added advantage of providing external means and percentages[1] against which the organization can compare itself. The evaluation should examine the groups and methods used to produce the statistics and determine their relevance for the organization.

The program evaluators should also reexamine (a) the items to see how well they really measured the areas of interest and (b) the organization's willingness to pay repeatedly for the service if the contract does not allow the organization to continue using the survey at no additional cost. These apparent monetary savings and external statistics may come with too many trade-offs. The proposed survey may fit the organization's needs about as well as an off-the-rack shirt fits a man with exceptionally long arms.

Questionnaire Quality

Much can be revealed about the quality of a survey program by systematically examining questionnaires. Adequate review and pretesting of questionnaires can render many problems moot before respondents see them. On the other hand, poorly developed questionnaires doom data gathering from the beginning. This chapter organizes questionnaire quality criteria into four categories: bad items, inadvertent mistakes, respondent inquiries and concerns, and international concerns.

Bad Items

All staff who have developed questionnaires and really evaluated their own work can remember a few bad items that somehow made it through extensive questionnaire pretesting and peer reviews and proofreading. The goal of pretesting and conducting reviews is to minimize the number of bad items that appear and correct problems before the item is used again.

The program evaluation should attempt to see whether certain minimum item-writing standards are met. One way to assess item quality would be to determine how well item writers adhered to Edwards, Thomas, Rosenfeld, and Booth-Kewley's (1997) general question-writing guidelines:

- Ask what you want to know (i.e., will the answer to this question tell the survey staff what it has been tasked to investigate?).
- Keep items simple and short (to avoid problems with reading level and comprehension).
- Ask about only one topic per item (to avoid the ambiguity that comes when analyzing double-barreled questions).

- Avoid ambiguous or vague questions (so that all respondents will interpret in the same way what is being asked).
- Use appropriate language (e.g., avoid acronyms and words that are meaningful to only part of the respondents)
- Avoid double negatives (e.g., "I do *not* support the idea of *not* allowing employees to work back-to-back shifts").
- Avoid biased items (e.g., that might presume the direction of an answer to a question such as "This organization has more opportunities for men than women").
- Take care with sensitive items (e.g., possibly ask about observed rather than the respondent's personal drug use).

Consistent violation of one or more of the guidelines suggests that future questionnaires need to be examined more closely before administration.

Questions that don't address the survey's purposes reflect another type of bad item. As a result, they are not used in briefings or reports, and their inclusion in the questionnaire may be a waste of organizational resources. Program evaluators can examine what proportion of the items in a questionnaire appeared in a briefing or report. Relative to shorter surveys, longer surveys cost more to duplicate, take longer to answer, may lead to higher nonresponse rates, and require more time to analyze.

Inadvertent Mistakes

Inadvertent mistakes may be minor or major, but they reflect poorly on the entire survey program because the questionnaire might be the only part of the process that respondents see. If respondents see something as minor as multiple typing errors, they could think little thought went into the whole survey process rather than attribute the errors to numerous last-minute changes that were rushed through to meet deadlines and address executives' concerns. Other types of inadvertent errors include incorrect skip patterns (i.e., instructions to move to another question without answering intermediate questions) and failing to list adequate alternatives (e.g., not having either an exhaustive set of options or a list of common answers followed by an "Other (specify)" option).

Although most mistakes can be avoided with ample pretesting and reviews, some errors might still occur. If inadvertent errors are found during the program evaluation, remedies to correct them should be provided. This type of evaluation is particularly important when a whole questionnaire or some of its items will be used again.

Respondent Inquiries and Concerns

Surveys are typically administered with a point of contact to answer inquiries about survey content and procedures. Examination of the concerns raised by employees could suggest changes across all surveys (e.g., concern about anonymity or confidentiality) or in a selected survey (e.g., a different login procedure for a Web survey).

If respondents continue to express the same concerns without seeing changes or receiving explanations on why the survey must be conducted as specified, response rates could be hurt.

To illustrate, one of the authors of this chapter completed a computerized organizational survey that was supposed to take only 30 minutes. Glitches in the computer program caused the author to spend nearly 90 minutes completing the survey. On three different sections of the survey, the computer failed to keep the author's responses, and the responses had to be re-entered. When the problem was reported to the point of contact, a generic reply was sent saying that the external survey developer would look into the problem. Apparently, the developer did not look into the problem because it remained when others reported similar problems days later.

International Concerns

As organizations add offices in other countries, survey specialists are confronted with additional concerns. The survey evaluation team needs to be especially alert to two of these concerns. First, if the survey was written in more than one language, the team should determine whether (a) the survey items and directions were translated into the additional language, (b) a different person translated the new version back to the original language, and (c) the two versions were compared for inconsistencies. Second, the team needs to determine whether the survey procedures met the legal standards present in the countries where the data were gathered. For example, the European Privacy Directive (95/46/EC) lays down common rules for those who collect, hold, or transmit personal data. Under this directive, data subjects are granted, among other things, access to the data, the right to know where the data originated, the right to have inaccurate data rectified, and the right to withhold permission to use their data in certain circumstances. In addition, certain demographic data, such as ethnic or racial origin, can be processed only with the explicit consent of the individual. If data are to be transferred to non-European Union countries, this directive includes provisions to ensure adherence to European Union rules. The U.S. Department of Commerce has developed a set of Safe Harbor Provisions in response to this directive to ensure the uninterrupted flow of data for organizations that agree to abide by certain constraints regarding the collection and dissemination of data.

Generalizability of Survey Findings

A critical aspect of all survey programs is being able to assess how well survey findings generalize or project to the population of interest, be it the whole organization or a subgroup such as employees in the organization's western region. Two indices—response rates and precision estimates—offer quantifiable measures related to generalizability.

Response Rates

Response rates are among the most frequently discussed measures of survey quality. In its most general form, a response rate is the number of eligible survey respondents who returned completed surveys divided by the number of eligible people surveyed. If 20 of 100 potential survey respondents returned completed surveys, the response rate is 20%. Differences in the formulas used to calculate this index could, however, cause response rates to differ artifactually. (See Council of American Research Organizations, 1982, for a detailed discussion of types of response rates.)

One frequently asked question is, "How high should the response rate be?" The National Center for Educational Statistics suggests 70% or higher for its surveys. This response rate is desirable, but researchers and practitioners have noted the decline of response rates over the last decade and a half (Kalton, 1988). Adding further confusion to the interpretation of response rates, many organizations refuse to divulge their response rates to people outside their organizations. A third point of confusion is that varying rates are obtained because of differences in the salience of the questionnaire content, demographics of the potential respondents, formulas used to calculate response rates, and so on. For example:

- Organizations with good employee relations will probably achieve higher rates than will organizations with poor employee relations.
- Organizations that are judicious in the use of surveys will probably have higher rates than will organizations that over-survey their people.
- Anonymously completed surveys will yield higher response rates than will surveys that ask respondents to identify themselves.
- Surveys of higher-level personnel typically yield higher rates than do surveys of rank and file workers.
- Surveys that assess topics of importance to respondents should elicit higher response rates than will other surveys.
- Surveys administered in person will result in higher response rates than will those administered through the mail.
- Surveys administered to groups on company time will almost always result in a higher response rate than will surveys completed at the respondents' leisure.

Survey response rates vary widely. Several consulting firms report that surveys administered on company time to scheduled groups typically yield response rates in excess of 80%. These same firms indicate that mail-in surveys often result in response rates below 50%. The U.S. Department of Defense routinely obtains response rates of around 55% on its large-scale surveys ($n = 40,000$ to $80,000$ persons) despite numerous, very elaborate, and costly follow-up contacts to solicit completed surveys. When response rates are low, program evaluation teams should determine whether nonresponse analyses (e.g., how well respondents' and population demographics matched) were performed. If so, the team should then determine what the analyses showed, what remedial steps were taken, and how unresolved problems or limitations were acknowledged in reports and briefings.

As a last cautionary note, program evaluators should consider long and hard before issuing a recommendation that the organization offer incentives (e.g., one hour off or a very small monetary payment) to increase response rates. Although marketing and polling surveyors find this a proven way to increase response rates, offering incentives could do long-term harm to an organization's survey program. The immediate positive effects of the incentives could wear off and require successively higher incentives to get the same response rate, and surveys that are administered without incentives might be viewed as less important and result in the return of proportionally fewer surveys. The big difference between the polling/marketing and organizational survey perspectives occurs because the former types of surveys do not need to continue surveying the same respondents over and over. Edwards et al. (1997) have listed other techniques for increasing response rates that the evaluation team might consider recommending.

Precision of Findings

Large organizations can often cut the costs of surveying the total organization or some large subunits if they gather data using a sample of the population of interest. Also, sampling can lessen a common negative effect of surveys—respondents' feelings that they are being surveyed to death. While some organizations continue to insist on the use of census surveying, a program evaluation should assess potential monetary and nonmonetary benefits associated with sampling, when applicable.

If a representative sample—rather than the population—has been surveyed, the precision associated with the resulting statistics needs to be evaluated. The precision of sample statistics might be indicated by statements such as "The sample findings are projectible to the population with ±5 percentage points at the 95% confidence interval." When a population has been surveyed, precision levels are a moot issue because a subgroup of the population is not being used to estimate what the population characteristic would have been had everyone been surveyed. (When nonrandom, judgmental sampling has been performed, precision levels should not be provided because it would be impossible to estimate how accurately the unrepresentative sample reflects the population.)

Just as representative samples can have too little precision, added precision can sometimes come at too great a cost. This can occur when responses are solicited from more people than an organization really needs. The extra people in the sample add unnecessary costs and place an undue burden on members who may already be over-surveyed.

As part of a lessons-learned review after each survey, survey staff should examine the findings and see whether the obtained level of precision was appropriate given the organization's objectives. In the spirit of cost-effectiveness, the evaluation team should ask, "Could the findings have been equally useful with a slightly larger margin of error?" An assessment of the trade-off between decreased precision versus a smaller sample size or lower costs should be conducted.

Also, a lessons-learned review of sample surveys should question whether the sample could have been designed better (e.g., with disproportional, stratified random sampling) to yield the same precision from a smaller sample. Basic sampling books (Henry, 1990) can assist the survey staff and program evaluators in determining an optimum sample size for simpler samples. For the evaluation of a complex sampling design, survey specialists might need to be contacted.

Data Analysis and Presentation of Findings

Data analysis and presentation of findings are closely linked as most of the presentation covers numerical summaries of the survey data. Therein lies a fine balancing act—using the limited types of statistics that will be meaningful to managers and other stakeholders while conveying the complex similarities, differences, and relationships found in the data. Program evaluators need to avoid being overly critical of the survey teams if they do not use the latest and most sophisticated statistical techniques. If managers don't understand the findings, they can't use them effectively.

Analyses and Statistics

In the initial stage of analysis, the survey staff should have checked the accuracy of the data being captured, regardless of whether it was captured by key entry, scanning, direct entry by the respondent with a computerized survey, or some other method. The program evaluators can check to see whether standard data-accuracy steps were completed. Minimal steps might include checking a sample of key-entered and scanned surveys in an electronic database against the original forms, looking for skip-pattern problems, making sure that reverse worded items are reverse scored before scale values and reliabilities are computed, and checking the programming used to capture the scanned and computerized surveys. Other methods might include looking at frequency/percentage distributions, means, and other descriptive statistics for "face validity." These statistics also probably served as the bases for many of the findings that will be presented to stakeholders.

The choice of statistics is ultimately a function of the stakeholders' minimum abilities and informational needs. Meeting these abilities and needs should have been a consideration during survey design. The evaluation team should be particularly concerned with the process that went into the selection of demographic breakdowns. These demographic breakdowns must support the informational needs of stakeholders and convey important ways in which employee opinions vary. At the same time, surveys that request too much demographic information may make anonymous respondents wonder whether they can be identified. Finally, evaluators of Web-based surveys should consider the ethical ramifications associated with collecting demographic information about employees (e.g., via a Web connect to a human resources information system) without the knowledge or consent of respondents.

Organizational survey data will often be summarized using percentages and means for the whole population (e.g., everyone in the organization), subgroups of the population (e.g., the marketing versus the manufacturing departments), and even subgroups within those subgroups (e.g., men and women in the marketing department examined separately). When a cross-tabulation is performed, it is imperative that any assurances of anonymity be upheld. The evaluation team might check this by determining whether any findings were reported on groups with fewer than 8–10 respondents.

Many analyses are conducted with collapsed variables (e.g., changing a 5-point satisfaction scale into 3 reporting categories, or the number of years worked at the organization into seniority groups). The survey program evaluation team can look at paper or electronic programs and printouts to determine whether the analyses were logically correct.

Some decision makers look for analyses beyond the descriptive level. Inferential statistics such as t-tests or analyses of variance are sometimes desired to answer questions pertaining to the significance of differences between groups. Similarly, correlational analyses are utilized to evaluate relationships between variables (e.g., between respondents' organizational commitment and intentions to leave). If these more advanced statistical analyses were used, evaluators should ask stakeholders to evaluate the extent to which the advanced, as well as the simpler, statistics met their informational needs.

Analysis of narrative answers to open-ended questions merits special mention because this typically requires rigorous procedures for coding comments into meaningful response categories. Evaluation teams can determine what types of training and coding materials were developed for the analysis of narrative answers. Also, the survey staff may have developed indices to document how well multiple coders agreed when evaluating the same comments.

A frequency distribution of responses is an effective way of summarizing written comments. Such content analyses can be expensive, but they are an effective way to analyze comments. Program evaluators should determine what, if anything, the survey team did with the narrative comments. Too often, such comments are requested (or given without requests), but they are not analyzed in the rush to provide findings quickly. Even though some respondents report a cathartic effect from writing about things that bother them, gathering narrative responses without systematically analyzing them is probably not an effective use of organizational resources.

Presenting Findings

A program evaluation of surveys must consider the extent to which stakeholders found the presentation of results to be useful, easily understood, and as appropriate, adding value to their interpretation. Evaluation teams can check whether survey findings were tailored to the audience. At the most strategic level, it is important that survey results be formatted and presented for senior executives in an abbreviated summary. For example, it is common for executives to focus on those survey items that were rated most and least favorably by the respondents. Top 10 and bottom 10 lists can be effectively utilized to enable this focus. This is most useful with reference to external statistics, or norms. Particularly when working with outside consultants, a brief narrative summary and recommendations section is often provided for executive review. Such an integration of findings should incorporate both quantitative and qualitative (i.e., written comments) data. The evaluation team can check recommendations to see whether they addressed the original survey goals.

Scale-level data may also be presented within an executive summary as a way to quickly capture the organization's overall strengths and priorities for improvement. In this regard, an overall "morale" or "commitment" index can be presented as a summary indicator. The quality of such indices should be evaluated to ensure that each index is comprised a sufficient number of appropriate items.

Managers and stakeholders at all levels have increasingly shown a preference for a graphic display of data, as opposed to tabular data. Bar graphs tend to be the best received. As an example, for a frequency distribution, the preference is often for a single stacked bar that represents the various response anchors (or favorability ratings) through different shadings and sums to 100%. The survey staff should be able to provide the evaluation team with a report of all items and, as appropriate, scale data. A transcription of written comments should also be provided in this data report.

The presentation of findings usually includes a series of meetings, moving from senior executives and decision makers to middle managers and finally to employees. These meetings are critical to the extent that they are the link between data and action. The quality of the facilitation in these meetings should be a primary focus of the program evaluation. Evaluation teams might obtain such documentation from computerized calendars and other documents.

Benchmarking and Best Practices

Benchmarking with surveys is usually considered in terms of establishing a relative standard against which survey findings may be viewed, but other types of benchmarks and best survey practices also provide important criteria for evaluating the survey program. As has previously been mentioned, participation in consortia offers a viable means for obtaining such information.

One mark of a high-quality survey is being able to put the findings in context. Relative to newer survey programs, organizations that have been using surveys for much longer have a greater likelihood that they have been using trend data in the presentation of findings. Evaluations of benchmarking could also address whether survey staff examined the convergence of survey findings with nonsurvey information from inside the organization. For example, the relationship between answers to organizational commitment survey items and turnover rates could have been examined for each of the organization's functional units (e.g., manufacturing and marketing).

Program evaluations addressing survey benchmarking should also determine whether staff placed the findings in even broader contexts. For example, a presentation of the organization's survey findings about satisfaction with pay might have included statistics from industry trade groups or the Bureau of Labor Statistics to show whether the organization's actual pay level was above the norm for similar industries, types of jobs, geographic regions, and so on.

Survey staff need to be aware of best practices in surveys even if these cannot currently be used in their organization. Changes in the costs, specialized equipment or software, and technical skills required for some survey procedures may rapidly alter the cost-benefit ratio for some previously unused best practices. For example, decreased software costs and less complex programming have greatly increased the viability of Web surveys. Thus, survey-process changes external to the organization must be considered in a survey program evaluation. This outward look at best practices allows the organization to evaluate how rapidly it has adapted to developments in the survey field.

Decisions and Changes Linked to Survey Findings

The goal for any survey should be much more than to gather information. The data should be gathered for concrete purposes that were identified during the initial survey planning. The survey evaluation team should assess what decisions were made after decision makers received the survey findings and what actions actually resulted from those decisions.

In assessing the usefulness of surveys, it is not enough to check whether survey staff and decision makers agreed about what the findings meant. The assessment should also look at what occurred later. These post-briefing steps are extremely important and lie almost solely in the hands of the decision makers. Thus, a full assessment of the survey program would need to answer the following politically sensitive questions.

- Did the results get fed back to the organizational members who were asked to respond?
- Did management make any decisions about what changes to institute as a result of the survey findings?
- Were the changes implemented?
- Was the link between survey findings and resulting changes conveyed to employees?
- How long was the period between the survey completion and the beginning of the change?

Documentation for this part of the evaluation can be obtained in interviews with and correspondence (e.g., e-mails, letter, and live or videotaped statements) from the organization's survey sponsor or upper management.

If employees can see that their responses matter and that their responses influence the organization's policies and programs, this linkage should result in positive side benefits such as increased response rates and higher morale. If organization members do not feel that their responses are going to influence the organization, potential respondents might adopt the attitude, "There's no use in answering and returning my survey. They never do anything with the information."

Timeliness and Cost

Reviewing timeliness and cost as the last two quality criteria is not meant to downplay their importance. Rather, they must be interpreted relative to all of the previously reviewed criteria. Internal or external survey staff would find it much easier to design and implement a state-of-the-art survey program if time and cost were not issues, but that is not the case in any organization. In an era when organizations are trying to do more with less, time and cost issues will be the foremost program quality considerations in the minds of many executives.

Rapidity With Which a Survey Can Be Conducted

Survey expertise and in-depth planning do not ensure that every survey will be briefed on time. Inevitably, some surveys will take longer than promised. Evaluations of survey-program timeliness should investigate the number and proportion of surveys that took longer than promised, the length of and reasons for the delays, and unanticipated resources that were added after the fact either to get or to attempt to deliver survey findings on time. A less often discussed timeliness issue is whether an on-time survey took longer than it should have. Survey developers could have built in so much time for unforeseen contingencies that they did the organization a disservice.

Getting a survey done within an agreed-upon time might be critical. In some cases, the impact of the survey findings is severely decreased if they arrive late. For example, survey-based testimony that must be presented to stockholders on a specified date requires that findings be available by that date. If the survey findings are not available on the specified date, important annual or longer term funding and program changes may either be delayed or made without information that would provide a firmer basis for changes or for maintaining the status quo.

Individuals who have little or no direct experience with organizational surveys are often surprised at how long the process can take, from determining that a survey should be conducted to reporting the survey results. Even though many survey steps can be done simultaneously to minimize the time between the start and the final report, thorough planning of the number of days and specific staff required for each step is critical to conducting a survey on time and with the anticipated budget. Edwards and Thomas's (1993) steps for novice survey developers are also applicable for evaluation teams interested in assessing timeliness and costs for the entire survey process.

Project planning software is very useful in survey planning because it can anticipate "free time" for the survey staff and allow them to perform other tasks. The software can also identify potential time- and commitment-related obstacles. Time-related obstacles might include vacations, holidays, and major organizational events that preclude involvement by staff. Similarly, commitment-related obstacles might include a survey developer's being designated to accomplish two 40-hour tasks in the same 5 days or mailing room staff not being available to print and distribute the surveys because they will be preparing and distributing tax statements to employees or annual reports to stockholders.

Review of the survey timelines may help program evaluators to identify what, if any, steps required initially unanticipated time and resources. These deviations can be used to recommend changes in the general survey process during the feeding back of program evaluation findings.

Table 18.1   Estimating Major Survey Costs

	Materials	Labor	Total
Survey staff time and travel			
Pretesting (participant time and possibly travel)			
Copies of the survey (or programming time for computer or Web-based surveys)			
Distribution and return processing (includes preliminary messages, surveys, and follow-ups)			
Physical distribution (e.g., assembling materials, and addressing and stuffing envelopes)			
Postage (if not done through interoffice mail) Processing returns			
Data capture (key entry, scanning, programming)			
Special software or equipment			
Survey completion time for respondents			
TOTAL			

Cost

Good surveys are rarely cheap. Few organizations will approach the estimated $1 million that it cost one government agency to conduct a 75,000-person 20-page survey, but organizational decision makers may be surprised at the full cost of a survey. A thorough accounting of survey costs needs to consider the expenses associated with the survey staff's time and travel, survey distribution and return, data entry/capture, special software for data analysis and presentation, and employee time during pretests and while completing the survey. Table 18.1 lists the most typical and expensive charges in conducting a survey. Evaluators can discuss these charges with the organization's accounting and human resources departments to arrive at the actual total costs of the survey program.

One of the most obvious costs associated with surveys is the expense of staff assigned to surveys either full- or part-time (e.g., to write and pretest items and perform actual data gathering). Foremost among organizational expenditures are the salary and benefits for the staff during the hours when they are occupied on survey-related tasks. Additional expenses are encountered when the staff travel to the organization's other locations for survey pretesting, data gathering, or briefings of employees regarding survey findings.

Another potentially major outlay is associated with preparing copies of the survey.

■ If the surveys are to be distributed on paper, the survey will need to be printed. While one- or two-page questionnaires copied on standard paper will cost little, longer surveys or surveys printed on special paper that can be optically scanned may cost $1 or more per questionnaire to print.

■ If a computerized survey is used, the costs of a programmer's salary and benefits must be considered. Also, a less quantifiable cost might come from bogging down or crashing the computer network if too many people attempt to access the survey at once. For example, when one organization asked its 3,500 employees to complete a skills inventory, its system would freeze for a minute at a time.

■ Distribution expenses will vary widely according to whether the questionnaires are administered in groups or individually and whether the surveys are on paper or computerized.

■ Assembling employees in a central location saves the costs of mailing paper surveys or questionnaires on diskettes, but it adds costs that are sometimes forgotten. More specifically, labor costs are associated with the time that it takes to travel to and from the survey location as well as to wait for the survey administration to start. Also, centralized data gathering at each location may require a travel budget for those responsible for administering the survey.

■ Surveys distributed on the Web or local network have almost no distribution costs. Even the addressing of notifications and passwords involves little staff time. Similarly, questionnaires delivered through company mail have minimal costs. The costs are primarily for the labor to address and stuff outgoing envelopes and to open envelopes when completed surveys are returned. Sending surveys to organization members via the U.S. mail is much more expensive. In addition to costs cited for using company mail, the company will incur postage charges for outgoing and returned surveys and the expense of two 1-time use envelopes. The cost of distributing surveys through the U.S. Postal Service multiplies if more than one mailing is sent to people in the survey population or sample who have not responded.

An often forgotten cost of conducting a survey is the lost labor time required to complete a survey. If it takes 20 minutes to complete and return a survey and an organization has 3,000 employees, that means that 1,000 hours (i.e., 125 days or about 50% of the days in one work year) of salaries and benefits are being paid to complete the survey. Thus, an evaluation of the survey program should consider whether needless items are routinely included in the survey. Even if organizations have only a few needless items on each survey, the cost can be surprisingly high when considered in the aggregate across all the surveys done in a given year.

A thorough accounting of all survey costs might result in a reevaluation of whether a survey is necessary. In some cases, management might decide that the costs are not worth the potential benefits, especially if the data can be gathered in other ways (e.g., from personnel records, grievances, and accident reports). In other cases, management might determine that several small surveys that were destined for the same population can be administered as a single larger survey. A third alternative might be to hire external consultants who specialize in organizational surveys to perform one or more of the survey steps if this might result in cost (or time) savings. Such a decision would, however, require the development of some firm in-house cost estimates to see if the consultants would be able to deliver all or part of the survey more cheaply. A program evaluation might be a first step to developing such cost estimates.

Summary and Conclusions

No single method or criterion for evaluating a survey program will fulfill the needs of all organizations. Therefore, the evaluation of an organization's survey program must begin with a thorough assessment of the needs and objectives of the program as well as an understanding of the resources available for the evaluation.

The intended impact of the evaluation must be considered from the very beginning. Increasingly, the data from survey programs are linked to important, specific organizational outcomes such as customer satisfaction, product quality, and employee turnover. A comprehensive evaluation program must consider how effective each survey was in helping the organization to achieve desired outcomes.

Note

1. These external statistics are rarely "norms." Rather, they are typically an aggregation of convenience samples from one or more populations. Comparisons against marginally relevant external statistics may do more harm than good. To illustrate, the external statistics might have been calculated from samples that were 70% white-collar employees, whereas the organization purchasing the survey is 80% blue collar. Comparisons to the external statistics might suggest one set of organizational changes, but the purchasing company may have acted very differently if it had had real norms and they had been relevant to its workforce. In surveys, it is common to find differences across organizational and demographic subgroups.

Appendix: Potential Information to Examine From Survey Archives

Survey title: _____

Sponsor: _____ Survey staff serving as survey point of contact: _____

Purpose(s): _____
_____

HOW LONG DID THE SURVEY TAKE AND HOW MUCH DID IT COST?

Date started: __ __ / __ __ / __ __   Cost/budget: $_____

Date fielded: __ __ / __ __ / __ __

Date briefed: __ __ / __ __ / __ __

Were formal timelines with milestones developed for the survey?   O Yes O No

Were the timelines generally met?   O N/A, no timelines O Can't tell O Yes O No

WHO COMPLETED THE SURVEY?

Population of interest:

O Whole organization   O Part(s) of the organization (*specify subgroups*): _____
_____

Census/sampling:

O Census   O Sample (*describe*):_____
_____

Organizational members' involvement:

_____ # who received a survey   _____ # who returned a completed survey

If nonresponse analysis performed, describe: _____

WHAT CHARACTERISTICS DID THE SURVEY POSSESS?

Length of survey:	**Complexity of survey:**
____ # of items (not just questions)	____ # of skip patterns used
____ Approximate time to complete a survey	____ Reading level of instructions
	____ Reading level of items

Quality of the items:

____ % of items poorly written (e.g., double-barreled, double negative, or insensitive)

____ Translation and re-translation back if survey was written in more than one language

WHAT WERE THE DISTRIBUTION AND ADMINISTRATION CONDITIONS?

Distribution method:	**Administration method:**	**Protection of responses:**
O Group administration	O Duplicated paper	O Identified
O Company mail	O Optical scan forms	O Confidential
O U.S. mail	O Telephone	O Anonymous
O Fax	O Computer	O Legal review for
O LAN		internal surveys
O Web		

WHAT KINDS OF STATISTICAL ANALYSES WERE PERFORMED ON THE DATA?

Type(s) of analyses conducted:

O   Frequencies/percentages for total database   O   Precision estimates (if sampling)

O   2-way crosstabs   O   Other statistics (*specify*)_____

O   Means   _____

O   Medians   _____

If sampling used, was weighting/software appropriate?   O   N/A, population   O   Yes   O   No

HOW WERE FINDINGS PRESENTED?

Variety for display of findings:

O   Word/bullet charts   O   Univariate graphs

O   Tables for univariate statistics   O   Bivariate graphs

O   Tables for bivariate statistics   O   Linear structural equation modeling

O   Tables with 3 or more variables   O   Other statistics (*specify*)_____

Did any findings report on groups of 8 or less?   O   Can't tell   O   Yes   O   No

WHAT DECISIONS AND ACTIONS WERE LINKED TO THE SURVEY FINDINGS?

Decisions linked to survey findings:

1. _____

2. _____

3. _____

Actions linked to survey findings:

1. _____

2. _____

3. _____

References

Council of American Research Organizations. (1982). *On the definition of response rates* (special report of the CASRO task force on completion rates, Lester R. Frankel, Chair). Port Jefferson, NY: Author.

Edwards, J. E., & Thomas, M. D. (1993). The organizational survey process: General steps and practical considerations. In P. Rosenfeld, J. E. Edwards, & M. D. Thomas (Eds.), *Improving organizational surveys: New directions, methods, and applications* (pp. 3–28). Thousand Oaks, CA: Sage.

Edwards, J. E., Thomas, M. D., Rosenfeld, P., & Booth-Kewley, S. (1997). *How to conduct organizational surveys: A step-by-step guide.* Newbury Park, CA: Sage.

Gallup, G. (1988, August). Employee research: From nice to know to need to know. *Personnel Journal,* pp. 42–43.

Henry, G. T. (1990). *Practical sampling.* Newbury Park, CA: Sage.

Kalton, G. (1988). Survey sampling. In S. Kotz, N. L. Johnson, & C. B. Read (Eds.), *Encyclopedia of statistical sciences* (Vol. 9, pp. 111–119). New York: John Wiley.

Morris, G. W., & LoVerde, M. A. (1993). Consortium surveys. In P. Rosenfeld, J. E. Edwards, & M. D. Thomas (Eds.), *Improving organizational surveys: New directions, methods, and applications* (pp. 122–142). Newbury Park, CA: Sage.

Weiner, S. P., & Schept, F. (1998). Alternative to surveys: Examples and benefits of qualitative research in organizational settings. In S. Rogelberg (Chair), *Surveys and more surveys: Addressing and dealing with oversurveying.* Symposium conducted at the 13th annual conference of the Society for Industrial and Organizational Psychology, Dallas, TX.

Suggested Readings in Surveys

Church, A. H., & Waclawski, J. (1998). *Designing and using organizational surveys.* Brookfield, VT: Gower.

Edwards, J. E., Thomas, M. D., Rosenfeld, P., & Booth-Kewley, S. (1997). *How to conduct organizational surveys: A step-by-step guide.* Newbury Park, CA: Sage.

Kraut, A. I. (Ed.). (1996). *Organizational surveys: Tool for assessment and change.* San Francisco: Jossey-Bass.

Robinson, J. P., Shaver, P. R., & Wrightsman, L. S. (Eds.). (1991). *Measures of personality and social psychological attitudes.* San Diego, CA: Academic.

Rosenfeld, P., Edwards, J. E., & Thomas, M. D. (Eds.). (1993). *Improving organizational surveys: New directions, methods, and applications* (pp. 3–28). Newbury Park, CA: Sage.

Rossi, P. H., Wright, J. D., & Anderson, A. B. (Eds.). (1983). *Handbook of survey research.* San Diego, CA: Academic.

CHAPTER 19

A Practical Guide to Evaluating Computer-Enabled Communications

J. Philip Craiger

Virginia Collins

Alex Nicoll

T he computer technology revolution has had a remarkable impact on the way individuals work and organizations do business, including the way they communicate. Once occurring solely by mail or telephone, communications now take place in many ways. Text and voice messages have been replaced by sophisticated messages composed of several types of media, transmitted to numerous recipients around the world in real time (i.e., without a perceptible delay).

As computer technology evolves it will continue to shape workplace communications, with most effects being constructive, improving the efficiency and effectiveness of workers. Nevertheless, the effective use of computer-enabled communication technologies requires an informed evaluation to determine which of the technologies provides the most appropriate fit to the needs of individuals, workgroups, and organizational units. Program evaluation is particularly relevant for an organization in which more and more workers are mobile: telecommuting from home, traveling, or are part of a geographically distributed workgroup. An evaluation is no simple task as the technologies vary along a number of dimensions that could be relevant in determining their satisfactory application in a variety of situations.

In this chapter we describe a strategy for evaluating computer-enabled communication technologies. This strategy will allow program evaluators to answer a number of important questions, the most important of which is, What communication technology, or technologies, best fit our organizational needs?

We begin by describing dimensions on which any communication technology can be evaluated. Next we discuss several strategies for choosing among a set of alternatives, that is, how information on these technologies can be combined into a summary index of goodness. We then describe several existing communication technologies that should be with us for some time. We conclude by describing organizational communication policies, providing guidelines on creating communication policies, including acceptable use policies and "netiquette," as well as guidelines for evaluating these communication policies.

Caveat. Before we describe our strategy we want to make clear that any evaluation of technology is best performed with a member of the organization's technical or computer staff as part of the evaluation team. Members of the technical staff are the subject matter experts; they understand the technology and will be able to comprehend the intricate details and terminology that will undoubtedly be used in the description of the technology.

Dimensions of Communication Technologies

We have been asked "What is the best way to provide communication between members of work groups?" Our answer is that "it depends." There is no one best way for members of geographically or temporally separated work groups to communicate, as different work contexts have different needs that require different solutions. Because there is no a priori way to identify the best technology for any particular context, we have devised a strategy that is applicable to any context or any organization. The key to this strategy is the identification of seven dimensions that are applicable to all communication technologies. Each dimension was selected based on its potential impact on the way members of an organizational unit communicate.

Dimensions

The seven dimensions are as follows.

Mobility. To what extent does the technology support the "mobile" worker? Does the technology limit a worker to a specific geographic location (e.g., the office or a specified conference area)? This is an important dimension because workers are increasingly mobile, partly driven by the creation of, as well as the reduced cost of, technologies that allow work to take place anywhere.

Additional questions to be addressed include these: Will additional training be required to use the new devices? Is the technology easy to use under any circumstances? Does the technology use standard protocols for communications, making sure that different devices will be able to "talk to" each other, that is, share information?

Broadcast flexibility. How flexible is the technology in terms of the number of potential recipients? Can a message be targeted to a specific subset of recipients? Preferred technologies will be more flexible, allowing messages to be broadcast to as many or as few recipients as needed.

Possible questions to be address include these: Does the technology allow for the broadcasting of messages to multiple remote locations? Can messages be targeted to a specific subgroup of recipients? If so, how easy or difficult is it to target messages to a specific subgroup?

Synchronicity/interactivity. Is the message received instantaneously, as with a phone conversation? Synchronous communications may support more interactivity between workers. Synchronous communications are critical when *immediate* feedback is desirable or required.

Additional questions to be addressed are these: Does the technology provide for synchronous communications? Can the technology be used in *both* synchronous and asynchronous modes? For instance, think of a phone—synchronous—combined with an answering machine—asynchronous.

Security. Does the technology support the sharing of information securely? For example, some governmental agencies have dedicated phone networks (e.g., the Defense Secure Network) and phones that encrypt messages so that discussions of a classified nature can be made. Does the technology support a way of securing the message so that the message cannot be surreptitiously intercepted? (For a nontechnical overview of computer security see Craiger & Burnham, 2001.)

Potential questions to be addressed are these: Does the technology provide for strong encryption (i.e., scrambling of the message's text that makes it difficult to decode)? Is the security transparent to the user (i.e., does the user need to worry about taking overt action to make a communication secure, or does the software automatically handle security)? Is security always "on," or is there a user selectable switch so that it can be turned off temporarily?

Persistence. Does the technology support the archiving of communications? Persistence provides an audit trail for corporate memory or legal situations.

The primary question to be addressed is this: In what formats can the communications be archived? Proprietary formats are undesirable because one never knows when a technology company will go belly-up.

Technology requirements. Different communications require different technology as well as support. Some communications can be built directly on the back of existing infrastructure, whereas others may require a significant investment in new technology.

Questions to be addressed include these: What technology is required to support the technology? Is sufficient technology available to support the needs of users? Can existing technology serve dual purposes?

Cost. What do the barebones and high-end versions of the system cost? Is the technology *cost-effective?* This can be an important factor for management, which may be looking for large return-on-investment. For example, technology-based training may have high start-up costs; however, reduced travel costs may make for a very cost-effective solution. Additional questions to be addressed with respect to cost include these: What costs are involved in building infrastructure, equipping employees, and maintaining the equipment? What will be the employee training costs, if any?

Groupware

Note that some systems combine two or more of these technologies into a single package and are called "groupware," computer-supported collaborative systems, or decision-support systems. These systems may combine, for example, e-mail and discussion groups, shared calendars, shared electronic white boards, and so on. Thus, groupware is flexible in that it provides multiple means of communicating among users.

Groupware is powerful, providing for a greater degree of functionality. We do not discuss groupware as a communication technology by itself but instead concentrate on those technologies that make up groupware software.

We now turn our attention to strategies for evaluating the appropriateness of a set of technologies. First we provide a brief description of evaluating communication needs. We then describe two strategies that can be employed in the evaluation and decision-making process and provide an example of how each would be conducted.

Evaluating Corporate Needs

It is very easy to overkill with technology—that is, using the most bleeding-edge technology (perhaps just because it's *available*)—when simpler and cheaper technology would do just as well. For example, it would make little sense to look at mobile solutions for employees in a documents processing department, whereas it might make a great amount of sense for sales staff. The effective use of technology requires that you determine your communication needs before identifying a technology to purchase or use. Below we provide a heuristic mapping between the dimensions described above and potential communication needs.

Mobility or mobile communication solutions are important when workgroup members are in different locations and there is a need for members to communicate, or when employees are mobile (teleworkers or those who travel frequently) and must maintain contact with headquarters.

Broadcast flexibility is important when there is a need to send messages to a subset of a larger group, or to an entire group of recipients, or to switch between different subsets of recipients.

Synchronicity/interactivity is important when immediate feedback is desirable or required. This may include either the need to get feedback for quick decisions or for creative activities such as brainstorming.

Security is important when there are monetary or other substantial consequences if unauthenticated or unauthorized users intercept messages.

Persistence is important when it is important that a corporate memory be established and preserved, or there are legal reasons for establishing an audit trail of a history of communications.

Although cost may *seem* to be a straightforward issue (the cheaper the better), this is not a guarantee. The costs of the technology must be weighed against the potential benefits it would bring. For instance, we know of cases in which the addition of computer technology, purchased to save time and money, has actually made workers much less productive—for example, changing an 8-minute manual task into a 30-minute computerized task. Any additional employee training required should not be overlooked.

The issue of technology requirements overlaps somewhat with the cost dimension. Some technology can be implemented within existing technology infrastructure, whereas others require the addition of new infrastructure. New infrastructure will mean additional costs, often substantial. The member of the technical staff on your evaluation team should be able to identify any new infrastructure required to support the new communications technology.

In summary, your evaluation team needs to identify your organization's requirements and then map them to the dimensions. At that time you should develop a rough estimate of the relative importance of the dimensions. This is important, as it is often desirable to use importance weightings in the decision strategies that we describe next.

Strategies for Selecting Among a Set of Alternatives

Whole books have been written about strategies for selecting among a set of alternatives. Given the limited number of pages we are allowed to devote to our subject, we have chosen two robust strategies that program evaluators may employ in a variety of situations. The first strategy is a compensatory model, and the second is a noncompensatory model.

Compensatory Model

The name "compensatory" indicates that high values on some dimensions compensate for lower values on other dimensions. The compensatory model assumes that (a) decision makers have a set of alternatives from which to choose; (b) the evaluators are seeking the best choice from among the set of alternatives; (c) each alternative can be rated on several dimensions; (d) these dimensions can be measured on a scale; and (e) where appropriate, each dimension can be differentially weighted to reflect its relative importance to a decision. Because this model is based on the linear model, it is assumed that statistical assumptions, such as the independence of dimensions, also hold, although the model has been shown to be fairly robust to the violation of these assumptions (Hogarth, 1988).

Ratings may be either subjective (e.g., preference ratings) or objective. For instance, evaluators may ask employees to rate the alternatives on a dimension according to their subjective preference or likeability using a 5-point Likert scale. Objective ratings may be calculated using objective data, such as cost, industry studies, ratings provided by subject matter experts in the field, and so on. Regardless of the type of rating, it is important that the ratings for all dimensions be reflected in the same scale range (1 to 5, 1 to 100, etc.) so that a dimension is not given undue weight because it has a larger scale or exhibits more variance due to the greater scale range.

The application of a multiplicative weighting factor allows the program evaluator to recognize that some dimensions may be more important than others. If a manager indicates that cost is more important than security, then the evaluator should be able to reflect this difference in importance by weighting cost more than security.

Weights typically, but are not required to, fall in the range from 0.0 to 1.0, and weights are usually normalized to 1.0 for statistical purposes (i.e., they sum to 1.0).

The compensatory model calculates a choice value C for alternative n (C_n) as

$$C_n = \sum_{i=1}^{n} X_i W_i$$

where x_i is the rating for dimension i and W_i is the relative weighting for dimension i.

The linear compensatory model has several attractive properties including these: a low value on one dimension can be compensated for by a higher value on another dimension, it is relatively robust from statistical assumptions (see Hogarth, 1988), and it is relatively straightforward to calculate.

Noncompensatory Model

There are several noncompensatory models from which to choose (see Plous, 1993; Hogarth, 1988). We have chosen to discuss the *conjunctive model* because we feel it will be useful in a variety of situations in which a compensatory model is not appropriate. The same assumptions hold for this model except minimum thresholds for dimensions are established where appropriate, and any alternatives not meeting the minimum threshold on a particular dimension are removed from the set of alternatives. The remaining alternatives in the set may then be subjected to a compensatory model analysis to determine the best of the remaining alternatives.

The conjunctive noncompensatory model is useful when a particular dimension(s) is so important that any deviation from a minimum threshold is cause to remove that choice from the set of alternatives. We can think of numerous instances when a noncompensatory model is more appropriate than a compensatory model. For instance, suppose a company is researching and developing a radical new breakthrough product with the potential for billions of dollars in sales. Because of the reality of corporate spying, the company must know that its communications are secure, with essentially a zero chance of anyone intercepting any communications. In this case, because a particular technology has a high rating on one dimension—say, it is very inexpensive—this would not compensate for the technology's inability to guarantee the company that communications could not be compromised. In this case, any alternative that exhibited less than the highest rating on the security dimension would be removed from the set of alternatives, no matter what their ratings were on any of the other dimensions.

Application of the Models

A simple example will illustrate each of the models. Table 19.1 is an abstract example with three alternatives, A, B, and C, and each of these can be characterized by dimensions X, Y, and Z. Each dimension for each alternative has been rated on the same scale, 1 to 5. Additionally, importance weights have been provided for each dimension (see Table 19.1, Note 1).

Results of the Compensatory Model

The results of the linear model suggest that the best choice is C, given that its weighted score is the highest (4.00). The example illustrates the model's compensatory nature in that the high score on dimension Z (5), multiplied by the high importance weight (.75), compensates for the low scores and low importance weights on dimensions X and Y.

Note that the use of the simple summated ratings (11, 8, and 8, respectively) would have suggested that the best choice was A. The use of simple summated ratings is often called "unit weighting," which essentially reduces to using no weights. Unit weighting is often desirable when there is no clear justification for assigning weights. A weighting system, however, allows us to assign differential importance to the dimensions, which clearly can make a difference in the outcome. Therefore, it is important that decision makers are careful and judicious in their selection and assignment of weights to dimensions.

Results of the Noncompensatory Model

The conjunctive noncompensatory model is essentially a two-step process. First, minimum thresholds are assigned to each dimension, where appropriate, and those

Table 19.1 Compensatory Model With Differential Weighting

	Alternatives					
	A		B		C	
	Raw	Weighted	Raw	Weighted	Raw	Weighted
	5	1.0	2	0.40	1	0.20
Dimension (weights)	5	0.25	3	0.15	1	0.05
	1	0.75	3	2.25	5	3.75
Summary Scores	11	2.00	8	2.80	8	4.00

Notes:

1. Weight for Dimension X = .20; Dimension Y = .05; Dimension Z = .75. Weights have been normalized so they sum to 1.0.

2. A raw score is an *unweighted* score. A weighted score is the raw score multiplied by the corresponding weight.

alternatives that do not meet or exceed these thresholds are removed from the set of alternatives. Second, either differential or unit weighting is applied to each of the ratings and then summed to determine the best alternative from the remaining set of alternatives.

In this example we will use unit weighting. Say that it is important that all three dimensions exhibit at least a score of "average" (e.g., a 3 on a scale of 1 to 5) to be deemed acceptable. Table 19.2 illustrates that although choice C has the highest summary score, it is eliminated given that its score on the dimension Y falls below the critical threshold value of 3. Of the two remaining choices A has a higher summated rating, and therefore is the preferred alternative.

Which Model to Use?

The choice of model will depend upon the needs of the program evaluator and the context in which it will be used. The noncompensatory model is applicable when a minimum threshold is required on a dimension. The compensatory model is appropriate when minimum thresholds are unnecessary and when it is appropriate that one dimension is able to compensate for another.

Prevalent Communication Technologies

Because our audience may include both technically sophisticated users as well as those who are not, we provide a brief description of existing communication technologies that will be with us for some time. We do not describe how these technologies are *implemented,* as this will undoubtedly change, but rather the general concept behind the technology. Also, we do not provide an evaluation of any of

Table 19.2   Noncompensatory Model With Unit Weighting

	Alternatives		
	A	B	C
	3	3	5
Dimensions	3	3	2
	4	3	5
Summary Score	10	9	12

Note: Minimum cutoff for dimension Y is 3

these technologies for the same reason; the actual implementations may change, rendering any evaluation we provide essentially obsolete.

We will begin our discussion with one of the more advanced technologies, videoconferencing.

Videoconferencing

Videoconferencing involves an interaction between two or more participants at different sites using computer networks to transmit video and audio data. In a two-person (point-to-point) video conferencing system, each user has an audio input and output device (e.g., microphone and speakers, respectively) and a video camera. As participants speak, their voices are carried over a network and delivered to another participant's computer. Whatever images appear in front of the video camera appear in a window on the other participant's computer monitor.

In contrast, multipoint videoconferencing allows three or more participants to sit in a virtual conference room and communicate as if they were sitting right next to each other. Until the 1990s, the hardware costs made videoconferencing prohibitively expensive for most organizations, but that situation is changing rapidly.

Figure 19.1 demonstrates a videoconference. The software displayed falls under the rubric of groupware because it provides more functionality than the broadcasting of video and audio. For example, multiple users at different remote locations may use a shared whiteboard, much the same as users within the same room can use a real, physical whiteboard. Each remote user can take control of the whiteboard, drawing pictures or typing text on the whiteboard with his or her mouse and "electronic ink," or may incorporate graphics or pictures.

This software also supports application sharing and collaboration, a feature that allows two or more users to use the same software while working at remote locations. In Figure 19.1 Philip (lower left) and Alex, located in different offices, are working simultaneously on an early version of this chapter's outline. The word processing software is running on Philip's computer, and surprisingly, Alex does not even have to have the same software installed on his computer. Yet Alex is able to make modifications to the same document in real time. Application sharing allows two or more

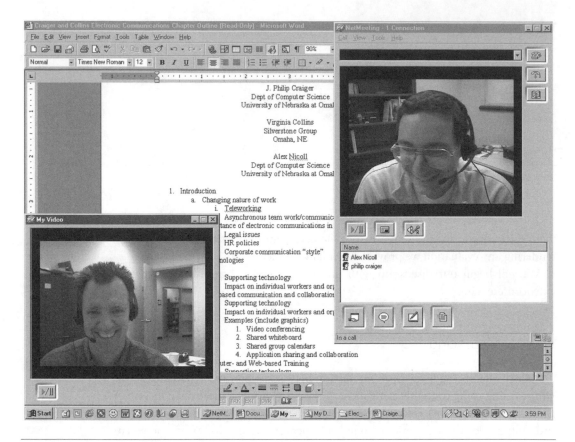

Figure 19.1   Videoconferencing

users to take turns controlling the software in an interactive fashion. It is almost as if the two were sitting in the same room and working alongside one another.

Larger companies are finding that videoconferencing provides a means of reducing travel costs. For example, Terry Milholland, a former CIO and vice president of Shared Services for the Boeing Co., indicated that Boeing used videoconferencing for meetings between its headquarters in Seattle and employees at satellite locations (T. Milholland, 1997, personal communication). The most often cited reasons for using videoconferencing include reduced air travel costs, employee time savings, and the ability to call "last-minute" meetings between employees at different locations.

Discussion Groups

A discussion group, sometimes called a *newsgroup,* is a collection of messages on a particular topic that are posted to an electronic bulletin board. A discussion group contains text-based discussion of a particular subject, such as politics, Dilbert, herbal cures, and so on. If one has access to a discussion group he or she

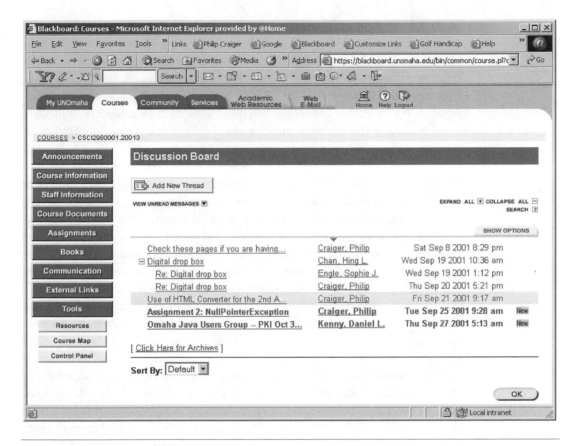

Figure 19.2   Discussion Group

may post a question or comment, to which others can reply. Companies can create a newsgroup to which only authenticated users, such as employees or customers, have access. Discussion groups used in this fashion allow employees or customers to provide text-based feedback, ideas, or comments to an organization regarding products, policies, or other matters. Figure 19.2 illustrates a discussion group used by university students to ask questions and share class-related information among all the students and instructor.

Discussion groups commonly operate in two modes. The first is an e-mail list format in which e-mail sent to a central address is redistributed to all the recipients on a specified list automatically, commonly called a "listserv." The second format is a server-based format used by the Usenet Newsgroups on the Internet—a central repository of information that is replicated to newsgroup servers, which can then be browsed and responded to by a user. All responses are automatically sent to the central repository, which then distributes them during the next replication cycle.

Discussion groups have proven to be highly interactive, as every member often has the ability to respond to every other member's comments. The openness of the media typically inspires a similar openness in the users.

Technology-Based Training

Technology-based training (TBT) is the use of computer technology to provide training content to workers. Technology may be used as an ancillary device along with traditional instructor-led training, or it may be used in place of conventional training. For example, technology-based methods such as computer- and Web-based training are becoming popular means of delivering training, supplanting the traditional instructor in many organizations.

Some may argue that computer-based and Web-based training are not communication technologies per se, or at least not to the same degree as e-mail and video-conferencing. However, we feel that this technology is important for several reasons. First, training, in essence, is a form of communication, regardless of whether it is delivered through a technological means. Second, more and more organizations are using TBT. Also, TBT is two-way communication given that workers interact with the training materials, and typically the results of the training are distributed back to management to determine the success of the training.

Computer-based training (CBT) is a type of TBT in which the worker learns by executing programs on a computer. It is particularly effective for training workers to use computer applications because the CBT can be integrated with the applications so that workers can practice using the application as they learn. Web-based training (WBT) is similar except the training materials are delivered to the trainee via the World Wide Web. CBT and WBT can be, and often are, composed of exactly the same training materials. Therefore, the primary difference is the *mode of delivery*. CBT is usually installed on a hard drive or a CD-ROM, and WBT is delivered through a Web browser running off a server. Hereon we will refer to both collectively as TBT.

One of the very attractive properties of TBT is that it supports distance learning; trainees can be freed from the constraints of geographical and temporal separation from a traditional place and time of training, that is, a corporate or training office where the trainee must be physically present in order to participate in training that is held during the weekday. With technology-based training a trainee can access materials from any place in the world as long as he or she has access to a computer with the appropriate software (CBT) or has Internet access (WBT). For example, Figure 19.3 demonstrates that a training video can be played on a wireless personal digital assistant.

TBT may consist of audio, video, graphics, and text, and therefore requires sufficient computing power to run efficiently. It supports all training strategies such as simulations, games, and drill-and-practice. TBT is becoming more popular as a training tool as we learn more about how to move training from the instructor-led classroom to the computer, and as workers are becoming increasingly mobile (Craiger, 2000).

Instant Messaging

Instant messaging (IM), also known as "Internet relay chat" or just "chat" for short, involves two or more users at remote locations typing messages that appear

Figure 19.3   Technology-Based Training

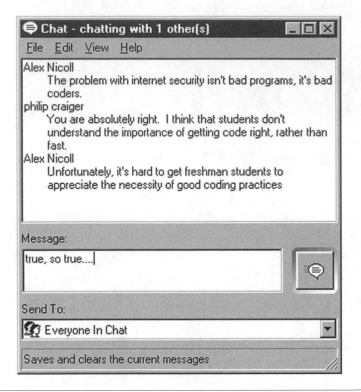

Figure 19.4 Chat

on the other remote users' screens instantaneously. IM supports real-time, interactive, synchronous communications. Figure 19.4 demonstrates IM. On the left side of the figure are the text-based conversations. Each line of text conversation is preceded by the user's "online" name. On the right is a list of names of users who are participating in the "chat room." As such, IM is similar to a phone conversation, only text has been replaced with audio. (Newer IM systems now support the transmission of both voice and text simultaneously.) Figure 19.4 illustrates a chat session between Philip and Alex.

"Chat" often conjures up pictures of teenagers communicating with peers late at night. Although this is sometimes the case, IM is increasingly used in organizations as a quick and efficient means of communicating with peers, bypassing the more obtrusive phone call. Moreover, researchers and developers are looking into the development of IM systems that support mobile workers by allowing them to track as well as contact peers using mobile devices, such as personal digital assistants (Tang et al., 2001). Research on patterns of use suggests that IM is often used to establish contact and decide whether it is a good time to interact, and that once contact is made, IM transitions to another communication channel such as phone, e-mail, or face-to-face conversation (Nardi, Whittaker, & Bradner, 2000).

Groupware often supports IM as an ancillary communication technology to videoconferencing. It may seem nonsensical to include such a low-end technology with videoconferencing. Consider, however, a situation in which you are participating in a videoconference but would like to privately share information with one of the other participants—just as you would whisper private information into the ear of a colleague at a meeting. This would be impossible using pure videoconferencing alone; however, the addition of IM allows two users to connect within a private "chat room" and send private messages back and forth while still participating in the videoconference.

Electronic Mail (E-mail)

E-mail is ubiquitous. We have found that that e-mail is replacing the phone as the preferred mode of communication. In many organizations almost everyone has an e-mail account assigned by the organization as well as a personal e-mail account.

Most non-urgent communications are handled by e-mail. The reasons are multiple. As with the telephone, almost everyone has a computer and an e-mail account. E-mail has an advantage over the telephone in that it can be searched (scanned) nonlinearly and quickly, whereas voice messages must be listened to serially (one by one). The third reason lies in the availability of the e-mail message for print copy. This final reason belies the belief in the paperless office, an evolution that has not materialized. People still like to hold documents in their hands, read from a print copy, and file like documents in a common location.

Corporate Web Sites

The corporate Web site is the final technology we discuss, and the only (essentially) one-way technology. Most readers should be familiar with Web sites and Web pages, the content that we view when we are on the World Wide Web. Web sites can provide a good channel for communications although the information flow is inherently in one direction, from the organization to the employee.

Many corporations use Web pages to distribute corporate policy or breaking news on products, services, and other matters to employees in a way that it cannot be overlooked: management forces the Web page that is the corporate home page to display first when the employees open a Web browser. A powerful feature of the corporate Web site is that information that once was either archived on paper alone or electronically on disparate computer systems (e.g., databases) can now be made accessible in electronic form through a corporate Web site.

Corporate Web sites are also used as two-way communications between customers and the company. Many corporate Web sites give customers the ability to submit questions or feedback via a Web site, such as through a form posted on a customer service Web page. This gives the customer some flexibility in the way they

Table 19.3   Percentage of Companies Monitoring Communications

Communication Process	Always Monitor	Sometimes Monitor
Internet Use	12%	62%
E-mail Use	7%	58%
Telephone Calls	2%	42%

provide feedback or submit questions; however, this should not be the only means as not everyone has access to the Web.

A new organizational practice is to incorporate a broad array of company services and resources on the company home page, thereby making it a "portal." The corporate portal then becomes the employee's primary tool for accessing important company information from a single starting point.

Computer-Enabled Communication: Impact and Policies

The increased accessibility afforded to individual workers does not come without issues and concerns for the organization. The Society for Human Resource Management (2000) polled 700 human resource managers to determine the extent to which companies are monitoring the various communication processes used by individual employees (Society for Human Resource Management, *http://www.shrm.org/surveys*, 2000). Table 19.3 shows findings from that poll.

The data support the perception that employers are watching their employees. Organizations are incorporating nonintrusive monitoring to manage these impressions. Software can scan for keywords and block e-mail that includes words identified as inappropriate to the work environment. Also, many companies trace which Internet sites have been accessed. Evaluation teams can assess such usage if the organization has policies and software that limit and monitor such access (see Acceptable Use Policies later in this chapter). For example, the team can look at monthly or quarterly trends for the number of e-mails blocked or the number of Web addresses to which the gatekeeper software denied access.

Evaluating Corporate Communications Policies

Although management may be the primary source of corporate technology policies, it is the technical staff that will be the primary source of ensuring compliance with the policies. Consequently, it is crucial that key members of the technical staff are included during the policy creation process to ensure that they have buy-in on the policy, and therefore motivation to ensure compliance, and that unenforceable policies are not mandated (e.g., attempting to enforce a policy that is impossible with the currently installed technology).

There are at least two formal corporate policies that every organization should have in place: an acceptable use policy and a policy on netiquette (i.e., online etiquette).

Acceptable Use Policies

Companies should have in place formal policies and corresponding documentation on the acceptable use of communication technologies. For instance, an *acceptable use policy* defines the kinds and amount of use that are considered permissible using the corporate network. Typical acceptable use policies contain the following proscriptions:

- Visiting Internet sites that contain obscene, hateful, or otherwise objectionable materials; sending or receiving any material that is obscene, defamatory, or intended to annoy, harass, or intimidate another person
- Sending and receiving unusually large e-mails or attachments; sending or forwarding electronic chain letters
- Spending time on nonbusiness purposes
- Soliciting e-mails that are unrelated to business activities or soliciting business for personal gain or profit
- Representing personal opinions as those of the business
- Using the Internet or e-mail for gambling or illegal activities
- Making or posting indecent remarks, proposals, or materials
- Uploading, downloading, or otherwise transmitting commercial software or copyrighted material in violation of its copyright
- Downloading any software or electronic files without implementing virus protection measures that have been approved or prescribed by management
- Intentionally interfering with normal operation of the network, including the propagation of computer viruses, or sustained high volume network traffic, which substantially hinders others in their use of the network
- Revealing or publicizing confidential or proprietary information, which includes, but is not limited to, databases and the information contained therein, computer software, computer network access codes, and student personal information
- Examining, changing, or using another person's files, output, or user name without explicit authorization

Netiquette

Companies should also have policies, documentation, and training on netiquette, the electronic version of etiquette. Netiquette training provides employees with ways of using acceptable language when initiating and responding to messages. This is necessary because the nonpersonal nature of communication technologies (especially e-mail) depersonalizes recipients. Like yelling at the

TV, writing a scathing e-mail does not have the same instant feedback and consequences as doing the same in person. A good source of netiquette guidelines can be found at the Netiquette Home Page (http://www.fau.edu/netiquette/net/netiquette.html).

Policies Regarding the Monitoring of Communications

Evaluation teams benchmark their policies and judge the extent to which behaviors in their organizations are problems by comparing their organizations against the findings for other organizations. The major concern for most of the surveyed human resources (HR) managers involves the Web sites that members visited while on the job. Abuse of Internet access at work includes employees conducting job searches for new employment (37%), shopping for personal items (40%), reading news (72%), making travel arrangements (45%), accessing stock market information (34%), and searching for information related to hobbies (37%) (Society for Human Resource Management, 2000). In a survey conducted by Vault.com in 2000, 80% of employers indicated that they had caught an employee surfing a non-work-related site at work, up from 54% the previous year (Vault.com, 2000).

Eleven percent of all participants in a 2000 Princeton Survey indicated that they knew someone who was either disciplined or fired because of the person's Internet use (Princeton Survey Research, 2000). Such disciplinary action is typical for violation of e-mail or Internet use policies. An evaluation team can review the violations, determine whether employees should have been disciplined, assess the frequency of occurrence and the equity of discipline, and decide whether policies need to be clarified and reemphasized. Dow Chemical Company examined the e-mail of several thousand employees in response to complaints regarding the distribution of pornographic and violent materials. This investigation led to the discharge of 50 employees and the suspension without pay of 200 additional employees (Business and Legal Reports, 2000).

Policies governing e-mail use have proliferated because of the occasional misuse of electronic mail. Most policies address the privacy issue head-on by stating that Internet access and e-mail are privileges and are restricted to business use. Some companies allow for private use with the caveat that "personal" does not imply "private." This approach stems from the Electronic Communications Privacy Act of 1986 (Washington State Bar, 2000), which mandates that all e-mail sent or received through a company's e-mail system is the property of the company and therefore subject to inspection. Most company policies indicate that all text and images can be disclosed to law enforcement or other third parties without prior sender or receiver consent. In addition, electronic communication should be considered to be a permanent record. The permanence of these records has been exploited in many high-profile court cases such as the Microsoft case in 2000 where records were retrieved and used as evidence in support of the government's case. Consequently, some companies are reexamining the advisability of archiving (backup or storage of) e-mail.

Conclusion

Notwithstanding the positive effects of computer-enabled communications throughout corporations large and small, the misuse of these technologies has caused some organizations to limit, or at least monitor, their use. New challenges and opportunities will present themselves as technologies change and workers' perceptions of corporate policies evolve. Organizations will have to walk a fine line in determining what and how communications and their associated technologies maximize the organization's profitability.

One way that organizations can influence policy is by selecting the most appropriate technology for a particular work context. If workers are given the appropriate tools for their jobs, then perhaps the need for defining the boundaries and scope as to how the technology can and cannot be used will no longer be necessary.

References

Business and legal reports. (2000). Online at www.blr.com/hr/online/newsletter/index.cfm?article=149

Craiger, J. P. (2000). Computer-based instruction. In M. Zeleny (Ed.), *International encyclopedia of business & management handbook of information technology* (pp. 649–657). London: Thompson International.

Craiger, J. P., & Burnham, B. (2001, April). Traveling in cyberspace: Computer security. *The Industrial and Organizational Psychologist, 38*(4), 130–141. Available online at http://www.siop.org/tip/backissues/TipApr01/18Craiger.htm.

Hogarth, R. (1988). *Judgement and choice.* New York: John Wiley.

Nardi, B., Whittaker, S., & Bradner, E. (2000). Interaction and outeraction: Instant messaging in action. *Proceedings of the Conference on Computer-Supported Cooperative Work (CSCW) 2000,* pp. 79–88.

Plous, S. (1993). *The psychology of judgment and decision making.* San Francisco: McGraw-Hill Higher Education.

Princeton Survey Research. (2000). *The Pew report, wired workers: Who they are, what they're doing online.* Online at http://www.pewinternet.org/reports/index.asp.

Society for Human Resource Management. (2000). *Workplace privacy survey.* Online at http://www.shrm.org/surveys.

Tang, J. C., Yankelovich, N., Begole, J., Van Kleek, M., Li, F., & Bhalodia, J. (2001). ConNexus to Awarenex: Extending awareness to mobile users. *Proceedings of the Special Interest Group in Computer-Human Interaction 2001,* pp. 221–228.

Vault.com. (2000) The second annual Survey of Internet Use in the Workplace. Online at http://www.vault.com.

Washington State Bar. (1999). The Electronic Communications and Privacy Act of 1986 and a Closer Look at the ABA Opinion on Unencrypted E-mail. Online at http://www.wsba.org/barnews/tech/greypunk/1999/07.htm.

Suggested Readings in
Computer-Enabled Communications

Flynn, N. (2001). *The e-policy handbook: Designing and implementing effective email, internet, and software policies.* New York: Amacom Books.

The Internet Advocate. (n.d.). Developing an acceptable use policy. Online at http://www.monroe.lib.in.us/~lchampel/netadv3.html.

The Netiquette Home Page. (n.d.) Online at http://www.fau.edu/netiquette/net/netiquette.html.

Wilcox, J.R. (2000). *Videoconferencing: The whole picture.* New York: CMP Books.

CHAPTER 20

Customer Service Programs

L. A. Witt

Paulette Henry

Margareta Emberger

As many companies face greater international competition, slower growth rates, and mature markets (Fornell, 1992), the challenge of identifying and maintaining sources of competitive advantage is becoming increasingly difficult. Corporations have a variety of means of creating competitive advantages in the marketplace. However, traditional means, such as cost, quality, and delivery convenience, are increasingly difficult to attain and maintain because of the availability and decreasing costs of technology. Therefore, creating a best-in-class customer experience has increasingly become a key component of corporate strategies (Berry, 1995).

The "service encounter" is an inevitable part of modern life, and customers are constantly expecting higher service standards. In order to create the best-in-class customer experience, organizations must have strong "customer service climates" (Schneider, White, & Paul, 1998) that yield strong customer service cultures, also referred to as customer care cultures. In other words, workers must understand, share, accept, and live the values underlying customer service, and supervisors and managers must understand, share, accept, and live the values underlying servant leadership (i.e., serving the servers). Organizations having procedures and practices that emphasize service as a top priority typically experience service quality as a result (Schneider, Gunnarson, & Niles-Jolly, 1994).

Customer service orientation is seen as key to competitive advantage even in organizations outside of the service sector, per se. Moreover, organizations have called for workers to treat internal clients and coworkers as important customer-like constituencies in order to enhance internal operating efficiencies. Even in business units whose main functions are not by nature interpersonal transactions (e.g., clerical, systems development, and production work units), adopting a customer service orientation toward fellow employees is expected.

Compared with implementing a new technological infrastructure, the decision to leverage customer service as a competitive advantage appears on the surface to be both inexpensive and relatively simple. Therefore, it has become increasingly popular. It falls as a responsibility of the human resources (HR) executive to create and maintain a strong customer service culture in the organization. Indeed, the primary role of the HR function in a large corporation is strategy-culture alignment. In this chapter, we focus on the evaluation of initiatives that are designed to link HR practices with customer care objectives.

Many companies see customer service as a responsibility of the marketing function. We emphasize that we are not focusing on programs that would be implemented in the marketing function, which typically are designed to influence consumer behavior. Rather, we are focusing on HR initiatives that are designed to influence the behavior of employees. Our aim in this chapter is to address issues unique to the evaluation of customer service programs. Accordingly, we discuss the role of the HR function in supporting customer service objectives. Then, we address the who, what, and why. By "who," we mean the stakeholders affected by the evaluation program. In terms of "what," we discuss appropriate evaluation criteria. Finally, we focus on the "why" with regard to empirically linking HR programs with customer service outcomes.

The Role of Human Resources in Customer Service

Because the customer service experience is largely a function of how the service providers treat the customer, human resources (HR) plays a central role in implementing programs that have impact on customer service. By strategically directing the major HR functions to focus on customer service behaviors, the HR team can mold the organization's culture in an attempt to achieve corporate service quality objectives. What programs can the HR staff undertake to increase customer service? The answer lies in aligning the practices of the basic HR functions with the customer service strategy. Are the HR functions working synergistically to yield employee behaviors that arrive at quality customer service? The recruiting, selection, succession planning, and promotion systems can place individuals whose abilities fit the job requirements and personalities fit the desired culture (i.e., person-job fit). The performance management and compensation systems can communicate expectations and provide incentives and rewards for job performance contributing to achievement of customer service targets. Training programs can establish alignment between core service competencies and emerging business objectives. Orientation programs can provide realistic job previews and orientation programs to socialize new hires into the customer care culture. Management development and mentoring programs can develop the managers into servant leaders.

To illustrate the role of HR programs in supporting customer care strategies, we cite as an example a hotel chain that relies on superior customer service as its primary source of competitive advantage. This company has formal and specific expectations for customer service behavior for it employees. These expectations define what "customer service orientation" means in the organization by establishing standards of etiquette appropriate for interpersonal transactions. These standards have two components. One involves "display rules" for emotional expression (e.g., cheerfulness on initial customer contact). Another involves guidelines for the degree of helpfulness, which in other companies may involve simple order-taking but in this one involves customization. Requiring a near-intimate knowledge of the customer's needs and the property's facilities and available services, customization involves developing nonstandard solutions to solve customer problems.

Several of this hotel chain's HR functions are designed to support their customer care strategy. Their HR team places a great emphasis on person-job fit. The notion of person-job fit implies that favorable outcomes occur when characteristics of an individual (e.g., personality, career orientation, ability) match or fit requirements of the job. A construct that has emerged to explain person-job fit in customer service jobs is "emotional labor." This refers to the effort expended to act consistent with display rules and prescribed levels of helpfulness. In cases of person-job fit, employees feel as though it is natural to comply with prescribed display and helpfulness protocol. In contrast, in cases of person-job misfit, employees must put forth considerable emotional labor to comply with prescribed protocol. Indeed, not everyone is cut out to be good at customer service. Some workers simply do not possess the needed levels of general mental ability (GMA) and/or social skill. For others, being helpful and nice over long periods at work in the face of difficulty and constraint causes angst, which leads to burnout, reduced effort, and turnover. Accordingly, this hotel chain emphasizes customer service skills in its recruiting, selection, succession planning, and promotion systems. They not only use customer service knowledge, skills, and abilities (KSAs) as criteria for selecting external candidates but also for promoting internal employees.

In hiring external candidates, they administer paper-and-pencil instruments that tap predispositions toward customer service and personal histories reflecting a likelihood of customer service orientation. Then, they invite candidates passing the paper-and-pencil instruments to sit through structured interviews that focus on customer service KSAs. In promoting internal candidates, they proactively use an enterprise-wide succession-planning system that identifies and further develops individual contributors who are likely to be effective at servant leadership and established managers who are ready for the next level of servant leadership. In other words, they have a pool of employees who are developed and ready for promotion. In addition, they use structured interviews that focus on customer service KSAs.

The hotel chain's HR team emphasizes selection and promotion processes because they have found that selecting and promoting the "right" people reduces the costs of training, turnover, and, most important, customer runoff. However, they also have directed other HR programs in the service of customer care. Their performance management system establishes for each employee customer service performance targets that are linked to business unit targets. It also provides a mechanism for designing individual development plans based on the company's list of customer care competencies; that is, they have a list of core competences reflecting customer service effectiveness that each employee is expected to develop. Congruently with the performance management system, the compensation system provides incentives and rewards for achievement of customer service targets. The company emphasizes training and orientation. To ensure that new hires learn "what matters" early on, they have an extensive orientation program that begins with in-class presentations on the first days of employment and ends with assignment of a peer mentor for each new hire. Technical training for employees at almost all levels consists of specific instruction of display rules and other guidelines for customer treatment. Employing a philosophy of servant leadership, the company provides development and mentoring programs for supervisors and managers. Basically, the company's idea is to treat the employees as customers, so that they are equipped to provide excellent service to the external customers.

Identifying Stakeholders (Who)

Customer service is not owned by any one business unit but actually by all. Therefore, successful evaluation teams avoid political problems by proactively communicating and working with representatives of all of the stakeholders affected by the evaluation.

Evaluators of the Customer Service Program

One of the critical early challenges is to identify membership of the evaluation team. For at least five reasons, an evaluation team composed of members representing multiple constituencies is helpful. First, the presence of the multidisciplinary perspectives improves the breadth and depth of issues raised. Second, having the key groups represented reduces the probability of political or territory-based resistance from those groups during implementation. Third, having members who control access to the data and understand the context of the data sources facilitates the data collection process. Fourth, because members of the evaluation team typically include those whose programs are being evaluated, having others on the team lessens the potential for conflicts of interest. The presence of multiple stakeholders adds credibility to the evaluation process and therefore to the results as well. We suggest that the evaluation team include representatives of staff departments, line departments, and external groups.

Staff Departments

The primary evaluators and primary source of customer service program evaluation information with regard to employee performance, employee attitudes, and perceptions of climate for service typically are the members of the internal HR staff. We have seen many cases in which evaluation teams consist primarily of HR professionals. However, other key staff areas are finance and marketing. Finance professionals direct the measurement of financial performance, while the marketing function provides data about consumer behavior.

Line Departments

Representatives of line management are necessary for identifying strategy, prioritizing criteria, and ensuring political support. They also are typically the gatekeepers of information critical to the evaluation. For example, the services delivery and operations functions can provide production data.

External Groups

Bringing in external consultants is sometimes necessary when specific technical expertise is needed. Bringing in external consultants may also help add credibility to the process. For example, some employees and customers may be reluctant to provide information to company employees but may be comfortable with external parties. Line managers may perceive results reported by external consultants as less likely to be tainted by proponents of internal organizational agenda. In some cases, however, the opposite can occur, as external consultants often identify from their sponsor what they want to find and then go find it. Their presence adds credibility to a process and outcome that was preordained. Thus, bringing in external consultants can be positive or negative. Customers are a rich source of ideas and can often ask questions that remain outside the imaginations of employees. Similarly, representatives of professional advisory boards and consumer protection agencies can provide external norms as well as sources of benchmarking targets. Union representatives can be very helpful, particularly when employee measurements will be included in the evaluation project.

Working With the Stakeholders

If the project team is composed of the important constituencies, then identifying the key stakeholders is typically a straightforward process that is conducted in the planning stages of the evaluation effort. However, as the programs are implemented and unanticipated groups are affected, it is important to revisit preliminary assessments of the stakeholders. It is imperative to communicate with and get "buy-in" from stakeholders outside of the evaluation team. HR directors know that managers resist well-designed performance management tools that enhance accountability. Most managers prefer very loose objectives for their business units (i.e., ones that cannot be easily measured) and will attempt to change the objectives as soon as they perceive that they cannot reach their targets (i.e., "criterion creep"). Similarly, most workers do not like to be held accountable for their performance failures, particularly when personal revenue is at stake. This phenomenon affects program evaluation. No one wants to be in a position in which his or her failure can be linked with measures of poor customer service, and organizational politics often comes into play to avoid accountability. We have seen many HR programs and evaluation efforts fail because of politics. Because customer service targets in various forms are often shared enterprise-wide, the potential for the emergence of political behavior is high.

While organizational politics cannot be eliminated, there are at least five actions that program evaluators can take to reduce the impact of politics on the evaluation effort. First is to meet privately with the key decision makers representing each stakeholder group. Savvy managers are unlikely to speak candidly in meetings. While unlikely to be fully informative and open even in one-on-one meetings, they are more likely to discuss or allude to deal-breakers in private. These one-on-one meetings should be conducted early in the process, and the evaluator should keep in touch with these individuals as often as appropriate. Second is to expect and plan for manifestations of internal territoriality and resistance along the way. We have often been amazed by program evaluators who face resistance based in hidden agendas and do not know what to do, often because they did not anticipate such reactions. Third is to consider carefully what information should not be reported. It may be unwise to report information that is accurate but at the same time will lead to heavy-handed resistance from a politically powerful decision maker and thus perhaps kill the program or evaluation effort. *Results should be considered in the context of what people will do with the information.* Fourth is to build an alliance with a senior executive who will be seen as a sponsor of the evaluation effort. Fifth is to network with other senior managers, even those not directly stakeholders in the current project. If your sponsor leaves the organization and you have no other senior-level allies, you and your evaluation efforts could be vulnerable.

Selecting the Evaluation Criteria (What)

Evaluation teams need to identify the desired outcomes of the programs; in the case of customer service programs this is not always easy. The bottom line is corporate or business unit financial performance. However, the links between customer service program implementation and financial performance are rarely direct and often confounded by illimitable other variables. Even the links between service quality and financial outcomes have still not been fully clarified (Greising, 1994).

The basic question to ask is this: "What are the outcomes of the customer service program that matter to the business and will tell us whether to continue the program?" To answer this question, we advocate data collection from two sources—internal customers (i.e., organization members) and external customers (i.e., consumers). In discussing the selection of evaluation criteria, we focus on five categories of HR programs—selection, performance management, technical service training, orientation, and management development.

Internal Customer Measures

Internal customer measures reflect criteria that are typically used to assess HR programs. We focus on performance management, technical service training, orientation, management development program effectiveness, and three sets of commonly used measures of selection—GMA, biodata, and personality. First, we discuss performance management and performance discipline data. "Performance management" refers to the performance appraisal system that is used to communicate performance expectations, performance feedback and evaluation, and developmental opportunities for improved performance. In contrast, performance discipline refers to the process by which managers confront dysfunctionally behaving employees (e.g., excessive tardiness and safety violations). Many HR information systems now permit enterprise-wide electronic storage and analyses of performance appraisal and performance discipline data. Second, we discuss employee attitudes. Third, we discuss medical incidents.

Performance Management and Performance Discipline Data

Performance management data can be used to assess all five of the HR programs that we listed. To illustrate the use of these data to validate a selection program, we cite as an example the call center unit of a financial services company that leverages superior customer service for competitive advantage. Call centers are often large rooms filled with customer service and/or sales workers interacting by phone with customers. In inbound call centers, workers receive calls (e.g., customer service representative). In outbound call centers, workers call the customers (e.g., collections agent). Workers are typically required to handle a high volume of calls every day and maintain a cheerful and helpful customer service approach in each transaction. Often, these transactions are scripted, with directions for beginning and ending conversations and cross-selling laid out by management. Such scripting may cause emotional dissonance. Moreover, for some workers, substantial levels of emotional labor are needed to remain "nice and helpful" when customers have significant, complex problems or become hostile. Individuals with little customer service training or who are by nature introverted may be likely to expend considerable emotional labor in inbound call center jobs, given the high volume of interpersonal transactions. They might spend even greater levels of emotional labor in outbound call center jobs, in which they would have to initiate interactions. This company has both in- and outbound call centers. For several years after starting-up the call centers, they experienced involuntary turnover of about 100% per year, long call wait times, and excessive customer complaints.

Eventually, call center management decided that they had hired the "wrong" people and approached HR to implement a new hiring protocol that would hire quick workers with the "right attitude." The HR team conducted a concurrent validation program comparing a timed GMA test, a custom-designed biodata survey, and two different personality measures. After administering the measures to the incumbent in- and outbound employees, they gathered hard criteria (e.g., calls per hour, off-the-phone time, sales in dollar value) and ratings from the respective call centers' quality monitors to assess core task performance. These measures were directly tied to the customer service objectives of the call centers, readily available in the company's operating system, and were included as part of the performance management system.

This brings us to a cautionary note: A problem with using data from legacy performance management systems is that the quality of the data is often unidimensional. By unidimensional, we mean that performance scores typically reflect either only core task performance or a global combination of various aspects of performance. Empirical work on the dimensionality of job performance suggests that the measurement of individual employee performance should be based on core task performance, job dedication, and interpersonal facilitation (e.g., Van Scotter & Motowidlo, 1996), all three of which reflect the degree of person-job fit. To this list, we add counterproductive behaviors (Bennett & Robinson, 2000), such as excessive whining, refusal to take direction, verbally abusing customers, and publicly making fun of coworkers. Unfortunately, the call center performance management system existing at the time did not include performance assessments of interpersonal facilitation, job dedication, and counterproductive behaviors. Therefore, the evaluation team developed an additional performance appraisal form for their research purposes only.

Another problem with using data from legacy performance management systems is that the quality of the data is typically poor. Data derived by managerial ratings have problems. For example, managers often have a political agenda (e.g., social promotion of undesirable employees and overly positive ratings of favored ones) as well as rating biases, such as leniency error, halo, and central tendency. A ubiquitous problem seems to be range restriction. We have found that many companies whose employees are rated on a 1 to 5 scale (1 being the lowest level of performance and 5 being the highest) have data suggesting that more than 85% of the employees are performing at a 3 or 4 level. With such range restriction, it is difficult to find meaningful correlations.

The evaluation team comparing the selection protocol also examined *performance discipline data*. It is very difficult to provide excellent customer service when you are not there to answer the phones. Accordingly, the evaluation team gathered tardiness and absenteeism data from the company's information system. They also gathered performance discipline incident reports of counterproductive behaviors.

Systematic examination of data collected from the *performance management system* can provide very helpful information. Examination of performance evaluation data across individuals and business units often yields patterns of performance deficiencies. Patterns of employee service failures can be indicative of problems with selection, succession planning, employee training, management development, and other HR-based customer service programs. For example, when 35% of the frontline employees receive "less-than-expected" evaluation scores on the timeliness of their delivery, then further investigation is warranted to determine what went wrong and what, if any, revisions to the customer service program are needed. Technology is permitting increasingly faster acquisition of these types of data. Returning to our call center example, that company conducts in real-time employee performance evaluation under the rubric of "customer service monitoring." First-line supervisors or quality control managers listen to live phone transactions between the employee and customer and record their observations immediately into the database. Within hours or days, patterns can be identified. It may seem obvious that data from the performance management system can be used as criteria to assess program effectiveness, but we are amazed at how many organizations do not make attempts to gather the data centrally for this purpose or systematically analyze the available data when centrally stored.

Employee Attitudes

We offer two reasons to support our suggestion that employee attitudes should be included as criteria of all five of the HR programs. First, empirical evidence clearly links employees' perceptions of their organization and customers' perceptions of quality of service (Schneider, Parkington, & Buxton, 1980). Organization members see problems before external customers do. Second, employees are customers of HR programs, as they rely on such programs to help them deliver service to not only external but also internal company customers. Schneider and Bowen (1995) argued that managers should recognize that how they manage internal design and operation issues may be visible to customers and affect their service-related perceptions, attitudes, and intentions. As we mentioned previously, managers are servant leaders who provide management services (i.e., resources, strategic direction, and professional development) to the frontline servers. There are three components of attitudes: feelings (i.e., affect), thoughts (i.e., cognitions), and behaviors.

Among the most commonly measured variables in organizational science is *job satisfaction*. Measures of job satisfaction assess feelings about the work experience. Much of the early work on job satisfaction was conducted with the implicit assumption that it was related to job performance. However, several decades of studies indicated that job satisfaction and job performance were not consistently related. Some HR professionals continue to argue that what matters most to job performance is GMA. GMA may account for much of the variance in global or core task performance among workers in nonservice jobs (Hunter, 1983), but we now know that job satisfaction and other manifestations of affect (i.e., mood on the job) are important to performance in service delivery (Schneider & Bowen, 1995). Workers very, very low in GMA may be relatively unable to solve customer problems, but high-GMA workers who manifest a bad mood are much more likely to create an unfavorable customer experience and thereby leave a lasting and negative impression on the customer. Therefore, we suggest that the job satisfaction of service workers may be an appropriate measure of customer service program effectiveness. High percentages of dissatisfied employees may reflect ineffective selection, succession planning, and promotion programs; that is, many of the employees may be experiencing stress because their personalities and abilities are not well suited for service work. High percentages of dissatisfied employees may also reflect poor management practices (e.g., failure to provide expectations, meaningful guidance, and courteous treatment), which are often addressed by performance management and management development programs. Low levels of satisfaction may also reflect frustration from the inability to meet customer expectations, which can be addressed by technical service training. Finally, dissatisfaction among workers who have been on the job less than a year may reflect a gap between their expectations of what the job and organization would be and what they discovered after working for a while; this may reflect inadequate orientation at the time of entry.

Other aspects of the employee experience appropriate for assessing HR practices influencing customer service program effectiveness may include perceptions of organizational support, organizational politics, fairness, and HR practices (e.g., training opportunities and adequacy, pay, benefits, etc.). These constructs reflect cognitions about the work experience. Thus, assessment of these issues can readily identify the effectiveness of customer service-related HR programs. However, we suggest that the most relevant measures of employee cognitions about the work experience are *climate for service* and *servant leadership*.

Organizations foster a climate for service by establishing practices that facilitate service delivery and by expecting and rewarding service excellence. Higher levels of customer service orientation result from a favorable perception of the organization's climate for service (Kelly, 1992). Schneider et al. (1998) defined climate for service in terms of employee perceptions of the practices, procedures, and behaviors relevant to customer service that are expected, supported, and rewarded. Research suggests that customer perception of service quality is high in business units in which the delivery efforts of the servers are well supported by the service of others (i.e., the level of internal service in the organization) and service employees receive performance feedback from the customers they serve (e.g., Johnson, 1996). In other words, customers report superior service from employees who experience their organization as one that supports them as people and supports excellence in service delivery. We cannot emphasize enough the utility of assessing climate for service as an index of customer service program effectiveness when it is relevant to do so. The specific issues addressed in climate for service surveys can be most helpful in ascertaining the reasons for success and failure in meeting service delivery objectives and customer service standards.

Managerial behaviors reflecting servant leadership have a significant impact on service delivery. The emphasis on total quality management fueled the use of upward feedback in the 1980s and 1990s. Upward feedback programs consist of using employee perceptions to evaluate managerial effectiveness. Programs that assess perceptions not only of employees but also of peers, internal and external customers, the boss, and the self are called "360-degree feedback." With the emphasis on servant leadership, some upward feedback measures are focusing specifically on behaviors affecting service delivery that can be addressed by performance management and management development programs. These programs are useful for managers providing service to both external and internal customers.

How can employee affect and cognitions be measured? *Employee attitude surveys* can be used to assess not only job satisfaction but also how the internal customers perceive the employee experience and servant leadership. Of course, focus groups, interviews, and other data collection techniques that identify issues of relevance prior to the development and dissemination of the survey should be employed to ensure that appropriate topics are included. That is critical to do. Without validation of content of the surveys (even individual items), the evaluation team is taking a risk that the survey may not be relevant. Climate for service is relatively new, and advances in its measurement continue to emerge. However, the items and dimensions are basically within the conceptual framework of organizational climate research. Upward feedback regarding servant leadership typically consists of obtaining ratings of supervisory performance from the rated supervisor and from his or her immediate manager and subordinates. Upward feedback processes are attractive as they (1) provide feedback from sources other than just the boss, (2) provide an opportunity for subordinates to provide feedback anonymously, and (3) are relatively inexpensive (Hazucha, Hezlett, & Schneider, 1993).

Survey administration requires consideration of at least five issues. First, organizations need to balance the need for information with the needs of employees to perform their job tasks. We have seen evaluation teams develop 30-page surveys requiring over two hours to complete. Such efforts annoy managers and workers alike. Second, employees who have completed surveys and have seen nothing done or reported in response to their expression of their concerns typically are not eager to respond to additional surveys. We have found this to be common and due to management either sitting on unfavorable results or thinking it unimportant to report the results to the line employees. Thus, we urge a devil's advocacy approach in the consideration of survey dissemination. Surveys should be used only when necessary, and feedback should be given as appropriate to the recipients. Whenever possible, policy decisions stemming from the survey results should be included in the feedback. Third, evaluation teams should be careful to monitor response rate. Managers typically are skeptical of surveys with low response rates, even those considered acceptable within the small community of employee survey researchers. Fourth, care needs to be given to the composition and selection of items. Evaluation teams need to use items that address issues for which corrective action can be taken. Asking questions about issues that are beyond management's ability to resolve only frustrates the respondents. Fifth, even before the survey is administered, interpretation guidelines need to be established. Such guidelines establish response targets linked to business targets. For example, one might consider as acceptable climate for service scores of around 45% favorable within 6 months of program implementation. However, 75% favorable might be considered as the minimum acceptable after 13 months. Without some interpretation guidelines, evaluation teams may find it difficult to understand the results. Upward feedback surveys require additional care. We recommend that such surveys permit data to be collected from all of the employees reporting to a manager. Some measures limit the number of contributors, which can lead to inaccurate results. In cases in which only three contributors are permitted, for example, managers may identify their favorite three supervisees as contributors.

The third component of employee attitudes is behavior. Perhaps the most relevant nonperformance behaviors are withdrawal behaviors. Premature involuntary turnover and instances of absenteeism and tardiness are important indices of HR program effectiveness. Employees vote with their feet! We urge caution in the assessment of turnover. Our experience suggests that turnover is typically measured by two dimensions—voluntary and involuntary. Whereas voluntary turnover reflects the employee's decision to leave the employer, involuntary turnover reflects the employer's decision for the employee to leave. This approach is flawed. Just as firms have unprofitable customers whom firms would like to encourage to go away, companies have unproductive employees. In other words, some employees add value; others destroy value. Thus, we encourage evaluation teams to assess overall involuntary turnover but to break down voluntary turnover into two categories: "desired" and "undesired" employees. What reflect poorly on the effectiveness of HR programs are high levels of involuntary turnover among all employees (of course, these are usually the undesired employees) and of involuntary turnover among the desired employees. The former reflects poorly on selection programs; the latter reflects poorly on the other HR programs. Of course, turnover rates need to be interpreted in light of the labor market. For example, in a tight labor market, low turnover of desired employees may not necessarily reflect successful HR programs.

Medical Incidents

Many managers at Walt Disney theme parks tell their employees that there is one thing that matters above all else. It is not guest satisfaction. It is not revenue. It is not speed of lines to rides. It is safety. Unsafe behavior can obviously derail efforts to deliver high-quality customer service. Therefore, we suggest that an important index of failure among HR programs supporting customer service can be medical incidents. Such incidents may not only include accidents (which may reflect violations of safety policy) but also problems associated with manifestations of employee stress (e.g., panic attacks, anxiety disorders). Evaluation teams need to look for unusually high levels of accidents and stress-related incidents. High levels may reflect not only poor management (e.g., sending employees out to serve customers in threatening weather) but also inadequate training and poor selection (i.e., hiring workers low in conscientiousness).

External Customer Measures

Customers see manifestations of both service-related and the HR-related organizational practices that we listed earlier, and they apply them in evaluating service quality (Bradley & Sparks, 2000). Consumer behavior is the measure of customer service that matters most. Commonly used measures include "wallet expansion," customer retention, requests for rework, referrals, and complaints. However, measures of customer satisfaction and perceptions of service quality are needed to predict and explain consumer behavior.

Wallet Expansion

An important benchmark of consumer behavior is the customer's decision to buy more services. Typically an outcome of both effective cross-selling and a favorable customer experience, the decision to expand the relationship with a services firm is a very profit-relevant criterion. In the financial services industry, this could be reflected in the customer who is happy with a basic checking account and later buys certificates of deposit, seeks financial advice, opens an estate account, and gets home, auto, and boat loans. In the wireless telecommunications industry, this could be reflected in a customer who is happy with a cellular phone account and later buys additional phones for family members or buys additional services (e.g., capability for downloading data from the Internet). Measurement of wallet expansion is often overlooked by program evaluators because many organizations have traditionally done a poor job of tracking it. However, like customer retention and referrals, it often reflects training programs and management practice. Customer retention, referrals, and wallet expansion can be linked to customer service and sales training programs that provide service providers with specific behavioral protocol for interacting with customers as well as performance management practices that develop and reinforce those behaviors. We have seen instances of increases in wallet expansion at stores simply because clerks trained in social skill made basic suggestions for additional services or products that fit well with the service or product being purchased.

Customer Retention

A common argument in the marketing industry is that it is substantially less expensive and easier to retain a current customer than it is to recruit new ones. For example, Rust and Zahorik (1993) reported that acquiring a new customer costs about five times more than it does to keep a current one. Moreover, new customers in some industries (e.g., life insurance) are unprofitable for a period of time after acquisition, and due to experience-curve effects, older customers can be served more efficiently (Zeithaml, Berry, & Parasuraman, 1996). Two other advantages of customer retention are opportunities for cross-selling and getting new ideas for business strategies. Therefore, customer retention and customer runoff are important. The former is often measured in terms of the percentage of customers who remain as customers, whereas the latter refers to the percentage of customers who discontinue service delivery or do not come back (i.e., when applying this phenomenon to employees, HR officials might label this as voluntary turnover).

Retaining customers can be critical to profit. Most consumers have experienced excellent marketing programs before delivery only to face disappointment later because the business emphasized recruitment of customers but not service delivery (Smith, Bolton, & Wagner, 1999). Many such businesses folded because of high customer runoff. However, a strong customer orientation is not always advantageous. It is sometimes desirable to run off certain customers. For example, in the financial services industry, 80% of the profit often comes from only 20% of the customers. Obviously, it is critical to retain these customers. However, financial services firms actually lose money on some customers. Those with free checking accounts or small balances who call the telephone banking unit and visit tellers frequently typically cost financial services firms quite a bit in transaction costs and provide little profit in return. Therefore, it is sometimes desirable from a profit perspective to encourage runoff. We mention this as it is important to place consumers into segments and focus on retention among the profitable or desired customers. Measuring all customer retention or runoff together may lead to inappropriate conclusions.

Referrals

When satisfied with service delivery, some customers will recommend the organization to potential customers. This has traditionally been very difficult to measure. Companies considering this a critical measure of consumer behavior have encouraged the reporting of referrals by compensating customers. When systematically collected, referral data can be helpful.

Requests for Rework and Complaints

Some consumer measures reflect poor performance on the part of the service provider. Such poor performance often reflects insufficient or ineffective training, which may reflect either technical (e.g., improperly installing a product or very slowly running a cash register) or interactional deficiencies (e.g., being perceived as rude to the customer). When dissatisfied with service delivery, some customers will request that the problem be fixed (i.e., rework). For example, hotel guests may request a different room, restaurant diners may request their meals to be prepared differently, and computer users may request a different set-up. Although a helpful way to identify consumer concerns, rework is expensive. Many organizations systematically collect these data; many do not. Similarly, when dissatisfied with service delivery, customers will complain to the services firm as well as warn other customers and potential customers. Complaint data are sometimes used as the primary criteria to evaluate customer service programs, but they seldom should be. Although useful information may come from tracking complaints when rework is impossible, the representativeness of the sample is often in question. However, when complaints come from a high percentage of the customers, tracking changes from the baseline number of complaints can be a useful criterion.

Customer Attitudes

Customer retention, wallet expansion, requests for rework, referrals, and complaints are good indices of the reactions of external customers to their customer experiences. Often utilized by marketing, sales, operations, and research and development units, these consumer behaviors affect profitability. However, with the possible exceptions of some referrals, complaints, and rework requests, consumer behaviors often do not provide the "why" underlying the behavior. Therefore, two of the most frequently used benchmarks of customer service initiatives are customer satisfaction and customer perceptions of service quality.

It is important to distinguish between perceptions of service quality and consumer satisfaction. Service quality perceptions are long-term beliefs (i.e., cognitions) about the standards of delivery. Expectations for service quality are specific and based on ideals or perceptions of excellence; they do not require experience. In contrast, feelings of satisfaction reflect affect, require experience, and reflect a large number of non-service-related issues (e.g., needs and perceptions of "fairness"). Measurement of both satisfaction and service quality perceptions is necessary to fully understand customer attitudes.

Common methods for measuring satisfaction and perceptions include asking external customers about the service they have received by structured phone and in-person interviews, focus groups, and standardized surveys. Data collected from these methods are helpful, as they permit understanding and prediction of consumer actions. An alternative is analyzing customer complaints as communicated through service workers. Often, the process of data collection itself presents real-time opportunities for addressing perceived wrongs and creating a loyal customer.

We emphasize that assessing perceptions of service quality is not a straightforward endeavor, as consumers have both a desired level of service (i.e., the level of service the customer hopes to receive) and an expected level of service (i.e., the minimum level of service the customer will accept). Moreover, services have at least three characteristics: (a) intangibility (i.e., there is rarely a uniform quality of service), (b) heterogeneity (i.e., performance tends to vary among different deliverers and consumers), and (c) inseparability (i.e., production and delivery of some services are inseparable). Service quality perceptions reflect consumer comparison of outcomes with expectations. Such perceptions reflect not only the outcome of a service—what is delivered—but also the process of service delivery—how it is delivered (Zeithaml et al., 1996).

Our focus, of course, would be on aspects of customer service and satisfaction that are affected by the human service providers. We emphasize that resource limitations, such as the number of service staff available, should be considered when interpreting customer attitudes. No waiting time, off-the-top-of-the-head knowledge of available inventory, and 100% availability of service providers are likely to be unrealistic service targets for most businesses. Therefore, it is imperative that the HR evaluation team identify the customer service targets established in the business line strategy and use those targets as a means of comparison with customer attitudes.

In summary, we revisit an observation offered two decades ago: Excellent companies listen to their customers so that they can improve service quality from the customer's viewpoint (Peters & Waterman, 1982). However, listening to both external and internal customers is needed to make sense of the impact of HR programs.

Linking HR Programs With Customer Service Outcomes (Why)

HR-based customer service programs have both direct and indirect effects on service quality and primarily indirect effects on customer reactions. We enjoin evaluators of customer service programs not only to assess multiple criteria but also to examine linkages between them. Moreover, we suggest that program evaluation efforts focus on relationships among multiple variables and differences between relevant business units. Examining linkages between the measures can lead to understanding of the effects of the programs. Similarly, demonstration of group differences (e.g., a bank branch with an unfavorable climate for service, poor customer service ratings, and low revenues versus one with a favorable climate for service, high customer service ratings, and exceptional revenues) presents a description in terms that managers typically use in thinking about their units. Hence, decision makers can see "why" the programs matter.

Accordingly, perhaps one of the most critical early steps in the evaluation process is to propose hypotheses, if not a model, to illustrate anticipated relationships to be tested. To illustrate how a model for service quality might look, we offer Figure 20.1 as an example. We list five categories of HR programs that could be developed to address strategy-customer care culture alignment issues—selection, performance management, technical service training, orientation, and management development. The effectiveness of each of these types of HR programs could be directly linked with measures of service quality performance. We also suggest that the effectiveness of each of these types of HR programs could be directly linked with employee attitudes, which we present in Figure 20.1 under the rubric of climate for service. The direct and indirect effects of the programs on delivery, customer behavior, and financial performance through climate for service could be assessed.

Development of such a model is helpful in at least three ways. First, it provides a conceptually explicit paradigm to guide the planning and measurement phases of the evaluation. Second, a model establishes in advance the analyses to be tested, reducing the probability of subsequent data mining. Third, it provides a picture and set of relationships for telling the story (i.e., reporting the relationships). The most rigorous evaluation efforts amount to very little when the evaluation team cannot "tell the story" and sell the results to decision makers.

We point to a study by Schneider et al. (1998) as an example of how researchers might link employee attitudes with consumer behavior. They looked at relationships between employee perceptions of climate for service and customer perceptions of service quality at over 100 bank branches. They tested relationships at the branch level of analyses, which is appropriate. The customer data were tied to the branches, not individual employees. With this design, they were able to (a) demonstrate the link between management practices (as reflected in climate for service scores aggregated at the branch level) and customer experiences, and (b) identify which branches were successful and which were not. This latter information permitted management to target resources to address the under-performing branches.

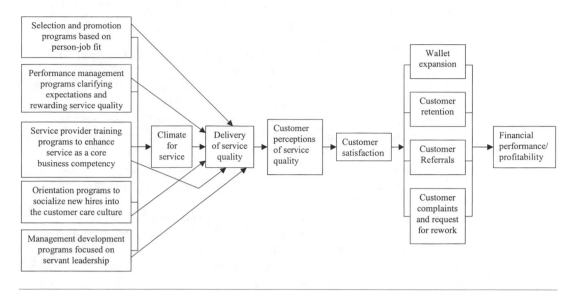

Figure 20.1   Climate for Service

The Schneider et al. (1998) design is both elegant and powerful in that it not only shows which business units have opportunities for changes in direction but also provides empirical evidence of how the employee perceptions matter. Unfortunately, a common practice is to report survey results but not report empirically how or why the survey results matter. Consultants with considerable experience in linking survey results with business relevant criteria have typically found that managers are much more likely to take the results seriously and to act on them when they are shown the links between the perceptions and feelings of their staff and important business outcomes. Many managers do not care what their employees think and feel. Many do. Most do when those thoughts and feelings affect business unit performance, as business unit performance is often tied to managerial compensation. The credibility of an evaluation project and usefulness of a program are greatly enhanced when the evaluation team demonstrates these links.

Summary

Evaluation of customer service programs follows much the same protocol and requires the same methodological rigor as evaluation of other HR initiatives. However, there are two key differences. First, customer service programs are typically not thought of as HR initiatives; evaluating them provides the HR team an opportunity to demonstrate the value that such evaluations can provide, but doing so requires a demonstration of the link between HR initiatives and customer care. Second, the evaluation criteria come from multiple sources, almost none of which are directly due to any one HR program. Hence, the evaluation of HR customer services programs is neither straightforward nor simple.

References

Bennett, R.J., & Robinson, S.L. (2000). Development of a measure of workplace deviance. *Journal of Applied Psychology, 85,* 349–360.

Berry, L. (1995). Relationship marketing of services–Growing interest, emerging perspectives. *Journal of the Academy of Marketing Science, 23,* 236–245.

Bradley, G. L., & Sparks, B. A. (2000). Customer reactions to staff empowerment: Mediators and moderators. *Journal of Applied Social Psychology, 30,* 991–1012.

Congram, C. (1991). Building relationships that last. In C. Congram (Ed.), *The AMA handbook of marketing for the service industries* (pp. 263–380). New York: AMACOM.

Fornell, C. (1992). A national customer satisfaction barometer: The Swedish experience. *Journal of Marketing, 56,* 6–21.

Greising, D. (1994, August 8). Quality: How to make it pay. *Business Week,* pp. 54–59.

Hazucha, J. F., Hezlett, S. A., & Schneider, R. J. (1993). The impact of 360-degree feedback on management skills development. *Human Resource Management, 32,* 325–351.

Hunter, J. E. (1983). A causal model of cognitive ability, job knowledge, job performance, and supervisor ratings. In F. Landy, S. Zedeck, & J. Cleveland (Eds.), *Performance measurement and theory* (pp. 257–266). Hillsdale, NJ: Lawrence Erlbaum.

Johnson, J. (1996). Linking employee perceptions of service climate to customer satisfaction. *Personnel Psychology, 49,* 831–851.

Kelley, S. W. (1992). Developing customer orientation among service employees. *Journal of the Academy of Marketing Science, 20,* 27–36.

Peters, T. J., & Waterman, R. H. (1982). *In search of excellence: Lessons from American's best run companies.* New York: Warner Books.

Rust, R., & Zahorik, A. (1993). Customer satisfaction, customer retention, and market share. *Journal of Retailing, 69,* 193–215.

Schneider, B., & Bowen, D. E. (1995). *Winning the service game.* Boston: Harvard Business School Press.

Schneider, B., Gunnarson, S. K., & Niles-Jolly, K. (1994). Creating the climate and culture of success. *Organizational Dynamics, 23,* 17–29.

Schneider, B., Parkington, J. J., & Buxton, V. M. (1980). Employee and customer perceptions of service in banks. *Administrative Science Quarterly, 25,* 252–267.

Schneider, B., White, S. S., & Paul, M. C. (1998). Linking service climate and customer perceptions of service quality: Test of a causal model. *Journal of Applied Psychology, 83,* 150–163.

Smith, A. K., Bolton, R. N., & Wagner, J. (1999). A model of customer satisfaction with service encounters involving failure and recovery. *Journal of Marketing Research, 36,* 356–372.

Van Scotter, J. R., & Motowidlo, S. J. (1996). Interpersonal facilitation and job dedication as separate facets of contextual performance. *Journal of Applied Psychology, 81,* 525–531.

Zeithaml, V. A., Berry, L. L., & Parasuraman, A. (1996). The behavioral consequences of service quality. *Journal of Marketing, 60,* 31–46.

Suggested Readings in Customer Service Programs

Czepiel, J. A., Solomon, M. R., & Surprenant, C. F. (1985). *The service encounter.* Lexington, MA: Lexington Books.

Grandey, A. A. (2003). When "the show must go on": Surface and deep acting as determinants of emotional exhaustion and peer-rated service delivery. *Academy of Management Journal, 46*, 86-96.

Headley, D. E., & Miller, S. J. (1993). Measuring service quality and its relationship to future consumer behavior. *Journal of Health Care Marketing, 13*, 32–41.

Kelley, S. W. (1992). Developing customer orientation among service employees. *Journal of the Academy of Marketing Science, 20*, 27–36.

PART VII

Health and Work/Life Balance

CHAPTER 21

Health and Safety Training Programs

Michael J. Burke

Jill Bradley

Harold N. Bowers

Occupational and public health and safety training is the systematic acquisition of knowledge, skills, or attitudes that results in improved safety performance. Health and safety training is a key element of human resource management and hazard prevention and control strategies within a myriad of industries. As human resource management practices aim at improving worker performance and productivity, health and safety training may be aligned with efforts to conduct work in a proper and efficient manner. In regard to hazard prevention and control strategies, health and safety training may be directed at meeting mandatory government regulations or voluntary standards specified in government guidelines and legislation. Here, the ultimate goals are protecting and promoting the health and safety of workers and the public.

Program evaluation plays a critical role in determining whether health and safety training has achieved its objectives. Training program evaluation is the means for modifying ongoing training to achieve desired results and for providing information to more effectively manage human resources and future training efforts. The general purpose of this chapter is to discuss health and safety training program evaluation within the context of a systems approach to training. A systems approach to training emphasizes the specification of instructional objectives, the alignment of training with these objectives, the development of measures associated with the instructional objectives, and the use of evaluation strategies to determine whether the objectives have been met. Given the importance of evaluating on-the-job behavior associated with health and safety training in critical skills occupations and high-reliability industries (e.g., hazardous waste work, firefighting, nuclear power, construction, mining, and manufacturing; see Cantor, 1992; Hofmann, Jacobs, & Landy, 1995) and the dearth of guidance concerning such assessments, emphasis is placed on recommendations for evaluating on-the-job behavior or actions associated with health and safety training.

The remainder of the chapter covers the following major items. First, a discussion of the key elements of a training system is presented. Second is an examination of the use of different types of measures for evaluating health and safety training including measures of attitudes, knowledge, behavior, and results associated with training. Third, guidelines and recommendations for assessing on-the-job behavior associated with health and safety training are discussed. Finally, issues concerning the transfer of health and safety training to the job are addressed.

A Systems Approach to Health and Safety Training

Assessing Training Needs and the Regulatory Nature of Health and Safety Training

The health and safety training systems approach outlined in Figure 21.1 provides a model with key elements and questions to be addressed. The model is heuristic in that it places emphasis on the derivation of instructional objectives and evaluation procedures. At the beginning, careful planning in the form of a needs assessment is necessary for a successful training program. All needs assessments address the basic question of "Who needs to do what and under what conditions?" A variety of analyses can be undertaken by training personnel or others to address this question including more traditional job/work analyses, job hazard analyses, analyses of performance problems and errors, examinations of records, examinations of training manuals, and interviews. In addition, walk-through observations of the organization or questionnaires used by the training evaluation team to assess trainee knowledge can aid in identifying safety training needs and establishing a baseline from which to compare pre-training knowledge and post-training knowledge (Caparez, Rice, Graumlich, Radike, & Morawetz, 1990). Finally, reports such as the Bureau of Labor Statistics work injury reports (Bureau of Labor Statistics, 1997) and National Institute for Occupational Safety and Health (NIOSH) investigative reports (e.g., see NIOSH, 1994) also acknowledge training needs for particular occupations and industries.

As part of a needs assessment, an examination of government legislation and guidelines is a necessity within both the United States and many other industrialized countries. For a number of occupations and industries within the United

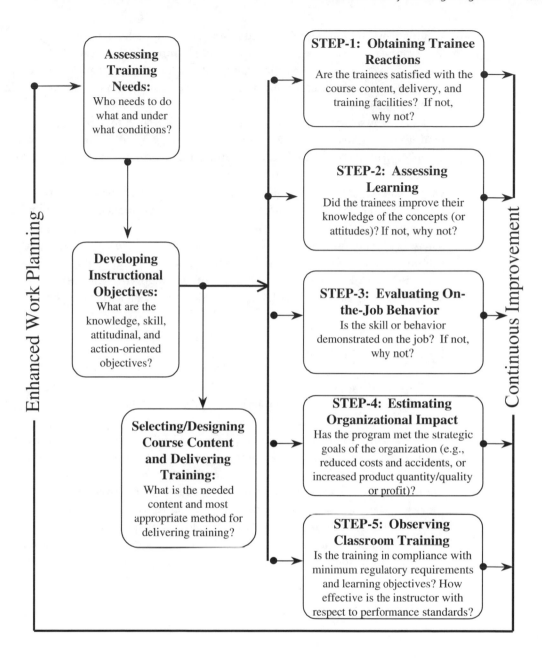

Figure 21.1   Health and Safety Training System With Safety Training Evaluation Procedures (STEPs)

States, the Occupational Safety and Health Administration (OSHA) has promulgated standards that explicitly require organizations to train employees in the health and safety aspects of their jobs such as hazard communication and emergency response. As an example, the HAZWOPER (Hazardous Waste Operation and Emergency Response) standard (29 CFR 1910.120) includes both competency requirements and minimum required hours spent in training. Refresher training is also required, and supervised field experience is strongly recommended. Personnel must complete worksite-specific training (e.g., on the company's emergency response plan) and task-specific training (e.g., about chemical or equipment hazards relevant to a specific job).

The OSHA standards vary across industries with respect to specifying the content of training, frequency and duration of training, need to document successful completion of the training program, and trainer qualifications. As discussed below, classroom observations are helpful for assessments of compliance of the training with OSHA regulatory requirements and learning objectives. In addition to OSHA, other government agencies ensure that employers are in compliance with more specific regulatory standards for health and safety training. For instance, the Mine Safety and Health Administration is responsible for overseeing the health and safety training of mine operators in relation to the Mine Safety and Health Act of 1977. Importantly, OSHA standards and those of other government agencies often contain useful information for developing action-oriented instructional objectives.

Developing Instructional Objectives

As pointed out in Figure 21.1, properly specified health and safety training objectives reflect four needed characteristics: knowledge (the facts that one knows), skills (the ability to carry out an action or series of coordinated actions), motivation (the choice to expend effort and persistence in the expenditure of effort at a particular level), and behavior (overt, visible activity in which an employee engages). Reduced accidents or illnesses are often the result of changes in employee knowledge, skills, motivation, and behavior. Training objectives related to these four characteristics should be specified with action verbs (e.g., to solve and to calculate) and include the desired level of proficiency subsequent to training.

As an example of the development of behavioral, action-oriented training objectives that are associated with regulatory materials, several objectives from the OSHA standards concerning hazardous waste operations (29 CFR 1920.120) are

To identify potential sources of chemical, physical, radiological, and biological hazards.

To control and maintain minor spills or releases.

To dispose of materials and/or equipment that poses a health risk.

Specifying health and safety training objectives with specific, action-oriented verbs will assist the evaluation team in the development of measures to evaluate the transfer of health and safety training to the job, a neglected area of health and safety training program evaluation that is discussed in detail below. In addition, spelling out other types of training objectives in terms of action verbs will also directly relate to the quality of other types of training program evaluation measures such as knowledge tests. Along with assisting in training program evaluation efforts, clearly specified behavioral objectives will directly determine the training content and delivery method.

Selecting and Designing Training Course Content and Delivering Training

The development of training materials (content) and selection of a training delivery method are largely based on the results of the needs assessment and training objectives. While the content of health and safety training may vary from basic instruction on the use of personal protective equipment to an emphasis on the development of advanced problem-solving skills, health and safety training often involves the use of multiple methods to deliver the content (e.g., a combination of methods such as lectures, role-playing, and behavioral simulations) (Burke & Sarpy, 2003). The use of multiple training methods often presents special issues for those who are involved in health and safety training program evaluation such as difficulty evaluating the efficacy of any particular training method and a concurrent need to focus on overall knowledge gained or procedural skills that are acquired (see Burke, Sarpy, Tesluk, & Smith-Crowe, 2002, for a detailed discussion of this issue).

As an example of health and safety training with varied content and delivered via multiple methods, Luskin, Somers, Wooding, and Levenstein (1992) described a learner-centered training program developed for state and municipal emergency responders, industrial emergency responders, hazardous waste site workers, and workers at treatment, storage, and disposal sites. The objectives of the training were to increase not only trainees' technical knowledge but also to improve planning, analyzing, and communication skills in order to empower workers and enable them to solve workplace health and safety problems on their own. Training methods included small group discussions, sharing work life experiences, hands-on practice, brief lectures, and responding to mock incidents. Results, based on trainee feedback sheets, written knowledge tests, and follow-up impact surveys, indicated that the overall program was effective in improving safety awareness and health and safety attitudes.

Enhanced Work Planning and Continuous Improvement Through Training Program Evaluation

Once the training program has been conducted, a recommendation is that training be evaluated in some manner to determine whether the instructional objectives have been achieved. As indicated in Figure 21.1, a series of questions that are tied to the various types of instructional objectives can be posed to determine the effectiveness of health and safety training. A variety of quantitative or qualitative study designs can be employed to generate useful information relative to these questions

(Goldstein & Ford, 2002). For a review of common study design options including examples of how various designs were employed by consortia, unions, and companies, we refer the reader to National Institute of Environmental Health Sciences' (NIEHS, 1997) resource guide for evaluating worker safety and health training.

The NIEHS (1997) guide, along with more detailed presentations of procedures for computing effect sizes due to training (see Morrow, Jarrett, & Rupinski, 1997), will assist program evaluators in making choices about possible study designs. Given situational constraints and opportunities related to implementing one or more study designs, program evaluators will likely have multiple design choices and in some cases less optimal choices. Nevertheless, information obtained for even less optimal designs (such as post-training information from one group without a comparison group) can provide useful feedback for modifying, where necessary, the training system including future training needs, objectives, course content, and course delivery. In this sense, training program evaluation is viewed as part of an ongoing process within a system aimed at effecting positive changes in worker knowledge, skills, motivation, and behavior. The quality of the evaluative information that is obtained from trainees, peers, supervisors, trainers, and program evaluators themselves directly relates to the success of future work planning efforts of this nature. Notably, in many health and safety training program evaluation efforts, labor unions often play a key role and place emphasis on the development and use of standardized tests of the knowledge gained from training.

Measures of Health and Safety Training Program Effectiveness

To address the effectiveness of health and safety training, a program evaluator will likely need to answer one or more of the evaluation questions posed in Figure 21.1. These questions were adopted from the Safety Training Evaluation Procedure (STEP) framework proposed by Burke, Sarpy, and colleagues (Burke et al., 2002; Sarpy & Burke, in press), in which each STEP requires a different type of measure or questionnaire. The first four questions or STEPS in Figure 21.1 are consistent with Kirkpatrick's (1996) levels of training program evaluation. The last STEP in Figure 21.1 is more unique to health and safety training and calls for classroom observations (STEP-5) to serve the purpose of obtaining independent (of the trainee) assessments of compliance of the training with OSHA regulatory requirements and learning objectives as well as independent evaluations of instructor effectiveness.

The first or trainee reaction level of assessment (STEP-1) typically involves asking the trainee questions about the course content, the course deliverer, and the training facility. Obtaining trainee reactions is a relatively quick, straightforward method and can provide useful information about the overall attitudes toward the usefulness of training. Trainee attitudes are important because prior experiences with training can affect the acceptance and efficacy of future training within the organization. Additionally, results based on trainee reactions may aid in revising

Table 21.1   Example Items for Obtaining Trainee's Reactions to Health and Safety Training

For each item, please circle the number that corresponds to your satisfaction level.

N/A Satisfied	Very Dissatisfied	Dissatisfied	Neither Dissatisfied nor Satisfied	Satisfied	Very Satisfied	
A. Course Content						
1. How well the course covered the topics you need to know	1	2	3	4	5	—
2. Amount of *hands-on* training opportunities	1	2	3	4	5	—
B. Presentation						
1. Instructor's skill in making the information clear	1	2	3	4	5	—
2. Use and quality of audio/visual presentations, graphics, etc.	1	2	3	4	5	—
C. Facility and Props						
1. Quality and appropriateness of the classroom	1	2	3	4	5	—
2. Appropriateness of the props for hands-on training	1	2	3	4	5	—

D. Additional Questions
1. What improvements (if any) would you like to see to the facility that would make your training more beneficial?
2. What improvements (if any) would you like to see to the props and other instructional aids to make your training more beneficial?
3. What improvements (if any) would you like to see to course content or delivery to make your training more beneficial?

Adapted from Sarpy and Burke (in press).

content and delivery for future training (Caparez et al., 1990). In particular, given the importance of behavioral simulations in health and safety training, program evaluators should consider the potential usefulness of trainee opinions of characteristics of the training facility. An example of a questionnaire used to obtain trainee reactions to various aspects of health and safety training is presented in Table 21.1.

Because reaction measures only assess trainee attitudes or perceptions about the effectiveness of training, more standardized assessments of trainee learning also are desirable. Another level of training program evaluation concerns the assessment of learning (STEP-2). These evaluations are intended to measure the extent to which the trainees acquired the principles, facts, techniques, and attitudes stated in the course objectives. Caparez et al. (1990) highlighted the usefulness of a pre-training knowledge test both as a tool to identify individuals in need of training and as a method of gauging the impact of training by comparing pre-training to post-training scores. Additional testing that takes place several weeks or months following training may be important in evaluating long-term changes in knowledge and in identifying needs for refresher training. The method for evaluating trainee proficiency (e.g., questionnaire, written test, or oral examination) in these areas and criteria for successful completion of the course are often determined by training providers. As noted above, in the case of health and safety training, unions often play a critical role in assessments of learning objectives.

Although knowledge tests and demonstrations of correct performance during training are indicators that learning has occurred, these assessments are not a guarantee that learned behavior will transfer beyond training to the job. Therefore, a thorough training program evaluation will include assessments of safety behaviors performed on the job (STEP-3). For instance, the use of behavior sampling as an effective evaluation tool was supported in a study of safety training for industrial lift truck operators (Cohen & Jensen, 1984). Behavior sampling is a procedure in which behaviors or actions to be observed are predefined, and the observer then watches one or more individuals for a specified period of time and records observed actions. Typically, the observer records whether the behavior or action was engaged in (e.g., wearing or not wearing ear protection). Unfortunately, many program evaluations fail to adequately measure behavioral changes on the job associated with health and safety training, even in a dichotomous behavioral sampling sense. STEP-3 procedures are discussed in more detail below for obtaining categorical or continuous assessments of behavioral changes associated with health and safety training.

Organizational results such as reductions in accidents, injury, disease, absenteeism, and health care claims make up another level of health and safety training program evaluation (STEP-4). For instance, Palchinsky-Magennis (1992) described how in-house reports of performance errors might indicate areas of training deficiency or lack of transferability of knowledge learned in training. Relatedly, Vojtecky and Schmitz (1986) emphasized the importance of maintaining thorough and accurate organizational data such as accident and absenteeism records. Archival data such as these can indicate what areas, if any, improved following training. Furthermore, Cohen and Colligan (1998) discussed how results-oriented criteria such as injury, illness, and cost data were employed in 32 health and safety training evaluation studies, with 28 studies producing positive results.

Although not widely recognized, procedures are available for estimating the incremental economic benefit of health and safety training (i.e., in terms of dollar gain or percentage improvement in output). To our knowledge, only one study (Morrow et al., 1997) has estimated the incremental gain in organizational profits resulting from a health and safety training program. All other evaluations of health and safety training concerning cost-benefit have focused exclusively on the cost reduction side. A possible reason that researchers and practitioners have focused almost solely on cost reductions associated with training is that estimates of the incremental benefit of health and safety training are, in part, dependent on estimates of change in on-the-job behavior due to training (e.g., Cascio, 2000). Given the need for estimates of change in on-the-job behavior to compute cost-benefit estimates and the dearth of well-developed measures for evaluating the transfer of health and safety training, more specific guidance and recommendations are presented below for developing measures to assess on-the-job behavior associated with health and safety training.

Prior to the discussion of recommendations for evaluating the transfer of training, the reader should note that Figure 21.1 includes a fifth level of training program evaluation: classroom observations (STEP-5). Classroom observations are a critical level of evaluation for health and safety training programs. Classroom observations serve the purpose of obtaining independent (of the trainee) assessments of compliance of the training with OSHA regulatory requirements and learning objectives as well as independent evaluations of instructor effectiveness. For instance, Sarpy, Vaslow, Burke, and Langlois (1997) presented a measure for evaluating 27 possible instructor behaviors organized according to categories of informing trainees of objectives, presenting the training material, eliciting trainee performance, enhancing retention and transfer, providing feedback, and assessing trainee performance. Measures for evaluating instructors can be produced in a similar manner to the recommendations for developing measures related to evaluating the transfer of training to the job.

Guidelines for Assessing On-the-Job Behavior (STEP-3) Associated With Health and Safety Training

As discussed above, certain groupings of jobs or occupations require high levels of procedural knowledge and skill to be performed safely, thus protecting the public, the environment, the organization, and the workers themselves (cf. Cantor, 1992; Hofmann et al., 1995). In many of these jobs and types of work, training objectives are specified in action-oriented terms similar to the examples presented in the section titled "Developing Instructional Objectives." Specifying training objectives in more specific action-oriented terms permits assessments of the extent to which such behaviors are properly demonstrated on the job. Yet, many training program evaluators and safety researchers evaluate only safety performance or the transfer of health and safety training with respect to very general or single-item measures (e.g., see Cheyne, Cox, Oliver, & Thomas, 1998; Lingard & Rowlinson, 1997). Typically, these latter assessments are self-reports of safe work behavior or supervisory assessments of employee safety performance.

Alternatively, some organizations will include items focusing on health and safety issues such as safety communication or safety compliance within organizational climate surveys (e.g., see Carroll, 1998; Flin, Mearns, O'Connor, & Bryden, 2000, for discussions of safety climate studies). Within these studies, employees often provide their own perceptions of organizational safety policies and management safety practices or rate their satisfaction with the respective policies and practices. That is, in contrast to reporting on the extent to which workers engage in actions or safe work behaviors, the focus of safety climate surveys is not on particular behaviors of employees.

Table 21.2   General Recommendations for Evaluating On-the-Job Behavior Associated With Health and Safety Training

Planning and Evaluation of On-the-Job Behavior

1. Determine which course(s) and individuals need to be evaluated and who will be the lead person on the evaluation effort.
2. Conduct one or more meetings with management personnel and union personnel (if necessary) to discuss the evaluation process and issues related to management and employee "buy-in."
3. Develop a draft proposal (summary) for conducting the evaluation and obtain input on the proposal from key stakeholders.
4. Meet with personnel to determine who will be responsible for notifying the participants and scheduling the administration of the training program evaluation surveys.

Developing and Administering Training Program Evaluation Forms

5. Identify terminal training course objectives and translate these into an initial list of behavioral statements.
6. Have subject matter experts review and comment on the initial list of behavioral statements.
7. Edit the initial list of behavioral statements, determine how the behavioral statements will be rated, determine who will rate the behavioral statements, develop open-ended questions, and develop a set (or sets for different rating sources) of preliminary survey instructions.
8. Pilot test the survey.
9. Revise the survey as needed for administration.
10. Administer the survey as needed (e.g., pre-training, post-training) to meet the requirements of the study (evaluation) design.

Analyzing Data, Following Up With Participants, and Reporting Results

11. Statistically analyze ratings of survey statements and content analyze comments related to open-ended questions.
12. Conduct follow-up focus group meetings with respondents to clarify both ratings of survey statements and comments related to open-ended questions.
13. Prepare final report.
14. Conduct evaluation close-out meetings with key stakeholders.

Single-item measures of safety performance or more general assessments of health and safety issues via safety climate surveys may be helpful for making an overall determination of the extent to which employees are engaging in safe work behaviors. These types of assessments, however, do not provide the specific information for determining whether training objectives have been met. The development of measures that are more directly tied to the objectives of training are necessary for obtaining useful feedback information and making decisions about particular training programs.

The general recommendations, summarized in Table 21.2, for evaluating on-the-job behavior associated with health and safety training are grouped into three areas: (a) planning an evaluation of on-the-job behavior, (b) developing and administering training program evaluation forms, and (c) analyzing data, following up with study participants, and reporting results. The recommendations made in these areas take into account professional guidelines for conducting assessments of on-the-job behavior and experiences of training program evaluators with respect to evaluating the transfer of health and safety training. The recommendations are advisory in nature and are intended to provide a frame of reference (guidelines) for addressing relevant issues arising from attempts to evaluate on-the-job behavior or actions associated with health and safety training.

Planning an Evaluation of On-the-Job Behavior

As part of an organization's ongoing evaluation planning efforts, an initial activity is determining which course(s) and individuals need to be evaluated and *who will lead* the evaluation effort. A suggestion is that only individuals who have academic training and practical experience in training program evaluation lead evaluations of on-the-job behavior associated with health and safety training.

Next, in many cases, *obtaining the support of top management and union personnel* is necessary for a successful assessment of on-the-job behavior associated with health and safety training. Often, there is a need to conduct one or more meetings with management personnel and relevant union personnel to discuss the evaluation process and issues related to management and employee "buy-in." In particular, any labor organizations that may have employees involved in the evaluation should be contacted. Key issues to be covered in such meetings are the goals of the evaluation effort, participation requirements, approximately when and where surveys would need to be completed, how evaluation results will be handled and communicated to management, assurances related to confidentiality or anonymity of responding, and next steps in the evaluation process.

The third activity in evaluation planning, *developing a draft proposal (or summary) and obtaining input on the proposal,* is highly recommended. Along with technical information related to the conduct of the evaluation effort, the proposal should incorporate information discussed above with a tentative timetable for completing the evaluation and a list of deliverables or products. Circulate (or discuss) the revised proposal to (with) key management and union personnel when appropriate for commentary and revise as needed for approval. As part of the approval process, a determination of who will be responsible for carrying out each phase of the evaluation is important. The development of a draft or working proposal may be particularly helpful with respect to obtaining final buy-in to the evaluation effort and a useful means for documenting expectations and responsibilities. The draft nature of such a proposal permits revisions and further discussion, when necessary, of sensitive items (e.g., confidential or anonymous responding to ensure union participation).

A particularly sensitive item related to evaluating the transfer of safety training is the need in some cases to use anonymous ratings to ensure union involvement in this process. The greatest concern is often with workers evaluating specific coworkers and the security of self- or peer appraisals of safety performance. To ensure union and line worker involvement in the evaluation process, Burke, Sarpy, and

Vaslow (1997) developed an anonymous coworker evaluation procedure. This evaluation procedure was characterized by having line workers rate the frequency to which a *typical* coworker exhibited safe work behaviors when required to do so. A typical coworker was defined as the usual employee whom the person worked with in the person's work group. The procedure was found to yield useful evaluative information and ratings that were consistent with supervisory ratings of specific employees.

Fourth, and a necessary activity, is *meeting with personnel* who will be responsible for notifying the participants and scheduling the administration of the surveys. Specific plans for how the participants will be notified and for administering the surveys should be part of these discussions. For supervisory surveys, lists with supervisors' names and the names of their subordinates should be provided to the lead person on the evaluation effort at this point.

Developing and Administering New Training Program Evaluation Forms

Assuming that training course objectives have been specified in behavioral (action-oriented) terms, the program evaluation team should translate these objectives into an initial list of behavioral statements or questionnaire items. Behavioral statements are typically written in the form of tasks that employees might engage in (e.g., uses the appropriate personal protective equipment as indicated by the site health and safety plan), with an action verb and a predicate. The action verb is typically written in present tense and the predicate identifies what is being acted upon (the object) and includes any qualifying conditions to communicate unambiguously what the task is.

In some cases, health and safety training and work are done to meet a general training need (e.g., to be in compliance with regulatory standards) and thus involve individuals from diverse sets of jobs and crafts (e.g., construction workers or hazardous waste workers). For these cases, a program evaluator may consider developing statements or items for use on the evaluation form that reflect actions that apply across the relevant types of work (e.g., uses applicable hazard controls and equipment such as ventilation, physical barriers, and remotely operated equipment). This step should also include a review of background materials on the measurement of performance for the types of work being considered as part of the evaluation effort. Another suggestion at this step is for the evaluation team to edit statements for clarity, eliminate redundancies, and cluster tentative statements into duty categories with definitions for the duty categories.

Subsequently, having subject-matter experts review and comment on the initial list of behavioral statements is desirable. In particular, supervisors, line workers, and training personnel can comment on the completeness and clarity of the list of behavioral statements as they pertain to the course objectives. Also, obtaining the input of industrial hygienists and health educators may be valuable with respect to the clarification of survey items. Importantly, given the jargon-laden nature of the fields of occupational and public health and safety training, obtaining line worker feedback on the understandability or clarity of possible survey items is critical for successful self- or peer appraisals.

Next, program evaluators may desire to pilot test a survey. Prior to the pilot test, the initial list of behavioral statements can be edited based on the input from various sources and a preliminary set of survey instructions can be written. The pilot test of the survey can be conducted with a small representative sample (e.g., 10 to 20 individuals) of those who will eventually participate in the evaluation.

Although there are many possible formats for measuring on-the-job behavior (see Guion, 1998), a frequency scale (ranging from never to always) may be particularly useful for rating the extent to which safe work behaviors are demonstrated (Latham & Wexley, 1981). An example of a part of a training program evaluation form (and a frequency scale) for assessing the extent to which employees exhibit trained behaviors is shown in Table 21.3. Forms such as the one presented in Table 21.3 can be modified as noted above to obtain anonymous coworker reports as well as modified to obtain self-reports of the extent to which one engages in safe work behaviors. In addition, a program evaluator can modify statements on such forms and have the statements rated with an alternative scale (e.g., an "effectiveness" scale).

After the pilot test, a training program evaluator will typically revise the survey as needed for administration. If a frequency scale is used for rating the behavioral statements, a suggestion is to include an NA (Not Applicable) response option on the survey (see Table 21.3), especially for supervisory assessments of employees' safety performance. Also, the inclusion of an open-ended question asking respondents to describe why certain behaviors were not exhibited as frequently as might be expected could yield highly beneficial diagnostic information. Responses to the latter question will be particularly helpful in determining whether factors extraneous to training are impacting the exhibition of safe work behaviors. In addition, responses to open-ended questions of this nature are useful for conducting follow-up interventions to enhance the transfer of learned behaviors.

As noted earlier in Table 21.2, surveys can be administered as needed (e.g., pre- and post-training) to meet the requirements of the evaluation design. When feasible, the surveys should be conducted at scheduled group meetings, so as not to interfere with work schedules and to increase response rates. For group administration of the surveys, there is often a need to ensure that the respondents will have adequate room to complete the surveys. Also, given literacy issues in some critical skills occupations, an adequate number of qualified survey administrators should be available to assist with the completion of group administered surveys.

In addition to asking an open-ended question about why certain behaviors were not exhibited as frequently as might have been expected, training program evaluators and management also might consider surveying respondents concerning their perceptions of general characteristics of the work environment (i.e., conducting a safety climate survey). As discussed in more detail below, this information will provide a more systematic assessment of work environment factors (e.g., management support, performance obstacles, and training opportunities) that might impact the demonstration of safe work behaviors.

Table 21.3   Example Items for Obtaining Supervisory Ratings of Employees' Safe Work Behavior

**FREQUENCY WITH WHICH
BEHAVIOR IS OBSERVED (IF REQUIRED)**

INSTRUCTIONS

**For the employee named below, please
rate how frequently you have observed
this employee engage in each behavior or
action over the last three months.**

Employee: _____

N/A Not Applicable (see instructions)
1. **Never**
2. **Almost never**
3. **Somewhat less than 50% of the time**
4. **About 50% of the time**
5. **Somewhat more than 50% of the time**
6. **Almost Always**
7. **Always**

Using Personal Protective Equipment: Using respiratory and protective clothing to shield or isolate individuals from chemical, physical, and biological hazards that may be encountered, when engineering and work controls are not feasible to control exposure.

1. Uses the appropriate personal protective equipment as indicated by the site health and safety plan.	☐ N/A ☐ 1 ☐ 2 ☐ 3 ☐ 4 ☐ 5 ☐ 6 ☐ 7
2. Correctly inspects and tests all personal protective equipment.	☐ N/A ☐ 1 ☐ 2 ☐ 3 ☐ 4 ☐ 5 ☐ 6 ☐ 7
3. Dons all personal protective equipment correctly.	☐ N/A ☐ 1 ☐ 2 ☐ 3 ☐ 4 ☐ 5 ☐ 6 ☐ 7
4. Doffs all personal protective equipment correctly.	☐ N/A ☐ 1 ☐ 2 ☐ 3 ☐ 4 ☐ 5 ☐ 6 ☐ 7
5. Correctly stores all personal protective equipment.	☐ N/A ☐ 1 ☐ 2 ☐ 3 ☐ 4 ☐ 5 ☐ 6 ☐ 7
6. When required, properly assists partner in checking, donning, and removing personal protective equipment or breathing apparatus.	☐ N/A ☐ 1 ☐ 2 ☐ 3 ☐ 4 ☐ 5 ☐ 6 ☐ 7
7. Appropriately communicates with other workers while wearing personal protective equipment.	☐ N/A ☐ 1 ☐ 2 ☐ 3 ☐ 4 ☐ 5 ☐ 6 ☐ 7
8. Properly performs work while wearing personal protective equipment.	☐ N/A ☐ 1 ☐ 2 ☐ 3 ☐ 4 ☐ 5 ☐ 6 ☐ 7
9. Conducts positive and negative pressure tests to ensure proper fit of air purifying.	☐ N/A ☐ 1 ☐ 2 ☐ 3 ☐ 4 ☐ 5 ☐ 6 ☐ 7

SOURCE: Adapted from Bruke, Sarpy, and Vaslow (1997).

Analyzing Data, Following Up
With Participants, and Reporting Results

Statistically analyzing ratings of survey statements and content analyzing comments related to open-ended questions require program evaluations with technical and content-matter expertise. Subsequent to these data analytic efforts, a recommendation is to plan follow-up meetings with respondents to clarify ratings of both survey statements and comments related to open-ended questions.

Although preparing a final report to document successes and failures is an obvious step, program evaluators are advised to obtain some form of peer review of a draft of the final report. Furthermore, either the final report in a condensed form should be circulated to key stakeholders (e.g., top management, union representatives) or close-out meetings should be held with key stakeholders. In either case, training program evaluators should discuss possible revisions to elements of the training system or how the results of the training program evaluation effort will be incorporated into subsequent work planning efforts.

The above process for developing, administering, and using measures of safe work behaviors is intended to be participatory in nature, with each stakeholder assumed to have interest in the transfer of health and safety training and the use of evaluation results to improve workplace health and safety. Although the process has been shown to produce useful measures for evaluating the transfer of safety training under such conditions, the measures do not necessarily have just a one-time use. The measures can be employed to monitor changes in safety performance over time and can also be used to measure and feed back safety performance results for developmental purposes on an individual basis.

Changes in behavior associated with training and, ultimately, the cost-effectiveness of training, may be caused or conversely suppressed by factors extraneous to training. For example, an unsupportive supervisor may prevent behavior change from occurring, whereas new technology or company policies might encourage the exhibition of safe work behaviors. In the following section, a discussion of some of the issues and factors that impact the transfer of training to the job is presented.

Issues Concerning the
Transfer of Health and Safety Training

Even when workers develop the necessary safety-related knowledge and skills from training, they may not apply new knowledge and skills on the job because of factors in their work environment that interfere with or fail to support their use (Smith-Crowe, Burke, & Landis, in press; Ford & Fisher, 1994). Various aspects of the work and organizational context such as work pressures and communication and coordination problems have been found to be associated with unsafe behaviors (Hofmann et al., 1995; Hofmann & Stetzer, 1996). For instance, when workers feel they are under pressure to complete a job quickly, they may engage in shortcut behaviors and bypass the use of safe work procedures. The result is that they may threaten their safety or the health and safety of their coworkers. In particular, the communication and coordination of work groups has been shown to influence safety through the development of norms about approaching coworkers engaged in unsafe behaviors, the degree to which safety is emphasized during work group meetings, and whether work is planned and coordinated in a way that allows for safe performance (Helmreich & Foushee, 1993). In short, efforts to improve health and safety in the workplace also need to focus attention on more systematic organizational and work environment diagnosis.

In effect, conditions in the immediate and broader work environment place an upper limit on the potential impact that health and safety training may have on the exhibition of safe work behaviors and reductions in workplace accidents and injuries. Understanding the impact of these work and organizational context factors on safety-related behaviors and outcomes is important for making decisions concerning how best to focus attention and resources to improve workplace safety.

As discussed above, specific information on immediate and broader workplace factors that facilitate or hinder the transfer of health and safety training can be gathered by means of open-ended questions on safety performance measures, interviews, and focus groups with employees, supervisors, and safety program officials and coordinators. These methods are particularly effective at identifying specific facilitating or hindering factors (e.g., work deadline pressures) and providing information on how such factors function to facilitate or interfere with the effective use of safety knowledge and skills (e.g., by causing workers to bypass proper safety precautions in order to complete work quickly). The information gathered through these qualitative means can be integrated into survey instruments that allow for more systematic assessments of worker perceptions of work environments. These types of surveys, typically referred to as work "climate" surveys, are particularly important for targeting aspects of the work environment that need improvement. In addition, the information gathered from a thorough assessment of worker perceptions of the work environment can be used as a baseline against which to measure future improvements in promoting health and safety in the workplace.

Conclusion

In summary, a systems framework for evaluating the effectiveness of health and safety training associated with clearly specified instructional objectives was presented (see Figure 21.1). Health and safety training program evaluation was discussed as a critical part of this closed-loop system. That is, health and safety training program evaluation generates answers to questions concerning how effective health and safety training is with respect to identified training objectives and provides the information for continuously improving training, enhancing work planning efforts, and identifying future training needs. An updated needs assessment is particularly important as safety training methods evolve and as employees' jobs and work procedures change over time. In this sense, training can be viewed as an evolving process and training program evaluation can be considered as a means for continuously improving workplace health and safety.

References

Bureau of Labor Statistics. (1997). *Occupational injuries and illnesses: Counts, rates, and characteristics, 1994* (Bulletin 2485). Washington, DC: U.S. Department of Labor.

Burke, M.J., & Sarpy, S.A. (2003). Improving safety and health through interventions. In L. Tetrick & D. Hoffman (Eds.), *Individual and organizational health.* (pp. 56-90). San Francisco: Jossey-Bass.

Burke, M. J., Sarpy, S.A., Tesluk, P.E., & Smith-Crowe, K. (2002). General safety performance: A test of a grounded theoretical model. *Personnel Psychology, 55,* 429–457.

Burke, M. J., Sarpy, S. A., & Vaslow, J. (1997). *A process for evaluating on-the-job behavior associated with training delivered at the HAMMER Training Center: The HAZWOPER demonstration project* (report prepared as part of the Year 3 Tulane/Xavier Universities HAMMER Project, Health and Training Reciprocity, U.S. Department of Energy, Richland, WA). New Orleans, LA: Tulane University/HAMMER Project.

Cantor, J. A. (1992). Evaluation of human performance in critical-skills occupations: Criteria and issues. *Performance Improvement Quarterly, 5,* 3–15.

Caparez, A., Rice, C., Graumlich, S., Radike, M., & Morawetz, J. (1990). Development and pilot evaluation of a health and safety training program for foundry workers. *Applied Occupational and Environmental Hygiene, 5,* 595–603.

Carroll, J. S. (1998). Safety culture as an ongoing process: Culture surveys as opportunities for enquiry and change. *Work & Stress, 12,* 272–284.

Cascio, W. F. (2000). *Costing human resources: The financial impact of behavior in organizations.* Cincinnati, OH: South-Western College Publishing.

Cheyne, A., Cox, S., Oliver, A., & Thomas, J. M. (1998). Modeling safety climate in the prediction of levels of safety activity. *Work & Stress, 12,* 255–271.

Cohen, A., & Colligan, M. J. (1998). *Assessing occupational safety and health training* (DHHS (NIOSH) Publication No. 98–145). Cincinnati, OH: National Institute for Occupational Safety and Health.

Cohen, H. H., & Jensen, R. C. (1984). Measuring the effectiveness of an industrial lift truck safety training program. *Journal of Safety Research, 15,* 125–135.

Flin, R., Mearns, K., O'Connor, P., & Bryden, R. (2000). Measuring safety climate: Identifying the common features. *Safety Science, 34,* 177–192.

Ford, J. K., & Fisher, S. (1994). The transfer of safety training in work organizations: A systems perspective to continuous learning. *Occupational Medicine, 9,* 241–259.

Goldstein, I. L., & Ford, J.K. (2002). *Training in organizations.* Belmont, CA: Wadsworth.

Guion, R. M. (1998). *Assessment, measurement, and prediction for personnel decisions.* Mahwah, NJ: Lawrence Erlbaum.

Helmreich, R. L., & Foushee, H. C. (1993). Why crew resource management? Empirical and theoretical bases of human factors training in aviation. In E. L. Weiner, B. G. Kanki, & R. L. Helmreich (Eds.), *Cockpit resource management* (pp. 3–45). New York: Academic Press.

Hofmann, D. A., Jacobs, R., & Landy, F. (1995). High reliability process industries: Individual, micro, and macro organizational influences on safety performance. *Journal of Safety Research, 26,* 131–149.

Hofmann, D. A., & Stetzer, A. (1996). A cross-level investigation of factors influencing unsafe behaviors and accidents. *Personnel Psychology, 49,* 307–339.

Kirkpatrick, D. L. (1996). Evaluation. In R. L. Craig (Ed.), *The ASTD training & development handbook* (pp. 294–312). New York: McGraw-Hill.

Latham, G. P., & Wexley, K. N. (1981). *Increasing productivity through performance appraisal.* Reading, MA: Addison-Wesley.

Lingard, H., & Rowlinson, S. (1997). Behavior-based safety management in Hong Kong's construction industry. *Journal of Safety Research, 28,* 243–256.

Luskin, J., Somers, C., Wooding, J., & Levenstein, C. (1992). Teaching health and safety: Problems and possibilites for learner-centered training. *American Journal of Industrial Medicine, 22,* 665–676.

Morrow, C. C., Jarrett, M. Q., & Rupinski, M. T. (1997). An investigation of the effect and economic utility of corporate-wide training. *Personnel Psychology, 50,* 91–119.

National Institute of Environmental Health Sciences. (1997). *Resource guide for evaluating worker training: A focus on safety and health.* Silver Spring, MD: NIEHS's National Clearinghouse for Worker Safety and Health Training for Hazardous Material, Waste Operations, and Emergency Response.

National Institute for Occupational Safety and Health (NIOSH). (1994). *Worker deaths in confined spaces. A summary of NIOSH surveillance and investigative findings (DHHS (NIOSH) 94-103).* Cincinnati, OH: National Institute for Occupational Safety and Health, Centers for Disease Control and Prevention, U.S. Department of Health and Human Services.

Palchinsky-Magennis, J. (1992). A training performance indicator model for monitoring the effectiveness of high-risk training. Reports of a study in progress. *Performance Improvement Quarterly, 5,* 44–55.

Sarpy, S. A., & Burke, M. J. (in press). Using Kirkpatrick's four-level training program evaluation framework. *Proceedings of the NIOSH National Conference on Workplace Safety & Health.* Cincinnati,OH: National Institute for Occupational Safety and Health.

Sarpy, S. A., Vaslow, J. B., Burke, M. J., & Langlois, E. C. (1997). *A multilevel process for evaluating training delivered at the HAMMER Training Center: The HAZWOPER demonstration project.* New Orleans, LA: Tulane University/HAMMER Project.

Smith-Crowe, K., Burke, M. J., & Landis, R. S. (in press). Organizational climate as a moderator of safety knowledge-safety performance relationships. In *Journal of Organizational Behavior.*

Vojtecky, M. A., & Schmitz, M. F. (1986). Program evaluation and health and safety training. *Journal of Safety Research, 17,* 57–63.

Recommended References in Health and Safety Training and Program Evaluation

Cohen, A., & Colligan, M. J. (1998). *Assessing occupational safety and health training* (DHHS (NIOSH) Publication No. 98-145). Cincinnati, OH: National Institute for Occupational Safety and Health (www.cdc.gov/niosh).

National Institute of Environmental Health Sciences. (1997). *Resource guide for evaluating worker training: A focus on safety and health.* Silver Spring, MD: NIEHS's Clearinghouse for Worker Safety and Health Training for Hazardous Material, Waste Operation, and Emergency Response (www.niehs.gov/wetp/clear.htm).

Occupational Safety and Health Administration. (1998). *Training requirements in OSHA standards and training guidelines* (OSHA Publication 2254). Washington, DC: U.S. Department of Labor, Occupational Safety and Health Administration.

Scannell, G. F. (1996). Occupational safety and health training. In R. L. Craig (Ed.), *The ASTD training & development handbook* (pp. 915–943). New York: McGraw-Hill.

CHAPTER 22

Work/Life Balance Policies and Programs

E. Jeffrey Hill

Sara P. Weiner

Why Evaluate Work/Life Policies and Programs?

The realities of a global economy, innovative business management, new work-facilitating technologies, and the advent of e-commerce have all combined to increase the challenge for individuals to simultaneously navigate the demands of paid work and personal/family life. Global competition coupled with skilled labor shortages, along with the intensity with which employees experience work/life difficulty, has given work/life programs a high priority in strategic business initiatives. Companies have instituted a variety of policies and programs to address these challenges. These programs are no longer primarily perceived as accommodations for the idiosyncratic needs of a relatively small group of employees, such as working mothers; rather, they are seen as part of a broad-based business imperative to meet the needs of all employees.

AUTHOR'S NOTE: The authors would like to thank Vjollca Kadi Martinson, a doctoral student in the BYU School of Family Life, for her research assistance. We also would like to thank Leslie Hammer at Portland State University and Alan Hawkins at Brigham Young University for their thoughtful comments on an earlier draft. We also greatly appreciate the helpful suggestions made by the editors.

An increase in work time, along with the rise in the proportion of dual-earner couples, creates a "time famine" in today's American families (Hochschild, 1997). For example, employees in the United States work the equivalent of three extra 40-hour weeks annually compared to a few years ago (Bond, Galinsky, & Swanberg, 1998). However, legislative bodies in European nations have championed the right of workers to have fulfilling personal and family lives by reducing work hours to 15%–30% fewer hours annually compared to those in the United States (International Labour Organization, 1999).

Work/life programs have been established in response to the need for greater flexibility to effectively manage work and personal/family life responsibilities. These programs are seen as integral to the ability of companies to attract and retain the best talent (Galinsky & Johnson, 1998). Retention is a particular focus because of the tight labor market and the expense of worker turnover, which can include costs of separation (e.g., exit interviews, accrued vacation, and continued benefits), position vacancy (e.g., temporary workers, overtime), recruiting, selection, and hiring (e.g., relocation or search fees), and new hire costs (e.g., orientation and training). In addition, there are indirect costs such as lost productivity of incumbents and other employees. These direct and indirect costs can total to between 41% and 241% of annual salary depending on the type of job (Corporate Leadership Council, 1998).

Despite the growing inclusion of work/life programs into corporate business strategy (see the appendix at the end of the chapter for a list of potential programs), there has been relatively little systematic evaluation of the effectiveness of these programs (Fried, 1999; Russell, 1997; Wilkie, 2001). Without establishing the business value of these programs through a cost-benefit analysis, senior managers are less likely to approve financial support. And although some work/life programs may be instituted without proof of their effectiveness, the long-term buy-in of senior through first-line management must be obtained to create the organizational culture required for these programs to be successful. Therefore, evaluation of work/life programs can ensure financial and cultural support for programs that have a positive effect on the business. After a brief historical overview, this chapter details the process for evaluating work/life policies and programs.

Historical Overview

Work/Family Focus on Child Care (1970s–1980s)

In the United States., the proportion of mothers with children under six years of age who work outside the home has increased from 15% in 1950, to 30% in 1970, to 62% in 1999 (U.S. Census Bureau, Table No. 659, 2000). In Canada, the labor force participation rate for women increased from 30% in 1960 to 59% in 1999. In 2000, 83% of all women in Norway between 25 and 55 years of age were employed (Haugland, 2001). Many early programs in the 1970s and 1980s in the United States focused on mothers with young children in the workforce such as childcare referral services, flexible starting and stopping times, and leaves for childbirth (Galinsky & Johnson, 1998).

Broad Work/Life Focus (1980s–1990s)

The concept of balancing "work and family" moved to "work/life balance" in the 1980s and 1990s with the recognition of the benefits of accommodating all employees' lives outside of work. A common innovation of the 1980s was the implementation of flextime (a degree of flexibility for most employees in starting, stopping, and break times) (Galinsky & Johnson, 1998).

There was also a move toward greater flexibility in leave-of-absence programs, including working part-time hours for family, education, or other approved personal needs. In the late 1980s and during the 1990s, flexi-place was introduced; it gave employees flexibility about where work is done through telecommuting or work-at-home programs (Hill, Miller, Weiner, & Colihan, 1998). These programs can result in substantial savings for companies. For example, after reducing real estate holdings and moving to a broader telecommuting model, IBM estimates it saves $75 million annually on real estate. The return on the investment was realized in the first year when expenses (telecommuting equipment) and savings (real estate) broke even (Apgar, 1998). Similarly, AT&T estimates a savings of $500 million since 1991 (Van Horn & Storen, 2000). In addition to significant financial savings for the company, increased flexibility in where the work gets done can include outcomes such as improved employee performance and commitment.

Work/Life Business Imperative (Late 1990s to the Present)

In recent years work/life balance has moved center stage as a critical business strategy, integral to attracting and retaining the best employees from an ever-decreasing labor pool and to facilitate maximum contribution on the job.

Demographic factors point to more pervasive dependent care needs for employees. As before, many employees have to arrange for the care of young children in order to come to work; indeed more than half of all employees in the United States have children under 18 (Bond et al., 1998). In addition, almost one-third of the employee population has some kind of elder care responsibility (Bond et al., 1998; Hill, Campbell, & Koblenz, 1997). For example, Clark and Weber (1997) reported that the number of elderly aged 65+ in the United States had increased to 13% of the total population in 1990 and is projected to increase to 23% by 2040. In addition, increasing numbers of employees have both childcare and elder care responsibilities, part of the "sandwich" generation. Geographic distance from relatives in need of assistance further complicates these responsibilities.

Women are more likely to have greater contributions to household income. As women around the globe make more money, their contribution to the family income becomes more important. In 1998 the average working wife in the United States added more than $26,500 per year to the household income compared to less than $8,000 per year in 1980 (in 1998 dollars) (U.S. Census Bureau, Table No. 748, 2000). In Sweden, the average wage for a woman is more than 90% of the wage for a male (Women & Men in Sweden: Facts and Figures, 2000).

Men are more likely to have childcare and housework responsibilities. Recent research has indicated that men are more likely to have work/life difficulties than in the past. Between 1977 and 1997, the number of housework hours reported by fathers in the United States increased from 14 to 21 hours per week and the number of childcare hours increased from 19 to 24 hours per week (Bond et al., 1998). The average work week for American men has also increased to 51 hours. In one study, 70% of fathers felt they spent too little time with their children (Bond et al., 1998). In another study, men were as likely as women to report work/life challenges (Hill, 1999). In Norway, men are more involved in childcare, with four weeks of paid leave reserved for men (Haugland, 2001).

Declining birthrate has led to labor shortages. Rapid technological advancements coupled with fewer labor market entrants have led to a critical labor shortage. Between 1960 and 1975, the birthrate in the United States declined. That resulted in more than one million fewer labor market entrants per year in this country in the late 1990s than in the mid-1980s (U.S. Census Bureau, Table No. 77, 2000). Norway is the only European country where the birthrate approaches replacement level (Haugland, 2001).

Workload is increasing in the United States. Technological sophistication has also contributed to increasing the work week in the United States. Between 1992 and 1997, the average U.S. work week increased from 43 to 47 hours, with men's hours increasing from 47 to 50 (Bond et al., 1998). In fact, the United States recently passed Japan as the developed country with the highest average number of annual hours worked while overall the work hours in Japan and Europe have been decreasing (International Labor Organization, 1999).

Legislation. Legislation also focuses attention on the issue. Norway's Marriage Act (1991) provides 42 weeks leave with full pay or 52 weeks with 80% pay for new parents; and four weeks are reserved for fathers (Sohlberg, 1999). The 1993 Family Medical Leave Act requires U.S. employers with 50 or more employees within a 75-mile radius to provide up to 12 weeks of unpaid leave per year for bona fide family reasons. After the leave, employers are required to place the employees in their previous or a comparable position.

Evaluating Work/Life Policies and Programs

In order to enhance the competitive advantage of a company, a focus on work/life that is aligned with the business strategy and driven by line management is indeed a business imperative. Therefore, in contrast to earlier times, these programs are now under greater scrutiny and need a sound evaluation methodology to demonstrate that they accomplish their objectives.

Evaluating work/life policies and programs is a relatively new discipline. In the past, evaluation typically has been unsystematic and based primarily on anecdotal evidence (Pruchno, Litchfield, & Fried, 2000). In today's environment, systematic evaluation of how well work/life initiatives are functioning and meeting their objectives is essential to the survival of the programs (Fried, 1999).

In this section, we examine the five steps necessary for systematic evaluation of work/life policies and programs in a corporate setting. These five steps are: identify objectives for the work/life initiative, determine the methods for gathering data, gather and analyze the data, link the data analysis to the bottom line, and recommend actions.

Step 1: Identify Objectives

When evaluating work/life policies and programs, objectives are identified on three levels: programmatic, organizational, and individual. Below are several work/life examples for each type of objective.

Programmatic objectives. These objectives examine the objectives for the programs themselves.

> P1. *Offer the best (or superior, or competitive, or average) work/life programs in the industry*—Decide whether the company needs to be THE leader, one of the leaders, or average in work/life policies and programs, and then act accordingly. This decision should be based on sound business strategy using a cost-benefit analysis approach.

> P2. *Promote work/life awareness*—Foster employee awareness so employees are fully aware of the programs available to them.

> P3. *Ensure work/life usage*—Determine whether employees for whom work/life programs are targeted actually use those programs.

> P4. *Improve continuously*—Determine whether users perceive the programs as helpful.

Organizational objectives. These objectives examine the link between the work/life programs and organizational outcomes.

> O1. *Improve recruiting*—Enhance the company's ability to attract and hire the best talent.

> O2. *Increase retention of the best talent*—Decrease attrition of key contributors.

> O3. *Motivate employees to contribute their best*—Facilitate the desire of employees to give extra effort and to focus their thoughts and energy on tasks beneficial to the organization.

O4. *Raise productivity*—Enable company employees to do more in less time and/or have fewer employees who are late or absent from work.

O5. *Move to a results-based culture*—Empower the organization to value a results-based culture in which work/life programs can be used without formal or informal penalty.

Individual objectives. These objectives examine the link between the work/life programs and individual outcomes.

I1. *Fulfillment on and off the job*—Empower company employees to find fulfillment both at work and in their personal/family lives.

I2. *Manageable workload*—Maintain workload levels so company employees feel that the amount of work they are expected to do is manageable.

I3. *Balance work and personal life*—See that the relative balance between work and personal/family life is such that work does not unduly interfere with personal life and personal life does not unduly interfere with a productive work life.

I4. *Seek synergy*—Foster the view that aspects of work can enhance personal/family life as well as that personal/family life can enhance work.

The purpose of implementing work/life policies and programs is to positively affect both organizational and individual outcomes. Identifying when the objectives are attained and when they are not is the heart of work/life evaluation.

Step 2: Determine Methods

The tools used in work/life evaluation are a set of analytical instruments often used in other business and social science research. There are quantitative methods that numerically document the results of work/life programs as they link to program objectives and business outcomes. There are also qualitative methods that evaluate perceptions of employees. We describe how these methods might be used to evaluate work/life policies and programs according to specific programmatic, organizational, and individual objectives. The contribution of work/life programs must also be evaluated in the context of other potential influences on outcomes. Causal linkages between work/life programs and outcomes are not usually direct; rather, they are typically moderated by job characteristics or by increasing the level of employee commitment (Fried, 1999; Russell, 1997). In addition, business outcomes such as attrition, absenteeism, or lateness can all be affected by the business environment such as new company leadership, better financial results, or an announcement of layoffs. Work/life program evaluation can demonstrate beneficial relationships of work/life programs to the business and to individuals and must be conducted while ensuring the context is considered.

Quantitative methods: Human resources (HR) databases. Data for evaluation of work/life policies and programs may exist in the company HR database. For example, the database often contains the number of participants using work/life programs such as leaves of absence, job sharing, and permanent part-time work. The database might also contain information needed to determine the demographic groups (e.g., gender, job type, and business unit) using these programs. Analyses may indicate where further communications may be needed on availability and support of using programs, or areas in the company in which the leaders are less likely to support work/life program usage than others.

In cases where the data are not available, a business case could be developed for inclusion of new items. For example, some employees work in a traditional office, others are mobile, and still others work from home. Adding a workplace indicator to the HR database would enable linkages to be made between work situation and performance, absenteeism, or lateness. If differences by work situation do exist, additional analysis or research could then be done to evaluate the facilitators or obstacles to achieving high performance.

One of the underlying reasons that work/life is becoming a strategic business issue involves the assumption that work/life programs and policies will contribute to attracting and retaining the best talent as discussed above. Attrition rates can be compared before and after implementation of programs. In addition, including a separation code for "work/life balance reasons" can identify the degree to which attrition is linked to work/life issues. After the implementation of programs, the frequency of that code as a primary reason for leaving can be tracked.

Quantitative methods: Surveys. Employee surveys are a common and effective quantitative method for gathering information to evaluate work/life programs. Asking some questions that can be compared with other organizations will indicate whether the results are best practice or average. The Mayflower Group (*www.mayflowergroup.org*) and the IT Survey Group (*www.itsg.org*) are examples of nonprofit consortiums in which normative databases of employee attitudes are available to members for benchmarking purposes, along with opportunities for formal and informal networking on a variety of HR topics. Another source of benchmarking data is the National Survey of the Changing Workforce (Bond et al., 1998) conducted every five years by the Families and Work Institute. It uses a nationally representative sample of workers in the United States (*www.familiesandwork.org*). Informal contacts at other companies or conferences such as the Association of Work Life Professionals (*www.awlp.org*) can also be very helpful.

In addition, there are numerous other helpful Web sites such as the Work-Family Researchers Electronic Network at *http://www.bc.edu/bc_org/avp/wfnetwork/*, the Center for Work and Family at *www.centerforworkandfamily.com,* the Gil Gordon site for information about telecommuting at *www.gilgordon.com,* and the U.S. Department of Labor site for U.S. policy and statistics at *www.dol.gov.*

Knowing how employee attitudes are changing over time is also critical in evaluating work/life policies and programs. For example, it may be that 40% of an employee population reports difficulty in work/life balance. That's bad news if last year's figure was 25%, but good news if it represents an improvement since last year's 50%.

In evaluating whether a program is effective, it is important to know how many employees actually belong to the group at whom the program is targeted (e.g., parents with young children). A work and life issues survey provides a great opportunity to obtain those data if they are not available in the HR database.

Whether an employee's partner is employed, the degree of that employment commitment, and whether the partner can provide dependent care during working hours is also valuable information to gather. For example, a targeted Work and Life Issues Survey at IBM found that, not surprisingly, work/life difficulty was more pronounced when employees belonged to dual-career couples and both partners had professional jobs (Hill et al., 1997).

Qualitative methods. Surveys and focus groups offer two valuable methods for gathering qualitative information. Surveys often generate open-ended write-in comments, a valuable source of qualitative comments. Sophisticated automated techniques for text mining can reduce the labor intensity of the content coding process (Bachiochi & Weiner, 2002). Including verbatim comments is a powerful way to amplify or clarify quantitative findings.

Focus groups provide an excellent opportunity to obtain rich data from a smaller number of employees. They are especially valuable in the evaluation of a pilot work/life program to identify the benefits and risks of the program and to ensure that a broader array of potential issues is uncovered for a follow-up survey.

Other options include conducting a "telefocus" group in which participants speak together on a conference call. In our experience the ideal number is up to three participants, plus one facilitator and one note-taker. Using online anonymous tools to facilitate discussion can also yield valuable qualitative data for evaluation. Bachiochi and Weiner (2002) provide more detailed guidance about conducting qualitative research, including more recent electronic solutions to use with employees in remote work locations.

Step 3: Gather and Analyze the Data

The purpose of evaluating each objective is to provide feedback about which portions of the work/life programs and policies should be enhanced, maintained, diminished, or eliminated. Evaluation also provides valuable information about new programs that might be implemented. The letter and number combination preceding each objective corresponds to those indicated in Step 1.

P1. *Offer the best (or superior, or competitive, or average) work/life programs in the industry.* One evaluation exercise is to benchmark work/life programs and identify gaps in work/life offerings based on their objectives. To aid in this task, we have included a list of potential programs in the appendix. A first step for U.S. companies could be to compare the programs offered with those offered by other U.S. companies. Of course the size of a company will influence the types of programs it can provide. Less traditional and more integrative programs (flextime, casual dress, etc.) may be more feasible for smaller companies and more desirable for newer entrants to the workforce.

P2. *Promote work/life awareness.* Level of awareness can be garnered in focus groups and by asking survey questions. One useful question is to ask "How did you first become aware of the [company's] _____?" and providing alternatives such as *company publication, Web site, coworker, manager, other (please explain),* or *I was not aware.*

P3. *Ensure work/life usage.* Sometimes, HR databases can provide usage rates (e.g., percentages and demographics of those using leaves of absence, part-time employment, or telecommuting). In addition, a question on a general survey could be used to measure usage. "[Company] offers a number of programs (e.g., flexible work hours, part-time employment, leaves of absence, and work-at-home) to help employees manage the demands of their work and personal/family lives. Which statement best describes your use of these programs?"
   a. I am aware of work/life programs and have used them.
   b. I am aware of work/life programs but have NOT used them.
   c. I am NOT aware of [company's] work/life programs.

P4. *Improve continuously.* Evaluating the helpfulness of programs might be assessed with using a 5-point scale varying from *extremely helpful* to *not at all helpful* and having two additional responses: *I am aware of the program, but have not used it* and *I have not heard of the program.* The question might be phrased, "Listed below are a number of [company's] programs. For each program YOU HAVE PERSONALLY USED, please indicate how helpful each has been in assisting you to better manage your work and personal/family life." The list would then include a separate item for each program (flextime, job sharing, part-time employment, etc.).

O1. *Improve recruiting.* Interviews with those who have declined the company's job offers can be used to determine the importance of work/life programs compared to other factors such as compensation, the job/skills match, or career opportunities. The degree to which work/life programs are promoted during recruiting, the perception of the programs themselves, and the perceived cultural support for using these programs could all be evaluated.

Another possibility is to compare recruit quality (e.g., grade point average or academic standing) before and after implementing a new recruiting campaign and compare with a control group. A company in a competitive campus hiring environment might emphasize its work/life environment and promote that as a compelling reason to choose the company. To evaluate this work/life initiative, baseline measures of recruiting quality and acceptance rates could be obtained for several campuses. The new campaign could be implemented on some of the campuses while similar campuses would continue to use recruiting methods without an emphasis on work/life programs. A reasonable decision then could be made about whether to expand the pilot. Fulfilling expectations of new recruits is essential to effective retention, so although recruiting success may improve with the new campaign, retention success may falter if the actual work/life environment does not meet the promises made during the campaign.

> O2. *Increase retention of the best talent.* If there is a work/life attrition code, the corporate work/life database can be an excellent source for work/life evaluation. Again, baseline measurements could be taken before undertaking a work/life initiative and compared periodically after the program is in place.

Another important step is to calculate the business benefit of such improvement in dollar figures. Galinsky and Johnson (1998) described one such example. Before implementing a new parental leave program, Aetna measured the attrition rate for new mothers after childbirth. They found that 23% of new mothers left the business, and those who left had higher performance ratings than those who returned to work. Aetna enacted three work/life programs: six months of parental leave, part-time work to transition to full time, and work/life training for supervisors. The turnover rate of new mothers was cut in half after implementation, to about 10% per year.

By calculating the cost of recruiting and training new hires versus the cost of implementing the programs, Aetna calculated a net return on investment of about $1 million a year. And, as cited above, the Corporate Leadership Council (1998) has estimated that turnover costs up to 241% of annual salary. For example, to replace an information technology professional with a $70,000 annual salary, the company will spend $123,300 on direct and indirect costs. If only 10 fewer professionals at this level left, the company could save over $1.2 million yearly.

Another way to anticipate problems is to use a survey to assess the employee's intention to leave the company as well as the reasons for potentially leaving. Intention to leave has been shown to be strongly correlated with actual turnover (Corporate Leadership Council, 1999). Not only can the absolute number of employees considering leaving be assessed and tracked (and compared to benchmarks if available), but correlations among survey question responses can show the strongest potential causes of dissatisfaction.

Other factors can be identified through qualitative research done in advance of the survey or other research available on the topic. The item wording may also be changed to assess negative "push" factors (dissatisfaction with factors at the current company) or positive factors either making it difficult to leave the current company or hard to resist an offer from a different company. If demographic questions are also asked in the survey such as latest performance appraisal rating or type of work, then analysis of responses for subgroups of employees the company most wants to retain is possible. In this case, retention factors for critical employees (e.g., high performers, technical professionals, and sales people) may be identified leading to appropriate targeted actions at the subgroup level. Caution is needed when analyzing demographics to ensure that the anonymity of individual respondents is not violated through the cross-tabulation of their responses.

A work and life issues survey at one large company revealed that inability to manage work and personal/family life was the primary or secondary reason top performers, engineers, consultants, and female executives would leave the business. This finding made a compelling case for a greater focus on work/life action (Galinsky & Johnson, 1998).

O3.   *Motivate employees to contribute their best.* Focus groups can provide insight about the extra effort employees are willing to give on tasks beneficial to the company. Performance effort should be measured by the end result rather than hours worked or face time (Russell, 1997). This type of information could be gathered with a standard 5-point agreement scale and a two-item question:

"To help [company] succeed, I am willing to put in a great deal of effort beyond my job requirements.

a.   I am able to focus my energy on tasks that are beneficial to [company].
b.   I am motivated to do my job to the best of my ability at [company]."

O4.   *Raise productivity.* Although it is challenging, directly linking work/life programs to productivity improvements is the ultimate goal of work/life evaluation. Proxy variables for productivity improvements could be absenteeism or lateness figures before and after communication about and implementation of the programs. Translating those figures into monetary savings can also be done. For example, if employees used flexibility programs instead of sick time for personal needs, a company can realize significant savings. A sick-day cost for an employee making $35,000 is $150 (using 260 work days as an average) (Russell, 1997).

One powerful example of linking a program to productivity was seen in IBM during implementation of a mobile workforce in the mid-1990s. IBM was dramatically reducing traditional office space for sales and services personnel and gave these employees the portable means to do their jobs (e.g., laptops, cell phones, and pagers). During the phased implementation, with a schedule built around lease expiration dates of office real estate, IBM conducted a survey among employees in offices that had implemented mobility and compared them to those still in a traditional office. Each group had the same jobs, targets, and sales environment. By taking advantage of this naturally occurring quasi-experiment, IBM was able to document a significant productivity increase using self-report survey data (Hill et al., 1998).

Instances of methodology with such a good control group will be limited, but there are several ways to evaluate the influence of work/life programs. One example is to use a survey for an evaluation of the effects of a telecommuting program on different aspects of the work environment and performance (scale: *very positive, positive, no effect, negative, very negative*):

    a. Effective communications in your work group

    b. Your career advancement in the company

    c. Your commitment/loyalty to the company

    d. Your morale

    e. Your motivation

    f. Your overall job satisfaction

    g. Your productivity

    h. The productivity of your work group

O5. *Move to a results-based culture.* The success of work/life programs depends on a supportive culture. Focus groups are a good way to assess whether the culture of the company supports the use of available programs. However, there are two caveats. First, focus groups are limited in their representativeness especially in large organizations. Second, if groups are selected from a subset of organizations within the company, the cultural assessment may reflect only management specific to that subset. A representative survey would be more effective at obtaining a broad measure of culture and assessing the first-level management supportiveness essential for the programs to succeed. For example, survey respondents might be asked how much they agree with two questions: "The environment in (company name) enables me to use the company's work/life options to successfully manage the demands of my work and personal/family life" and "My manager is helpful to me in family or personal emergencies." By comparing responses by business unit or different demographic subgroups, valuable evaluative information can be obtained and actions can be taken to address any cultural barriers.

I1. *Fulfillment on and off the job.* This issue is something readily assessed in focus groups but more precisely measured using survey items. Because of the hesitation to report feeling less than successful in either one's work or personal life, a 7-point scale from *extremely successful* to *extremely unsuccessful* is preferred over a 5-point scale that may result in range restriction of responses. The multi-item question is this:

All in all, how successful do you feel in each of the following:

    a. Your work life

    b. Your personal and/or family life

    c. Managing the demands of your work and personal/family life

I2. *Manageable workload.* Workload is a key factor in an employee's ability to manage work and personal/family life responsibilities. One approach to evaluation is to ask about the number of hours worked. In some countries, there are legal restrictions regarding asking about hours worked, so be sure to check with legal counsel. In addition, it is most important to understand whether the perception of the hours worked is acceptable. The two issues can be explored by the following questions and answer alternatives:

"Do you have a workload problem?" (answered *yes* or *no*) and "The amount of work I am expected to do on my job is . . ." (answered with a 5-point scale: *far too much* to *far too little* with *about right* as the midpoint).

I3. *Balance work and personal life.* In evaluating the relative balance between work and personal/family life, the perception of employees as reported in work/life surveys is perhaps the best measure. Understanding the effects of spillover from work to family as well as from family to work is important. Many studies (Russell, 1997; Bond et al., 1998) report that the work-to-family spillover is more detrimental than the reverse. One broad measure is, "How easy or difficult is it for you to successfully manage the demands of your work and your personal/family life?" using the anchors *very easy, easy, neither easy nor difficult, difficult, very difficult.*

Questions can also be worded to address the spillover effect either assessing negative spillover from the job to family/personal life or vice versa using a frequency scale such as *never, rarely, sometimes, often, very often.* The questions might be either "Because of my job, it has been difficult for me to have enough time for my family or important people in my life" or "Because of my family or personal life, it has been difficult for me to do as good a job at work as I could."

"Point in time" survey questions can also be used to evaluate trends over time. Here is an example: "Compared to two years ago, is it easier or more difficult for you to manage the demands of your work and your personal/family life?" (answered with a 5-point scale: *much easier* to *much more difficult* and a neutral midpoint).

I4. *Seek synergy.* A new work/life paradigm (Friedman, Christensen, & DeGroot, 1998) recognizes that work can enhance personal/family life and that personal/family life can enhance life at work. A paradigm shift may be needed in the concept of "balance"— from a point that if one aspect of life takes priority at a moment in time then by definition the scale is unbalanced to a point that work and personal life are seen as complementary rather than competing priorities, with success in one often leading to success in the other (Friedman et al., 1998). The authors pointed to "three mutually reinforcing principles" (p. 120) for managers: (a) clearly communicate the important business priorities and clarify each employee's personal priorities; (b) support the personal/family life of the employee— recognizing that life outside of work contributes to making that person whole—and ensure that there are boundaries where necessary; and (c) continuously explore new ways to get the work done—to enhance performance and ensure time for employees' personal lives, which can contribute to that performance. In the new paradigm, the goal is not balance but rather a synergy between the demands and rewards in all aspects of one's life, coalescing for greater total satisfaction and success.

Step 4: Link Analysis to Bottom-Line Measures

The next step of work/life program evaluation is to make financial calculations to build a business case for determining which work/life programs should be adopted, modified, or eliminated. To evaluate work/life initiatives in financial terms, it is best to use standard accounting procedures such as return on investment (ROI) or break-even analysis.

ROI. ROI is the bottom line measurement used most frequently to establish the value of work/life programs (Cohen & Trompeter, 1999). ROI evaluates which of several competing investment possibilities will yield the greatest financial benefit to the company. ROI can be thought of as a logical step following four levels of evaluation: reactions, learning, behavioral transfer, and organizational outcomes of training (Philips, 1997). ROI percentage is calculated by dividing the net program benefits by the program costs multiplied by 100 (Phillips, 1997). For example, say that the objective of a new work/life initiative is to reduce the turnover of female professionals. The program implemented may include telecommuting, a paid-parental leave program, and concierge services for a total cost of $1.4 million. Further, assume that an evaluation has shown that the program cut the attrition of female professionals by 20 women. Assuming an average turnover cost of twice annual salary and an average salary of $60k, the total cost savings is $120k per person, or $2.4 million. The net savings is $1 million or total cost savings ($2.4 million in savings) – investment cost ($1.4 million in costs). Therefore, the net ROI is 71% or "net benefits" ($1 million) / "investment cost" ($1.4 million).

Break-even analysis. Break-even analysis calculates how many employees need to participate in a program to justify the cost. The formula for calculating the break-even point is costs / contribution (savings or income) per person. For example, if the cost of a telecommuting program is $500,000 and the net value of increased productivity and loyalty resulting from the program is $25,000 per employee, then the break-even point is 20 employees ($500,000 / $25,000). In other words, the break-even point would be when 20 employees had decided to use the telecommuting program. Every additional telecommuter would contribute to a positive ROI.

Step 5: Make Recommendations
Based on the Work/Life Evaluation

After completing Steps 1–4, recommendations for change in work/life programs and their implementation will be based on data related to organizational and individual outcomes. New programs may be needed, or old programs modified or eliminated. It is also wise to include a plan for the next evaluation in the recommendations. Making recommendations will not result in change unless monitored actively. Therefore, periodic monitoring to ascertain how well the recommendations are being implemented can lead to adjustments that will make the decisions more effective.

We have now explained all five recommended steps in the evaluation of work/life policies and programs. Here is a fictional case study to bring it all together:

NBI Case Study

NBI enterprises, an employer of 2,500 in the United States and Australia, strives to be a leader in its industry. NBI's vice president of Workforce Management, Ms. Jean Bergstrom, wants NBI to be a leader in work/life policies and practices to enable the company to attract and retain the best talent while contributing to the bottom line. Ms. Bergstrom believes instituting these programs is socially responsible. In addition, she feels work/life policies and programs make career advancement, especially into executive ranks, less difficult on employees' personal/family lives.

Before Implementing Work/Life Initiative

Step 1: Identify objectives of work/life initiative. Ms. Bergstrom got top-level support for the following five objectives:

1. Make NBI one of the leaders in work/life policies and programs
2. Increase retention of key employees, especially professional women
3. Improve productivity
4. Decrease stress experienced by employees as they navigate work and personal/family life
5. Offer programs that employees want and will use

Step 2: Determine methods. The degree to which these methods were met was assessed using a variety of methods.

1. Benchmark the work/life practices of peer companies.
2. Obtain before and after measures of attrition rates and performance appraisal ratings from company HR database.
3. Obtain before and after measures of productivity (e.g., percentage of targets met by division) from the company business results.
4. Add questions to the annual employee survey asking employees' intention to leave the company, perception of productivity, perceptions about degree of current stress, and perceptions about how the level of stress has changed in the last year. In addition, add questions about awareness, use, and evaluation of NBI work/life programs and policies.

5. Using all data, calculate a bottom line return on investment (ROI) analysis.

Implement the Work/Life Initiative

After conducting a benchmark survey of work/life practices, it was determined that for NBI to be one of the work/life leaders many new programs and policies were needed. These new programs and polices included job sharing, telecommuting, 12 months' paid parental leave after birth or adoption (at 50% salary), and a concierge service (subsidized, easy access services such as dry cleaning, grocery shopping, car repair, etc.). Measures were gathered before implementation of the work/life initiatives from the HR database as well as by adding work/life questions to the company's annual employee survey: attrition rate was 10% for the 1,500 male professionals and 18% for the 1,000 professional women.

After Implementing Work/Life Initiative

Step 3: Gather and analyze work/life data. One year after implementing the work/life initiative, more data were gathered. The annual attrition rate had dropped: for professional women, from 18% to 12%; for men, from 10% to 9%. Survey results showed a decrease in employees reporting they intended to leave NBI, an increase in self-reported productivity, and a decrease in self-reported stress levels. Employees also reported high levels of awareness and satisfaction with the leave program, job sharing, and telecommuting. However, relatively few knew about the concierge services. In addition, very few (about 100 of those eligible) were using telecommuting and write-in comments indicated that the reason could be the perception that face-time was still important to career progression.

Step 4: Bottom line return on investment analysis. It was found that investments (costs) in the work/life initiative totalled $4.05 million:

1. Job sharing: additional benefits, change to the payroll program, etc.—$400k
2. Telecommuting: additional hardware, software, telecommunications costs —100 @ $6k per employee = $600k
3. Paid leave: additional salaries—$2.8 million
4. Concierge services: vendor contract—$2,500 @ $20 year per employee = $50k
5. Miscellaneous costs (including evaluation costs): $200k

Assumption: Average cost to recruit and train a new professional employee is $140k (2x salary = $140k)
Quantitative program benefits (retention savings) documented.

1. Attrition of professional women before w/l initiative: 18% rate x 1,000 employees = 180
   Attrition of professional women after w/l initiative: 12% rate x 1,000 employees = 120
   Net difference: 60 positions x $140k to replace = $8.4 million
2. Attrition of professional men before w/l initiative: 10% rate x 1,500 employees = 150
   Attrition of professional men after w/l initiative: 9% rate x 1,500 employees = 135
   Net difference of 15 positions x $140k to replace = $2.1 million

Program benefits (retention savings): $8.4 million (professional women) + $2.1 million (professional men) = $10.5M

Net program benefits (program benefits − program costs)/ program costs = % ROI: Attrition savings ($10.5M) − program costs ($4.05M)/program costs ($4.05M) = ROI (1.59) x 100 = 159%

Step 5: Make recommendations based on evaluation. In this case, the clear quantitative benefits of the work/life initiatives to the bottom line were much greater than the costs. Specifically, an ROI of 159% was documented. In addition, NBI employees reported two highly desirable outcomes: increased productivity and decreased stress. Based on the evaluation, Ms. Bergstrom recommended the following to NBI senior management:

1. Move forward with more work/life initiatives. Seek to become THE industry leader in the work/life area.
2. Publicize the concierge and telecommuting programs through a variety of internal communications channels.
3. Initiate actions for moving from a "face-time" to a "results-oriented" culture.
4. Monitor progress of recommended actions closely.
5. Repeat evaluation steps in one year and make adjustments as indicated.

Summary

Work/life policies and programs are no longer perceived as primarily accommodative; rather, they are integral to the business strategy in meeting objectives for recruiting, retention, and productivity. In this chapter, we have examined five steps necessary for systematic evaluation of work/life policies and programs in a corporate setting. First, clearly identifying objectives is fundamental to evaluation. Second, choosing a sound methodology is critical, and several quantitative and qualitative methods were presented for gathering data against which the objectives are measured. Third, selecting methods for data collection and interpretation were described. The fourth step, simultaneously the most difficult and most important step, is linking the data analysis to the bottom line by using an accounting measure accepted by the business. Finally, using the data analysis to take appropriate actions for the business is the ultimate goal.

By conducting systematic evaluation of work/life programs and policies, an organization can determine whether desired outcomes of improved recruiting, greater retention, and enhanced productivity will be achieved, thus meeting the needs of business to make a profit and the needs of employees to have a satisfying work and personal/family life.

References

Apgar, M. (1998, May–June). The alternative workplace: Changing where and how people work. *Harvard Business Review, 76*(3), 121–136.

Bachiochi, P. D., & Weiner, S. P. (2002). Qualitative data collection and analysis. In S. G. Rogelberg (Ed.), *Handbook of research methods in industrial and organizational psychology.* London: Blackwell.

Bond, J. T., Galinsky, E., & Swanberg, J. E. (1998). *The 1997 national study of the changing workforce.* New York: Families and Work Institute.

Clark, J. A., & Weber, K. A. (1997). *Challenges & choices: Family relationships—elderly care giving.* [Online]. Available: http://muextension.missouri.edu/xplor/hesguide/huanrel/gh6657.htm

Cohen, J., & Trompeter, G. (1999). Measuring impact on the bottom line: Applying accounting measures to work/life initiatives. In *Metrics manual: Ten approaches to measuring work/life.* Boston, MA: Boston College Center for Work and Family.

Corporate Leadership Council. (1998). *Workforce turnover and firm performance: The new business case for employee retention.* Washington, DC: The Corporate Advisory Board.

Corporate Leadership Council. (1999). *The compelling offer: Salient findings from a quantitative analysis of the career preferences and decisions of high value employees.* Washington, DC: Corporate Executive Board.

Fried, M. (1999). Evaluation: Using a participatory approach. In *Metrics manual: Ten approaches to measuring work/life.* Boston, MA: Boston College Center for Work and Family.

Friedman, S. D., Christensen, P., & DeGroot, J. (1998, November–December). Work and life: The end of the zero-sum game. *Harvard Business Review, 76*(6), 119–129.

Galinsky, E., & Johnson, A. A. (1998). *Reframing the business case for work-life initiatives.* New York: Families and Work Institute.

Haugland, V. S. (2001, February). *Family politics for a new generation.* Paper presented at the Family Life Lecture, Brigham Young University, School of Family Life, Provo, UT.

Hill, E. J. (1999, April). *Turning work/life research into change: The case for workforce flexibility.* Symposium presented at the annual conference of the Society for Industrial and Organizational Psychology, Atlanta, GA.

Hill, E. J., Campbell, A., & Koblenz, M. (1997, April). *The art of employee surveys: Using surveys for organizational change.* Presented at the 1997 Conference Board Work and Family Conference in New York.

Hill, E. J., Miller, B. C., Weiner, S. P., & Colihan, J. (1998). Influences of the virtual office on aspects of work and work/life balance. *Personnel Psychology, 51,* 667–683.

Hochschild, R. (1997). *The time bind: When work becomes home and home becomes work.* New York: Metropolitan Books.

International Labour Organization. (1999, September 6). *Americans work longest hours among industrialized countries, Japanese second longest.* [Online]. Available: http://www.ilo.org/public/english/bureau/inf/pr/1999/29.htm

Phillips, J. J (1997). *Return on investment in training and performance improvement programs.* Houston, TX: Gulf.

Pruchno, R., Litchfield, L., & Fried, M. (2000). *Measuring the impact of workplace flexibility.* Boston, MA: Boston College Center for Work and Family.

Russell, G. (1997). *Guide to evaluating work and family strategies.* Commonwealth of Australia: Canberra.

Sohlberg, R. (1999). *Business policy/social policy: Filling the gaps.* Paper presented at the 1999 Conference Board Work and Family Conference, New York.

U. S. Census Bureau. (2000). *Statistical abstract of the United States.* Washington, DC: Author.

Van Horn, C. E., & Storen, D. (2000). *Telework & the new workplace of the 21st Century. Telework: Coming of age?* [Online]. Available: http://www.dol.gov/dol/asp/public/telework/p1_1.htm

Wilkie, S. (2001, February). *Going global: Developing a work/life vision and strategy.* Presentation given at the annual conference of the Association of Work/Life Professionals, Orlando, FL.

Women & men in Sweden: Facts and figures. (2000). [Online]. Available: http://www.scb.se/eng/befovalfard/levnadsforhallanden/jamstalldhet/publikation.asp

Suggested Readings in Work/Life Balance Policies and Programs

Cohen, J., & Trompeter, G. (1999). Measuring impact on the bottom line: Applying accounting measures to work/life initiatives. In *Metrics manual: Ten approaches to measuring work/life.* Boston, MA: Boston College Center for Work and Family.

Fried, M. (1999). Evaluation: Using a participatory approach. In *Metrics manual: Ten approaches to measuring work/life.* Boston, MA: Boston College Center for Work and Family.

Friedman, S. D., Christensen, P., & DeGroot, J. (1998, November–December). Work and life: The end of the zero-sum game. *Harvard Business Review, 76*(6), 119–129.

Galinsky, E., & Johnson, A. A. (1998). *Reframing the business case for work-life initiatives.* New York: Families and Work Institute.

Pruchno, R., Litchfield, L., & Fried, M. (2000). *Measuring the impact of workplace Flexibility.* Boston, MA: Boston College Center for Work and Family.

Appendix: List of Work/Life Programs

Flexible Work Arrangements:	*Percentage of U.S. Companies Offering:*
Traditional Flextime (change starting and quitting times periodically)	68%
Daily Flextime (change starting and quitting times on a daily basis)	24%
Gradual Return to Work After Childbirth or Adoption	81%
Flexibility in Moving from Full- to Part-Time Work	57%
Job Sharing	38%
Occasional Work-at-Home	55%
Regular Work-at Home	33%
Time Off to Attend School and Childcare Functions	88%

Leaves

Maternity Leave for Childbirth and Early Infant Care (minimum of 12 weeks of unpaid, job-guaranteed time off required by the FMLA)	91%
Pay During Maternity Leave (wage replacement for at least part of leave beyond vacation days, accrued sick days, or other paid personal time off)	53%
Paternity Leave for Fathers (minimum of 12 weeks of unpaid, job-guaranteed time off required by the Family Medical Leave Act)	90%
Pay During Paternity Leave (wage replacement for at least part of leave beyond accrued vacation days, sick days, or other paid personal time off)	13%
Leave for Adoption and Foster Care Placement (minimum of 12 weeks of unpaid, job-guaranteed time off required by the FMLA)	90%
Pay During Adoption and Foster Care Leave (wage replacement for at least part of leave)	13%
Leave to Care for Seriously Ill Children (minimum of 12 weeks of unpaid, job-guaranteed time off required by the FMLA)	93%
Time for Mildly Ill Children (paid time off without losing vacation days)	49%

Childcare Assistance

Childcare Resource and Referral	36%
On- or Near-Site Childcare	9%

Vouchers or Direct Subsidies for Childcare	5%
Dependent Care Assistance Plans (flexible spending accounts, employees can set aside wages on a pretax basis to reimburse up to $5,000 a year in childcare or other qualified dependent-care expenses)	50%
Reimbursement of Childcare Costs for Working Late	4%
Reimbursement of Childcare Costs for Travel	6%
Childcare for School-Age Children on Vacation	6%
Backup of Emergency Care (when regular childcare arrangements fall apart)	4%
Sick Childcare (care for mildly ill children of employees)	5%

Elder Care Assistance

Elder Care Resource and Referral Services	23%
Long-Term Care Insurance for Family Members	9%

Programs for the Teenage Children of Employees

After School Programs	1%
Seminars/Workshops	2%
Summer Programs	<1%
Employee Assistance Programs	5%
Referral Information Services	1%
Scholarship Programs/Educational Assistance	1%
Counseling	3%

Helping Employees Resolve Family Problems

Employee Assistance Programs (help employees deal with problems that may affect their work or personal life)	56%
Work/Life Seminars (workshops or seminars on parenting, child development, care of the elderly, or work/family problems)	25%

Company Efforts to Develop Supportive Supervisors

Work/Life Training (train supervisors to respond to employees' work-family needs)	43%
Expanding Performance Evaluations to Include Management of Work/Life Issues	44%
Training to Manage Diversity	62%
Career Counseling of Management/Leadership Training Program for Women	22%

Health of Employees and their Families

Personal Health Insurance for Full-Time Workers	97%
Personal Health Insurance for Part-Time Workers	33%
Health Insurance With Family Coverage	95%
Paid Health Insurance for Family Coverage	87%
Health Care Coverage for Unmarried Partners	14%
Wellness Programs for Employees and Their Families	51%
Lactation Space and Storage at Work	37%

Benefits to Enhance Economic Security

Temporary Disability Insurance (typically partial replacement of pay until long-term Social Security Disability Insurance commences)	70%
Company-Paid Temporary Disability Insurance	85%
Pension With Guaranteed Benefits	48%
401(k) or 403 (b) Retirement Plan	90%
Company Contributions to Retirement Plan	91%
Scholarships or Other Educational Assistance for Children of Employees	24%

SOURCE: Galinsky, E. & Bond, J. T. (1998). *The 1998 business work-life study: A sourcebook.* New York: Families and Work Institute. *http://www.familiesandwork.org.*

PART VIII

Issues Spanning Human Resources Programs

CHAPTER 23

Evaluation of Human Resource Information Systems

Jeffrey M. Stanton

Timothy V. Nolan

John R. Dale

I n most large organizations, human resource information systems (HRISs) provide the technology backbone supporting the complete body of human resource (HR) functions. In this role, HRISs play a critical part in the operation of each component of HR. Additionally, by integrating across business processes HRISs provide organizations with control, forecasting, and planning tools that supersede simple computerization of HR functions. For these reasons, effective use of HRISs in organizations contributes to overall organizational effectiveness. Unfortunately, the complexity and nearly infinite customizability[1] of HRISs make suboptimal implementations of these systems common, if not typical. As with other technologies, HRISs require careful, regular scrutiny to ensure continued benefit. This chapter overviews strategies and procedures involved in evaluation of existing HRISs. After reading this chapter, managers and HR professionals should have the knowledge to plan their own HRIS evaluation project. Students and researchers reading this chapter may better understand the complexity of HRISs and research opportunities for evaluating the organizational impacts of these systems.

HRIS is one critical element in enterprise resource planning (ERP) systems. ERP systems comprise multiple, interlinked software modules that allow businesses to manage and control their various processes. In the year 2000, the software firm SAP claimed ERP installations in more than 13,000 organizations worldwide; more than 50 other vendors also provide HRISs (see Bancroft, Seip, & Sprengel, 1998; Bilbrey, 1999; Blain & Dodd, 1999, for more on HRIS and ERP). Large or small, these HRIS systems implement a common core of data entry, processing, analysis, and reporting functions. The data include applicant information, employee profiles, salaries and wages, benefits and insurance, equal employment opportunity data, time and attendance, and employee evaluations. Systems vary in the richness of analysis, reporting, and integration with other systems inside and outside of the organization. HRISs also vary in user interfaces, automation, scalability, security considerations, reliability, and the degree and methods of customization.

Basic benefits of HRISs include the ability to keep large quantities of employee-related records organized and available for analysis and reporting in paperless form. In larger organizations, HRISs can also provide advantages such as cost reduction (less data entry, less rework) and greater employee engagement (better service, one-stop service). A leap in capabilities occurs, however, when one includes tools that extract meaningful patterns from the data. As a simple example, with simultaneous analysis of recruiting data and employee records, some firms have discovered that particular recruiting sources provide employees who collectively have a much higher likelihood of turnover in the first year than do employees from other sources. Subsequent efforts to discover causes of higher turnover in this group might eventually reduce hiring and training expenses.

Organizations cannot realize useful capabilities such as these without associated costs. Besides the expense of purchasing or leasing software and hardware, an organization must hire, train, and compensate staff to manage and maintain its information systems (ISs). Further, benefits described above have the largest positive impact when many managers use the tools, share the data, run the analyses, and generate the reports. Whether these managers work in or out of the HR department, they all require training. In the largest organizations, where a high degree of customization is usually required, initial HRIS installation costs (including software, consulting, internal staff, etc.) can easily reach $50 million and require more than a year to implement. For medium-sized organizations, systems with limited customization can be installed for $100,000 or less. Ongoing costs (e.g., licensing fees, support contracts, facilities costs) must also be factored into considerations of the long-term effectiveness of HRISs. For highly customized, complex systems, annual upkeep can exceed $1 million. Of course, part of these costs would be incurred regardless of whether a firm uses an HRIS embedded in an ERP or a piecemeal system, because some system functions (e.g., tracking affirmative action goals) require staff and resources either way. While planners and developers try to make a strong business case for the anticipated benefits of HRISs, the reality that subsequently arrives may too often fall short of this ideal. Figure 23.1 depicts this situation as a cost-benefit comparison over time. The top half of the figure shows the ideal scenario, in which benefits of the new system begin to accrue within a

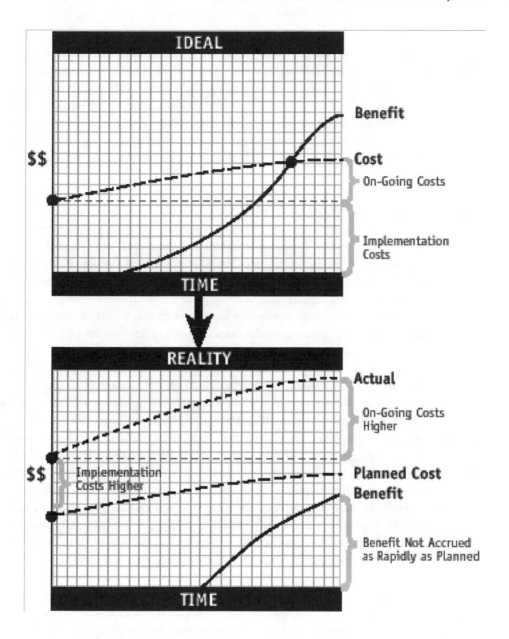

Figure 23.1   Contrasting Cost-Benefit Scenarios

relatively short time frame. In contrast, the bottom half of Figure 23.1 shows what happens in most organizations: Costs over time substantially exceed the planned amounts whereas benefits take much longer to manifest than expected.

The remainder of this chapter provides a framework for systematically examining the costs and benefits of HRIS with the goal of evaluating the effectiveness of existing systems. Armed with an evaluation of strengths and weaknesses of an existing HRIS, managers and HR professionals can make informed decisions on how to improve effectiveness. We examine the evaluation of HRIS from three perspectives: research methods, evaluators, and criteria. In our discussion of methods, we describe various strategies for finding out how the HRIS is working. In considering different evaluators, we examine the options and weigh the advantages of self-study versus having an outside agent conduct the research. Finally, we examine criteria for judging effectiveness and strategies for integrating criteria to satisfy multiple stakeholders.

Brief Historical Overview of HRISs

Before presenting the three major elements of the chapter, we believe it important to briefly overview the evolution of HRISs to provide context for our discussion of evaluation strategies. In his book on HRIS, Alfred Walker (1993) provided a history of HR computing beginning with the expensive but primitive systems available in the 1950s. These systems primarily supported payroll functions, though gradual specialization led to the capture of more and more employee information throughout the 1950s and 1960s. Two developments in the 1960s motivated the creation of specialized HR systems. First, affordable mainframes put general purpose computing into many large organizations. Second, civil rights legislation and related developments in employment law created new reporting requirements. In the 1970s and 1980s, a new generation of HRISs emerged with the introduction of cheaper computers and prepackaged software that made HRIS available for even the smallest firms. Low-cost networking simplified distribution of functions throughout the organization. At this stage, however, HRISs still comprised only computerized record keeping and reporting.

From the 1980s to now, forces converged to make HRIS more complex and critical. Economic considerations compelled mergers, acquisitions, and downsizing, each with an associated movement of employees. The 1980s also saw a push for total quality management, reengineering, and process improvement. These moves required streamlined processes (e.g., enter data once) and integration (e.g., of applicant tracking with equal employment opportunity reporting). At the same time, HR departments were often scaled back and more functions were outsourced. Increased use of menu-based benefits and compensation plans also forced HRISs to become more complex. Lastly, globalization of large firms resulted in larger databases and complex processing and reporting functions to cope with the cultural and regulatory issues of many different countries.

Fortunately, another recent trend emerged to make the situation more tractable, if not simpler. Specifically, growth of the Internet and the World Wide Web made remote access and control of HRIS functions increasingly feasible (e.g., for self-service benefits). Another result of the popularity of the Web has been the emergence of application service providers. These providers take outsourcing to a new level by taking over day-to-day installation, maintenance, upgrading, backup, and related operations of HRIS's and providing Web-based interfaces to all HRIS functions.

Application service providers cannot alleviate all of the details and complexity of the HRIS (e.g., employees still need training on how to use it), but they can hide, at a price, many of the technical challenges of the in-house HRIS. The following list summarizes the functions provided by modern HRIS/ERP systems and application service providers:

■ Workforce planning: HRISs provide tools for mapping organizational structure, describing jobs and families of jobs, planning work teams and larger groups, understanding current and future scheduling and resource allocation needs, and implementing succession planning.

■ Recruiting and selection: HRISs can post open positions, track recruiting activities/results, track applicants' progress through the selection process, and store/evaluate screening data (e.g., scanned resumes). One large retail firm has placed kiosks in its stores and some Web developers have created turnkey packages to conduct these activities on the Internet.

■ Performance tracking: HRISs can detail the activities and effectiveness of every employee using performance management systems that include supervisor or 360-degree evaluations; results of certification, licensure, continuing education, and post-training assessments; and skill profiles that reveal areas of strength and developmental needs.

■ Compensation/benefits: In addition to administering salary, wages, payroll, bonuses, benefits, and insurance, HRISs capture and process data related to business travel, expense reimbursement, and taxes. An important trend here is increasing self-service: Employees use Web interfaces to manage their own benefits, record travel activities, and file expense reports.

■ Compliance: Federal and state governments repeatedly increment regulatory reporting requirements, particularly for large organizations. HRIS supports automated processing and reporting of equal employment opportunity data and a plethora of related rules and legislation.

Note that at this writing few organizations have implemented all of these functions, and fewer still have done so within an integrated ERP framework. Many organizations have implemented functions individually, and many are working toward higher degrees of integration. Large national and multinational organizations based in the United States, the Pacific Rim, and the European Union have made the most extensive progress on such integration, but firms in other developed countries are not far behind. Progress toward integration sometimes proceeds slowly, often because the complexity and difficulty preclude making a clear business case for further investment. Some organizations now circumvent this difficulty by using application service providers. As mentioned above, however, such moves do not erase the problems of running an effective HRIS. Because of the challenges of integration and outsourcing, it is important for all organizations to periodically evaluate the status and success of their HRIS with an eye toward enhancing system benefits. The frequency of such evaluations depends on the rapidity of change in the organization's industry and environment. Even in the slowest moving industries, however, continuing advances in computing make three years the *outermost* limit for evaluation frequency. Program evaluations of recently implemented HRISs should typically be conducted within a year of first rollout and at one- to two-year intervals after that.

Primary Research
Strategies for Evaluating an HRIS

Program evaluation shares many similarities with other kinds of research: A researcher or a team of researchers conducts the evaluation by using an appropriate research method and measuring a meaningful set of criteria. This section describes program evaluation strategies as applied to analysis of the effectiveness of a HRIS; later sections consider teams of evaluators and varieties of evaluation criteria. As described elsewhere in this book, the strategy for program evaluation depends on the type of information that is needed to make appropriate, accurate decisions on changing and improving a program.

Although different experts conceive program evaluation differently, one perspective posits three general strategies for evaluation: goals-based, process-based, and outcome-based (see Clarke, 1999, for more on program evaluation). These categories overlap: Often a combination of strategies works better than one or another implemented singularly. In a goals-based framework, evaluation comprises understanding how well the current status of the program, in this case the operation and maintenance of the HRIS, matches a set of predetermined goals; it is also possible to evaluate HRIS achievements relative to other similar HRISs in a normative approach. In either case, one might consider a goals-based evaluation as an assessment of the degree to which the actual benefits of the HRIS matched those predicted in the original business case. In process-based evaluation, the focus is on the workflow and activities that exist in the HRIS, rather than on its status at one point in time. Process-based evaluations are appropriate for systems that have evolved over a substantial period of time. Ultimately there may be no one person who fully understands the operation of the system, the workflow it imposes on its administrators, or the complete set of inputs and outputs that the system processes. In such cases, process-based evaluation serves a documentation function by ascertaining exactly what the HRIS does and how it does it. Outcome-based evaluation focuses on the value obtained by program stakeholders. There is usually a diverse audience of stakeholders and their demands on the HRIS may differ widely and in some cases conflict. Thus, in contrast to goals-based evaluation when good data can tell you whether you've met your goals, the results of an outcome-based evaluation may contain contradictory results with some parties well served and others are poorly served.

Assessors Who Can Conduct HRIS Evaluations

In addition to selecting the appropriate strategies for evaluating the HRIS, identifying appropriate assessors is critical to conducting a program evaluation. Optimally, assessors should come from both inside and outside the organization—that is, there should be a mixture of both *internal* and *external* assessors. The following section provides a description of each group and their respective advantages and disadvantages.

Internal Groups

Perhaps the most obvious group to assess an HRIS implementation is the group using the system most frequently—HRIS staff. These are the individuals who enter, process, or view data within the system. They are the individuals who generate reports, analyze system data, manage interfaces with other systems, and provide or receive data from the rest of the organization. The advantage of having this group assess HRIS is that they are content experts with respect to HRIS operation. Moreover, they are the people who may have knowledge of earlier systems and their associated strengths and weaknesses; they are in the best position to compare the present with the past. Additionally, HRIS staff often possess a great deal of knowledge regarding other systems such as "bolt-on" or auxiliary systems used in concert with the HRIS. Finally, this group may understand the needs and concerns of people in the organization at-large.

The advantages that HRIS staff bring to the assessment process may come at a price. First, the staff may be threatened by the change implied by the evaluation process. For example, program evaluation may highlight needs for a new system. The new system may bring functions that displace reliance on the staff's current knowledge and skills. For this reason HRIS staff may be negatively predisposed toward the evaluation process and thus may provide biased data or interpretations. Customized bolt-on systems may also engender pride-of-ownership among HRIS staff because of the time and effort that were required to make these auxiliary components work smoothly. The potential demise of such systems can be another source of bias. A final caution is that HRIS staff can be overly biased toward the HR functions of the system, without adequate consideration for how well the system supports the needs of other stakeholders in the business unit. Overall then, we believe that HRIS staff can best serve a process-based program evaluation because of their extensive knowledge of how things currently work. Although HRIS staff may also provide useful information for a goals-based evaluation, their perspective on the full range of stakeholders is often too limited to provide complete information for an outcome-based evaluation.

A second group of internal assessors to consider is an internal audit group (i.e., individuals not from HR or IS departments). The advantage that this group may bring to evaluation is an unbiased perspective on the existing system. Internal groups generally conduct rigorous and attentive data collection and analysis efforts. These advantages increase the likelihood of discovering important problems with an HRIS. Despite these advantages, internal audits can also be overly negative; that is, they focus heavily on the problems and not on what is working well. Further, internal auditors may not propose useful solutions because of lack of content area expertise. One important consideration to weigh when bringing internal auditors into the assessment process is whether the high level of rigor they can provide is warranted—colloquially described, "Are you trying to hunt mice with an elephant gun?" Although internal auditors can generate quality assessments, sole reliance on such groups for a program evaluation can provide an unbalanced picture. We recommend internal auditors for goals-based evaluation because of their ability to thoroughly evaluate HRIS operations in an unbiased manner. Internal auditors are a less likely solution for process-based evaluation because HRIS staff members have better knowledge. Internal auditors may provide an overly negative view of stakeholder benefits in an outcome-based evaluation.

External HRIS Experts

The previous section described a number of advantages of using internal staff to conduct HRIS program evaluation, but concerns about objectivity may prompt consideration of external evaluators as well. One may consider hiring a consultant, from either an established consulting firm or a university institute, if concerns exist about the ramifications of having in-house staff conduct an evaluation of their own HRIS. External consultants have the advantage of neutrality and may also have specific skills and experience to defuse highly charged situations in which different stakeholders have divergent ideas about the strategies and goals of the evaluation. Regardless of the source of the consultant, the support of top management for the evaluation provides the keystone for a successful project conducted by an external party.

Consulting firms, if chosen judiciously, often have an advantage over individual consultants or university institutes in their ability to bring extensive resources and experience to bear on the program evaluation and any subsequent intervention that occurs. A large consulting firm can also bring an important advantage in situations in which the evaluation generates extensive bad news. The larger the firm, the less dependent they are on any one particular client. Possibly then, in truly troubled situations, these larger firms may have the capability of providing brutal honesty when it is required. These advantages come at a price: Consulting firms, as for-profit entities, must charge market rates. As with other professional services, one also pays a higher price for higher quality. One pitfall to avoid in working with an established consulting firm is that they may have a cookbook strategy for evaluation that does not fit the specific situation of the organization under evaluation. One should carefully pre-qualify any strategy that contains a hint of one size fits all.

Sole proprietor consultancies and faculty from university departments or institutes provide another source of program evaluators. Under less market pressure than commercial consulting firms, these individuals may provide a more economical approach to an evaluation project. Individual consultants may also have less interest in reusing a cookie cutter approach with each new client. One key difference between sole proprietors and university faculty is that the former may strongly depend on a client's continued business for their livelihood and this may color the judgments and language they use during the evaluation and in reports. Another difference is that a university institute may contain a broad range of expertise from which a client may choose, whereas an individual consultant is less likely to span multiple specialty areas.

External evaluators, depending upon their expertise, can develop process-, goals-, or outcome-based evaluations. With regard to process- and goals-based evaluations, external evaluators must have the capability of developing a solid and positive working relationship with the HRIS staff in order to ensure the opportunity to obtain detailed data on current HRIS processes and functions. For outcome-based evaluations, external evaluators must have upper management support to ensure effective cooperation of all relevant stakeholder groups.

Consortium Participation

A final source of evaluators lies in participation in a professional consortium. Such participation can provide the opportunity to compare the performance of one's own organizational ISs with those of other organizations. The greatest value, of course, comes from comparison with the practices of organizations that are known to be doing things right, that is, best practices benchmarking. Hundreds of professional consortia exist, usually organized for a specific industry or organizational function, and many groups offer a menu of benchmarking services to their member organizations. One of the best known of these organizations, the Mayflower Group, is a consortium about 50 of the largest U.S. based companies whose purpose is the collection, analysis, and exchange of employee opinion data. Many lesser known consortia also exist, and some of these are targeted at HR functions and organizational use of information technologies. Choosing among the possibilities requires research and decision making beyond the scope of this chapter, but one useful starting point for materials on best practices studies comes from the American Productivity and Quality Center *(www.apqc.org)*. The Center is a nonprofit organization that serves as a focal point for hundreds of benchmarking studies of U.S. organizations. Their Web site provides executive summaries of all studies accomplished so far. In closing, be aware that many consulting firms have benchmarking databases that provide similar benefits to participation in a consortium.

Criteria for Judging HRIS Quality

The foregoing discussion has considered general research methods and the individuals or groups that organizations can choose to conduct an evaluation of an HRIS. The third component, appropriate criteria, is the linchpin that determines the success or failure of the evaluation project. The choice of a criterion comprises *what to measure* (e.g., stakeholder satisfaction), *how to measure* it (e.g., with surveys), and *how to understand* what the measurements mean (e.g., in reference to norms). An excellent team of evaluators can use a great research strategy; but if it fails to measure meaningful criteria, measure criteria inappropriately, or interpret measurements incorrectly the program evaluation will fail. In the worst case scenario, the evaluation will fail by recommending the wrong course of action for improving the HRIS.

The easiest mistake to make in choosing criteria is to choose based on availability or how easily criteria can be obtained. For example, one might easily check with the IS department to find the clock speed of servers running HRIS software. This clock speed is readily quantified (e.g., in MHz), can be understood easily by anyone who has used a computer, and can quickly be compared to similar numbers in other business units. The obvious problem is that server clock speed is a trivial and nearly meaningless criterion, with little relationship even to how fast HRIS software runs, let alone other considerations such as reliability, security, uptime, or stakeholder satisfaction. This example illustrates the importance of choosing criteria based on their meaningfulness rather than their convenience.

Meaningfulness derives from the values of the organization's stakeholders. If one organization values careful cost accounting, forecasts of return on investment, and other financial considerations, then a selection of cost and benefit criteria, measured in dollars, may provide the most meaning. Others may benefit most from examining a set of HRIS stakeholder satisfaction criteria. Indeed most successful organizations value these and many other concerns, so a diverse mix can facilitate the most effective evaluation. Nonetheless, because the mixture of criteria and the emphasis on different measures will vary substantially from organization to organization, the evaluation team should always invest time and effort to ascertain the values of the organization. At the same time, many would agree that certain fundamental values apply across all organizations. HRISs and other types of computing systems must possess certain basic characteristics to be functional in any organization: Such systems must be reliable, must be secure, must be put to use by employees, and must provide added value above doing similar work manually.

A final consideration in choosing criteria is to plan how they function as a set. Evaluators must pursue several, sometimes contradictory goals here. First, the criteria as a set should be inclusive, that is, they should include measures that are meaningful to each and all of the relevant stakeholders. The flip side of inclusiveness is deficiency. A set of criteria is deficient if it fails to include all the relevant dimensions of HRIS performance. A common example of deficiency occurs in evaluations that measure technical and financial data but fail to include stakeholder measures: HRIS usage, stakeholder satisfaction with the system, expertise of system administrators, training needs, and so forth. Next, a set of criteria must avoid contamination, or, if contaminated, must compensate for the extraneous factor. An example of a contaminated criterion would be to measure the latency or response time of HRIS functions over a virtual private network. For example, intranet traffic, Internet congestion, and software incompatibilities that HRIS system administrators cannot control may adversely affect response latency. One would have to measure these influences separately and include them as compensatory factors in calculating response times. Finally, evaluators should strive for modest but not excessive redundancy among criteria. Multiple measures of a particular performance dimension allow triangulation on the issue of interest. For example, when assessing satisfaction, evaluators often use stakeholder surveys, but another measure of satisfaction can be obtained by examining complaint logs. Each measure provides a somewhat different take on satisfaction.

With these general considerations in mind, we now turn to a discussion of specific criteria. We have organized these into several functional groups: financial, infrastructure, technical, reaction, and value-added. We close the next section with a review of benchmarking criteria, which incorporate measures that have been normalized for comparison across different organizations. Table 23.1 provides an overview of all of the functional groups of criteria, categories within those groups, and specific measures for each category.

Financial Criteria

Financial criteria for evaluating an HRIS comprise a combination of initial installation costs and ongoing ownership costs. Together these represent the total cost of ownership and are thus an important element in program evaluation. If total cost of ownership were not in proportion to the ongoing or total benefits obtained from the system, then it would be difficult to justify the system's continuation. Ideally, total cost of ownership is more than fully offset by benefits.

Because monetary measures are easy to grasp, financial indicators have evident appeal for communicating costs and benefits of an HRIS. Evaluators must beware, however, of the pitfalls in measuring IS performance in dollars. Too often, either in up-front planning or ongoing maintenance, relevant measures such as staff time, training, and forced upgrades of related systems are not systematically documented; thus true costs of the HRIS are never really known. One reference point that sometimes helps address this gap is the original HRIS business case (see Remenyi, 1999, for more about IT business cases). A firm's archives may contain the case that was developed prior to the implementation of a specific IS or cases may have been developed more recently to justify upgrades or changes. Although business cases usually intend to *sell* an idea and might not be the most accurate source of *evaluative* information, they can help organize a financial evaluation of an HRIS. Specifically, the most accurate element of a case often pertains to the system that was operative at the time the case was written (i.e., how things worked then and how much it used to cost). Thus, the original HRIS case often contains baseline financial measures just prior to the new system or upgrade. The case guides what could be measured *now;* it also provides a point of reference to assess change.

In most IS projects, initial costs are often much higher than anticipated. In almost all cases, this is because the initial budget was based on an unrealistic timeline and because the complexity of the system was underestimated. Actual installation costs can vary from many millions for the most complex and largest organizations to less than $100,000 for a small, single-site operation. Specific cost categories include hardware, software, forced upgrades to related systems, training

Table 23.1   Taxonomy and Summary of Program Evaluation Criteria

Functional Groups	Categories	Specific Measures
Financial	Initial installation	Hardware; software; forced upgrades; training; professional services; and staff time
	Ongoing ownership costs	Compensation, benefits, continuing education; software licensing and support; hardware leasing, maintenance, and depreciation costs; rent; telecommunications charges; lost productivity; and software and hardware upgrades
Human Infrastructure	Qualifications of internal IS/HRIS	Previous experience; relevant training; and objectively measured skills, knowledge, and tacit knowledge
	Qualifications of contractors and consultants	Same as above
	Structure of IS or HRIS department	Percentage of staff time on HRIS; other responsibilities of HRIS staff; other constituencies to whom HRIS people are responsible; reporting relationships (i.e., layers to get to the IS director); talent mix of HRIS staff; and availability of ombudsman for HRIS problems
	Management/ leadership assessment	360-degree evaluation; traditional performance appraisal
Technical	System utilization	Logs of database access; Web page connections and hits; software diagnostic outputs; peak use load; and average user load
	Downtime	Isolate downtime problems due to HRIS and non-HRIS (e.g., telecommunications) causes
	Response latency	On Web-based and non-Web-based interfaces
	Reliability	Error correction; fail-safe performance; backup systems; and data accuracy
	Data security	Remote access; physical security; authentication; access control
	System architecture	Integration with other enterprise systems (e.g., amount of third party software, custom programming, telecommunications, and custom hardware); and *absence* of connections between relevant systems
Reactions	Perceptual measures	Perceived reliability, security, system response speed, accuracy, user friendliness, feature richness
	Overall satisfaction	Assessed directly; solicited suggestions; and logs of suggestions and complaints
Value-added	Reporting	Utility/quality of custom reporting
	Decision making	Historical quality of decisions and forecasts; and support for future decision making and forecasting (on staffing, training, re-engineering, etc.)

Functional Groups	Categories	Specific Measures
	Self-service	Number and availability of functions
	Automation	Hand work in periodic processing cycles and required/standard reports
	Work group management	Performance evaluation and project-based staff placements
Benchmarking	Financial	Divide raw costs by full-time equivalents, number of new hires, or number of employment transactions (transfers, terminations, promotions, etc.)
	Functional	Staff size or labor time involved in standard report preparation, data entry, and processing tasks
	Balanced scorecard	Composites of financial and nonfinancial criteria

of system administrators and other users, professional services, and staff time (salary, fringes, overhead charges, and opportunity costs). For the purposes of evaluation, the best way to obtain these financial data is through the accounting department. Ideally, when the project was initiated, job or charge codes were established and time was charged to these. If such codes were not used, then these financial data must be estimated from other sources. Depending on the level of accuracy needed, this can be relatively simple (estimate the number of people involved over a certain time frame, add up the consulting bills, and add in the software and hardware costs). If more accuracy is required, then a professional financial audit may be required. Even a professional audit may not be 100% accurate. For example, staff may have purchased new equipment to improve HRIS operations but included these costs invisibly in the operation budget (i.e., rather than in a development or upgrade budget). In such cases, one may have difficulty finding these costs.

This example illustrates the difficulty in pinpointing the other element of total cost of ownership: ongoing costs. We recommend investigating ongoing costs of compensation, benefits, and continuing education for HRIS and some relevant non-HRIS staff; software licensing and support fees; hardware leasing, maintenance, and depreciation costs; rent on physical space occupied by HRIS hardware and staff; telecommunications charges for communicating internally and with remote sites; lost productivity due to maintenance downtime; and costs of software and hardware upgrades. Almost all of this information should be available from the accounting department or the HRIS/IS department. In all likelihood, these costs will be scattered throughout the accounting system and will need to be aggregated.

To best evaluate the HRIS based on financial information, it is important to compare the information to some baseline or benchmark such as the original business case, but we do not recommend comparing this information to that of other organizations (also see our discussion of benchmarking criteria below). Implementation of an HRIS depends on too many variables (many of which are subtle; e.g., organizational culture), and comparisons between organizations are not always meaningful.

Human Infrastructure

The operation of any IS depends on the continuing activities of people who manage, support, secure, maintain, and upgrade the system. Thus, assessing the skills and abilities of these people can be an important component in an HRIS program evaluation. Given the dynamic business environment typical to most organizations, the human infrastructure that supports an HRIS and other ISs provides the capability of flexible response that is critical to maintaining system effectiveness. This section describes criteria of staff quality that HRIS evaluators should consider incorporating into their program evaluation.

Qualifications of internal HRIS/IS staff may be readily available from the HRIS itself or can be ascertained by self-report methods such as surveys. Useful measures include previous experience, relevant training (college degrees, postgraduate work, and self-learning), and objectively measured skills and knowledge (e.g., through certification programs). In multinational organizations, foreign language knowledge and cross-cultural communication skills may figure prominently in HRIS departmental success. Qualifications of contractors and consultants can be obtained in a similar fashion to those of internal staff. Obtaining detailed information about the qualifications of hardware and software vendors (particularly their support staff) or outsourcing firms can be considerably more difficult, however. Depending upon the nature of the relationship with these outside entities, it may be more fruitful to have internal staff describe or rate their experiences working with these groups. Any vendor whose staff is consistently rated as lacking expertise or being difficult to work with should be examined as a possible weak element in the HRIS/IS infrastructure. A final consideration pertains to staff members' tacit knowledge—the unspoken wisdom often acquired from working over a period of time in the present environment. This tacit knowledge cannot be assessed by examining paper credentials but is nonetheless extremely valuable in ensuring the smooth operation of any IS.

An additional set of measures that is often overlooked derives from the organizational structure of the IS or HRIS department. If a general IS department supports the HRIS, then one critical measure is the percentage of staff time dedicated to working on the HRIS. For those who work on the HRIS, what other responsibilities do they have? To how many other constituencies in the organization are they responsible? Relatedly, examining the subdepartments and reporting relationships within the IS department can be instructive. For example, if all individuals who specialize in HRIS must go through multiple layers to get to the IS director, this could be indicative of the low status of HRIS issues within the IS department. This point also underscores the importance of an appropriate mix of staff whose primary assignment is to the HRIS. Too many technicians and too few managers or vice versa can cause problems. Additionally, it is helpful if one HRIS manager serves as the ombudsman for HRIS problems. If stakeholders throughout the organization feel secure in knowing to whom they can turn with questions or problems about the HRIS, this can enhance stakeholder satisfaction and increase effective usage.

As a closing note about human infrastructure, we also wish to underscore the importance of effective IS management. In his book on management of information technology functions, Robert Thierauf (1994) emphasized the importance of management controls over information technology people, processes, and systems. While his book's total quality management orientation may overemphasize the notion of control, we strongly agree that effective managers in IS and information technology are a critical factor in the success of an HRIS and other organizational ISs. Thus in addition to assessing staff training, organizational structure, and allocation of staff time to HRIS duties, we also recommend assessing the effectiveness of leaders in this area. Leadership effectiveness in HRIS groups is particularly important when the group must serve a diverse constituency of customers (i.e., across business functions, company locations, and/or cultures). The most comprehensive strategy for leadership assessment is a professionally designed and implemented 360-degree evaluation, but when time or resources are limited, traditional performance evaluations of IS managers may suffice.

Technical Quality of System Functioning

A substantial proportion of HRIS staff time focuses on ensuring continued effective system operations. For the purposes of program evaluation, operational effectiveness can be measured by collecting technical data about the quality of HRIS functions. Such technical data include system utilization, downtime, response latency, reliability, and data security, as well as system architecture issues such as integration with other enterprise systems. This section details a variety of technical criteria that reflect quality of HRIS functioning.

At the most basic level, evaluators should obtain system utilization data—logs of database access, Web page connections and hits, software diagnostic outputs, and so forth—to develop a picture of peak and average usage loads. Average load should not approach theoretical limits (e.g., for the number of simultaneous users or connections) nor should it be extremely low. Very high averages may indicate impending undercapacity (i.e., not enough resources for the typical set of users), whereas low averages may indicate that people are simply not using the system to the extent that they should. Peak information can be helpful in scheduling system maintenance and in planning incentives that encourage people to use systems at off-peak times.

Other important measures of effectiveness can be more difficult to obtain but are arguably more important than utilization. From a user's point of view, if the system is unavailable for any reason, it is clearly useless. The difficulty in measuring downtime is that myriad problems can interfere with user access, and not all of them are localized in the HRIS and IS departments. Telecommunications problems, in particular, contribute substantially to system downtime. When the system is available, users care about speed and features. Simple response speed can be measured easily in some cases (see the caveat above about telecommunication delays), but important sequences of user functions can be harder to measure without careful study across multiple users (particularly if users differ much in their levels of expertise).

Note that reliability is a more general concept than downtime; the former also encompasses error correction, fail-safe performance, backup systems, and data accuracy. Although error-correcting telecommunications and data storage techniques have substantially eliminated data errors in transmission and storage, the human-computer interface is still an important source of data errors. As an example, consider entering personal data such as names and addresses into an HRIS database. An intelligent interface uses zipcode look up to automatically insert city names. In contrast, simpler interfaces without these features permit entry of erroneous data.

Modern HRISs contain huge amounts of sensitive data that, in the wrong hands, could severely compromise personal privacy and competitive advantage. Further, large HRIS systems used in multinational organizations must often conform to the mandated security controls of countries that are more restrictive than the United States in this regard (e.g., the European Union countries). Because almost all organizational ISs are distributed or permit remote access, security, authentication, access control, and encryption are critical functions. With HRIS, the variety of information stored and the large set of different audiences for which that information is intended make security highly complex. Assessing that complexity and ascertaining how easily the security can be breached requires a careful and professional audit. The parameters of such an audit are beyond the scope of this chapter, but three primary considerations are (a) making sure that the HRIS is protected from malicious external attack, (b) making sure that friendly authorized users have the right mix of permissions to perform their tasks, and (c) ensuring adequate staff training on privacy and related data protection issues. This latter point deserves emphasis: Many, if not most, security lapses and privacy violations occur as a result of human action rather than technical failures.

One final technical area from which useful criteria can be obtained is by examining linkages to other enterprise systems. For instance, effective use of project planning software requires making assumptions about the availability of staff to fill certain roles in the project. Does incorporating these assumptions require separate steps and manual work to obtain information from HRIS, or are the two systems mated together in a way that allows data to flow easily from one to the other? From a conceptual standpoint, more complete or seamless integration between different enterprise computing systems is desirable. It is often difficult, however, to translate this conceptual criterion into something measurable. Integration between computing systems often requires third party software, custom programming, telecommunications, and custom hardware. In one sense, then, the complexity of the integration can be measured by the amount of resources required to connect the distinct systems. Additionally, it is also important to capture the *absence* of connections between relevant systems.

Reactions

Some information technology researchers have argued that the actual technical characteristics of an IS matter less than how users perceive them. For example, two ISs may have identical mean time between failures but fail in different ways. One system allows a soft landing so that it can save work sessions before the system crashes, whereas another system crashes without a warning or the opportunity to save or retrieve work in progress. Clearly, perceptions of these systems will differ substantially even though simple measures of reliability reflect no difference. This example illustrates that user perceptions of system functioning have incremental value beyond hard measures. Roughly six criteria can capture perceived system functioning. Evaluators should query perceived reliability, security, system response speed, accuracy, user friendliness, and feature richness. In addition to these individual perceptual measures, evaluators should also measure overall satisfaction. Overall satisfaction can be assessed directly with questions about how much stakeholders like the system but can also be tapped indirectly by soliciting suggestions or examining logs of suggestions and complaints.

Value-Added Functions

Beyond considerations of how stakeholders perceive the HRIS, the organization's interests are best served by a system that adds value to various business processes. It is a common supposition in program evaluation that the ultimate criterion for any program lies in the value it provides to stakeholders. In the case of an HRIS, such value must accrue over and above what could be obtained without the HRIS, or with an alternative solution having known characteristics (e.g., whatever was used before the current HRIS was installed). Here the historical overview of HRISs (that appeared at the beginning of this chapter) provides useful context about the value-added functions of an HRIS. Specifically, early HRISs provided value to organizations by organizing records that formerly existed only in paper form and by providing reporting functions in compliance with government regulations. Current HRISs vastly supersede these basic storage and reporting functions. Many managers now see the HRIS as a critical strategic element in understanding, predicting, and controlling business processes. To a large degree, these three issues—understanding, predicting, and controlling—are a function of the degree of integration between the HRIS and other ERP systems. Although integration is not a value-added function in itself, this point underscores the importance of assessing intersystem integration (as described in the discussion of technical system functioning above).

An HRIS facilitates understanding current business processes in a variety of ways. For example, a sophisticated analysis of salary and benefits across operating units combined with financial and accounting data can provide a detailed picture of the relative efficacy of the different operating units. Thus, one value-added criterion is the utility and quality of HRIS custom reporting. On a related note, because strategic planning involves forecasting future business conditions, another value-added criterion is the historical quality of predictions contained in HRIS reports. To make this idea more concrete, consider the planning stages that preceded the opening of a facility last year. One element of those plans comprised predictions of staffing needs for the new facility. Assuming that those needs were forecast with the assistance of then-current HRIS data, a key indicator of value-added would be how well the actual staffing needs of the facility matched the predictions derived from the HRIS.

In more general terms, this example illustrates that, at its best, an HRIS provides management with support for any decisions that involve consideration of future staffing, training, re-engineering, compensation, and benefits. When reviewed retrospectively over recent time periods (i.e., 1–5 years), the quality of such decisions provides a key indicator of HRIS utility. Naturally, decision quality usually derives from a variety of factors beyond HRIS data and reporting, and it is important in evaluating an HRIS not to construe poor decisions as necessarily indicative of a poor HRIS. The inverse is less likely to hold true, however. It is rare to make good decisions consistently when informed by bad data.

An HRIS often purports to provide value-added functions to stakeholder groups other than managers. For example, the move toward self-service benefits functions attempts to provide useful services to some employees while reducing transaction costs within some HR departments. Careful analysis is warranted of whether such services simply transfer workload out of HR and into the rest of the organization. For workers within HR departments, an HRIS can also provide value-added functions by automating repetitive functions such as monthly or weekly processing cycles and report generation. Finally for line managers (i.e., individuals without strategic planning responsibilities), an HRIS can provide a variety of workgroup management functions such as performance evaluation and flexible, project-based staff placements. In some cases, the simple evidence that a value-added function has been used implies a benefit for the stakeholder. In other cases, however, a more precise and meaningful way of assessing the value of the function is through a stakeholder survey. Note that assessing value-added functions differs from previously described queries about perceived ease of use, reliability, and so forth, in that it focuses on the intrinsic value of HRIS services to particular stakeholder groups. For example, a project-based staff placement system may be easy to use, simple, and reliable, but the most important question is whether the manager feels it gives her the ability to get a new project up and running quickly and with the right mix of people.

Benchmarking and Best Practices Criteria

Benchmarking criteria do not necessarily differ from those discussed above except with regard to adjustments that make the criteria comparable across organizations. For example, in the earlier section concerning financial criteria, one gross measure that was described was the annual staff cost of maintaining the HRIS. This raw number may have meaning to managers well versed in the organization and its practices, but the number provides little basis for comparison with other organizations. As the core purpose of benchmarking is comparing performance across organizations, some adjustment must occur to make the raw financial data comparable across firms. The typical strategy is to divide cost figures by the number of employees (or full-time equivalents), by the number of new hires, or by the number of employment transactions (transfers, terminations, promotions, etc.).

Note that financial benchmarks, even when adjusted for number of full-time equivalents, may not always serve as a useful basis of comparison between organizations.

A hypothetical example illustrates this point. "ChangeCorp" has 40,000 employees working in 70 sites. Over the years, ChangeCorp has invested heavily in its information technology infrastructure and has worked hard on developing its employees' change management skills. Similarly, "SolidCo" has 42,000 employees at 60 sites. In contrast to ChangeCorp, however, SolidCo is a top-down driven organization whose employees are not as open to change as the employees of ChangeCorp. Likewise, SolidCo has not invested as strongly as ChangeCorp in maintaining and building IS infrastructure. In comparing IS installation costs of these two organizations, the difference in existing IS infrastructure, number of employees, number of locations, and so forth would normally be figured into financial assessments. However, the difference in employee acceptance of change likely would not be noted, but it would have a major impact on installation time frame and costs. It is unclear whether the resulting benchmarking comparisons would be useful for managers in either firm. At a minimum, the dissimilarity between the firms seems to potentially obscure the interpretation of the benchmarking figures.

Nonfinancial measures can be compared across organizations by examining core HRIS functions that all systems perform. For example, all large U.S. organizations work within the same framework of equal employment opportunity reporting requirements. HR departments must generate annual reports of applicant pool composition, hiring results, and so forth. Even in the most sophisticated HRIS, such reports are not entirely automatic, and thus there is always labor involved in report preparation. The labor investment for this and other common tasks can serve as the basis for comparisons across different organizations' HRISs. Likewise common data entry, editing, and processing tasks are activities accomplished by all HRISs and therefore can also be compared across organizations.

As a final note about benchmarking, a popular trend has emerged in the use of balanced scorecard measures. Such measures usually consist of a composite of financial and nonfinancial criteria scaled to a common metric and combined through weighted averaging. The resulting summary scores then rank or rate participating firms. Although the philosophy behind balanced scorecard strategies has merit—that is, including financial and nonfinancial performance in an evaluation—the measures can be problematic as a result of the scoring and scaling techniques applied to the component criteria. From a measurement standpoint, combining unlike measures into summary scores can obscure the useful variability in those scores and thus provide less information than a simple comparison of the component measures might offer. If a consulting or benchmarking firm provides a balanced scorecard, make sure that results can also be compared on the individual criteria that make up the balanced scorecard composites.

Integrating Criteria and Reporting Evaluation Results

In general, reporting results of an evaluation study of an HRIS differs little from reporting any other type of research project. The major difference is that program evaluation reports conclude with concrete recommendations for action that might not appear in typical scientific research reports. A scientific report might touch on implications, but a program evaluation results in a directive to continue a program, discontinue a program, or modify a program. With an HRIS, analogous action plans might be to keep using a particular software vendor, quit using that vendor and find a new solution, or integrate the HRIS in some new way with other elements of the ERP system. Aside from inclusion of extensive action plans, evaluation reports must always contain the standard elements of a research report: abstract or executive summary; introductory material; a description of research methods, including measurement techniques and descriptions of who participated in the evaluation; and a description and discussion of the results obtained.

This latter element provides the most substantial challenge to most evaluators because of the complexity of interpreting a complex set of results for the wide variety of audiences—from programmers to board members—that may read the report. Although a complete discussion of this topic is beyond the scope of this chapter, we offer several points we consider important. First, we cannot overstress the importance of understanding the value systems at work in the host organization. Each organization has a unique and distinctive culture that comprises sets of valued perspectives, goals, and end states. Of particular relevance to the evaluation of HRISs and other ISs, some organizations value technical sophistication, others value financial analysis, and still others care strongly about impacts on people—particularly internal and external customers. Whatever the organization values, the synthesis of evidence that occurs in a report must reflect that value system if the report's message is to be properly understood by the audience.

Next, it is critical to balance the reporting of HRIS strengths and weaknesses. Failures are ubiquitous in the area of IS development, but failures are rarely so complete that there is nothing to be learned or no benefit to be salvaged from the wreckage. Conversely, even the most successful implementation of an HRIS contains flaws that can be rectified. Further, success is fleeting: Changing business conditions require upgrades and improvements to an HRIS that a successful evaluation report can help to shape and clarify. Thus, any successful evaluation report carefully balances critiques and kudos to ensure that the organization can build on current HRIS strengths and address areas in need of further development.

As a final recommendation, we suggest avoiding the temptation to oversimplify or homogenize the interpretation of the evaluation's results. In an earlier section, we stressed the importance of collecting data on multiple criteria and allowing for some degree of overlap among criteria. If one follows this approach, it is not uncommon to obtain some results that appear contradictory. Rather than whitewashing such contradictions, we suggest using them as a way of highlighting the complexity of ISs and the multiple perspectives that different stakeholders may take in the evaluation of an HRIS and other ISs. The concerns we expressed about balanced scorecard systems are apropos here as well. Competent HRIS program evaluation is best served by reporting and helping readers to understand the complexity of an HRIS, rather than by hiding the complexity and assuming that one's strategy for doing so is appropriate. In essence, then, we suggest that an HRIS evaluation should educate decision makers about the status of a system and its stakeholders to a sufficient degree that they can understand and make choices among the possible action plans that follow the evaluation's completion.

As the adoption of ERP systems continues to increase the level of technology integration in medium and large organizations, we expect that the importance of effective HRIS functioning will increase for managers, employees, and other stakeholders. At the same time, the complexity of HRIS will grow as more firms operate in the distributed, global business environment that the diffusion of the Internet and other globalization forces create. Taken together, these two trends suggest that regular and rigorous program evaluations of HRISs (and other ERP modules) will provide an increasingly critical ingredient in overall business effectiveness.

Note

1. Customizable software systems provide users with functions that suit their particular needs, but such customizations also tend to vastly increase support costs because of the emergence of hidden defects, incompatibilities, and other problems that are introduced by customization.

References

Bancroft, N. H., Seip, H., & Sprengel, A. (1998). *Implementing SAP R/3: How to introduce a large system into a large organization.* Greenwich, CT: Manning.

Bilbrey, D. (1999). *Peoplesoft administrator's guide.* San Francisco: Sybex.

Blain, J., & Dodd, B. (1999). *Administering SAP R/3: The HR-human resources module.* Indianapolis, IN: Que.

Clarke, A. (1999). *Evaluation research: An introduction to principles, methods, and practice.* London: Sage.

Remenyi, D. (1999). *IT investment: Making a business case.* Oxford: Butterworth Heinemann.

Thierauf, R. J. (1994). *Effective management and evaluation of information technology.* Westport, CT: Quorum.

Walker, A. J. (1993). *Handbook of human resource information systems: Reshaping the human resource function with technology.* New York: McGraw-Hill.

Suggested Readings in HRIS Program Evaluation

Boulmetis, J., & Dutwin, P. (2000). *The ABCs of evaluation: Timeless techniques for program and project managers.* San Francisco: Jossey-Bass.

Davenport, T. H. (2000). *Mission critical: Realizing the promise of enterprise systems.* Boston: Harvard Business School Press.

Web Resources

- American Productivity and Quality Center (www.apqc.org)
- Balanced Scorecard Institute (www.balancedscorecard.org)

- Human Resources Benchmarking Association (www.hrba.org)
- International Association for Human Resource Information Management (www.ihrim.org)
- ISWORLD: Reference database of IS survey instruments (www.ucalgary.ca/~newsted/constructs.htm; or www.isworld.org/isworld/ isworldtext.html)

CHAPTER 24

Global Human Resource Metrics

Helen De Cieri

John W. Boudreau

What is the logic underlying global human resources (HR) measurement in your organization? In your organization, do you measure the contribution of global HR programs to organizational performance? Do you know the most competitive employee mix—that is, the proportion of expatriates versus local employees, for your business units? (How) do you measure the cost and value of the different types of international work performed by your employees?

In the globalized economy, organizations increasingly derive value from human resources, or *talent* as we shall also use the term here (Boudreau, Ramstad, & Dowling, in press). The strategic importance of the workforce makes decisions about talent critical to organizational success. Informed decisions about talent require a strategic approach to measurement. However, measures alone are not sufficient, for measures without logic can create information overload, and decision quality rests in substantial part on the quality of measurements. An important element of enhanced global competitiveness is a measurement model for talent that articulates the connections between people and success, as well as the context and boundary conditions that affect those connections.

This chapter proposes a framework within which existing and potential global HR measures can be organized and understood. The framework reflects the premise that measures exist to support and enhance decisions, and that strategic decisions require a logical connection between decisions about resources, such as talent, and the key organizational outcomes affected by those decisions. Such a framework may provide a useful mental model for both designers and users of HR measures.

We illustrate how this framework can be applied by using a range of practical measurement examples. While our analysis is supported by examples of practical applications drawn from survey reports and interviews with key managers in several multinational companies, our key sources are these:

- Cargill, Incorporated, an international marketer, processor, and distributor of agricultural, food, financial, and industrial products and services with 97,000 employees in 59 countries.
- *Global Relocation Trends 2001 Survey Report* (2002) sponsored by GMAC Global Relocation Services, National Foreign Trade Council (NFTC), and SHRM Global Forum. Respondents to this survey were 150 HR executives, 83% of whom were employed in multinational enterprises with U.S. headquarters.

Talentship: A Decision Science for HR

HR metrics are often evaluated by asking clients and key decision makers for their opinions about measures. This is in stark contrast to the approach taken in fields such as finance, in which the focus is on the key organizational outcomes of the measures. This is not to argue against the possible use of subjective judgments, attitudes, and even nonquantitative measures in HR. We acknowledge that more mature and organizationally powerful decision sciences such as finance, marketing, and operations management rely on some "soft" measures and that they are not immune from subjectivity and alternative interpretations. However, it is important that the field of HR avoid accepting virtually any measurement method, criterion, and stakeholder perspective that someone feels might be useful. To do so would create measurement systems with less credibility and value. Rather, we are suggesting that HR measurement strive to reflect a deep and logical connection between talent and key organizational outcomes, just as finance does for monetary resources and marketing does for customer resources.

Recognizing that a significant future challenge for global organizations will be to develop and enhance their ability to link talent to global strategic success, Boudreau et al. (in press) have proposed that it is necessary to fully develop a decision science for global talent. This requires models that are logical, rich, and relevant for understanding talent. The complexity in the people side of decision making is due in part to the absence of a model for organizing measurement. The field of HR management needs to develop a decision science or model to support decisions about people.

Boudreau and Ramstad (see 2002a, 2002b) coined the term *talentship* to refer to this emerging decision science, capturing the distinction between the decision science of talent and the professional practice of HR management. Talentship is to HR as finance is to accounting and as marketing is to sales. Talentship is the decision science that improves organizational performance by enhancing decisions that affect or depend on people. Talentship builds on HR management practices and measures, and goes further to create a framework of tools that enhances decisions. These decisions may cover a broad range of areas, such as individual choices about whether to take an international assignment as a development opportunity or global HR policies about decisions for international career development (Boudreau & Ramstad, 2002a; Boudreau et al., in press).

It is well recognized by academics and practitioners in the accounting and management fields that in the new economy, traditional corporate measurement systems must include measurement of intangible assets (Boudreau & Ramstad, 2002a). In the field of strategic HR management, scholars (e.g., Boudreau, 1998; Boudreau & Ramstad, 2002a) have noted the importance of understanding the value of talent. We propose here that such logic is essential to understanding, building, and using global HR measurements.

HR professionals need to adopt a framework for metrics of human performance that will enable effective decisions to be made regarding people and success in organizations. Boudreau and Ramstad (2002a) viewed this as essential for the success of any HR measurement system. Measurement of global HR should enable the HR function to create and manage HR interventions to achieve outcomes for the organization, customers, and employees. Further, the HR interventions need to be evaluated by objective metrics. Such a transformative process is a necessary element for elevating the HR function to an equal footing with other functional areas of the multinational enterprise[1] (MNE) and develops the long-term support within the organization for HR policies and practices that are evidence based and scientifically evaluated (Boudreau & Ramstad, 1997; Murphy & Zandvakili, 2000).

A Strategic Approach to the Measurement of Global HR

MNEs face many complex HR issues and sometimes conflicting pressures for global integration and local differentiation (Schuler, Dowling, & De Cieri, 1993). For MNEs, there are specific and unique challenges related to the development of talent as part of a strategic approach to HR. Achieving a balance between global coordination (integration) and local responsiveness (differentiation) is important. This balance may vary depending on the strategic context, resources and processes, and pivotal talent that are relevant in a particular situation (Boudreau et al., in press).

Global HR typically includes all HR programs conducted in MNEs across national borders. These may include global shared services, worldwide training programs, expatriation programs, and so on. Research and practice in global HR has largely focused on the management of expatriation, although there is increasing recognition of the need for strategic decision making about global HR (see Dowling, Welch, & Schuler, 1999). Global HR management requires a flexible measurement framework to fit a great variety of situations, because managing across national boundaries requires attention to and measurement of additional context and boundary conditions.

The involvement of HR managers in strategic decision making is important. However, research in MNEs has noted that leaders of non-HR functions may be reluctant to include the global HR function in strategic decisions, arguing that HR specialists often complicated decision making (Stroh & Caligiuri, 1998). Although making decisions relating to people is difficult and complex, this aspect of decision making is critical and it is likely to affect not only HR policies and practices but overall organizational performance as well. We argue that there is an imperative for global leaders to rigorously incorporate talent into their strategic planning and decisions. For HR to contribute to that process requires sophisticated measures that are clearly and logically linked to the key competitive concerns of strategic leaders, business managers, and key constituents.

Three key challenges are important for the measurement of global HR programs:

■ *Global-local balance.* MNE management must focus simultaneously on global performance (the whole of the MNE) *and* subsidiary or regional performance (the parts). MNEs require generic measures that make sense across global operations, complemented by specific measures able to detect subtle differences among locations.

■ *Comparability of data.* Performance evaluation data obtained from one subsidiary/region may not be comparable with that obtained from another because of local differences. It is important to decide which data are comparable and which are unique.

■ *Geographic dispersion.* Separation by time and distance complicates judgments about the degree of fit between subsidiary performance and the long-term strategy of the MNE. With regard to global HR, distance may hamper connections between HR programs and organizational performance or even prevent such connections from being made. MNEs require measures that are not only financial; a balance between long- and short-term orientation, rather than a short-term focus on profits, may be required.

A Model for Global HR Metrics

A well thought-out framework for measurement acts as both a guide and a benchmark for evaluating the contribution of the organization's talent to strategy implementation (Becker, Huselid, & Ulrich, 2001; Stroh & Caligiuri, 1998) and provides a valid and systematic justification for resource allocation decisions. We advocate a strategic mental model that provides an actionable logic (Boudreau, Dunford, &

Ramstad, 2000) to analyze relationships between talent and the global context for MNEs, as shown in Figure 24.1. Our framework identifies the links between the external and organizational (i.e., internal) context for MNEs, the central linking elements related to talent, and MNE concerns and goals. This model should enhance our ability to address questions such as these: Which HR approach is most appropriate to deal with the dynamic and volatile industry, as well as national and regional contexts encountered by MNEs? Which HR approach is most appropriate to optimize the strategic circumstances of MNEs? In posing such questions, we are mindful that it is inappropriate to simplify the nature of HR investments and suggest that there exists a single optimal HR architecture for managing all employees worldwide. Instead, HR investment will vary according to different business needs and subsidiaries may have a variety of different strategies within the parent company (Lepak & Snell, 1999). This is precisely the reason that a general template should be more useful than any single measurement approach. Given the complexity and diversity of issues in global HR, there is a need for an approach to measurement that provides a useful generic framework, but one that can be customized to reflect the particular measurement and business logic of the appropriate business unit, industry, or regional context.

Our framework as shown in Figure 24.1 integrates two models: the Strategic HR in MNEs model (De Cieri & Dowling, 1999) and the HC BRidge™ Model[2] (Boudreau & Ramstad, 2002a). Figure 24.1 shows the linking elements of the HC BRidge Model combined with the contextual elements of strategic HR in MNEs. The resulting framework shows the external and organizational (i.e., internal) factors that impact talent in MNEs, as well as the often conflicting pressures for global coordination (integration) and local responsiveness (differentiation). Identifying the links to MNE concerns and goals, or execution, is often a challenging task for strategic HR but nonetheless important. It is important to acknowledge that our model provides a somewhat simplified representation of the dynamic inter-relationships between the elements shown in these various boxes. For example, "industry characteristics" (an external factor) also are a core aspect of sustainable strategic success (a linking element). Similarly, "inter-organizational networks" and "MNE structure" (organizational factors) may be viewed as global versions of the linking element "talent pools and structures."

The logic underlying our framework should help global HR managers to identify enhanced measurement opportunities or synergies across the various boxes shown in the framework. With this logic, MNEs should be able to identify gaps in their measurement approaches and develop a systematic approach that enables strategic connections to be made. In several of the MNEs investigated for this chapter, various elements of global HR are measured, but in a piecemeal or unconnected way. For example, a vast array of measures may be used to determine the efficiency of expatriation, yet the MNE may lack the measures, or the connections, for other elements, such as intra-organizational networks or aligned actions.

To support and elaborate on the decision model of Figure 24.1, Table 24.1 provides a list of illustrative metrics that may be utilized for global HR. In the following sections, we outline the elements of this model and describe how this model can be

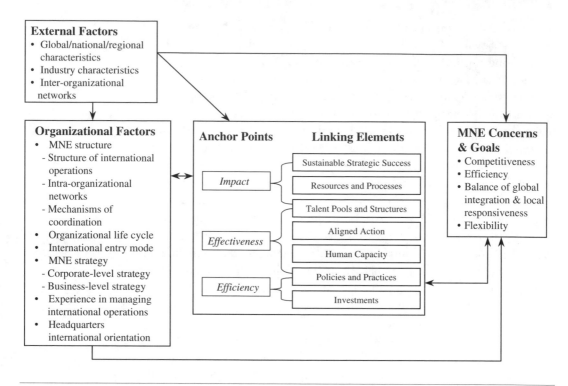

Figure 24.1   Global HR Model, incorporating the HC BRidge™ Model

SOURCE: Adapted from Boudreau, J. W. 2000. *Global Strategic Success through Human Capital Value,* CAHRS, Cornell University, NY. Reprinted with permission.

applied, using the metrics shown in Table 24.1. Our aim is to provide examples that will assist organizations and HR professionals to understand the challenges facing global HR and to develop knowledge of the analytical tools that may be used.

The metrics shown in Table 24.1 are drawn from the wide array of possible approaches available for measuring global HR elements. We have selected measures that appear to have the greatest applicability to global HR elements. These include traditional evaluation of HR programs, utility analysis, financial efficiency measures of HR operations, benchmark surveys, HR activity and best practice indices, the balanced scorecard, and financial statement augmentation. This is not an exhaustive list of metrics. For a more detailed discussion of the growing array of alternative measurement tools available to organizational decision makers, see Boudreau and Ramstad (2002a). Each approach may be useful for different purposes or circumstances; each has advantages and disadvantages.

Still, not every measurement approach is equally effective and appropriate for all situations. Recognizing that there is no "one best way" should not abdicate the obligation of HR scholars and leaders to build and use measures that effectively identify and enhance the key strategic talent decisions (Boudreau & Ramstad, 2002b). Thus, Figure 24.1 and Table 24.1 provide not only a measurement taxonomy but, we hope, a point of departure for further enhancements to the logic underlying those measures and their ability to articulate the key strategic connections. Only through

(*Text continues on page 502*)

Table 24.1 Illustrative Measures of Global HR

Elements of Global HR	*Illustrative Measures*
External Factors	
• **Global/national/regional characteristics**	Benchmark survey, statistical databases, intelligence reports, legislation for
• Political	• government instability
• Social	• changing social values
• Economic	• inflation, recession
• Technological	• Internet capabilities
• Legal	• equal opportunity legislation
• Environmental	• environmental hazards
• **Industry characteristics**	
• Industry size	• Number of competitors
• Industry life cycle stage	• Size (sales) of competitors
• Factors influencing profitability	• Market maturity
• Changing players in the market (e.g., new entrants)	• Projections of market growth or decline
	• Relative pricing power and margins
	• Financial capital migration
• **Inter-organizational networks**	
• Network relationships	• Extent of trust among network members
• Human and social capital	• Quality, type, and quantity of network relationships
	• Importance of the network to each partner organization
	• Extent of communication and knowledge sharing among network members
Organizational Factors	
• **MNE structure**	
• Structure of international operations	• Extent of inefficiency and duplication across business units
• Intra-organizational networks	• Extent of interdependence among business units
• Mechanisms of coordination	• Extent of business units' reliance on headquarters
	• Trust, quality, type, and quantity of relationships among organizational units
	• Extent of communication and knowledge sharing among network members
	• Extent of bureaucratic vs. cultural controls
• **Organizational life cycle stage**	
	• Age of organization
	• Age of products
• **International entry mode**	
	• Extent of control in joint ventures
	• Percentage of firm ownership in joint ventures

(Continued)

Table 24.1 Continued

Elements of Global HR	Illustrative Measures
	• Percentage of joint venture managers who are expatriates • Number of local vs. expatriate employees
• **MNE strategy** • Corporate-level strategy • Business-level strategy	• Organizational global or multidomestic capabilities • Quality (e.g., relative number of service and product failures compared to competitors, percentage of global units achieving ISO or other quality certifications, total global and regional budgets for training in quality processes) • Cost leadership (e.g., cost controls, reduction of input costs, cost of materials and labor, operating efficiency) • Innovation (e.g., new product development, extent of research and development activity) • Speed (e.g., time for product/service to reach markets) • Customer responsiveness (e.g., product/ service customization for local markets) • Constituent relations (e.g., maintenance of relationships with regulatory agencies)
• **Experience in managing international operations**	• MNE experience in international business (e.g., years of operation by region or country, the historical proportion of manufacturing, service and sales by region or country) • Senior management years of prior experience in international business (e.g., length of service of senior management by countries or regions) • Managerial competencies such as flexibility, openness, and cultural sensitivity
• **Headquarters international orientation**	• Extent of ethnocentrism • Headquarters corporate culture maintained in foreign units • Proportion of non parent-country managers achieving headquarters positions, • Number of specific regional innovations adopted by headquarters for application throughout the world

Elements of Global HR	Illustrative Measures
Linking Elements	
• **Impact**	
• Sustainable strategic success	• Stock price
	• Earning per share
	• Economic value added
	• Growth (sales, earning, and employees)
	• Ratings of managers' leadership and talent management capability
• Resources and processes	• New products
	• Brand awareness
	• Supply-chain analysis
	• Speed
	• Cycle time
	• Balanced scorecard
	• Service processes
	• Total quality
• Talent pools and structures	• Results of performance differences (e.g., sales and delays)
	• Customer satisfaction with employee service
	• Performance, perceptions by constituents and, number of key constituent contacts of employees in the talent pool
	• Number of employees in the talent pool
• **Effectiveness**	
• Aligned action	• Expatriates' and repatriates' acquisition and diffusion of knowledge across the MNE
	• Performance ratings
	• Monitoring against objectives
	• Behavioral feedback
	• Customer reports
• Human capacity	• Capability (competencies, skills, test scores, certifications)
	• Opportunity (territory potential, customer contacts, reporting relationships, new markets/products)
	• Motivation (pay-performance relationships, pay-performance awareness, shared values and commitment, "fit" of needs and rewards)
	• Changes in attitudes among expatriates
	• Expatriate job satisfaction
• **Efficiency**	
• Policies and Practices	• Audits of HR programs
	• Index of the number of HR practices
	• Benchmark HR practices against leaders

(Continued)

Table 24.1 Continued

Elements of Global HR	Illustrative Measures
• Investments	• Time to fill positions • Cost per recruitment advertisement • Benefit cost per headcount • HR staff per total staff • Expatriate assignment costs • Expatriate training costs • Expatriate and repatriate retention/attrition rates • Vendor cost per month for outsourced activities
• **MNE concerns and goals** • **Competitiveness** • **Efficiency**	• Market share • Benchmark organizational performance against leaders • Extent and outcomes of global project teamwork
• **Balance of global integration & local responsiveness** • **Flexibility**	• Response time for decision making • Capability to switch production across locations

such logical frameworks can we hope to guide the HR field toward improved measurement, not simply more measures.

External Factors Influencing Global HR Metrics

The first box in Figure 24.1 shows that there is a wide range of external factors that are important influences for global HR measurement. These include global, national, and regional characteristics; industry characteristics; and inter-organizational networks. Metrics for each of these factors are listed in Table 24.1.

With regard to *global, national,* or *regional characteristics,* a wide array of data pertaining to political, social, economic, and technological factors is available for MNEs to collect and analyze. Measurement of these external factors may be conducted in several ways, including benchmark surveys of national social conditions, such as surveys of employment practices, consumer preferences, or social values. Government reports, nongovernmental organization (NGO) reports, and expert consultancy reports are major sources of political and economic intelligence. For example, the International Programme on the Elimination of Child Labour (IPEC), initiated by the International Labour Organization, is a 90-country alliance against child labor. A wide range of NGOs throughout the world work actively with IPEC, on activities including development and maintenance of statistical databases, sets of good management practices and manuals, guidelines, and training materials. Another useful source of information is the A. T. Kearney/*Foreign Policy Magazine* Globalization Index, which attempts to measure the impact of globalization in 50 developed countries and key emerging markets worldwide. At a national or regional level, detailed information is essential for investment and performance decisions. For example, political risk analysis calculates the relative risk of elements such as political instability in a given country or region. Many MNEs utilize the services of external vendors who collate information from various sources and provide reports to the MNE on locations of interest. One of the MNE managers interviewed explained that her company uses an external vendor in conjunction with analysis provided by local management and an in-house risk assessment unit; this MNE has substantial numbers of employees in volatile locations.

Analysis of external factors has numerous implications for global HR management. For example, many MNEs provide salary premiums to expatriate employees on assignment in volatile locations; decisions about salary premiums rely upon accurate information about the location. Any MNE with plans for investment in Indonesia would need to evaluate the political risk associated with government instability, civil unrest, violence, and threats of balkanization. Several MNEs, concerned about security and corruption, have abandoned Indonesian operations.

Industry characteristics may be measured using collection and analysis of information about factors such as key competitors and potential market share, supplier relationships, and customer perspectives. Industry analysis seeks to identify and understand the forces that influence the industry, such as the industry size and life cycle stage, factors influencing profitability, and changing players in the market (such as new entrants). For MNEs, industry analysis may need to include several levels: local (parent and host country), national, regional, and global industry levels. Industry surveys (for example, see *Breaking New Ground*, 2002) and competitor intelligence reports can be used to gather metrics such as the number and size of competitors, market maturity, projections for market growth or decline, relative pricing power and margins, and financial capital migration.

Inter-organizational networks may be complex relationship webs that are difficult to analyze and measure. Inter-organizational networks may be based upon personal relationships and trust; nonbinding social contracts that may be, nevertheless, long-term, pervasive, and strong in nature. Networks may include parent country managers and employees, host country managers and employees, host country governments, and investors. At the core of network management is an emphasis on talent that must recognize that knowledge, power, perceived trustworthiness, expertise, and social bonds are often person-specific rather than organization-specific. Measures for networks include collection and analysis of HR data using methods such as questionnaires, interviews, and behavioral observation. There is a wide array of measures for knowledge that could be utilized in networks, relevant to the stock or flow of knowledge and to enabling processes related to the knowledge stock or flow (Boudreau, in press). Human and social capital data to be collected may include elements such as the level of trust between network members; quality, type, and quantity of relationships; and the importance of the network to each member organization. These metrics can be utilized as part of a global HR measurement framework.

For example, the International Network for Acid Prevention (INAP) brings together mining companies that wish to work collaboratively to reduce the impact of acid drainage, a significant environmental issue in the global mining industry. A key measure of networking for INAP is the maintenance of communication programs, including a Web site to facilitate knowledge sharing and networking activities on specific research projects. Outcomes credited to knowledge sharing in the network member organizations since the inception of INAP in 1998 include cost savings in millions of dollars. Referring back to Figure 24.1, this knowledge sharing may also be viewed as a global version of the linking element "human capacity," because it utilizes employees' capability and opportunity for networking.

Organizational Factors Influencing HR in MNEs

Organizational factors refer to characteristics that are outside the HR area but may also have important influences on the MNE's global HR. Several methods may be used to measure these factors, and such measures can be developed to work within a global HR measurement framework.

MNE structure may influence global HR in several ways, particularly via the way in which *international operations* are structured. For example, the level of decision making in the MNE is an important consideration. Decision making centralized at corporate headquarters may lead to outcomes quite different from decisions devolved to business units. The structural relationships between business units, including the extent of duplication or interdependence, may be important metrics. *Intra-organizational networks* may be subject to the same conditions as those networks external to the MNE. Again, important characteristics include the trust between network members; quality, type, and quantity of relationships; and communication and knowledge sharing between network members. Metrics to assess the *mechanisms of coordination* may vary from highly formalized bureaucratic rules to cultural norms entrenched via socialization of employees to the organizational culture.

Models of *organizational life cycle stages* vary, but in general, the life cycle of a typical organization is argued to comprise four identifiable although possibly overlapping stages: birth, growth, maturity, and decline (and/or revival). Theory and research indicate that the organizational life cycle stage will be an important influence on HR practices (see, for example, Milliman, Von Glinow, & Nathan, 1991). Organizational life cycle stages may be measured by examining the organizational age, the age of key products/services, and projections for organizational growth or decline.

International entry mode, also known as the mode of foreign market service, has been examined extensively by researchers and practitioners. The evidence shows that green-field (new) operations take longer than acquisitions or joint ventures to provide a financial return on investment. In the long term, surviving green-field operations outperform the other modes. Recent research suggests, however, that the opportunities for transfer of knowledge and learning in international joint ventures may provide an HR benefit beyond the outcomes achievable in green-fields or acquisitions. Examples of measures related to international entry mode include the extent of ownership or control in a joint venture, the percentage of joint venture managers who are expatriates, or the number of local versus expatriate employees.

MNE strategy may be measured in several ways. First, the approach to global markets may be explored by assessing the organization's capability for global integration or multidomestic differentiation. Are business decisions made with a local focus or does the organization think globally for every decision? Second, the source of sustainable strategic success may be measured, for example, with metrics for dimensions of differentiation. Traditional dimensions of differentiation include price quality, innovation, speed, or customer responsiveness, but differentiation may also encompass dimensions such as relationships with key constituents or distribution and support functions (Boudreau et al., 2000).

Research has indicated that the extent of *international business experience* held by the managers, measured by their years of international experience and their level of cross-cultural competencies, will be positively correlated with MNE organizational success (Dowling et al., 1999). Examples of possible measures include the MNE's years of operation by region or country, the MNE's historical proportion of manufacturing, service, and sales by region or country, and the length of service of senior management by countries or regions. Also, managerial competencies such as flexibility, openness, and cultural sensitivity will enhance global organizational performance (Dowling et al., 1999).

Further, the *international orientation of MNE headquarters* can have important implications for HR practices and global performance. In particular, ethnocentrism in the headquarters orientation and among senior management in MNEs, reinforced by dissemination of a strong headquarters culture, has been shown to be associated with poorer global organizational performance (Caligiuri & Stroh, 1995). Examples of specific measures for headquarters' international orientation include the proportion of nonparent country nationals employed in headquarters management positions or the number of regional innovations adopted by headquarters for application throughout the world. Typical of the situation in many MNEs, a global HR manager in a U.S.-based MNE explained that the company is "U.S.-centric but it is well-recognized that expatriate assignments are an important and strategic part of career development." Some MNEs have moved to reinforce this in HR policies and practices. For example, Daimler Chrysler's strategy to develop global leaders at senior levels of the organization includes a "2×2×2" policy: a requirement that executives speak at least two languages, have worked in at least two of the 12 business units, and have worked in at least two countries. Beyond this, "soft skills" such as flexibility and openness are deemed to be essential for managers in a global context. These measures have interesting potential for applications to global leadership; perhaps items such as knowledge of languages, countries, and business units, combined with a selection of soft skills might form the basis of an index for global leadership, which could be customized for a particular MNE's requirements.

Linking Elements

The central part of Figure 24.1 shows the HC BRidge Model (Boudreau et al., 2000; Boudreau & Ramstad, 2002a), which articulates the seven links between contextual elements (external and organizational factors) and organizational performance outcomes. The seven linking elements are anchored by three points: impact, effectiveness, and efficiency. In the sections below we present illustrative metrics for these linking elements and analyze the advantages and disadvantages of the various approaches underlying the metrics.

Impact

The upper three elements of the HC BRidge Model—sustainable strategic success, resources and processes, and talent pools and structures—comprise the impact section of the framework. *Sustainable strategic success* refers to competitive advantage as well as success factors such as corporate social responsibility. As shown in Table 24.1, sustainable strategic success can be measured by stock price, earning per share, economic value added, or growth figures reported in financial statements. In addition, financial statements can be augmented with managers' reports of intangible assets. For example, the annual reports of many MNEs include at least some reporting of assets like the leadership and talent management capabilities of their managers. This emphasis on intangible assets should not only focus on management, but rather should include all employees, to develop a global "line of sight," which encourages recognition of how individual employee behaviors relate to the strategic objectives of the organization (Boudreau & Ramstad, 2002a).

Although the financial statement augmentation approach may be appealing to financial analysts and perhaps to shareholders, there are significant limitations. First, there is no generally accepted method of reporting HR investments. Second, as the focus is usually on firm-level numbers, the difficulties of developing financial reporting for global HR programs may be substantial and this approach is likely to be limited in its ability to inform decisions about HR investments. Finally, this approach reveals little about the decision-making logic underlying the connections between HR investments and outcomes (Boudreau & Ramstad, 2002a).

Resources and processes are the transformation elements that enable an organization to add value (see Boudreau et al., in press, for more detail). Resources and processes can be measured by new products, brand awareness, supply-chain analysis, speed, cycle time, service processes, and total quality. The balanced scorecard can provide a tool to measure several of the linking elements, particularly with regard to impact elements such as resources and processes. This approach seeks to measure how the organization or the HR function meets objectives in four areas: customers, financial markets, internal processes, and learning and growth. Cargill uses an adaptation of the balanced scorecard throughout their operations worldwide. Boudreau and Ramstad (2002a) pointed out that a vast array of global HR measures could be categorized into the balanced scorecard and a key benefit is that this approach is well known to many managers. There is also potential for flexibility, as software can allow users to "drill" or "cut" HR measures to support their own analysis questions. A potential concern with the balanced scorecard, however, is that naïve users may misinterpret or misanalyze the information (see Boudreau & Ramstad, 2002b).

The term *talent pools and structures,* rather than jobs, is used to focus on contribution rather than administration (Boudreau & Ramstad, 2002a, 2002b). Measures of talent pools may include constituent relations or customer satisfaction with employee service. For example, the maintenance of positive relations with local government or other officials is an important process for many MNEs. The maintenance role may reside in no one individual but may encompass local managers and employees with personal contact, as well as those formally assigned the jobs of negotiating and maintaining such relationships. Measures may include the performance, perceptions by constituents, and number of key constituent contacts of these individuals. Even though there may be no particular "job" of government relations, these employees comprise a talent pool whose work collectively (and perhaps collaboratively) affects government and constituent relations.

Effectiveness

Effectiveness articulates how HR policies and practices connect to changes in the aligned actions of the talent pools. Aligned actions refer to the behaviors of those in the pivotal talent pools that make the largest difference in the elements of competitive success. For example, employees undertaking expatriation assignments or short-term forms of international work acquire knowledge to be diffused throughout the MNE (Kamoche, 1996). Measures for these aligned actions include performance reviews, behavioral feedback, and customer reports. Boudreau et al. (in press) provide a detailed example of pre-sales engineers who were identified as key mediators in relationships between engineers in one country and salespeople in the United States, even though their job description might not have included that aligned action. Recognition and measurement of the pivotal contribution of the pre-sales engineers had several implications, such as the strategic justification for HR investments (e.g., development and reward programs) to enhance their actions as "diplomats" in their organization.

The *Global Relocation Trends 2001 Survey* (2002) found that to save expatriation costs (particularly for U.S. expatriates) companies increasingly rely on short-term expatriate assignments and use those assignments for development purposes. Measured in terms of cost savings and the amount of time of expatriate experience created, this appears sound. However, it is frequently the long-term expatriates who exhibit the aligned action of sharing their acquired knowledge and experience throughout the MNE, because longer-term expatriates not only have greater experience but also more status within the organization. Measures that specifically focus on this sort of information sharing behavior are required to clearly evaluate these trade-offs.

Effectiveness also links changes in the key talent pools and structures to *human capacity,* including the impact of HR interventions on the capability, opportunity, and motivation necessary to support aligned actions. Measures of capability may include competencies, such as test scores or skill acquisition. Measures of opportunity include territory potential or customer relationships. Motivation may be measured by attitude surveys, organizational values shared by employees, or perceived "fit" between employee needs and their rewards. Potential measures for expatriate management might include changes in attitudes among expatriates or expatriate job satisfaction.

The effectiveness area includes many elements of utility analysis measurement for HR programs, which requires assessments of variables such as knowledge, skills, and performance transformed into dollar values and offset with estimated costs (Boudreau, 1991; Boudreau & Ramstad, 2002a).

Utility analysis provides a wide array of possible approaches for estimating the possible returns on HR program investments. This approach to analysis provides useful logic and rigor. A criticism of utility analysis, however, is that the complexity and assumptions may reduce its credibility and usefulness in applications to global HR programs (Boudreau & Ramstad, 2002a).

Efficiency

The resources expended in managing the impact and effectiveness of global HR are linked to the resulting HR *policies and practices* and *investments* via the efficiency anchor. Although many traditional HR measurement approaches concentrate primarily on efficiency measures, and these are useful, they must be embedded within the context of impact and effectiveness to avoid misinterpretation. For example, calculation of the cost of sending one expatriate on assignment must be considered in the organizational context. It has been estimated that a three-year expatriate assignment may cost US$1 million or more for an employee with a base salary of US$75,000 to US$100,000. Besides salary, additional direct costs may include housing allowance, cost of living allowances, education costs for children, home leave, shipping or storage of household goods, host country taxes, hardship premiums, danger pay, mobility allowances, and income taxes. Indirect costs may include changes to organizational and client relationships or changes for the expatriate's family members, such as disruption of a spouse's career. Further, "expatriate failure" or premature return of an expatriate is a potentially high-cost problem, with direct costs such as replacement expenses and indirect costs such as loss of market share and damaged international relationships (Dowling et al., 1999). What are the alternatives? What value will be created through this assignment? How can expatriate assignments be best managed to achieve optimal outcomes, for individuals and the MNE?

Of course, a complete answer to these questions awaits further research, but we would propose that organizations that focus solely on expatriate costs may well overlook significant potential value and either underutilize expatriates or deploy them improperly. For example, expatriate costs can likely be minimized by using the least expensive assignments, keeping them of short duration, and taking few risks of potential client or operations damage from poor performance. However, our framework suggests a more systematic view that would pose questions and attempt to measure connections between expatriate practices and the human capacity, aligned action, contribution to key talent pools linked to core processes and resources, and eventually to sustainable strategic success. For example, if organizations desire to build competitive success in environments where long-run relationships are key and to develop leaders who have learned to operate in environments of high importance and significant potential, it may well be that expatriate assignments to "hardship" (and thus expensive) locations, of longer duration, and specifically targeted to high-risk and high-return situations may be precisely the way to build the necessary human capacity for the future. This sort of logic is often hinted at but seldom articulated in detail and even more rarely measured. We would suggest that a measurement framework such as that developed here may be a starting point to more complete analysis for decisions such as expatriation.

Measures for *policies and practices* have relied to some extent on HR activity and best practice indices, which measure the association between a collection of HR activities and changes in organizational outcomes such as profits and shareholder value creation (Becker & Huselid, 1998; Cappelli & Neumark, 2001). In terms of Figure 24.1, HR activity and best practice indices aim to link the *policies and practices* element with *sustainable strategic success.*

The best practice approach has been adopted in many MNEs. The focus has tended to be on specific HR activities, testing for relationships with specific actions and performance outcomes. For example, Caligiuri and Stroh's (1995) study of HR executives in 60 MNEs found the most successful companies had HR functions that performed better in three areas: developing global leadership through cross-cultural assignments, making HR a strategic partner in global business, and ensuring flexibility in all HR programs and processes. Their analysis suggested a positive relationship between the financial success of an organization and its HR performance in these three areas.

Although HR activity and best practice indices may provide a more direct approach than utility analysis, Boudreau and Ramstad (2002a) pointed out that the research results for this approach should be treated with caution, as the causal mechanisms and direction of relationships may be unclear. This lack of clarity may lead to incorrect conclusions or actions.

Cargill administers to all employees an annual global HR survey of over 100 items related to HR policies and practices. This measure enables correlation of global HR policies and practices with organizational performance and identifies national differences in the policies and practices that predict organizational performance. Annual data collection and analysis in an organization of over 90,000 employees worldwide is a substantial undertaking. Their findings indicate that some 9% of the variance in global organizational performance is explained by HR programs. Although this figure represents a small proportion of the total, the organization's efforts are noteworthy, given the complex linkages between HR practice and organizational performance. Referring again to Figure 24.1, we note that such measurements also provide a useful platform for the intermediate linking elements between HR practices and financial outcomes.

Measures for *investments* have relied to some extent on traditional evaluation of HR programs. Although this has potential to provide a rich source of information on program effects, statistical results may not be easily translated into organizational goals. To utilize expatriation management as an example, many MNEs focus their HR efforts on the technical management of expatriates rather than encompassing strategic implications of expatriation. Hence, their expatriate HR measures focus on expatriate relocation costs such as housing, compensation and benefits, and family allowances. The most commonly used measures appear to be limited to the costs of expatriate selection, pre-departure training, and expatriate allowances and benefits—in sum, a restricted range of expatriate HR program elements are evaluated, if at all. Despite the substantial investment required for expatriation, surveys indicate a lack of measurement of expatriate and repatriate attrition rates. For example, the *Global Relocation Trends 2001 Survey* (2002) found that 49% of respondent organizations did not know the attrition rate of expatriates.

The HR investment metrics draw to some extent upon financial efficiency measures of HR operations. This measurement approach involves systems for calculating costs of HR programs and HR functions, with a variety of dollar- or time-based ratios for activities such as staffing, compensation, and expatriation. The focus of this category of measures is on calculating dollar-based indicators of HR operations and comparing these standardized indicators across organizations (Boudreau & Ramstad, 2002a, 2002b).

Although several aspects of global HR have been measured in this way (e.g., expatriate selection and pre-departure training), reports indicate that relatively few organizations gather comprehensive efficiency measures for global HR activities. The matter of expatriate return on investment (ROI) provides an example. According to the *Global Relocation Trends 2001 Survey* (2002), "there is no universal understanding of the meaning of ROI, and there are few mechanisms in place for measuring it accurately" (p. 9). It is interesting to note that the *Global Relocation Trends 2001 Survey* (2002) found that MNEs that have partially or wholly outsourced their expatriation programs are better able to monitor costs, value, and performance of international assignments. The logic of our framework suggests enhanced measures of expatriation to improve the identification and utilization of value that may exist there. We propose that, at the very least, expatriate ROI should involve some measures of repatriate retention and career development, knowledge sharing via global networking, or costs of expatriate and repatriate attrition. Although expatriation is probably the area of global HR in which most would agree the greatest measurement has occurred, evidence suggests that expatriate measurement in many MNEs has been largely focused on the element of HR investments. Our framework provides both a general template and specific measures that might raise attention to the linking elements of effectiveness and impact of expatriation.

Outcomes: MNE Concerns and Goals

MNEs have numerous strategic concerns and goals, which may include the development and maintenance of transnational HR management systems, world-class HR management status, competitiveness, efficiency, balance of global integration and local responsiveness, and flexibility. These organizational outcomes are related to each of the preceding elements in our framework and thus overlap to some extent. They may be viewed as global organizational outcomes of the other elements shown in Figure 24.1. For example, following Schuler et al. (1993), measures for *competitiveness* may include market share, and measures for *efficiency* include benchmark surveys of organizational performance against leaders. In addition, we note that either category may utilize measures we discussed earlier, related to industry or to MNE strategic dimensions of differentiation. The MNE's *balance between global integration and local responsiveness* may be measured by assessments of the extent and outcomes of global project teamwork, or by measurement of the response time for decision making. Finally, measures of the MNE's *flexibility* may include determination of the organizational capability to switch production across locations. These organizational outcomes may also be viewed as global outcomes of the linking elements shown in Figure 24.1.

Summary and Conclusions

The metrics we have discussed provide important contributions to the overall development and understanding of global HR measurement. In our review of global HR research and current practice, we found evidence that these measurement approaches are being applied to global HR in MNEs. However, even when an approach is being applied, there are evident constraints and challenges. To deal with the limitations of these measures, many MNEs use several of these measures in parallel. For example, Cargill uses several measures for their global HR measurement, including cost-benefit analysis, the balanced scorecard, and HR indices correlated with organizational performance. Indeed, we propose that the metrics are maximally useful when embedded in the decision model. MNEs that better understand the connection between human resources and strategic success on a global basis will win. To date, however, there appear to be relatively few examples of MNEs that understand and act to build this connection in tangible ways.

In this chapter, we have built upon the context of talentship, or decision-based HR, to articulate a framework for the measurement of global HR. We hope that the framework will help the practice of global HR metrics to move beyond the tendency to emphasize efficiency, the focus on expatriation measurement, the tantalizing correlations between global HR practices and financial outcomes that suggest the promise of better measurement, and the apparent situation in which even organizations with relatively extensive measurement could benefit from a logical model that connects practices, talent, and global strategic success. Our framework aims to reflect a strong and deep logical connection between resources, decisions, and organizational outcomes, to increase the impact, efficiency, and effectiveness of global HR.

Notes

1. We define a multinational enterprise (MNE) as any enterprise that carries out transactions in or between two sovereign entities, operating under a system of decision making that permits influence over resources and capabilities, where the transactions are subject to

influence by factors exogenous to the home country environment of the enterprise (Sundaram & Black (1992, p. 733).

2. HC BRidge™ is a trademark of the Boudreau-Ramstad Partnership.

References

Becker, B., & Huselid, M. (1998). High performance work systems and firm performance: A synthesis of research and managerial implications. *Research in Personnel and Human Resource Management, 16,* 53–101.

Becker, B., Huselid, M., & Ulrich, D. (2001). *The HR scorecard: Linking people, strategy and performance.* Boston, MA: Harvard Business School Press.

Boudreau, J. W. (1991). Utility analysis for decisions in human resource management. In M. D. Dunnette & L. M. Hough (Eds.), *Handbook of industrial and organizational psychology* (Vol. 2, pp. 621–745). Palo Alto, CA: Consulting Psychologists Press.

Boudreau, J. W. (1998). Strategic human resource management measures: Key linkages and the PeopleVANTAGE model. *Journal of Human Resource Costing and Accounting, 3,* 21–40.

Boudreau, J. W. (in press). Strategic knowledge measurement and management. In S. Jackson, M. Hitt & A. DeNisi (Eds.), *Managing knowledge for sustained competitive advantage: Designing strategies for effective human resource management.* San Francisco, CA: Jossey-Bass.

Boudreau, J. W., Dunford, B., & Ramstad, P. M. (2000). *The human capital "impact" on e-business: The case of Encyclopedia Britannica* (CAHRS working paper 00–05). Ithaca, NY: Cornell University.

Boudreau, J. W., & Ramstad, P. M. (1997). Measuring intellectual capital: Learning from financial history. *Human Resource Management, 36,* 343–356.

Boudreau, J. W., & Ramstad, P. M. (2002a). Strategic I/O psychology and the role of utility analysis models. In W. Borman, D. Ilgen, & R. Klimoski (Eds.), *Handbook of psychology: Vol. 12, Industrial and organizational psychology* (Chap. 9, pp. 193–221). New York: Wiley.

Boudreau, J. W., & Ramstad, P. M. (2002b). *Strategic HRM measurement in the 21st century: From justifying HR to strategic talent leadership* (CAHRS working paper 02–15). Ithaca, NY: Cornell University.

Boudreau, J. W., Ramstad, P. M., & Dowling, P. J. (in press). Global talentship: Toward a decision science connecting talent to global strategic success. In W. Mobley & P. Dorfman (Eds.), *Advances in global leadership* (Vol. 3). Stamford, CT: JAI Press/Elsevier Science.

Breaking new ground: The final report of the Mining, Minerals, and Sustainable Development Project, 2002. London: Earthscan Publications.

Caligiuri, P. M., & Stroh, L. K. (1995). Multinational corporation management strategies and international human resources practices: Bringing IHRM to the bottom line. *International Journal of Human Resource Management, 6,* 494–507.

Cappelli, P., & Neumark, D. (2001). Do "high-performance" work practices improve establishment-level outcomes? *Industrial and Labor Relations Review, 54,* 737–775.

De Cieri, H., & Dowling, P. J. (1999). Strategic human resource management in multinational enterprises: Theoretical and empirical developments. In P. M. Wright, L. D. Dyer, J. W. Boudreau, & G. T. Milkovich (Eds.), *Research in personnel and human resources management: Strategic human resources management in the twenty-first century* (Supplement 4, pp. 305–327). Stamford, CT: JAI Press.

Dowling, P. J., Welch, D. E., & Schuler, R. S. (1999). *International HRM: Managing people in a multinational context* (3rd ed.). Cincinnati, OH: South-Western.

Global Relocation Trends 2001 Survey Report. (2002, February). Sponsored by GMAC Global Relocation Services, National Foreign Trade Council (NFTC), and SHRM Global Forum.

Kamoche, K. (1996). The integration-differentiation puzzle: A resource capability perspective in international human resource management. *International Journal of Human Resource Management, 7,* 230–44.

Lepak, D. P., & Snell, S. (1999). The human resource architecture: Towards a theory of human capital allocation and development. *Academy of Management Journal, 24,* 31–48.

Milliman, J., Von Glinow, M. A., & Nathan, M. (1991). Organizational life cycles and strategic international human resource management in multinational companies: Implications for congruence theory. *Academy of Management Review, 16,* 318–339.

Murphy, T. E., & Zandvakili, S. (2000). Data- and metrics-driven approach to human resource practices: Using customers, employees and financial metrics. *Human Resource Management, 39,* 93–105.

Schuler, R. S., Dowling, P. J., & De Cieri, H. (1993). An integrative framework of strategic international human resource management. *Journal of Management, 19,* 419–459.

Stroh, L. K., & Caligiuri, P. M. (1998). Strategic HR: A new source for competitive advantage in the global arena. *International Journal of Human Resource Management, 9*(1), 1–17.

Sundaram, A. K., & Black, J. S. (1992). The environment and internal organization of multinational enterprises. *Academy of Management Review, 17,* 729–757.

Suggested Readings in Global HR Metrics

Boudreau, J. W., Dunford, B., & Ramstad, P. M. (2000). *The human capital "impact" on e-business: The case of Encyclopedia Britannica* (CAHRS working paper 00–05). Ithaca, NY: Cornell University.

Boudreau, J. W., & Ramstad, P. M. (2002). Strategic I/O psychology and the role of utility analysis models. In W. Borman, D. Ilgen, & R. Klimoski (Eds.), *Handbook of psychology: Vol. 12, Industrial and organizational psychology* (Chap. 9, pp. 193–221). New York: Wiley.

De Cieri, H., & Dowling, P. J. (1999). Strategic human resource management in multinational enterprises: Theoretical and empirical developments. In P. M. Wright, L. D. Dyer, J. W. Boudreau, & G. T. Milkovich (Eds.), *Research in personnel and human resources management: Strategic human resources management in the twenty-first century* (Supplement 4, pp. 305–327). Stamford, CT: JAI Press.

Dowling, P. J., Welch, D. E., & Schuler, R. S. (1999). *International HRM: Managing people in a multinational context* (3rd ed.). Cincinnati, OH: South-Western.

Florkowski, G. W., & Schuler, R. S. (1994). Auditing human resource management in the global environment. *International Journal of Human Resource Management, 5,* 827–851.

CHAPTER 25

Strategic Planning for Human Resources

Edward J. Kelleher

F. Stephen Cobe

S trategic planning[1] (SP) in business organizations can be viewed from three perspectives: corporate, line of business, and functional levels. Corporate-level strategy is aimed at ensuring the long term (i.e., 5 years or more) success and survival of the organization whereas line of business strategy is aimed at allowing business units to compete successfully in the marketplace on a short term (i.e., 1 to 2 years) basis. At the functional level of strategy, the management of each function (e.g., finance, human resources research and development (R&D), marketing, operations, and (RD)), is responsible for developing and maintaining policies and programs to implement the corporate and line of business level strategies. The effectiveness of these policies and programs is generally assessed by benchmarking (comparing the function's success in implementing corporate and business strategy to the performance of the same function in competitive firms). In addition, the development and maintenance of each program must be cost-effective. Functional strategy is guided by a need to allocate resources by "cherry-picking" actions that will be reflected in improved performance of the organization. It is essential that programs to which firms commit significant resources be prioritized to focus on actions that are mission-critical (i.e., are required for the firm's long-term survival). The effectiveness of functional strategies, HR strategy in particular, is subject to many contingencies.

Key Strategic Planning Issues for HR

Over the last two decades, strategic planning in business organizations has undergone a shift in emphasis from an environmental orientation (Porter, 1980, 1985) in which environmental factors such as the intensity of competition were seen as the basis for successful strategies to a resources orientation (Grant, 1991; Hamel & Prahalad, 1994; Lado, Boyd, & Wright, 1992; Robins & Wiesma, 1993) in which the distinctive or core competencies possessed by individual companies are seen as major determinants of the success of strategies and companies. The development and maintenance of distinctive and core competencies is an issue that poses both opportunities and challenges for the HR function.[2]

A second issue of importance to the HR function is its role in the implementation of corporate and business-level strategy. The design of organizational structures to support strategy, the development and maintenance of reward systems that will provide incentives to meet strategic goals, the design of organizational interventions needed to effectively manage change, and the sourcing of HR needed to develop and maintain distinctive competencies are crucial elements in the successful implementation of strategy.

A third issue the HR function must address is its role in formulating corporate and business-level strategies. The choice between chase and steady-state staffing strategies, the design of reward systems that respond to individual business units' needs at differing stages of the product life cycle, the choice between union avoidance and union acceptance strategies, and the designation of internal versus outsourced HR programs (e.g., tuition refund programs vs. corporate universities) are all critical determinants of the cost and quality components of a firm's overall performance.

The Strategic Planning–HR Interface

The initial challenge to the HR function lies in establishing an interface with strategic planning. Although virtually all firms participate in what is called the "strategic management process," they do so with differing degrees of formality, with varying levels of management hierarchical involvement, and with different time horizons. Furthermore, to determine an appropriate HR-SP interface, it is necessary to be able to recognize both the stage of the firm's strategic management evolution and its strategic planning orientation. To fail to do so significantly increases the risk of failure.

A McKinsey & Associates study (Glueck, Kaufman, & Walleck, 1980) has identified four evolutionary stages of strategic management through which firms pass as they develop: financial planning, forecast-based planning, externally oriented planning, and strategic management.

- The financial planning stage typifies small businesses in which the development of strategy is usually restricted to the chief executive officer (CEO) and other officers. These firms tend to focus on the budgeting process and the forecasting of revenues is accomplished by canvassing the company's sales force for estimates.

■ The forecast-based planning stage extends the time horizons covered in the stage one budgeting process. It is frequently initiated in response to recognition of a need for capital expenditure planning. Forecasting becomes more sophisticated, relying on statistical projections to improve accuracy in allocating resources. Strategy development is still generally the province of the firm's officers. There is a tendency for the planning process to degenerate into rewrites of last year's plan.

■ The externally oriented planning stage begins when the emphasis in planning shifts from improving trend-based forecasting to identifying customer needs and market shifts. At this point, scenario-based planning begins, and the opportunity for participation in strategic planning tends to increase for both the marketing and the HR functions. This stage typically provides an opportunity for general managers of business units to impact the strategic planning process.

■ The strategic management stage is reached when the firm merges its strategy development and management into a single process. The firm's strategy is directly linked to operational decisions. This is accomplished through (a) the comprehensive involvement of managers at all levels in the organization; (b) the establishment of a comprehensive, flexible strategy development process; and (c) the assimilation into the corporate culture of top management support for the strategic management process.

Strategic Planning Orientations

In large business organizations, the HR-SP interface is likely to be molded by one of the four following orientations, or strategic planning models (Brummel, 1997). An understanding of these options is essential not only in pursuing an appropriate interface but also in the execution of HR's organizational design responsibilities.

Business Paramount

This model exists where the corporate structure is decentralized and planning focuses on short-term performance. Strategy is delegated to operating divisions provided they meet overall financial performance targets. This model is most frequently used in conglomerate firms. There are two structural options for this model.

1. The strategic planning department provides direction through the development of planning assumptions but is largely passive in the process. Plans are developed upward from the business units with strategic planning aggregating divisional plans into an overall corporate plan.

2. There is no strategic planning department. Instead, a task force drawn widely from across business units comes together to review strategic objectives and

develop new strategic priorities. This provides bottom-up input into the planning process to ensure coherence and alignment across business in a widely dispersed organization.

Corporate Command

This model is characterized by a centralized power structure and short-term performance focus. It may be viewed as a top-down command structure. Short-term performance targets may be either negotiated or imposed on business units. Financial planning and budgeting are focal issues for corporate-level plans. There are two options for the role of the strategic planning function.

1. Strategic planners may be actively involved in plan content, not only in providing planning assumptions, but in challenging business unit targets and operating plans. The challenge role may extend to monitoring the ongoing performance of business units and may provide the CEO with specific business analyses and research to support this monitoring.

2. Strategic planners may serve as facilitators of the planning process, bringing corporate and business managers together to develop plans, budgets, and performance targets. In this role, planning serves to reconcile and resolve conflicts but is not an active participant in the power structure of the organization.

Corporate Strategies

This model is encountered where a strong centralized management exists that focuses on long-term strategy development. Creating and maintaining synergies between business units through sharing of technologies, distribution channels, and managerial skills is an overriding goal for top management. Strategies are developed by top management and are then supported by plans for finance, marketing, operations, and R&D. The HR function is expected to establish functional plans and cost-effective programs aimed at implementing these long-term strategic plans. The strategic planning function is an influencer that may frame key issues and strategic options; ensure the integration of strategies with plans, budgets, and actions by coordinating and consolidating business unit plans; and design performance measurements that are not limited to financial considerations alone. This model supports strategic thinking[3] throughout the organization, but the top-down orientation of the model creates process barriers for the injection of new ideas.

Strategic Networks

This model focuses on long-term strategy development within a decentralized structure. Business units and corporate management have a joint leadership responsibility in establishing strategic objectives, developing long-term strategies, and setting the direction of the organization. Participation in planning is widespread, so that management operates as a network, focusing on the strategic management process and building strategic capacity. The strategic planning function has two key roles:

1. Facilitation by building communications networks to obtain key inputs and to increase commitment to successful implementation of strategy, as well as designing and coordinating the planning process itself.

2. Participation in the process by providing research and analysis on key topics and challenging key business assumptions to ensure objectivity in decision making.

In this model, the HR function is responsible for designing implementation programs, providing research and analysis on the expected impact of various program options, and participating in the development of distinctive and core competencies. The development of these competencies is achieved by identifying mission-critical skills and designing programs to develop and disperse these skills throughout the organization. Given the differences between these four models in expectations for the HR function and in opportunities for its participation in the strategic management process, the identification of the prevailing orientation within the organization is an appropriate point of departure to establish the HR-SP interface.

The Strategic Management Process

As shown in Figure 25.1, strategic management is a cyclical process with six stages:

1. Environmental scanning: In this stage, management constantly scans the firm's environment for changes (especially discontinuous ones) in technology, customer needs and expectations, competitor initiatives and responses, geopolitical shifts, governmental regulations, societal expectations, currency fluctuations, and any other variables that indicate opportunities for, or threats to, the firm and its businesses.

2. Situational assessment: In the second stage, management examines the firm's recent and current performance, assesses the sustainability of the firm's unique competencies and strategic positioning, and attempts to reconcile the firm's strengths and weaknesses with opportunities and threats from the environment.

3. Goal and objective setting: At this stage, management sets or revises long-term objectives and short-term goals for the firm, including criteria for the measurement of future performance. Some firms formulate a mission statement setting forth the firm's present and targeted product-market alignments and any distinctive or core competencies the firm must develop to achieve long-term sustainable competitive advantage.

4. Strategy development: Based on the foregoing analysis and management's assumptions about the emergence of alternative future scenarios, management

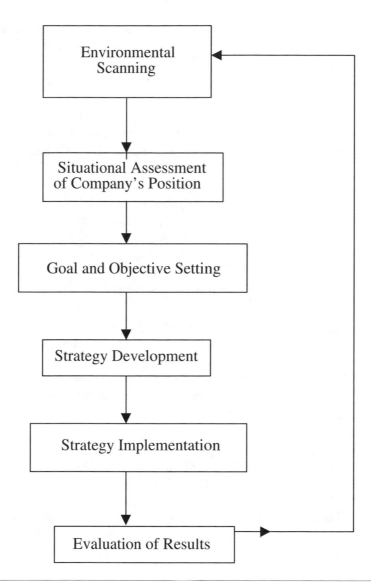

Figure 25.1   The Strategic Management Process

establishes corporate- and business-level strategies aimed at the goals and objectives defined in the previous stage of the process.

5. Implementation of strategy: During this stage, the strategies and plans of action developed in the foregoing stages are set into motion. This includes changes in organization structure, corporate culture, leadership, and reward systems. The HR function is typically responsible for developing and implementing programs and policies to manage these changes.

6. Evaluation of results: At regular intervals, ranging from monthly to annually, measurements are collected and reported to management to determine progress

against goals and objectives. These measurements allow management to make mid-course corrections in situations for which mileposts and interim goals are not being met. The measurements also serve to focus management's attention on the specific behaviors that are measured and on the time horizons allowed to reach specific goals.

One area of concern for the measurement process is that management tends to ignore long-term objectives if progress is measured on a short-term basis. This is particularly true when the organization's reward system attaches executive bonuses to short-term performance. In this case, strategy is subordinated to tactics. In this context, Douglas Ivester, CEO (and former CFO) for the Coca-Cola Company, has stated, "If we ever begin making decisions based on one-year results, you should sell the (Coca-Cola) stock" (Sellers, 1999).

HR Roles in the Strategic Management Process

There are four key roles in the strategic management process for the HR function: (a) program development and administration to implement corporate and business strategies; (b) development and implementation of HR strategies; (c) participation in change management through organizational development interventions; and (d) assessment of the impact of acquisitions or mergers on the firm's distinctive and core competencies.

Role 1: Implementation of Corporate and Business Strategies and HR Program Development

The implementation of corporate and business-level strategies requires appropriate program development from all functions within the organization. Typically, these programs are structured to fit into the framework of a strategic plan. The HR function is expected to provide input to this plan and to participate in its implementation through actions such as designing an organizational structure that will support corporate strategy, developing HR plans to forecast staffing needs, developing compensation and benefits programs that are responsive to specific product life cycle (PLC) stage requirements, or establishing job rotation programming to transfer technology and other components of distinctive competencies across lines of business within the organization. The thrust of program development for HR, as for all other functions, will be affected by management's selection of a strategy implementation model.

A number of strategy implementation process models (i.e., the commander, change, cultural, collaborative, champion, and collaborative-champion models) are in common usage (Bourgeois & Brodwin, 1984; Kelleher, 2001). These models differ in terms of the locus of strategy development, the locus of responsibility for implementation, the role of top management, the approach to decision making employed, the information requirements of the model, and the environment in which the model is applicable. A summary of the features of these models is

Table 25.1   Characteristics of Strategy Implementation Models

Characteristics	Commander	Change	Cultural
Locus of Strategy Development	Top management originates strategy	Top management originates strategy	Dependent on specific culture
Locus of Strategy Implementation Responsibility	Middle- and lower-level management	Middle- and lower-level management	Middle and lower level management
Role of Top Management	Originate strategy and set policy	Originate strategy and specify implementation mechanisms	Set mission and objectives; infuse culture
Role of Middle Management	Follow policy to implement strategy	Create programs needed to implement strategy	Dependent on specific culture
Methods Emphasized	Analytical methods (especially financial); use of policy to create guidelines for implementation	Organizational structure design; control system (e.g., performance measurement and reward systems)	Infuse corporate culture to guide implementation
Requirements of Model	Current, accurate information; analytical reports	Long lead time is needed to set up and communicate control system	Long lead time is needed to create cultural norms, procedures, and standards
Applicable Climate	Stable, slow rate of environmental change	Stable, slow rate of environmental change	Dependent on degree to which responsiveness to change is infused into the culture

Characteristics	Collaborative	Champion	Collaborative/Champion
Locus of Strategy Development	Top management originates strategy	Middle management originates strategy	Top management originates corporate level strategy; middle management originates business level strategy
Locus of Strategy Implementation Responsibility	Top-level management	Middle- and lower-level management	Top-, middle-, and lower-level management
Role of Top Management	Top management team originates corporate-level strategy	Top management establishes mission and serves as review board for middle management strategic proposals	Set mission and objectives, originate corporate-level strategy; serve as review board for middle management strategic proposals

(Continued)

Table 25.1   Continued

Characteristics	Collaborative	Champion	Collaborative/Champion
Role of Middle Management	Follow policy to implement strategy	Originate business-level strategy to pursue objectives and mission established by top management	Originate business-level strategy to pursue objectives and mission established by top management
Methods Emphasized	Consensus decisions	Valuation of and resource allocation to business strategies	Literative interactions between top and middle management
Requirements of Model	Top management competence in strategic management	SBU* level autonomy and competence in strategic management	Competence in strategic management at all management levels
Applicable Climate	Complex, turbulent environment	Complex, turbulent environment	Complex, turbulent environment

Note: A SBU is Strategic Business Unit (also known as Line of Business)

presented in Table 25.1. Comparison of these models in terms of the relationship between the locus of strategy design and the locus of strategy implementation leads to the observation that the commander, change, culture, and collaborative models tend to have a "top-down" orientation to the development of strategy whereas the champion model necessitates a "bottom-up" orientation. In contrast, the collaborative-champion model provides for two-way communication and multilevel interaction in both the development and the implementation of strategy.

Implementation Roles in HR

■ Under the commander model, the HR function is usually expected to issue policy guidelines concerning employment qualification standards, eligibility requirements for compensation and benefits programs, and disciplinary procedures. Input to strategic plans tends to focus on supplying labor cost information and identifying alternative programs for sourcing and training personnel. HR planning is likely to be limited to succession planning for key middle management and executive positions

■ Under the change model, the role of the HR function usually expands to include the design of organizational structures and linkage of reward systems to organizational goals. HR planning may be extended to include forecasting of overall staffing needs and the establishment of an HR information system to determine the adequacy of available internal candidates to fill anticipated job vacancies. Finally, organizational development programs such as team building and survey feedback may be required to facilitate organizational change.

■ In firms adopting the cultural model, the HR function is characteristically expected to design programs that reflect the values and expectations of the prevailing corporate culture. These programs tend to be evaluated against criteria that emanate from the firm's corporate mission statement, and both program launches and modifications are usually subject to widespread review and require design stage input from decision makers and influencers throughout the organization.

■ In situations in which the collaborative model has been adopted by an organization, the HR function tends to play a consulting role to provide input on organizational designs, development and maintenance of distinctive competencies, and program development to implement corporate-level strategy. The extent to which HR is responsible for the maintenance of implementation programs will vary, depending on the orientation of the firm's top management.

■ Under the champion model, the HR function characteristically provides inputs to business unit-level plans and proposals to identify programs and costs of implementation of business-level strategies. Input on team-based organizational designs, reward systems that are tailored to product life cycle stages, and transfer of distinctive competencies across business units are of paramount concern.

■ The collaborative-champion model may require HR management to cover its full range of capabilities. HR will need to be able to function both in consulting and program designing roles and in integrating corporate- and business-level strategies and programs. Identification of opportunities to leverage distinctive competencies across business units tends to require both environmental scanning and an extensive HR management information system.

Testing the Implementation Models

Although data from comparative empirical testing of these models is lacking, a *reality check* can be applied to the models based on their anticipated adequacy of handling of five implementation problems found by Alexander to differentiate between high- and low-level success in implementation of strategy in 93 Fortune 1000 level firms (Alexander, 1985). Alexander's study identified the following problems as key factors in this differentiation:

■ Key implementation tasks and activities were not originally defined in enough detail.

■ Problems requiring top management involvement were not communicated to them fast enough.

■ Changes in roles and responsibilities of key employees were not clearly defined.

- Key formulators of the strategic decision did not play an active enough role in implementation.
- Major problems surfaced during implementation that had not been identified beforehand.

An examination of the six implementation models in terms of the reality check criteria identified by Alexander indicates the following:

The *commander model* is characterized by top management's definition of organizational objectives, use of analytical frameworks such as corporate planning models in strategic decision making, and attempts to guide strategy implementation through policy while assigning implementation to lower levels of management. The model appears vulnerable to all five criterion problems for these reasons:

- Lack of input to strategy development by implementers, resulting in an insufficiently detailed definition of key implementation tasks and in a limited ability to anticipate problems during the strategy development process.
- Emphasis on top-down communications, resulting in inadequate communication about problems requiring top management involvement.
- Over-reliance on policy as an implementation vehicle, resulting in avoidance of implementation responsibility of strategy developers.

The *change model,* an extension of the commander model, is typically used to implement a new strategy. The model is characterized by reliance on organizational structure changes, incentive systems, measurement of performance to guide strategy implementation, and efforts to change corporate culture. This model has been characterized as the traditional business policy approach (Bourgeois & Brodwin, 1984). Comparison of the model with the criteria derived from Alexander's study reveals the following shortcomings:

- Due to centralized, top-down decision making, the change model risks failing to identify problems prior to strategy implementation.
- Due to limited input from implementers, key implementation tasks may be insufficiently defined during strategy development.

The *cultural model* is characterized by the infusion of culture to guide efforts of individuals within the organization toward a corporate mission that is established by top management. The model emphasizes the use of shared implementation. Through cross-referencing of the model with the criteria used here, the following deficiencies in the model are detected.

- Communications to top management are likely to be slow and filtered when resistance exists to ideas that diverge from cultural expectations.
- The cultural model requires a long lead time to create cultural support for implementation of new strategies, thus creating increased vulnerability to any problems not anticipated during strategy development.

The *collaborative model* focuses on consensus decision making within the top management team. The model relies both on analytical analyses and on brainstorming to get multiple inputs reflecting different perspectives on strategy-related issues. The model also relies on top management commitment obtained through participation to guide implementation. The collaborative model's shortcomings include these:

- Limited input from lower levels of management may result in inability to identify problems prior to implementation.
- Limited input from lower levels of management increases the likelihood of insufficiently defined tasks during strategy development.

The *champion model* is typified by "bottom-up" presentation of strategic proposals to top management by middle management "champions." These proposals are responsive to the corporate objectives and mission established by top management. Top management reviews the proposals, valuates them, and selects proposals to be funded. Although this model serves to gain input and commitment from a broader spectrum of levels of management, it is subject to the following criticisms:

- Champions may filter information on potential problems in order to sell their proposals, resulting in failure to identify problems prior to implementation.
- The model does not provide a clear mechanism for the coordination of the proposals but assumes that they will collectively result in the development of corporate-level strategy.

The *collaborative-champion model* is aimed at multilevel strategy development in which top management establishes objectives and mission, collaborates on the development of corporate strategy, and interacts with middle management to valuate and coordinate the allocation of resources to business-level strategic endeavors. Middle management is responsible for the development and implementation of business-level strategy. Strategy development is approached on an iterative basis, allowing for interaction between corporate and business unit-level management at each iteration. The multilevel interaction provided by the model provides the opportunity to reveal potential problems, to improve task definition, to result in communication of changes in roles and responsibilities to key employees, and to create an awareness of problems requiring top management attention during the process of strategy development. To capitalize upon this opportunity, the existence of broad-based strategic management competency in both top and middle management is required.

Program Development Models

Historically, the program development model most frequently used in HR, marketing, and research and development is the life cycle model (alternately referred to as the product life cycle model or the organizational life cycle model). This model assumes that there are five stages in the life of a business unit: introduction, growth, shakeout, maturity, and decline. In particular, HR programs addressing compensation and benefits issues have attempted to tailor reward system features to differences in available capital resources and competitive issues encountered by the business unit as it passes through each of these five stages (Balkin & Gomez-Mejia, 1987; Gerhart & Milkovich, 1992; Lawler, 1981, 1983; Milkovich & Newman, 1988; Salter, 1973).

An alternative contingency approach, the environmental uncertainty model has been proposed as a basis for designing pay plans (Rockmore, 1991; Rockmore & Jones, 1996). The environmental uncertainty model matches pay plan features to executive perceptions of uncertainty in the organization's task environment. Research comparing the effectiveness of pay plans whose development has been based on the two models indicates that the environmental uncertainty model is more useful than the life cycle model in developing pay plans that are related to the performance of a given business unit (Rockmore, Zimmerer, & Green, 1998).

Role 2: HR Strategies

HR shares responsibility with other functions of the organization for the development and implementation of both corporate- and business-level strategy. The following two schematics, which reflect the differences between corporate- and business-level strategy in time horizons and in the extent of resource commitment, can provide guidelines for HR strategy development.

Corporate-level strategy has been conceptualized in terms of various developmental stages models (Christensen, Andrews, & Bauer, 1978; Joyce, 1999; Kelleher & Cotter, 1982; Moore, 1996; Steiner, 1969; Wasson, 1978). In this context, an extension of the Scott-Wrigley-Rumelt conceptualization (Christensen et al., 1978; Kelleher & Cotter, 1982; Salter, 1970), referred to here as the Corporate Development Stages Model, may prove useful.

Corporate Development Stages Model

This schematic postulates four sequential stages of corporate development, as follows:

- *Entrepreneurial*—at stage 1, the organization is small, with a single core business and limited resources, so that a corporate-level strategy of concentration is necessitated. (A concentration strategy typically consists of focusing the firm's resources on a single activity in the industry's value chain and shifting resource allocation gradually from product development to market development to market penetration.) The firm's organizational structure may consist of a single manager supervising all other employees. The strategic thrust of the firm at this stage focuses on assembling the components of its desired distinctive competencies.

- *Specialization*—at stage 2, the organization has grown larger, so that a group of managers will be needed to carry out the key activities of the business. The firm still has a single core business and operates at a single stage of the industry value

Table 25.2   Corporate Development Stages and HR Strategy

Corporate Development Stage	Core Competency Strategic Thrust	HR Strategy
Entrepreneurial	Assemble components of core competencies	Recruit experienced personnel from supplier firms
Specialization	Integrate components of core competencies	*Virtual company staffing*—Retain specialists to develop distinctive competencies; outsource nonkey functions
Expansion	Transfer core competencies to management/professional personnel	Train and retain *cadre of key managers and professionals:* steady state staffing (manufacturing); chase staffing (services), and outsource nonkey functions. (Chase staffing = hiring & firing of temporary personnel.)
Product-Market	Leverage core competencies (transfer core competencies to additional organizational businesses)	Allocate cadre to business units to transfer core competencies: *low-cost work force*—low-tech and service businesses (2-tiered staffing and automation of production) and *specialized work force*—high-tech and professional service business (cadre of professionals with outsourcing of nonkey functions

chain. The firm still pursues a concentration strategy, supported by a functional organizational structure. The business' strategic thrust characteristically shifts to integrating the components of its desired distinctive competencies.

■ *Expansion*—in stage 3, the firm attempts to grow its core business by adding to its product line, increasing its market coverage, and increasing its coverage of the activities in the industry value chain. The firm's corporate-level strategy may shift to one or more of the following: geographic expansion (including expansion into overseas markets), horizontal integration (merger with, or acquisition of, another firm pursuing the same core business), or vertical integration (usually through the acquisition of a supplier or distributor). The firm's organization structure is typically divisionalized along customer focus, geographical, or product lines. This necessitates the transfer of the firm's distinctive competencies to management and professional personnel throughout the organization.

■ *Product-Market*—stage 4 companies develop multiple product lines and distribution channels, sell to targeted market segments, and tend to be organized into business units. The firm pursues a diversification strategy, usually leveraging

Table 25.3   HR Competitive Strategy Matrix

		Resource Locus	
		Internal	**External**
Strategic Thrust	**Differentiation through innovation**	Provide consultation and program development	Scan the environment to identify opportunities
	Cost control through standardization	Maintain services and audit policy compliance	Selectively outsource program administration

technology, production process, or distribution channel capacity across lines of business. At this point, the company attempts to leverage its distinctive competencies across lines of business. To the extent this is possible, the firm will have succeeded in establishing core competencies.

At each of the foregoing stages, the corporate development model reveals overriding objectives for all key functions. To respond to these objectives (which correspond to changes in corporate strategy), a sequence of HR functional strategies may be pursued. These are summarized in Table 25.2.

Each HR strategy described in Table 25.2 must be accompanied by appropriate program development actions in order to ensure successful implementation. Consequently, alternative programs (of both internal and external origin) should be identified and compared through a cost-benefits analysis. At the business strategy level, each line of business usually pursues a competitive strategy that is formulated to have a multifunctional scope. In general, competitive strategies focus on either a sequence of product innovation followed by product differentiation in the marketplace, or a sequence of process innovation to improve quality and reduce costs followed by pricing-focused competition in the marketplace. In stage 4, diversified firms, synergy (e.g., sharing of technology and/or distribution channels and management skills) may be added to the process innovation-price competition sequence. Generic competitive strategy options for the HR function are summarized in Table 25.3, that follows.

Role 3: HR Participation in Change Management

In order to improve performance or to respond to discontinuous changes in the company's environment, firms are periodically required to alter their strategies and business models. In turn, modifications in organizational structure, in control and reward systems, and in leadership may be required. Management of these changes is necessary to ensure a smooth transition and to achieve the goals and objectives toward which the strategies are ultimately directed. Existing programs and policies that do not support the modifications specified by management must be revised or replaced. These actions are likely to result in a conflict with the firm's corporate culture, which tends to preserve the status quo. A number of unsuccessful attempts by chief executive officers to deal with this conflict have been documented, including Thomas Vanderslice at GTE, Archie McCardell at International Harvester, and Gil Amelio at Apple Computers. As of the writing of this chapter, an effort by Carlton (Carly) Fiorina, CEO at Hewlett Packard, is being made to address the obsolescence of "the Hewlett-Packard Way," Hewlett Packard's widely touted corporate culture.

In organizations anticipating such changes, the HR function may be expected to provide interventions through the application of organizational development techniques. In particular, the combination of top management team building with strategic plan development and the modification of corporate cultures through reorganization (i.e., redesigning corporate structures and facilitating changes in leadership) are often required to successfully implement corporate-level strategy.

Both the collaborative and collaborative-champion implementation models rely on the effectiveness of a cooperatively interacting team of top managers. When a decision to adopt either of these models has been made, HR may be expected to facilitate the change. Typically, such a facilitation entails providing a diagnostic survey of the management group involved and identifying a consultant to introduce a team-building exercise aimed at identifying appropriate actions to respond to the survey results.

Changes in a firm's culture are typically achieved through corporate reorganization. This entails the use of changes in organization design, changes in managerial personnel and their assignments, and modification of organizational information and control systems to reinforce these changes. The HR function may be expected to source candidates for management positions from within and without the firm, to assist in orientation of newly appointed management personnel, to disseminate information to employees regarding changes in policy and procedures, and to monitor the emergence of new group norms through employee attitudinal surveys as the reorganization takes place. Fulfilling these expectations may require the development of new HR programs or the modification of existing ones.

Role 4: HR Participation in Acquisitions and Mergers

The HR function's participation in acquisition and merger activity may be segregated into before and after-the-fact responsibilities. The after-the-fact responsibilities typically entail alignment of HR programs among the components of the newly integrated organization. The before-the-fact responsibilities include an audit of the HR to be integrated, an assessment of the degree of management strategic fit (based on the synergy of the managerial and professional skills underlying the other firm's distinctive competencies with those of the present firm), and provision of related risk, cost, and benefits information to top management and the strategic planning function. An assessment of the skills underlying a firm's distinctive competencies can be structured in terms of a four-layered structural model of human competence (Spencer & Spencer, 1993).

Layer 1 of the human competence structure is concerned with observable skills and knowledge related to a task to be performed. These can be identified through a job analysis, can be learned in professional and technical training courses, and often serve as the basis for professional certification. Layer 2 consists of behavioral skills that are not job-specific. These include communications and relationship-building skills, general technical insights, problem solving, and basic approaches to work. These behaviors can be learned through individual mentoring and feedback, which is a lengthy and therefore relatively expensive process. Layer 3 consists of the values, standards, and ethics of the person concerned and how they relate to the expectations of the firm or a relevant professional group. This layer includes a professional frame of reference and includes the person's internalization of professional standards of performance. Acceptance by a professional group requires commitment to these values and standards. The first three layers of the human competence structure are referred to as the professional qualification of the person. Layer 4 consists of personal characteristics that are difficult to perceive or assess. It includes factors such as self-perception, motivation, sources of inspiration, and commitment to results. The Spencer model views these aspects of competence as providing the basis for exceptionally high levels of performance. The Spencer model can be used to define and structure a universe of human competencies from which the skills underlying a firm's distinctive competency can be identified. This is accomplished by conducting a systems task analysis to determine the component tasks in the overall process required to provide the firm's market offering. The task analysis results serve as the basis for a job analysis to pinpoint the skills necessary to carry out the task activities. The task and job analysis procedures required to accomplish this have been described elsewhere (Black et al., 1995; Chapanis, 1996; Hanser, 1995; Meister, 1985; Sanders & McCormick, 1993; Vallerie, 1978).

Evaluation of HR Strategy

HR strategy can be evaluated through the use of self-audits, benchmarking comparisons with other organizations, or achievement of expected values of organizational performance. These evaluation alternatives have different costs, benefits limitations, and methodologies.

Self-Audit Questionnaire for HR Strategy

The questionnaire shown in Form 25.1 can be used to structure a self-audit of HR strategy in terms of the models and concepts covered in the present chapter. This process has three results. First, sequentially answering the questions identifies the degree of alignment among corporate-level, business-level, and HR strategies. Second, accessing the HR strategy models set forth in the present chapter provides a check on the degree to which HR strategy selection will support corporate- and business-level strategies. Third, this procedure identifies the HR program development needed to successfully implement appropriate HR strategies. When answering these questions, the user should refer to the various models presented in the foregoing chapter to obtain guidelines for the decisions entailed in answering each question.

Form 25.1   HR Strategy Self-Audit Questionnaire

1. What is your organization's corporate strategy?_____
   (e.g., concentration, geographic expansion, horizontal integration, vertical integration, or diversification).

2. Is your organization's corporate-level strategy being implemented successfully, so that the organization's long-term goals are being met?_____

3. What business-level strategies are being used to support your organization's corporate-level strategy?_____
   (e.g., continuous product innovation, continuous process innovation, synergy, product differentation, or low-cost leadership).

4. Are your organization's business-level strategies being implemented successfully, so that the organization's short-term goals are being met?_____

5. At which stage of corporate development is your organization?_____
   (e.g., entrepreneurial, specialization, expansion, or product-market).

6. Is your HR strategy properly matched to this stage of development?_____

7. Is your HR program development model appropriate to manage the competencies of the organization's human resources at this stage of development?

   _____

8. What is the strategic thrust of your organization's business units?_____
   (e.g., innovation/differentiation vs. standardization to control costs/compete on price).

9. What is your HR competitive strategy?_____
   (e.g., consult, scan, maintain, or outsource).

10. Is your HR competitive strategy consistent with your organization's business-level strategic thrust?_____

11. How effective is the implementation of your organization's HR corporate strategy, your HR competitive strategy, and your corresponding program development? (compare HR management ratings with top management ratings on a 10-point scale).

12. If this implementation is not satisfactory, what corrective actions will you take to deal with the shortfall?_____

HR Strategy Benchmarking

Benchmarking is a process of comparing measures of costs and performance in one organization with those of other organizations. The goals of this process include ensuring that decisions are made based on mission-critical factors and that actions resulting in higher-than-average costs result in higher-than-average levels of performance. Although the factors that are mission-critical for a given organization will

---

Box 25.1   Generalized Benchmark Measures

---

1. Organization's revenue per employee versus industry median revenue per employee
2. Organization's net income per employee versus industry median net income per employee
3. Organization's annual turnover rate versus industry average turnover rate
4. Organization's median salary for key jobs versus industry median salary for key jobs
5, Organization's cost of benefits per employee for key jobs versus industry median cost of benefits for key jobs
6. Ratings of organization's customer service effectiveness versus ratings of customer service of competitors
7. HR function budget as percentage of organization's revenue versus industry average HR function budget as percentage of revenues

---

vary somewhat between industries, there are some measures that generalize across industries. The factors that are mission-critical across industries include those in Box 25.1.

Box 25.2 on information sources can provide an organization with benchmarking or baseline data on the generalized mission-critical factors and others:

A comprehensive benchmarking of an organization's HR strategy and its associated impact on performance are likely to require the use of several of the foregoing sources to glean the information needed to form appropriate baselines for comparison.

Achievement of Expected Values of Performance

The remaining alternative for the evaluation of HR strategy lies in comparing expected values of performance with actual values of performance. An example of this alternative is available through organizational participation in the Strategic Planning Institute's PIMS (Profit Impact of Market Strategy) model program. The PIMS model was developed at General Electric Corporation by Harvard University faculty members in 1960, and then spun off to the Strategic Planning Institute in Cambridge, Massachusetts. PIMS is a regression model with a database of over 3,000 business units from more than 450 companies. The model generates several different reports that relate strategy and resources variables to measures of performance including ROI (return on investment).

One of the reports generated by the model projects expected values of ROI for a strategy based on a given level of resource allocation. Differences between the expected value and the subsequent actual value are attributed to the performance of the general manager of the business unit. Recommendations from the PIMS

Box 25.2 Benchmarking Sources

1. Published data from annual reports, 10K reports, or industry statistics
2. Proprietary data from databases established and maintained by industry associations or management consulting intermediaries
3. Customer service ratings surveys conducted by Consumer Reports or trade magazines
4. Participation in the Human Resources Benchmarking Association (HRBA) (see the HRBA Web site at http://hrba.org)
5. Participation in Best Practices, LLC Human Resources Benchmarking (see the Best Practices Web site at http://www.best-in-class.com/expertise/human resources.htm)

---

model use performance above the expected value of ROI as a basis for awarding management bonuses. Although it is not a standard feature of the PIMS model, this procedure could be extended to the HR function through a partial regression or discriminant function analysis model.

Conclusions

Fulfillment of the four foregoing roles provides the HR function with opportunities for extensive participation in the strategic management process. Determination of the appropriate focus for the HR function at a given time will depend on the (McKinsey model) stage of development attained by the firm, on the orientation of the strategic planning function, and on the strategy implementation model in use by the firm.

Evaluation of HR strategy can be achieved through (a) the use of a self-audit questionnaire to test the appropriateness of the alignment of HR strategy with corporate- and business-level strategies, supported by the use of the HR strategy models to provide decision guidelines; (b) the use of benchmarking the HR function's performance against the performance of other organizations; and (c) the comparison of expected and actual performance through a partial regression or discriminant function analysis model. Because these procedures allow both before-the-fact and after-the-fact assessment, a combination of the self-audit with benchmarking is recommended.

Notes

1. Strategic planning is a process for developing and implementing strategies.

2. Distinctive competencies may be operationally defined as "the ability of a firm to integrate skills, technology and other resources to produce a market offering which is unique and preferred over those of other firms by prospective customers" (Meyer, 1991). When a

distinctive competency can be shared across multiple lines of business it becomes a core competency (Hamel & Prahalad, 1994).

3. Strategic thinking may be defined as knowing when a discontinuity occurs, developing a response, and taking appropriate action.

References

Alexander, L. D. (1985). Successfully implementing strategic decisions. *Long Range Planning, 18*(3), 91–97.

Balkin, D. B., & Gomez-Mejia, L. R. (1987). Toward a contingency theory of compensation strategy. *Strategic Management Journal, 8*(4), 169–182.

Black, J. B. et al. (1995). *Using a knowledge representations approach to cognitive task analysis.* Proceedings of the 1995 National Convention of the Association for Educational Communications and Technology, AECT.

Bourgeois, L. J., & Brodwin, D. R. (1984). Strategic implementation: Five approaches to an elusive phenomenon. *Strategic Management Journal, 5,* 241–264.

Brummel, A. (1997, September). *The future of corporate planning.* Transcripts of the Global Business Network Canada Meeting on the Future of Corporate Planning.

Chapanis, A. (1996). *Human factors in systems engineering.* New York: Wiley.

Christensen, C. R., Andrews, K. R., & Bower, J. L. (1978). *Business policy.* Homewood, IL: Irwin.

Gerhart, B., & Milkovich, G. T. (1992). Employee compensation: Research and practice. In M. D. Dunnette & L. M. Hough (Eds.), *Handbook of industrial and organizational psychology* (2nd ed., pp. 481–569). Palo Alto, CA: Consulting Psychologists Press.

Glueck, F., Kaufman, S., & Walleck, A. (1980, July-August). Strategic management for competitive advantage. *Harvard Business Review,* 154–161.

Grant, R. M. (1991, Spring). The resource-based theory of competitive advantage: Implications for strategy formulation. *California Management Review, 33,* 114–135.

Hamel, G., & Prahalad, C. K. (1994). *Competing for the future.* Boston, MA: Harvard Business School Press.

Hanser, L. M. (1995). *Traditional and cognitive job analyses as tools for understanding the skills gap.* National Center for Research in Vocational Education, University of California, Berkeley.

Joyce, W. T. (1999). Megachange: How today's leading companies have transformed their workforces. Boston, MA: Free Press.

Kelleher, E. J. (2001). *Strategic analysis: Conceptualizing, formulating, and valuating competitive strategy.* Unpublished manuscript, San Jose State University, San Jose, CA.

Kelleher, E. J., & Cotter, K. L. (1982). An integrative model for human resource planning and strategic planning. *Human Resource Planning, 5*(1), 15–27.

Lado, A. A., Boyd, N. C., & Wright, P. (1992). A competency based model of sustainable competitive advantage: Toward a conceptual integration. *Journal of Management, 18,* 77–91.

Lawler, E. E. (1981). *Pay and organization development.* Reading MA: Addison-Wesley.

Lawler, E. E. (1983). Strategic design of reward systems. In C. Fombrun, N. Tichy, & M. DeVanna (Eds.), *Strategic human resource management* (pp. 127–147). New York: Wiley.

Meister, D. (1985). *Behavioral analysis and measurement methods.* New York: Wiley.

Meyer, A. D. (1991). What is strategy's distinctive competence? *Journal of Management, 17*(4), 821–833.

Milkovich, G. T., & Newman, J. M. (1988). *Compensation.* Homewood, IL: Irwin.

Moore, J. F. (1996, 3rd Quarter). The four stages of a business: Life cycle lessons from nature. *Strategy and Business,* Booze Allen and Hamilton Reprint No. 96305.

Porter, M. (1980). *Competitive strategy.* Cambridge, MA: Free Press.

Porter, M. (1985). *Competitive advantage.* Cambridge, MA: Free Press

Robins, J., & Wiesma, M. (1993). A resource-based approach to the multibusiness firm: Empirical analysis of portfolio interrelationships and corporate financial performance. *Strategic Management Journal, 16,* 277–299.

Rockmore, B. W. (1991). *Exploring the relationship between pay plan design and firm performance within varying task environments.* Unpublished doctoral dissertation, University of Georgia, Athens.

Rockmore, B. W., & Jones, F. F. (1996). Business investment strategy and firm performance: A comparative examination of accounting and market-based measures. *Managerial Finance, 22*(8), 44–56.

Rockmore, B. W., Zimmerer, T. W., & Green, R. F. (1998). Which is the better explanation for the relationship between pay plan design and firm performance: Life cycle or environmental uncertainty? *Western Decision Science Institute's Annual Conference Proceedings II,* Reno, NV.

Salter, M. S. (1970). Stages of corporate development. *Journal of Business Policy, 1*(1), 23–27.

Salter, M. S. (1973, March–April). Tailor incentive compensation to strategy. *Harvard Business Review,* 159–174.

Sanders, M. S., & McCormick, E. J. (1993). *Human factors in engineering and design* (7th ed.). New York: McGraw-Hill.

Sellers, P. (1999, July 19). Crunch time for Coke. *Fortune.*

Spencer, L. M., & Spencer, S. M. (1993). *Competence at work,* New York: Wiley.

Steiner, G. A. (1969). *Top management planning.* New York: Macmillan.

Vallerie, L. L. (1978). *Survey of task analysis methods* (Research Note RN80–17). Alexandria, VA: Army Research Institute.

Wasson, G. R (1978). Dynamic competitive strategy and product life cycles. Austin Press.

Suggested Readings in HR Strategy

Ansoff, I. (1990). *Implanting strategic management* (2nd ed.). Hertfordshire, UK: Prentice-Hall.

Chandler, A. A. (1992). *Strategy and structure* (2nd ed.). Cambridge, MA: MIT Press.

Charan, R. (2001). *What the CEO wants you to know.* New York: Crown.

Nonaka, I., Ichijo, K., & Von Krogh, G. (2000). *Enabling knowledge creation.* New York: Oxford University Press.

Prosci HRLC. (n.d.). Innovative practices in human resources: Benchmarking reports from 67 companies. Web site at *Hrservices@prosci.com.*

Glossary

Definitions of Technical and Statistical Terms Commonly Used in HR Program Evaluations

Chet Robie

Nambury S. Raju

The purpose of this chapter is to provide readers with brief, simple definitions of various technical and statistical terms commonly used in human resource (HR) program evaluations. These technical and statistical terms are presented alphabetically and arranged in the following manner: (a) technical or statistical term, (b) a general operational or conceptual definition, with examples where appropriate, (c) pointers to any related technical or statistical terms that are also covered in this appendix, and (d) typically one or more citations where readers can find additional information on the primary (and related) terms.

Adaptive testing is a form of computerized testing in which successive items are chosen for administration based on an item's psychometric quality and an examinee's responses to prior items. (Wainer et al., 2000)

Analysis of covariance (ANCOVA) is analogous to ANOVA with one major exception; it controls for variation in the dependent variable due to an outside variable. This is done prior to the examination of mean differences across the variable(s) of interest. *See also* **analysis of variance**. (Kirk, 1995; Winer, Brown, & Michels, 1991)

Analysis of variance (ANOVA) assesses whether mean differences on a dependent (or outcome) variable exist across two or more levels of one or more independent (or predictor) variables. Levels of the independent variable are typically different groups in the typical application of the ANOVA method. *See also* **F-test** and **t-test**. (Kirk, 1995; Winer et al., 1991)

Attenuation refers to the effect of unreliability on a statistic or a parameter. The correlation between observed predictor and criterion measures is affected adversely by the unreliability associated with the predictor and the criterion. *See also* **reliability**. (Cascio, 1991; Guion, 1998)

Beta coefficients are standardized optimal weights that denote the unique strength of the relationship between a given predictor variable and the variable being predicted. In a multiple regression analysis, a linear relationship between an optimally weighted group of predictor variables and an outcome or a criterion variable is calculated. *See also* **multiple regression analysis.** (Cohen, Cohen, West, & Aiken, 2003; Guion, 1998)

Bias in coverage—The extent to which subgroups of a target population participate differentially in a program. (Rossi, Freeman, & Lipsey, 1999)

Bias in ratings can be encountered in several forms during a program evaluation. Some of these are defined below.

> **Halo effect (bias)** is consistently conceptualized as a rater's failure to discriminate among conceptually distinct and potentially independent aspects of a ratee's behavior (Saal, Downey, & Lahey, 1980). For example, a supervisor may rate a bank teller high on all aspects of his or her job because the supervisor knows that the employee has excellent public relations with clients. *See also* **leniency effect** and **severity effect.** (Cascio, 1991)
>
> **Leniency effect (bias)**—The tendency of some raters to rate all ratees higher (i.e., in a positive direction) than is warranted by the ratees' behavior (Vance, Winne, & Wright, 1983). Such raters are called the "easy" raters. *See also* **halo effect** and **severity effect.** (Cascio, 1991)
>
> **Severity effect (bias)**—The tendency of some raters to rate all ratees lower (i.e., in a negative direction) than is warranted by the ratees' behavior (Vance, Winne, & Wright, 1983). Such raters are called "tough" raters. *See also* **halo effect** and **leniency effect.** (Cascio, 1991)

Causal modeling is a representation of causal relationships, usually with mediators. It is the specification of models that use both indicators and underlying variables (i.e., structural equation models) to make inferences about the latent variables based on the covariances of the observed indicators (Bollen, 1989). Causal modeling is an innovative quantitative technique that is typically used to make causal inferences with nonexperimental data. *See also* **experimental (versus nonexperimental) design** and **structural equation modeling.** (Byrne, 1998)

Ceiling effect—Responses on a variable closely approach the maximum possible response so that further increases are difficult to obtain. *See also* **floor effect** (Shadish, Cook, & Campbell, 2002).

Change measurement includes a wide array of methods to measure the degree to which some HR-related phenomenon (e.g., performance, attrition, attitudes) shifts across two or more time points. It is generally recommended to measure the phenomenon of interest with multiple measures and at more than two time points so that the most sophisticated methodological technology can be used and the strongest inferences made. (Cook & Campbell, 1979)

Chi-square test is a test used with data measured on a nominal scale (i.e., frequency, categorical, or count data). It is typically used to assess goodness of fit or the relationship between two variables. *See also* **levels of measurement** and **goodness of fit**. (Conover, 1998)

Cluster analysis is an alternative technique to factor analysis; it is designed to examine the structure or relationships of objects or people to one another. *See also* **factor analysis** and **multidimensional scaling**. (Everitt, 1980)

Comparison group—In an experiment, a group that is compared with a treatment group and that may receive either an alternative treatment or no intervention. *See also* **control group** and **treatment group**. (Shadish et al., 2002)

Confidence interval is sample-derived statistic that represents an estimated range of values in which a population parameter (e.g., a mean or percentage) is likely to fall with a given level of likelihood (e.g., 95% or 99% of the time). For example, the 95% confidence interval for the correlation ($r = .10$) between job satisfaction and job performance in a sample of workers may be reported as $.10 \pm .05$. *See also* **correlation**. (Kirk, 1990)

Confirmatory factor analysis (CFA) consists of a set of techniques that allows one to specify and test the structure of the relationships among objects and people (i.e., test a factor analytic model). Essentially, the test compares the actual inter-relations of the variables with the interrelations of the variables that are reproduced (i.e., estimated) from the CFA model. Models that most closely reproduce the interrelations among the variables are considered the best. *See also* **factor analysis** and **structural equation modeling**. (Byrne, 1998)

Confounding factors—Extraneous variables resulting in observed effects that obscure or exaggerate the true effects of an intervention. (Rossi et al., 1999)

Construct is a theoretical concept or abstraction aimed at organizing and making sense of our environment. Examples of constructs are anxiety, motivation, mental ability, attitude, self-esteem, interest, frustration, and altruism. (Pedhazur & Schmelkin, 1991)

Control group—In an experiment, this term typically refers to a comparison group that does not receive a treatment but that may be assigned to a no-treatment condition, to a wait list for treatment, or sometimes to a placebo intervention group. *See also* **comparison group** and **treatment group**. (Shadish et al., 2002)

Correlation is a measure of the linear relationship between two variables. A correlation coefficient can vary between -1.00 and $+1.00$. The degree or level of relationship is indicated by the absolute value of the correlation (i.e., .40 indicates a stronger relationship than does .25, and $-.50$ and $+.50$ indicate the same degree of relationship). The sign associated with the correlation signifies the direction of the relationship. In a positive correlation, the values of one variable would increase if the values of the other variable increased. In a negative correlation, the values of one variable would decrease if the values for the other variable increased. (Cohen et al., 2003)

Correlation matrix consists of a table of numbers in which each value represents the relationship (i.e., correlation) between each pair of variables in a study. *See also* **correlation**. (Cohen et al., 2003)

Cross-sectional design is a research approach in which two or more cohorts are observed or studied simultaneously. For example, comparing job satisfaction of U.S.-based employees with that of non-U.S.-based employees of a global organization is an example of a cross-sectional design. (Kirk, 1995)

Cross-validation is a process that uses multiple samples to estimate and compare multiple regression analysis parameters across samples. More specifically, the procedure entails (a) deriving weights for optimally predicting an outcome variable in one sample (called the "holdout group"), (b) applying the weights to predict the outcome variable in another sample (called the "weighting group"), (c) obtaining predicted criterion scores for each person in the holdout group, and (d) correlating predicted criterion scores with actual criterion scores for persons in the holdout group. A high, statistically significant correlation coefficient indicates that the regression equation is useful for individuals other than those on whom the equation was developed (Gatewood & Feild, 2001). *See also* **multiple regression analysis** (Guion, 1998)

Cut-off score (cut score) is a minimum value that examinees/applicants must attain to be chosen for further consideration in a selection process. (Guion, 1998)

Degrees of freedom is the number of restrictions placed upon a set of scores (e.g., performance rating for men or women). In general, a single degree of freedom is "lost" every time a parameter like a mean is estimated (e.g., two degrees of freedom are lost when the means of men and women are estimated separately). (Kirk, 1990)

Differential item functioning (DIF) is a popular method designed to examine whether items measure their intended constructs across groups. *See also* **construct** and **measurement equivalence**. (Raju, Laffitte, & Byrne, 2002)

Discriminant analysis is a statistical procedure for predicting group membership (e.g., quit or stay) with measured variables (e.g., job satisfaction). Classification (or prediction) efficiency is measured by examining the match between observed percentages in each group with those predicted by the measured variables. (Tatsuoka, 1988)

Effect size indicates the degree to which a predictor measure is related to an outcome measure or the degree of difference between treatment groups on a measure of interest. Two popular effect sizes are the standardized difference (or *d*) score and the correlation coefficient. A *d* score is the difference between two treatment group means divided by the groups' weighted or pooled standard deviation. *See also* **correlation**. (Hedges & Olkin, 1985; Hunter & Schmidt, 1990)

Error—Several types of errors are encountered in program evaluation. Some of these are defined below.

> **Measurement error** is variation in (test, attitude, etc.) scores of an individual from one occasion to the next and/or on different sets of items drawn from the same content domain. These fluctuations in scores are generally assumed to be random. (Anastasi, 1988)
>
> **Sampling error** is the difference between the sample statistic and the population parameter. For example, the mean score from a sample reflects not only the population mean from which the sample is drawn but also the specific individuals included in the sample and the size of the sample. The difference between the sample mean and the population mean is called the sampling error of the sample mean. The variation in the sample-based mean scores is commonly referred to as the sampling variance of the mean. (Kirk, 1990)
>
> **Type I error rate** is the probability of rejecting the null hypothesis when it is actually true. That is, it is the probability of concluding that the population parameter is non-zero when in fact it is zero. *See also* **null hypothesis** and **Type II error rate**. (Kirk, 1990)
>
> **Type II error rate** is the probability of retaining the null hypothesis when it is actually false. That is, it is the probability of concluding that the population parameter is zero when in fact it is non-zero. *See also* **Type I error rate** and **statistical power**. (Kirk, 1990)

Experimental (versus nonexperimental) design is a research approach in which (a) one or more treatment groups are compared to a control group and (b) participants are randomly assigned to the groups. A control group and random assignment minimize the likelihood that unrecognized variables influenced the observed effect(s) of the independent variable(s) on the dependent variable. *See also* **control group** and **treatment group** (Kirk, 1995; Winer et al., 1991)

F-test is a statistical test used to investigate, for example, whether the averages of two or more groups differ from one another. As with the *t*-test, the *F*-test can involve groups that have been assigned to one or more levels of the independent variable (i.e., within-groups or between-groups *F*-test). *See also* **t-test, analysis of covariance**, and **analysis of variance**. (Kirk, 1995; Winer et al., 1991)

Factor analysis is a procedure for summarizing the relations among variables. By identifying the interrelations among variables, a researcher is able to identify "factors" or constructs that consist of multiple variables. *See also* **cluster analysis** and **multidimensional scaling**. (Gorsuch, 1983; Kline, 1993; Tatsuoka, 1988)

Floor effect—Responses on a variable closely approach the minimum possible response so that further decreases are difficult to obtain. *See also* **ceiling effect** (Shadish et al., 2002)

Focus group—A small panel of persons selected for their knowledge or perspective on a topic of interest that is convened to discuss the topic with the assistance of a facilitator. The discussion is usually recorded and used to identify important themes or to construct descriptive summaries of views and experiences on a focal topic. (Rossi et al., 1999)

Goodness of fit assesses how well observed data match the expected distributional properties, identified from either a theoretical model or prior empirical research. For example, the square of a multiple correlation (R^2) expresses the goodness of fit (or strength) of the linear relationship between a set of predictors and a performance measure. *See also* **correlation**. (Pedhazur & Schmelkin, 1991)

Hawthorne effect is a change in an outcome variable (e.g., productivity) that occurs as a result of individuals receiving some type of different treatment, even if the treatment itself has no actual effect. *See also* **treatment group**. (Roethlisberger, 1939)

Hierarchical linear modeling—The decomposition of variance in a given variable based on levels of other variables that are nested within each other. For example, how much variation in job satisfaction can be accounted for by the individuals, versus the team they work in, versus the organization in which they work. *See also* **variance**. (Raudenbush & Bryk, 2002)

Interaction—How the effect of one variable on a second variable changes as a function of the level of a third variable (e.g., voluntary turnover is related to profit losses most strongly when the average performance ratings of those who leave are high). (Kirk, 1995)

Internet applications—The Internet can be used to quickly and efficiently gather HR program evaluation information (Simsek & Veiga, 2001; Stanton & Rogelberg, 2001). Recent research has generally shown that data gathered through the Internet is comparable to that gathered from more traditional means such as paper and pencil. (Penny, 2003; Stanton, 1998)

Item response theory (IRT)—A group of methods that relate responses to items to the underlying construct or constructs that the items are designed to measure. One or several parameter estimates can be used to characterize these relations, depending on the complexity of the chosen model. IRT methods have been designed for dichotomous (e.g., yes/no) and polytomous (e.g., disagree, neutral, agree) item response formats and multiple constructs (e.g., spatial and verbal skills). (Hambleton, Swaminathan, & Rogers, 1991)

Latent variables—An unobserved, theoretical construct is referred to as a latent variable. For example, intelligence is a latent variable, but a score on an intelligence test is an indicator of the construct of intelligence. *See also* **structural equation modeling**. (Byrne, 1998)

Levels of measurement—This refers to the properties of a scale: nominal scale (with no special meaning to the numerical values attached), ordinal scale (increases in numerical values are ordered but equal increases do not necessarily reflect equal increases in the construct being measured), interval scale (an ordinal scale in which equal increases in numerical values reflect equal increases in the construct being measured), and ratio scale (an interval scale in which zero means an absence of the property under investigation).

Levels of transfer—A framework used to classify the degree to which training has had its intended effect(s). The following framework consists of four levels ranging in degree of evaluative rigor: reactions, learning, behavior, and results. Reactions consist simply of trainees' self-report of quality of various dimensions of the training. Learning usually consists of a post-training test of the degree to which the trainee has mastered the material contained in the training exercises. Behavior usually consists of measuring some form of on-the-job behavior that is related to the training. Finally, the most difficult level of transfer to measure is whether the training has translated into demonstrable results that benefit the organization. (Kirkpatrick, 1998)

LISREL—Stands for linear structural relations, and it is a computer program used in structural equation modeling. *See also* **structural equation modeling.** (Byrne, 1998)

Logistic regression—Similar to regression analysis in which the dependent (or criterion) variable is dichotomous or categorical. *See also* **multiple regression analysis** (Cohen et al., 2003)

Longitudinal design—A longitudinal design or study refers to any design or study in which the same persons are observed at two or more times. *See also* **cross-sectional design.** (Kirk, 1995)

Mean—The average score.

Measurement equivalence—Measurement equivalence is the general term for any set of techniques that are designed to examine whether a given set of variables or items taps the constructs they are designed to measure in a similar way across different groups, situations, or contexts. *See also* **differential item functioning.** (Raju et al., 2002)

Median—The score that divides a distribution of scores in half.

Mediator—A third variable that comes between a cause and effect and that transmits the causal influence from the cause to the effect. *See also* **moderator.** (Shadish et al., 2002)

Meta-analysis—A group of methods designed for secondary analysis of data. Studies are the unit of analysis instead of individuals. (Hedges & Olkin, 1985; Hunter & Schmidt, 1990; Lipsey, 2001)

Moderator—An independent variable interacts with another independent variable in predicting a third (outcome) variable. For example, if the relationship between cognitive ability and job performance varies as a function of gender, then gender is considered a moderator. *See also* **mediator.** (Cascio, 1991; Guion, 1998)

Multidimensional scaling—Alternative techniques to factor analysis that are designed to examine the structure of objects or people. *See also* **cluster analysis** and **factor analysis.** (Davison, 1983)

Multiple regression analysis—A form of analysis that results in an equation that denotes the optimal linear relation between a group of variables (i.e., predictor variables) with one other variable (i.e., outcome variable). Many variants of the analysis exist; however, the basic parameter estimates of interest are the weights for each of the predictor variables that denote the unique (i.e., other variables held constant) strength of the relation between a given predictor variable and the outcome variable. (Cohen et al., 2003; Guion, 1998)

Multivariate analysis of variance (MANOVA)—Analogous to ANOVA with the exception that it allows for the simultaneous analysis of mean differences across levels of an independent variable(s) on multiple dependent variables. (Tatsuoka, 1988)

Needs assessment—An evaluative study that answers questions about the social conditions a program is intended to address and the need for the program. (Rossi et al., 1999).

Non-normal/skewed distribution—A distribution that is not bell shaped; this typically takes the form of scores falling either more heavily on the lower side of the distribution (positive skew) or scores falling more heavily on the upper side of the distribution (negative skew). Other non-normal distributions are possible such as a bimodal distribution in which scores fall heavily in the lower and upper thirds of the distribution. *See also* **normal distribution.** (Kirk, 1990)

Nonparametric statistics—A branch of statistics in which the assumption about the shape of the distribution of a variable in the population is not needed. (Cohen et al., 2003)

Normal distribution—A distribution of scores characterized by a bell shape in which most scores fall in the middle of the distribution and few scores fall in the extremes of the distribution. *See also* **non-normal/skewed distribution.** (Kirk, 1990)

Null hypothesis testing—A special case of significance testing in which a hypothesis of "no difference" is evaluated. *See also* **significance testing.** (Kirk, 1990)

Parametric statistics—A branch of statistics in which the shape of the distribution of a variable in the population is assumed known. For example, test scores are generally assumed to be normally distributed in a population of interest. *See also* **nonparametric statistics** and **normal distribution.** (Cohen et al., 2003)

Path analysis—A form of structural equating modeling in which only measured variables are involved. *See also* **causal modeling** and **structural equation modeling.** (Cohen et al., 2003)

Population—In statistics, a population is the totality of objects or individuals about which inferences are to be made through a sampling study. (Winer et al., 1991)

Profile analysis—A method of analysis that compares the shape of one individual's (or a group's) profile of scores on a set of scales to that of another individual's (or group's) profile of scores. (Tatsuoka, 1988)

Program evaluation—the use of research procedures to systematically investigate the effectiveness of social intervention programs that are adapted to their political and organizational environments and designed to inform social action in ways that improve social conditions. (Rossi et al., 1999).

Qualitative approaches—Qualitative approaches to data gathering and interpretation usually involve collecting non-numerical data; this does not preclude later organization of the data in a numerical fashion. A variety of qualitative approaches can be taken to aid inquiry in the area of HR program evaluation. *See also* **quantitative approaches.** (Patton, 1990)

Quantitative approaches—Quantitative approaches involve variables or constructs that can be measured numerically. *See also* **qualitative approaches.** (Kirk, 1990; Patton, 1990)

Quasi-experimental designs—The term is generally applied to designs that assign participants to treatments primarily based on self-selection or administrative considerations. Various methods can be used to help aid in inferences of causality with the use of these designs without the option of randomly assigning participants to treatments. *See also* **experimental designs.** (Cook & Campbell, 1979)

Random sampling—A method of drawing samples from a specified population so that every possible sample of a particular size is equally likely to be chosen. (Winer et al., 1991)

Range restriction—Refers to a restricted distribution of scores. For example, in a selection program, all applicants will generally have scores on the predictor, but criterion measures are only available for those that are ultimately hired. The distribution of predictor scores for the latter group (the hired group) is said to be restricted because typically the low-scoring applicants are not hired. (Cascio, 1991)

Rank-order correlation—A measure of correlation used on data that are clearly ordinal in nature (e.g., the relation between employee performance rankings and job level). *See also* **correlation.** (Kirk, 1990)

Reliability—Reliability is the extent to which scores are replicable upon repeated sampling of items and/or occasions. Several types of reliability exist and can be differentiated based on what they sample. The types of reliability estimates defined here range from 0.00 to 1.00 with higher values denoting higher levels of reliability. *See also* **internal consistency reliability, inter-rater reliability, parallel forms reliability, and test-retest reliability.** (Anastasi, 1988)

> **Reliability, internal consistency**—A type of reliability estimate based on a single administration of a test/questionnaire with a sampling of items. Groups of items (i.e., scales) that are internally consistent tend to be responded to in a similar manner. (Anastasi, 1988)
>
> **Reliability, inter-rater**—A type of reliability estimate based on the sampling of raters. A scale is administered to at least two raters who have observed a

given ratee's behavior; the correlation between raters' scores is then computed. *See also* **reliability**. (Guion, 1998)

Reliability, parallel forms—The correlation between two forms of a test or scale that are designed to measure the same construct(s) is used as an estimate of test/scale reliability. *See also* **reliability**. (Anastasi, 1988)

Reliability, test-retest—The correlation between two administrations of the same test to the same subjects is commonly referred to as the test-retest reliability. *See also* **internal consistency, inter-rater,** and **parallel form reliabilities**. (Anastasi, 1988)

Return on investment (ROI)—ROI is a popular form of cost-benefit analysis. If the cost of a training program is $100,000 and the increased revenue due to increased productivity is $200,000, then the ROI is (operational results/training costs or $200,000/$100,000) = 2 or two dollars returned for every dollar spent on the training program. (Cascio, 2000; Robinson & Robinson, 1989)

Sample—A sample is a (proper) subset of individuals or objects from a population of individuals or objects. (Kirk, 1990)

Significance testing—The term used for describing a general class of tests that are designed to ascertain the degree to which a result may be due to random fluctuation or is replicable across repeated sampling of a given population. *See also* **null hypothesis testing**. (Kirk, 1990)

Stakeholders—Individuals, groups, or organizations having a significant interest in how well a program functions—for instance, those with decision-making authority over it, funders and sponsors, administrators and personnel, and clients or intended beneficiaries. (Rossi et al., 1999)

Standard deviation—The degree to which scores deviate from the mean (i.e., the degree to which scores differ from one another). (Kirk, 1990)

Statistical power—The probability of rejecting a false null hypothesis at a given Type I error rate, sample size, and effect size. *See also* **null hypothesis, Type I error,** and **effect size**. (Kirk, 1995; Winer et al., 1991)

Structural equation modeling—A set of analytic techniques that relate factors (or constructs) to one another in a "para-causal" system (also referred to as path analysis). Inferences of causality are strengthened with structural equation models when they are combined with a causal or experimental design. *See also* **experimental (versus nonexperimental) design** and **path analysis**. (Byrne, 1998)

t-test—A statistical method used to investigate whether the average scores of two groups differ. The groups may be independent (each group is exposed to only one treatment or is representative of one level of the variable) or dependent (each group is exposed to both levels of the treatment or is representative of both levels of the variable). *See also* *F*-**test** and **analysis of variance**. (Kirk, 1995)

Treatment group—In an experiment, the group that receives the intervention of interest. *See also* **comparison group** and **control group**. (Shadish et al., 2002)

Utility theory—A theory derived from economic models that attempts to quantify in "objective," usually dollar terms, the impact of a given HR intervention on the organization. (Cascio, 2000)

Validity—The degree to which a score actually measures what it purports to measure. Several types of validity exist and range from primarily qualitative to primarily quantitative. As with reliability estimates, judgment should not replace strict decision rules should not replace judgment when interpreting numerical estimates of validity. (Guion, 1998)

> Concurrent (criterion-related) validity—Form of validation strategy in which incumbents are utilized; predictor and criterion scores are *concurrently* (i.e., at the same time) correlated with one another to arrive at an approximated prediction equation. (Gatewood & Feild, 2001)
>
> Construct validity—The degree to which a test/questionnaire actually measures the phenomenon it purports to measure. In construct validity assessment, correlational methods are typically used to examine relations with other measures that are hypothesized to (a) correlate strongly with the measure of interest, and (b) possess near-nonexistent relations with measures that the measure should not be correlated with. For example, if a new personality test has strong correlations with another well-established personality test but also with a well-established cognitive ability test, it may not purely be measuring personality; in other words, its construct validity may be in question. The degree to which the results support the hypotheses is the degree to which "construct validity" is said to exist. *See also* **validation**. (Guion, 1998)
>
> Content validity—The degree to which a measure encompasses an appropriately representative sample of the construct (i.e., phenomenon) domain. Several quantitative measures of content validity exist; however, content validity is typically built in to measures through professional judgment and thus assumed to be adequate. *See also* **validation**. (Guion, 1998)
>
> Convergent validity—The degree to which different methods designed to measure the same construct appear to *converge* on the construct. For example, a high correlation between a paper-and-pencil measure of need for achievement and a projective technique for measuring need for achievement would constitute evidence of convergent validity. (Campbell & Fiske, 1959)
>
> Criterion-related validity—Several forms of criterion-related validity exist. The basic notion behind this form of validity is to use correlational or multiple regression analyses to examine relations between a single (or group) of predictors (e.g., interview scores or a training course) and a single (or group) of outcome variables (e.g., performance appraisal ratings or post-training test results). *See also* **validation**. (Guion, 1998)

Discriminant validity—The degree to which similar methods designed to measure different constructs appear to *diverge*. For example, if need for achievement and need for power are both being measured by paper-and-pencil methodology, discriminant validity would be evidenced by a low correlation coefficient between the measured variables. (Campbell & Fiske, 1959)

External validity is concerned with the generalizability of research findings from one population to other populations of objects/subjects. *See also* **internal validity**. (Cook & Campbell, 1979)

Face validity—The degree to which the instrument, measure, or test *appears* to measure what it says it is measuring. (Anastasi, 1988)

Internal validity is concerned with accurately concluding that a variable of interest (an independent variable) is responsible for the variation in an outcome (dependent) variable. *See also* **external validity**. (Cook & Campbell, 1979)

Predictive (criterion-related) validity—Form of validation strategy in which applicants are utilized; applicants are tested and predictor and criterion scores are correlated at some later date. In practice, at least five forms of the predictive validity design exist. (see Guion & Cranny, 1982)

Validity generalization—A form of meta-analysis in which the mean and standard deviation of effect sizes (correlations) in a given group of studies are examined. If the mean of the effect sizes is non-zero (in the expected direction) and the variation among the effect sizes is minimal [after the variance in artifacts (sample size, reliability of the measures, etc.) has been accounted for], validity is said to generalize. *See also* **effect size**. (Hunter & Schmidt, 1990)

Variable, dependent is the variable that is used to assess the effects of an independent variable. For example, if a cognitive ability test is used to predict job performance, then job performance becomes the dependent variable. *See also* **independent variable**. (Winer et al., 1991)

Variable, independent—Any hypothesized or suspected causal event under investigation is called an independent variable. For example, if a cognitive ability test is used to predict job performance, then cognitive ability is called the independent variable. *See also* **dependent variable**. (Kirk, 1995)

Variance—The degree to which scores deviate from the mean (i.e., the degree to which scores differ from one another). Variance is the square of the standard deviation. *See also* **standard deviation**. (Kirk, 1990)

z-score is a type of standardized data value that is measured in the number of standard deviations the value is from the mean. A positive z-value indicates the value is larger than the mean and a negative z-value indicates that the value is smaller than the mean. *See also* **mean** and **standard deviation**. (Kirk, 1990)

z-test—A test used to investigate whether a sample mean differs from a population mean. *See also* **t-test** and **F-test**. (Kirk, 1990)

References

Anastasi, A. (1988). *Psychological testing* (6th ed.). New York: Macmillan.

Bollen, K. A. (1989). *Structural equations with latent variables.* New York: Wiley.

Byrne, B. M. (1998). *Structural equation modeling with LISREL, PRELIS, SIMPLIS: Basic concepts, applications, and programming.* Mahwah, NJ: Lawrence Erlbaum.

Campbell, D. T., & Fiske, D. W. (1959). Convergent and discriminant validation by the multitrait-multimethod matrix. *Psychological Bulletin, 56,* 81–105.

Cascio, W. F. (1991). *Applied psychology in personnel management.* Englewood Cliffs, NJ: Prentice Hall.

Cascio, W. F. (2000). *Costing human resources: The financial impact of behavior in organizations* (4th ed.). Cincinnati, OH: South-Western.

Cohen, J., Cohen, P., West, S. G., & Aiken, L. S. (2003). *Applied multiple regression/correlation analysis for the behavioral sciences.* Mahwah, NJ: Lawrence Erlbaum.

Conover, W. J. (1998). *Practical nonparametric statistics* (3rd ed.). San Francisco: Jossey-Bass.

Cook, T. D., & Campbell, D. T. (1979). *Quasi-experimentation: Design and analysis issues for field settings.* Boston, MA: Houghton Mifflin.

Davidson, M. L. (1983). *Multidimensional scaling.* New York: Wiley.

Everitt, B. S. (1980). *Cluster analysis* (2nd ed.). New York: Halstead Press.

Gatewood, R. D., & Feild, H. S. (2001). *Human resource selection* (5th ed.). Fort Worth: Dryden Press.

Gorsuch, R. L. (1983). *Factor analysis* (2nd ed.). Hillsdale, NJ: Lawrence Erlbaum.

Guion, R. M. (1998). *Assessment, measurement, and prediction for personnel decisions.* Mahwah, NJ: Lawrence Erlbaum.

Guion, R. M., & Cranny, C. J. (1982). A note on concurrent and predictive validity designs: A critical reanalysis. *Journal of Applied Psychology, 67,* 239–244.

Hambleton, R. K., Swaminathan, H. R., & Rogers, J. (1991). *Fundamentals of item response theory.* Thousand Oaks, CA: Sage.

Hedges, L. V., & Olkin, I. (1985). *Statistical methods for meta-analysis.* Orlando, FL: Academic Press.

Hunter, J. E., & Schmidt, F. L. (1990). *Methods of meta-analysis.* Beverly Hills, CA: Sage.

Kirk, R. E. (1990). *Statistics: An introduction* (3rd ed.). Fort Worth, TX: Holt, Rinehart and Winston.

Kirk, R. E. (1995). *Experimental design: Procedures for the behavioral sciences* (3rd ed.). Pacific Grove, CA: Brooks/Cole.

Kirkpatrick, D. L. (1998). *Evaluating training programs: The four levels* (2nd ed.). San Francisco: Berrett-Koehler.

Kline, P. (1993). *An easy guide to factor analysis.* London: Routledge.

Lipsey, M. W. (2001). *Practical meta-analysis.* Thousand Oaks, CA: Sage.

Patton, M. Q. (1990). *Qualitative evaluation and research methods* (2nd ed.). Newbury Park, CA: Sage.

Pedhazur, E. J., & Schmelkin, L. P. (1991). *Measurement, design, and analysis: An integrated analysis.* Hillsdale, NJ: Lawrence Erlbaum.

Penny, J. A. (2003). Exploring differential item functioning in a 360-degree assessment: Rater source and method of delivery. *Organizational Research Methods, 6,* 61–79.

Raju, N. S., Laffitte, L. J., & Byrne, B. M. (2002). Measurement equivalence: A comparison of methods based on confirmatory factor analysis and item response theory. *Journal of Applied Psychology, 87,* 517–529.

Raudenbush, S. W., & Bryk, A. S. (2002). *Hierarchical linear models: Applications and data analysis methods.* Thousand Oaks, CA: Sage.

Robinson, D. G., & Robinson, J. C. (1989). *Training for impact: How to link training to business needs and measure the results.* San Francisco: Jossey-Bass.

Roethlisberger, F. J. (1939). *Management and the worker; an account of a research program conducted by the Western Electric Company, Hawthorne Works, Chicago.* Boston, MA: Harvard University Press.

Rossi, P. H., Freeman, H. E., & Lipsey, M. W. (1999). *Evaluation: A systematic approach* (6th ed.). Thousand Oaks, CA: Sage.

Saal, F. E., Downey, R. G., & Lahey, M. A. (1980). Rating the ratings: Assessing the psychometric quality of rating data. *Psychological Bulletin, 88,* 413–428.

Shadish, W. R., Cook, T. D., & Campbell, D. T. (2002). *Experimental and quasi-experimental designs for generalized causal inference.* New York: Houghton Mifflin.

Simsek, Z., & Veiga, J. F. (2001). A primer on internet organizational surveys. *Organizational Research Methods, 4,* 218–235.

Stanton, J. M. (1998). An empirical assessment of data collection using the Internet. *Personnel Psychology, 51,* 709–725.

Stanton, J. M., & Rogelberg, S. G. (2001). Using internet/intranet web pages to collect organizational research data. *Organizational Research Methods, 4,* 200–217.

Tatsuoka, M. M. (1988). *Multivariate analysis: Techniques for educational and psychological research* (2nd ed.). New York: Macmillan.

Vance, R. J., Winne, P. S., & Wright, E. S. (1983). A longitudinal examination of rater and ratee effects in performance rating. *Personnel Psychology, 36,* 609–630.

Wainer, H., Dorans, N. J., Eignor, D., Flaughter, R., Green, B. F., Mislevy, R. J., Steinberg, L., & Thissen, D. (2000). *Computer adaptive testing: A primer* (2nd ed.). Mahwah, NJ: Lawrence Erlbaum.

Winer, B. J., Brown, D. R., & Michels, K. M. (1991). *Statistical principles in experimental design* (3rd ed.). New York: McGraw-Hill.

Index

About the Editors

Jack E. Edwards is an assistant director in the Defense Capabilities and Management area of the U.S. General Accounting Office in Washington, D.C., where he conducts program evaluations on military human resources. He has also served as an assistant director in GAO's Office of Applied Research Methods where he provided methodological assistance to teams evaluating a wide array of national security programs. His other prior positions include chief of the Personnel Survey Branch at the Defense Manpower Data Center, science adviser to the Chief of Naval Personnel, personnel research psychologist at the Navy Personnel Research and Development Center, and tenured associate professor of industrial/organizational psychology at the Illinois Institute of Technology. He has over 100 publications and presentations examining practical and theoretical concerns for a wide range of human resources issues: program evaluation, survey methods, attitude measurement, personnel selection, performance appraisal, leadership, diversity, and utility analysis. He has published two other books: *How to Conduct Organizational Surveys: A Step-by-Step Guide* (Sage, 1997) and *Improving Organizational Surveys: New Directions, Methods, and Applications* (Sage, 1993). He received his Ph.D. from Ohio University in 1981.

John C. Scott is vice president and co-founder of Applied Psychological Techniques (APT), a human resources consulting firm that specializes in the design and validation of selection and assessment technologies, staffing for organizational change, performance management, and employment litigation support. Prior to co-founding APT, John was a managing principal for the New York office of HRStrategies, where he directed consulting services in the areas of selection development and validation, skills assessment, survey design, performance management, and executive assessment. He was formerly a senior research psychologist for Wisconsin Electric Power Company and held an adjunct faculty position at the University of Wisconsin. Earlier, he managed the abilities test product line at the Riverside Publishing Company and directed the development and nationwide standardization of the *Stanford-Binet Intelligence Scale*, 4th edition. He has served on the program and review committees for Division 14 of the American Psychological Association, is an editorial board member for SIOP's Professional Practice book series, and is a frequent presenter in the area of selection and assessment. He received his Ph.D. from the Illinois Institute of Technology in 1985.

Nambury S. Raju is a Distinguished Professor in the Institute of Psychology and a senior scientific adviser at the Center for Research and Service at the Illinois Institute of Technology, Chicago, Illinois. Prior to joining academia in 1978, he worked at Science Research Associates from 1961 to 1978, specializing in test development and validation. He has strong interests in personnel selection and psychometrics, especially in the areas of reliability, selection and validation, item bias, validity generalization/meta-analysis, and utility of organizational interventions. He served on the Department of Defense Advisory Committee on Military Personnel Testing from 1989 to 1992. He recently served on a National Academy of Science Committee to evaluate the National Assessment of Educational Progress (NAEP). He currently serves on nine editorial boards including *Educational and Psychological Measurement, Applied Psychological Measurement, Journal of Applied Psychology, Personnel Psychology, Psychological Balletin, International Journal of Selection and Assessment,* and *Organizational Research Methods.* He has over 150 publications and presentations and is a Fellow of APA and SIOP. He received his Ph.D. from the Illinois Institute of Technology in 1974.

About the Contributors

Seymour Adler is senior vice president of Aon Consulting's Talent Solutions Consulting practice. He is responsible for directing a team that develops and implements integrated solutions for selection, assessment, training, development, and performance management in the private and public sectors. He received his Ph.D. in industrial/organizational psychology from New York University. In addition to his 30 years of experience as a consultant, he has served on the faculties of Purdue University, Tel Aviv University, and Stevens Institute of Technology; he is currently an adjunct professor at New York University. He is a Fellow of the Society of Industrial and Organizational Psychology, has served as president of the Metropolitan New York Applied Psychology Association, and was awarded the 2002 Certificate of Merit for innovations in HR assessment by the International Personnel Management Association Assessment Council.

Mary Dunn Baker, Ph.D., is senior vice president and senior research economist at ERS Group in Tallahassee, Florida. She specializes in statistical analyses to determine how hiring, promotion, termination, compensation, and other employment practices relate to gender, race/ethnicity, age, and other demographic characteristics. In addition to analyzing employment practices for litigation support and testifying as an expert witness, she estimates the value of economic losses and designs programs to monitor the outcomes of employment decision-making processes for public and private organizations.

Janet L. Barnes-Farrell has several years of experience conducting research and consulting on the development and evaluation of effective performance appraisal systems. She has published numerous articles and book chapters on this topic. She is associate professor in the Department of Psychology at the University of Connecticut, where she currently serves as the director of the graduate program in industrial/organizational psychology.

Wendy S. Becker is assistant professor of management at the University at Albany. Her research involves examining how organizations change, including team interventions and team processes. Current research interests also include new greenfield plants and the impact of high-performance work practices.

John W. Boudreau (Ph.D., Purdue University) is professor of human resource studies at Cornell University. His research won the Academy of Management's Organizational Behavior New Concept and Scholarly Contribution awards. He consults with companies worldwide including Boeing, Bristol-Myers Squibb, Citigroup, GE, IBM, Novartis, Schering-Plough, Shell International, Sun Microsystems, the United Nations, Verizon, and Williams-Sonoma. He was an architect and the first visiting director of Sun Microsystems' unique R&D Laboratory for Human Capital. A Fellow of the National Academy of Human Resources, he has published more than 40 books and articles, translated into Chinese, Czech, and Spanish. His work has been featured in the *Wall Street Journal*, *Fortune, Business Week, Training,* and *Human Resources Management.*

Harold N. Bowers is the facility and safety training manager for Pacific Northwest National Laboratory and is a program manager in the Engineering and Environmental Analysis Group. His primary professional and research focus has been the integration of health and safety management and the development and management of occupational health and safety training.

Jill Bradley is a research assistant at Tulane University. Her primary research focus is on the fit of persons to organizations.

Marilyn Buckner is president of National Training Systems, Inc.—an Atlanta-based company that specializes in innovative solutions to leadership development, succession planning, and change challenges in organizations. As an HR consultant, she uses simulations, a variety of assessments, and a systems approach to solving business problems. Prior to founding NTS a decade ago, she was the head of corporate and international HRD for The Coca-Cola Company. She has received several awards from Georgia State University and ASTD for her professional achievements. She is also the immediate past president of a global nonprofit association of human resource executives—The Human Resource Planning Society. Many of her clients are Fortune 500 companies for which she has implemented unique leadership development solutions.

Michael J. Burke is the A. B. Freeman Distinguished Professor of Organizational Behavior at Tulane University. His research and practice efforts in health and safety training have focused on the meaning and measurement of safety performance, the relationship between safety knowledge and safety performance, and the role of safety climate in the transfer of health and safety training.

William C. Byham, Ph.D., is co-founder, chairman, and CEO of Development Dimensions International (DDI), a worldwide premiere human resources training and consulting company. His major accomplishments include championing the application of the assessment center method worldwide, including two books and more than 50 articles and papers; developing the first behavior-based interviewing system, Targeted Selection®; authoring 20 books including Zapp!® The Lightning of Empowerment, a seminal book about empowerment (it has sold more than 4.5 million copies); and developing the Acceleration Pool^{SM} method of succession management—a radically new method of developing leaders. He co-authored the book *Grow Your Own Leaders* with Audrey Smith and Matthew Paese.

Jeanne M. Carsten, Ph.D., is currently development director of assessment and evaluation for the retail businesses of JPMorgan Chase Bank. She is responsible for assessing employee learning and evaluating employee and organizational development programs, including job analysis, competency modeling, and strategic evaluation.

Peter Y. Chen (Ph.D. in industrial and organizational psychology, University of South Florida, 1991) is currently an associate professor in the psychology program at Colorado State University. He teaches graduate seminars in personnel psychology, occupational health psychology, and statistics. He also provides consulting services in the areas of job analysis, competency model development, training, and workplace violence prevention.

Allan H. Church, Ph.D., is a director of organization and management development at PepsiCo Inc., where he is responsible for driving the 360-degree feedback and Organizational Health survey processes. Previously he spent nine years as an external OD consultant with Warner Burke Associates, and several years prior to that with IBM. He received his Ph.D. in organizational psychology from Columbia University, and is the author of over 100 articles, 12 book chapters, and 4 books.

F. Stephen Cobe is currently president of Omniplex, Ltd., a software development startup, specializing in sophisticated, state-of-the-art business strategy analysis. Prior to this activity, he was, for 15 years, principal in the management consulting firm of Welti, Cobe and Associates. He has worked in the strategic planning function for the American Red Cross (national organization), Conrail, and Southern Pacific Railway. He has an MBA from the Wharton School of Business and a B.A. from Stanford University.

Virginia Collins is a senior consultant with the SilverStone Group with over 15 years' experience in human resources management. She has research experience in the areas of decision processes, computerized communication process, individual differences and problem solving, executive assessment, emotional intelligence, creativity, and leadership.

J. Philip Craiger is an associate professor of computer science in the College of Information Science and Technology at the University of Nebraska at Omaha. He is involved in teaching and research in the areas of human-computer interaction, ubiquitous and pervasive computing, and the interaction of human behavior and computer security.

Steven F. Cronshaw is a professor in the department of psychology at the University of Guelph, Guelph, Ontario, Canada, and a principal consultant with the Guelph Centre for Organizational Research. His specialty area of research, graduate teaching, and consulting is industrial/ organizational psychology.

John R. Dale, Ph.D., is a principal in The Continuous Learning Group, Inc. As leader of e-Business initiatives, he has led many successful projects involving technology implementation including corporatewide knowledge management and document management systems.

David Dalsky is a doctoral student in cross-cultural psychology at the University of Mississippi.

E. Jane Davidson is associate director of The Evaluation Center at Western Michigan University and director of WMU's new interdisciplinary Ph.D. in evaluation. The program spans several colleges in the university and is based in the internationally recognized Evaluation Center. She specializes in applying evaluation techniques in organizational settings to build competitive advantage. She received her Ph.D. in organizational behavior (with an emphasis on evaluation) from Claremont Graduate University in California and has several years' experience working in both internal and external evaluation and HR consulting roles in both the public and private sectors.

Helen De Cieri (Ph.D., University of Tasmania) is an associate professor of human resource management in the Department of Management, Monash University (Australia). Her academic experience includes appointments in Australia, China, Hong Kong, Malaysia, and the United States. Her teaching, research, and consulting interests are concerned with global and strategic HR management. She has published over 60 journal articles and monographs. She is the past editor of the *Asia Pacific Journal of Human Resources* (1996–2002).

Margareta Emberger received her M.B.A. from the University of New Orleans.

Andrew J. Falcone is the director of research and development for Applied Measurement Professionals, Inc., a Kansas City, Missouri, area consulting firm that specializes in the development and validation of certification and licensure examinations. He received his Ph.D. in industrial/organizational psychology from the Illinois Institute of Technology in Chicago, Illinois, in 1985.

Sidney A. Fine is a retired industrial/organizational psychologist whose career was divided between the Department of Labor (job analyst and research director for development of the Occupational Classification System of the Dictionary of Occupational Titles) and consultant, researcher, and teacher in the private and institutional sector of the economy. He is the originator of Functional Job Analysis.

Bruce M. Fisher is director of the Center for Research and Service and adjunct professor at the Illinois Institute of Technology, Chicago. Before taking that position, he was a principal in a human resource consulting firm.

Michael M. Harris is professor of management in the College of Business Administration at the University of Missouri-St. Louis. He has written several articles and book chapters, has made various professional presentations regarding recruitment, and regularly conducts workshops on recruiting and hiring.

Paulette Henry is general manager, Scotia Service, of the Bank of Nova Scotia–Jamaica, Ltd., which is headquartered in Kingston, Jamaica, West Indies. Her enterprisewide responsibilities include customer service and customer satisfaction across financial and product sectors. Previously, she was a faculty member in the School of Communications, Howard University

E. Jeffrey Hill has a master's of organizational behavior from Brigham Young University and a Ph.D. in family life from Utah State University. He is currently an associate professor of marriage, family, and human development at BYU with a research emphasis in how flexible work arrangements affect the family and how aspects of family life affect the workplace.

Anna Sigismund Huff is director of the Advanced Institute for Management (AIM), an initiative funded by the ESRC and EPSRC and visiting professor at London Business School. She received an M.A. in sociology and a Ph.D. in Management from Northwestern University, and has been on the faculty at UCLA, the University of Illinois, and the University of Colorado. Her research interests focus on strategic change, both as a dynamic process of interaction among firms and as a cognitive process affected by the interaction of individuals over time. She is a strategy editor for the book series Foundations in Organization Science (Sage Publications) and serves on the editorial boards of the *Strategic Management Journal,* the *Journal of Management Studies,* the *British Journal of Management, Management Learning,* and the electronic journal, M@n@gement. In 1998–1999 she was president of the Academy of Management, an international organization of over 12,000 scholars interested in management issues.

Edward J. Kelleher is professor of organization and management in the College of Business at San Jose State University. His research interests are focused on quantitative methods and strategic management. He has also taught at Seattle University and the University of Wisconsin. Prior to his academic career, he held management and executive-level positions with IBM's publishing subsidiary, S. C. Johnson, and Bendix Corporation. He earned his Ph.D. degree at the Illinois Institute of Technology.

Kurt Kraiger is McFarlin Professor of Psychology and director of graduate programs in industrial/organizational psychology at the University of Tulsa. He received his Ph.D. in industrial organizational psychology from Ohio State University in 1983. He is a Fellow in the Society for Industrial-Organizational Psychology, and currently serves on the Committee for Human Factors for the National Academy of Science. He is a nationally known expert in the areas of training and training evaluation who has consulted on training evaluation for a number of Fortune 500 companies. He has also edited or co-edited two applied books on training: *Creating, Implementing, and Managing Effective Training and Development Systems in Organizations,* and *Improving Training Effectivenes in Work Organizations.* He is currently conducting research on computer-based instruction, training evaluation, and organizational climate.

Autumn D. Krauss is a doctoral student in industrial and organizational psychology at Colorado State University. Her research interests include occupational health and safety, labor unions, and personnel training and development.

Dan Landis is an affiliate professor of psychology at University of Hawaii-Hilo and emeritus professor of psychology and director emeritus, Center for Applied

Research and Evaluation, University of Mississippi. He is coeditor of the *Handbook of Intercultural Training* (2nd ed., Sage, 1996) and currently editor-in-chief of the *International Journal of Intercultural Relations.*

Elliot D. Lasson, Ph.D., is a personnel analyst supervisor for the state of Maryland in the Office of Personnel Services and Benefits. He also is on the faculty at the University of Baltimore in the Division of Applied Psychology and Quantitative Methods. He earned his Ph.D. in industrial/organizational psychology from Wayne State University in Detroit, Michigan.

Russell Lobsenz, Ph.D., is manager of consulting services for viaPeople, Inc., where he is responsible for developing and implementing enterprisewide performance management systems. Prior to joining viaPeople, he worked as an internal consultant, designing employee assessment systems, for the Federal Bureau of Investigation, Bell Atlantic Corporation, and Square D Company.

Manuel London is associate provost for enrollment management and professor of management and policy at the State University of New York at Stony Brook. He received his Ph.D. from the Ohio State University in industrial and organizational psychology. He taught at the University of Illinois at Champaign for 3 years. He was then a researcher and human resource manager at AT&T for 12 years before moving to Stony Brook. He has written extensively on the topics of 360-degree feedback, career dynamics, and management development. His books include *Job Feedback: Giving, Seeking, and Using Feedback for Performance Improvement, 360 Degree Feedback: A Tool and Process for Continuous, Self-Directed Management Development* (co-edited with Walter Tornow), and *Leadership Development: Paths to Self-Insight and Professional Growth.* He is a consultant for business and government organizations in the areas of career planning and development, performance management systems, human resource forecasting and planning, and organizational change.

Angela M. Lynch is a managing consultant in IBM's Business Consulting Services, specializing in organizational change initiatives. She also has worked in IBM's Global Employee Research Department.

John E. Mathieu is a Northeast Utilities Scholar and professor of management at the University of Connecticut. His current research interests include models of training effectiveness, team and multiteam processes, and cross-level models of organizational behavior. In particular, his recent work has focused on how team composition influences team performance trajectories over time, how team training and other interventions enhance team effectiveness, and how teams-of-teams coordinate their joint efforts.

Scott B. Morris, Ph.D., is associate professor of industrial/organizational psychology at Illinois Institute of Technology. He has published and presented many articles on the validation, legal defensibility, and fairness of personnel selection systems.

Alex Nicoll is a senior technology research fellow in the department of Computer Science, College of Information Science and Technology, at the University of

Nebraska at Omaha. He is involved in research in wireless security, systems management, and ubiquitous and pervasive computing.

Timothy V. Nolan, Ph.D., is a consultant with The Continuous Learning Group, Inc., specializing in change leadership, performance improvement, and leadership behavior. He has done organizational change work with companies such as Bristol-Myers Squibb, Bayer Corporation, Bechtel, and The Weather Channel. Prior to joining CLG, he worked as a change consultant for county government and as a college admissions counselor.

David B. Peterson is senior vice president and global practice leader for coaching services at Personnel Decisions International. He received his Ph.D. from the University of Minnesota, specializing in industrial/organizational and counseling psychology. An expert on coaching, executive development, and how organizations can create strategic advantage through learning and development, he has been quoted in the *Wall Street Journal, Fortune, Business Week, Sloan Management Review, Washington Post,* and *USA Today.* With his colleague Mary Dee Hicks, he has authored two best-selling books, *Development FIRST: Strategies for Self-Development* (1995) and *Leader as Coach: Strategies for Coaching and Developing Others* (1996).

Andrew Pettigrew is associate dean research and professor of Strategy and Organisation at Warwick Business School, Warwick University. Between 1985 and 1995 he founded and directed the Centre for Corporate Strategy and Change. He has held previous academic positions at Yale University, London Business School, and Harvard Business School, where in the academic year 2001 he was a visiting professor.

He is a fellow of both the Academy of Management and The British Academy of Management. He was the first chairman of the British Academy of Management (1987–1990) and then president (1990–1993). In 1998 he was elected a Founding Academician of the Academy of the Social Sciences. In 2001 he was elected the Distinguished Scholar of the Academy of Management, the first European scholar to be so honored. His latest books include the *Handbook of Strategy and Management,* coedited with Howard Thomas and Richard Whittington (2001, London: Sage); and Pettigrew, A. M., Whittington, R., Martin, L., Sanchez-Runde, C., van den Bosch, F., Ruigrok, W., & Numagami, T. (Eds.), *Innovative Forms of Organizing: International Perspectives* (2003, London: Sage).

Miguel A. Quiñones is associate professor of psychology and management at Rice University. He co-edited *Training for a Rapidly Changing Workplace: Applications of Psychological Research,* has published extensively in the area of training and development, and has consulted with public and private industry on human resource related issues.

Chet Robie is assistant professor of management and organizational behavior in the School of Business and Economics at Wilfrid Laurier University in Waterloo, Ontario, Canada. His research interests can be characterized as quite broad with publications in expatriate selection and training issues, multi-source ratings, assessment centers, personality testing, leadership, business ethics, psychometrics, job satisfaction, and shiftwork. He serves as an ad hoc reviewer for six journals. He earned his Ph.D. from Bowling Green State University.

Dale S. Rose is president of 3D Group, a Berkeley, California-based consulting firm dedicated to helping organizations make data-driven decisions. He is an expert in workplace measurement, program evaluation, and assessment-based leadership development. In addition to working with many small and large companies to translate evaluation results into organizational effectiveness, he has published on a range of topics including program evaluation, 360-degree feedback, and workplace surveys. He received his Ph.D. in industrial/organizational psychology from DePaul University in Chicago.

Paul Rosenfeld is a personnel research psychologist at the Navy Personnel Research Studies and Technology (NPRST), Department of the Navy Personnel Command. He is currently the NPRST Washington, D.C., liaison and principal investigator on the Navy and Marine Corps Equal Opportunity/Sexual Harassment Surveys. He coedited *Hispanics in the Workplace* (Sage, 1992) and coauthored *How to Conduct Organizational Surveys* (Sage, 1997).

Rob Silzer is managing director of HR Assessment and Development Inc. For the past 25 years he has consulted with managers and executives in over 100 organizations focusing on executive leadership selection and development, succession planning, and strategically driven HR practices and systems. He recently edited the book *The 21st Century Executive: Innovative Practices for Building Leadership at the Top* (2002) and with Dick Jeanneret coedited the book *Individual Psychological Assessment: Predicting Behavior in Organizational Settings* (1998). He holds a Ph.D. in industrial/organizational psychology and counseling psychology from the University of Minnesota. He has served as president of Metropolitan New York Applied Psychology Association, president of PDI–New York, senior director of Human Resources at Fieldcrest-Cannon Inc., adjunct professor at the University of Minnesota and New York University, and a member of the editorial board for *Personnel Psychology.*

Jeffrey M. Stanton, Ph.D., is the author of more than 20 articles and chapters on organizational research methods and impacts of information technology on organizations. He is assistant professor at Syracuse University's School of Information Studies and he directs the NSF-funded Syracuse Information Systems Evaluation project. He has more than 17 years of experience in business and consulting.

Stephen D. Steinhaus, Ph.D., is the principal of Human Resource Alignment Consulting, Ltd. (HRA). His prior experiences include managing director at SHL and Corporate Industrial Psychologist at Ameritech. He has provided consulting solutions to numerous organizations in the public and private sectors. His expertise and experience are primarily in the areas of human resource analytics, strategy, and assessment. He has developed and implemented human resource impact analyses using a variety of theoretical and practical models.

Scott Tonidandel is assistant professor of psychology at Davidson College. His research focuses on personnel psychology and research design and analysis, and he has consulted with organizations on a variety of training-related interventions.

Sara P. Weiner has a Ph.D. in industrial and organizational psychology from the University of Connecticut and has been with IBM's Global Employee Research department for over 12 years. Her research has included attraction and retention of critical talent, career opportunity, downsizing, telecommuting, and work and personal life balance, with an emphasis on linking employee opinions to worldwide and local strategic business decisions.

L. A. Witt is an associate professor of management at the University of New Orleans. He was a human resources director with Barnett Banks, Inc. in Jacksonville, Florida, prior to joining the faculty of the department of management at the University of New Orleans. He has published research articles in such journals as *Journal of Applied Psychology* and *Personnel Psychology* on topics including organizational politics, social skill, and personnel selection.